# Turkey

How do democratic societies maintain the balance between civil rights and security while continuing the fight on global terrorism? This work raises this issue and presents one country, Turkey, and its struggle to implement laws to combat terrorism and comply with the European Union's civil rights standards.

A collection of materials that reflect the legal responses in combating terrorism is an essential volume in any academic and professional collection as it provides a case-specific reference point in the fields of European Union (EU) politics, law, and international relations. *Turkey* contains translations, contextual notes, and explanations from the editors of over 112 Turkish and EU documents covering martial law, Kurdistan Workers' Party (PKK) terror, Turkey–EU relations, Human Rights, and Turkish reforms. This resource book enables the reader to gauge Turkey's prospects for success in establishing an effective government that at the same time protects the rights of the individual.

This book will prove a valuable source for students and researchers of international politics, international relations, and security studies.

**Yonah Alexander** is Co-Director of the Inter-University Center for Legal Studies at the International Law Institute, Washington, DC. He is also Director of the Inter-University Center for Terrorism Studies, and Senior Fellow at Potomac Institute and the George Washington University, USA.

**Edgar H. Brenner** is Co-Director of the Inter-University Center for Legal Studies, Washington DC, as well as Legal Counsel to the Inter-University Center for Terrorism Studies, USA.

**Serhat Tutuncuoglu Krause** currently practices law in New York City, USA. He also holds an M.A. degree from University of Notre Dame in Peace Studies.

# Turkey

Terrorism, civil rights, and the European Union

**Edited by Yonah Alexander,
Edgar H. Brenner and
Serhat Tutuncuoglu Krause**

LONDON AND NEW YORK

First published 2008
by Routledge
2 Park Square, Milton Park, Abingdon, Oxfordshire OX14 4RN
Simultaneously published in the USA and Canada
by Routledge
711 Third Avenue, New York, NY 10017
First issued in paperback 2014
*Routledge is an imprint of the Taylor and Francis Group, an informa business*

© 2008 Yonah Alexander, Edgar H. Brenner and Serhat T. Krause

Typeset in Baskerville by
Taylor & Francis Books

All rights reserved. No part of this book may be reprinted or reproduced or utilised in any form or by any electronic, mechanical, or other means, now known or hereafter invented, including photocopying and recording, or in any information storage or retrieval system, without permission in writing from the publishers.

*British Library Cataloguing in Publication Data*
A catalogue record for this book is available from the British Library

*Library of Congress Cataloging in Publication Data*
Turkey : terrorism, civil rights and the European Union
/ edited by Yonah Alexander, Edgar H. Brenner and
Serhat Tutuncuoglu Krause.
p.cm.
Includes bibliographical references and index.
ISBN 978-0-415-44163-6 (hardback : alk. paper) – ISBN 978-0-203-93628-3 (e-book : alk. paper) 1. Civil rights–Turkey. 2. Terrorism–Turkey. 3. European Union–Turkey. I. Alexander, Yonah. II. Brenner, Edgar H. III. Tutuncuoglu, Serhat.
KKX2460.T868 2007
341.242'409561–dc22
2007024708

ISBN 978-0-415-44163-6 (hbk)
ISBN 978-1-138-01136-6 (pbk)
ISBN 978-0-203-93628-3 (ebk)

# Contents

| | |
|---|---|
| About the editors | xii |
| List of illustrations | xiii |
| Foreword | xiv |
| Preface | xv |

**1 Turkey: country information** — 1

Document no. 1: General information — 3
Document no. 2: Historical overview — 4
Document no. 3: Maps — 10

**2 1980 Military coup, martial law and state of emergency, and a new Constitution** — 13

Document no. 4: 1980 Coup D'Etat — 15
Document no. 5: Martial law and state of emergency in Turkey — 17
Document no. 6: Introduction to anti-terrorism measures in the Republic of Turkey — 19
Document no. 7: Martial Law Act of 13 May 1971 — 22
Document no. 8: Constitutional history of Turkey — 38
Document no. 9: The Constitution of the Republic of Turkey — 43
Document no. 10: State of Emergency Law of October 25, 1983 — 90

**3 Emergence of the PKK and Turkey's legal responses to terrorism** — 101

Document no. 11: PKK terror — 103
Document no. 12: Martial law/state of emergency proclamations — 105
Document no. 13: State of emergency — regional governor's powers — 107
Document no. 14: Turkey's August 6, 1990, notice of derogation from rights enshrined in Articles 5, 6, 8, 10, 11, and 13 of the European Convention on Human Rights in conformity with Article 15 of the Convention — 109
Document no. 15: State of Emergency — Regional Governor's additional powers Governor and of the state of emergency of December 16, 1990 — 110

vi  *Contents*

*Document no. 16: Turkey's January 3, 1991, Notice of Derogation from Rights Enshrined in Articles 5, 6, 8, 10, 11, and 13 of the European Convention on Human Rights in conformity with Article 15 of the Convention* .... 115
*Document no. 17: Anti-Terrorism Law (law to fight against terrorism)* .... 117
*Document no. 18: Comment on the law to fight against terrorism, Law no. 3713* .... 125
*Document no. 19: Turkey's May 12, 1992, notice of derogation from rights enshrined in Article 5 of the European Convention on Human Rights in conformity with Article 15 of the convention* .... 132
*Document no. 20: Other laws used against terrorism* .... 133

## 4   European system of Human Rights and fundamental freedoms — **139**

*Document no. 21: Introductory comment* .... 141
*Document no. 22: The Council of Europe Convention for the Protection of Human Rights and Fundamental Freedoms (European Convention of Human Rights), as amended by Protocol no. 11* .... 143
*Document no. 23: European Court of Justice, Fundamental Rights and the European Convention on Human Rights* .... 160

## 5   European Community and Human Rights — **163**

*Document no. 24: European Community (EC) the Single European Act* .... 165
*Document no. 25: ECJ: ERT v. Pliroforissis et al.* .... 167
*Document no. 26: EC Declaration on Human Rights Conclusion of the Luxembourg European Council (28–29 June 1991)* .... 170
*Document no. 27: Resolution of the EC Council and of the Member States meeting in the Council on Human Rights, Democracy and Development (28 November 1991)* .... 173

## 6   European Union and Human Rights — **177**

*Document no. 28: Treaty on European Union (Maastricht Treaty)* .... 179
*Document no. 29: Copenhagen European Council Presidency conclusions, 21–22 June 1993* .... 182
*Document no. 30: European Union agreements with third countries and the Human Rights clause* .... 185
*Document no. 31: Cannes European Council Presidency conclusions, 26 and 27 June 1995* .... 196
*Document no. 32: European Union briefings on the 1996 Intergovernmental Conference: Fundamental Rights* .... 200
*Document no. 33: Consolidated version of the Treaty on European Union (as amended by the Treaty of Amsterdam Amending the Treaty on European Union, the Treaties Establishing The European Communities and Related Acts)* .... 208
*Document no. 34: Declaration of the European Union on the occasion of the 50th Anniversary of the Universal Declaration on Human Rights, Vienna, 10 December, 1998* .... 213

Contents vii

## 7 Turkey–EU relations: 1963–94: The Ankara agreement, emergence of Turkey's Human Rights record as a problem     217

*Document no. 35: Turkey–EU brief history*     219
*Document no. 36: Agreement establishing an association between the European Economic Community and Turkey, 12 September 1963*     223
*Document no. 37: ECtHR: France, Norway, Denmark, Sweden and The Netherlands v. Turkey (1982) ["friendly settlement" proceedings]*     227
*Document no. 38: European Commission's 1989 opinion on Turkey's request for accession to the Community*     229
*Document no. 39: The Council of Europe Parliamentary Assembly (PACE) Resolution 985 (1992) on the situation of Human Rights in Turkey*     234
*Document no. 40: Public statement on Turkey by the Council of Europe European Committee for the Prevention of Torture (1992)*     238
*Document no. 41: [European Parliament (EP)] Resolution on the trial of members of the Turkish Grand National Assembly*     249
*Document no. 42: [European Parliament] resolution on the trial of Turkish members of Kurdish origin of the Turkish Grand National Assembly*     251

## 8 Customs Union decision and the first implications of the Human Rights problems     253

*Document no. 43: EP [European Parliament] Resolution on the draft agreement on the conclusion of a customs union between the EU and Turkey*     255
*Document no. 44: [European Parliament] Resolution on the visit of the troika to Ankara and the Turkish military intervention in northern Iraq*     257
*Document no. 45: PACE [Council of Europe Parliamentary Assembly] Recommendation 1266 (1995) on Turkey's military intervention in northern Iraq and on Turkey's respect of commitments concerning constitutional and legislative reforms*     259
*Document no. 46:* ECtHR-Yagci and Sargin v. Turkey     261
*Document no. 47: The Bill pertaining to amending the Preamble and some of the Articles of the Constitution of the Republic of Turkey, 23 July 1995*     268
*Document no. 48: Amendment to Article 8 of the Turkish Anti-Terrorism Law*     274
*Document no. 49: [European Parliament] Decision on the unblocking of the EU–Turkey Joint Parliamentary Committee*     279
*Document no. 50: [European Parliament] Legislative resolution on the proposal for a council decision relating to a common position by the community in the EC–Turkey association council on implementing the final phase of the Customs Union*     280
*Document no. 51: [European Parliament] Resolution on the Human Rights situation in Turkey*     281
*Document no. 52: Decision No. 1/95 of the EC–Turkey Association Council of 22 December 1995 on implementing the final phase of the Customs Union*     284

viii    *Contents*

**9   After the Customs Union decision: problems persist:
1996–98**  **287**

*1996*  289

Document no. 53: PACE [Council of Europe Parliamentary Assembly] Recommendation 1298 (1996) on Turkey's respect of commitments to constitutional and legislative reforms (follow-up to Recommendation 1266 (1995))  289

Document no. 54: [European Parliament] Resolution on Human Rights and the situation in Turkey  291

Document no. 55: Editors' comment on other EP resolutions in 1996  293

Document no. 56: ECtHR — Aksoy v. Turkey  295

Document no. 57: Editors' comment on other ECtHR cases in 1996  316

*1997*  318

Document no. 58: Editors' comment on relevant 1997 ECtHR cases in which Turkey was a party  318

Document no. 59: Law of March 1997 amending the Code of Criminal Procedure (CMUK)  321

Document no. 60: Luxembourg European Council Presidency Conclusions (12–13 December 1997) and its aftermath  323

*1998*  327

Document no. 61: Cardiff European Council Presidency Conclusions (15–16 June 1998)  327

Document no. 62: ECtHR — Incal v. Turkey  329

Document no. 63: List of some decisions rendered by the ECtHR in 1998 in which Turkey was a party  351

Document no. 64: [European Parliament] Resolution on the commission reports on developments in relations with Turkey since the entry into force of the Customs Union  352

Document no. 65: [European Parliament] Resolution on the communication from the Commission to the Council and the European Parliament on the further development of relations with Turkey and on the communication from the Commission to the Council: European Strategy for Turkey — The Commission's initial operational proposals  356

**10  1999 Helsinki European Council and European Union
membership perspective for Turkey**  **361**

Document no. 66: Council of Europe Committee on the Honouring of Obligations and Commitments by Member States of the Council of Europe. Honouring of Obligations and Commitments by Turkey, 15 January 1999  363

Document no. 67: ECtHR Judgments in Thirteen Cases against Turkey  372

Document no. 68: 1999 Regular Report from the European Commission on Turkey's progress towards accession  380

Document no. 69: Helsinki European Council Presidency Conclusions (10–11 December 1999)  395

Contents ix

## 11 After Helsinki: initial developments — 2000     397

Document no. 70: Editors' comment on capture of Abdullah Öcalan, the leader
of the PKK     399
Document no. 71: [European Parliament] Briefing no. 7: Turkey and relations
with the European Union     401
Document no. 72: ECtHR — Kilic v. Turkey     404
Document no. 73: [European Parliament] Resolution on the 1999 Regular Report
from the Commission on Turkey's Progress Towards Accession     418

## 12 Turkish reforms on Civil Rights begin — 2001     423

Document no. 74: European Council Regulation (EC) no. 390/2001 of 26
February 2001 on Assistance to Turkey in the Framework of the Pre-Accession
Strategy, and in Particular on the Establishment of an Accession Partnership     425
Document no. 75: Turkey–EU Association Council Decision of 8 March 2001
on the Principles, Priorities, Intermediate Objectives and Conditions Contained
in the Accession Partnership with the Republic of Turkey     428
Document no. 76: Turkish National Programme for the Adoption of the Acquis     434
Document no. 77: 3 October 2001 Amendments to the Constitution of the
Republic of Turkey     449
Document no. 78: Editors' comment on developments related to the European Court
of Human Rights (ECtHR) in 2001     463
Document no. 79: PACE [Council of Europe Parliamentary Assembly] Resolution
no: 1256 (2001): Honouring of Obligations and Commitments by
Turkey     465
Document no. 80: Republic of Turkey Secretariat General of European Affairs
Studies within the framework of National Programme: Comparison Chart
between the Accession Partnership, NPAA, and the 2001 Regular Report     470
Document no. 81: Editors' additional comment     477
Document no. 82: Measures taken by the Republic of Turkey against terrorism —
2001 Report to the United Nations Security Council     478

## 13 Turkey's progress on Human Rights: changes in anti-terrorism-related laws: 2002–3     489

2002     491
Document no. 83: Harmonisation package (1)     491
Document no. 84: Harmonisation package (2)     502
Document no. 85: Council of Europe Guidelines on Human Rights and the
Fight Against Terrorism     508
Document no. 86: Editors' comment on ECtHR decisions in 2002 and PACE
[Council of Europe Parliamentary Assembly] Resolution no. 1297 (2002):
Implementation of Decisions of the European Court of Human Rights by
Turkey     513
Document no. 87: Harmonisation package (3)     515

x  Contents

    *Document no. 88: Editors' comment on European Council Declarations of 2002 and the Copenhagen European Council Presidency Conclusions 2003*    532
        534
    *Document no. 89: Harmonisation package (4)*    534
    *Document no. 90: Harmonisation package (5)*    540
    *Document no. 91: ECtHR* — Ocalan v. Turkey    542
    *Document no. 92: Council of Europe: the Committee of Ministers Response to PACE Recommendation no. 1576 and other ECtHR developments in 2003*    566
    *Document no. 93: EU–TR Association Council Decision of 19 May 2003 on the Principles, Priorities, Intermediate Objectives and Conditions Contained in the Accession Partnership with Turkey*    569
    *Document no. 94: Harmonisation package (6)*    573
    *Document no. 95: Turkey's 2003 Revised National Programme for the Adoption of the* Acquis    578
    *Document no. 96: Harmonisation package (7)*    585
    *Document no. 97: European Council Decisions in 2003*    591

## 14 Year of evaluation for Turkey to start EU accession negotiations — 2004    593

*Document no. 98: Introductory comment*    595
*Document no. 99: Checklist on the status of legislative changes in the political criteria section of the 2001 and 2003 National Programme for the Adoption of the* Acquis    599
*Document no. 100: Constitutional amendments of 7 May 2004*    607
*Document no. 101: Brussels European Council Presidency Conclusions, 17–18 June 2004*    609
*Document no. 102: PACE [Council of Europe Parliamentary Assembly] Resolution 1380 (2004): Honouring of Obligations and Commitments by Turkey*    610
*Document no. 103: Communication from the Commission to the Council and the European Parliament: recommendation of the European Commission on Turkey's progress towards accession*    616
*Document no. 104: European Commission 2004 Regular Report on Turkey's progress towards accession*    624
*Document no. 105: [European Parliament] Resolution on the 2004 Regular Report and the recommendation of the European Commission on Turkey's Progress Towards Accession*    659
*Document no. 106: Brussels European Council Presidency conclusions, 16–17 December 2004*    666

## 15 Quo Vadis? After 2004: European Union membership still a rough path    669

*Document no. 107: Issues arising from Turkey's membership perspective*    671
*Document no. 108: Developments in 2005 through press reports*    677

*Contents* xi

*Document no. 109: Common future of the EU and Turkey: roadmap for reforms and negotiations* 683
*Document no. 110: Critical developments in Turkey in 2005 and 2006* 686
*Document no. 111: Problems in the European Union: European constitution and the fading support* 692
*Document no. 112: Terror activities after December 2004 and re-emergence of the Kurdistan Workers' Party (PKK)* 699
*Document no. 113: ECtHR* — Ocalan v. Turkey 717
*Document no. 114: Negotiating framework (Luxembourg, 3 October 2005)* 720
*Document no. 115: European Commission 2006 Regular Report on Turkey's Progress Towards Accession* 724

*Notes* 742
*Bibliography* 756
*Glossary* 770
*Index* 771
*Index of documents* 780

# About the editors

**Yonah Alexander** is Co-Director of the Inter-University Center for Legal Studies at the International Law Institute in Washington DC. He is also Senior Fellow and Director, International Center for Terrorism Studies at the Potomac Institute for Policy Studies and Director, Inter-University Center for Terrorism Studies. Formerly a Professor and Director of Terrorism Studies at the State University of New York and The George Washington University, Dr. Alexander was educated at the University of Chicago and Columbia University. He conducted research and lectured extensively in Turkey since the 1970's. He has written or edited over ninety-five books, focusing on international affairs, terrorism and the Middle East. His 2008 publications include *The Evolution of US Counterterrorism Policy [Three Volumes]* with Michael B. Kraft and *The New Iranian Leadership: Ahmadinejad, Terrorism, Nuclear Ambition and the Middle East* with Milton Hoenig.

**Edgar H. Brenner** is Co-Director of the Inter-University Center for Legal Studies at the International Law Institute in Washington DC and is Legal Counsel to the Inter-University Center for Terrorism Studies. He is a graduate of the Yale Law School and is a member of the District of Colombia Bar and of the Bar of the Supreme Court of the United States. He has lectured on legal responses to terrorism and counter-terrorism policy issues at such venues as The George Washington University, the University of Michigan Law School and the Universities of Bahcesehir and Marmara Law Schools in Istanbul, Turkey. He is Co-Editor with Yonah Alexander of *Legal Aspects of Terrorism in the United States [Four Volumes]*, *The United Kingdom's Legal Response to Terrorism*, *U.S. Federal Legal Responses to Terrorism*, and *Terrorism and the Law*.

**Serhat Tutuncuoglu Krause** was born in Istanbul, Turkey. Mr. Krause attended high school at Istanbul Robert College and graduated with a degree in International Relations from Istanbul Koc University. He then completed a Master's Degree in Peace Studies from the University of Notre Dame after which he taught "Introduction to Political Science" and "Diplomacy" courses at Istanbul Bilgi University. Mr. Krause obtained his law degree from Catholic University Columbus School of Law, *magna cum laude*, and currently is an attorney practicing in New York City. He has researched and written in various capacities about international law, terrorism and civil rights. Mr. Krause is the author of *Turkey's New Law on Associations: Promising but not Tested*.

# Illustrations

Document no. 3: Map 1: Turkey — 10
Document no. 3: Map 2: Areas of Kurdish population — 11
Document no. 3: Map 3: Turkey in its region — 12
Document no. 5: Martial law and state of emergency in Turkey — 17
Document no. 22: Convention for the Protection of Human Rights and Fundamental Freedoms (dates given in form of day/month/year) — 158
Document no. 63: List of decisions rendered by the ECtHR in 1998 in which Turkey was a party — 351
Document no. 80: Republic of Turkey Secretariat General of European Affairs Studies within the framework of National Programme: Comparison Chart between the Accession Partnership, NPAA, and the 2001 Regular Report — 470
Document no. 99: Checklist on the status of legislative changes in the political criteria section of the 2001 and 2003 National Programme for the Adoption of the *Acquis* — 599
Document no. 111: Problems in the European Union: European constitution and the fading support — 692

# Foreword

I wish to commend the editors on what is a monumental achievement: a compendium of documents, which is at the same time a compendium of commentary on many of the documents, and a work of history. While dealing with the framework of Turkish law, policy and practice to enable Turkey to cope with terrorism, it is really much more. It presents the record of the evolution of Turkey, principally since 1980, with respect to its civil and Human Rights, and its determined relationship with the European Union, itself undergoing considerable evolution.

I am an admirer of Turkey and its progress from Ottoman times to the present. The record presented in this volume, of the simultaneous response to terrorism, a changing society, and the requirements of the European Union, is rich and fascinating.

This book demonstrates once again the prodigious scholarship of which Professors Alexander and Brenner and their colleagues are capable. I welcome this text.

Don Wallace, Jr.
Professor of Law, Georgetown University Law Center, and Chairman, International Law Institute; of counsel. Morgan. Lewis and Bockius, Washington, D.C; BA, Yale College; LLB, Harvard Law School

# Preface

At the end of World War I, the Ottoman Empire was divided among the Allied victors, and the territory that now constitutes Turkey was occupied by French, Italian, and Greek forces. These Allied forces were ousted by a successful nationalist campaign for independence in the period 1918–23, led by Mustafa Kemal (later called "Atatürk," father Turk). Following Kemal's victory in the War of Independence, modern Turkey was founded and proclaimed a republic in 1923 with Mustafa Kemal Atatürk as the country's first president.

Atatürk's main aspiration for Turkey was ascension to the level of contemporary civilizations, meaning modernization, democratization, and Westernization of Turkish society and Turkey's political and legal systems. Accordingly, Atatürk led Turkey through a drastic revolution, breaking the Imperial decadent past. Under Atatürk's presidency, the country implemented wide-ranging social, legal, and political reforms, dispensed with the feudal caliphate structure, and embraced secularism as a basic tenet of state policy.

After World War II and during the Cold War, Turkey aligned with the Western Bloc and was a founding member of the United Nations, as well as a member of the North Atlantic Treaty Organization (NATO), the Council of Europe, and the Organization for European Cooperation and Development (OECD) and an associate member of the Western European Union. However, this alignment did not necessarily translate into the perfect adoption of the values promoted through these newly established institutions such as democracy and Human Rights.

Yet, in conformity with the enunciated direction of the country and having entered into very close cooperation with Western Europe in the political realm, it was logical for Turkey to attempt to complete this alignment in the economic area. Thus, in July 1959, shortly after the creation of the European Economic Community (EEC) in 1958, Turkey made its first application to join the EEC. The EEC's response to Turkey's application was to suggest the establishment of an association relationship until Turkey's circumstances permitted its accession. However, the military coup of 1960 (seeking to restore law and order in the country), temporarily froze the relationship between the EEC and Turkey. In the aftermath of the coup, negotiations ensued and culminated in the signature of the Agreement Creating an Association between the Republic of Turkey and the European Economic Community (the "Ankara Agreement") on September 12, 1963.

The Ankara Agreement established three phases of a Customs Union, which served as an instrument to foster additional integration of Turkey into the EEC. Moreover, the Agreement formalized the possibility of Turkey becoming a member of the EEC, particularly through Article 28, stating "[a]s soon as the operation of this Agreement has advanced far enough to justify envisaging full acceptance by Turkey of the obligations arising out of the Treaty establishing the Community, the Contracting Parties shall examine the possibility of the accession of Turkey to the Community."

Unfortunately for Turkey, the aforementioned deterioration of Euro-Turkish relations as a result of the 1960 military coup was not the last such instance. In the following years, Euro-Turkish relations were paralyzed owing to periods of Turkish instability and two military coups in 1971 and 1980, as well as Turkey's intervention in Cyprus in 1974. Indeed, the then constituted European Community (EC) did not normalize its relations with Ankara until the return to civilian politics in 1983 following the 1980 coup.

After 1983, progress resumed with new momentum. Encouraged by the developments, Turkey reapplied for full membership to the EC on 14 April 1987 in accordance with Article 237 of the EEC Treaty, which gave any country with land in the European continent the right to do so. The ruling body of the EC, the European Council, forwarded Turkey's application to the executive body of the EC, the Commission, for the preparation of an Opinion. In 1989, the European Commission found Turkey eligible for full membership, yet deferred the in-depth analysis of Turkey's application until the emergence of a more favorable environment for both Turkey and the Community. As for the unfavorable factors for the Community, the Opinion stated that, because establishment of the Single Market was a priority, it could not contemplate enlargement at that time.

As for Turkey, the Commission gave both economic and political reasons and recommended progress as foreseen in the Ankara Agreement in particular under Article 28 of the Agreement. The Commission also noted "the negative effects" of the dispute between Greece and Turkey and "the situation in Cyprus". At the same time, the Commission made recommendations for Turkey to carry out further political, economic, and social reforms before the opening of accession negotiations. The EC Council endorsed the Commission's opinion in 1990.

By 1990 a separatist Kurdish insurgency in Southeastern Anatolia, which had begun in 1984, had dominated the Turkish political scene. At the turn of the decade, the political and social focus was on combating the insurgency, which employed the shape of terrorism. In order to respond to the rising threat and fight the secessionist terrorism, Turkey adopted a series of legal and practical measures, in addition to already existing legal mechanisms, at the expense of certain fundamental civil rights. The 1982 Constitution and other laws adopted following the military coup already provided for fighting terrorism while to a certain extent compromising Human Rights and fundamental freedoms. Supported by public opinion, and following the suggestions of the military and security forces, the government initially adopted several decrees, which introduced measures derogating from certain principles of the European Convention on Human Rights. Additionally, the Turkish Grand National Assembly adopted the Law to Fight Terrorism in 1991 (Anti-Terrorism Law [ATL]). With the legal framework ready in the early 1990s, the military and security forces flexed their strength and the result was a sacrifice of many fundamental Human Rights and freedoms, especially in Southeastern Anatolia. Furthermore, the State Security Court system permitted imposition of harsher sentences on those accused of "terrorist" crimes as opposed to "ordinary" crimes.

In the meantime, the EC began to transform itself into a political body, the European Union (EU). The new Union was founded on the principles of democracy, the rule of law, and Human Rights. When the Maastricht Treaty came into force (in 1983), the corollary was a declaration in the Copenhagen European Council that "membership [to the EU] require[d] that the candidate country has achieved stability of institutions guaranteeing democracy, the rule of law, Human Rights and respect for and protection of minorities." Further requirements included respect of fundamental rights, as guaranteed by the European Convention on Human Rights, existence of a viable market economy, and the capacity to adopt the *acquis communautaire* (the common rules, standards, and policies that make up the body of EU law). This development was indeed a result of years of accumulating recognition that certain fundamental rights were principles upon which the community was founded, and, as would be seen in the following years, this recognition was irreversible and progressive.

If the rise of Human Rights and fundamental freedoms in the EU agenda did not alarm Turkey at first, its impact was definitely felt in the following years throughout EU–Turkey relations. In 1995, when it was time to complete the EU–Turkey Customs Union, the European Parliament (EP) refused to give its consent because of Human Rights abuses in Turkey. In response to this refusal, Turkey amended its Constitution and the ATL. When finally the EP consented to the establishment of a customs union between the EU and Turkey, it attached a Human Rights reservation to the relations.

In the following years, the pressure on Turkey to improve its Human Rights practices intensified. The European Court of Human Rights (ECtHR) in numerous petitions ruled against Turkey, finding it in violation of various Human Rights. The EP repeatedly chastised Turkey's Human Rights record, and the Council of Europe Parliamentary Assembly (PACE) over the years voiced its concern over Turkey's Human Rights practices and its compliance with ECtHR judgments. Turkey responded to these reports by pointing out that these Human Rights abuses were exaggerated and, even when valid, the abuses could be explained by the ongoing terrorism in the country.

Turkey's arguments were rarely accepted and the improvement of its Human Rights record became a precondition of its membership to the EU. Accordingly, in the Luxembourg European Council, Turkey's candidacy was deferred once more mainly because of its failure to fulfill the political Copenhagen criterion (Human Rights, rule of law, and protection of minorities). Ankara considered this decision as unjust and biased since, in Luxembourg, former communist countries and Cyprus were included in the list of candidates. To express its dissatisfaction with the decision, Ankara initially suspended political dialogue with the EU. Some months later, both Turkey and the EU decided to restore the bilateral relationship. In 1998, the European Commission prepared its first regular report on Turkey, which emphasized Turkey's failure to comply with the political criteria as the main obstacle to Turkey's candidacy.

Even when, owing to changing political conditions in the EU, Turkey was recognized as a "candidate State destined to join the Union on the basis of the same criteria as applied to the other candidates" in the Helsinki European Council in December 1999, the start of accession negotiations was deferred. The stated reason for this non-uniform treatment was again Turkey's shortcomings in the areas of "stability of institutions guaranteeing democracy, the rule of law, Human Rights and respect for and protection of minorities."

Thereafter, relations between the EU and Turkey became more predictable in the sense that the EU demanded improvements in Turkey's Human Rights practices and Turkey, motivated by prospective EU membership and benefiting from decreasing terrorism, complied.

In 2001, Turkey adopted the "Turkish National Programme for the Adoption of the Acquis," (NPAA) in which it promised the EU to undertake major legislative reforms, some in the short term (1–2 years) and some in the medium term (3–5 years). Shortly thereafter, Turkey amended more than one-fifth of the 177 articles of the 1982 Constitution. The amendments introduced new provisions in line with the priorities of the 2001 NPAA, such as freedom of thought and expression, prevention of torture, strengthening of democracy and civilian authority, freedom and security of the individual, right to privacy, the inviolability of the domicile, freedom of communication, freedom of residence and movement, freedom of association, and gender equality.

Starting in 2002, Turkey adopted seven legislative packages amending more than one code or law at a time, such as the Penal Code, the Press Law, the Law on Associations, the Law on Political Parties, and the ATL. The so-called "Harmonization Packages" were Turkey's attempts to redress shortcomings vis-à-vis the political criteria and to improve the Human Rights situation as quickly as possible. During this time, Turkey also signed or ratified a number of international conventions and agreements in order to participate more fully in the development of international Human Rights instruments (treaties, conventions, etc.).

In the meantime, pressure from the EP, EU, ECtHR, and PACE ensued, now focusing on the implementation of the Harmonization Packages. To comply with these demands, Turkey adopted several mechanisms for monitoring the implementation of legislative changes, and relevant Ministries issued a number of circulars in order to facilitate the effective implementation of the legislative reforms.

Finally, in December 2004, the Helsinki European Council decided that Turkey had improved the stability of institutions guaranteeing democracy, the rule of law, Human Rights, and respect for and protection of minorities. Deciding that Turkey was then in compliance with the minimum requirements of the political Copenhagen criterion, the European Council declared that accession negotiations could begin by late 2005. However, as a caveat, the Council decision stated that the negotiations could take a very long time and were not necessarily determinative of Turkey's EU membership.

*Turkey: Terrorism, Civil Rights, and the European Union* presents the story briefly stated above through the most significant public and legal documents. The focus is on Turkish laws used against terrorism, including those of a repressive nature, and the European Union's perception of these laws, as well as how and why these laws were amended to comply with European civil rights standards. This volume does not address other economic and political explanations for the troubled course of EU–Turkey relations over the years. The reader should keep in mind that economic issues, Cyprus, and territorial disputes between Turkey and Greece were also important factors in EU–Turkey relations. To demonstrate the importance of these issues, reference to portions of the Helsinki European Council's Presidency Conclusions will suffice.

> [The candidate states] must share the values and objectives of the European Union as set out in the Treaties. In this respect the European Council stresses the principle of peaceful settlement of disputes in accordance with the United Nations Charter and urges candidate States to make every effort to resolve any outstanding border disputes and other related issues. Failing this they should within a reasonable time bring the dispute to the International Court of Justice.
>
> The European Council underlines that a political settlement will facilitate the accession of Cyprus to the European Union. If no settlement has been reached by the completion of accession negotiations, the Council's decision on accession will be made without the above being a precondition. In this the Council will take account of all relevant factors.

Thus, an interested reader should consult the numerous publications that exist to understand the impact of these issues.

Limited and focused in its scope, this volume provides current background statistics and information about Turkey. Chapter 1 also outlines Turkey's twentieth century history through a narrative of the main points of political transition, its evolution into a modern democracy, and the effects of terrorism on this process.

Chapter 2 focuses on the military coup of 1980, the first counterterrorism measures, such as the imposition of martial law, taken by this state, and traces the evolution of the Turkish Constitution until the mid-1980s.

Chapter 3 presents the emergence of the Kurdish terrorism insurgency — the Kurdistan Workers' Party (PKK) — and Turkey's response to its activities. It later presents the incompatibility of certain counterterrorism measures with the European Convention on Human Rights. To provide all the dimensions of this issue, Chapter 4 documents the mechanisms through which Human Rights and fundamental freedoms initially gained importance and eventually became the founding blocks of the European Union. Chapters 5 and 6 details the role of

Human Rights in the EU by presenting documents intrinsic to the development of the EU's Human Rights policy.

Chapter 7 covers the era from 1963 to 1994—from the Ankara Agreement to the signing of the Customs Union Treaty. This part contains documentation of the problems that were posed by Turkey's Human Rights record to complete a thirty-two-year process. Chapter 8 focuses on the years following the signing of the 1995 Customs Union Treaty and presents documentation regarding the continuous damaging effect of the Human Rights situation in Turkey and what Turkey did in an attempt to achieve membership of the EU. As Human Rights issues have functioned as a serious impediment to Turkey's accession process, Chapter 9 provides additional Human Rights-related documents from the years 1996–98, including European resolutions and ECtHR court materials.

The 1999 Helsinki European Council Presidency Conclusions, various progress reports, and documents that reflect European encouragement of Turkish reforms are presented in Chapter 10. Chapter 11 covers events and documents from the year 2000 including ECtHR case reports, which motivated Turkey to initiate reforms in 2001, as offered in Chapter 12. Chapters 12 and 13 reflect the impact of the EU's demands on Turkey to improve its Human Rights record an assortment of relevant materials: EU documents demanding improvements and making these improvements a precondition of accession negotiations; and Turkish documents changing various laws that were in place to improve Human Rights while fighting terrorism.

Chapter 14 outlines Turkey's significant progress and effort in aligning itself with European Human Rights standards. It presents the December 2004 Brussels European Council Presidency Conclusions and other documents, which reflect Europe's attitude towards Turkey's membership and provide recommendations for improvements.

The final chapter includes documents to answer the question of where EU–Turkey relations are headed after the December 2004 Brussels European Council. It provides a range of documents to answer what legal measures can be expected to counter terrorism, and to improve Human Rights and fundamental freedoms; presents the most up-to-date developments in the areas of EU–Turkey relations; and incorporates a summary of the recent events in Turkey relating to Human Rights, the Kurdish issue, terrorist incidences, and counterterrorism measures.

To present the importance of Human Rights issues between the EU and Turkey, and to show the impact of the EU's "compliance with political Copenhagen precondition criteria," this volume contains 115 edited documents (most of which are from official sources) and 28 documents of commentary proposed by the editors. Where official documents were not available, or not translated into English, we either translated such documents or described them. Also, the text contains the editors' comments at certain points where the editors felt that such comments would either be helpful to the reader or would serve to explain related developments. These comments are based on either scholarly and well-supported articles or original documents.

Finally, owing to the number of documents included in this volume, we had to edit fiercely. In edited documents "\*\*\*" signifies major redactions, whereas an ellipsis ( ... ) is used for minor exclusions. The reader may also find it useful to consult the glossary since many of the acronyms and other terms used vary in form.

## Postscript

It is customary to update manuscripts before the page proofs are finalized and the book is being printed. This volume is no exception. Since the original draft was completed in December 2006, the editors decided to prepare a postscript focusing on 2007 developments before the scheduled publication in March 2008. A general review of both the domestic and international press coverage of significant events related to the Turkish political and security issues during the past year is bound to discover a proliferation of articles with the following headlines selected at random:

- Tensions in Turkey in advance of presidential elections
- Turkish judiciary at war with the AKP government to defend its independence
- Turkey's election a struggle over identity
- Turkish Radio and TV council issues warning to Turkish radio stations for broadcasting Islamic messages and calling for jihad
- Turkey reinforces Iraq border
- Iraq: Kurdistan province leader Massoud Al-Barazani warns Turkey not to interfere over Kirkuk
- Turkey and Iraq sign terrorism deal amid border row
- Turkey plays Mideast mediator
- Turkey needs to let NATO safeguard the Black Sea
- Greek Cypriot veto a myth
- Turkey lashes out at U.S. lawmakers for the Armenian 'Genocide' Resolution

On the basis of the typical aforementioned headlines, as well as numerous other articles and reports from governmental and non-governmental sources during 2007, what emerged were several significant developments in four major areas:

1. Political

In April, Foreign Minister Abdullah Gül was nominated by the AKP as their candidate for the Turkish Presidency. His selection was rejected by the political opposition and the heads of the Turkish Army. Additionally, hundreds of thousands of ordinary citizens demonstrated in Istanbul to express their support for the separation of state and religion and protested the apparent Islamization of Turkey. The following month, after a parliamentary deadlock over the candidacy of Gül, the incumbent president, Ahmet Necdet Sezer, was allowed to retain his office until the country elected a successor. As a result of the July 2007 election for the Grand National Assembly, which resulted in an increase in the popular vote for the AKP, Gül was able to win the presidential election against other opposition candidates. Although he became the first politician with an Islamic background to serve as the head of state since the creation of the modern Turkish Republic in 1923, the new president immediately pledged loyalty to both democracy and secularism. Finally, in October a referendum on the popular election for the Turkish Presidency was approved by 69% of the electorate, confirming the constitutional reforms of the AKP enacted earlier in the year.

2. PKK Terrorism and Response Strategies

It is not surprising that Turkey, a prime victim of terrorism over the past forty years, has once again become deeply concerned with security threats from both the PKK as well as other secular and Islamic extremists. In the last year the PKK intensified its attacks within the country against civilian and military targets. For instance, the militant Kurdistan Freedom Falcons claimed responsibility for bomb attacks in Istanbul and other locations in which nine people died and scores were injured. Additionally, extremists targeted Turkey's democratic structures; an armed attack on judges at the Council of State (the highest administrative court) resulted in the death of one judge and the wounding of four others.

Although the PKK announced a unilateral ceasefire on October 1, 2007, terrorism has escalated, particularly as a result of attacks originating from Kurdish terrorist bases in Northern Iraq. In response to the intensification of hostilities across the border, Turkey undertook successive air strikes and deployed troops against Kurdish terrorist targets inside Iraq. Apparently, Turkey's military actions were sanctioned by the United States which provided to its NATO ally the actionable intelligence required for such operations.

A few of Turkey's non-military response strategies in 2007 were also noteworthy. For instance, the Turkish Parliament revised the Law to Fight Terrorism, essentially broadening classification of crimes punishable as terrorism offenses. Additionally, Turkey ratified both the First Optional Protocol to the International Covenant on Civil and Political Rights (ICCPR) and the Second Optional Protocol to the ICCPR, aiming at the abolition of the death penalty.

To be sure, these and other measures have led to legal and diplomatic problems, including criticism by various Western governments and private bodies of Turkey's allegedly poor Human Rights record. Many were particularly concerned regarding restrictions on the freedom of expression, resulting in prosecutions brought under Article 30 of the Turkish Penal Code (TPC) which criminalizes denigration of "Turkishness," the Republic, and the institutions of the State. However most of these cases, such as that of Nobel Prize-winning novelist Orhan Pamuk, ended in acquittal.

3. EU Relations and the Accession Process

During 2007, Turkey and the EU continued negotiations in connection with several issues, including implementation of the Turkish roadmap for EU accession, enterprise and industry, financial control and statistics, health and consumer protection, and trans-European transport. These discussions went forward, although somewhat slowed, despite two major obstacles. One relates to the unique disposition of France as expressed by President Nicholas Sarkozy, eroding Turkey's accession process. The second was undertaken by the Greek Cypriot government who threatened to block accession talks if Turkey failed to open its seaports and airports to Cyprus and recognize the Cyprus government.

Another positive development during 2007 was the finding of the Parliamentary Assembly of the Council of Europe (PACE) that the general elections in Turkey were "transparent, professional, and efficient."

4. The Armenian Genocide Case

In January 2007, United States Congressman Adam Schiff (D, CA-29), with a substantial Armenian constituency, introduced with 211 other co-sponsors in the U.S. House of Representatives, the non-binding "Affirmation of the United States Record on the Armenian Genocide Resolution" (H.Res. 106). In March, the Senate Majority Whip Richard Durbin (D-IL) also introduced a resolution similar to the House's version on the Armenian Genocide in the U.S. Senate.

Although President George W. Bush opposed these congressional actions and Secretary of State Condoleezza Rice refused to accept the issue of genocide as a fact, the House Foreign Affairs Committee passed H.Res. 106 in a 27 to 21 committee vote. Turkey saw this development as a low-point in its relations with the United States and therefore there were worries about broader consequences for the alliance. Ankara had long called for an international commission to investigate the World War I era events. In the interim, the non-binding Resolution has stalled in Congress.

In light of the developments that took place in 2007, the question arises; what is the outlook on several key issues affecting Turkey in 2008 and beyond? Although no forecast can be definitive because of multiple domestic and international unknowns, three assumptions have a high degree of certainty. First, the AKP, under Prime Minister Recep Tayyip Erdoğan and President Abdullah Gül, remain in power until the next general elections in 2011. Second, the United States will continue to provide Turkey with important strategic and tactical intelligence relevant for fighting the PKK, most importantly ending cross-border attacks from Northern Iraq. Third, the Turkey EU accession process will advance as the country's economic reform efforts and its Human Rights policies are expected to make further progress.

As this book is being finalized in January 2008, a number of items in the economic sphere should also be noted: Turkey, Syria, and Iraq agreed on joint water development projects; Iran decided to build new pipelines designed to carry its natural gas to the Turkish market; and future plans to establish nuclear energy stations in Turkey, which would also enrich uranium, are currently being discussed within government ministries.

Finally, the editors wish to acknowledge the contributions of some of the individuals and institutions that participated in this academic project during the past four years. We are most appreciative of the continuing support of Professor Don Wallace, Chairman of the International Law Institute, for his guidance and for the "Foreword" to this volume. Thanks are also due to Michael S. Swetnam, Chairman and CEO of the Potomac Institute for Policy Studies, who provided office space and facilities to our staff who worked on some aspects of the manuscript. Thanks are due to several research assistants including Jack Baber, Brett Wallace, Steven Lockfield, and Jennifer Zewin and the most recent interns, Steve Mathany and Jeremy Becker. Special gratitude also goes to Janet Brenner for her superb editorial contribution.

This book is dedicated to the Turkish victims of terrorism with the hope that the motto of the founder of the modern Republic, Mustafa Kemal Atatürk, "peace at home, peace in the world," will ultimately become a reality.

# 1 Turkey: country information

# Document no. 1

**General information**

Turkey is one of the largest non-Arab Muslim countries with its territory and population on two continents — Asia and Europe — separated by the Bosporus. As a democracy with a predominantly Muslim population, which borders the Middle East, the Balkans and the Black, Aegean, and Mediterranean seas, it is a strategic partner not only for its neighbors but also for the United States and Europe. With a total area of 780,588 square kilometers and a population of over 70 million (est. 2006), the country is significantly larger than others near it. Ankara, the capital, is located in the heart of Anatolia, and Istanbul — the center of economy and culture — has one of the largest populations — over 12 million (est. 2008) — of all European cities[1].

Turkey has a fairly young population with a median age of roughly 28.3 (est. 2006). Eighty percent of its inhabitants are ethnically Turkic-speaking people, while the rest consider themselves to be Kurdish, Zaza, Arab, Georgian, Circassian, Armenian, Greek, Jewish, and others. Despite the significant Kurdish population (close to 20 percent), Turkish is the only officially recognized language. Because eight-year education is now compulsory, full literacy has been attained by about 87.4 percent (est. 2004) of its people.

As over one-third of the population is employed in agriculture in a land dotted by remote and barren regions, poverty and economic inequality is a reality. Political leaders have struggled to transform Turkey's economy and boost its gross national income per capita by developing strong industrial and service sectors with 22.8 percent and 41.2 percent labor force employment, respectively.[2]

Despite the manifold problems the country faces, it has managed to emerge as a progressive nation with a modernized society after years of turbulence, and to create itself out of a crumbling and occupied Ottoman Empire. Its national ethic emphasizes secular government, women's rights, and economic growth. Ranking ninety-second on the Human Development Index,[3] there is room for improvement, which it has been trying to accomplish by taking bold steps towards accession into the European Union, among other measures. While Turkey faces challenges such as neighboring turbulent regions, combating secessionist movements, and corruption, when weighed against its twentieth century experience it has taken significant steps in achieving the status of a modern and civilized nation.

# Document no. 2

### Historical overview[4]

The allied forces partitioned the declining Ottoman Empire after World War I. While turbulence appeared to have abated elsewhere, all was not quiet in Anatolia. Under the leadership of Mustafa Kemal Pasha ("Atatürk"), the Turkish people rose up and demanded independence from their occupiers. This nationalist movement expelled the allies and abolished the Ottoman Sultanate.

In 1923, Kemal declared Turkey an independent republic and promised sweeping political, social, and economic reforms. On assuming office, Atatürk initiated a series of radical reforms of the country's political, social, and economic life that were aimed at rapidly transforming Turkey into a modern state. A secular legal code, modeled along European lines, was introduced that completely altered laws affecting women, marriage, and family relations. Women's rights eventually included universal suffrage in 1934.

Atatürk also urged his fellow citizens to look and act like Europeans. Turks were encouraged to wear European-style clothing and surnames were adopted. Likewise, Atatürk insisted on cutting links with the past that he considered anachronistic. Titles of honor were abolished. The wearing of the fez, which had been introduced a century earlier as a modernizing reform to replace the turban, was outlawed because it had become, for the nationalists, a symbol of the reactionary Ottoman regime.

The ideological foundation of Atatürk's reform program became known as Kemalism. Its main points were enumerated in the "Six Arrows" of Kemalism: republicanism, nationalism, populism, reformism, etatism (statism), and laicism (secularism). These were regarded as "fundamental and unchanging principles" guiding the republic and were written into Turkey's new 1924 Constitution,[5] proclaimed by the Grand National Assembly to replace the 1876 document that had served as the legal framework of the republican government. The principle of republicanism — that "sovereignty is vested in the nation" and not in a single ruler — was included in the Constitution.

Displaying considerable ingenuity, Atatürk set about reinventing the Turkish language and recasting Turkish history in a nationalist mold. The President himself went out into the park in Ankara on Sunday, the newly established day of rest, to teach the Latin alphabet adapted to Turkish as part of the language reform. Socially, Kemal's policy skimmed on the rhetoric of populism and

Turkish classless all-inclusiveness, and encompassed not only the notion that all Turkish citizens were equal but that all of them were Turks. What remained of the *millet* system that had provided communal autonomy to other ethnic groups[6] was abolished. Reformism legitimized the radical means by which changes in Turkish political and social life were implemented, and etatism emphasized the central role reserved to the state in directing the nation's economic activities. This concept was cited particularly to justify state planning of Turkey's mixed economy and large-scale investment in state-owned enterprises. An important aim of Atatürk's economic policies was to prevent foreign interests from exercising undue influence on the Turkish economy.

In the reform process, the national hero Kemal secured his hold over the citizenry and limited foreign influence by positioning the state as the headmaster of the fledgling nation-building process and using the Six Arrows tactfully. Republicanism gave birth to "representative" practice, nationalism supported Turkish sovereignty and defined Turkish identity, and laicism — the total separation of state and religion — defined the political structure.

Of all the Kemalist reforms, the exclusion of Islam from an official role in the life of the nation shocked Atatürk's contemporaries most profoundly. The abolition of the Caliphate ended any connection between the state and religion. The Islamic religious orders were suppressed, *madrasas*[7] were closed, public education was secularized, and the *sharia*[8] was revoked. These changes required readjustment of the entire social framework of the Turkish people. Despite subsequent protests, Atatürk conceded nothing to the traditionalists.

According to some commentators, Atatürk's success can largely be attributed to his favoritism and use of the military, through which he was able to institute reforms. As Kemal believed that authoritarianism was necessary before the people could be trusted to make safe and progressive choices at the polls, he governed a single-party state, with the Republican People's Party (CHP) founded to promote his ideas and legitimize his rule, from inside a unicameral legislature — the Grand National Assembly.[9] Kemal also encouraged the founding of an opposition party, the Democratic Party (DP), and forced several officials to join it to counter him in government. Later, some DP members, such as Adnan Menderes, became significantly influential political figures.[10]

The venerated leader died in 1938, but his policies remained consistent through his right-hand man, his chief lieutenant Ismet Inönü. Turkey maintained a neutral position until the last days of World War II, when it too declared war on the Axis powers and was allowed to participate in the Conference on International Organization during which the United Nations Charter was drafted in 1945.[11] In 1950, 88 percent of the eligible electorate went to the polls. The DP won a sweeping majority under a very different banner of reform. Under Menderes, the DP government attempted to promote privatization and a push toward industrial-sector activities. Turkey also joined NATO in 1952.

These reforms produced a rift not only in the government but in the populace as well. The CHP's and DP's inability to compromise was reflected by civil unrest caused by students and factions throughout Turkey. The government used the military to enforce martial law. As a result, the armed forces took it as their responsibility to enforce order and fix the political crisis — a pattern developed for years to come. Furthermore, the leading military figures believed that the DP government had strayed too far from Atatürk's socialist principles; they therefore staged the first military coup in 1960.

The Council for National Unity was established as an interim non-civilian governing body. General Cemal Gursel sought to return control of the government to a civilian body. While the military has always maintained that the return to civilian democracy was all along the goal, some commentators believe that he intended to return the power to civilians because a civilian-controlled institution would be better prepared to manage Turkey's deepening financial problems such as rises in debt and inflation. An interim civilian legislature drafted a new constitution, which passed in national referendum in 1961. It created a bicameral Grand National Assembly, a formal separation of powers,[12] and elections were held.

Ismet Inönü was chosen in 1961 as Prime Minister but was unable to secure a majority or form a coalition in government. The 1965 election brought in the Justice Party (Adalet Partisi; AP); and Suleyman Demirel became Prime Minister. He encouraged reforms: religious tolerance, a mixed state-directed economy, increased privatization, and foreign investment. The pro-Western attitude sparked a nationalist, agrarian-orientated, and a religiously conservative reaction in the form of political parties such as the Nationalist Action Party (MHP). The AP lost its majority in the next election and the late 1960s and 1970s were scarred by violence as the "Grey Wolves," the ultra-nationalist Nationalist Movement Party's (MHP) armed youth movement, clashed with far-left communist factions. The political and social unrest continued into 1971 with outbreaks of violence among students and trade unions, and by Kurdish separatists.

The DP and AP had promised reforms and civil peace, but factional infighting prevented the government from taking effective action. Therefore, the military put pressure on the government by threatening to stage another coup in 1971. This time, an "above-party" government was created primarily for the purpose of suppressing the violence through oppressive martial measures.[13]

The 1973 oil shock hit all corners of the world; the Turkish economy was not excluded. In the face of growing political and economic tension, Greece staged a coup in Cyprus in 1974, which Turkey interpreted as a threat to the Turkish minority on the island. Both sides sent troops, and, after days of battle and a collapse in peace negotiations, a line was drawn apportioning the island into Greek and Turkish states. While Turkey continues to assert a right to the northern portion, the international arena does not recognize its claim.

On the mainland, the government was deadlocked without a clear majority. The political struggle inside the legislature overflowed into the streets once more. Left and right groups clashed in universities, sectarian violence in the southern city of Kahramanmaras inflamed the situation as Sunni and Alevi Muslims fought each other; meanwhile, the Kurds began to voice their own concerns. The government again imposed martial law. Finally, in 1979, Demirel returned by popular election to form a technocratic government and imposed draconian martial laws restricting unions and public assembly.

Military leaders were still dissatisfied since these steps had not been taken to mollify the factional disputes and address the social unrest. By August 1980, almost 2000 people had died as a result of clashes between the left- and right-wing factions since the beginning of the year — regardless of the extension of martial law in twenty out of the sixty-seven provinces. Despite an economic stabilization package from the International Monetary Fund (IMF), the armed forces staged another coup in 1980 to clamp down on the fighting once more in an attempt to bring back the concepts behind Kemalism. The coup leaders formed the Council of National Security (CNS), which implemented martial law throughout all of Turkey. Political parties were banned and some influential left-orientated leaders were killed. Over 123,000 people were put behind bars; some were tortured and/or executed. As a consequence of government efforts to suppress civil disorder through martial law,[14] economic activity was disrupted in all rural areas. The Kurdish population, living largely in one of the most impoverished areas of Turkey, suffered exponentially.

Overall, it can be inferred that Kemal's first wave of reforms was productive and beneficial in comparison with the declining Ottoman Empire. All the other alterations ended in violence because each step toward "modernization" created an even larger rift in government. The evidently warring ideologies of a nationalized state-run versus a private export-driven economy transposed themselves into political parties that had diametrically opposing conceptions of a novel Turkish state that refused to concede to each other. This resulted in uncontrollable violence for which the government repeatedly prescribed an ineffective policy and used martial law imposed by the military.

Historically, the military pledged itself to Kemalism and believed in its methodology: controlled reform in the hands of the government. Therefore, when problems arose, the armed forces overstepped their democratic bounds in their attempts to reassert the concept.[15] They would temporarily bandage the political wound through coups followed by oppressive martial law. As the military leaders were not equipped to take on the pressing issue of integrating Turkey into the modern world economy, the inevitable return of civilian rule brought with it another wave of instability.

In 1982, the Turkish people voted for the third constitution prepared by the 1980 coup makers, which extended the powers of the President inter alia: a seven-year term and power to appoint the Prime Minister.[16] A 10 percent threshold on party seats was instituted[17] to streamline the post-election government-forming process. Under Turgut Ozal, the Motherland Party (MP) won the 1983 election and the leader managed to bring about cogent reforms with the assistance of the previously granted IMF package.

The Turkish economy of the 1980s was significantly more successful than that of the 1970s. The country's economic stability can be attributed to fiscal austerity measures and other conditions prescribed by the IMF. While purchasing power fell and inflation rose, the industrial sector grew and so in turn did exports. The country began to overhaul its infrastructure, and Turkey began to assume its role as an intermediary between Europe and the Middle East.

Yet not all factions were satisfied; the Kurdistan Workers' Party (PKK), an organization internationally recognized as a terrorist group, began a terrorist guerrilla campaign in 1984 with the goal of a separate Kurdistan. They attacked Turks in Kurdish neighborhoods, government targets, and pro-government co-ethnics. During the Gulf War in 1991, the PKK established its base of operations in northern Iraq. As violence escalated in the southeastern region, the government imposed martial law. Additionally, it passed stringent anti-terrorism legislation, known as the Anti Terrorism Law (ATL).

The PKK was not the only violently active party. In addition to some far-left terrorist organizations, Armenian terrorist groups such as the Armenian Secret Army for the Liberation of Armenia (ASALA) and the Justice Commandos of the Armenian Genocide (JCAG) began to stage attacks in the 1970s and 1980s. They justified their use of violence as revenge for the "alleged"[18] Armenian genocide of 1915–17.[19] It is estimated that, during the period from 1973 to 1985, various Armenian terrorist groups committed over 200 terrorist attacks on Turkish targets in Turkey and abroad.[20]

Ozal died in 1993. The prime minister and leader of the True Path Party (DYP) at the time — Suleyman Demirel — was elected by the Turkish Grand National Assembly as the country's next President for a full seven-year term. In turn, Tansu Ciller became the first female prime minister as the new leader of the DYP. She pushed for additional progressive reforms such as increasing privatization and a relationship with the EU. While her policies brought some success, she was unable to cement a coalition. The 1995 elections brought in a more conservative, Islam-orientated coalition government. It lost ground in the next election, as Turkish citizens voted along secular party lines. While the prime ministerial position has been transferred over half a dozen times since, the office of the President has remained a stable position for guidance and decision-making.

In 1999, after a number of deadly terrorist attacks, the PKK declared a unilateral cease-fire in 1999 after the capture of its leader, Abdullah Ocalan. As the terrorist organization predictably asserted that their demands for Kurdish autonomy were not met, they annulled the truce in June of 2004. Since 1984, PKK attacks and clashes with government troops have culminated in the death of over 30,000 people to date. The recent increase in insurgency and the possibility of a Turkish incursion into northern Iraq to fight the PKK has transformed accession negotiations into a challenging prospect for both Turkey and the EU. Ahmet Necdet Sezer's[21] term as the tenth President of Turkey expired in 2007, and Abdullah Gul, former minister of Foreign Affairs, who is regarded as Islamist in some circles, was elected as the new president.

As this brief overview suggests, while Turkey has a strong potential to grow and improve its democracy, there are numerous problems that Turkey might face in the future. The international community and particularly the EU will watch for developments as Turkey plays the balancing act of protecting its own citizens from terrorism, maintaining international Human Rights standards, and expanding and developing its economy, while negotiating for full EU membership.

## References and further information

*Modern Turkey* at http://www.naqshbandi.org/ottomans/modern.htm

Talip Kucukcan. State, Islam, and religious liberty in modern Turkey: reconfiguration of religion in the public sphere. *Brigham Young University Law Review*, 2003, 475.

*The Library of Congress, Country Studies: Turkey* (1995) at http://lcweb2.loc.gov/frd/cs/trtoc.html (last visited March 2, 2005).

*Turkey: Country Studies* at http://lcweb2.loc.gov/frd/cs/trtoc.html

*United Kingdom Home Office Country Information and Policy Unit, Country Assessment: Turkey (April 2001)* at http://www.ecoi.net/pub/dh697/01377tur.html (last visited March 2, 2005).

# Document no. 3

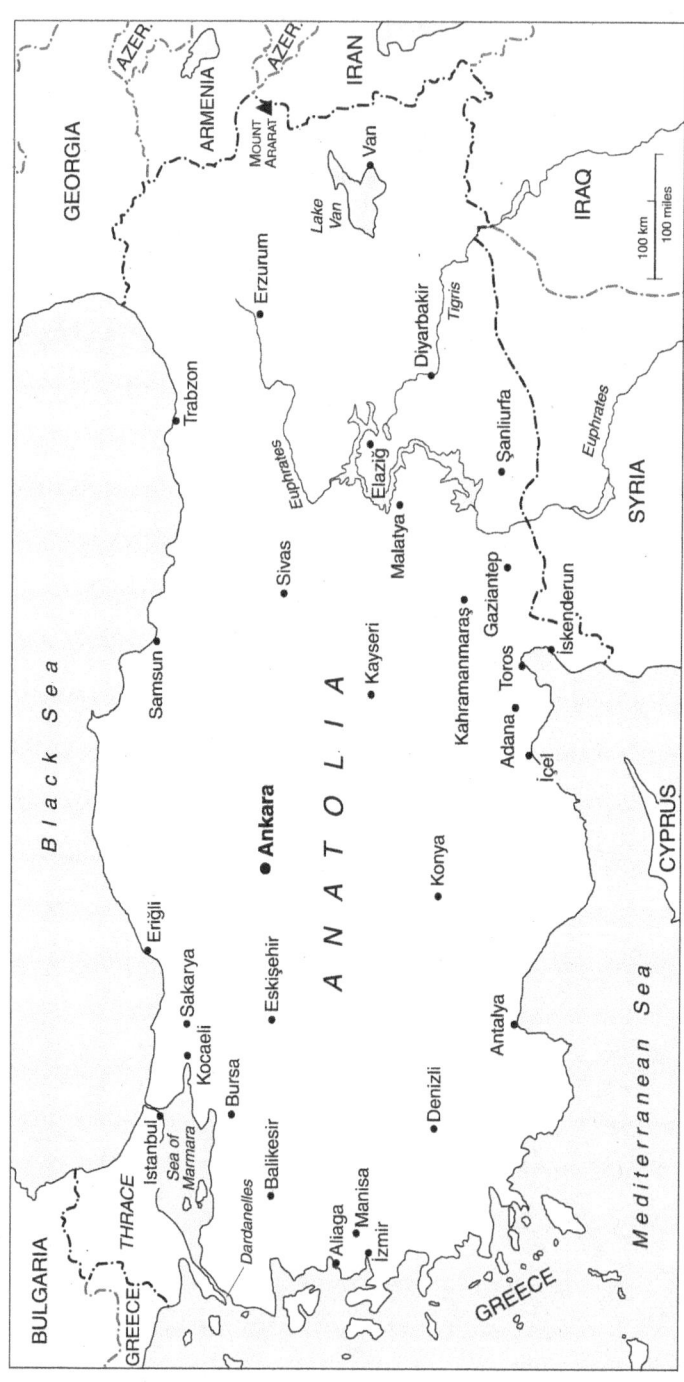

Map 1 Turkey.

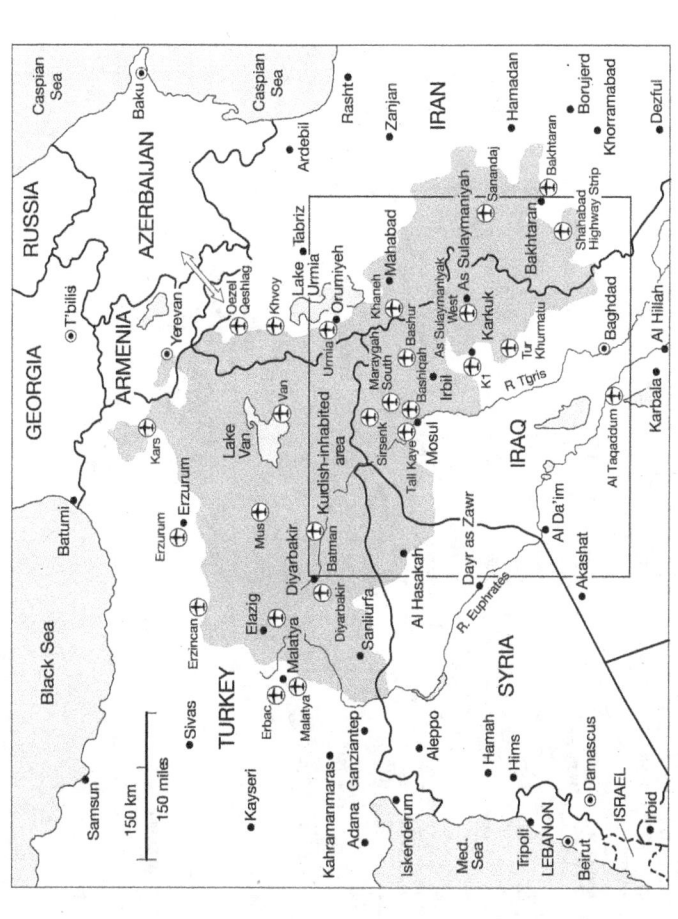

*Map 2* Areas of Kurdish population.

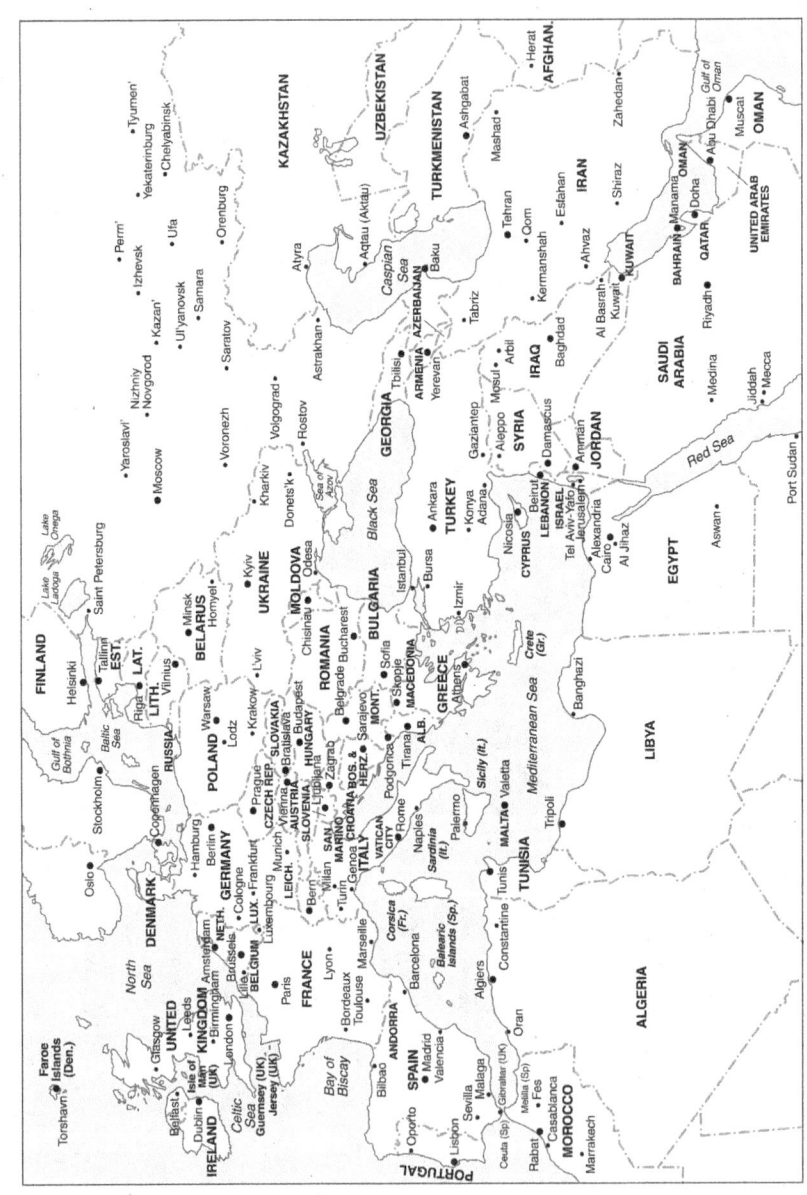

*Map 3* Turkey in its region.

# 2 1980 Military coup, martial law and state of emergency, and a new Constitution

# Document no. 4

## 1980 Coup D'etat

***Chairman of the Military Chiefs of Staff General Kenan Evren's radio address to the nation on September 12, 1980: Military Communiqué no. 1[1]***

Honorable Turkish Nation ... The government of the Republic of Turkey, as you have witnessed in recent years, faces physical and serious hostile attacks against its regime and independence by the provocations of domestic and foreign foes. [As a result] the state and its principal organs have been rendered inoperative, constitutional organs have become obsolete and silent, and political parties with their intransigent attitude have failed to form the prerequisite consensus to save the nation and have failed to take necessary precautions.

In short, the state has been left powerless and made impotent. Honorable Turkish nation, under such conditions, the Turkish Armed Forces, to protect the Republic of Turkey, have decided to take absolute control of the whole country in the name of the Turkish Nation by the power bestowed upon it by Law on Internal Affairs of the Armed Forces. We expect citizens to silently remain at their homes, listen to their radios and televisions, become aware of further Communiqués, obey orders and trust the Turkish Armed Forces which has spawned from it.

*Editors' comment*: At about 6 o'clock in the morning, Chief of Staff Kenan Evren addressed the Turkish nation with the preceding speech. When the speech was delivered, the National Security Council had already abolished the government, the Senate and the Parliament, and curfew and martial law all around the country had been imposed starting at 05:00. In the aftermath of the coup, the Constitution was rendered invalid; the activities of political parties were suspended; the immunities of members of the Parliament and the Senate were lifted; former political leaders, thousands of suspected terrorists, and political extremists were all detained; large caches of weapons and ammunition were captured; all trade unions and associations were closed; and all foreign travel was suspended. For Kenan Evren's radio and television address on September

12, 1980, at 13:00 explaining the reasons for the coup in detail, see http://www.cunta.org/12eylul/6.htm (available in Turkish); for an article written right after the coup, see Feroz Ahmad, Military intervention and the crises in Turkey, *MERIP Reports*, January 1981, pp. 5–24; see also Ben Lombardi, Turkey: the return of reluctant generals? *Political Science Quarterly*, Summer 1997, pp. 191–215.

# Document no. 5

## Martial law and state of emergency in Turkey[2]

| Province | Martial law | State of emergency |
|---|---|---|
| Adana | 12.26.78–11.19.85 | 11.19.85–3.19.87 |
| Adıyaman | 4.26.79–11.19.85 | 11.19.85–3.19.86 |
| Afyon | 9.12.80–7.19.84 | – |
| Ağrı | 4.20.80–11.19.85 | 11.19.85–3.19.87 |
| Amasya | 9.12.80–7.19.84 | 7.19.84–3.19.85 |
| Ankara | 12.26.78–7.19.85 | 7.19.85–11.19.86 |
| Antalya | 9.12.80–3.19.85 | 3.19.85–7.19.87 |
| Artvin | 9.12.80–7.19.85 | 7.19.85–3.19.86 |
| Aydın | 9.12.80–7.19.84 | 7.19.84–11.19.84 |
| Balıkesir | 9.12.80–7.19.84 | 7.19.84–11.19.84 |
| Bilecik | 9.12.80–3.19.84 | – |
| Bartın | 8.28.91 | 5.16.90–10.2.97 |
| Bingol | 12.26.78–3.19.86 | 3.19.86–10.2.97 |
| Bitlis | 9.12.80–3.19.84 | 3.19.84–.19.84; Reimposed 3.19.93–10.2.97 |
| Bolu | 9.12.80–7.19.84 | – |
| Burdur | 9.12.80–3.19.84 | – |
| Bursa | 9.12.80–3.19.85 | 3.19.85–3.19.86 |
| Canakkale | 9.12.80–3.19.84 | 3.19.84–7.19.84 |
| Cankırı | 9.12.80–3.19.84 | 3.19.84–11.19.84 |
| Corum | 9.12.80–7.19.84 | 7.19.84–7.19.85 |
| Denizli | 9.12.80–11.19.84 | 11.19.84–3.19.85 |
| Diyarbakır | 4.26.79–7.19.87 | 7.19.87–11.30.02 |
| Edirne | 9.12.80–7.19.85 | 7.19.85–11.19.85 |
| Elazig | 12.26.78–3.19.86 | 3.19.86–3.19.93 |
| Erzincan | 12.26.78–4.20.80; 9.12.80–87.19.85 | 7.19.85–11.19.85 |
| Erzurum | 12.26.78–11.19.85 | 11.19.85–3.19.86 |
| Eskisehir | 9.12.80–11.19.84 | 11.19.84–3.19.85 |
| Gaziantep | 12.26.78–11.19.85 | 11.19.85–3.19.86 |
| Giresun | 9.12.80–11.19.84 | 11.19.84–3.19.85 |
| Gümüshane | 9.12.80–3.19.84 | 3.19.84–11.19.84 |

*continued*

## 18  *Military coup, martial law and state of emergency*

| Province | Martial law | State of emergency |
|---|---|---|
| Hakkari | 4.26.79–7.19.87 | 7.19.87–7.30.02 |
| Hatay | 2.20.80–11.19.85 | 11.19.85–3.19.87 |
| Icel | 9.12.80–3.19.85 | 3.19.85–7.19.86 |
| Istanbul | 12.26.78–11.19.85 | 11.19.85–11.19.88 |
| Izmir | 2.20.80–7.19.85 | 7.19.85–11.19.86 |
| K. Maraş | 12.26.78–3.19.85 | 3.19.85–11.19.85 |
| Kars | 12.26.78–11.19.85 | 11.19.85–11.19.86 |
| Kastamonu | 9.12.80–3.19.84 | 3.19.84–7.19.84 |
| Kayseri | 9.12.80–11.19.84 | – |
| Kırklareli | 9.12.80–3.19.84 | – |
| Kırşehir | 9.12.80–3.19.84 | 3.19.84–11.19.84 |
| Kocaeli | 9.12.80–3.19.85 | 3.19.85–11.19.85 |
| Konya | 9.12.80–11.19.84 | – |
| Kutahya | 9.12.80–3.19.84 | – |
| Malatya | 12.26.78–3.19.85 | 3.19.85–3.19.86 |
| Manisa | 9.12.80–11.19.84 | 11.19.84–3.19.85 |
| Mardin | 4.26.79–7.19.87 | 7.19.87–11.29.96 |
| Mugla | 9.12.80–7.19.84 | – |
| Mus | 9.12.80–3.19.84 | – |
| Nevsehir | 9.12.80–7.19.84 | – |
| Nigde | 9.12.80–7.19.84 | 7.19.84–11.19.84 |
| Ordu | 9.12.80–7.19.85 | 7.19.85–7.19.86 |
| Rize | 9.12.80–7.19.84 | 7.19.84–3.19.85 |
| S. Urfa | 12.26.78–3.19.86 | 3.19.86–3.19.87 |
| Sakarya | 9.12.80–7.19.84 | 7.19.84–3.19.85 |
| Samsun | 9.12.80–3.19.85 | 3.19.85–7.19.85 |
| Siirt | 4.26.79–7.19.87 | 7.19.87–11.30.99 |
| Sinop | 9.12.80–3.19.84 | 3.19.84–7.19.84 |
| Sivas | 12.26.78–2.26.80; 9.12.80–3.19.85 | 3.19.85–7.19.86 |
| Sirnak | 5.16.90 | 5.16.90–11.30.02 |
| Tekirdag | 9.12.80–7.19.84 | – |
| Tokat | 9.12.80–3.19.85 | 3.19.85–7.19.85 |
| Trabzon | 9.12.80–3.19.85 | 3.19.85–7.19.85 |
| Tunceli | 4.26.79–3.19.86 | 3.19.86–7.30.02 |
| Usak | 9.12.80–11.19.84 | 11.19.84–3.19.85 |
| Van | 9.12.80–3.19.87 | 3.19.87–7.30.00 |
| Yozgat | 9.12.80–7.19.84 | |
| Zonguldak | 9.12.80–3.19.85 | 3.19.85–7.19.85 |

# Document no. 6

## Introduction to anti-terrorism measures in the Republic of Turkey[3]

In the Turkish example of the fight against terrorism, preventive measures providing security forces with almost unfettered power have been predominant. Focusing on domestic terrorism, especially against the Kurdish Workers' Party (PKK), these measures, authorized by the Constitution and respective laws, introduced strict regimes in areas under the threat of terrorism.

## Proclamation of a state of emergency and martial law

Within the framework of preventive measures, the most important legal instruments were probably the proclamation of a state of emergency and martial law in affected areas. These declarations enabled the government to issue decrees having force of law to monitor publications of the press, establish a Special Governor, and introduce other measures.

The Constitution codifies the conditions for declaration of a state of emergency or martial law through articles 199–122. In addition to the Constitution, the Martial Law Act and the State of Emergency Act delineate the procedures to be followed, the manner in which freedoms can be restricted or suspended, and the powers given to the executive authority of the state of emergency rule or martial law area.

These powers were extensively used in the regions in which intense terror activity took place. States of emergency rule or martial law were declared in different cities over the course of time. Since these declarations were only temporarily valid, the Turkish Parliament periodically declared either martial law or state of emergency rule in certain cities.

Furthermore, by the power given in the Constitution to issue decrees having force of law, respective Councils of Ministers first issued a decree establishing the office of a Special Governor (decree having force of Law no. 285 of July 20, 1987) and then enlarged the powers of the Governor with Decree 430 of December 15, 1990. Under these decrees, the Special Governor had jurisdiction over eight provinces and was empowered to evacuate villages, permit or prohibit gatherings and strikes, hire and fire civil servants, and regulate the import of goods into the region. He possessed substantial powers of censorship with regards to the press coverage of the regions. This also included control over imports of press outputs and the banning of "unwanted persons" from the area. Moreover, he was only directly accountable to the Council of Ministers, who were entitled to direct the provincial governors in matters of government and even control the coordination of police and gendarmerie activities.

### *Enlarging the powers of the security forces*

The responsibility for maintaining security and order in Turkey's rural areas was transferred to the gendarmerie in 1983 with Law no. 2803 of March 10, 1983. Drawn from the conscripts and headed by professional officers, the institution thereafter performed police duties in rural areas where police infrastructure did not exist. By article 9(1) of the aforementioned law, the gendarmerie was given the power to substitute for the civil servant in his absence. In addition to that, another decree made possible the use of the gendarmerie by the Special Governor.

Furthermore, in order to coordinate and optimize the fight against terrorism, a "Counter-Terrorism and Warfare Office" was established in 1986. This was complemented by the founding of the "Special Warfare Office" by a decree. The members of these offices were placed under the authority of the Ministry of Interior and its members conducted covert operations under deep cover.

## Civilians used

In the mid-1980s, with an amendment to the law called the "Rural Communities Act" (Law no. 442 of April 27, 1924), a rural community protection system was formed in villages (and thirty-seven cities) in the areas affected by terrorism.

These units, acting as village guards, were trained, armed, and paid by the government. Mobilization of locals, mostly ethnic Kurds, proved to be effective in preventing logistical support to PKK and protecting facilities such as factories, pipelines, or oil fields, as well as secluded villages.

## Repentance laws

The base of terrorist organizations in Turkey has been closely connected to the socio-economic structure. Thus, many teenagers, in the absence of a welcoming government and worsening economic conditions, became members of terror organizations. To break the cycle and to enable the new PKK conscripts to rejoin the society, numerous repentance laws were passed.

In these laws passed in 1985, 1988, 1990, 1992, 1995, and 1999, the members of the PKK who had only committed minor offenses or no crimes and who were willing to contribute to the resolution of crimes attributed to the PKK were granted immunity or considerably reduced sentences.

However, despite granting immunity, these laws excluded members of the command structure, or those PKK members who had killed members of security forces. In short, it can be said that these laws provided both carrots and sticks for PKK members.

## Article 221

"(1) No penalty shall be imposed on any founders or administrators of the organization who dissolve or initiate dissolution of the organization by providing information prior to any investigation being launched into the formation of a criminal organization, or prior to any crime being committed to further the organization's aims.

(2) No penalty shall be imposed on any organization member who notifies the authorities of their voluntary dissociation from the organization without having participated in any offence committed by the organization.

(3) No penalty shall be imposed on any organization member apprehended before participating in any crime committed by the organization provided that they repent and provide information likely to lead to the dissolution of the organization or the apprehension of its members.

(4) Penalties for the offence of establishing, administering or becoming a member of a criminal organization shall not be imposed on any person who is the founder, administrator or member of a criminal organization or who is not a member but who commits crimes on behalf of the organization or who assists the organization knowingly and willingly provided that they surrender voluntarily and provide information concerning the structure and activities of the organization. Where the person provides such information after being apprehended, the penalty imposed for the crime shall be reduced by one third to three fourth.

(5) Anyone who benefits under provisions for effective contrition shall be subject to probation for a term of one year. The term of probation may be extended for up to three years.

# Document no. 7

## Martial Law Act of 13 May 1971[4]

### *Chapter one: General principles*

*Proclamation of martial law*

*Article 1.* The proclamation of martial law under Article 124 of the Turkish Constitution and the notifications detailing the districts or provinces in which and the duration for which it shall remain in force shall be made public by such media as may be deemed appropriate by the Ministry of Internal Affairs.

*Enforcement of martial law*

*Article 2.* 1. The duties and powers of police forces concerned with general security and public safety shall, in districts coming within the scope of a martial law proclamation, be transferred to the martial law command. The entire police force in such districts shall be placed under the authority of the Martial Law Commander.

2. The police forces in districts under martial law shall report to the concerned military authorities for the discharge of their duties connected with martial law and to judicial and administrative authorities for the discharge of their other duties.

3. The National Intelligence Organization shall cooperate with the martial law command.

4. The Martial Law Commander shall exercise the duties and powers vested in him by this Act through the local police and military units placed under his command. Both in times of peace and in emergencies the Martial Law Commander shall ask the garrison commander of his district or the garrison commander of the district nearest to him to place under his command as many such units as he may consider necessary. Such a request shall be complied with immediately.

5. The Martial Law Commander may change the postings of both the police and military personnel within the boundaries of his district. He may deploy military personnel to reinforce police forces whenever circumstances warrant it.

In such circumstances, the executive personnel shall continue to perform their duties in the capacity of advisors under the command of the Martial Law Commander.

6. Orders relating to the execution of services shall be carried out by the governmental agencies and organizations within the district.

7. Except with the permission of the Martial Law Commander, the resignation or retirement formalities of personnel serving under the martial law command or of those who have been given assigned similar duties may not be finalized nor can such personnel be assigned a new posting for as long as martial law remains in force.

8. [Inserted by Decree 2301 of September 19, 1980, and amended by Decree 2766 of December 28, 1982] Any order of the Martial Law Commander relating to the appointment or dismissal of civil servants — within the framework of the relevant laws — whose services are deemed [superfluous] or whose continuance in office is deemed to be injurious to the general security, public safety and public order of the region, and to the discharge or removal from office of personnel in the local administration shall be immediately executed. The provisions of the Law on the Retirement Pension Fund of the Turkish Republic and of the Law on Other Social Security Organizations to which these are subject shall apply. Employees and other public officials and workers employed in public services so discharged shall not be re-employed in the public services. In respect of orders related to persons who come within the scope of Article 21 of the present law, the provisions contained in the respective laws apply.

## Duties and authorities

*Article 3.* 1. [Amended by Decree 2301] The Martial Law Commander is charged with the preservation and promotion of the general security, public safety and public order in areas where martial law is in force. He is furthermore authorized to take the following measures if necessary.

a. To search: lodgings; all types of premises including those belonging to associations, political parties, trade unions and clubs; business premises; establishments belonging to persons (real or artificial, including autonomous corporations) and their dependents; all kind of covered and open spaces; and to intercept letters, cables and other consignments and search them as well as persons, without a warrant, application or demand for such acts, and to seize articles likely to be of evidentiary value or are liable to forfeiture.
b. To impose censorship on, restrict or interrupt any radio or television broadcasts or telecommunications.
c. [Amended by Laws 2301 and 2766] To control all verbal, written and pictorial communications, films or sound transmissions, publications, correspondence, letters, cables and other consignments; to ban or impose censorship on all kinds of newspapers, periodicals and books, and on the

printing or distribution of other publications; to prohibit the possession, or carrying into a martial law region of more than one copy of such publications; to seize all kinds of documents including books, periodicals, newspapers, brochures, posters, pamphlets, placards, records, tapes as well as broadcasting and communication media and to close down printing houses and record and tape manufacturing workshops; to take necessary measures to destroy those articles deemed by the martial law command to be objectionable or to return them to their owners if it is decided that they should not be confiscated; and to require special authorization for the publication of new newspapers and periodicals.

d. [Amended by Decree 2836 of June 3, 1983] To control the movement of individuals convicted of offenses against public order, individual freedom, public safety or state forces, or for murder or assault and battery, and those who are under general surveillance or have no fixed address in areas where martial law is in force or are suspects; to relocate persons found to be carrying out activities injurious to the general security and public order and to bar them entry to certain areas under martial law or to prohibit their settlement in such areas; and to deport those whose presence is deemed to be harmful to places outside areas where martial law is in force.

Those deported on the grounds that their activities are deemed to be injurious to the general security and public order may be ordered to remain outside the areas where martial law is in force for a period determined by the Martial Law Commander not exceeding five years and they may be compelled to reside in a place specified by the Ministry of the Interior;

e. To prohibit the storage, preparation, production or transportation of all kinds of arms, ammunition, bombs, explosives, radioactive materials or gases and to order the delivery of these items and of articles, tools and instruments used in the fabrication or production thereof; to carry out searches for such articles and seize them.

f. [Amended by Decree 2301] To ban or impose restrictions on trade union activities such as strikes, lock-outs, [balloting], etc.; to prohibit, prevent or take appropriate measures against destructive activities, pillages, illegal occupation [of premises], boycotts, slow-downs, interferences with the freedom to work, illegal closures of workplaces, etc.

g. [Amended by Decree 2362 of March 12, 1982] To prohibit or impose restrictions on meetings, whether held in covered places or in the open, and on demonstrations; to fix and assign places for such meetings and to control them; to require permission for the establishment of new associations, trust funds and organizations founded on the basis of official deeds; to ban the activities of all kinds of associations, trust funds and other organizations or subject such activities to the requirement of prior permission.

h. [Amended by Law 2301] To control, as and when necessary, commercial and industrial establishments producing, fabricating, storing, transporting or selling essential goods; to take appropriate legal action against persons hoarding such materials, selling them at exorbitant prices, stopping or slowing

i. [Amended by Decree 2301] To control or close down restaurants, clubs, casinos, cafes, beer houses, taverns, theaters, cinemas, night clubs, gambling saloons, hotels, motels, camping sites and other similar places and to determine and limit the hours during which they shall remain open.
j. To take necessary measures relating to the control of land, sea and air traffic and to restrict or prohibit for security purposes the entry and exit of transportation vehicles.
k. To impose restrictions on entry into and exit from areas where martial law is in force.
l. To impose restrictions on the movement of people; to impose curfews; and, as and when necessary, to introduce appropriate civil defense measures.
m. [Amended by Decree 2301] To compel all public and private establishments in areas under martial law to take appropriate measures; and, if necessary, to requisition the premises, vehicles and personnel of the Treasury, state economic enterprises and establishments and organizations of the local administration, municipality and banks.
n. To execute the decisions of the Council of Ministers relating to martial law.
o. [Amended by Decree 2301] To suspend temporarily the education and training carried out in primary and secondary schools and in universities; and to require concerned individuals and committees of such establishments to lift or shorten any such suspension of educational activities.
p. [Amended by Decree 2301] To order the severing of relations between students who have been deported from areas under martial law after their presence in such areas has been deemed harmful, and their educational or training establishments; and to require the concerned authorities to apply the special rules and regulations of such establishments.
q. [Added by Decree 259 of July 25, 1986; Amended by Law 3310 of September 3, 1986] Where the incidents which led to the declaration or continuation of martial law under Article 122 of the Constitution occur in the border areas of the Turkish Republic and where those responsible for such incidents are established to have taken refuge in neighboring countries, to plan and put into execution, within the context of agreements entered into with such neighboring countries, operations beyond Turkey's frontiers on a limited scale using, as appropriate, land, air or naval forces, each time with the permission of the government and the Chief of the General Staff, with a view to apprehending the culprits or rendering them ineffective.

2. In the exercise of the abovementioned powers, regard shall be had to the constitutional provisions relating to the privileges and immunities recognized by international law for diplomatic representatives and delegations and to [legislative privileges].

*Authorization to use weapons*

*Article 4.* [Amended by Decree 2301] 1. Members of the Armed Forces, the police forces and other security personnel under the command of the Martial Law Commander are authorized to use weapons upon the occurrence of any event or condition necessitating the use of weapons in accordance with the provisions of the Turkish Armed Forces (Internal Service) Act and Regulations, the Law on Powers and Duties of the Police and the Law on the Organization and Duties of the Gendarmerie to which they are subject in the execution of their tasks.

2. Members of the security forces on duty are authorized to fire directly at their targets without hesitation should the latter fail to heed their orders or if their orders are reciprocated with fire or if such it is necessary to do so in legitimate self-defense.

3. All personnel authorized to use weapons are subject to the provisions of paragraphs V and VI of Article 87 of the Turkish Armed Forces (Internal Service) Act [Law 211] and of Article 3 of the Law on the Prevention of Offenses Against Law and Order [Law 1481]. Any investigation ordered into their conduct shall be carried out without them being detained.

4. Orders made by the Martial Law Commander involving the use of weapons by the abovementioned personnel for the preservation of public order and of lives and property shall be announced through the appropriate media.

## Chapter two: Organs

*Martial Law Commander and his assistants*

*Article 5.* 1. A commander who has served or is serving at a rank not below that of a corps commander or equivalent may be appointed as Martial Law Commander by a decree signed by the Prime Minister and ratified by the President. Such appointment shall be upon the nomination of the Ministry of National Defense pursuant to a proposal by the Chief of General Staff.

2. Having regard to the area where martial law has been declared and to the scale of events necessitating such declaration, a sufficient number of assistant Martial Law Commanders may be appointed in accordance with the abovementioned procedure. It shall be made clear in their appointment orders whether or not the Martial Law Commander or his assistants shall continue to hold their previous posts as well.

3. The Martial Law Commander, having regard to the exigencies of the situation, may transfer his own powers to any of his assistants either wholly or in part.

4. [Amended by Decree 2342 of November 14, 1980] Where martial law is declared in a number of districts or on a country-wide scale, cooperation and coordination for the various martial law commands shall be provided by the Office of General Staff.

*Obligations of the Martial Law Commander*

*Article 6.* [Amended by Decree 2342] The Martial Law Commander shall report to the Chief of General Staff in regard to his duties and powers; however, in relation to the execution of military duties, the general provisions to which he is subject shall apply.

*Acting Martial Law Commander*

*Article 7.* In the event of the Martial Law Commander having to leave the district where martial law is in force or cannot exercise his functions for any other reason, an Acting Martial Law Commander shall be appointed by the [Chief of] General Staff. However, if the period for which the Martial Law Commander cannot exercise his functions exceeds fifteen days, he shall be replaced at the earliest convenient date.

*Headquarters*

*Article 8.* 1. Simultaneously with the declaration of martial law, a martial law headquarters shall be set up, having regard to the requirements of the situation. The posts in the martial law command shall have been created in advance by the Office of the General Staff and officers, non-commissioned officers and civilian personnel duty appointed to these posts in sufficient numbers.

2. Personnel appointed to the abovementioned posts are required to start work within twenty-four hours of receipt of their appointment orders and to report to duty [as soon as possible.]

*Units*

*Article 9.* Military units in sufficient numbers shall be placed at the disposal of the Martial Law Commander by the Chief of General Staff for the effective execution of martial law operations.

*Legal advisors*

*Article 10.* [Government] legal advisors and assistant legal advisors shall, whenever martial law is in force, serve as legal advisors to the Martial Law Commander besides discharging their functions under the law governing their appointment.

*Martial law courts*

*Article 11.* 1. Military courts in sufficient numbers shall be established within martial law districts in localities to be determined by the Ministry of National Defense under Law 353 dated October 25, 1963. These courts shall be known as the martial law courts of the area where they are set up and shall be assigned numbers if there is more than one in each area.

2. [Added by Decree 2342] Among the offenses falling within the jurisdiction of these courts, cases involving offenses carrying a punishment of imprisonment for up to five years or less shall be tried by a single member of the court who is a professional judge. However, this rule shall not apply to cases involving persons mentioned in Article 21 of this Act or senior military officers.

3. [Added by Decree 2342] Where a case involves several offenses committed by a single accused, it shall be tried by the tribunal having jurisdiction to try the offense carrying the severest punishment. The same rule would apply to cases involving a link between various acts.

4. [Amended by Decree 2301] The legal advisor, the military judge, the military prosecutor and their assistants shall, on the opinion of the Chief of General Staff, be appointed from among candidates nominated by a committee made up of the chief of personnel and legal advisor in the Office of the General Staff, the chief of personnel and legal advisor to the command from which such personnel are drawn, and the Chief of the Military Judicial Affairs in the Ministry of National Defense.

5. The provisions of Article 16 of Law 357 dated October 26, 1963, concerning military judges and prosecutors shall continue to apply. However, where the absence of a judge or prosecutor exceeds a continuous period of more than a month, he shall not be entitled to the protection of those provisions.

6. A sufficient number of member officers shall be appointed to the martial law courts in accordance with the procedure for appointment of military officer judges and on the proposal of the [Office of] General Staff.

7. During a state of war, if the Chief of General Staff considers it necessary, the military courts functioning within a district where martial law is in force or where military operations are under way may assume the functions of martial law courts. In such cases, the Ministry of National Defense shall determine the jurisdiction of such courts and, where there is more than one military court, designate a particular court or courts to act as martial law court or courts.

### Chapter three: Martial law courts

*Actions to be taken pending the formation of martial law courts*

*Article 12.* [Amended by Decree 2301] 1. Pending the formation of martial law courts by the Martial Law Commander, the military prosecutors and military courts functioning in the area where an offense has been committed, and in their absence prosecutors of the Republic and courts of justice, shall perform the functions of military prosecutors and martial law courts.

*Acts within the context of circumstances warranting the declaration of martial law*

*Article 13.* [Amended by Decree 2301]

- a. Persons who are charged with having committed, during a period of three months from the date of declaration of martial law, offenses relating to events

that gave rise to the declaration of martial law in an area where martial law is in force or offenses listed in Article 12 of Law 6136 concerning Firearms, Knives and Other Instruments, amended by Decree 2249, and
b. persons who have committed offenses falling within the jurisdiction of martial law courts and offenses relating to the same general and common purpose shall be tried by martial law courts even if such offenses may have been committed outside the boundaries of the areas where martial law is in force.

2. The Martial Law Commander is, however, empowered to refer cases which, in his opinion, fall outside the jurisdiction of the martial law courts to the appropriate judicial authorities.

3. The prosecutors of the Republic, military prosecutors, military tribunals or courts of justice to whom cases are sent by the Martial Law Commander shall not plead lack of competence or lack of jurisdiction to deal with them. Such cases shall be dealt with under the provisions of existing law.

*Jurisdiction over offenses committed by martial law personnel*

Article 14. 1. Offenses committed by personnel serving under the martial law command while on duty or during their term of office shall be tried by martial law courts.

2. In such cases the investigation is carried out *ex officio* and the provisions relating to judicial proceedings contained in their respective laws do not apply.

3. [Amended by Decree 2301] Offenses committed by military personnel serving under the martial law command shall be tried by martial law courts. The Martial Law Commander may, in respect of personnel under his command, [also] apply *ex officio* the disciplinary and administrative sanctions permissible under the relevant laws or make recommendations to the appropriate authorities and committees for dealing with such offenders within the framework of the relevant legislation.

*Powers and duties of martial law courts*

Article 15. [Amended by Decree 1728 of May 15, 1973, and Decree 2301] 1. Persons committing any of the following offenses in areas where martial law is in force shall be tried by martial law courts regardless of their rank, title or office, subject only to the provisions of Article 21 of this Act:

a. Offenses committed against the identity of the state mentioned in Chapters 1, 2 and 4 of Section I of the Second Book of the Turkish Penal Code.
b. Provoking, or [conspiring to commit], offenses mentioned in Chapters 1 and 2 of Section V of the Second Book of the Turkish Penal Code.
c. Counterfeiting of public seals, stamps, etc. mentioned in Chapter 2 of Section VI of the Second Book of the Turkish Penal Code.

d. Crimes committed against public safety mentioned in Section VII of the Second Book of the Turkish Penal Code.
e. Offenses of pillage, stopping individuals with criminal intent and kidnapping mentioned in Chapter 2 of Section X of the Second Book of the Turkish Penal Code.
f. [Amended by Law 2301] Offenses mentioned in the following Articles of the Turkish Penal Code: 179, 180, 188, 191, 192, 201, 228, 234, 235, 236, 241, 242, 248, 249, 254, 255, 256, 257, 258, 260, 264, 266, 268, 271, 296, 448, 449, 450, 451, 452, 516 [except the sub-paragraphs relating to proceedings conducted on the filing of a complaint]; offenses mentioned in Articles 517, 536 and 537 of the said Code and those mentioned in Law 6136 concerning Firearms, Knives and Other Instruments.
g. Offenses mentioned in Articles 390 and 391 of the Turkish Penal Code and spiriting away of any kind of equipment, installation or cable intended for telecommunications and belonging to the Telephone and Telegram General Management or to the Turkish Armed Forces.
h. Offenses mentioned in Articles 55, 56, 57, 58, and 59 of the Military Penal Code.
i. Offenses mentioned in Articles 75, 93, 95, and 96 and in the second paragraph of Article 148 and in Article 160 of the Military Penal Code.
j. Offenses committed through the press whose prosecution does not require [the formal lodging of] complaints and offenses whose prosecution does not necessitate personal actions.
k. Offenses arising from infringements of the Law on the Freedom of Assembly and Demonstrations.
l. Cases relating to the closing down of associations, trade unions and professional organizations as provided for under the relevant legislation. (The provisions of Law 648 concerning the closure of political parties is excepted.)

2. [Amended by Decree 2301] The authorities to whose attention any of the abovementioned offenses are drawn shall send the papers relating to the preliminary investigation to the Martial Law Commander as soon as possible. The Martial Law Commander shall thereupon transfer the file to the appropriate military prosecutor for necessary action.

3. [Amended by Decree 2301] The Martial Law Commander may however transfer to the civil judicial authorities such cases as should in his opinion not be tried by martial law courts.

4. [Added by Decree 2301] The prosecutors of the Republic, military prosecutors and courts to whom the Martial Law Commander has sent cases for trial shall not plead lack of jurisdiction or competence. The provisions of existing law shall apply to the disposal of such cases.

5. [Added by Decree 2301; amended by Decree 3195 of May 3, 1985] The Martial Law Commander may keep persons accused of any of the abovementioned offenses under detention pending charge or pending a decision on whether they should be tried by a martial law court. The maximum period of

detention in such cases shall not exceed fifteen days. However, if it is not possible to produce the accused before a judge within the said period of fifteen days on account of lengthy investigations or determination of evidence, the accused shall be produced before the competent judge at the conclusion of such investigation or within thirty days, whichever is earlier. If the accused is not produced before the judge at the conclusion of the first fifteen-day period, the martial commander of the said period shall determine whether they shall be produced before the judge or not. Unless there is a justifiable reason such as the emergence of new evidence, such a power of review shall not be exercisable more than once in respect of the same individual on the same grounds.

*Offenses and penalties*

*Article 16.* [Amended by Decree 2301] 1. Persons acting in contravention of measures adopted by the Martial Law Commander in areas where martial law has been declared, failing to abide by any orders or instructions [issued by the Martial Law Commander], intentionally giving false information about their identity or refusing to provide proof of their identity when demanded to do so are liable to be punished with imprisonment for between three months and one year.

2. Persons spreading or conveying unfounded or exaggerated news or rumors with intent to create unrest or panic among the public are liable to be punished with imprisonment for between six months and two years and with a monetary fine of not less than five thousand lira. If the offense is committed in collusion with a foreigner the term of imprisonment shall not be less than one year and the fine not less than five thousand lira. If the offense is committed by the press or other mass media those responsible (directly and indirectly) shall be liable to a double punishment.

3. [Amended by Decree 2766] Persons deported from areas where martial law is in force re-entering such areas or entering areas where they have been forbidden entry, and persons failing to notify the security authorities in their new places of residence of their previous domiciles or of the address to which they intend to move shall be liable to be punished with imprisonment for between two months and four months for a first offense and for between four months and one year for a second or subsequent offense.

*Provisions relating to determined punishments*

*Article 17.* [Amended by Decrees 2301 and 2766] 1. Punishments and fines awardable by martial law courts for offenses mentioned in Article 15 of this Act relating to the declaration and operation of martial law and in Additional Article 4 are hereby increased. Such increase shall be up to two times and not less than one-third of the terms of imprisonment or amounts of fine specified for each offense. For offenses committed against martial law personnel the punishments shall stand doubled. However the punishment inflicted shall not exceed the maximum prescribed for a particular offense.

2. Punishments imposed by martial law courts cannot be commuted to fines or to any other measures specified in the law nor can they be deferred.

3. [Added by Decree 2342] The provisions of Article 59 of the Turkish Penal Code may not be applied in appropriate cases involving good conduct by the accused during his trial.

*Procedure to be applied [by martial law courts]*

*Article 18.* [Amended by Decree 2301]

a. The competence of martial law courts to try cases involving offenses committed outside areas in which martial law is in force shall be determined and announced by the Ministry of National Defense upon declaration of martial law.
b. [Amended by Decree 2342] The decision as to whether or not an accused is to be kept in detention or continued detention, as the case may be, pending investigation of his case shall be made by one of the judges of the martial law court. Appeals against such a decision shall be heard by a judge of the military court functioning under Articles 74 and 75 of the Law on the Establishment of Military Courts and Trial Procedures (Law 353) and under Article 19 of this Act.
The same provision applies to decisions concerning searches and seizures.
c. The identities of informers reporting crimes falling under the jurisdiction of martial law courts shall not be disclosed unless they consent to it or unless the scope of the denunciation [sic] constitutes a crime in itself.
d. The prosecutor of the Republic or military prosecutor shall inform the Martial Law Commander as soon as he comes to know or takes cognizance of a fact which indicates that an offense falling within the purview of the martial law courts has been committed. The Martial Law Commander may, if he deems fit, have the prosecutor of the Republic or military prosecutor carry out the preliminary investigation at the place where the offense has been committed.
e. Where an offense is committed outside the territorial jurisdiction of a martial law court, the military prosecutor of the martial law may ask the prosecutor of the Republic or military prosecutor to carry out the preliminary investigation at the place where the offense has been committed.
In such cases the preliminary investigation shall be carried out expeditiously. Prosecutors of the republic or military prosecutors charged with carrying out investigations specified in paragraphs (d) or (e) above shall have recourse to the local military courts and civil courts of justice for decisions and orders that may be necessary for their investigations.
f. The orders of military prosecutors issued in accordance with Article 98 of the Law on the Establishment of Military Courts and Trial Procedures (Law 353) shall be carried out within twenty-four hours.
g. During investigations and initiation of legal proceedings in respect of offenses falling within the jurisdiction of martial law courts, the provisions of

supplementary Article 4 of the Code of Criminal Procedure (added by Decree 1696) shall apply.

h. The martial law court may rule in appropriate cases that the trial should be held elsewhere for reasons of security or to secure an expeditious outcome.

i. Even if the circumstances mentioned in Article 126 of the Law on the Establishment of Military Courts and Trial Procedures (Law 353) may not exist, the witnesses and experts may be heard by a substitute judge or rogatory judge.

j. In martial law courts, a rogatory court or court of a substitute judge, shorthand or other technical means may be used to record the proceedings. The record that is later drawn up based on such a transcript shall be signed by the committee of judges or the rogatory judge as well as the secretary drawing up the record in evidence of the fact that the contents thereof reflect the proceedings accurately. The original shorthand or other notes or tapes shall be preserved.

k. [Amended by Decree 2342] Adjournments in cases tried by martial law courts shall not at any time exceed thirty [continuous] days.

To enable the military prosecutor or his proxy to prepare his indictment and the accused or his lawyer to prepare their defense against the indictment a maximum period of fifteen days shall be given [by the martial law court]. This period may be extended to one month in cases where fifteen or more individuals are involved.

Where legal provisions entailing a punishment lighter than that prescribed for the offense mentioned in the indictment are canvassed [at the trial], the trial may not be adjourned only to enable the preparation of additional defenses.

l. Where cases falling within the jurisdiction of martial law courts involve offenses for which the maximum punishment prescribed by law is imprisonment for a term not exceeding three years, the trial may be held in the absence of an [absconding] accused.

m. Investigations and prosecution of offenses committed against members of the armed forces and of other security forces charged with the maintenance of public security and peace as on September 12, 1980, shall be conducted within the framework of [this Act] regardless of the location and time limits provided in Articles 1 and 4 of the Law on the Procedure for Flagrant Offenses (Law 3005).

n. [Amended by Decree 2362] The imposition of fines, whether alone or in conjunction with other penalties, and penal sanctions involving the restriction of individual freedom for up to six months (inclusive) cannot be appealed by those convicted.

They can, however, be the subject of an appeal by the Martial Law Commander or where the commander or the chief of an organization under whose jurisdiction the military courts have been set up or the prosecutor of a province deems it necessary to send such cases to the courts of justice or other military courts. In such a case the accused and his defending lawyer, if any, and the military prosecutor shall have a week to present the grounds for appeal.

In addition to the provisions set out in this Act, the Law on the Establishment of Military Courts and Trial Procedures (Law 353) and the provisions relating to a state of war in the said law shall apply in martial law courts. If martial law has not been declared on account of a state of war the provisions of the Law on the Establishment of Military Courts and Trial Procedures relating to a state of war shall not apply.

o. [Added by Decree 2651 of April 4, 1982] In martial law courts [it shall suffice] for the military prosecutor to read out a summary of the indictment disclosing the identity of the accused, the description of the act which is alleged to constitute an offense, the legal consequences of such an act, and the provisions of law applicable to the case.

p. [Added by Decree 2651] In cases involving more than one accused, where some of the accused are not concerned with part of the trial, the court may rule that they be excluded from such hearings. However, if during such hearings matters involving all the accused are discussed, the relevant part of the proceedings shall be made known to the excluded accused before they are included in subsequent hearings.

Also, during preliminary proceedings in cases involving several accused, the senior judge of the court may have some of them summoned to remain present [at subsequent hearings].

*Remedies and the examining authority*

*Article 19.* The Martial Law Commander shall have all the powers and authority of a commander of the military corps or the chief military authority under whose command a martial law court has been set up. If within a district there is more than one martial law court, the revising authority to entertain appeals from decisions of either court shall be the martial law court nearest to the court that pronounced the decision in question.

*Priority in revision by the Military Court of Appeal*

*Article 20.* [Amended by Decree 1728] Sentences pronounced by martial law courts and appealed from shall be finalized within two months [from the date of pronouncement of the sentence] at the latest in accordance with the last paragraph of Article 217 of Law 353 as amended by Law 1596.

*Authorization for prosecution*

*Article 21.* [Amended by Decree 1728] Authorization for prosecution of offenses covered by this Act shall be granted by the following persons or bodies:

a. where the accused is a member of the Council of Ministers or a member of the Grand National Assembly of Turkey, by the Assembly;
b. where the accused is a general or admiral, by the Chief of General Staff;
c. where the accused is an under-secretary, by the Prime Minister or the Minister [of the department] concerned;
d. where the accused is a governor or district governor, by the Ministry of the Interior;
e. where the accused is the President or a spokesman of the President, a member of the Constitutional Court, the Court of Appeal, the Council of State, Military Court of Appeal, Military Supreme Administrative Court, Supreme Council of Judges or of the Court of Audit, the Chief Prosecutor of the Republic, the Chief Military Prosecutor of the Military Court of Appeal, a judge or deputy judge or prosecutor of the Republic or an official of similar rank, or a military officer judge, by the committee or authority specified in the relevant law governing their office. Such accused are also subject to the appropriate procedures laid down in such law.

If the authorized committee or authority does not allow the Martial Law Commandership to prosecute any of the abovementioned persons, their cases shall be dealt with in accordance with the appropriate law.

Legal principles concerning diplomatic immunity shall be respected.

*Offenses whose prosecution require special authorization*

Article 22. [Amended by Decree 2632 of March 12, 1982] Except for an infringement of Article 158 of the Turkish Penal Code, for offenses specified in this Act and whose prosecution would require special authorization, no authorization is required [sic].

*Powers and authority of the martial law courts on the termination of martial law*

Article 23. [Amended by Decree 2301] 1. Even after martial law is lifted, the martial law courts shall continue to perform their functions and exercise their authority pending the final disposal of cases being tried by them.

The command under the order of which these courts will continue to function shall be determined by the Law on Establishment of Military Courts and Trial Procedures (Law 353). The courts shall continue to apply the provisions of this Act.

2. The number of martial law courts and of military judges, prosecutors and officers serving in them may be increased as and when required.

3. Cases requiring no public [sic] action and cases in respect of which trials have been suspended shall be transferred to the appropriate [civilian] authorities to be dealt with [suitably].

## Chapter four: General state of war

\*\*\*

## Chapter five: Miscellaneous articles

\*\*\*

*Additional Article 1.* [Added by Decree 2310 of October 8, 1980] 1. Regardless of the time-limits and territorial restrictions mentioned in Article 13 above, in accordance with Articles 13 and 15 the military courts functioning under the martial law command of the area where the general headquarters of a political party is domiciled [situated] is hereby authorized to conduct investigations into and try cases involving the administrators and members at all levels of such political party, executives and members of affiliated organizations who commit crimes triable [sic] by martial law courts, and administrators and members of other organizations and associations suspected of having relations with such political party.

2. The Martial Law Commander may however transfer to the concerned [civilian] judicial or other authorities cases which in his opinion do not warrant trial by the martial law courts.

3. No authority to whom cases referred to in the foregoing paragraph have been sent can reject them, nor can any judicial authority plead lack of competence to try them.

*Additional Article 2.*

\*\*\*

5. The launch of disciplinary proceedings, imposition of disciplinary sanctions and investigation and prosecution of service-related offenses in respect of personnel seconded to martial law duty shall be determined by the relevant laws governing their appointment and continuation in service and not by this Act. However, if permission is granted under those laws for the initiation of any of the abovementioned measures, after the investigations are carried out by the military justice inspector, the file shall be sent to the Ministry of Justice.

\*\*\*

*Additional Article 3.* [Added by Decree 2342] No action for annulment shall be brought in the courts for the administrative acts of the martial law command carried out in accordance with the powers conferred by this Act. Civil liability based on the personal fault of personnel serving in the martial law command cannot be asserted.

*Additional Article 4.* [Added by Decree 2354 of December 8, 1980; Amended by Decree 2682 of June 17, 1982] 1. Persons involved in smuggling of a nature likely to endanger the political, financial, economic, military or administrative security of the state and their accessories (including accessories after the fact) shall be tried by the martial law courts regardless of any time-limits. Such persons shall be tried in a martial law court of competent jurisdiction determined by the Ministry of National Defense and announced in the Official Gazette under Article 13 of this Act.

2. The jurisdictional provisions concerning smuggling covered by Articles 13 and 15 of this Act shall be inapplicable.

3. During investigation and prosecution for smuggling as provided in paragraph (1) above, the Law on Prohibition and Prosecution of Smuggling (Law 1918) and special provisions relating to smuggling contained in other laws shall be applied by the martial law command, military prosecutors, and martial law courts.

4. The Martial Law Commander may transfer to the appropriate judicial authorities such cases involving crimes provided in paragraph (1) above, which in his opinion do not warrant trial by the martial law courts.

5. The prosecutors of the Republic, military prosecutors, courts of justice or military courts to whom cases are sent by the Martial Law Commander as provided in the foregoing paragraph shall not plead lack of competence or lack of jurisdiction to try them. With regard to case files sent in such manner the provisions of this Act shall apply.

\*\*\*

*Additional Article 7.* [Added by Decree 2439 of March 24, 1981] 1. Detainees or convicts held in detention centers shall promptly be handed over to the Martial Law Commander or military prosecutor upon being requested to do so in writing by the Martial Law Commander in connection with investigations being carried out by the martial law authorities.

2. Such persons who have been handed over to the abovementioned authorities shall be returned to their original detention centers at the end of the investigations. The time spent by them outside their detention centers shall be included in the overall time spent by them in detention.

3. If, while in the custody of the abovementioned authorities, the order of detention or execution passed against such persons is revoked or modified or completed, the Martial Law Commander and the office of the military prosecutor shall be notified.

*Additional Article 8.* [Added by Decree 2836] If a file relating to an offense which in the opinion of the Martial Law Commander does not warrant trial by the martial law courts is sent to an appropriate judicial authority in accordance with Articles 13 or 15 or Additional Article 4 of this Act, and it subsequently transpires that the case is directly connected to another case being tried by a martial law court or to an investigation being carried out by a military prosecutor, then on being so ordered by the said martial law court or military prosecutor, it shall be sent to such a court or prosecutor by the [civil] judicial authority.

*Additional Article 9.* [Added by Decree 3423 of March 31, 1988] Upon the lifting of martial law persons arrested by the martial law authorities and detained in military prisons shall be transferred to civil prisons after suitable agreement has been reached between the Ministry of Justice and the Ministry of National Defense. Such persons shall be subjected to the regime applicable to civil prisons.

\*\*\*

# Document no. 8

### Constitutional history of Turkey[5]

#### Constitutional movements during the Ottoman period

Constitutional movements during the Ottoman period commenced towards the end of the eighteenth century. During the period 1789–1808, Sultan Selim the Third envisaged the formation of an advisory assembly, called the Meclis-i Meshveret, within the context of the New System (called the Nizam-i Cedid). [This is] seen as a major step towards a constitutional government system.

The "Sened-i Ittifak," or Charter of Alliance, is seen as the first important document from the point of view of a constitutional order. Whilst the 1808 charter restricted the Sultan's exercise of power, it also delegated some authorities to a senate body, called the Ayan. The charter is a significant document as it was also recognized by the Sultan.

The Tanzimat Reform era commenced with the issue of the decree entitled "Gulhane Hatt-i Humayun" in 1839. The subjects of the Ottoman Padishah were assured that their basic rights would be respected.

The documents are especially significant for their recognition of equal rights in education and in government administration for those of Christian persuasion, exemplifying egalitarian principles. The 1875 document entitled the "Ferman-i Adalet," or the Imperial Edict on Justice, provided for independence of the judicial courts and ensured the safety of judges.

The most important step along the road to the rule of law was made with the introduction of the 1876 "Kanun-i Esasiye," or Constitution, which also started the period known as the "First Meshrutiyet," or First Constitutional Period. The basic concept in the 1876 constitution is that, although somewhat restrictive in the exercise of powers, it nevertheless, for the first time, recognized a parliamentary system. This constitution has provisions covering basic rights and privileges, the independence of courts and the safety of judges, among other aspects.

After the 1876 Constitution had been in effect for one year, the "Second Meshrutiyet" period laid the foundations of a parliamentary system by adopting the 1876 Constitution with some amendments made thereto.

## The constitutional system during the War of Independence

When the Turkish Grand National Assembly congregated on April 23, 1920, this in itself marked a unique and important change in the exercise of sovereignty.

During the Ottoman reign, the workings of Parliament were to an extent the use by delegation of the powers of the ruler in the legislative process. In contrast, in the case of the workings of the Turkish Grand National Assembly, all authority was vested in Parliament itself.

The Constitution of January 20, 1921, is called the "Constitution Law," and when compared with the Ottoman legal system contains a radically new concept. According to this concept, whilst the power to legislate belongs to Parliament, the executive powers can only be exercised by an "executive council" to be elected by majority vote from among the members of Parliament.

According to this "Law of Constitution," differences of opinion and disagreements between ministers are to be resolved in Parliament. In addition to this, the changing of ministers is also counted among the powers of Parliament ... On the other hand, the government itself was vested with the power to dissolve Parliament or to "renew the election of the Assembly."

In this system, which did not have a "Head of State," the members of Independence Tribunals were also elected from among the members of the Assembly.

An important step was taken to establish a Council of Ministers with more freedom of movement when a motion that the form of the state should be "Republic" was enacted on October 29, 1923; the President of the Republic was to be elected from among the members of the Assembly for one term of office. According to law, the President would select the Prime Minister from among the members of the Parliament. In turn, the Prime Minister would select the other Ministers from among the members of Parliament and, finally, the President would submit the whole of the Council of Ministers for the approval of Parliament.

## The 1924 Constitution

The 1924 Constitution provided for the continuation of the system of parliamentary government. Powers of both legislation and execution were held by Parliament. Whilst Parliament had the right to monitor and if necessary to bring down the Government, neither the President nor the Government could dissolve Parliament.

Although under the provisions of the 1924 Constitution, executive powers could be exercised only by the President or the Council of Ministers, the 1924 Constitution contained elements of both the parliamentary system and governmental executive powers. In this manner, whilst Parliament directly exercised legislative powers, a separation of powers did exist in view of the exercise of executive power. Furthermore, the principle of collective responsibility of the

Council of Ministers to Parliament and the concept of the President not being vested with political responsibility were embodied in the 1924 Constitution.

The judicial and executive powers were clearly separated. Independent courts exercise judiciary powers on behalf of the nation.

The 1924 Constitution was amended in 1937; the six main principles of the Republican Peoples' Party program, republicanism, nationalism, populism, statism, secularism, and reformism, remained enshrined in the Constitution itself as basic qualities of the state.

## *The 1961 Constitution*

The 1924 Constitution represented a mixed system somewhere between parliamentary governments and a parliamentary model. The 1961 Constitution brought about further developments in the parliamentary system.

The Legislature was a bi-cameral Parliament. One chamber was the National Assembly consisting of 450 deputies elected by universal suffrage. The other was the Republican Senate, composed of 150 Senators elected by universal suffrage and fifteen Senators who were appointed by the President. In addition, the members of the National Unity Committee and former Presidents of the Republic were lifetime Senators. In the functioning of the legislative process, the National Assembly had final say over the two houses.

In the exercise of executive power, the President symbolically represented the unity and integrity of the State, and the Prime Minister and other Ministers make up the Council of Ministers, who bore political responsibility in the use of this power.

The Prime Minister was appointed by the President from among the members of the Turkish Grand National Assembly. The Ministers were appointed by the Prime Minister and presented to the President for his ratification.

The 1961 Constitution fully separated the judiciary from the executive and the legislature, thereby clearly operating the separation of powers principle. In this system, details regarding the security of judges as well as matters related to full freedom and independence of the courts and the positions of the judges were turned over to the "High Commission for Judges," whose members were elected from among the judges of the Supreme Court.

Furthermore, the concept of the "Constitutional Court" was first introduced with the 1961 Constitution.

## *The 1982 Constitution*

Whilst the 1982 Constitution continued the basic structure of the 1961 Constitution, it nevertheless made significant changes in several areas.

The Republican Senate was abolished in the 1982 Constitution.

In order to make the workings of the legislature easier and to prevent deadlocks from occurring in the election of the Speaker of the House, the quorum was reduced to one-third of the total number of members. The taking of decisions was by majority of those present, but with the provision that this may not be less than one-quarter-plus-one of the total number of members.

The 1982 Constitution provided the executive with powers that derived directly from the Constitution itself, provided that the executive actions taken did not conflict with the law.

The Constitution regulated the election of the President so that, should the first two ballots, to be at least three days apart, not produce the required majority of two-thirds of the total number of members, then an absolute majority in the third ballot would suffice to elect the President. Should it happen that the third ballot also failed to produce the required results, then a fourth ballot had to be held to determine between the two candidates with the highest number of votes. Should the fourth ballot again fail, then parliamentary elections had to be renewed.

The 1982 Constitution also provided that a State Audit Board functioned as a Constitutional body, appointed by the President and reporting to the President.

A supplementary provisional article in the Constitution also stipulated that the National Security Council would become the Presidential Council for a period of six years following the date the Turkish Grand National Assembly commenced to function.

According to a constitutional provision, the President could, upon the proposal of the Prime Minister, terminate the holding of office of any Minister.

The powers of the judiciary were limited and restrictions brought regarding the monitoring of laws with respect to their form were brought into effect.

This was especially so in connection with issues related to the Constitution and its legal administration, and whether or not new laws were framed according to the principles contained in the Constitution.

## *Additional comment on the 1982 Constitution*[6]

In stark contrast to the 1961 Constitution, the 1982 Constitution had the main purpose of strengthening political power, not liberty or democracy. Therefore, the State was placed at a position superior to the individual and the society, and the individual and society were made to depend upon the State. Furthermore, even though the 1982 Constitution declared Turkey to be a liberal democracy, it substantially restricted the means of achieving a true liberal democracy. Rights given in several provisions of the Constitution were subsequently taken back in later provisions. It was similar neither to liberal–democratic constitutions nor to the young Mediterranean democratic constitutions (Spain, Greece). The main sources of the Constitution were 1971 and 1973 Amendments to the 1961 Constitution, and the codes and orders already promulgated by the National Security Council (the Government and the Parliament of the military rule era).

Under the 1982 Constitution, a very large number of repressive codes enacted by the National Security Council regarding political life and the security field were declared to be exempt from judicial review by the Constitutional Court. Even though referrals were made to the European Human Rights

Convention, words were selectively placed or left out to guarantee state superiority over legal review. Judicial reviews of decisions of certain institutions such as the Supreme Military Council, the Supreme Council of Judges and Public Prosecutors, and the Presidency were forbidden. The military was given a predominant place in the political process by the formation of the "National Security Council." Additionally, the administrative authority of universities was destroyed.

# Document no. 9

## The constitution of the Republic of Turkey[7]

Preamble
Part one — General Principles
    I.    Form of the State
    II.   Characteristics of the Republic
    III.  Integrity of the State, official language, flag, national anthem, and capital
    IV. Irrevocable provisions
    V.    Fundamental aims and duties of the State
    VI.   Sovereignty
    VII.  Legislative power
    VIII. Executive power and function
    IX.   Judicial power
    X.    Equality before law
    XI.   Supremacy and binding force of the Constitution

Part two — Fundamental rights and duties
    Chapter one — General provisions
        I.    Nature of fundamental rights and freedoms
        II.   Restriction of fundamental rights and freedoms
        III.  Prohibition of abuse of fundamental rights and freedoms
        IV. Suspension of the exercise of fundamental rights and freedoms
        V.    Status of aliens
    Chapter two — The rights and duties of the individual
        I.    Personal inviolability, material and spiritual entity of the individual
        II.   Prohibition of forced labor
        III.  Personal liberty and security
        IV. Privacy and protection of private life
            A. Privacy of the individual's life
            B. Inviolability of domicile
            C. Freedom of communication
        V.    Freedom of residence and movement
        VI.   Freedom of religion and conscience

- VII. Freedom of thought and opinion
- VIII. Freedom of expression and dissemination of thought
- IX. Freedom of science and arts
- X. Provisions relating to the press and publication
  - A. Freedom of the press
  - B. Right to publish periodicals and non-periodicals
  - C. Protection of printing facilities
  - D. Right to use mass media other than the press which are owned by public corporations
  - E. Right of rectification and reply
- XI. Rights and freedoms of assembly
  - A. Freedom of association
  - B. Right to hold meetings and demonstration marches
- XII. Right of property
- XIII. Provisions relating to the protection of rights
  - A. Freedom to claim rights
  - B. Guarantee of lawful judge
  - C. Principles relating to offenses and penalties
- XIV. Right to prove an allegation
- XV. Protection of fundamental rights and freedoms

Chapter three — Social and economic rights and duties
- I. Protection of the family
- II. Right and duty of training and education
- III. Public interest
  - A. Utilization of the coasts
  - B. Land ownership
  - C. Protection of agriculture, animal husbandry, and persons engaged in these activities
  - D. Expropriation
  - E. Nationalization
- IV. Freedom to work and conclude contracts
- V. Provisions relating to labor
  - A. Right and duty to work
  - B. Working conditions and right to rest and leisure
  - C. Right to organize labor unions
  - D. Activities of labor unions
- VI. Collective bargaining, right to strike, and lock-out
  - A. Right of collective bargaining
  - B. Right to strike, and lock-out
- VII. Guarantee of fair wage
- VIII. Health, the environment, and housing
  - A. Health Services and conservation of the environment
  - B. Right to housing
- IX. Youth and sports
  - A. Protection of youth

           B. Development of sports
- X. Social security rights
  - A. Right to social security
  - B. Persons requiring special protection in the field of social security
  - C. Turkish nationals working abroad
- XI. Conservation of historical, cultural, and natural wealth
- XII. Protection of arts and artists
- XIII. The extent of social and economic rights

Chapter four — Political rights and duties
- I. Turkish citizenship
- II. Right to vote, to be elected, and to engage in political activity
- III. Provisions relating to political parties
  - A. Forming parties, membership and withdrawal from membership in a party
  - B. Principles to be observed by political parties
- IV. Right to enter the public service
  - A. Entry into the public service
  - B. Declaration of assets
- V. National service
- VI. Obligation to pay taxes
- VII. Right of petition

Part three — Fundamental organs of the Republic

Chapter one — Legislative power
- I. The Turkish Grand National Assembly
  - A. Composition
  - B. Eligibility to be a deputy
  - C. Election term of the Turkish Grand National Assembly
  - D. Deferment of elections to the Turkish Grand National Assembly, and by-elections
  - E. General administration and supervision of the elections
  - F. Provisions relating to membership
    1. Representing the nation
    2. Oath-taking
    3. Activities incompatible with membership
    4. Parliamentary immunity
    5. Loss of membership
    6. Application for annulment
    7. Salaries and allowances
- II. Functions and power of the Turkish Grand National Assembly
  - A. General provisions
  - B. Introduction and debate of the laws
  - C. Promulgation of laws by the President of the Republic
  - D. Ratification of international treaties
  - E. Authorization to enact decrees having force of law

F. Declaration of state of war and authorization to permit the use of armed forces
III. Provision relating to the activities of the Turkish Grand National Assembly
    A. Convening and adjournment
    B. Bureau of the assembly
    C. Rules of procedure, political party security affairs
    D. Quorums required for sessions and decisions
    E. Publicity and publication of debates
IV. Ways of collecting information and supervision by the Turkish Grand National Assembly
    A. General provisions
    B. Interpellation
    C. Parliamentary investigation

Chapter two — executive
I. President of the Republic
    A. Qualifications and impartiality
    B. Election
    C. Oath
    D. Duties and powers
    E. Presidential accountability and non-accountability
    F. Deputation for the President of the Republic
    G. General Secretariat of the President of the Republic
    H. State Supervisory Council
II. Council of Ministers
    A. Formation
    B. Taking office and vote of confidence
    C. Vote of confidence while in office
    D. Functions and political responsibilities
    E. Formation of ministries, and ministers
    F. Provisional Council of Ministers during elections
    G. Regulations
    H. Calling elections for the Turkish Grand National Assembly by the President of the Republic
    I. National defense
        1. Offices of Commander-in-Chief and Chief of the General Staff
        2. National Security Council
III. Procedure governing emergency rule
    A. States of emergency
        1. Declaration of a state of emergency on account of a natural disaster or serious economic crisis
        2. Declaration of a state of emergency on account of widespread acts of violence and serious deterioration of public order
        3. Rules relating to the states of emergency
    B. Martial law, mobilization, and state of war

IV. Administration
    A. Fundamentals of the administration
        1. Integral unity and public legal personality of the administration
    B. Recourse to judicial review
    C. Organization of the administration
        1. Central administration
        2. Local administrations
    D. Provisions relating to public servants
        1. General principles
        2. Duties and responsibilities, and guarantees during disciplinary proceedings
    E. Institutions of higher education and their higher bodies
        1. Institutions of higher education
        2. Superior bodies of higher education
        3. Institutions of higher education subject to special provisions
    F. Radio and television administration and news agencies with State connection
    G. The Atatürk High Institution of Culture, Language, and History
    H. Public professional organizations
    I. Department of Religious Affairs
    J. Unlawful orders

Chapter three — Judicial power
    I. General provisions
        A. Independence of the courts
        B. Security of tenure of judge and public prosecutors
        C. Judges and public prosecutors
        D. Publicity of the hearings and verdict justification
        E. Organization of courts
        F. Courts of the Security of the State
        G. Supervision of judges and public prosecutors
        H. Military Justice
    II. Higher courts
        A. The Constitutional Court
            1. Organization
            2. Termination of membership
            3. Functions and powers
            4. Functioning and trial procedure
            5. Annulment action
            6. Time limit for annulment action
            7. Contention of unconstitutionality before other courts
            8. Decisions of the Constitutional Court
        B. The High Court of Appeals
        C. Council of State
        D. Military High Court of Appeals
        E. High Military Administrative Court of Appeals

          F. Jurisdictional Conflict Court
    III.   Supreme Council of Judges and Public Prosecutors
    IV. Audit Court

Part four — Financial and economic provisions
    Chapter one — Financial provisions
        I.    Budget
            A. Preparation and implementation of the budget
            B. Debate on the budget
            C. Principles governing budgetary amendments
            D. Final account
            E. Auditing of State economic enterprises
    Chapter two — Economic provisions
        I.    Planning
        II.   Supervision of markets and regulation of foreign trade
        III.  Exploration and exploitation of natural resources
        IV. Forests and the inhabitants of forest villages
            A. Protection and development of forests
            B. Protection of the inhabitants of forest villages
        V.    Promotion of cooperatives
        VI.   Protection of consumers, small traders, and craftsmen
            A. Protection of consumers
            B. Protection of small traders and craftsmen

Part five — Miscellaneous provisions
    I. Preservation of reform laws

Part six — Provisional articles
    Sixteen Provisional articles

Part seven — Final provisions
    I. Amendment of the Constitution, participation in election and referendum
    II. Preamble and headings of articles
    III. Entry into force of the Constitution

## Preamble

Following the operation carried out on September 12, 1980, by the Turkish Armed Forces in response to a call from the Turkish Nation, of which they form an inseparable part, at a time when the approach of a separatist, destructive, and bloody civil war unprecedented in the Republican era threatened the integrity of the eternal Turkish Nation and motherland and the existence of the sacred Turkish State.

    This CONSTITUTION was prepared by the Consultative Assembly, given final form by the Council of National Security, which are the legitimate representatives of the Turkish Nation, and adopted, approved, and directly enacted by the Turkish Nation.

And is entrusted for safekeeping by the Turkish Nation to the patriotism of its democracy-loving sons and daughters, in order that it may be understood to embody the IDEAS, BELIEFS and RESOLUTIONS set forth below and be interpreted and implemented accordingly, commanding respect for, and absolute loyalty to, its letter and spirit:

- The direction of the concept of nationalism as outlined by Atatürk, the founder of the Republic of Turkey, its immortal leader and unrivalled hero; and in line with the reforms and principles introduced by him.
- The determination to safeguard the everlasting existence, prosperity and material and spiritual well-being of the Republic of Turkey, and to ensure that it attains the standards of contemporary civilization, as a full and honorable member of the world family of nations.
- Recognition of the absolute supremacy of the will of the nation, and of the fact that sovereignty is vested fully and unconditionally in the Turkish Nation and that no individual or body empowered to exercise it on behalf of the nation shall deviate from democracy based on freedom, as set forth in the Constitution and the rule of law instituted according to its requirements.
- The understanding that separation of powers does not imply an order of precedence among the organs of State, but reflects a civilized division of labor and mode of cooperation restricted to the exercise of specific State powers, and that supremacy is vested solely in the Constitution and the laws.
- The determination that no protection shall be afforded to thoughts or opinions contrary to Turkish National interests, the principle of the existence of Turkey as an indivisible entity with its State and territory, Turkish historical and moral values, or the nationalism, principles, reforms and modernism of Atatürk, and that, as required by the principle of secularism, there shall be no interference whatsoever of sacred religious feelings in State affairs and politics.
- The understanding that it is the birthright of every Turkish citizen to lead an honorable life and develop his material and spiritual resources under the aegis of national culture, civilization and the rule of law, through the exercise of the fundamental rights and freedoms set forth in this Constitution, in conformity with the requirements of equality and social justice.
- The recognition that all Turkish citizens are united in national honor and pride, in national joy and grief, in their rights and duties towards their existence as a nation, in blessings and in burdens, and in every manifestation of national life, and that they have the right to demand a peaceful life based on absolute respect for one another's rights and freedoms, mutual love and fellowship, and the desire for, and belief in, "Peace at home, peace in the world."

## Part one — General principles

### I. Form of the State

*Article 1.* The Turkish State is a republic.

## II. Characteristics of the Republic

*Article 2.* The Republic of Turkey is a democratic, secular and social State governed by the rule of law; bearing in mind the concepts of public peace, national solidarity, and justice; respecting Human Rights; loyal to the nationalism of Atatürk, and based on the fundamental tenets set forth in the Preamble.

## III. Integrity of the State, official language, flag, national anthem, and capital

*Article 3.* The Turkish State, with its territory and nation, in an indivisible entity. Its language is Turkish.

Its flag, the form of which is prescribed by the relevant law, is composed of a white crescent and star on a red background.

Its national anthem is the "Independence March."

Its capital is Ankara.

## IV. Irrevocable provisions

*Article 4.* The provision of Article 1 of the Constitution establishing the form of the State as a Republic, the provisions in Article 2 on the characteristics of the Republic, and the provision of Article 3 shall not be amended, nor shall their amendment be proposed.

## V. Fundamental aims and duties of the State

*Article 5.* The fundamental aims and duties of the State are: to safeguard the independence and integrity of the Turkish Nation, the indivisibility of the country, the Republic and democracy; to ensure the welfare, peace, and happiness of the individual and society; to strive for the removal of political, social, and economic obstacles which restrict the fundamental rights and freedoms of the individual in a manner incompatible with the principles of justice and of the social State governed by the rule of law; and to provide the conditions required for the development of the individual's material and spiritual existence.

## VI. Sovereignty

*Article 6.* Sovereignty is vested in the nation without reservation or condition.

The Turkish Nation shall exercise its sovereignty through the authorized organs as prescribed by the principles laid down in the Constitution.

The right to exercise sovereignty shall not be delegated to any individual, group, or class. No person or agency shall exercise any State authority which does not emanate from the Constitution.

## VII. Legislative power

*Article 7.* Legislative power is vested in the Turkish Grand National Assembly on behalf of the Turkish Nation. This power cannot be delegated.

## VIII. Executive power and function

*Article 8.* Executive power and function shall be exercised and carried out by the President of the Republic and the Council of Ministers in conformity with the Constitution and the laws.

## IX. Judicial power

*Article 9.* Judicial power shall be exercised by independent courts on behalf of the Turkish Nation.

## X. Equality before law

*Article 10.* All individuals are equal without any discrimination before the law, irrespective of language, race, color, sex, political opinion, philosophical belief, religion, and sect, or any such considerations.

No privilege shall be granted to any individual, family, group, or class.

State organs and administrative authorities shall act in compliance with the principle of equality before the law in all their proceedings.

## XI. Supremacy and binding force of the Constitution

*Article 11.* The provisions of the Constitution are fundamental legal rules binding upon legislative, executive and judicial organs, and administrative authorities and other agencies, and individuals.

Laws shall not be in conflict with the Constitution.

# Part two — Fundamental rights and duties

## Chapter one — General provisions

### I. Nature of fundamental rights and freedoms

*Article 12.* Everyone possesses inherent fundamental rights and freedoms which are inviolable and inalienable.

The fundamental rights and freedoms also include the duties and responsibilities of the individual towards society, his family, and other individuals.

### II. Restriction of fundamental rights and freedoms

*Article 13.* Fundamental rights and freedoms may be restricted by law, in conformity with the letter and spirit of the Constitution, with the aim of safeguarding the indivisible integrity of the State with its territory and nation, national sovereignty, the Republic, national security, public order, general peace, the public interest, public morals and public health, and also for specific reasons set forth in the relevant articles of the Constitution.

General and specific grounds for restrictions of fundamental rights and freedoms shall not conflict with the requirements of the democratic order of society and shall not be imposed for any purpose other than those for which they are prescribed.

The general grounds for restriction set forth in this article shall apply for all fundamental rights and freedoms.

### III. Prohibition of abuse of fundamental rights and freedoms

*Article 14.* None of the rights and freedoms embodied in the Constitution shall be exercised with the aim of violating the indivisible integrity of the State with its territory and nation, of endangering the existence of the Turkish State and Republic, of destroying fundamental rights and freedoms, of placing the government of the State under the control of an individual or a group of people, or establishing the hegemony of one social class over others, or creating discrimination on the basis of language, race, religion or sect, or of establishing by any other means a system of government based on these concepts and ideas.

The sanctions to be applied against those who violate these prohibitions, and those who incite and provoke others to the same end shall be determined by law.

No provision of this Constitution shall be interpreted in a manner that would grant the right of destroying the rights and freedoms embodied in the Constitution.

### IV. Suspension of the exercise of fundamental rights and freedoms

*Article 15.* In times of war, mobilization, martial law, or state of emergency the exercise of fundamental rights and freedoms can be partially or entirely suspended, or measures may be taken, to the extent required by the exigencies of the situation, which derogate the guarantees embodied in the Constitution, provided that obligations under international law are not violated.

Even under the circumstances indicated in the first paragraph, the individual's right to life, and the integrity of his material and spiritual entity, shall be inviolable except where death occurs through lawful acts of warfare and execution of death sentences; no one may be compelled to reveal his religion, conscience, thought or opinion, nor be accused on account of them; offenses and penalties may not be made retroactive, nor may anyone be held guilty until so proven by a court judgment.

\*\*\*

## Chapter two — The rights and duties of the individual

### I. Personal inviolability, material and spiritual entity of the individual

*Article 17.* Everyone has the right to life and the right to protect and develop his material and spiritual entity.

The physical integrity of the individual shall not be violated except under medical necessity and in cases prescribed by law; he shall not be subject to scientific or medical experiments without his consent.

No one shall be subjected to torture or ill-treatment; no one shall be subjected to penalty or treatment incompatible with human dignity.

The cases of carrying out of death penalties under court sentences, the act of killing in self-defense, the occurrences of death as a result of the use of a weapon permitted by law as a necessary measure in cases of: apprehension, or the execution of warrants of arrest, the prevention of escape of lawfully arrested or convicted persons, the quelling of a riot or insurrection, the execution of the orders of authorized bodies during martial law or state of emergency are outside of the provision of paragraph 1.

\*\*\*

### III. Personal liberty and security

*Article 19.* Everyone has the right to liberty and security of person.

No one shall be deprived of his liberty except in the following cases where procedure and conditions are prescribed by law: execution of sentences restricting liberty and the implementation of security measures decided by courts, apprehension or detention of a person as a result of a court order or as a result of an obligation upon him designated by law; execution of an order for the purpose of the educational supervision of a minor or for bringing him before the competent authority; execution of measures taken in conformity with the relevant legal provision for the treatment, education, or correction in institutions of a person of unsound mind, an alcoholic or drug addict or vagrant or a person spreading contagious diseases, when such persons constitute a danger to the public; apprehension or detention of a person who enters or attempts to enter illegally into the country or concerning whom a deportation or extradition order has been issued.

Individuals against whom there are strong indications of having committed an offense can be arrested by decision of a judge solely for the purposes of preventing escape, or preventing the destruction or alteration of evidence as well as in similar other circumstances which necessitate detention and are prescribed by law. Apprehension of a person without a decision by a judge shall be resorted to only in cases when a person is caught in the act of committing an offense or in cases where delay is likely to thwart justice; the conditions for such apprehension shall be defined by law.

Individuals arrested or detained shall be promptly notified, and in all cases in writing, or orally, when the former is not possible, of the grounds for their arrest or detention and the charges against them; in cases of offenses committed collectively this notification shall be made, at the latest, before the individual is brought before the judge.

The person arrested or detained shall be brought before a judge within forty-eight hours and within fifteen days in the case of offenses committed collectively, excluding the time taken to send him to the court nearest to the place of seizure. No one can be deprived of his liberty without the decision of a judge after the expiry of the above specified periods. These periods may be extended during a state of emergency, under martial law or in time of war.

Notification of the situation of the person arrested or detained shall be made to the next of kin, except in cases of definite necessities pertaining to the risks of revealing the scope and subject of the investigation compelling otherwise.

Persons under detention shall have the right to request to be tried with a reasonable time or to be released during investigation or prosecution. Release may be made conditional on the presentation of an appropriate guarantee with a view to securing the presence of the person at the trial proceedings and the execution of the court sentence.

Persons deprived of their liberty under any circumstances are entitled to apply to the appropriate judicial authority for speedy conclusion of proceedings regarding their situation and for their release if the restriction placed upon them is not lawful.

Damages suffered by persons subjected to treatment contrary to the above provisions shall be compensated for according to law, by the State.

## IV. Privacy and protection of private life

### A. PRIVACY OF THE INDIVIDUAL'S LIFE

*Article 20.* Everyone has the right to demand respect for his private and family life. Privacy of individual and family life cannot be violated. Exceptions necessitated by judiciary investigation and prosecution are reserved.

Unless there exists a decision duly passed by a judge in cases explicitly defined by law, and unless there exists an order of an agency authorized by law in cases where delay is deemed prejudicial, neither the person nor the private papers, nor belongings of an individual shall be searched nor shall they be seized.

### B. INVIOLABILITY OF DOMICILE

*Article 21.* The domicile of an individual shall not be violated. Unless there exists a decision duly passed by a judge in cases explicitly defined by law, and unless there exists an order of an agency authorized by law in cases where delay is deemed prejudicial, no domicile may be entered or searched, or the property therein seized.

C. FREEDOM OF COMMUNICATION

*Article 22.* Everyone has the right to freedom of communication.

Secrecy of communication is fundamental.

Communication shall not be impeded nor its secrecy be violated, unless there exists a decision duly passed by a judge in cases explicitly defined by law, and unless there exists an order of an agency authorized by law in cases where delay is deemed prejudicial.

Public establishments or institutions where exceptions to the above may be applied will be defined by law.

*V. Freedom of residence and movement*

*Article 23.* Everyone has the right to freedom of residence and movement.

Freedom of residence may be restricted by law for the purpose of preventing offenses, promoting social and economic development, ensuring sound and orderly urban growth, and protecting public property; freedom of movement may be restricted by law for the purpose of investigation and prosecution of an offense, and prevention of offenses. A citizen's freedom to leave the country may be restricted on account of the national economic situation, civic obligations, or criminal investigation or prosecution.

Citizens may not be deported, or deprived of their right of entry into their homeland.

\*\*\*

*VII. Freedom of thought and opinion*

*Article 25.* Everyone has the right to freedom of thought and opinion.

No one shall be compelled to reveal his thoughts and opinions for any reason or purpose; nor shall anyone be blamed or accused on account of his thought and opinions.

*VIII. Freedom of expression and dissemination of thought*

*Article 26.* Everyone has the right to express and disseminate his thought and opinion by speech, in writing, or in pictures or through other media, individually or collectively. This right includes the freedom to receive and impart information and ideas without interference from official authorities. This provision shall not preclude subjecting transmission by radio, television, cinema, and similar means to a system of licensing.

The exercise of these freedoms may be restricted for the purposes of preventing crime, punishing offenders, withholding information duly classified as a State secret, protecting the reputation and rights and the private and family life of others, or protecting professional secrets as prescribed by law, or ensuring the proper functioning of the judiciary.

No language prohibited by law shall be used in the expression and dissemination of thought. Any written or printed documents, phonograph records, magnetic or video tapes, and other means of expression used in contravention of this provision shall be seized by a duly issued decision of a judge or, in cases where delay is deemed prejudicial, by the competent authority designated by law. The authority issuing the seizure order shall notify the competent judge of its decision within twenty-four hours. The judge shall decide on the matter within three days.

Provisions regulating the use of means of disseminating information and ideas shall not be interpreted as a restriction of the freedom of expression and dissemination unless they prevent the dissemination of information and thoughts.

## IX. Freedom of science and arts

*Article 27.* Everyone has the right to study and teach freely, explain, and disseminate science and arts and to carry out research in these fields.

The right to disseminate shall not be exercised for the purpose of changing the provisions of Articles 1, 2, and 3 of this Constitution.

The provisions of this article shall not preclude regulation by law of the entry and distribution of foreign publications in the country.

## X. Provisions relating to the press and publication

*A. Freedom of the press* *Article 28.* The press is free, and shall not be censored. The establishment of a printing house shall not be subject to prior permission and to the deposit of a financial guarantee.

Publication shall not be made in any language prohibited by law.

The State shall take the necessary measures to ensure the freedom of the press and freedom of information.

In the limitation of freedom of the press, Articles 26 and 27 of the Constitution are applicable.

Anyone who writes or prints any news or articles which threaten the internal or external security of the State or the indivisible integrity of the State with its territory and nation, which tend to incite offense, riot or insurrection, or which refer to classified State secrets and anyone who prints or transmits such news or articles to others for the above purposes shall be held responsible under the law relevant to these offenses. Distribution may be suspended as a preventive measure by the decision of a judge, or in the event delay is deemed prejudicial, by the competent authority designated by law. The authority suspending distribution shall notify the competent judge of its decision within twenty-four hours at the latest. The order suspending distribution shall become null and void unless upheld by the competent judge within forty-eight hours at the latest.

No ban shall be placed on the reporting of events, except by the decision of a judge issued to ensure proper functioning of the judiciary, within the limits to be specified by law.

Periodical and non-periodical publications may be seized by the decision of a judge in cases of ongoing investigation or prosecution of offenses prescribed by law; and, in situations where delay could endanger the indivisible integrity of the State with its territory and nation, national security, public order or public morals, and for the prevention of offense by order of the competent authority designated by law. The authority issuing the seizure order shall notify the competent judge of its decision within twenty-four hours at the latest. The seizure order shall become null and void unless upheld by the competent court within forty-eights hours at the latest.

The general common provisions shall apply when seizure and confiscation of periodicals and non-periodicals for reasons of criminal investigation and prosecution take place.

Periodicals published in Turkey may be temporarily suspended by court sentence if found guilty of publishing material which contravenes the indivisible integrity of the state with its territory and nation, the fundamental principles of the Republic, national security, and public morals. Any publication which clearly bears the characteristics of being the continuation of the suspended periodical is prohibited; and shall be seized by a decision of judge.

B. RIGHT TO PUBLISH PERIODICALS AND NON-PERIODICALS

*Article 29.* Publication of periodicals or non-periodicals shall not be subject to prior authorization or to the deposit of a financial guarantee.

To publish a periodical it shall suffice to submit the information and documents prescribed by law to the competent authority designated by law. If the information and documents submitted are found to be in contravention of law, the competent authority shall apply to the appropriate court for suspension of publication.

The publication of periodicals, the conditions of publication, the financial resources, and rules relevant to the profession of journalism shall be regulated by law. The law shall not impose any political, economic, financial, and technical conditions obstructing or making difficult the free dissemination of news, thought, or beliefs.

Periodicals shall have equal access to the means and facilities of the State, other public corporate bodies, and their agencies.

C. PROTECTION OF PRINTING FACILITIES

*Article 30.* A printing press or its annexes duly established as a publishing house under law shall not be seized, confiscated, or barred from operation on the grounds of being an instrument of crime, except in cases where it is convicted of offenses against the indivisible integrity of the State with its territory and nation, against the fundamental principles of the Republic or against national security.

D. RIGHT TO USE MASS MEDIA OTHER THAN THE PRESS WHICH ARE OWNED BY PUBLIC CORPORATIONS

*Article 31.* Individuals and political parties have the right to use mass media and means of communication other than the press owned by public corporations. The conditions and procedures for such use shall be regulated by law.

The law shall not impose restrictions preventing the public from receiving information or forming ideas and opinions through these media, or preventing public opinion from being freely formed, on grounds other than the general restrictions set forth in Article 13.

\*\*\*

*XI. Rights and freedoms of assembly*

A. FREEDOM OF ASSOCIATION

*Article 33.* Everyone has the right to form associations without prior permission.

Submitting the information and documents stipulated by law to the competent authority designated by law shall suffice to enable an association to be formed. If the information and documents submitted are found to contravene the law, the competent authority shall apply to the appropriate court for the suspension of activities or dissolution of the association involved.

No one shall be compelled to become or remain a member of an association. The formalities, conditions, and procedures governing the exercise of freedom of association shall be prescribed by law.

Associations shall not contravene the general grounds of restriction in Article 13, nor shall they pursue political aims, engage in political activities, receive support from or give support to political parties, or take joint action with labor unions, with public professional organizations or with foundations.

Associations deviating from their original aims or conditions of establishment, or failing to fulfill the obligations stipulated by law, shall be considered dissolved.

Associations may be dissolved by the decision of a judge in cases prescribed by law. They may be suspended from activity by the competent authority designated by law pending a court decision in cases where delay endangers the indivisible integrity of the State with its territory and nation, national security or sovereignty, public order, the protection of the rights and freedoms of others, or the prevention of crime.

Provisions of the first paragraph of this article shall not prevent imposition of restrictions on the rights of Armed Forces and Security Forces officials and civil servants to form associations, or the prohibition of the exercise of this right.

This article shall apply equally to foundations and other organizations of the same nature.

B. RIGHT TO HOLD MEETINGS AND DEMONSTRATION MARCHES

*Article 34.* Everyone has the right to hold unarmed and peaceful meetings and demonstration marches without prior permission.

The competent administrative authority may determine a site and route for the demonstration march in order to prevent disruption of order in urban life.

The formalities, conditions, and procedures governing the exercise of the right to hold meetings and demonstration marches shall be prescribed by law.

The competent authority designated by law may prohibit a particular meeting and demonstration march, or postpone it for not more than two months in situations where there is a strong possibility that disturbances may arise which would seriously upset public order, where the requirement of national security may be violated, or where acts aimed at destroying the fundamental characteristics of the Republic may be committed. In cases where the law forbids all meetings or demonstration marches in districts of a province for the same reasons, the postponement may not exceed three months.

Associations, foundations, labor unions, and public professional organizations shall not hold meetings or demonstration marches exceeding their own scope and aims.

\*\*\*

*XIII. Provisions relating to the protection of rights*

A. FREEDOM TO CLAIM RIGHTS

*Article 36.* Everyone has the right of litigation either as plaintiff or defendant before the courts through lawful means and procedure.

No court shall refuse to hear a case within its jurisdiction.

B. GUARANTEE OF LAWFUL JUDGE

*Article 37.* No one may be tried by any judicial authority other than the legally designated court.

Extraordinary tribunals with jurisdiction that would in effect remove a person from the jurisdiction of his legally designated court shall not be established.

C. PRINCIPLES RELATING TO OFFENSES AND PENALTIES

*Article 38.* No one shall be punished for any act which did not constitute a criminal offense under the law in force at the time it was committed; no one shall be given a heavier penalty for an offense than the penalty applicable at the time when the offense was committed.

The provisions of the above paragraph shall also apply to the statute of limitations on offenses and penalties and on the results of conviction.

Penalties, and security measures in lieu of penalties, shall be prescribed only by law.

No one shall be held guilty until proven guilty in a court of law.

No one shall be compelled to make a statement that would incriminate himself or his legal next of kin, or to present such incriminating evidence.

Criminal responsibility shall be personal.

General confiscation shall not be imposed as penalty.

The administration shall not impose any sanction resulting in restriction of personal liberty. Exceptions to this provision may be introduced by law regarding internal order of the Armed Forces.

No citizen shall be extradited to a foreign country on account of an offense.

\*\*\*

*XV. Protection of fundamental rights and freedoms*

*Article 40.* Everyone whose constitutional rights and freedoms are violated has the right to request prompt access to the competent authorities.

Damages incurred by any person through unlawful treatment by holders of public office shall be compensated by the State. The State reserves the right of recourse to the official responsible.

## Chapter three — Social and economic rights and duties

\*\*\*

*II. Right and duty of training and education*

*Article 42.* No one shall be deprived of the right of learning and education.

The scope of the right to education shall be defined and regulated by law.

Training and education shall be conducted along the lines of the principles and reforms of Atatürk, on the basis of contemporary science and education methods, under the supervision and control of the State. Institutions of training and education contravening these provisions shall not be established.

The freedom of training and education does not relieve the individual from loyalty to the Constitution.

Primary education is compulsory for all citizens of both sexes and is free of charge in state schools.

The principles governing the functioning of private primary and secondary schools shall be regulated by law in keeping with the standards set for state schools.

The State shall provide scholarships and other means of assistance to enable students of merit lacking financial means to continue their education. The State shall take necessary measures to rehabilitate those in need of special training so as to render such people useful to society.

Training, education, research, and study are the only activities that shall be pursued at institutions of training and education. These activities shall not be obstructed in any way.

No language other than Turkish shall be taught as mother tongue to Turkish citizens at any institutions of training or education. Foreign languages to be taught in institutions of training and education and the rules to be followed by

## C. RIGHT TO ORGANIZE LABOR UNIONS

*Article 51.* Workers and employers have the right to form labor unions and employers' associations and higher organizations, without prior permission, in order to safeguard and develop their economic and social right and the interests of their members in their labor relations.

In order to form unions and their higher bodies, it shall suffice to submit the information and documents prescribed by law to the competent authority designated by law. If this information and documentation is not in conformity with law, the competent authority shall apply to the appropriate court for the suspension of activities or the dissolution of the union or the higher body.

Everyone shall be free to become a member of, or withdraw from membership in, a union.

No one shall be compelled to become a member, remain a member, or withdraw from membership of a union.

Workers and employers cannot hold concurrent membership in more than one labor union or employers' association.

Employment in a given workplace shall not be made conditional on being, or not being, a member of a labor union.

To become an executive in a labor union or in higher organizations of them it is a prerequisite condition that the workers should have held the status of a laborer for at least ten years.

The status, the administration, and the functioning of the labor unions and their higher bodies should not be inconsistent with the characteristics of the Republic as defined in the Constitution, or with democratic principles.

## D. ACTIVITIES OF LABOR UNIONS

*Article 52.* Labor unions, in addition to being under the general restrictions set forth in Article 13, also shall not pursue a political cause, engage in political activity, receive support from political parties or give support to them, and shall not act jointly for these purposes with associations, public professional organizations, and foundations.

The fact of engaging in labor union activities in a workplace shall not justify failure to perform one's work.

The administrative and financial supervision of labor unions by the State, and their revenues and expenditures, and the method of payment of membership dues to the labor union, shall be regulated by law.

Labor unions shall not use their revenues beyond the scope of their professional aims, and shall keep all their funds in State banks.

## VI. Collective bargaining, right to strike, and lock-out

A. RIGHT OF COLLECTIVE BARGAINING

*Article 53.* Workers and employers have the right to conclude collective bargaining agreements in order to regulate reciprocally their economic and social position and conditions of work.

The procedure to be followed in concluding collective bargaining agreements shall be regulated by law.

More than one collective bargaining agreement at the same place of work for the same period shall not be concluded or put into effect.

B. RIGHT TO STRIKE, AND LOCK-OUT

*Article 54.* Workers have the right to strike if a dispute arises during the collective bargaining process. The procedures and conditions governing the exercise of this right and the employer's recourse to a lock-out, the scope of both actions, and the exceptions to which they are subject shall be regulated by law.

The right to strike, and lock-out, shall not be exercised in a manner contrary to the principle of goodwill to the detriment of society, and in a manner damaging to national wealth.

During a strike, the labor union is liable for any material damage caused in a workplace where the strike is being held, as a result of deliberate negligent behavior by the workers and the labor union.

The circumstances and places in which strikes and lock-outs may be prohibited or postponed shall be regulated by law.

In cases where a strike or a lock-out is prohibited or postponed, the dispute shall be settled by the Supreme Arbitration Board at the end of the period of postponement. The disputing parties may apply to the Supreme Arbitration Board by mutual agreement at any stage of the dispute.

The decisions of the Supreme Arbitration Board shall be final and have the force of collective bargaining agreement.

The organization and functions of the Supreme Arbitration Board shall be regulated by law.

Politically motivated strikes and lock-outs, solidarity strikes and lock-outs, occupation of work premises, labor go-slows, production decreasing, and other forms of obstruction are prohibited.

Those who refuse to go on strike shall in no way be barred from working at their workplace by strikers.

\*\*\*

## Chapter four — Political rights and duties

*I. Turkish citizenship*

*Article 66.* Everyone bound to the Turkish State through the bond of citizenship is a Turk.

The child of a Turkish father or a Turkish mother is a Turk. The citizenship of a child of a foreign father and a Turkish mother shall be defined by law.

Citizenship can be acquired under the conditions stipulated by law, and shall be forfeited only in cases determined by law.

No Turk shall be deprived of citizenship, unless he commits an act incompatible with loyalty to the motherland.

Recourse to the courts, against the decisions and proceedings related to the deprivation of citizenship, shall not be denied.

*II. Right to vote, to be elected, and to engage in political activity*

*Article 67.* In conformity with the conditions set forth in the law, citizens have the right to vote, to be elected, and to engage in political activities independently or in a political party, and to take part in a referendum.

Elections and referendums shall be held under the direction and supervision of the judiciary, according to the principles of free, equal, secret, direct, universal suffrage, and public counting of the votes.

All Turkish citizens entering the age of twenty in the year of election and referendum shall have the right to vote in elections and take part in a referendum, the months and days of the age not taken into account.

The exercise of these rights shall be regulated by law.

Conscripts serving in the Armed Services, students in military schools, and detainees and convicts in prisons cannot vote.

*III. Provisions relating to political parties*

A. FORMING PARTIES, MEMBERSHIP AND WITHDRAWAL FROM MEMBERSHIP IN A PARTY

*Article 68.* Citizens have the right to form political parties, and to join and withdraw from them in accordance with the established procedure. To become a member of a party, one must be over twenty-one years of age.

Political parties are indispensable elements of the democratic political system.

Political parties shall be founded without prior permission and shall pursue their activities in accordance with the provisions set forth in the Constitution and law.

The statutes and programs of political parties shall not be in conflict with the indivisible integrity of the State with its territory and nation, Human Rights, national sovereignty, and the principles of the democratic and secular Republic.

Political parties whose aim is to support and to set up the domination of a class or group, or any kind of dictatorship, cannot be formed.

Political parties shall not organize and function abroad, shall not form discriminative auxiliary bodies such as women's or youth branches, nor shall they establish foundations.

Judges and prosecutors, members of higher judicial organs, members of the teaching staff at institutions of higher education, members of the Higher Education

Council, civil servants in public organizations and corporations, and other public servants who are not considered to be laborers by virtue of the services they perform, students, and members of the Armed Forces shall not become members of political parties.

B. PRINCIPLES TO BE OBSERVED BY POLITICAL PARTIES

*Article 69.* Political parties shall not engage in activities outside the lines of their statutes and programs, and shall not contravene the restrictions set forth in Article 14 of the Constitution; those that contravene them shall be dissolved permanently.

Political parties shall not have political ties and engage in political cooperation with associations, unions, foundations, cooperatives, and public professional organizations and their higher bodies in order to implement and strengthen their party policies, nor shall they receive material assistance from these bodies.

The internal functioning and the decisions of political parties shall not be contrary to the principles of democracy.

The auditing of political parties shall be carried out by the Constitutional Court.

The Office of the Chief Public Prosecutor shall examine, with priority, the conformity of the status and programs of new parties and of the status of their founders in view of the Constitution and the law; and shall also follow their activities.

The dissolution of political parties shall be decided by the Constitutional Court after the filing of a suit by the Office of the Chief Public Prosecutor of the Republic.

The founding members and administrators at every level of a political party which has been permanently dissolved shall not become founding members, administrators, or comptrollers of a new political party; nor shall any new political party be founded, the majority of whose members are former members of a political party previously dissolved.

Political parties shall not receive assistance in kind or cash from foreign states, international organizations, associations, and groups in foreign countries, nor shall they take orders from these bodies, or participate in their decisions and activities which are prejudicial to the independence and territorial integrity of Turkey. Political parties contravening the provisions of this paragraph shall also be dissolved permanently.

The formulation and activities, supervision, and dissolution of political parties shall be regulated by law within the abovementioned provisions.

*IV. Right to enter the public service*

A. ENTRY INTO THE PUBLIC SERVICE

*Article 70.* Every Turk has the right to enter the public service.

No criteria other than the qualifications for the office concerned shall be taken into consideration for recruitment into the public service.

***

# Part three — Fundamental organs of the Republic

## Chapter one — Legislative power

*I. The Turkish Grand National Assembly*

\*\*\*

B. ELIGIBILITY TO BE A DEPUTY

*Article 76.* Every Turk over the age of thirty is eligible to be a deputy.

Persons who have not completed their primary education, who have been deprived of legal capacity, who have failed to perform compulsory military service, who are banned from public service, who have been sentenced to a prison term totaling one year or more excluding involuntary offenses, or to a heavy imprisonment; those who have been convicted for dishonorable offenses such as embezzlement, corruption, bribery, theft, fraud, forgery, breach of trust, fraudulent bankruptcy; and persons convicted of smuggling, conspiracy in official bidding tender, or purchases, of offenses related to the disclosure of State secrets, of involvement in ideological and anarchistic activities, and incitement and encouragement of such activities, shall not be elected deputies, even if they have been pardoned.

Judges and prosecutors, members of the higher judicial organs, members of the teaching staff at institutions of higher education, members of the Higher Education Council, employees of public institutions and agencies who have the status of civil servants, other public employees not regarded as laborers on account of the duties they perform, and members of the Armed Forces shall not stand for election or be eligible to be a deputy unless they resign from office.

\*\*\*

F. PROVISIONS RELATING TO MEMBERSHIP

*1. Representing the nation*
*Article 80.* Members of the Turkish Grand National Assembly represent not merely their own constituencies or constituents but the Nation as a whole.

*2. Oath-taking*
*Article 81.* Members of the Turkish Grand National Assembly, on assuming office, shall take the following oath:

> I swear upon my honor and integrity, before the great Turkish nation, to safeguard the existence and independence of the State, the indivisible integrity of the country and the Nation, and the absolute sovereignty of the Nation; to remain loyal to the supremacy of law, to the democratic and secular Republic, and to Atatürk's principles and reforms; not to deviate

from the ideal according to which everyone is entitled to enjoy Human Rights and fundamental freedoms under peace and prosperity in society, national solidarity and justice, and loyalty to the Constitution.

\*\*\*

*4. Parliamentary immunity*
Article 83. Members of the Turkish Grand National Assembly shall not be liable for their votes and statements concerning parliamentary functions, for the views they express before the Assembly, or, unless the Assembly decides otherwise on the proposal of the Bureau for that sitting, for repeating or revealing these outside the Assembly.

A deputy who is alleged to have committed an offense before or after the election shall not be arrested, interrogated, detained, or tried unless the Assembly decides otherwise. This provision shall not apply in cases where a member is caught in the act of committing a crime punishable by a heavy penalty and in cases subject to Article 14 of the Constitution if an investigation has been initiated before the election. However, in such situations the competent authority shall notify the Turkish Grand National Assembly immediately and directly.

The execution of a criminal sentence imposed on a member of the Turkish Grand National Assembly either before or after his election shall be suspended until he ceases to be a member; the statute of limitations does not apply during the term of membership.

Investigation and prosecution of a re-elected deputy shall be subject to the renewed waiver of immunity by the Assembly.

Political party groups in the Turkish Grand National Assembly shall not hold discussions or take decisions regarding parliamentary immunity.

*5. Loss of membership*
Article 84. The loss of membership by deputies shall be decided by an absolute majority of the total number of members in respect of deputies who resign, who are convicted of an offense precluding election to the Turkish Grand National Assembly, who are deprived of their legal capacity, who resign from their party in order to join another party, or take up a ministerial post in the Council of Ministers other than a provisional ministerial post during the election period who assume a function incompatible with membership, or who failed to attend without excuse, five meetings in a period of one month.

A deputy who resigns from his party shall not be nominated as a candidate in the following elections by the central organs of any party existing at the time of his resignation.

The membership of a deputy, whose acts and statements are cited in a judgment of the Constitutional Court as having caused the dissolution of a political party and that of other deputies who belonged to the party on the date when the action for dissolution was brought, shall end when the Presidency of the Turkish Grand National Assembly is notified of the dissolution order.

## 6. Application for annulment

*Article 85.* If the Turkish Grand National Assembly decides to waive the parliamentary immunity of a member or disqualify him from membership, the member concerned or any member of the Turkish Grand National Assembly may, within a week of the decision, appeal to the Constitutional Court for the decision to be annulled on the grounds that it is contrary to the Constitution or to the Rules of Procedure of the Assembly. The Constitutional Court shall decide on the appeal within fifteen days.

\*\*\*

## II. Functions and power of the Turkish Grand National Assembly

### A. GENERAL PROVISIONS

*Article 87.* The functions and powers of the Turkish Grand National Assembly comprise the enactment, amendment, and repeal of laws; the supervision of the Council of Ministers and the ministers; authorization of the Council of Ministers to issue governmental decrees having force of law on certain matters; debating and approval of the budget draft and the draft law of the final accounts; making decisions regarding printing of currency and declaration of war; ratifying international agreements, deciding on the proclamation of amnesties and pardons, excluding those who have been convicted for activities set out in Article 14 of the Constitution; confirming death sentences passed by the courts; and exercising the powers and executing the functions envisaged in the other articles of the Constitution.

\*\*\*

### C. PROMULGATION OF LAWS BY THE PRESIDENT OF THE REPUBLIC

*Article 89.* The President of the Republic shall promulgate the laws adopted by the Turkish Grand National Assembly within fifteen days.

He shall, within the same period, refer to the Turkish Grand National Assembly for further consideration laws which he deems unsuitable for promulgation, together with a statement of his reasons. Budget laws shall not be subject to this provision.

If the Turkish Grand National Assembly adopts in its unchanged form the law referred back, the President of the Republic shall promulgate it; if the Assembly amends the law which was referred back, the President of the Republic may again refer back the amended law to the Assembly.

Provisions relating to Constitutional amendments are reserved.

### D. RATIFICATION OF INTERNATIONAL TREATIES

*Article 90.* The ratification of treaties concluded with foreign states and international organizations on behalf of the Republic of Turkey shall be subject to adoption by the Turkish Grand National Assembly by a law approving the ratification.

Agreements regulating economic, commercial, and technical relations, and covering a period of no more than one year, may be put into effect through promulgation, provided they do not entail any financial commitment by the state, and provided they do not infringe upon the status of individuals or upon the property rights of Turkish citizens abroad. In such cases, these agreements must be brought to the knowledge of the Turkish Grand National Assembly within two months of their promulgation.

Agreements in connection with the implementation of an international treaty, and economic, commercial, technical, or administrative agreements which are concluded depending on an authorization given by law shall not require approval by the Turkish Grand National Assembly. However, agreements concluded under the provision of this paragraph and affecting the economic or commercial relations and private rights of individuals shall not be put into effect unless promulgated.

Agreements resulting in amendments to Turkish laws shall be subject to the provisions of the first paragraph.

International agreements duly put into effect carry the force of law. No appeal to the Constitutional Court can be made with regard to these agreements, on the ground that they are unconstitutional.

E. AUTHORIZATION TO ENACT DECREES HAVING FORCE OF LAW

*Article 91.* The Turkish Grand National Assembly may empower the Council of Ministers to issue decrees having force of law. However, the fundamental rights, individual rights, and duties included in the First and Second Chapter of the Second Part of the Constitution and the political rights and duties listed in the Fourth Chapter cannot be regulated by decrees having force of law except during periods of martial law and states of emergency.

The empowering law shall define the purpose, scope, principles, and operative period of the decree having force of law, and whether more than one decree will be issued within the same period.

Resignation or fall of the Council of Ministers or expiration of the legislative term shall not cause the termination of the power conferred for the given period.

When approving a decree having force of law before the end of the prescribed period, the Turkish Grand National Assembly shall also state whether the power has terminated or will continue until the expiry of the said period.

Provisions relating to the decrees having force of law issued by the Council of Ministers meeting under the chairmanship of the President of the Republic, in time of martial law or states of emergency, are reserved.

Decrees having force of law shall come into force on the day of their publication in the Official Gazette. However, a later date may be indicated in the decree as the date of entry into force.

Decrees are submitted to the Turkish Grand National Assembly on the day of their publication in the Official Gazette.

Laws of empowering and decrees having force of law which are based on these shall be discussed in the committees and in the plenary session of the Turkish Grand National Assembly with priority and urgency.

Decrees not submitted to the Turkish Grand National Assembly on the day of their publication shall cease to have effect on that day and decrees rejected by the Turkish Grand National Assembly shall cease to have effect on the day of the publication of the decision in the Official Gazette. The amended provisions of the decrees which are approved as amended shall go into force on the day of their publication in the Official Gazette.

\*\*\*

## Chapter two — Executive

*I. President of the Republic*

A. QUALIFICATIONS AND IMPARTIALITY

*Article 101.* The President of the Republic shall be elected for a term of office of seven years by the Turkish Grand National Assembly from among its own members who are over forty years of age and who have completed their higher education or from among Turkish citizens who fulfill these requirements and are eligible to be deputies.

The nomination of a candidate for the Presidency of the Republic from outside the Turkish Grand National Assembly shall require a written proposal by at least one-fifth of the total number of members of the Assembly.

The President of the Republic cannot be elected for a second time.

The President-elect, if a member of a party, shall sever his relations with his party and his status as a member of the Turkish Grand National Assembly shall cease.

\*\*\*

C. OATH

*Article 103.* On assuming office, the President of the Republic shall take the following oath before the Turkish Grand National Assembly:

> In my capacity as President of the Republic I swear upon my honor and integrity before the Turkish Grand National Assembly and before history to safeguard the existence and independence of the State, the indivisible integrity of the country and the nation and the absolute sovereignty of the nation, to abide by the Constitution, the rule of law, democracy, the principles and reforms of Atatürk and the principles of the secular Republic, not

to deviate from the ideal according to which everyone is entitled to enjoy Human Rights and fundamental freedoms under conditions of national peace and prosperity and in a spirit of national solidarity and justice, and to do my utmost to preserve and exalt the glory and honor of the Republic of Turkey and perform without bias the functions that I have assumed.

D. DUTIES AND POWERS

*Article 104.* The President of the Republic is the Head of the State. In this capacity he shall represent the Republic of Turkey and the unity of the Turkish Nation; he shall ensure the implementation of the Constitution, and the regular and harmonious functioning of the organs of State.

To this end, the duties he shall perform, and the powers he shall exercise, in accordance with the conditions stipulated in the relevant articles of the Constitution are as follows:

a. Those relating to legislation:
   To deliver, if he deems it necessary, the opening address of the Turkish Grand National Assembly on the first day of the legislative year,
   To summon the Turkish Grand National Assembly to meet, when necessary,
   To promulgate laws,
   To return laws to the Turkish Grand National Assembly to be reconsidered,
   To submit to referendum, if he deems it necessary, legislation regarding the amendment of the Constitution,
   To appeal to the Constitutional Court for the annulment in part or entirety of certain provisions of laws, decrees having force of law, and the Rules of Procedures of the Turkish Grand National Assembly on the grounds that they are unconstitutional in form or in content,
   To call new elections for the Turkish Grand National Assembly.
b. Those relating to the executive functions:
   To appoint the Prime Minister and to accept his resignation,
   To appoint and dismiss ministers on the proposal of the Prime Minister,
   To preside over the Council of Ministers or to call the Council of Ministers to meet under his chairmanship whenever he deems it necessary,
   To accredit representatives of the Turkish State to foreign states and to receive the representatives of foreign states to the Republic of Turkey,
   To ratify and promulgate international treaties,
   To represent the Office of the Commander-in-Chief of the Turkish Armed Forces on behalf of the Turkish Grand National Assembly,
   To appoint the Chief of the General Staff,
   To call the National Security Council to meet,
   To preside over the National Security Council,
   To proclaim martial law or state of emergency, and to issue decrees having force of law, in accordance with the decisions of the Council of Ministers under his chairmanship,

To sign decrees,

To remit, on grounds of chronic illness, disability, or old age, all or part of the sentences imposed on certain individuals,

To appoint the members and the chairman of the State Supervisory Council,

To instruct the State Supervisory Council to carry out enquiries, investigations, and inspections,

To appoint the members of the Higher Education Council,

To appoint rectors of universities.

c. Those relating to the judiciary:

To appoint the members of the Constitutional Court, one-fourth of the members of the Council of State, the Chief Public Prosecutor and the Deputy Chief Public Prosecutor of the High Court of Appeals, the members of the Military High Court of Appeals, the members of the Supreme Military Administrative Court, and the members of the Supreme Council of Judges and Public Prosecutors.

The President of the Republic shall also exercise powers of election and appointment, and perform the other duties conferred on him by the Constitution and laws.

E. PRESIDENTIAL ACCOUNTABILITY AND NON-ACCOUNTABILITY

*Article 105.* All Presidential decrees except those which the President of the Republic is empowered to enact by himself without the signatures of the Prime Minister and the minister concerned, in accordance with the provisions of the Constitution and other laws, shall be signed by the Prime Minister, and the ministers concerned. The Prime Minister and the ministers concerned shall be accountable for these decrees.

No appeal shall be made to any legal authority, including the Constitutional Court, against the decisions and orders signed by the President of the Republic on his own initiative.

The President of the Republic may be impeached for high treason on the proposal of at least one-third of the total number of members of the Turkish Grand National Assembly, and by the decision of at least three-fourths of the total number of members.

\*\*\*

H. STATE SUPERVISORY COUNCIL

*Article 108.* The State Supervisory Council, which shall be established attached to the Office of the Presidency of the Republic with the purpose of performing and furthering the regular and efficient functioning of the administration and its observance of law, will be empowered to conduct upon the request of the President of the Republic all enquiries, investigations, and inspections of all public bodies and organizations, all enterprises in which those public bodies and organizations share more than half of the capital, public professional organizations, employers' associations and labor unions at all levels, and public benefit associations and foundations.

The Armed Forces and all judicial organs are outside the jurisdiction of the State Supervisory Council.

The members and the Chairman to be designated from among the member of the State Supervisory Council shall be appointed by the President of the Republic from among those with the qualifications set forth in the law.

The functioning of the State Supervisory Council, the term of office of its members, and other matters relating to their status shall be regulated by law.

\*\*\*

*II. Council of Ministers*

\*\*\*

I. NATIONAL DEFENSE

\*\*\*

*2. National Security Council*
*Article 118.* The National Security Council shall be composed of the Prime Minister, the Chief of the General Staff, the Ministers of National Defense, Internal Affairs, and Foreign Affairs, the Commanders of the Army, Navy, and the Air Force, and the General Commander of the Gendarmerie, under the chairmanship of the President of the Republic.

Depending on the particulars of the agenda, Ministers and other persons concerned may be invited to meetings of the Council and their views be heard.

The National Security Council shall submit to the Council of Ministers its views on taking decisions and ensuring necessary coordination with regard to the formulation, establishment, and implementation of the national security policy of the State. The Council of Ministers shall give priority consideration to the decisions of the National Security Council concerning the measures that it deems necessary for the preservation of the existence and independence of the State, the integrity and indivisibility of the country, and the peace and security of society.

The agenda of the National Security Council shall be drawn up by the President of the Republic taking into account the proposals of the Prime Minister and the Chief of the General Staff.

In the absence of the President of the Republic, the National Security Council shall meet under the chairmanship of the Prime Minister.

The organization and duties of the General Secretariat of the National Security Council shall be regulated by law.

### III. Procedure governing emergency rule

A. STATES OF EMERGENCY

\*\*\*

**2. Declaration of a state of emergency on account of widespread acts of violence and serious deterioration of public order**
*Article 120.* In the event of the emergence of serious indications of widespread acts of violence aimed at the destruction of the free democratic order established by the Constitution or of fundamental rights and freedoms, or serious deterioration of public order because of acts of violence, the Council of Ministers, meeting under the chairmanship of the President of the Republic, after consultation with the National Security Council, may declare a state of emergency in one or more regions or throughout the country for a period not exceeding six months.

**3. Rules relating to the states of emergency**
*Article 121.* In the event of a declaration of a state of emergency under the provisions of Articles 119 and 120 of the Constitution this decision shall be published in the Official Gazette and shall be submitted immediately to the Turkish Grand National Assembly for approval. If the Turkish Grand National Assembly is in recess, it shall be summoned immediately. The Assembly may alter the duration of the state of emergency, extend the period for a maximum of four months each time at the request of the Council of Ministers, or may lift the state of emergency.

The financial, material, and labor obligations which are to be imposed on citizens in the event of the declaration of state of emergency under Article 119, and, applicable according to the nature of each kind of state of emergency, the procedures as to how fundamental rights and freedoms shall be restricted or suspended in line with the principles of Article 15, how and by what means the measures necessitated by the situation shall be taken, what sort of powers shall be conferred on public servants, what kind of changes shall be made in the status of officials, and the procedure governing emergency rule shall be regulated by the Law on State of Emergency.

During the state of emergency, the Council of Ministers meeting under the chairmanship of the President of the Republic may issue decrees having force of law on matters necessitated by the state of emergency. These decrees shall be published in the Official Gazette, and shall be submitted to the Turkish Grand National Assembly on the same day for approval; the time limit and procedure for their approval by the Assembly shall be indicated in the Rules of Procedure.

B. MARTIAL LAW, MOBILIZATION, AND STATE OF WAR

*Article 122.* The Council of Ministers, under the chairmanship of the President of the Republic, after consultation with the National Security Council, may declare martial law in one or more regions or throughout the country for a period not exceeding six months, in the event of widespread acts of violence which are more dangerous than the cases necessitating a state of emergency and which are aimed at the destruction of the free democratic order or the fundamental rights and freedoms embodied in the Constitution; or in the event of war, the emergence of a situation necessitating war, an uprising, or the spread of violent and strong rebellious actions against the motherland and the Republic, or widespread acts of violence of either internal or external origin threatening the indivisibility of the country and the nation. This decision shall be published immediately in the Official Gazette, and shall be submitted for approval to the Turkish Grand National Assembly, on the same day. If the Turkish Grand National Assembly is in recess, it shall be summoned immediately. The Turkish Grand National Assembly may, when it deems necessary, reduce or extend the period of martial law or lift it.

During the period of martial law, the Council of Ministers meeting under the chairmanship of the President of the Republic may issue decrees having force of law on matters necessitated by the state of martial law.

These decrees shall be published in the Official Gazette and shall be submitted for approval to the Turkish Grand National Assembly on the same day. The time limit and procedures for their approval by the Assembly shall be indicated in the Rules of Procedure.

Extension of the period of martial law for a maximum of four months each time shall require a decision of the Turkish Grand National Assembly. In the event of a state of war, the limit of four months does not apply.

In the events of martial law, mobilization, and state of war, the provisions to be applied and conduct of affairs, the relations with the administration, the manner in which freedoms are to be restricted or suspended, and the obligations to be imposed on the citizens in a state of war, or in the event of emergence of a situation necessitating war, shall be regulated by law.

The Martial Law Commanders shall exercise their duties under the authority of the Office of the Chief of the General Staff.

*IV. Administration*

A. FUNDAMENTALS OF THE ADMINISTRATION

*Article 123.* The administration forms a whole with regard to its structure and functions, and shall be regulated by law.

The organization and functions of the administration are based on the principles of centralization and local administration.

Public corporate bodies shall be established only by law, or on the authority expressly granted by law.

*Article 124.* The Prime Ministry, the ministries, and public corporate bodies may issue bylaws in order to ensure the application of laws and regulations relating to their particular fields of operation, provided that they are not contrary to these laws and regulations. The law shall designate which bylaws are to be published in the Official Gazette.

## B. RECOURSE TO JUDICIAL REVIEW

*Article 125.* Recourse to judicial review shall be open against all actions and acts of the administration.

The acts of the President of the Republic in his own competence, and the decisions of the Supreme Military Council, are outside the scope of judicial review.

In suits filed against administrative acts, a statute of limitations shall start from the date of written notification.

Judicial power is limited to the verification of the conformity of the actions and acts of the administration with law. No judicial ruling shall be passed which restricts the exercise of the executive function in accordance with the forms and principles prescribed by law, which has the quality of an administrative action and act, or which removes discretionary powers.

If the implementation of an administrative act would result in damages which are difficult or impossible to compensate, and at the same time this act is clearly unlawful, then a stay of execution may be decided upon, stating the reasons therefore.

The law may restrict the issuing of stay of execution orders in cases of state of emergency, martial law, mobilization, and state of war, and for reasons of national security, public order, and public health.

The administration shall be liable to compensate for damages resulting from its actions and acts.

\*\*\*

## E. INSTITUTIONS OF HIGHER EDUCATION AND THEIR HIGHER BODIES

\*\*\*

*2. Superior bodies of higher education*
*Article 131.* The Higher Education Council shall be established to plan, organize, administer, and supervise the education provided by institutions of higher education, to orient the activities of teaching, education, and scientific research, to ensure the establishment and development of these institutions in conformity with the objectives and principles set forth by law, to ensure the effective use of the resources allotted to the universities, and to plan the training of the teaching staff.

The Higher Education Council is composed of members appointed by the President of the Republic from among the candidates who are nominated by the Council of Ministers, the Chief of the General Staff and the universities, and in accordance with the numbers, qualifications and procedure prescribed by law, priority being given to those who have served successfully as faculty members or rectors, and of members directly appointed by the President of the Republic himself.

The organization, functions, authority, responsibility, and operating principles of the Council shall be regulated by law.

\*\*\*

### F. RADIO AND TELEVISION ADMINISTRATION AND NEWS AGENCIES WITH STATE CONNECTION

*Article 133.* Radio and television stations shall be established only by the State, and shall be administered by an impartial corporate body.

The law shall provide that broadcasts are made in a manner to safeguard the existence and independence of the Turkish State, the indivisible integrity of the country and the nation, the peace of society, public morals, and the fundamental characteristics of the Republic as outlined in Article 2 of the Constitution; and it shall observe the principle of impartiality in the administration and supervision of the Corporation, in the formation of its administrative organs, and in all radio and television broadcasts.

The principles governing the selection, treatment, and presentation of news and programs, the fulfillment of the task to aid the national culture and education, the principles of ensuring the accuracy of the news, and the election, functions, and responsibilities of the organs shall be regulated by law.

The provisions of paragraph 2 above shall also apply to those news agencies having the character of state economic enterprises and to those receiving financial aid from the State or other public corporate bodies.

\*\*\*

## Chapter three — Judicial power

*I. General provisions*

#### A. INDEPENDENCE OF THE COURTS

*Article 138.* Judges shall be independent in the discharge of their duties; they shall give judgment in accordance with the Constitution, law, and their personal conviction conforming with the law.

No organ, authority, office, or individual may give orders or instructions to courts or judges relating to the exercise of judicial power, or send them circulars, make recommendations, or suggestions.

No question shall be asked, debate held, or statement made in the Legislative Assembly relating to the exercise of judicial power concerning a case under trial.

Legislative and executive organs and the administration shall comply with court decisions; these organs and the administration shall neither alter them in any respect nor delay their execution.

#### B. SECURITY OF TENURE OF JUDGE AND PUBLIC PROSECUTORS

*Article 139.* Judges and public prosecutors shall not be dismissed or retired before the age prescribed by the Constitution; nor shall they be deprived of their salaries, allowances or other rights relating to their status, even as a result of the abolition of court or post.

Exceptions indicated in law relating to those convicted for an offense requiring dismissal from the profession, those who are definitely established as unable to perform their duties on account of ill health, and those determined unsuitable to remain in the profession are reserved.

C. JUDGES AND PUBLIC PROSECUTORS

*Article 140.* Judges and public prosecutors shall serve as judges and public prosecutors of courts of justice and of administrative courts. These duties shall be carried out by career judges and public prosecutors.

Judges shall discharge their duties in accordance with the principles of the independence of the courts and the security of tenure of judges.

The qualifications, appointment, rights and duties, salaries, and allowances of judges and public prosecutors, their promotion, temporary or permanent change of their duties or posts, the initiation of disciplinary proceedings against them and the subsequent imposition of disciplinary penalties, the conduct of investigation concerning them and the subsequent decision to prosecute them on account of offenses committed in connection with, or in the course of, their duties; the conviction for offenses or instances of incompetence requiring their dismissal from the profession, their in-service training, and other matters relating to their personnel status shall be regulated by law in accordance with the principles of the independence of the courts and the security of tenure of judges.

Judges and public prosecutors shall exercise their duties until they complete the age of sixty-five; the age limit, promotion, and the retirement of military judges shall be prescribed by law.

Judges and public prosecutors shall not assume official or public functions other than those prescribed by law.

Judges and public prosecutors shall be attached to the Ministry of Justice insofar as their administrative functions are concerned.

Those judges and public prosecutors working in administrative posts of the justice service shall be subject to the same provisions as other judges and public prosecutors. Their categories and grades shall be determined according to the principles applying to judges and public prosecutors, and they shall enjoy all the rights accorded to judges and public prosecutors.

D. PUBLICITY OF THE HEARINGS AND VERDICT JUSTIFICATION

*Article 141.* Court hearings shall be open to the public. It may be decided to conduct all or part of the hearings in closed session only in cases where required absolutely for reasons of public morality or public security.

Special provisions shall be provided in the law with respect to the trial of minors.

The decisions of all courts shall be made in writing with a statement of justification.

It is the duty of the judiciary to conclude trials as quickly as possible and at the minimum cost.

E. ORGANIZATION OF COURTS

*Article 142.* The organization, functions and jurisdictions of the courts, their functioning, and trial procedures shall be regulated by law.

F. COURTS OF THE SECURITY OF THE STATE

*Article 143.* Courts of the Security of the State shall be established to deal with offenses against the indivisible integrity of the State with its territory and nation, the free democratic order, or against the Republic whose characteristics are defined in the Constitution, and offenses directly involving the internal and external security of the State.

The Court of the Security of the State shall consist of a President, two regular and two substitute members, one public prosecutor, and a sufficient number of deputy public prosecutors.

The President, one regular and one substitute member and the public prosecutor from among first category judges and public prosecutors; one regular and one substitute member from among first category military judges; and deputy public prosecutors from among public prosecutors of the Republic and military judges shall be appointed in accordance with procedures prescribed by their special laws.

The President, members and substitute members, and public prosecutors and deputy public prosecutors of the Court of the Security of the State shall be appointed for four years; those whose term of office expires may be reappointed.

The High Court of Appeals is the competent authority to examine appeals against the verdicts of the Court of the Security of the State.

Other provisions relating to the functioning, the duties and jurisdiction, and the trial procedures of the Court of the Security of the State shall be prescribed by law.

In the event of declaration of martial law within the regions under the jurisdiction of a Court of the Security of the State, the latter may be transformed, in accordance with the provisions prescribed by law, into a Martial Law Military Tribunal with jurisdiction restricted to these regions.

G. SUPERVISION OF JUDGES AND PUBLIC PROSECUTORS

*Article 144.* Supervision of judges and public prosecutors with regard to the performance of their duties in accordance with laws, regulations, bylaws, and circulars (administrative circulars, in the case of judges), investigation into whether they have committed offenses in connection with, or in the course of, their duties, whether their behavior and attitude are in conformity with their status and duties, and, if necessary, inquiry and investigations concerning them shall be made by judiciary inspectors with the permission of the Ministry of Justice. The Minister of Justice may request the investigation or inquiry to be conducted by a judge or public prosecutor who is senior to the judge or public prosecutor to be investigated.

H. MILITARY JUSTICE

*Article 145.* Military justice shall be exercised by military courts and military disciplinary courts. These courts shall have jurisdiction to try military personnel for military offenses, for offenses committed by them against other military personnel or in military places, or for offenses connected with military service and duties.

Military courts also have jurisdiction to try non-military persons for military offenses specified in the special law; and for offenses committed while performing their duties specified by law, or against military personnel on military places specified by law.

The offenses and persons falling within the jurisdiction of military courts in time of war or under martial law, their organization, and the appointment, where necessary, of judges and public prosecutors from courts of justice to military courts shall be regulated by law.

The organization of military judicial organs, their functions, matters relating to the status of military judges, relations between military judges acting as military prosecutors, and the office of commander under which they serve shall be regulated by law in accordance with the principles of the independence of courts and the security of tenure of judges and with the requirements of military service. Relations between military judges and the office of commander under which they serve, regarding the requirements of military service apart from the judicial functions, shall also be prescribed by law.

*II. Higher courts*

A. THE CONSTITUTIONAL COURT

*1. Organization Article 146.* The Constitutional Court shall be composed of eleven regular and four substitute members.

The President of the Republic shall appoint two regular and two substitute members from the High Court of Appeals, two regular and one substitute member from the Council of State, and one member each from the Military High Court of Appeals, the High Military Administrative Court and the Audit Court, three candidates being nominated for each vacant office by the Plenary Assemblies of each court from among their respective presidents and members, by an absolute majority of the total number of members; the President of the Republic shall also appoint one member from a list of three candidates nominated by the Higher Education Council from among members of the teaching staff of institutions of higher education who are not members of the Council, and three members and one substitute member from among senior administrative officers and lawyers.

To qualify for appointments as regular or substitute members of the Constitutional Court, members of the teaching staff of institutions of higher education, senior administrative officers and lawyers shall be required to be over the age of forty and to have completed their higher education, or to have served at least fifteen years as a member of the teaching staff of institutions of higher education or to have worked actually at least fifteen years in public service or to have practiced as a lawyer for at least fifteen years.

The Constitutional Court shall elect a President and Deputy President from among its regular members for a term of four years by secret ballot and by an absolute majority of the total number of members. They may be re-elected at the end of their term of office.

The members of the Constitutional Courts shall not assume other official and private functions, besides their main functions.

*2. Termination of membership*
Article 147. The members of the Constitutional Court shall retire on reaching the age of sixty-five.

Membership in the Constitutional Court shall terminate automatically if a member is convicted of an offense requiring his dismissal from the judicial profession; it shall terminate by a decision of an absolute majority of the total number of members of the Constitutional Court if it is definitely established that he is unable to perform his duties on account of ill health.

*3. Functions and powers*
Article 148. The Constitutional Court shall examine the constitutionality in respect of both form and substance of laws, decrees having force of law, and the Rules of Procedure of the Turkish Grand National Assembly. Constitutional amendments shall be examined and verified only with regard to their form. However, no action shall be brought before the Constitutional Court alleging the unconstitutionality as to the form or substance of decrees having force of law, issued during a state of emergency, martial law, or in time of war.

The verification of laws as to form shall be restricted to consideration of whether the requisite majority was obtained in the last ballot; the verification of constitutional amendments shall be restricted to consideration of whether the requisite majorities were obtained for the proposal and in the ballot, and whether the prohibition on debates under urgent procedure was complied with. Verification as to the form may be requested by the President of the Republic or by one-fifth of the members of the Turkish Grand National Assembly. Applications for annulment on the grounds of defect in form shall not be made more than ten days after the date on which the law was promulgated; nor shall objection be raised.

The President of the Republic, members of the Council of Ministers, presidents and members of the Constitutional Court, of the High Court of Appeals, of the Council of State, of the Military High Court of Appeals, of the High Military Administrative Court of Appeals, their Chief Public Prosecutors, Deputy Public Prosecutors of the Republic, and the presidents and members of the Supreme Council of Judges and Public Prosecutors, and of the Audit Court shall be tried for offenses relating to their functions by the Constitutional Court in its capacity as the Supreme Court.

The Chief Public Prosecutor of the Republic or Deputy Chief Public Prosecutor of the Republic shall act as public prosecutor in the Supreme Court.

The judgments of the Supreme Court shall be final.

The Constitutional Court shall also perform the other functions given to it by the Constitution.

*4. Functioning and trial procedure*
Article 149. The Constitutional Court shall convene with its President and ten members, and shall take decisions by absolute majority. Decision of annulment of Constitutional amendments shall be taken by a two-thirds majority.

The Constitutional Court shall give priority to the consideration of, and to decisions on, applications for annulment on the grounds of defect in form.

The organization and trial procedures of the Constitutional Court shall be determined by law; its method of work and the division of labor among its members shall be regulated by the Rules of Procedure made by the Court.

The Constitutional Court shall examine cases on the basis of files, except where it acts as the Supreme Court. However, when it deems necessary, it may call on those concerned and those having knowledge relevant to the case to present oral explanations.

*5. Annulment action*
Article 150. The President of the Republic, parliamentary groups of the party in power and of the main opposition party and a minimum of one-fifth of the total number of members of the Turkish Grand National Assembly shall have the right to apply for annulment action to the Constitutional Court, based on the assertion of the unconstitutionality of laws in form and in substance, of decrees having force of law, of Rules of Procedure of the Turkish Grand National Assembly or of specific articles or provisions thereof. If more than one political party is in power, the right of the parties in power to apply for annulment action shall be exercised by the party having the greatest number of members.

*6. Time limit for annulment action*
Article 151. The right to apply for annulment directly to the Constitutional Court shall lapse sixty days after the publication in the Official Gazette of the contested law, the decree having force of law, or the Rules of Procedure.

*7. Contention of unconstitutionality before other courts*
Article 152. If a court which is trying a case finds that the law or the decree having force of law to be applied is unconstitutional, or if it is convinced of the seriousness of a claim of unconstitutionality submitted by one of the parties, it shall postpone the consideration of the case until the Constitutional Court decides on this issue.

If the court is not convinced of the seriousness of the claim of unconstitutionality, such a claim together with the main judgment shall be decided upon by the competent authority of appeal.

The Constitutional Court shall decide on the matter and make public its judgment within five months of receiving the contention. If no decision is reached within this period, the trial court shall conclude the case under existing legal provisions. However, if the decision on the merits of the case becomes final, the trial court is obliged to comply with it.

No allegation of unconstitutionality shall be made with regard to the same legal provision until ten years elapse after the publication in the Official Gazette of the decision of the Constitutional Court dismissing the application on its merits.

*8. Decisions of the Constitutional Court*
*Article 153.* The decisions of the Constitutional Court are final. Decisions of annulment cannot be made public without a written statement of reasons.

In the course of annulling the whole or a provision of laws or decrees having force of law, the Constitutional Court shall not act as a lawmaker and pass judgment leading to new implementation.

Laws, decrees having force of law, or the Rules of Procedure of the Turkish Grand National Assembly or provisions thereof shall cease to have that effect from the date of publication in the Official Gazette of the annulment decision. Where necessary, the Constitutional Court may also decide on the date on which the annulment decision shall come into effect. That date shall not be more than one year from the date of the publication of the decision in the Official Gazette.

In the event of the postponement of the date on which an annulment decision is to come into effect, the Turkish Grand National Assembly shall debate and decide with priority on the draft bill or a law proposal, designed to fill the legal void arising from the annulment decision.

The annulment decision cannot have retroactive effect.

Decisions of the Constitutional Court shall be published immediately in the Official Gazette, and shall be binding on the legislative, executive, and judicial organs, on the administrative authorities, and on persons and corporate bodies.

B. THE HIGH COURT OF APPEALS

*Article 154.* The High Court of Appeals is the last instance for reviewing decisions and judgments given by courts of justice and which are not referred by law to other judicial authority. It shall also be the first and last instance for dealing with specific cases prescribed by law.

Members of the High Court of Appeals shall be appointed by the Supreme Council of Judges and Public Prosecutors from among the first category of judges and public prosecutors of the Republic of the courts of justice, or those considered to be members of this profession, by secret ballot and by an absolute majority of the total number of members.

The first President, first Deputy Presidents and heads of division shall be elected by the Plenary Assembly of the High Court of Appeals from among its own members, for a term of four years, by secret ballot and by an absolute majority of the total number of members; they may be re-elected at the end of their term of office.

The Chief Public Prosecutor of the Republic and the Deputy Chief Public Prosecutor of the Republic of the High Court of Appeals shall be appointed by the President of the Republic for a term of four years from among five candidates nominated for each office by the Plenary Assembly of the High Court of Appeals from among its own members by secret ballot. They may be re-elected at the end of their term of office.

The organization, the functioning, the qualifications, and procedures of election of the President, Deputy Presidents, the heads of division and members and the Chief Public Prosecutor of the Republic and the Deputy Chief Public Prosecutor of the Republic of the High Court of Appeals shall be regulated by law in accordance with the principles of the independence of courts and the security of tenure of judges.

C. COUNCIL OF STATE

*Article 155.* The Council of State is the last instance for reviewing decisions and judgments given by administrative courts and which are not referred by law to other administrative courts. It shall also be the first and last instance for dealing with specific cases prescribed by law.

The Council of State shall try administrative cases, give its opinions on draft legislation submitted by the Prime Minister and the Council of Ministers, examine draft regulations and the conditions and contracts under which concessions are granted, settle administrative disputes, and discharge other duties as prescribed by law.

Three-fourths of the members of the Council of State shall be appointed by the Supreme Council of Judges and Public Prosecutors from among the first category administrative judges and public prosecutors, or those considered to be of this profession; and the remaining one-fourth of the members by the President of the Republic from among officials meeting the requirements designated by law.

The President, Chief Public Prosecutor, Deputy President, and heads of division of the Council of State shall be elected by the Plenary Assembly of the Council of State from among its own members for a term of four years by secret ballot and by an absolute majority of the total number of members. They may be re-elected at the end of their term of office.

The organization, the functioning, the qualifications, and procedures of election of the President, the Chief Public Prosecutor, the Deputy Presidents and the heads of division and the members of the Council of State shall be regulated by law in accordance with the principles of the specific nature of the administrative jurisdiction, and of the independence of the courts and the security of tenure of judges.

D. MILITARY HIGH COURT OF APPEALS

*Article 156.* The Military High Court of Appeals is the last instance for reviewing decisions and judgments given by military courts. It shall also be the first and last instance for dealing with specific cases designated by law concerning military personnel.

Members of the Military High Court of Appeals shall be appointed by the President of the Republic from among three candidates nominated for each vacant office by the Plenary Assembly of the Military High Court of Appeals from among military judges of the first category, by secret ballot and by an absolute majority of the total number of members.

The President, Chief Public Prosecutor, second presidents, and heads of division of the Military High Court of Appeals shall be appointed according to rank and seniority from among the members of the Military High Court of Appeals.

The organization, the functioning of the Military High Court of Appeals, and disciplinary and personnel matters relating to the status of its members shall be regulated by law in accordance with the principles of the independence of the courts and the security of tenure of judges and with the requirements of military service.

### E. HIGH MILITARY ADMINISTRATIVE COURT OF APPEALS

*Article 157.* The High Military Administrative Court of Appeals shall be the first and last instance for the judicial supervision of disputes arising from administrative acts and actions involving military personnel or relating to military service, even if such acts and actions have been carried out by civilian authorities. However, in disputes arising from the obligation to perform military service, there shall be no condition that the person concerned be a member of the military body.

Members of the High Military Administrative Court of Appeals who are military judges shall be appointed by the President of the Republic from a list of three candidates nominated for each vacant office by the President and members of the Court, who are also military judges, by secret ballot and by an absolute majority of the total number of such members, from among military judges of the first category; members who are not military judges shall be appointed by the President of the Republic from a list of three candidates nominated for each vacant office by the Chief of the General Staff from among officers holding the rank and qualifications prescribed by law.

The term of office of members who are not military judges shall not exceed four years.

The President, Chief Public Prosecutor and head of division of the Court shall be appointed from among military judges according to rank and seniority.

The organization and functioning of the High Military Administrative Court of Appeals, its procedure, disciplinary affairs, and other matters relating to the status of its members shall be regulated by law in accordance with the principles of the independence of the courts and the security of tenure of judges with the requirements of military service.

### F. JURISDICTIONAL CONFLICT COURT

*Article 158.* The Jurisdictional Conflict Court shall be empowered to deliver final judgments in disputes between courts of justice, and administrative and military courts concerning their jurisdiction and decisions.

The organization of the Jurisdictional Conflict Court, the qualifications of its members and the procedure for their election, and its functioning shall be regulated by law. The Office of President of this Court shall be held by a member delegated by the Constitutional Court from among its own members.

Decisions of the Constitutional Court shall take precedence in jurisdictional disputes between the Constitutional Court and other courts.

*III. Supreme Council of Judges and Public Prosecutors*

*Article 159.* The Supreme Council of Judges and Public Prosecutors shall be established and shall exercise its functions in accordance with the principles of the independence of the courts and the security of tenure of judges.

The President of the Council is the Minister of Justice. The Undersecretary to the Minister of Justice shall be an *ex officio* member of the Council. Three regular and three substitute members of the Council shall be appointed by the President of the Republic for a term of four years from a list of three candidates nominated for each vacant office by the Plenary Assembly of the High Court of Appeals from among its own members and two regular and two substitute members shall be similarly appointed from a list of three candidates nominated for each vacant office by the Plenary Assembly of the Council of State. They may be re-elected at the end of their term of office. The Council shall elect a Deputy President from among its regular members.

The Supreme Council of Judges and Public Prosecutors shall deal with the admission of judges and public prosecutors of courts of justice and of administrative courts into the profession, appointments, transfers to other posts, the delegation of temporary powers, promotion, and promotion to the first category, the allocation of posts, decisions concerning those whose continuation in the profession is found to be unsuitable, the imposition of disciplinary penalties and removal from office. It shall take final decisions on proposals by the Ministry of Justice concerning the abolition of a court or an office of judge or public prosecutor, or changes in the jurisdiction of a court. It shall also exercise the other functions given to it by the Constitution and laws.

There shall be no appeal to any judicial instance against the decisions of the Council.

The functioning of the Council and methods of performing its duties, the procedure governing election and working methods, and the principles relating to the examination of objections within the Council shall be regulated by law.

The Minister of Justice is empowered to appoint judges and public prosecutors with their consent to temporary or permanent functions in the central offices of the Ministry of Justice.

The Minister of Justice may, in cases where delay is deemed prejudicial, confer temporary powers on judges or public prosecutors to prevent the disruption of services, subject to the approval of the Supreme Council of Judges and Public Prosecutors at its first meeting thereafter.

## IV. Audit Court

*Article 160.* The Audit Court shall be charged with auditing, on behalf of the Turkish Grand National Assembly, all the accounts relating to the revenue, expenditure, and property of government departments financed by the general and subsidiary budgets, with taking final decisions on the acts and accounts of the responsible officials, and with exercising the functions required of it by law in matters of inquiry, auditing, and judgment. Parties concerned may file a single request for reconsideration of a final decision of the Audit Court within fifteen days of the date of written notification of the decision. No applications for judicial review of such decisions shall be filed in administrative courts.

In the event of a dispute between the Council of State and the Audit Court concerning decisions on matters of taxation or similar financial obligations and duties, the decision of the Council of State shall take precedence.

The organization, functioning and auditing procedure of the Audit Court, the qualifications, appointment, duties and powers, rights and obligations of its members, other matters relating to their personnel status, and the security of tenure of the President and members shall be regulated by law. The procedure for auditing, on behalf of the Turkish Grand National Assembly, of State property in possession of the Armed Forces shall be regulated by law in accordance with the principles of secrecy required by National Defense.

\*\*\*

# Part five — Miscellaneous provisions

## *I. Preservation of Reform Laws*

*Article 174.* No provision of the Constitution shall be construed or interpreted as rendering unconstitutional the Reform Laws indicated below, which aim to raise Turkish society above the level of contemporary civilization and to safeguard the secular character of the Republic, and which were in force on the date of the adoption by referendum of the Constitution of Turkey.

1. Act no. 430 of March 3, 1340 (1924), on the Unification of the Educational System.
2. Act no. 671 of November 25, 1341 (1925), on the Wearing of Hats.
3. Act no. 677 of November 30, 1341 (1925), on the Closure of Dervish Convents and Tombs, the Abolition of the Office of Keeper of Tombs and the Abolition and Prohibition of Certain Titles.
4. The principle of civil marriage according to which the marriage act shall be concluded in the presence of the competent official, adopted with the Turkish Civil Code no. 743 of February 17, 1926, and Article 110 of the Code.

5. Act no. 1288 of May 20, 1928, on the Adoption of International Numerals.
6. Act no. 1353 of November 1, 1928, on the Adoption and Application of the Turkish Alphabet.
7. Act no. 2590 of November 26, 1934, on the Abolition of Titles and Appellations such as Efendi, Bey or Pasa.
8. Act no. 2596 of December 3, 1934, on the Prohibition of the Wearing of Certain Garments.

## Part six — Provisional articles

*Provisional Article 1.* On the proclamation, under lawful procedure, of the adoption by referendum of the Constitution as the Constitution of the Republic of Turkey, the Chairman of the Council of National Security and Head of State at the time of the referendum shall assume the title of President of the Republic and shall exercise the constitutional functions and powers of the President of the Republic for a period of seven years. The oath he took as Head of State on September 18, 1980, shall remain valid. At the end of the period of seven years the election for the Presidency of the Republic shall be held in accordance with the provisions set forth in the Constitution.

The President of the Republic shall also hold the chairmanship of the Council of National Security formed on December 12, 1980, under Act no. 2356, until the convening of the Turkish Grand National Assembly and the formation of the Bureau of the Assembly following the first general elections.

If the Presidency of the Republic falls vacant for any reason before the Turkish Grand National Assembly convenes and assumes its functions at the end of the first general elections, the most senior member of the Council of National Security shall act as President of the Republic and shall exercise all his constitutional functions and powers until the convening of the Turkish Grand National Assembly and its election of a new President of the Republic in accordance with the provisions of the Constitution.

*Provisional Article 2.* The Council of National Security formed on December 12, 1980, under Act no. 2356 shall continue to exercise its functions under Act no. 2324 on the Constitutional Order and Act no. 2485 on the Constituent Assembly until the convening of the Turkish Grand National Assembly and the formation of the Bureau of the Assembly following the first general elections held under the Political Parties Act and the Elections Act prepared in accordance with the Constitution.

After the adoption of the Constitution, Article 3 of Act no. 2356 relating to the procedure for filling a seat on the Council of National Security, which falls vacant for any reason, shall cease to apply.

After the Turkish Grand National Assembly has convened and assumed its functions, the Council of National Security shall become the Presidential Council for a period of six years, and the members of the Council of National Security shall acquire the title of members of the Presidential

Council. The oath they took on September 18, 1980, as members of the Council of National Security shall remain valid. Members of the Presidential Council shall enjoy the rights and immunity conferred by the Constitution on members of the Turkish Grand National Assembly. The legal existence of the Presidential Council shall terminate on the expiry of the period of six years.

The following functions of the Presidential Council shall be as follows:

a. To examine laws adopted by the Turkish Grand National Assembly and submitted to the President of the Republic concerning: the fundamental rights and freedoms and duties, the principle of secularism, the preservation of the reforms of Atatürk, national security and public order set forth in the Constitution, the Turkish Radio and Television Corporation, International Treaties, the sending of Armed Forces to foreign countries and the stationing of foreign forces in Turkey, emergency rule, martial law and the state of war, and other laws deemed necessary by the President of the Republic, within the first ten days of the period of fifteen days granted to the President of the Republic for his consideration.
b. On the request of the President of the Republic and within the period specific by him:
To consider and give an opinion on matters relating to the holding of new general elections, the exercise of emergency powers and the measures to be taken during a state of emergency, the management and supervision of the Turkish Radio and Television Corporation, the training of youth and the conduct of religious affairs.
c. According to the request of the President of the Republic, to consider and investigate matters relating to internal or external security and such other matters as are deemed necessary, and to submit its findings to the President of the Republic.

\*\*\*

*Provisional Article 15.* No allegation of criminal, financial, or legal responsibility shall be made, nor shall an application be filed with a court for this purpose in respect of any decisions or measures whatsoever taken by: the Council of National Security formed under Act no. 2356 which will have exercised legislative and executive power on behalf of the Turkish Nation from September 12, 1980, to the date of the formation of the Bureau of the Turkish Grand National Assembly which is to convene following the first general elections; the governments formed during the term of office of the Council; or the Consultative Assembly which has exercised its functions under Act no. 2485 on the Constituent Assembly.

The provisions of the above paragraphs shall also apply in respect of persons who have taken decisions and adopted or implemented measures as part of the implementation of such decisions and measures by the administration or by the competent organs, authorities, and officials.

No allegation of unconstitutionality shall be made in respect of decisions or measures taken under laws or decrees having force of law enacted during this period or under Act no. 2324 on the Constitutional Order.

***

# Document no. 10

## State of Emergency Law of October 25, 1983[8]

*Part one — general provisions*

*Purpose*

*Article 1.* The purpose of this Act, in case of:

a. natural disasters, dangerous epidemic diseases, or serious economic crises; or
b. the appearance of serious indications resulting from widespread acts of violence designed to eliminate the free democratic order established by the Constitution or fundamental rights and freedoms or violent actions causing serious deterioration of public order, is to determine the declaration of a state of emergency and the procedures to be applied in states of emergency.

*Scope*

*Article 2.* This Act covers provisions of the declaration of a state of emergency; the financial, material, and working obligations imposed on citizens during states of emergency declared in the case of natural disaster, dangerous epidemic diseases, or serious economic crises. Provisions shall differ for each type of state of emergency concerning how fundamental rights and freedoms shall be limited or suspended; how and in which way necessary measures shall be taken; what sort of powers shall be given to public service officials; what changes shall be made in the position of officials; and administrative procedures of emergency.

*Declaration of states of emergency*

*Article 3.* 1. The Council of Ministers assembled under the chairmanship of the President shall declare a state of emergency:

a. whenever there is in existence one or more natural disasters, dangerous epidemic diseases, or serious economic crisis;

b. whenever there appear serious indications resulting from widespread acts of violence which are aimed at destroying the free democratic order or fundamental rights and freedoms, or violent acts causing serious deterioration to public order, after consultation with the National Security Council, in one or more regions or throughout the country for a period not exceeding six months.

2. The state of emergency decision shall be published in the Official Gazette and immediately submitted for approval of the Turkish Grand National Assembly. If the Turkish Grand National Assembly is in recess, it shall be summoned to meet immediately. The Assembly may amend the duration of the state of emergency. On a request from the Council of Ministers, the Assembly may prolong the duration each time for a period not exceeding four months, or it may terminate the state of emergency.

3. The Council of Ministers, after declaring a state of emergency in accordance with provision (b) above, shall also consult the National Security Council before making a decision on questions related to the prolongation of the duration, alteration of the scope, or termination of the state of emergency.

4. The reasons for the decision to declare a state of emergency, its duration, and scope shall be broadcast on Turkish radio and television and, if the Council of Ministers deems it necessary, also disseminated through other media.

Decrees having the force of law

*Article 4.* During a state of emergency, the Council of Ministers meeting under the chairmanship of the President of the Republic may issue decrees having the force of law on matters necessitated by the state of emergency without complying with the restrictions and procedures laid down in Article 91 of the Constitution. Decrees having the force of law shall be published in the Official Gazette and submitted to the Turkish Grand National Assembly for approval.

## Part two — obligations and measures to be taken

*Chapter one [obligations and measures to be taken in natural disasters and dangerous epidemic diseases]*

\*\*\*

*Chapter two [obligations and measures to be taken in the event of serious economic crises]*

\*\*\*

*Chapter three — measures to be taken in the case of violence*

MEASURES

*Article 11.* Whenever a state of emergency is declared in accordance with Article 3 (1)(b) to protect general security, safety, and public order and to prevent the spread of acts of violence, in addition to the measures taken in accordance with Article 9, the following measures may be taken:

a. imposition of a limited or full curfew;
b. prohibition of any kind of assembly or procession or movement of vehicles in certain places or within certain hours;
c. authorization of officials to search persons, their vehicles, or property and to seize goods deemed to have evidentiary value;
d. imposition of obligation to carry identity cards by those living in or entering regions which are declared to be under a state of emergency;
e. prohibition of, or imposition of obligation to require permission for, the publication (including issuance of reprints and editions) and distribution of newspapers, magazines, brochures, books, etc.; prohibition of importation and distribution of publications published or reprinted outside regions declared to be under a state of emergency; and confiscation of books, magazines, newspapers, brochures, posters, and other publications of which publication or dissemination has been banned;
f. control and, if deemed necessary, restriction or prohibition of every kind of broadcasting and dissemination of words, writings, pictures, films, records, sound, and image bands (tapes);
g. taking or increase of special security measures for internal security of banks and sensitive public and private establishments;
h. control and, if deemed necessary, suspension or prohibition of the exhibition of all kinds of plays and films;
i. prohibition of the carrying or conveying of all types of weapons and projectiles, including those licensed by the state;
j. prohibition, or the imposition of a requirement to obtain prior permission, for the possession, preparation, manufacture, or conveying of all types of ammunition, bombs, destructive materials, explosives, radioactive materials, and corrosive, caustic or ulcerating chemicals, and all kinds of poisons, suffocating gases and other similar material; and confiscation of, or demand to submit [to the state], goods, instruments and tools used in the preparation or manufacture of the aforesaid items;
k. prohibition of persons or groups of persons believed to be disrupting public order or public security from entering the concerned region, expulsion of such persons or groups from the region, or imposition of a requirement on them to reside in or enter specified places in the region;
l. prohibition, restriction, or regulation of the entry [of people] into and exit from establishments or institutions deemed essential for the security of the region;
m. prohibition of, postponement of, or imposition of a requirement to obtain permission for assemblies and demonstrations in both enclosed and open spaces; regulation of the time and place of permitted assemblies and demonstrations; and supervision, and if deemed necessary dispersal, of all kinds of permitted assemblies;

n. [As amended by Decree 3076 dated November 14, 1984] Postponement of, or imposition of a requirement to obtain permission for, the retrenchment of labor for periods exceeding three months, except in cases of termination or cancellation of labor contracts at the request of workers, dismissal on grounds of immoral behavior or breach of good faith, retrenchment on health grounds, or normal retirement;

o. [As amended by Decree 3076 dated November 14, 1984] Suspension of the activities or associations for periods not exceeding three months, after considering each individual case;

[As amended by Decree 3076 dated November 14, 1984] Postponement of decisions to enforce strikes and lock-outs for up to a maximum of one month;

p. [Introduced by Decree 3310 dated September 3, 1988] Planning and execution of operations, in so far as they may be necessary, beyond the borders of Turkey to capture or incapacitate persons who, having carried out [disruptive] actions in Turkey, have sought refuge in a neighboring country. Such operations shall be carried out by the competent military commander, using the Army, Navy, and Air Force, after obtaining the requisite permission from the Council of Ministers through the Office of the Chief of General Staff, at the request of regional governors, and within the framework of agreements arrived at between the Government of Turkey and that of the neighboring country concerned. This power shall only extend to an emergency declared under Article 121 of the Constitution.

## Part three — organs and implementation

*Chapter one — Organs*

COORDINATION

*Article 12.* [As amended by Decree 3432 dated April 21, 1988]

1. Whenever a state of emergency is declared, coordination will be provided by the office of the Prime Minister or a ministry designated by the Prime Minister.

2. For this purpose, a States of Emergency Coordination Council shall be established by the representatives of ministries related to the cause of the state of emergency declared. The ministries, which constitute this Council, may designate a unit for the same purpose within the central administration or for a special unit.

3. The constitution and functions of the States of Emergency Coordination Council shall be provided for by a regulation to be promulgated.

\*\*\*

STATES OF EMERGENCY COUNCIL AND OFFICES

*Article 13.* 1. Within the region in respect of which a state of emergency is declared, the State of Emergency Council shall be constituted with the following membership: the regional governor as the Chairman, the governors of provinces, directors of public establishments and the garrison commander or an authorized representative of the commander. The functions of this Council shall be to supervise the application of measures taken and to evaluate [their efficacy]. The tasks of the Regional Governance and its institutions shall remain unaffected.

2. If the regional governor deems it necessary, or if the state of emergency is declared in one province, a State of Emergency Bureau shall be established in the center of the province and in the districts. The provincial bureau shall be presided over by the governor of the province or by a person designated by the governor, and the district bureau shall be presided over by the governor of the district.

3. While the state of emergency is in force, except for personnel employed in the civil and administrative judiciary and in the organization of the military, any public service employee designated by his director may be seconded to the abovementioned bureau and Councils together with his staff.

4. The constitution, powers, procedures, and principles of States of Emergency Councils and Bureau shall be determined by regulations.

*Chapter two — implementation of states of emergency*

IMPLEMENTATION OF STATES OF EMERGENCY

*Article 14.* 1. The duty of and authority for implementing states of emergency shall belong to:

a. the governor of a province, if the state of emergency covers one province;
b. the regional governor, if the state of emergency is declared in more than one province administratively connected to a regional governance;
c. the regional governors, with coordination and cooperation being provided by the office of the Prime Minister, if the state of emergency is declared throughout the country or in provinces within the jurisdiction of more than one regional governor.

All the necessary powers shall be exercised by the abovementioned functionaries.

2. Regional governors may transfer, totally or partially, their duties and powers, to the governors of provinces covered by a state of emergency.

NOTIFICATION AND APPLICATION OF OBLIGATIONS

*Article 15.* 1. General obligations shall be announced through every kind of mass media. If necessary, specific obligations shall be notified to [affected] persons in written form and in urgent cases notification may be made orally but confirmed in writing later.

2. Upon such notification, persons under obligation shall deliver moneys, real estate, or movables subject to the obligation to the authorities within a specified

period and according to specified procedure; if they are under an obligation to do labor, they may be required to start work on a specified day and time.

ESTABLISHING REPAYMENT OBLIGATIONS

*Article 16.* 1. An official document shall be issued to persons whose property has been requisitioned or used, or who have been required to perform compulsory labor.

2. Payment shall be made to persons under labor or material obligation upon submission of the said document to the relevant authorities. The State of Emergency Councils or Bureau shall determine the price, rent, remuneration, or compensation payable to the person for the property requisitioned or labor performed, having regard to local market rates.

3. In the event of a delay in payment or payment by installments, the amount repaid shall include interest at the official rate.

4. Affected persons may, in accordance to the general provisions of the law, apply to the civil judiciary if they dispute the price, rent, remuneration, or compensation determined by the Emergency Councils or Bureau.

PROPERTY REQUISITIONED FOR A TEMPORARY PERIOD

*Article 17.* 1. Transportation vehicles and other property which are requisitioned for a temporary period shall be returned to their owners when such obligation has terminated.

2. The procedures for implementation of the provisions of Article 16 and of this Article shall be notified in the regulations.

RETURN OF GOODS BELONGING TO PUBLIC ESTABLISHMENTS

*Article 18.* Real estate, movables, and unused materials belonging to government departments having their own budget, government departments dependent on the general budget, state economic enterprises and institutions connected to them, and local administrative organs, shall be returned to them. No price, rent, remuneration, or compensation shall be payable to such establishments.

EXCEPTIONS

*Article 19.* 1. The provisions of ... Article 11 (c) shall not apply to the civil judiciary and military institutions and to judges, prosecutors and military personnel.

2. In imposing obligations and taking measures, the provisions of international law which recognize diplomatic privileges and legislative immunities shall be complied with.

**Part four**

\*\*\*

#### DEMAND OF FORCE

*Article 21.* 1. Regional governors of regions where a state of emergency has been declared in accordance with Article 3(1)(b) of this Act shall try to contain and prevent existing or potential social disturbances in their regions with the use of forces under their command or with the use of security forces specially organized for this purpose.

2. If they are unable to prevent, or are satisfied that it is impossible to prevent, such incidents or to implement the necessary measures with the abovementioned forces, they may apply to other regional governors in the area requesting for assistance from the security forces of those regions. The Ministry of the Interior shall also be notified of this situation.

3. If all these measures are considered inadequate, or if a regional governor is faced with urgent and extraordinary circumstances, he may request aid from the highest military commandership in his region.

4. Any of the abovementioned demands of the regional governor shall be met by the authorities without delay.

5. If a regional governor demands aid from the military, such action shall be carried out in accordance with the following procedure:

a. In urgent cases the demand may be made orally but confirmed in writing later.
b. The military force demanded to meet potential [incidents], of such strength as may be determined by the military commandership after consultation with the governor of the province in question, shall be made ready for deployment in an appropriate place or places.

   If military force is demanded to meet urgent and extraordinary events, the duties assigned by the regional governor shall be carried out immediately under the orders and directions of the appropriate commander and in accordance with the provisions of the Turkish Armed Forces Internal Service Act and the competence recognized for the security forces to provide general security.
c. The rules of cooperation and coordination between the security forces and the military units, which come to assist [in the abovementioned circumstances], and the principles governing their command structure shall be determined jointly by the regional governor and the highest military commander in the concerned region. However, if certain tasks are carried out together by the security forces and the military units, which come to assist, decisions regarding their command and administration shall be taken by the commander of the military or the most-senior commander of the military on duty.
d. The expenses necessitated in the use of military units shall be provided by appropriation in the budget of the Ministry of the Interior without awaiting an order for payment.

#### DEMANDS FOR AID AND FORCES BY GOVERNORS OF PROVINCES

*Article 22.* 1. ***

b. The governors of provinces in whose territories a state of emergency has been declared under Article 3 (1)(b) of this Act shall try to contain or prevent existing or potential incidents by the use of force at their disposal. If they are unable to do so, or are satisfied that it is impossible for them to do so, or if they are unable to implement any of the measures adopted to deal with the situation, they shall apply to the appropriate regional governor for additional reinforcements of security forces. The security forces sent for this purpose will function under the command of the provincial governor.

2. If the governor of a province is faced with urgent and extraordinary circumstances or needs to take urgent measures pending the arrival of forces requisitioned by him as above, he may demand aid from the nearest military commandership. He shall also notify the regional governor and the Ministry of the Interior of such a situation.

3. The demands of a governor mentioned above shall be met immediately.

4. Whenever a demand is made by the governor of a province for aid from the military, the provisions of Article 21 of this Act shall apply. In such cases the duties and powers of the regional governor shall be exercised by the governor of the province.

COMPETENCE ON THE USE OF ARMS

*Article 23.* 1. During the pendency of a state of emergency, security forces and special security forces shall, in carrying out their duties, have the authority to use arms if one of the conditions laid down in statutes governing the use of arms exists.

2. In the case of a state of emergency declared under Article 3 (1)(b) of this Act, the security forces on duty may fire [on a person or a group of persons] if an order to surrender is not obeyed or if there is an attempt at armed resistance or if the security forces have to act in the interests of legitimate self-defense.

3. The provisions of Article 87 (V) and (VI) of the Turkish Armed Forces Internal Service Act and Article 3 of the Law on the Prevention of Offenses Against Law and Order (Law 1481) shall be applicable to all personnel using arms. Furthermore, investigations against such personnel shall be carried out without them being detained.

4. The orders given by a regional governor or the governor of a province in accordance with this Article permitting security force personnel to use arms to protect the authority of the state or their lives or property shall be proclaimed by appropriate means.

## Part five — jurisdiction, procedure, and penal provisions

JURISDICTION AND PROCEDURE IN A STATE OF EMERGENCY

*Article 24.* 1. Except for crimes falling within the jurisdiction of State Security Courts or Military Courts, all crimes committed in areas under a state of emergency shall be subject to the jurisdiction of the civil judiciary.

2. The investigation and prosecution of crimes regulated by this Act shall be carried out in accordance with the Law of Legal Procedure on Flagrant Offenses (Law 3005) irrespective of the location or time of the crime.

PENAL PROVISIONS

*Article 25.*

\*\*\*

B. Within areas where a state of emergency has been declared in accordance with Article 3 (1)(b) of this Act:

1. anyone whose actions constitute a breach of the measures taken by a regional governor or the governor of a province in accordance with the authority provided in this Act or in other statutes, or who disobeys orders or does not carry out the requirements of such orders, or who intentionally provides false proof of identity or refuses to provide proof of identity when demanded, is liable, in addition to the punishment prescribed for such actions in ordinary criminal law, to imprisonment for between one and six months;

2. anyone who acts in a manner which would constitute a breach of clause (A)(2) of this Article shall be liable to a penalty which shall be double the penalty mentioned in the foregoing clause. [Clause (A)(2): anyone who spreads or conveys false or exaggerated news or information with intent to create panic among the public shall be liable to additional punishment of imprisonment for between three months and one year and a minimum fine of five thousand Turkish liras. If such crime is committed by a person in association with a foreigner, the additional term of imprisonment shall not be for less than one year together with a fine of thirty thousand liras. If the crime involves publication and/or the use of broadcasting media, the penalty shall be doubled and imposed on both the person primarily responsible for the crime and anyone else connected with its commission.]

EXTENSION OF CUSTODY

*Article 26.* In cases involving a state of emergency declared in accordance with Article 3 (1)(b) of this Act, the custody periods prescribed in the Code of Criminal Procedure (Article 128) may be doubled on a written request made by the Public Prosecutor [to] a civil or investigation court judge if damage is likely to result from any delay.

## Part six — miscellaneous provisions

\*\*\*

PUBLICATION OF DECISIONS

*Article 31.* Decisions taken under this Act, the publication of which is obligatory or deemed necessary by the competent authorities, shall be published and disseminated to the nation free of charge by Turkish radio and television and in the Official Gazette and by the mass media under the control of the local administration. Any requirements of the competent authorities in this regard shall be met immediately.

APPLICATION OF DISCIPLINARY PENALTIES

*Article 32.* 1. The regional governor or the governor of a province, whether in the normal course of their duties or if specifically empowered in this regard, shall be entitled to impose directly the disciplinary penalties of reproach, warning, and docking of wages on all public personnel except the military and judiciary, if such personnel do not perform or discharge the duties assigned to them or disobey orders. In doing so the governor shall have regard to the gravity of the offense and not to the fact of whether the offending action necessitated a disciplinary penalty in accordance with the disciplinary regulations.

2. The regional governor or the governor of a province may also apply the penalty of docking of wages to public personnel not covered by clause (1) of this Article and to other persons whose services are requisitioned if they act in like manner. The governor shall determine the amount of the penalty which shall be between one-thirtieth and one-eighth of the employee's monthly salary.

PROHIBITION AGAINST ISSUING STAY ORDERS

*Article 33.* The issuing of stay orders against the administrative acts of governors performed in accordance with the authority vested in them shall be prohibited.

REGULATIONS

*Article 34.* Regulations provided for in this Act shall be made within a period of three months from the date of promulgation of this Act and brought into force by the Council of Ministers by publication in the Official Gazette.

***

# 3 Emergence of the PKK and Turkey's legal responses to terrorism

# Document no. 11

**PKK terror**[1]

Established in 1978, the PKK (Kurdistan Workers' Party) started its armed struggle in 1984 after a preparatory period of numerous murders and attacks, with the objective of the establishment, through armed struggle, of an independent Kurdistan within Turkey's borders.

Since 1984, PKK's terrorist activities resulted in the death of more than 30,000 Turkish citizens, among whom were innocent civilians, teachers, and other public servants, many deliberately murdered.

In its history, the terrorist organization also employed suicide-bombing methods, waged mainly by women terrorists in Turkey, and kidnapped foreign tourists in southeastern Anatolia in the early 1990s. In order to damage Turkey's economy, the organization also set forests in Turkey's tourist resorts on fire.

Following the arrest of its leader, Abdullah Ocalan, in 1999, the organization started claiming that it had switched its strategy to peaceful methods and would pursue political struggle from then on.

In accordance with this policy of appearing as a born-again legitimate organization and to convince the international community accordingly, the organization changed its name to KADEK (Kurdistan Freedom and Democracy Congress) in April 2002, alleging that the PKK had fulfilled its historical mission and would now like to be accepted as a political organization.

In October 2003, the organization underwent another name change to KONGRA-GEL (Kurdistan Peoples' Congress). The decision was made public by a press statement in Iraq on November 15, 2003.

However, despite the name changes, the leading members of the organization remain the same. Today, PKK/KONGRA-GEL is still headed by Abdullah Ocalan, with Zübeyir Aydar — a former member of the "Kurdish National Congress," an affiliate of PKK — its president. Furthermore, founders and leading figures of the PKK, such as Murat Karayilan and Cemil Bayik, continue to assume leading roles in the organization. Many of the leading figures of PKK/KONGRA-GEL are internationally recognized criminals.

Moreover, notwithstanding these two name changes and the so-called strategy change of 1999, the organization did not undergo changes on substantial issues such as decommissioning of arms and it continued to carry out attacks, mainly in southeastern Anatolia but not on the scale of pre-1999 period.

PKK/KONGRA-GEL also keeps its militants and recruits new ones. PKK militants did not surrender to justice, not even to benefit from the provisions of the "Law on Reintegration into Society" that came into force on August 6, 2003 (for a period of six months) and that provided amnesty to those members of a terrorist organization who were not involved in any crimes.

The organization's recent declaration of May 29, 2004, alleging an end to a so-called unilateral cease-fire that the organization claims to have been implementing since September 1999 and stating that it would, by June 1, 2004, respond to any offense with a rationale of self-defense, is yet another open revelation of the organization's terrorist nature.

Presently [as of November 1, 2006], it is estimated that there are a total of 5,000 PKK/KONGRA-GEL terrorists, the majority of whom are in northern Iraq where the organization's headquarters are situated.

Given this picture, the organization's arguments for a policy change can be defined as merely make-up.

# Document no. 12

## Martial law/state of emergency proclamations[2]

### Resolution no. 37 of March 12, 1987

In the seventy-sixth session of the Turkish Grand National Assembly on March 12, 1987, the resolution of the Cabinet dated March 11, 1987, that the martial law declared on September 12, 1980, throughout the country [which has since been continued in five provinces for four months] be amended as follows:

1. that it be revoked in Van province with effect from 17:00 hours on March 19, 1987; and
2. that it be re-extended for four months in the provinces of Diyarbakir, Hakkari, Mardin, and Siirt with effect from 17:00 hours on March 19, 1987, has been ratified.

\*\*\*

### Resolution no. 38 of March 12, 1987

In the seventy-sixth session of the Turkish Grand National Assembly on March 12, 1987, the following decision made by the cabinet on March 11, 1987, has been ratified at its request:

The state of emergency which had been extended for four months in eight provinces on November 19, 1986

1. has been revoked in the provinces of Adana, Agri, Hatay, and Sanliurfa with effect from 17:00 hours on March 19, 1987; and
2. has been re-extended in the provinces of Bingol, Elazig, Istanbul, and Tunceli with effect from 17:00 hours on March 19, 1987.

\*\*\*

## Having the force of Law no. 426 of May 18, 1990

In accordance with Article 121 of the Constitution and Article 4 of Law no. 2935, Decree 285 has been amended by the Cabinet chaired by the President on May 18, 1990, as follows:

*Article 1.* The provinces of Batman and Sirnak have been added to the list of provinces mentioned in the Article 1 of Decree 285 dated July 10, 1987, and the provisions of Decree 424 apply to those provinces as well.

*Article 2.* This Decree comes into force on the date it is issued.

# Document no. 13

**State of emergency — regional governor's powers**

*Descriptive summary of the content of the decrees which have the Force of Law, Decrees 424 and 425 of May 10, 1990[3]*

A. By virtue of the decrees having Force of Law Nos 424 and 425 on the state of emergency region, the State of Emergency Region Governorship has been empowered with the following additional powers.

1. The Ministry of the Interior, upon the proposal of the Governor of the state of emergency region, can temporarily or permanently ban the publication (regardless of the location of the printing press) which is prone to cause a serious disruption in the public order of the region or excitement of the local people or to handicap the security forces in performing their duties by misinterpreting the regional activities. This also includes, if necessary, the power to order the closure of the printing press concerned.
2. The Governor of the state of emergency region can order persons who continuously violate the general security and public order to settle at a place to be specified by the Ministry of the Interior outside the state of emergency region for a period which shall not exceed the duration of the state of emergency. At their request, the persons concerned may receive financial aid from the Development and Support Fund. The particulars for this assistance shall be determined by the Ministry of the Interior.
3. The Governor of the state of emergency region (or the delegated provincial Governor) can suspend (up to three months) or require prior permission for certain labor dispute-related activities such as strike and lockout.
4. The Governor can also ban, or take preventive measures against, certain activities such as destruction, looting, boycotting, slowing down of work, restricting the freedom of work, and closing down of business.
5. The Governor of the state of emergency region can order the temporary or permanent evacuation, change of place, or regrouping of villages, grazing fields and residential areas for reasons of public security.

6. The Governor of the state of emergency region can order the relevant public institutions in the state of emergency region to transfer permanently or temporarily to other positions their public officials who are deemed to be harmful to general security and public order; the concerned public official shall remain subject to the provisions of the special law on civil service applicable to him.

B. No legal claims of criminal, pecuniary, or legal nature can be brought against, nor can any legal steps be taken with, the judicial authority for this purpose in respect of any decision taken or any act performed by the Minister of the Interior, the Governor of the emergency region, and other governors when exercising the power under the Decree 424 having force of law.

C. No interim decision to suspend the execution of an administrative act can be taken during proceedings of an administrative suit which has been filed against the act(s) performed when exercising the power given by the Law of Emergency no. 2935 to the Minister of the Interior, the Governor of the state of emergency region, and the provincial governors.

D. The suit of nullity cannot be filed against administrative acts performed by the Governor of the state of emergency region when exercising the power given to him under the decree having Force of Law no. 285.

# Document no. 14

**Turkey's August 6, 1990, notice of derogation from rights enshrined in Articles 5, 6, 8, 10, 11, and 13 of the European Convention on Human Rights in conformity with Article 15 of the Convention[4]**

1. The Republic of Turkey is exposed to threats to its national security in South East Anatolia which have steadily grown in scope and intensity over the last months so as to amount to a threat to the life of the nation in the meaning of Article 15 of the Convention.
   During 1989, 136 civilians and 153 members of the security forces have been killed by acts of terrorists, acting partly out of foreign bases. Since only the beginning of 1990, the numbers are 125 civilians and 96 members of the security forces.
2. The threat to national security is predominantly occurring in provinces[5] of South East Anatolia and partly also in adjacent provinces.
3. Because of the intensity and variety of terrorist actions and in order to cope with such actions, the Government has not only to use its security forces but also take appropriate steps to cope with a campaign of harmful disinformation of the public, partly emerging from other parts of the Republic of Turkey or even from abroad and with abuses of trades union rights.
4. To this end, the Government of Turkey, acting in conformity with Article 121 of the Turkish Constitution, has promulgated on May 10, 1990, the decrees with Force of Law Nos 424 and 425. These decrees may in part result in derogating from rights enshrined in the following provisions of the European Convention for Human Rights and Fundamental Freedoms: Articles 5, 6, 8, 10, 11, and 13. A descriptive summary of the new measures is attached hereto. The issue of their compatibility with the Turkish Constitution is presently pending before the Constitutional Court of Turkey.
5. The Government of Turkey will inform the Secretary General of the Council of Europe when the measures referred to above have ceased to operate.
6. This notification is given pursuant to Article 15 of the European Convention on Human Rights

\*\*\*

# Document no. 15

**State of emergency — regional governor's additional powers**

*Decree Having Force of Law concerning the additional measures to be taken during the term of the office of the State of Emergency Regional Governor and of the state of emergency of December 16, 1990[6]*

Adoption of the Decree Having Force of Law concerning additional measures to be taken during the pendency of the state of emergency declared on the grounds of the spread of acts of violence and serious disturbances to public order was decided on December 15, 1990, by the Council of Ministers, which was convened and chaired by the President of the Republic under powers conferred by Article 121 of the Constitution and Article 4 of Law 2935 dated October 25, 1983.

*Article 1.* The State of Emergency Regional Governorship which was created by Decree 285 dated July 10, 1987, and, during the pendency of the state of emergency, the State of Emergency Regional Governor with the provinces under his jurisdiction, shall exercise the powers conferred on a Provincial Governor in Law 2935 dated October 25, 1983, and those duties and powers conferred on governors in the Law on Provincial Administration, Code of Penal Procedure, and other laws that are concerned with matters specified in Article 1 of Decree 285, and discharge their duties accordingly. The following additional measures may also be taken for the purpose of preserving the general security, peace, and public order and preventing acts of violence from becoming widespread:

a. The State of Emergency Regional Governor or a provincial governor in a region under a state of emergency may prohibit, or subject to the obtaining of prior permission, the printing, duplicating, publishing, or distribution of any printed work, book, magazine, newspaper, brochure, poster, or other similar printed matter, and the entry into and distribution within the region of those that are printed or duplicated outside the region, those which are likely to cause a serious disturbance of public order in the region or agitation among the population of the region, or to prevent the security forces from discharging their duties properly by falsely depicting the activities in the region or reporting untruthful news. If confiscation of any such book, magazine, newspaper, brochure, poster, or other similar matter that are prohibited herein is not sufficient, the Minister of the Interior shall, on the recommendation of or in consultation with, the State of Emergency Regional Governor issue a written notice of warning to the owners and/or editors responsible for such publications to cease or withdraw from circulation their publications, regardless of whether the publications were printed within or outside the concerned region. If the publication or distribution of such publications continues in spite of the warning, he may prohibit their printing, duplication, publication, or distribution for a stated or indefinite period and order the closure of the printing press that prints them for up to ten days, if necessary, and for up to one month if the owners or editors concerned persist in such conduct.

b. For reasons of general security and public order in the provinces where a state of emergency is in force, persons who request to be moved for settlement elsewhere, or who engage in harmful activities either voluntarily or involuntarily, or who are known or likely to disturb public order may be moved or expelled, as the case may be, from the region at the discretion of the State of Emergency Regional Governor for a period not exceeding the period for which the state of emergency is in force. Where appropriate, such persons may be provided financial support from the Development and Support Fund according to criteria specified by the Ministry of the Interior and on the condition that they live at a definite place.

c. Persons who reside in areas where the State of Emergency Regional Governor exercises the powers conferred by paragraph (h) of clause (2) of Article 4 of Decree 285 or who, having resided in such areas, had to leave their homes previously for reasons of safety of life or property and whose employment is considered a necessity following investigations made, may, if they so request, be provided with residence within or outside the concerned state of emergency region. Such persons may be provided with financial support from the Development and Support Fund for their resettlement or may be provided with a job. For this purpose, the posts listed in the annexed table have been authorized and allocated for use by the Ministry of the Interior. The Council of Ministers is authorized to increase the number of such posts by no more than 25 percent. Appointment of relevant persons to these posts shall be ensured on the basis of a joint decision by way of altering of the classes, titles, and grades of the posts by the Ministry of the Interior wherever necessary, provided that the hierarchical structure is not disturbed. Such persons may be transferred to assigned public departments or organizations with their posts and/or positions. Their wages and other statutory benefits shall be provided by such organizations. The Ministry of the Interior has been authorized to create a maximum of 40,000 posts of workers for those who qualify as workers among such persons. The said Ministry shall specify the conditions for the utilization of such posts and positions, the qualifications for appointment, whether an examination shall be held or not, the return of the posts and positions to the Ministry when they become vacant for any reason, and other matters. The provisions of Settlement Law (no. 2510 dated June 14, 1934) may be applied in appropriate cases concerning residence or where requested by those concerned.

*Article 2.* The State of Emergency Regional Governor may prohibit, or subject to the obtaining of prior permission, such trades union activities as the exercise of strike and lock-out rights, expression of will and referendum [balloting]. He may also prohibit or prevent such acts as destruction, looting, occupation, boycotts, go-slows, restrictions on the right to work, and closing down of workplaces, and take any other preventive measures as is deemed necessary in the provinces that are listed in Decree 285 and where a state of emergency has been declared for the duration of the emergency.

*Article 3.* In the provinces where a state of emergency has been declared, and during the duration of the emergency, the State of Emergency Regional Governor:

a. may order relevant institutions or organizations that public personnel whose employment is deemed pernicious and whose services may be detrimental to the province or provinces under his jurisdiction in terms of security, peace, and public order be relocated or assigned work outside the province or provinces under his jurisdiction, temporarily or permanently. Such orders shall be complied with immediately. The provisions in their own special laws shall be applied in respect of such personnel;

b. may request the local office of the Chief Prosecutor of the Republic to start legal proceedings for offenses concerning acts that led to the declaration of the state of emergency, and the Chief Prosecutor of the State Security Court to start legal proceedings for offenses that fall within the jurisdiction of the State Security Court, and all such requests shall be complied with. Identities of those who inform about offenses that fall within the jurisdiction of the State Security Courts shall not be revealed without their consent or unless the content of the information does not constitute an offense in itself;

c. Those prisoners or detainees who need to be questioned in the course of any investigation concerning offenses that led to the declaration of the state of emergency may be taken from the penal enforcement institution (prison) or custody center upon a recommendation by the State of Emergency Regional Governor, a request by the Chief Prosecutor of the Republic, or a decision by a judge, for a period not exceeding ten days at a time. Such periods shall be considered to be spent in prison or in other custody. The prisoner or detainee may request that his state of health on departure from and return to the prison or custody center be ascertained by medical examination. If the decision to hold such a person in custody is revoked or if the prisoner's term of imprisonment expires during such removal for questioning, the matter shall immediately be reported to the Office of the Chief Prosecutor for the Republic in the territory where such person is kept;

d. may order general searches on roads or residential places, searches on houses, workplaces, and their annexes as well as on non-public places belonging to private parties, where a request to the police to carry out such searches may lead to delays which may be prejudicial, or where for other reasons he deems such action to be necessary;

e. may make recommendations for investment concerning the economic, social, and cultural development of provinces in the region in exercise of his functions;

f. is obliged to effect coordination and cooperation with the General Directorate of the Turkish Radio and Television Corporation, the Ministry of the Interior, and the General Secretariat of the National Security Council on broadcasts concerning the provinces falling within the state of emergency region or affecting the region;

g. may request that statements, bulletins, and declarations prepared by the Office of the Regional Governor concerning activities carried out within his territorial jurisdiction be transmitted *in toto* by the Turkish Radio and Television Corporation.

*Article 4.* The relevant provisions concerning the other powers conferred on the Minister of the Interior and the transfer of powers incorporated in the last two paragraphs of Article 4 of Decree 285 shall also be valid in respect of powers concerning additional measures introduced by this decree.

*Article 5.* If, during the term of a State of Emergency Regional Governance created by Decree 285 and during the pendency of a state of emergency, the courts order the payment of indemnity under the provisions of the Turkish Civil Code and the Law on Liabilities following a demand for redress of personal damage by officers and authorities whose personal rights have been attacked through publications concerning them, regardless of whether such publications are printed within or outside the state of emergency region and adjacent provinces, but establishing a link to the measures taken, practices adopted, powers used, or decisions made in a state of emergency region or in adjacent provinces, the amount of such indemnity shall not be less than 75 percent of, in the case of periodicals, the amount of actual total sales volume in the previous period and, in the case of publications of a non-periodical nature or newly published periodicals, the amount of the previous month's average sales of the best-selling daily periodical.

*Article 6.* If offenses of defamation described in Article 480 of the Turkish Penal Code are committed by the publication of untrue articles, reports, news items, photographs, or documents or by the reporting of any incident or document in a distorted manner concerning personnel or authorities, regardless of whether such publication occurs within a state of emergency region or outside but establishing a link to the measures taken, practices adopted, powers used, or decisions made in a state of emergency region under the relevant legislation or decrees, those guilty shall, in addition to the penalties prescribed in the said Articles, be liable to a heavy fine ranging from one hundred million liras to two hundred million liras. Where such offenses are committed by such periodicals as are specified in Article 3 of the Press Law no. 5680 dated July 15, 1970, the said penalties shall also extend to the proprietors of the concerned publications. One half of the fine (which shall not be less than one hundred million liras) shall also be levied on the editors of such publications. The application of this Article is subject to a separate complaint made in this regard. If no such complaint is filed, the untruthfulness of a published report cannot be investigated *sua sponte*. Any complaint must be filed within the time limit specified in Article 490 of the Turkish Penal Code. In the case of offenses of defamation described in Articles

158, 159, and 268 of the Turkish Penal Code being committed in a manner contemplated under the first and second paragraphs of this Article, those found guilty under the said Articles shall also be punished according to the terms of the abovementioned paragraphs. In cases where Article 481 of the Turkish Penal Code is applied, the provisions of this Article may not be applied.

*Article 7.* In the provinces listed in Decree 285 and where a state of emergency is in force, those guilty of an offense described in Article 125 of the Turkish Penal Code and those who are liable to the punishment set out in Article 169 thereof, shall be liable to a one-fold increase in the punishment.

*Article 8.* No criminal, financial, or legal responsibility may be claimed against the Minister of the Interior, the State of Emergency Regional Governor, or a provincial governor within a state of emergency region in respect of any of their decisions or acts connected with the exercise of the powers entrusted to them by this decree, and no application may be made to any judicial authority to this end. This is without prejudice to the rights of individuals to claim indemnity from the State for damage suffered by them without cause.

*Article 9.* In cases where acts aimed at disturbing the integrity of the State, its territory or the nation, threatening the existence of the Turkish State and Republic, or destroying fundamental rights and freedoms show a tendency to spread to neighboring provinces, the powers entrusted to the Minister of the Interior and the State of Emergency Regional Governor by this Decree shall be exercised by them in such provinces also.

*Article 10.* Provisions of Law 2935 dated October 25, 1983, and Decree 285 dated July 10, 1987, are hereby reserved.

\*\*\*

# Document no. 16

**Turkey's January 3, 1991, Notice of Derogation from Rights Enshrined in Articles 5, 6, 8, 10, 11, and 13 of the European Convention on Human Rights in conformity with Article 15 of the Convention**[7]

1. I have the honor to refer to the Notice of Derogation made by the Republic of Turkey in conformity with Article 15 of the European Convention on Human Rights on August 6, 1990.

2. The said Notice of Derogation referred to Decrees with Force of Law Nos 424 and 425, and was accompanied by a Descriptive Summary of the contents of the said decrees. I hereby inform you that a Decree with Force of Law no. 430 has been enacted by the Council of Ministers of Turkey on December 16, 1990, to replace Decree 424. A Descriptive Summary of the new Decree and the amendments it has introduced to the previous rules is attached hereto. This Descriptive Summary should replace part of the Descriptive Summary attached to the Notice of Derogation referred to above.

3. This notification is made in conformity with Article 15, paragraph 3, of the European Convention on Human Rights.

### *Descriptive Summary of Decree with Force of Law no. 430*

1. The powers of the Governor of the state of emergency under Decree with Force of Law no. 425 have been limited to the region where a state of emergency is in force. Thus, the adjacent provinces have been excluded from the competence of the Governor.

2. The special powers given to the Governor of the state of emergency by virtue of Decree with Force of Law no. 425 have been restricted to measures dealing with terrorist activities aiming at the destruction of fundamental rights and freedoms.

3. The powers of the Minister of the Interior relating to banning any publication or ordering the closure of the printing press (regardless of the location) is restricted. According to the new provision, the Minister of the Interior has at first to issue a warning to the owner or the publisher of the publication. If the

owner or the publisher continues to print or distribute the controversial issue, then the Minister concerned may temporarily or permanently ban the publication and, if necessary, may also order the closure of the printing press for a maximum period of ten days, which may, however, be extended to one month in case of repetition. No maximum period for closure of the printing press has been stipulated by the (abrogated) Decree 424 (compare paragraph A(1) of the Descriptive Summary attached to the Notice of Derogation of August 6, 1990).

4. The authority of the Governor of the state of emergency to order persons to settle at a specified place outside the state of emergency region has been restricted by virtue of the new decree. The persons who are expelled from the state of emergency region are not obliged to settle in a specified place. Hence, they will be free to choose their residence out of the region except when they request financial aid. In this case they have to settle at a specified place (see paragraph A(2) of previous Descriptive Summary).

5. Referring to the paragraphs A(3, 4, 5, and 6) of the Descriptive Summary of August 6, 1990 (which are related to strikes, lock-out, and some other activities of labor unions, evacuation and regrouping of villages, transfer of public officials to other posts or positions), it should be noted that the adjacent provinces have been excluded by virtue of the new decree.

6. As to paragraph 8 of the previous Descriptive Summary, a new clause has been included in the new decree safeguarding the right to file an action against the administration (State) for loss or damages arising out of the performance of the acts taken under the emergency measures.

# Document no. 17

**Anti-Terrorism Law (ATL)**[8]

*Part one — definition of terrorism and terrorist offenses*

*Definition of terrorism*

*Article 1.* 1. Terrorism is any kind of act done by one or more persons belonging to an organization with the aim of changing the characteristics of the Republic as specified in the Constitution, its political, legal, social, secular, and economic system, damaging the indivisible unity of the State with its territory and nation, endangering the existence of the Turkish State and Republic, weakening or destroying, or seizing the authority of the State, eliminating fundamental rights and freedoms, or damaging the internal and external security of the State, public order, or general health by means of pressure, force and violence, terror, intimidation, oppression, or threat.

2. An organization for the purposes of this law is constituted by two or more persons coming together for a common purpose.

3. The term "organization" also includes formations, associations, armed associations, gangs, or armed gangs as described in the Turkish Penal Code and in the provisions of special laws.

*Terrorist offenders*

*Article 2.* 1. Any member of an organization, founded to attain the aims defined in Article 1, who commits a crime in furtherance of these aims, individually or in concert with others, or any member of such an organization, even if he does not commit such a crime, shall be deemed to be a terrorist offender.

2. Persons who are not members of a terrorist organization, but commit a crime in the name of the organization, are also deemed to be terrorist offenders and shall be subject to the same punishment as members of such organizations.

*Terrorist offenses*

*Article 3.* Offenses defined in Articles 125, 131, 146, 147, 148, 149, 156, 168, 171, and 172 of the Turkish Penal Code are terrorist offenses.

*Offenses committed for terrorist purposes*

*Article 4.* In applying this law offenses defined in:

a. Articles 145, 150, 151, 152, 153, 154, 155, 169, and the second paragraph of Article 499 of the Turkish Penal Code and
b. offenses defined in Article 9, part (b), (c), and (e) of Law 2845 on the Foundation and Criminal Procedure at State Security Courts are terrorist offenses if they are committed for terrorist purposes as described in Article 1.

*Increase of sentences*

*Article 5.* Penalties of imprisonment and fines imposed according to the respective laws for those committing crimes as described in Articles 3 and 4 above shall be increased by one-half. In doing so the penalties may exceed the maximum penalty for that or any other crime. However, in the case of rigorous imprisonment the penalty may not exceed thirty-six years', in case of [ordinary] imprisonment twenty-five years', and in case of light imprisonment ten years' imprisonment.

*Disclosure and publication*

*Article 6.* 1. Those who announce that the crimes of a terrorist organization are aimed at certain persons, whether or not such persons are named, or who disclose or publish the identity of officials on anti-terrorist duties, or who identify such persons as targets shall be punished with a fine of between five and ten million Turkish liras.

2. Those who print or publish leaflets and declarations of terrorist organizations shall be punished with a fine of between five and ten million Turkish liras.

3. Those who, in contravention of Article 14 of this law, disclose or publish the identity of informants shall be punished with a fine of between five and ten million Turkish liras.

4. If any of the offenses defined above are committed by periodicals as described in Article 3 of Press Law no. 5680 their publishers shall be punished additionally by the imposition of fines as follows: for periodicals published at less than monthly intervals the fine shall be 90 percent of the average real sales of the previous month; for periodicals issued monthly or at longer intervals the fine shall be 90 percent of the real sales of the previous issue; for printed works that are not periodicals or periodicals which have just entered the market the fine shall be 90 percent of the monthly sales of the best-selling daily periodical. In any case the fine shall not be less than fifty million Turkish liras. Editors in charge of such periodicals shall be punished with half the sentences imposed on their publishers.

*Terrorist organizations*

*Article 7.* 1. Under reservation of provisions in Articles 3 and 4 and Articles 168, 169, 171, 313, 314, and 315 of the Turkish Penal Code those who found organizations as specified in Article 1 under any name or who organize and lead activities in such organizations shall be punished with imprisonment of between five and ten years and with a fine of between two hundred million and five hundred million Turkish liras; those who join these organizations shall be punished with imprisonment of between three and five years and with a fine of between one hundred million and three hundred million Turkish liras.

2. Those who assist members of organizations constituted in the manner described above or make propaganda in connection with such organizations shall be punished with imprisonment of between one and five years and with a fine of between fifty million and one hundred million Turkish liras, even if their offense constitutes a separate crime.

3. Where assistance is provided to such organizations in the form of buildings, premises, offices, or extensions of associations, foundations, political parties, professional or workers' institutions, or their affiliates, or in educational institutions or students' dormitories or their extensions, the punishments mentioned in paragraph 2 shall be doubled.

4. In addition, activities of associations, foundations, trades unions and similar institutions found to have supported terrorism shall be banned and the institutions may be closed down by a court's decision. Assets of these institutions will be confiscated.

5. If the offense of propaganda in connection with an organization as mentioned in paragraph 2 is committed by a periodical as defined in Article 3 of the Press Law no. 5680, its publishers shall be punished additionally with the following amounts of fine: for periodicals issued at less than monthly intervals the fine shall be 90 percent of the average real sales for the previous month; for printed works that are not periodicals or periodicals that have just entered the market the fine shall be 90 percent of the monthly sales of the best-selling daily periodical. In any case the fine shall not be less than one hundred million Turkish liras. Editors in charge of such periodicals shall be punished with half the sentences awarded to publishers and a sentence of between six months' and two years' imprisonment.

*Propaganda against the indivisible unity of the State*

*Article 8.* 1. Written and oral propaganda and assemblies, meetings, and demonstrations aimed at damaging the indivisible unity of the Turkish Republic with its territory and nation are forbidden, regardless of the methods, intentions, and ideas behind such activities. Those conducting such activities shall be punished with a sentence of between two and five years' imprisonment and with a fine of between fifty million and one hundred million Turkish liras.

2. If the offense of propaganda as mentioned in the foregoing paragraph is committed by a periodical as defined in Article 3 of the Press Law no. 5680, its publishers shall be punished additionally by the following amounts of fine:

for periodicals issued at less than monthly intervals the fine shall be 90 percent of the average real sales of the previous month; for printed works that are not periodicals or periodicals that have just entered the market the fine shall be 90 percent of the monthly sales of the best-selling daily periodical. In any case the fine shall not be less than one hundred million Turkish liras. Editors in charge of such periodicals shall be punished with half the sentences awarded to publishers and a sentence of between six months' and two years' imprisonment.

## Part two — criminal procedure

*Competent court*

*Article 9.* Offenses within the scope of this law are to be tried in state security courts; and for those committing one of these crimes or participating in these crimes, the provisions of this law and the Law 2845 on The Foundation and Criminal Procedures at State Security Courts shall be applied.

*Representation by and contacts with a lawyer*

*Article 10.* In applying this law:

a. the defendant and interveners may be represented by a maximum of three lawyers;
b. the defendant in pre-trial detention or convicts may have contact with a lawyer under the supervision of a detention center or prison official.

*Length of detention*

*Article 11.* People detained for offenses under this law shall be presented before a judge within forty-eight hours [of their arrest]; in case of collective crimes, within fifteen days excluding the time it takes to bring the suspect from the place of detention to the nearest court.

*Testimonies of interrogators/investigators*

*Article 12.* Police chiefs and officers interrogating suspects and witnesses of crimes within the scope of this law or writing reports about the event or facts may, if necessary, testify in court as witnesses. However, if they are called to testify, their testimony shall be taken in a closed hearing.

*Suspension and commutation of sentences to fines*

*Article 13.* Sentences imposed under this law cannot be commuted to a fine, converted to other measures or suspended.

## Non-disclosure of the identity of informants

*Article 14.* The identity of those providing information about crimes or criminals within the scope of this law shall not to be disclosed, unless the informant has given permission or the nature of the information constitutes a crime by the informant.

## Trial without imprisonment

*Article 15.* 1. Where chiefs and officers of police and intelligence or other officials engaged in fighting terrorism are publicly prosecuted for crimes allegedly committed during the course of their duty, they shall be tried without being detained.

2. Where chiefs and officers of police and intelligence or other officials engaged in fighting terrorism are publicly prosecuted for crimes allegedly committed during the course of their duty, they shall be represented by a maximum of three lawyers whose fees shall be paid by the relevant institution [to which they were attached] regardless of the amount of fees charged by the lawyers.

3. Where chiefs and officers of police and intelligence or other officials engaged in fighting terrorism are alleged to have committed crimes during the course of their duty, the provisions of the Law on Prosecution of Civil Servants shall be applied in case of offenses involving negligence and similar failures, except offenses of murder or attempted murder.

## Part three — execution of sentences

### Execution of sentences and holding of pre-trial detainees

*Article 16.* 1. The sentences of those convicted under the provisions of this law shall be executed in special penal institutions built with rooms each capable of holding between one and three persons.

2. In such institutions, free visits may not be allowed. Contacts between the convicts and communication with other convicts may be prevented.

3. Those convicts who have served at least one-third of their sentences with good conduct and have less than three years to serve before becoming entitled to conditional release may be transferred to other closed penal centers.

4. Those held in pre-trial detention for crimes within the scope of this law shall be kept in detention centers as described in paragraph 1. The provisions of paragraph 2 shall also apply to pre-trial detainees.

### Conditional release

*Article 17.* 1. Those convicted under this law shall be released conditionally: after thirty-six years' imprisonment if, having been sentenced to death, their death penalty is not ratified by the Grand National Assembly of Turkey; after thirty years' imprisonment if they were sentenced to life imprisonment; or after they have served three-fourths of their terms of imprisonment in all other cases, if they have served their sentences with good conduct [and have applied for such release].

2. Those who may have escaped during pre-trial detention or as convicts, or may have attempted to escape, or were convicted for insurrection against the prison administration and who as a disciplinary punishment have been awarded a sentence of solitary confinement shall not benefit from conditional release, even if their disciplinary punishment has been lifted.

3. Convicts under the provisions of this law who commit another crime under this law after their sentence has been confirmed shall not benefit from conditional release.

4. The provisions of paragraph 1 and 2 of Article 19 and additional Article 2 of Law 647 on the Execution of Sentences shall not be applied to such convicts.

*Construction of prisons and detention centers*

*Article 18.* For the construction of prisons, detention centers, and custodial buildings according to Article 16 of this law, the provisions of Article 89 of Law 2886 on Public Tender will be applied.

## Part four — miscellaneous provisions

*Rewards*

*Article 19.* 1. Those, to be specified by the Ministry of the Interior, who help to apprehend criminals under this law or provide information about their whereabouts or identity shall be entitled to a financial reward according to Law 1481 on the Prevention of Certain Crimes against Public Order.

2. The Ministry of the Interior shall take measures to protect those receiving a reward.

*Measures of protection*

*Article 20.* 1. The State shall take necessary protective measures for officials involved in fighting terrorism or anarchy and officials of the judiciary, intelligence, administration, and military who carry out such duties, police chiefs and officers, the Director-General and deputy Director-General for Prisons and Detention Centers, prosecutors and directors of prisons and detention centers for the detention of terrorists, judges and prosecutors of state security courts and others performing such duties, those who may become or have been made targets for terrorist organizations, and witnesses and informants who assist in the exposure of such crimes.

2. Such protective measures shall include plastic surgery to change physical appearance, alteration of registration records, driving licenses, matrimonial

certificates, degrees and other documents, arrangement of military service, rights of movable and immovable property, and protection of social security and other rights.

3. In applying these measures the Minister of the Interior and other institutions involved shall be bound by all rules of secrecy.

4. The rules for protective measures shall be specified in guidelines to be prepared by the Prime Minister's Office.

5. Those mentioned above are entitled to use arms in order to protect themselves, their spouses, and children against attacks by terrorists, even if they have left service.

*Pension for invalids and support for widows and orphans*

*Article 21*. Where an official is injured, left disabled, dies, or is killed as a result of being exposed to terrorist activities in the course of his duty at home or abroad, even if he has [subsequently left service], the provisions of Law 2330 on Monetary Compensation and Pension shall be applied. In addition:

a. The total of the pension for invalids, or the spouse and orphans of those killed and entitled to a pension, may not be less than the pension of their colleagues on duty; if pensioners are killed the monthly payment for their spouse and orphans may not be less than their monthly pension according to the relevant law. In case of deficiency the difference shall be paid by the social security institutions and reimbursed by the Treasury.
b. Those left invalid while benefiting from public accommodation at home or abroad, and the spouse and orphans of those killed and entitled to a pension (except those living in houses specially provided under the Law of Public Housing), shall continue to benefit from public accommodation for one year. Those who after that year leave such public housing and those not benefiting from public accommodation and those living in specially provided houses shall on application be paid rent by the State for accommodation within the country for a period of ten years. Those living in especially provided accommodation abroad shall on application be paid the rent payable abroad for one year by the State.
c. As regards benefiting from accommodation loans, the provisions of additional Article 9 of Law 2559 on the Duties and Competence of the Police shall be applied; those provisions shall also be applicable to invalids or their spouses and, where their partners are not alive or have remarried, to their children.
d. Invalids, spouses, and the minor children of those killed in circumstances mentioned above shall be entitled to travel free of charge on State railroads, city maritime lines and on public transport. If the spouses or orphans cease to be entitled to a pension under the provisions of the laws on social security, they shall not be entitled to any of the rights provided in this Article.

*Support for other people suffering losses from terrorism*

*Article 22.* Citizens who are not civil servants, but suffer from terrorist activities with loss of life or property shall get special support from the Social Welfare and Solidarity Fund. The scope and amount of the support will be determined by the local authorities administering the fund.

## Part five — Temporary provisions

\*\*\*

*Provisions repealed*

*Article 23.* [The following laws:]

a. Law 2 on High Treason;
b. Law 6187 on the Protection of Freedom of Conscience and Meetings;
c. Articles 140, 141, 142, and 163 of the Turkish Penal Code no. 765;
d. Article 5, chapters 7 and 8, and Article 6, chapter 2, of Law 2908 on Associations; and
e. Law 2932 on Broadcasts and Publications in Languages other than Turkish

are hereby repealed.

*Entry into force*

*Article 24.* This law shall enter into force on the date of its publication.

*Implementation*

*Article 25.* This law shall be implemented by the Council of Ministers.

# Document no. 18

**Comment on the law to fight against terrorism, Law no. 3713**

*The Constitutional Court's perspective*[9]

*Reasons for the enactment of the [ATL]*

The reasons for the preparation and enactment of the [ATL] are explained by the Government as follows:

> Terrorism has been threatening societies and nations since the early times of history. In our century, terrorism has spread. Terror has succeeded in small nations and then after, emboldened by these successes, terror activities have spread all around the world.
>
> Terrorism has ceased to be a mere threat but has become a clear and present danger. States sponsoring terrorism has enabled it to grow and gain an international dimension.
>
> \*\*\*
>
> The fight against terrorism needs to be at the forefront of any Government's agenda because it spreads by manipulating circumstances. The nature of terrorism obliges countries to have effective, intelligent, and determined mechanisms and programs ready to fight terrorism at all times.
> It is well known that our country [Turkey] has been the target of terrorism for many years because of its geographic location. ...
>
> \*\*\*
>
> While countries and governments evaluate terrorism within the confines of democratic rules, terrorism functions without respecting any rules. In order to achieve world peace and to prevent suffering, terror needs to be eradicated ideologically, legally, and in practice ...

The struggle against terrorism requires balancing certain rights and requirements. Therefore, while fighting against a course of action which has no respect for any of the fundamental rights recognized by the Constitution [1982] and which has adopted violence as the means of terrorism, laws need to enable expression and organization of non-violent ideas in order to reach the level of contemporary requirements of democracy.

\*\*\*

[In order to accomplish the goals stated above] This law defines terrorism, introduces new mechanisms to try and punish terrorist activities, contains provisions to secure the authorities engaged in the struggle, and replaces some of the laws that restrict freedom of expression with laws that enable non-violent thoughts to be expressed. ...."

*The structure of the law, its scope and the rules introduced by the law*

The [ATL] introduces new rules in trying, punishing, and executing terrorist crimes as well as annulling or amending certain other laws already in force.

The law is composed of five parts. The first part defines terrorism, terrorist organization, and terrorist. In doing so, the first part defines certain crimes in the Turkish Penal Code (TPC) as terrorist crimes. The second part regulates some special mechanisms to try terrorist crimes. The third part states the special sentencing times to be applied in crimes falling under the law. The fourth part regulates rewards, remedies, and protection mechanisms for the public officials engaged in the struggle against terrorism and those helping authorities. The fifth part contains temporary articles for crimes committed before April 8, 1991.

*Unconstitutionality of certain provisions of the Act*

1. Article 1:
   A. The meaning and the scope of the Article:
   This article defines terrorism and terrorist organizations. The first paragraph of the article requires three conditions for an act to be a terrorist act.

a. The first requirement is that the act be done by means of pressure, force and violence, terror, intimidation, oppression, or threat. The concepts of force and violence, and intimidation, are well-defined in Turkish law. ... However, the concepts of pressure, oppression, threat, or terror have not been used extensively in Turkish law. ...

   Our assessment of the meaning of these concepts shows that these [concepts] are either synonyms or have very close meanings. Most of the time it might be hard to discern under which one of these concepts an act falls. ... Therefore, it would suffice to state that the existence of one of these means of action would create a terrorist crime provided that other requirements are met.

\*\*\*

b. The second requirement for an act to be defined as terror is the goal orientation. It is possible to assess the goal orientation requirement under five headings:

    aa. To change the characteristics of the Republic of Turkey as specified in the Constitution [its political legal, social, secular, and economic system, and the characteristics of the Republic enunciated in Article 2 of the Constitution and by way of reference in the Preamble] ...

    bb. To damage the indivisible unity of the State with its territory and nation, and to endanger the existence of the Turkish State and Republic: [The Court decided that the provisions of the TPC (Articles 125, 146, 147, 149, 168, 171, and 141/4 and 142/3 replaced by Article 7 and 8 of the Act) state what falls under this heading.]
\*\*\*

    cc. To weaken, destroy or seize the authority of the State: [The Court stated that Articles 146, 147, and 149 of the TPC also address crimes falling under this crime as well as Articles 150, 152, 153, 154, and 155.]
\*\*\*

    dd. To eliminate fundamental rights and freedoms: [The Court stated that Articles 174 (political freedoms), 175 (religious freedom), 179–92 (personal freedom), 193–94 (inviolability of the residence), 195–200 (protection of confidentiality), and provisions related to freedom to work contain these fundamental rights and freedoms. However, the Court expressed that Article 1 of the [ATL] mentions eliminating these freedoms whereas the TPC considers acts falling short of elimination as crimes, and, therefore, Article 1 is narrower in scope.]
\*\*\*

    ee. To damage the internal and external security of the State, public order, or general health: [The Court stated that the crimes that damage the external security are enunciated in the Law on Formation and Criminal Procedure of State Security Courts, and in Article 125–45 of the TPC. With regards to crimes that damage the internal security, the Court listed Articles 146–62 (acts against State forces), 369–83 (arson, purposeful flooding, and other crimes likely to create significant damage), and 384–93 (acts against transfer and military vehicles) of the TPC. Finally, concerning crimes that damage public order or general health, the Court stated that most of the crimes in Articles 125–45 of the TPC also create conditions that damage public order in addition to Articles 311–14 of the TPC (crimes against public order). The Court also added that crimes against the public order were not limited to the TPC but could also be found in the Law on Gatherings and Demonstrations, the Law on Trades Unions, the Law on Strikes and Slowing of Jobs, and the Law on Associations. As for crimes against public health, the Court stated that contaminating food or water constituted typical examples, but that the crime also included spreading diseases.]

\*\*\*

c. The third requirement for an act to be classified as a terrorist act is that it should be committed by a person or a group of people who are members of an organization. In cases where the same act is committed by individuals, the law does not apply. However, according to the last paragraph of Article 2 of the [ATL], individuals who commit crimes in the name of an organization even though they are not members of the organization would be guilty of terrorist crimes. For purposes of this law, an organization is formed when two or more people gather around the same aim. Organizations also include those groups described in the TPC and other laws [such as platforms, associations, and all armed groupings].

\*\*\*

The organization concept in the [ATL] also creates some other crimes not connected to Article 1. For example, according to Article 2, an organization member is an organizational criminal regardless of his participation in the organization's activities. Also Article 7 criminalizes establishing, organizing, managing, promoting, becoming a member of such an organization, or aiding and abetting such an organization's member(s).

\*\*\*

*Editors' note:* As the Constitutional Court's analysis shows, the definition of terrorism in the ATL consists of three components: goal orientation, means, and group focus. The extensive "goal orientation" component of the definition in the ATL, aside from referring to the Constitution within the definition, also integrates non-listed parts of the Constitution as well as numerous provisions of the TPC. Thus the relevant constitutional and TPC provisions form an integral part of the definition and must be read together. However, it should be noted that there is a difference between the TPC and the ATL; whereas the TPC requires concrete acts to establish guilt, the ATL only requires intent.

The "group focus" component of the ATL's definition of terrorism requires "belongingness" to an organization. However, the definition of an organization does not carry any ideological traits. Thus the definition does not only apply to associations with specific ideological goals, but covers all organizations. When read in combination with the aims given in the definition of terrorism, the lack of the requirement of "ideological focus" to constitute an organization permits any group allegedly possessing the stated proscribed aims to fall within the scope of the law.

*Terrorist offenses*[10]

With respect to possible terrorist offenses, the ATL differentiates between three types of terrorist acts. The first category is defined in Article 3 and these constitute absolute terrorist acts—crimes considered as terrorism at all times. The second type of terrorist acts are defined in Article 4 and consist of crimes enumerated in the TPC and elsewhere. However, these crimes do not constitute terrorist acts per se but only when they are committed with the intent stated in Article 1. The third type of terrorist acts, as stated in Article 7(1) of the ATL, consist of establishing terrorist organizations. ATL also contains an additional base that triggers the application of the anti-terror law: crimes that are not terrorist acts, but which nevertheless indirectly further terrorism.

*Absolute Terrorist Acts (Article 3):* Offenses defined in Articles 125, 131, 146, 147, 148, 149, 156, 168, 171, and 172 of the TPC.

*Article 125 of the TPC:* An act with the purpose of placing the control of the whole or a portion of the Turkish territory under foreign sovereignty, or an act threatening the unity of the State, or an act to bring about secession of a territory under the control of the State.

*Article 131 of the TPC:* Destruction or temporary incapacitation of the vessels, airplanes or any air machinery, transportation tools, roads, facilities, depots, or other military equipment under the control of the Turkish Armed Forces (TAF) or State Security Forces.

*Article 146 of the TPC:* Intentional attempts to breach the "Main Structure Law of 1921" and intentionally attempting to force the Turkish Grand National Assembly to annul itself or stop it from fulfilling its duties.

*Article 147 of the TPC:* Preventing the Council of Ministers from fulfilling their duties, or encouraging others to take action to prevent it from properly functioning.

*Article 148 of the TPC:* Drafting or arming citizens as soldiers to work under the authority of a foreign state or for the benefit of a foreign state without the approval of the State.

*Article 149 of the TPC:* Provoking the public to revolt against the government or arming the public against each other by using numbing, suffocating or burning gases, or by using explosive materials.

*Article 156 of the TPC:* Attempting to assassinate or assassinating the President of the Republic.

*Article 168 of the TPC:* Forming an armed organization or gang to commit the crimes stated in Articles 125, 131, 146, 147, 149, and 156, or leading an organization or a branch of it formed with the prohibited crimes in those articles.

*Article 171 of the TPC:* Conspiring to privately commit the crimes stated in Articles 125, 131, 146, 147, 149, and 156.

*Article 172 of the TPC:* Provoking the public in public meeting areas to commit the crimes stated in Articles 125, 131, and 156 or in Articles 146, 147, and 149.

Acts which are considered as terrorist acts if committed for terrorist purposes described in Article 1 of the ATL (Article 4): Articles 145, 150, 151, 152, 153, 154, 155, 169, and the second paragraph of Article 499 of the Turkish Penal Code, and offenses defined in Article 9, parts (b), (c) and (e) of Law 2845 on the Foundation and Criminal Procedure at State Security Courts.

*Article 145 of the TPC:* Desecrating or damaging the Turkish flag or any other insignia of the State's sovereignty.

*Article 150 of the TPC*: Manufacturing, producing, transporting, hiding, or importing [smuggling] weapons, ammunition, knives, bombs, or related flammable, destructive, or deadly materials for a criminal group.

*Article 151 of the TPC*: Failure to immediately inform competent authorities upon becoming aware of any of the crimes stated in Articles 146–50.

*Article 152 of the TPC*: Seizing control of a military unit, base, facility, naval unit, or a public settlement, or not obeying the orders to leave a military settlement in excess of official capacity or without an excuse accepted by the government.

*Article 153 of the TPC*: Inciting soldiers to disobey the law, disavow their oath, or neglect military duties.

*Article 154 of the TPC*: Distributing materials aimed to incite the public to commit the crimes stated in Articles 152 and 153.

*Article 155 of the TPC:* Publishing articles inciting people to break the law or harm the security of the country, or preparing publications or suggestions that make people unwilling to serve in the military or delivering speeches to that end in public meetings or gathering places — except in circumstances indicated in the aforementioned articles.

*Article 169 of the TPC:* Aiding and abetting organizations formed to commit the crimes stated in Articles 125, 131, 146, 147, 149, and 156.

*Article 499/2 of the TPC:* Kidnapping individuals to force state officials to take or not to take an action in a given area or issue.

*Article 9*, subsections (b), (c), and (e) of Law 2845 on the Foundation and Criminal Procedure of State Security Courts (SSC):

*Subsection b*: Crimes stated in the Law on Weapons, Knives and Other Devices (Law no. 6136); production, possession, transfer of explosives or firing a weapon at public gathering places to create fear or panic (TPC 264); production or import of narcotics (TPC 403), if committed as a group.

*Subsection c*: Acts that were initially the reasons for Declaration of a State of Emergency in accordance with Article 120 of the Constitution if committed in state of emergency declared regions.

*Subsection e*: Article repealed in February 1993.

*Editors' additional note on terrorist offenses:* The ATL also introduces a strict liability system for people forming organizations falling within the definition given in Article 1, and for people becoming members of such organizations or giving assistance to members of such organizations (Article 7/1). In addition to the category "Crime of Establishing a Terrorist Organization," provided in Article 7/1, the ATL also establishes that the law is applicable in some crimes that are not terrorist acts by themselves but which nevertheless indirectly further terrorism (see Articles 6/1, 6/2, 6/3, 7/2, 7/4, 8/1, and 14 of the ATL).

*Editors' note on Competent Courts:*[11] Article 9 of the ATL declares that State Security Courts (SSC) are the competent tribunals to try terrorist crimes. Although disbanded in 2004, SSCs formed one of the most important aspects of Turkey's struggle with terrorism. Formed by Law 2845 in 1983 in accordance with Article 143 of the Constitution, SSCs comprised a system of special courts operating throughout Turkey (in eight centers, some with multiple chambers), which dealt with offenses against the indivisible integrity of the state within its territory and nation, the free democratic order, or against the Republic whose characteristics are defined in the Constitution, offenses directly involving the internal and external security of the State (Article 1), and crimes falling under the ATL. SSCs consisted of a president, two full members, a substitute, a prosecutor, and deputy prosecutors (Articles 3 and 4). The president, one full member, and one substitute were civilians (Article 5). The other full member was a military judge. SSCs differed from regular courts in a variety of ways; most significant of which were the number of judges, the use of military judges and prosecutors, the use of stricter procedures than ordinary criminal courts, and reliance on a special investigative arm of the security forces. A number of features of the SSC and their envious protection of the State raised questions regarding the availability of a fair trial to defendants tried within the system and the independence of such courts, i.e. the participation of a military judge on every SSC panel, and special procedures that afford fewer protections for defendants than do procedures in Turkey's ordinary criminal courts (extended periods of incommunicado detention, limitations on lawyers representing defendants in the SSCs). Thus, SSC trials have been the subject of numerous European Court of Human Rights (ECtHR) applications; almost all were resolved against Turkey. As a consequence of the mounting pressure from the ECtHR and the EU, first the military judge was removed from the SSC panel during Abdullah Ocalan's trial in 2001, and, second, in 2004, the SSCs were abolished with an amendment to the Constitution.

*Editors' final note on the ATL:* As the preceding analysis suggests, the application of the ATL in any crime meant that the accused individual would come into a legal system that was rather different than the ordinary criminal justice system. The main aspect of the ATL system was the SSC jurisdiction and increased penalties (Articles 5, (6/4), 7/3, 7/5, and 8/2) that could not be commuted to a fine, converted to other measures, or suspended (Article 13).

# Document no. 19

**Turkey's May 12, 1992, notice of derogation from rights enshrined in Article 5 of the European Convention on Human Rights in conformity with Article 15 of the convention[12]**

1. I have the honor to refer to the Notice of Derogation and the Notice of Information made by the Republic of Turkey in conformity with Article 15 of the European Convention for the Protection of Human Rights and Fundamental Freedoms on August 6, 1990, and 3 January 1991, respectively.

2. As most of the measures described in the decrees which have the Force of Law Nos 425 and 430 that might result in derogating from rights guaranteed by Articles 5, 6, 8, 10, 11, and 13 of the Convention are no longer being implemented, I hereby inform you that the Republic of Turkey limits henceforward the scope of its Notice of Derogation with respect to Article 5 of the Convention only. The derogation with respect to Articles 6, 8, 10, 11, and 13 of the Convention is no longer in effect; consequently, the corresponding reference to these Articles is hereby deleted from the said Notice of Derogation.

# Document no. 20

### Other laws used against terrorism[13]

#### Turkish Penal Code (Law no. 765, adopted March 1, 1926)

*Article 158* — (amended: 1961/235)

Whoever insults the President of the Republic face-to-face or through cursing shall face a heavy penalty of not more than three years.

If the insulting or cursing happens in the absence of the President of the Republic, those who commit the crime will be liable to imprisonment of between one and three years. Even if the name of the President of the Republic is not directly mentioned, allusion and hint shall be considered as an attack made directly against the President if there is presumptive evidence beyond a reasonable doubt that the attack was made against the President of Turkey.

If the crime is committed in any published form, the punishment will increase from one-third to one-half.

*Article 159* — (amended:1961/235)

Those who publicly insult or ridicule the moral personality of Turkishness, the Republic, the Parliament, the Government, State Ministers, the military or security forces of the state, or the Judiciary will be punished with a penalty of no less than one year and no more than six years of maximum security imprisonment. ...

If insulting Turkishness is carried out in a foreign country by a Turk the punishment given will be increased from one-third to one-half.

*Article 311* — Inciting to commit a crime, threatening with the goal of inciting panic and fear — (amended: 1953/6123); (amended: 1981/2370)

One who publicly incites the commission of a crime shall be punished in the ways below.

1. If the penalty of the felony incited is higher than the duration of the heavy penalty, a heavy imprisonment of between three and five years.
2. If limited heavy imprisonment or imprisonment is necessary, it will be from three months' to three years' imprisonment in accordance with the type of crime.
3. In other circumstances, a heavy fine of between 1,000 and 5,000 lira will be applied.

(Amendment: 1981/2370)
If the incitement occurs by various means of mass media, sound tapes, records, films, papers, periodicals, or with other press instruments, or by writings written by hand and then multiplied and printed or distributed, or by signs or written announcements hung, the heavy imprisonment and fines which will be determined according to the paragraphs above will be doubled.

*Article 312* — (amended: 1981/2370)
One who openly praises an action considered criminal under the law or speaks positively about it or incites people to disobey the law shall be sentenced from six months to two years of imprisonment and to a heavy fine of between 2,000 and 10,000 lira.

One who openly incites people to enmity and hatred by pointing to class, racial, religious, confessional, or regional differences will be punished by imprisonment of between one and three years and a heavy fine of between 3,000 and 12,000 lira. If the incitement is done in a way that could possibly be dangerous for public security, the punishment given to the perpetrator is increased from one-third to one-half.

Penalties given to those who carry out crimes in the paragraphs written above by means outlined in the second paragraph of Article 311 will be increased accordingly.

## Political Parties Law (no. 2820, adopted April 26, 1982)

*Article 81*: Preventing the creation of minorities
Political parties:

a. cannot put forward that minorities exist in the Turkish Republic based on national, religious, confessional, racial, or language differences. . . .;
b. cannot by means of protecting, developing, or disseminating language or cultures other than the Turkish language and culture through creating minorities in the Republic of Turkey have the goal of destroying national unity or be engaged in activities to this end;
c. cannot use a language other than Turkish in writing and printing party statutes or programs, at congresses, at meetings in open air or indoor gatherings; at meetings, and in propaganda, cannot use or distribute placards, pictures, phonograph records, voice and visual tapes, brochures and statements written in a language other than Turkish; cannot remain indifferent to these actions and acts committed by others; however, it is possible to translate party statutes and programs into foreign languages other than those forbidden by law.

## The Law concerning the Founding and Broadcasts of Television and Radio (no. 3984, adopted April 13, 1994)

*Article 4*: Broadcasting principles
Radio and television broadcasts are to be carried out in the understanding of public service according to the principles below.
Broadcasts cannot be contradictory to the following:

a. the existence and independence of the Turkish Republic, the indivisible unity of the state with its territory and nation;
b. the national and spiritual values of society. ...;
d. the general morality, civil peace, and structure of the Turkish family ...

Must be conducted in accordance with:

h. the general goals and basic principles of Turkish national education and the development of national culture;
i. fairness and objectivity in broadcasting and the fundamental principle of respect for the law; ...
l. to present news in a speedy and correct way;
m. the principle that broadcasts will not be made that have a negative effect on the physical, intellectual, mental, and moral development of children and youth ...; and
t. radio and television broadcasts will be made in Turkish; however, for the purpose of teaching or of imparting news those foreign languages that have made a contribution to the development of universal cultural and scientific works can be used.

## Foreign Language Education and Teaching Law (no. 2923)

*Article 2*

a. The mother tongue of Turkish citizens cannot be taught in any language other than Turkish. ...
c. Taking into consideration the view of the National Security Council, the Council of Ministers by its decision will determine in Turkey what foreign languages can be taught.

## Decision no. 92/2788, Official Gazette, March 20, 1992

2 — ... It had been decided by the Council of Ministers on March 4, 1992, that in official and private courses education and teaching are to be made in the following languages: English, French, German as well as Russian, Italian, Spanish, Arabic, Japanese, and Chinese.

## The law concerning fundamental provisions on elections and voter registries (no. 298, adopted April 26, 1961)

*Article 58*

... It is forbidden to use any other language or script than Turkish in propaganda disseminated in radio or television as well as in other election propaganda.

## Press Law (no. 5680, adopted July 15, 1950)

*Article 1*

The press is free.

The publishing of printed works is subject to the written directives in this law.

*Article 16*: Criminal responsibility for crimes committed by means of the press (amended 1983/2950)

1. The responsibility for crimes committed in periodicals belongs, together with the person who caused the crime, whether the writer, news writer, artist, or caricaturist, to the periodical's responsible editor. However, punishments depriving liberty given to responsible editors without regard to their duration shall be converted to monetary fines. .... Responsible editors cannot be punished with security detention.

2. The responsible editor is not required to give the name of writers, news writers, artists, or caricaturists who publish with a pen name or alias. Without regard to the first paragraph, the responsibility for a writing, or a news report, or a picture, or a caricature, where the author of a work is not clear or where the author's names is not revealed in a true manner by the responsible editor at the latest during the first court interrogation, shall fall to the responsible editor as if he were the person who through writing, or news writing, or making a picture or caricature caused the crime.

3. The responsible editor is not responsible for writings, news, pictures, or caricatures published by the periodical's owner without his approval. Under such circumstances, the legal responsibility of the responsible editor belongs to the person who publishes the writing, news, picture, or caricature.

4. In crimes that are committed in publications that are not defined as periodicals [books], the legal responsibility belongs to the publisher together with the writer, translator, or artist. However, regardless of the duration, all verdicts giving the penalty of imprisonment for the publisher shall be converted to fines. Computation of the fine is based on the amount mentioned in the Law no. 647 on the Execution of Penalties, Article 4, paragraph 1. Publishers are not to be penalized with security detention.

In the case where the author of the printed work published as a non-periodical is not identified, the responsibility belongs to the publisher without regard to the aforementioned articles. In the case when the work is published without the knowledge and consent of its writer, translator, or artist, only the publisher becomes responsible as if the one who created the work.

When the abovementioned persons are not identified or a case in a Turkish court is not opened against them, the responsibility belongs to the seller and distributor when the publisher is not known.

In quotations that are made in publications published in Turkey without the consent of the owner, the responsibility belongs to the one who made the quote.

If publication is made in any language prohibited by law, the relevant articles which envision converting into monetary fines and of not giving a penalty of placing under security detention shall not be applied.

*Article 31* (amended 1983/2950)

The entry or distribution into Turkey of works published in a foreign country that contradict the indivisible unity of the state with its territory and nation, national hegemony, the existence of the Republic, national security, public order, general law and order, the common good, general morality, or health can be outlawed by a decision of the Council of Ministers.

## Provincial Administration Law (no. 5442, adopted June 10, 1949)

*Article 2/d/2* (amended 1959:7267)

Village names that are not Turkish and give rise to confusion are to be changed in the shortest possible time by the Ministry for the Interior after receiving the opinion of the Provincial Permanent Committee.

## Police Duty and Responsibility Law (no. 2559, adopted July 4, 1934)

*Article 8* (amended: 1985/3233)

If the police are in possession of incontrovertible evidence and by order of the district's highest civil servant, areas where plays are conducted, presentations given, films or videos shown that will damage the indivisible unity of the state with its territory and nation, constitutional order, or general security or common morality can be closed by the police or have their activities stopped.

If the reason for the closing or ceasing of activities requires a legal investigation by the state, the investigation file shall be immediately given to the judiciary. ...

## The law concerning crimes committed against Atatürk (no. 5816, adopted July 25, 1951)

*Article 1*

Anyone who publicly insults or curses the memory of Atatürk shall be imprisoned with a heavy sentence of between one and three years.

A heavy sentence of between one and five years shall be given to anyone who destroys, breaks, ruins, or defaces a statue, bust, or monuments representing Atatürk or the grave of Atatürk.

Anyone who encourages others to commit the crimes outlined in the paragraphs above will be punished as if committing the crime.

*Article 2*

If the crimes outlined in the first article are committed by a group of two or more individuals, or publicly, or in public districts or by means of the press will have the penalty imposed increased by a proportion of one-half.

If the crimes outlined in the second paragraph of the first article are committed using force ... the penalty will be doubled. ...

# 4 European system of Human Rights and fundamental freedoms

# Document no. 21

### Introductory comment[1]

The Treaty of Rome of 1957, establishing the European Community (EC), did not specifically mention Human Rights, although several parts of the Treaty contained Human Rights-related clauses. In its Preamble, the Treaty notes the Member States' resolution to "pool their resources to preserve and strengthen peace and liberty" and calls "upon the other peoples of Europe who share their ideal to join in their efforts." In ex-Article 7 (the articles were renumbered with the Amsterdam Treaty), the Treaty states that "[t]he internal market shall comprise an area without internal frontiers in which the free movement of goods, persons, services and capital is ensured. ... " Ex-Article 119 contains the principle of equal pay for men and women and ex-Article 51 contains the principle of equal treatment for immigrant workers. From these limited rights, it can be seen that the Treaty of Rome's Human Rights-related provisions concerned mainly economic subjects.

Despite the fact that Human Rights seem to have been of minuscule importance in the foundation of the European Community, the European Union (EU) has consistently tried to formulate a document that makes fundamental Human Rights a part of EU law, particularly through two mechanisms: accession to the European Convention on Human Rights (ECtHR) or the adoption of a separate EC bill of rights.

To create a separate EC fundamental rights document, "[t]he European Parliament (EP) adopted a Resolution in 1973 'concerning the protection of the fundamental rights of Member States' citizens when Community law was drafted' and another in 1977 'on the granting of special rights to the citizens of the European Community.' The EP issued a declaration of political principle on the definition of fundamental rights on 10 February 1977, which was subsequently adopted by the Council and Commission. In a 1979 Resolution, the EP urged EC accession to the European Convention and envisaged the drafting of a European Charter of Civil Rights. Further Resolutions in 1983 and 1984 emphasised the need to incorporate fundamental Human Rights in the EC in a constitutional manner and, in 1989, the EP proposed the adoption of a declaration of fundamental rights as part of a 'Constitution' for the EU."[2]

However, such a document failed to materialise until the official proclamation of the EU Charter of Fundamental Rights in the European Council Nice Summit in December 2000. In the absence of such a document, the 1950 ECtHR was the main legal instrument for safeguarding such rights in Europe. Although the EU was not a party to the Convention, through a combination of factors (declarations, European Court of Justice (ECJ) decisions, and positions taken by member states), the ECtHR became a very important part of the EU system.

# Document no. 22

**The Council of Europe Convention for the Protection of Human Rights and Fundamental Freedoms (European Convention of Human Rights), as amended by Protocol no. 11[3]**

The text of the Convention had been amended according to the provisions of Protocol no. 3 (ETS no. 45), which entered into force on 21 September 1970, of Protocol no. 5 (ETS no. 55), which entered into force on 20 December 1971, and of Protocol no. 8 (ETS no. 118), which entered into force on 1 January 1990, and comprised also the text of Protocol no. 2 (ETS no. 44) which, in accordance with Article 5, paragraph 3 thereof, had been an integral part of the Convention since its entry into force on 21 September 1970. All provisions which had been amended or added by these Protocols are replaced by Protocol no. 11 (ETS no. 155), as from the date of its entry into force on 1 November 1998. As from that date, Protocol no. 9 (ETS no. 140), which entered into force on 1 October 1994, is repealed and Protocol no. 10 (ETS no. 146) has lost its purpose.

The governments signatory hereto, being members of the Council of Europe,

Considering the Universal Declaration of Human Rights proclaimed by the General Assembly of the United Nations on 10 December 1948;

Considering that this Declaration aims at securing the universal and effective recognition and observance of the Rights therein declared;

Considering that the aim of the Council of Europe is the achievement of greater unity between its members and that one of the methods by which that aim is to be pursued is the maintenance and further realisation of Human Rights and fundamental freedoms;

Reaffirming their profound belief in those fundamental freedoms which are the foundation of justice and peace in the world and are best maintained on the one hand by an effective political democracy and on the other by a common understanding and observance of the Human Rights upon which they depend;

Being resolved, as the governments of European countries which are likeminded and have a common heritage of political traditions, ideals, freedom, and the rule of law, to take the first steps for the collective enforcement of certain of the rights stated in the Universal Declaration,

Have agreed as follows:

## Article 1 [1] — Obligation to respect Human Rights

The High Contracting Parties shall secure to everyone within their jurisdiction the rights and freedoms defined in Section I of this Convention.

*Section I* [1] — Rights and freedoms

## Article 2 [1] — Right to life

1. Everyone's right to life shall be protected by law. No one shall be deprived of his life intentionally save in the execution of a sentence of a court following his conviction of a crime for which this penalty is provided by law.
2. Deprivation of life shall not be regarded as inflicted in contravention of this article when it results from the use of force which is no more than absolutely necessary:
   a. in defence of any person from unlawful violence;
   b. in order to effect a lawful arrest or to prevent the escape of a person lawfully detained;
   c. in action lawfully taken for the purpose of quelling a riot or insurrection.

## Article 3 [2] — Prohibition of torture

No one shall be subjected to torture or to inhuman or degrading treatment or punishment.

## Article 4 [1] — Prohibition of slavery and forced labour

1. No one shall be held in slavery or servitude.
2. No one shall be required to perform forced or compulsory labour.
3. For the purpose of this article the term "forced or compulsory labour" shall not include:
   a. any work required to be done in the ordinary course of detention imposed according to the provisions of Article 5 of this Convention or during conditional release from such detention;
   b. any service of a military character or, in case of conscientious objectors in countries where they are recognised, service exacted instead of compulsory military service;
   c. any service exacted in case of an emergency or calamity threatening the life or well-being of the community;
   d. any work or service which forms part of normal civic obligations.

## Article 5 [1] — Right to liberty and security

1. Everyone has the right to liberty and security of person. No one shall be deprived of his liberty save in the following cases and in accordance with a procedure prescribed by law:

a. the lawful detention of a person after conviction by a competent court;
b. the lawful arrest or detention of a person for non-compliance with the lawful order of a court or in order to secure the fulfilment of any obligation prescribed by law;
c. the lawful arrest or detention of a person effected for the purpose of bringing him before the competent legal authority on reasonable suspicion of having committed an offence or when it is reasonably considered necessary to prevent his committing an offence or fleeing after having done so;
d. the detention of a minor by lawful order for the purpose of educational supervision or his lawful detention for the purpose of bringing him before the competent legal authority;
e. the lawful detention of persons for the prevention of the spreading of infectious diseases, of persons of unsound mind, alcoholics or drug addicts, or vagrants;
f. the lawful arrest or detention of a person to prevent his effecting an unauthorised entry into the country or of a person against whom action is being taken with a view to deportation or extradition.
2. Everyone who is arrested shall be informed promptly, in a language which he understands, of the reasons for his arrest and of any charge against him.
3. Everyone arrested or detained in accordance with the provisions of paragraph 1.c of this article shall be brought promptly before a judge or other officer authorised by law to exercise judicial power and shall be entitled to trial within a reasonable time or to release pending trial. Release may be conditioned by guarantees to appear for trial.
4. Everyone who is deprived of his liberty by arrest or detention shall be entitled to take proceedings by which the lawfulness of his detention shall be decided speedily by a court and his release ordered if the detention is not lawful.
5. Everyone who has been the victim of arrest or detention in contravention of the provisions of this article shall have an enforceable right to compensation.

## *Article 6 [3] — Right to a fair trial*

1. In the determination of his civil rights and obligations or of any criminal charge against him, everyone is entitled to a fair and public hearing within a reasonable time by an independent and impartial tribunal established by law. Judgment shall be pronounced publicly but the press and public may be excluded from all or part of the trial in the interests of morals, public order or national security in a democratic society, where the interests of juveniles or the protection of the private life of the parties so require, or to the extent strictly necessary in the opinion of the court in special circumstances where publicity would prejudice the interests of justice.
2. Everyone charged with a criminal offence shall be presumed innocent until proved guilty according to law.

3. Everyone charged with a criminal offence has the following minimum rights:
   a. to be informed promptly, in a language which he understands and in detail, of the nature and cause of the accusation against him;
   b. to have adequate time and facilities for the preparation of his defence;
   c. to defend himself in person or through legal assistance of his own choosing or, if he has not sufficient means to pay for legal assistance, to be given it free when the interests of justice so require;
   d. to examine or have examined witnesses against him and to obtain the attendance and examination of witnesses on his behalf under the same conditions as witnesses against him;
   e. to have the free assistance of an interpreter if he cannot understand or speak the language used in court.

## *Article 7[4] — No punishment without law*

1. No one shall be held guilty of any criminal offence on account of any act or omission which did not constitute a criminal offence under national or international law at the time when it was committed. Nor shall a heavier penalty be imposed than the one that was applicable at the time the criminal offence was committed.
2. This article shall not prejudice the trial and punishment of any person for any act or omission which, at the time when it was committed, was criminal according to the general principles of law recognised by civilised nations.

## *Article 8 [1] — Right to respect for private and family life*

1. Everyone has the right to respect for his private and family life, his home, and his correspondence.
2. There shall be no interference by a public authority with the exercise of this right except such as is in accordance with the law and is necessary in a democratic society in the interests of national security, public safety or the economic well-being of the country, for the prevention of disorder or crime, for the protection of health or morals, or for the protection of the rights and freedoms of others.

## *Article 9 [1] — Freedom of thought, conscience, and religion*

1. Everyone has the right to freedom of thought, conscience, and religion; this right includes freedom to change his religion or belief and freedom, either alone or in community with others and in public or private, to manifest his religion or belief, in worship, teaching, practice, and observance.
2. Freedom to manifest one's religion or beliefs shall be subject only to such limitations as are prescribed by law and are necessary in a democratic society in the interests of public safety, for the protection of public order, health or morals, or for the protection of the rights and freedoms of others.

## Article 10 [1] — Freedom of expression

1. Everyone has the right to freedom of expression. This right shall include freedom to hold opinions and to receive and impart information and ideas without interference by public authority and regardless of frontiers. This article shall not prevent States from requiring the licensing of broadcasting, television, or cinema enterprises.
2. The exercise of these freedoms, since it carries with it duties and responsibilities, may be subject to such formalities, conditions, restrictions or penalties as are prescribed by law and are necessary in a democratic society, in the interests of national security, territorial integrity or public safety, for the prevention of disorder or crime, for the protection of health or morals, for the protection of the reputation or rights of others, for preventing the disclosure of information received in confidence, or for maintaining the authority and impartiality of the judiciary.

## Article 11 [5] — Freedom of assembly and association

1. Everyone has the right to freedom of peaceful assembly and to freedom of association with others, including the right to form and to join trades unions for the protection of his interests.
2. No restrictions shall be placed on the exercise of these rights other than such as are prescribed by law and are necessary in a democratic society in the interests of national security or public safety, for the prevention of disorder or crime, for the protection of health or morals, or for the protection of the rights and freedoms of others. This article shall not prevent the imposition of lawful restrictions on the exercise of these rights by members of the armed forces, of the police, or of the administration of the State.

## Article 12 [1] — Right to marry

Men and women of marriageable age have the right to marry and to found a family, according to the national laws governing the exercise of this right.

## Article 13 [1] — Right to an effective remedy

Everyone whose rights and freedoms as set forth in this Convention are violated shall have an effective remedy before a national authority notwithstanding that the violation has been committed by persons acting in an official capacity.

## Article 14 [1] — Prohibition of discrimination

The enjoyment of the rights and freedoms set forth in this Convention shall be secured without discrimination on any ground such as sex, race, colour, language, religion, political or other opinion, national or social origin, association with a national minority, property, birth, or other status.

## Article 15 [1] — *Derogation in time of emergency*

1. In time of war or other public emergency threatening the life of the nation any High Contracting Party may take measures derogating from its obligations under this Convention to the extent strictly required by the exigencies of the situation, provided that such measures are not inconsistent with its other obligations under international law.
2. No derogation from Article 2, except in respect of deaths resulting from lawful acts of war, or from Articles 3, 4 (paragraph 1) and 7 shall be made under this provision.
3. Any High Contracting Party availing itself of this right of derogation shall keep the Secretary General of the Council of Europe fully informed of the measures which it has taken and the reasons therefor. It shall also inform the Secretary General of the Council of Europe when such measures have ceased to operate and the provisions of the Convention are again being fully executed.

## Article 16 [1] — *Restrictions on political activity of aliens*

Nothing in Articles 10, 11, and 14 shall be regarded as preventing the High Contracting Parties from imposing restrictions on the political activity of aliens.

## Article 17 [6] — *Prohibition of abuse of rights*

Nothing in this Convention may be interpreted as implying for any State, group, or person any right to engage in any activity or perform any act aimed at the destruction of any of the rights and freedoms set forth herein or at their limitation to a greater extent than is provided for in the Convention.

## Article 18 [1] — *Limitation on use of restrictions on rights*

The restrictions permitted under this Convention to the said rights and freedoms shall not be applied for any purpose other than those for which they have been prescribed.

*Section II* [7] — European Court of Human Rights

## Article 19 — *Establishment of the Court*

To ensure the observance of the engagements undertaken by the High Contracting Parties in the Convention and the Protocols thereto, there shall be set up a European Court of Human Rights, hereinafter referred to as "the Court." It shall function on a permanent basis.

## Article 20 — *Number of judges*

The Court shall consist of a number of judges equal to that of the High Contracting Parties.

## Article 21 — Criteria for office

1. The judges shall be of high moral character and must either possess the qualifications required for appointment to high judicial office or be jurisconsults of recognised competence.
2. The judges shall sit on the Court in their individual capacity.
3. During their term of office the judges shall not engage in any activity which is incompatible with their independence, impartiality, or with the demands of a full-time office; all questions arising from the application of this paragraph shall be decided by the Court.

## Article 22 — Election of judges

1. The judges shall be elected by the Parliamentary Assembly with respect to each High Contracting Party by a majority of votes cast from a list of three candidates nominated by the High Contracting Party.
2. The same procedure shall be followed to complete the Court in the event of the accession of new High Contracting Parties and in filling casual vacancies.

## Article 23 — Terms of office

1. The judges shall be elected for a period of six years. They may be re-elected. However, the terms of office of one-half of the judges elected at the first election shall expire at the end of three years.
2. The judges whose terms of office are to expire at the end of the initial period of three years shall be chosen by lot by the Secretary General of the Council of Europe immediately after their election.
3. In order to ensure that, as far as possible, the terms of office of one-half of the judges are renewed every three years, the Parliamentary Assembly may decide, before proceeding to any subsequent election, that the term or terms of office of one or more judges to be elected shall be for a period other than six years but not more than nine and not less than three years.
4. In cases where more than one term of office is involved and where the Parliamentary Assembly applies the preceding paragraph, the allocation of the terms of office shall be effected by a drawing of lots by the Secretary General of the Council of Europe immediately after the election.
5. A judge elected to replace a judge whose term of office has not expired shall hold office for the remainder of his predecessor's term.
6. The terms of office of judges shall expire when they reach the age of 70.
7. The judges shall hold office until replaced. They shall, however, continue to deal with such cases as they already have under consideration.

## Article 24 — Dismissal

No judge may be dismissed from his office unless the other judges decide by a majority of two-thirds that he has ceased to fulfil the required conditions.

## Article 25 — *Registry and legal secretaries*

The Court shall have a registry, the functions and organisation of which shall be laid down in the rules of the Court. The Court shall be assisted by legal secretaries.

## Article 26 — *Plenary Court*

The plenary Court shall:

a. elect its President and one or two Vice-Presidents for a period of three years; they may be re-elected;
b. set up Chambers, constituted for a fixed period of time;
c. elect the Presidents of the Chambers of the Court; they may be re-elected;
d. adopt the rules of the Court, and
e. elect the Registrar and one or more Deputy Registrars.

## Article 27 — *Committees, Chambers, and Grand Chamber*

1. To consider cases brought before it, the Court shall sit in committees of three judges, in Chambers of seven judges, and in a Grand Chamber of seventeen judges. The Court's Chambers shall set up committees for a fixed period of time.
2. There shall sit as an *ex officio* member of the Chamber and the Grand Chamber the judge elected in respect of the State Party concerned or, if there is none or if he is unable to sit, a person of its choice who shall sit in the capacity of judge.
3. The Grand Chamber shall also include the President of the Court, the Vice-Presidents, the Presidents of the Chambers, and other judges chosen in accordance with the rules of the Court. When a case is referred to the Grand Chamber under Article 43, no judge from the Chamber which rendered the judgment shall sit in the Grand Chamber, with the exception of the President of the Chamber and the judge who sat in respect of the State Party concerned.

## Article 28 — *Declarations of inadmissibility by committees*

A committee may, by a unanimous vote, declare inadmissible or strike out of its list of cases an application submitted under Article 34 where such a decision can be taken without further examination. The decision shall be final.

## Article 29 — *Decisions by Chambers on admissibility and merits*

1. If no decision is taken under Article 28, a Chamber shall decide on the admissibility and merits of individual applications submitted under Article 34.

2. A Chamber shall decide on the admissibility and merits of inter-State applications submitted under Article 33.
3. The decision on admissibility shall be taken separately unless the Court, in exceptional cases, decides otherwise.

## Article 30 — Relinquishment of jurisdiction to the Grand Chamber

Where a case pending before a Chamber raises a serious question affecting the interpretation of the Convention or the protocols thereto, or where the resolution of a question before the Chamber might have a result inconsistent with a judgment previously delivered by the Court, the Chamber may, at any time before it has rendered its judgment, relinquish jurisdiction in favour of the Grand Chamber, unless one of the parties to the case objects.

## Article 31 — Powers of the Grand Chamber

The Grand Chamber shall:

a. determine applications submitted under either Article 33 or Article 34 when a Chamber has relinquished jurisdiction under Article 30 or when the case has been referred to it under Article 43; and
b. consider requests for advisory opinions submitted under Article 47.

## Article 32 — Jurisdiction of the Court

1. The jurisdiction of the Court shall extend to all matters concerning the interpretation and application of the Convention and the protocols thereto which are referred to it as provided in Articles 33, 34, and 47.
2. In the event of dispute as to whether the Court has jurisdiction, the Court shall decide.

## Article 33 — Inter-State cases

Any High Contracting Party may refer to the Court any alleged breach of the provisions of the Convention and the protocols thereto by another High Contracting Party.

## Article 34 — Individual applications

The Court may receive applications from any person, non-governmental organisation or group of individuals claiming to be the victim of a violation by one of the High Contracting Parties of the rights set forth in the Convention or the protocols thereto. The High Contracting Parties undertake not to hinder in any way the effective exercise of this right.

### Article 35 — *Admissibility criteria*

1. The Court may deal with the matter only after all domestic remedies have been exhausted, according to the generally recognised rules of international law, and within a period of six months from the date on which the final decision was taken.
2. The Court shall not deal with any application submitted under Article 34 that:
   a. is anonymous; or
   b. is substantially the same as a matter that has already been examined by the Court or has already been submitted to another procedure of international investigation or settlement and contains no relevant new information.
3. The Court shall declare inadmissible any individual application submitted under Article 34 which it considers incompatible with the provisions of the Convention or the protocols thereto, manifestly ill-founded, or an abuse of the right of application.
4. The Court shall reject any application which it considers inadmissible under this Article. It may do so at any stage of the proceedings.

### Article 36 — *Third-party intervention*

1. In all cases before a Chamber or the Grand Chamber, a High Contracting Party, one of whose nationals is an applicant, shall have the right to submit written comments and to take part in hearings.
2. The President of the Court may, in the interest of the proper administration of justice, invite any High Contracting Party which is not a party to the proceedings or any person concerned who is not the applicant to submit written comments or take part in hearings.

### Article 37 — *Striking out applications*

1. The Court may at any stage of the proceedings decide to strike an application out of its list of cases where the circumstances lead to the conclusion that:
   a. the applicant does not intend to pursue his application; or
   b. the matter has been resolved; or
   c. for any other reason established by the Court, it is no longer justified to continue the examination of the application.

   However, the Court shall continue the examination of the application if respect for Human Rights as defined in the Convention and the protocols thereto so requires.
2. The Court may decide to restore an application to its list of cases if it considers that the circumstances justify such a course.

### Article 38 — *Examination of the case and friendly settlement proceedings*

1. If the Court declares the application admissible, it shall:

a. pursue the examination of the case, together with the representatives of the parties, and, if need be, undertake an investigation, for the effective conduct of which the States concerned shall furnish all necessary facilities;
b. place itself at the disposal of the parties concerned with a view to securing a friendly settlement of the matter on the basis of respect for Human Rights as defined in the Convention and the protocols thereto.
2. Proceedings conducted under paragraph 1.b shall be confidential.

## Article 39 — Finding of a friendly settlement

If a friendly settlement is effected, the Court shall strike the case out of its list by means of a decision which shall be confined to a brief statement of the facts and of the solution reached.

## Article 40 — Public hearings and access to documents

1. Hearings shall be in public unless the Court in exceptional circumstances decides otherwise.
2. Documents deposited with the Registrar shall be accessible to the public unless the President of the Court decides otherwise.

## Article 41 — Just satisfaction

If the Court finds that there has been a violation of the Convention or the protocols thereto, and if the internal law of the High Contracting Party concerned allows only partial reparation to be made, the Court shall, if necessary, afford just satisfaction to the injured party.

## Article 42 — Judgments of Chambers

Judgments of Chambers shall become final in accordance with the provisions of Article 44, paragraph 2.

## Article 43 — Referral to the Grand Chamber

1. Within a period of three months from the date of the judgment of the Chamber, any party to the case may, in exceptional cases, request that the case be referred to the Grand Chamber.
2. A panel of five judges of the Grand Chamber shall accept the request if the case raises a serious question affecting the interpretation or application of the Convention or the protocols thereto, or a serious issue of general importance.
3. If the panel accepts the request, the Grand Chamber shall decide the case by means of a judgment.

### Article 44 — Final judgments

1. The judgment of the Grand Chamber shall be final.
2. The judgment of a Chamber shall become final:
   a. when the parties declare that they will not request that the case be referred to the Grand Chamber; or
   b. three months after the date of the judgment, if reference of the case to the Grand Chamber has not been requested; or
   c. when the panel of the Grand Chamber rejects the request to refer under Article 43.
3. The final judgment shall be published.

### Article 45 — Reasons for judgments and decisions

1. Reasons shall be given for judgments as well as for decisions declaring applications admissible or inadmissible.
2. If a judgment does not represent, in whole or in part, the unanimous opinion of the judges, any judge shall be entitled to deliver a separate opinion.

### Article 46 — Binding force and execution of judgments

1. The High Contracting Parties undertake to abide by the final judgment of the Court in any case to which they are parties.
2. The final judgment of the Court shall be transmitted to the Committee of Ministers, which shall supervise its execution.

### Article 47 — Advisory opinions

1. The Court may, at the request of the Committee of Ministers, give advisory opinions on legal questions concerning the interpretation of the Convention and the protocols thereto.
2. Such opinions shall not deal with any question relating to the content or scope of the rights or freedoms defined in Section I of the Convention and the protocols thereto, or with any other question which the Court or the Committee of Ministers might have to consider in consequence of any such proceedings as could be instituted in accordance with the Convention.
3. Decisions of the Committee of Ministers to request an advisory opinion of the Court shall require a majority vote of the representatives entitled to sit on the Committee.

### Article 48 — Advisory jurisdiction of the Court

The Court shall decide whether a request for an advisory opinion submitted by the Committee of Ministers is within its competence as defined in Article 47.

### Article 49 — *Reasons for advisory opinions*

1. Reasons shall be given for advisory opinions of the Court.
2. If the advisory opinion does not represent, in whole or in part, the unanimous opinion of the judges, any judge shall be entitled to deliver a separate opinion.
3. Advisory opinions of the Court shall be communicated to the Committee of Ministers.

### Article 50 — *Expenditure on the Court*

The expenditure on the Court shall be borne by the Council of Europe.

### Article 51 — *Privileges and immunities of judges*

The judges shall be entitled, during the exercise of their functions, to the privileges and immunities provided for in Article 40 of the Statute of the Council of Europe and in the agreements made thereunder.

*Section III* [8, 9] — Miscellaneous provisions

### Article 52 [1] — *Inquiries by the Secretary General*

On receipt of a request from the Secretary General of the Council of Europe any High Contracting Party shall furnish an explanation of the manner in which its internal law ensures the effective implementation of any of the provisions of the Convention.

### Article 53 [1] — *Safeguard for existing Human Rights*

Nothing in this Convention shall be construed as limiting or derogating from any of the Human Rights and fundamental freedoms which may be ensured under the laws of any High Contracting Party or under any other agreement to which it is a Party.

### Article 54 [1] — *Powers of the Committee of Ministers*

Nothing in this Convention shall prejudice the powers conferred on the Committee of Ministers by the Statute of the Council of Europe.

### Article 55 [1] — *Exclusion of other means of dispute settlement*

The High Contracting Parties agree that, except by special agreement, they will not avail themselves of treaties, conventions, or declarations in force between them for the purpose of submitting, by way of petition, a dispute arising out of the interpretation or application of this Convention to a means of settlement other than those provided for in this Convention.

## Article 56 [10] — Territorial application

1 [11]. Any State may at the time of its ratification or at any time thereafter declare by notification addressed to the Secretary General of the Council of Europe that the present Convention shall, subject to paragraph 4 of this Article, extend to all or any of the territories for whose international relations it is responsible.

2. The Convention shall extend to the territory or territories named in the notification as from the thirtieth day after the receipt of this notification by the Secretary General of the Council of Europe.

3. The provisions of this Convention shall be applied in such territories with due regard, however, to local requirements.

4 [2]. Any State which has made a declaration in accordance with paragraph 1 of this article may at any time thereafter declare on behalf of one or more of the territories to which the declaration relates that it accepts the competence of the Court to receive applications from individuals, non-governmental organisations or groups of individuals as provided by Article 34 of the Convention.

## Article 57 [1] — Reservations

1. Any State may, when signing this Convention or when depositing its instrument of ratification, make a reservation in respect of any particular provision of the Convention to the extent that any law then in force in its territory is not in conformity with the provision. Reservations of a general character shall not be permitted under this article.

2. Any reservation made under this article shall contain a brief statement of the law concerned.

## Article 58 [1] — Denunciation

1. A High Contracting Party may denounce the present Convention only after the expiry of five years from the date on which it became a party to it and after six months' notice contained in a notification addressed to the Secretary General of the Council of Europe, who shall inform the other High Contracting Parties.

2. Such a denunciation shall not have the effect of releasing the High Contracting Party concerned from its obligations under this Convention in respect of any act which, being capable of constituting a violation of such obligations, may have been performed by it before the date at which the denunciation became effective.

3. Any High Contracting Party which shall cease to be a member of the Council of Europe shall cease to be a Party to this Convention under the same conditions.

4 [12]. The Convention may be denounced in accordance with the provisions of the preceding paragraphs in respect of any territory to which it has been declared to extend under the terms of Article 56.

### Article 59 [13] — Signature and ratification

1. This Convention shall be open to the signature of the members of the Council of Europe. It shall be ratified. Ratifications shall be deposited with the Secretary General of the Council of Europe.
2. The present Convention shall come into force after the deposit of ten instruments of ratification.
3. As regards any signatory ratifying subsequently, the Convention shall come into force at the date of the deposit of its instrument of ratification.
4. The Secretary General of the Council of Europe shall notify all the members of the Council of Europe of the entry into force of the Convention, the names of the High Contracting Parties who have ratified it, and the deposit of all instruments of ratification which may be effected subsequently.

Done at Rome this 4th day of November 1950, in English and French, both texts being equally authentic, in a single copy which shall remain deposited in the archives of the Council of Europe. The Secretary General shall transmit certified copies to each of the signatories.

[1]  Heading added according to the provisions of Protocol no. 11 (ETS no. 155).
[2]  Heading added according to the provisions of Protocol no. 11 (ETS no. 155).
[3]  Heading added according to the provisions of Protocol no. 11 (ETS no. 155).
[4]  Heading added according to the provisions of Protocol no. 11 (ETS no. 155).
[5]  Heading added according to the provisions of Protocol no. 11 (ETS no. 155).
[6]  Heading added according to the provisions of Protocol no. 11 (ETS no. 155).
[7]  New Section II according to the provisions of Protocol no. 11 (ETS no. 155).
[8]  Heading added according to the provisions of Protocol no. 11 (ETS no. 155).
[9]  The articles of this Section are renumbered according to the provisions of Protocol no. 11 (ETS no. 155).
[10] Heading added according to the provisions of Protocol no. 11 (ETS no. 155).
[11] Text amended according to the provisions of Protocol no. 11 (ETS no. 155).

[12] Text amended according to the provisions of Protocol no. 11 (ETS no. 155).
[13] Heading added according to the provisions of Protocol no. 11 (ETS no. 155).

Convention for the Protection of Human Rights and Fundamental Freedoms (dates given in form of day/month/year) CETS No.: 005[4]
Opening for signature: Place: Rome   Date: 4/11/1950
Entry into force:   Conditions: 10 ratifications.   Date: 3/9/1953
Status as of: 3/3/2005

| States | Signature | Ratification | Entry into force | Notes | R. | D. | A. | T. | C.O. |
|---|---|---|---|---|---|---|---|---|---|
| Albania | 13/7/1995 | 2/10/1996 | 2/10/1996 | | | | | | |
| Andorra | 10/11/1994 | 22/1/1996 | 22/1/1996 | | X | X | | | |
| Armenia | 25/1/2001 | 26/4/2002 | 26/4/2002 | | X | | | | |
| Austria | 13/12/1957 | 3/9/1958 | 3/9/1958 | | X | | | | |
| Azerbaijan | 25/1/2001 | 15/4/2002 | 15/4/2002 | | X | X | | | |
| Belgium | 4/11/1950 | 14/6/1955 | 14/6/1955 | | | | | | |
| Bosnia-Herz. | 24/4/2002 | 12/7/2002 | 12/7/2002 | | | | | | |
| Bulgaria | 7/5/1992 | 7/9/1992 | 7/9/1992 | | | | | | |
| Croatia | 6/11/1996 | 5/11/1997 | 5/11/1997 | | X | | | | |
| Cyprus | 16/12/1961 | 6/10/1962 | 6/10/1962 | | | | | | |
| Czech Republic | 21/2/1991 | 18/3/1992 | 1/1/1993 | 17 | X | | | | |
| Denmark | 4/11/1950 | 13/4/1953 | 3/9/1953 | | | | | | |
| Estonia | 14/5/1993 | 16/4/1996 | 16/4/1996 | | X | | | | |
| Finland | 5/5/1989 | 10/5/1990 | 10/5/1990 | | X | | | | |
| France | 4/11/1950 | 3/5/1974 | 3/5/1974 | | X | X | X | | |
| Georgia | 27/4/1999 | 20/5/1999 | 20/5/1999 | | | | | | |
| Germany | 4/11/1950 | 5/12/1952 | 3/9/1953 | 30 | X | | X | | |
| Greece | 28/11/1950 | 28/11/1974 | 28/11/1974 | 29 | | | | | |
| Hungary | 6/11/1990 | 5/11/1992 | 5/11/1992 | | | | | | |
| Iceland | 4/11/1950 | 29/6/1953 | 3/9/1953 | | | | | | |
| Ireland | 4/11/1950 | 25/2/1953 | 3/9/1953 | | X | | | | |
| Italy | 4/11/1950 | 26/10/1955 | 26/10/1955 | | | | | | |
| Latvia | 10/2/1995 | 27/6/1997 | 27/6/1997 | | | | | | |
| Liechtenstein | 23/11/1978 | 8/9/1982 | 8/9/1982 | | X | | | | |
| Lithuania | 14/5/1993 | 20/6/1995 | 20/6/1995 | | X | | | | |
| Luxembourg | 4/11/1950 | 3/9/1953 | 3/9/1953 | | | | | | |
| Malta | 12/12/1966 | 23/1/1967 | 23/1/1967 | | X | X | | | |
| Moldova | 13/7/1995 | 12/9/1997 | 12/9/1997 | | X | X | | | |
| Monaco | 5/10/2004 | | | | X | | | | |
| Netherlands | 4/11/1950 | 31/8/1954 | 31/8/1954 | | | | | X | |
| Norway | 4/11/1950 | 15/1/1952 | 3/9/1953 | | X | | | | |
| Poland | 26/11/1991 | 19/1/1993 | 19/1/1993 | | | | | | |
| Portugal | 22/9/1976 | 9/11/1978 | 9/11/1978 | | X | | | | |
| Romania | 7/10/1993 | 20/6/1994 | 20/6/1994 | | X | | | | |
| Russia | 28/2/1996 | 5/5/1998 | 5/5/1998 | | X | | | | |

*continued*

| States | Signature | Ratification | Entry into force | Notes | R. | D. | A. | T. | C. | O. |
|---|---|---|---|---|---|---|---|---|---|---|
| San Marino | 16/11/1988 | 22/3/1989 | 22/3/1989 | | X | X | | | | |
| Serbia and Mont. | 3/4/2003 | 3/3/2004 | 3/3/2004 | | X | X | | | | |
| Slovakia | 21/2/1991 | 18/3/1992 | 1/1/1993 | 17 | X | | | | | |
| Slovenia | 14/5/1993 | 28/6/1994 | 28/6/1994 | | | | | | | |
| Spain | 24/11/1977 | 4/10/1979 | 4/10/1979 | | X | X | | | | |
| Sweden | 28/11/1950 | 4/2/1952 | 3/9/1953 | | | | | | | |
| Switzerland | 21/12/1972 | 28/11/1974 | 28/11/1974 | | | | | | | |
| FYROM | 9/11/1995 | 10/4/1997 | 10/4/1997 | | | | | | | |
| Turkey | 4/11/1950 | 18/5/1954 | 18/5/1954 | | | | | | X | |
| Ukraine | 9/11/1995 | 11/9/1997 | 11/9/1997 | | X | | | | | |
| United Kingdom | 4/11/1950 | 8/3/1951 | 3/9/1953 | | | | | | X | X |

Total number of signatures not followed by ratifications: 1
Total number of ratifications/accessions: 45

**Notes** (17) Dates of signature and ratification by the former Czech and Slovak Federal Republic. (29) Ratification 28/03/1953 — denunciation with effect on 13/06/1970. (30) Ratification by Saarland 14/01/1953 — Saarland became an integral part of Germany on 01/01/1957.

a. Accession: s, signature without reservation as to ratification; su, succession; r, signature "ad referendum"; R., reservations; D., declarations; A., authorities; T., territorial application; C., communication; O., objection.

Comment: Turkey signed Protocol no. 6 only recently and it entered into force on December 1, 2003.

# Document no. 23

**European Court of Justice, Fundamental Rights and the European Convention on Human Rights[5]**

Through a series of rulings starting in the late 1960s, the European Court of Justice (ECJ) gradually created certain fundamental rights and integrated the European Convention into the body of European Community (EC)/European Union (EU) law, at least as a source, which guided and inspired fundamental right determinations.

In a ruling in 1969, *Stauder v. Ulm*,[6] the ECJ implied that Human Rights considerations were inherent in EC law when it stated that "interpreted in this way the provision at issue contains nothing capable of prejudicing the fundamental Human Rights enshrined in the general principles of community law and protected by the Court."

In 1970, in the *Internationale Handelsgesellschaft*,[7] the ECJ decided that "respect for fundamental rights form[ed] an integral part of the general principles of law protected by the Court of Justice," and those rights had to be "inspired by the constitutional traditions common to member states, and [had to be] ensued within the [Community] framework."

In 1974, in the *Nold* case,[8] the ECJ reinforced the holding of the *Internationale Handelsgesellschaft* and stated (though not the European Convention specifically) that, in addition to constitutional traditions of member states, "international treaties for the protection of Human Rights on which the member states have collaborated or which they are signatories [could] supply guidelines which should be followed within the framework of the Community law."

In 1975, *Rutili v. Ministre de l'intérieur*,[9] the ECJ explicitly referred to the European Convention when it ruled that "the concept of public policy must, in the community context and, where, in particular, it is used as a justification for derogating from the fundamental principles of equality or treatment and freedom of movement for workers, be interpreted strictly, so that its scope cannot be determined unilaterally by each member state without being subject to control by the institutions of the Community." The Court then stated that "taken as a whole, these limitations placed on the powers of member states in respect of control of aliens are a specific manifestation of the more general principles enshrined in Articles 8, 9, 10 and 11 of the European Convention ... which provide in identical terms, that no restrictions in the interest of national security or public safety shall be placed on the rights secured by the above quoted articles other than such are necessary for the protection of those interests 'in a democratic society.'"

In addition to the examples of fundamental rights recognised, the ECJ ruled on numerous individual situations recognising numerous fundamental rights over the years. These included human dignity (*Casagrande*, 1974), principle of equality (*Klöckner-Werke* AG, 1962), non-discrimination (*Defrenne v. Sabena*, 1976), freedom of association (*Confédération syndicale, Massa*, etc., 1974), freedom of religion and beliefs (*Prais*, 1976), protection of private life (*National Panasonic*, 1980), medical secrecy (*Commission v. Germany*, 1992), rights of property ownership (*Hauer*, 1979), freedom to engage in an occupation (*Hauer*, 1979), freedom of trade (*Intern. Handelsgesellschaft*, 1970), economic freedom (*Usinor*, 1984), freedom of competition (*France*, 1985), respect for family life (*Commission v. Germany*, 1989), right to effective protection by the courts and fair procedure (*Johnston v. Chief Constable of the Royal Ulster Constabulary*, 1986; *Pecastaing v. Belgium*, 1980), inviolability of the home (*Hoechst AG v. Commission*, 1989), and freedom of opinion and publication (*VBVB, VBBB*, 1984).[10]

In these decisions, Human Rights were considered to be an "indirect source of Community law, and the rights protected had to be within the EC system and within the jurisdiction of the ECJ for the ECJ to act.[11] However, as the similarity of the recognised fundamental rights to the rights in the European Convention indicates, the European Convention was a major source in deciding what the fundamental rights are. Indeed, the referral to the European Convention by the ECJ in deciding on fundamental rights elevated the Convention to a level where "its provisions are given effect as 'general principles' of EC law."[12] Since, by virtue of Article 220 (ex-Article 164) "[t]he Court of Justice [had to] ensure that in the interpretation and application of [the Treaty Establishing the EC] the law is observed," "the standards of the European Convention [in a way became] part of EC law."[13] The consequence of ECJ rulings upholding Human Rights in the Community was "when the Institutions adopt legislation they [had to] also comply with international provisions, particularly the standards of the ECtHR."[14]

# 5 European Community and Human Rights

# Document no. 24

## European Community (EC) the Single European Act[1]

### 1. Preamble

HIS MAJESTY THE KING OF THE BELGIANS, HER MAJESTY THE QUEEN OF DENMARK, THE PRESIDENT OF THE FEDERAL REPUBLIC OF GERMANY, THE PRESIDENT OF THE HELLENIC REPUBLIC, HIS MAJESTY THE KING OF SPAIN, THE PRESIDENT OF THE FRENCH REPUBLIC, THE PRESIDENT OF IRELAND, THE PRESIDENT OF THE ITALIAN REPUBLIC, HIS ROYAL HIGHNESS THE GRAND DUKE OF LUXEMBOURG, HER MAJESTY THE QUEEN OF THE NETHERLANDS, THE PRESIDENT OF THE PORTUGUESE REPUBLIC, HER MAJESTY THE QUEEN OF THE UNITED KINGDOM OF GREAT BRITAIN AND NORTHERN IRELAND,

MOVED by the will to continue the work undertaken on the basis of the treaties establishing the European communities and to transform relations as a whole among their states into a European union, in accordance with the solemn declaration of Stuttgart of 19 June 1983,

RESOLVED to implement this European Union on the basis, firstly, of the Communities operating in accordance with their own rules and, secondly, of European cooperation among the signatory States in the sphere of foreign policy and to invest this Union with the necessary means of action,

*DETERMINED to work together to promote democracy on the basis of the fundamental rights recognised in the constitutions and laws of the Member States, in the Convention for the Protection of Human Rights and Fundamental Freedoms and the European Social Charter, notably freedom, equality, and social justice,* [emphasis added]

CONVINCED that the European idea, the results achieved in the fields of economic integration and political cooperation, and the need for new developments correspond to the wishes of the democratic peoples of Europe, for whom the European Parliament, elected by universal suffrage, is an indispensable means of expression,

AWARE of the responsibility *incumbent upon Europe to aim at speaking ever increasingly with one voice and to act with consistency and solidarity in order more effectively to protect its common interests and independence, in particular to display the principles of democracy and compliance with the law and with Human Rights to which they are attached,* so that together they may make their own contribution to the preservation of international peace and security in accordance with the undertaking entered into by them within the framework of the *United Nations Charter,* [emphasis added]

DETERMINED to improve the economic and social situation by extending common policies and pursuing new objectives, and to ensure a smoother functioning of the Communities by enabling the institutions to exercise their powers under conditions most in keeping with Community interests,

\*\*\*

HAVE DECIDED to adopt this Act and to this end have designated as their Plenipotentiaries:

\*\*\*

# Document no. 25

**ECJ: *ERT v. Pliroforissis et al.*[2]**

\*\*\*

1. By judgment of 11 April 1989, which was received at the Court on 16 August 1989, the Monomeles Protodikeio Thessaloniki [Thessaloniki Regional Court], in proceedings for interim measures, referred to the Court for a preliminary ruling under Article 177 of the EEC Treaty several questions on the interpretation of the EEC Treaty, in particular Articles 2, 3(f), 9, 30, 36, 85, and 86, and also of Article 10 of the European Convention for the Protection of Human Rights and Fundamental Freedoms for November 1950 in order to determine the compatibility with those provisions of a national system of exclusive television rights.

2. Those questions were raised in proceedings between Elliniki Radiophonia Tileorassi Anonimi Etairia (hereinafter referred to as "ERT"), a Greek radio and television undertaking, to which the Greek State had granted exclusive rights for carrying out its activities, and Dimotiki Etairia Pliroforissis (hereinafter referred to as "DEP"), a municipal information company at Thessaloniki, and S. Kouvelas, Mayor of Thessaloniki. Notwithstanding the exclusive rights enjoyed by ERT, DEP and the Mayor, in 1989, set up a television station which in that same year began to broadcast television programs.

\*\*\*

5. Since it took the view that the case raised important questions of Community law, the national court stayed the proceedings and referred the following questions to the Court of Justice for a preliminary ruling:

1. Does a law which allows a single television broadcaster to have a television monopoly for the entire territory of a Member State and to make television broadcasts of any kind is consistent with the provisions of the EEC Treaty and of secondary law [?]

\*\*\*

9. Whether and to what extent the grant by law to a single broadcaster of a television monopoly for the entire national territory of a Member State, with the right to make television broadcasts of any kind, is compatible today with the social objective of the EEC Treaty (Preamble and Article 2), the constant improvement of the living conditions of the peoples of Europe and the rapid raising of their standard of living, and with the provisions of Article 10 of the European Convention for the Protection of Human Rights of 4 November 1950.

10. Whether the freedom of expression secured by Article 10 of the European Convention for the Protection of Human Rights of 4 November 1950, and the abovementioned social objective of the EEC Treaty, set out in its Preamble and in Article 2, impose per se obligations on the Member States, independently of the written provisions of Community law in force, and if so what those obligations are."

\*\*\*

9. The ninth and tenth questions are concerned with an examination of the monopoly situation in the field of television in the light of Article 2 of the Treaty and Article 10 of the European Convention on Human Rights.

\*\*\*

Article 10 of the European Convention on Human Rights

41. With regard to Article 10 of the European Convention on Human Rights, referred to in the ninth and tenth questions, it must first be pointed out that, as the Court has consistently held, fundamental rights form an integral part of the general principles of law, the observance of which it ensures. For that purpose the Court draws inspiration from the constitutional traditions common to the Member States and from the guidelines supplied by international treaties for the protection of Human Rights on which the Member States have collaborated or of which they are signatories (see, in particular, the judgment in Case C-4/73 *Nold v. Commission* [1974] ECR 491, paragraph 13). The European Convention on Human Rights has special significance in that respect (see in particular Case C-222/84 *Johnston v. Chief Constable of the Royal Ulster Constabulary* [1986] ECR 1651, paragraph 18). It follows that, as the Court held in its judgment in Case C-5/88 *Wachauf v. Federal Republic of Germany* [1989] ECR 2609, paragraph 19, the Community cannot accept measures which are incompatible with observance of the Human Rights thus recognised and guaranteed.

42. As the Court has held (see the judgment in Joined Cases C-60 and C-61/84 *Cinéthèque v. Fédération Nationale des Cinémas Français* [1985] ECR 2605, paragraph 25, and the judgment in Case C-12/86 *Demirel v. Stadt Schwaebisch Gmund* [1987] ECR 3719, paragraph 28), it has no power to examine the compatibility with the European Convention on Human Rights of national rules which do not fall within the scope of Community law. On the other hand, where such rules do

fall within the scope of Community law, and reference is made to the Court for a preliminary ruling, it must provide all the criteria of interpretation needed by the national court to determine whether those rules are compatible with the fundamental rights the observance of which the Court ensures and which derive in particular from the European Convention on Human Rights.

43. In particular, where a Member State relies on the combined provisions of Articles 56 and 66 in order to justify rules which are likely to obstruct the exercise of the freedom to provide services, such justification, provided for by Community law, must be interpreted in the light of the general principles of law and in particular of fundamental rights. Thus the national rules in question can fall under the exceptions provided for by the combined provisions of Articles 56 and 66 only if they are compatible with the fundamental rights the observance of which is ensured by the Court.

44. It follows that in such a case it is for the national court and, if necessary, the Court of Justice to appraise the application of those provisions having regard to all the rules of Community law, including freedom of expression, as embodied in Article 10 of the European Convention on Human Rights, as a general principle of law the observance of which is ensured by the Court.

45. The reply to the national court must therefore be that the limitations imposed on the power of the Member States to apply the provisions referred to in Articles 66 and 56 of the Treaty on grounds of public policy, public security, and public health must be appraised in the light of the general principle of freedom of expression embodied in Article 10 of the European Convention on Human Rights.

\*\*\*

# Document no. 26

### EC Declaration on Human Rights Conclusion of the Luxembourg European Council (28-29 June 1991)[3]

*The European Council adopted the declaration in Annex V, which should guide the future work of the Community and its Member States.*

Recalling the 1986 declaration of Foreign Ministers of the Community on Human Rights (21 July 1986), the European Council reaffirms that respecting, promoting, and safeguarding Human Rights is an essential part of international relations and one of the cornerstones of European cooperation as well as of relations between the Community and its Member States and other countries. In this regard the European Council stresses its attachment to the principles of parliamentary democracy and the primacy of law.

The European Council welcomes the considerable progress made in recent years in the field of Human Rights, and the advances in democracy in Europe and throughout the world, particularly in certain developing countries. It welcomes the growing prominence of demands of peoples for freedom and democracy throughout the world.

They deplore, however, the persistence of flagrant violations of Human Rights in many countries. The Community and its Member States undertake to pursue their policy of promoting and safeguarding Human Rights and fundamental freedoms throughout the world. This is the legitimate and permanent duty of the world community and of all States acting individually or collectively. They recall that the different ways of expressing concern about violations of rights, as well as requests designed to secure those rights, cannot be considered as interference in the internal affairs of a State and constitute an important and legitimate part of their dialogue with third countries. For their part, the Community and its Member States will continue to take up violations wherever they occur.

The European Community and its member States seek universal respect for Human Rights. Many international instruments have been elaborated in the last decades, first among which rank the Universal Declaration of Human Rights and the Covenants on civil and political rights and on economic, social, and cultural rights. No specific provision based on national, cultural, or religious factors can validly be invoked to detract from the principles established by these instruments. The European Council calls on all States to become a party to the international instruments in force.

In the field of Human Rights, the effective and universal implementation of existing instruments and the strengthening of international mechanisms of control is a priority. The Community and its Member States will continue to work for the efficient functioning of such mechanisms in their administrative, organisational, and financial aspects. Moreover, they undertake, in the context of these mechanisms, to push for an improvement in the transparency of procedures. The European Council is well disposed towards the possibility of enabling individuals to be involved in the protection of their rights. The European Council calls for the cooperation of States with the intergovernmental organisations to which they belong in monitoring the implementation of Human Rights, in particular in the framework of the Commissions created by UN agreements and in regional institutions.

Tensions and conflicts arising from flagrant and systematic violations of Human Rights and fundamental freedoms in one country or in a specific region are often a threat to international peace and security.

The protection of minorities is ensured in the first place by the effective establishment of democracy. The European Council recalls the fundamental nature of the principle of non-discrimination. It stresses the need to protect Human Rights whether or not the persons concerned belong to minorities. The European Council reiterates the importance of respecting the cultural identity as well as rights enjoyed by members of minorities which such persons should be able to exercise in common with other members of their group. Respect of this principle will favour political, social, and economic development.

The European Council recalls the indivisible character of Human Rights. The promotion of economic, social and cultural rights, as of civil and political rights, and of respect for religious freedom and freedom of worship, is of fundamental importance for the full realisation of human dignity and of the legitimate aspirations of every individual. Democracy, pluralism, respect for Human Rights, institutions working within a constitutional framework, and responsible governments appointed following periodic, fair elections, as well as the recognition of the legitimate importance of the individual in a society, are essential prerequisites of sustained social and economic development.

The European Council deplores the fact that countless people in the world are victims of hunger, illness, illiteracy, and extreme poverty and are thus deprived of the most basic economic and social rights. It notes moreover that special attention should be paid to the most vulnerable categories of people, for example, children, women, old people, migrants, and refugees.

The European Council believes that it is an affront to human dignity to deny help to victims in emergency situations or in extreme distress, particularly in cases of violence against innocent civilians and refugees. To the victim's need for humanitarian assistance corresponds a duty of solidarity of the States concerned and of the international community.

All lasting development should be centred on man as the bearer of Human Rights and beneficiary of the process of development. Violations of Human Rights and suppression of individual freedoms impede an individual from participating in and contributing to this process. Through their policy of cooperation and by including clauses on Human Rights in economic and cooperation agreements with third countries, the Community and its Member States actively promote Human Rights and the participation, without discrimination, of all individuals or groups in the life of society, bearing in mind particularly the role of women.

The Council of Europe plays a leading role in the field of Human Rights with its expertise, its numerous projects in this field, training and educational activities, and programs of cooperation with the countries of Central and Eastern Europe which possess or are seeking to possess democratic institutions. Under its aegis, the European Convention on the Protection of Human Rights and Fundamental Freedoms, given the binding character of its norms and the strictness and reliability of its provisions of control, is both an advanced, effective system of protection and a point of reference for other regions of the world. The European Council welcomes the readiness of the Council of Europe to put its experience at the service of the CSCE [Conference on Security and Cooperation in Europe].

The Community and its Member States stress the importance they attach to the human dimension of the CSCE process, to its important contribution to democratic reforms in Europe, and to its considerable influence on the development of Human Rights in the European space. The European Council recalls the prospects opened up by the Final Document of the Copenhagen Conference in 1990 and the commitments undertaken when the Paris Charter was adopted. The mechanism of the Conference on the Human Dimension reflects participating States' conviction that upholding undertakings in the Human Rights field is the legitimate concern of the whole international community.

Individuals and non-governmental organisations throughout the world are making valuable and courageous contributions to safeguarding and promoting Human Rights. The European Council pays tribute to this commitment and deplores the fact that defenders of Human Rights are too often the first victims of the arbitrary treatment which they denounce.

It calls on all States to enhance the attachment of their publics to the cause of Human Rights through educational programs, and by allowing non-governmental organisations [NGOs] free access to information and free distribution of information on Human Rights. By drawing the attention of the public at large to governments' failings, the NGO's contribute significantly to the protection of individuals and the promotion of Human Rights in general.

The European Council reiterates the commitment of the Community and its Member States to support and promote in regional and international bodies that respect for Human Rights and fundamental freedoms without which peace and lasting security cannot be established.

# Document no. 27

**Resolution of the EC Council and of the Member States meeting in the Council on Human Rights, Democracy and Development (28 November 1991)**[4]

1. The Council recalls the European Council Resolution of 29 June 1991, which stated that respect for Human Rights, the rule of law and the existence of political institutions which are effective, accountable, and enjoy democratic legitimacy are the basis for equitable development. It also recalls the 1986 Declaration of Foreign Ministers of the Community on Human Rights (21 July 1986) and reaffirms that respecting, promoting, and safeguarding Human Rights is an essential part of international relations and one of the cornerstones of European cooperation as well as of relations between the Community and its Member States and other countries. In this regard it stresses its attachment to the principles of representative democracy, of the rule of law, of social justice, and of respect for Human Rights.

2. The Council shares the analysis contained in the Commission's communication of 25 March 1991, and acknowledges that Human Rights have a universal nature and it is the duty of all States to promote them. At the same time, Human Rights and democracy form part of a larger set of requirements in order to achieve balanced and sustainable development. In this context, account should be taken of the issue of good governance as well as of military spending.

The Council considers it important that the Community and its Member States should have a common approach aimed at promoting Human Rights and democracy in developing countries. Such an approach would improve the cohesion and consistency of initiatives taken in this field. The objective of the present resolution is to formulate concrete guidelines, procedures, and lines of action.

3. The Community and its Member States recognise the necessity of a consistent approach towards Human Rights, democracy, and development in their cooperation with developing countries. Development cooperation is based on the central place of the individual and has, therefore, in essence to be designed with a view to promoting — in parallel with economic and social rights — civil and political liberties by means of representative democratic rule that is based

on respect for Human Rights. They endorse, on the basis of these principles, the following approaches, instruments, and activities.

4. The Community and its Member States will give high priority to a positive approach that stimulates respect for Human Rights and encourages democracy. An open and constructive dialogue between them and the governments of developing countries can make a very important contribution to the promotion of Human Rights and democracy. Various initiatives can be undertaken, for example, through active support for:

- countries which are attempting to institute democracy and improve their Human Rights performance;
- the holding of elections, the setting-up of new democratic institutions, and the strengthening of the rule of law;
- the strengthening of the judiciary, the administration of justice, crime prevention and the treatment of offenders;
- promoting the role of NGOs and other institutions which are necessary for a pluralist society;
- the adoption of a decentralised approach to cooperation;
- ensuring equal opportunities for all.

At the request of the Commission or one of the Member States, the possibility of increased assistance to developing countries in which substantive positive changes in Human Rights and democracy have taken place will be examined.

5. The Council stresses the importance of good governance. While sovereign States have the right to institute their own administrative structures and establish their own constitutional arrangements, equitable development can only effectively and sustainably [sic] be achieved if a number of general principles are adhered to: sensible economic and social policies, democratic decision-making, adequate governmental transparency and financial accountability, creation of a market-friendly environment for development, measures to combat corruption, as well as respect for the rule of law, Human Rights, and freedom of the press and expression. The Community and Member States will support the efforts of developing countries to advance good governance and these principles will be central in their existing or new development cooperation relationships.

6. While, in general, a positive and constructive approach should receive priority, in the event of grave and persistent Human Rights violations or the serious interruption of democratic processes, the Community and its Member States will consider appropriate responses in the light of the circumstances, guided by objective and equitable criteria. Such measures, which will be graduated according to the gravity of each case, could include confidential or public *démarches* as well as changes in the content or channels of cooperation programs and the deferment of necessary signatures or decisions in the cooperation process or, when necessary, the suspension of cooperation with the States concerned.

The Member States and the Commission will exchange immediate information concerning such measures and consider joint approaches in reaction to violations. They will be informed in such cases through the EPC [European Political Cooperation] communication network and particular cases may be further discussed within the Council framework.

7. The Community's response to violations of Human Rights will avoid penalising the population for governmental actions. Rather than simply discontinuing development cooperation, the Community and the Member States may adjust cooperation activities with a view to ensuring that development aid benefits more directly the poorest sections of the population in the country, for example through non-governmental or informal networks, while at the same time establishing a certain distance vis-à-vis the government concerned. Such adjustment will focus on the choice of partners of projects and of the type of cooperation programs. In all cases, however, humanitarian and emergency aid, which directly benefit vulnerable populations, will continue to be made available.

8. The Council welcomes the efforts undertaken in recent years by developing countries to move towards democracy. It is recognised that governments have to build the political, economic, and social structures to support democracy and that this is a gradual process which will sometimes take a relatively long period. The Community and its Member States will support the process and hold regular informal exchanges of views on the best possible course of action in order to achieve lasting results as speedily as possible.

9. The Council attaches very great importance to the question of military spending. Excessive military expenditure not only reduces the funds available for other purposes, but can also contribute to increased regional tensions and violations of international law, as well as often being meant and used for purposes of internal repression and denial of universally recognised Human Rights.

Moreover, in a period in which donor countries are engaged in a process leading to levels of armament not exceeding sufficiency levels, development cooperation with governments which maintain much larger military structures than needed will become difficult to justify. In the dialogue with their partners in developing countries, the Community and its Member States will stress the negative effects of excessive military spending on the development process. They will consider adopting concrete measures in their cooperation in order to encourage developing countries to reduce their military expenditure, which is often excessive in relation to their legitimate security needs, and simultaneously to implement development projects of an economic and social nature, with particular emphasis on the education and health sectors. With this in mind, they may consider increasing support for countries which achieve substantial reductions in their military expenditure, or reducing support for countries which fail to do so. The Council recognises the need for restraint and transparency in the transfer of conventional weapons to developing countries. It will further examine the question of military spending by developing countries along these lines. The Community and its Member States will request countries with which development cooperation relationships are maintained to cooperate voluntarily with the new UN [United Nations] register of arms transfers.

10. The Community and its Member States will explicitly introduce the consideration of Human Rights as an element of their relations with developing countries; Human Rights clauses will be inserted in future cooperation agreements. Regular discussions on Human Rights and democracy will be held, within the framework of development cooperation, with the aim of seeking improvements.

In order to facilitate timely support by the Community for initiatives in developing countries aiming at the promotion of respect for Human Rights and the encouragement of democracy and good governance it is intended to expand resources devoted to these ends within the overall allocations available for development. Sound activities in Third World countries promoting Human Rights and democracy, both by governments and by non-governmental entities, will be eligible for financial support. The Community and its Member States undertake in addition to integrate the promotion of respect for Human Rights and the advancement of democracy in their future cooperation programs.

The Commission will transmit an annual report to the Council on the implementation of this resolution.

In addition to the consultations and meetings which can be convened as stipulated in paragraphs 4, 5, and 6, a meeting will be held annually by representatives of the Commission and Member States to consider policies and specific lines of action to further enhance respect for Human Rights and establishment of representative democratic rule.

# 6 European Union and Human Rights

# Document no. 28

### Treaty on European Union (Maastricht Treaty)[1]

*Preamble*

HIS MAJESTY THE KING OF THE BELGIANS, HER MAJESTY THE QUEEN OF DENMARK, THE PRESIDENT OF THE FEDERAL REPUBLIC OF GERMANY, THE PRESIDENT OF THE HELLENIC REPUBLIC, HIS MAJESTY THE KING OF SPAIN, THE PRESIDENT OF THE FRENCH REPUBLIC, THE PRESIDENT OF IRELAND, THE PRESIDENT OF THE ITALIAN REPUBLIC, HIS ROYAL HIGHNESS THE GRAND DUKE OF LUXEMBOURG, HER MAJESTY THE QUEEN OF THE NETHERLANDS, THE PRESIDENT OF THE PORTUGUESE REPUBLIC, HER MAJESTY THE QUEEN OF THE UNITED KINGDOM OF GREAT BRITAIN AND NORTHERN IRELAND,

RESOLVED to mark a new stage in the process of European integration undertaken with the establishment of the European Communities,

RECALLING the historic importance of the ending of the division of the European continent and the need to create firm bases for the construction of the future Europe,

CONFIRMING their attachment to the principles of liberty, democracy, and respect for Human Rights and fundamental freedoms and of the rule of law,

DESIRING to deepen the solidarity between their peoples while respecting their history, their culture, and their traditions,

DESIRING to enhance further the democratic and efficient functioning of the institutions so as to enable them better to carry out, within a single institutional framework, the tasks entrusted to them,

RESOLVED to achieve the strengthening and the convergence of their economies and to establish an economic and monetary union including, in accordance with the provisions of this Treaty, a single and stable currency,

DETERMINED to promote economic and social progress for their peoples, within the context of the accomplishment of the internal market and of reinforced cohesion and environmental protection, and to implement policies ensuring that advances in economic integration are accompanied by parallel progress in other fields,

RESOLVED to establish a citizenship common to nationals of their countries,

RESOLVED to implement a common foreign and security policy including the eventual framing of a common defence policy, which might in time lead to a common defence, thereby reinforcing the European identity and its independence in order to promote peace, security, and progress in Europe and in the world,

REAFFIRMING their objective to facilitate the free movement of persons, while ensuring the safety and security of their peoples, by including provisions on justice and home affairs in this Treaty,

RESOLVED to continue the process of creating an ever closer union among the peoples of Europe, in which decisions are taken as closely as possible to the citizen in accordance with the principle of subsidiarity,

IN VIEW of further steps to be taken in order to advance European integration,

HAVE DECIDED to establish a European Union and to this end have designated as their Plenipotentiaries:

\*\*\* [Signatories]

WHO, having exchanged their full powers, found in good and due form, have agreed as follows.

\*\*\*

## *Article B*

The Union shall set itself the following objectives:

- to promote economic and social progress which is balanced and sustainable, in particular through the creation of an area without internal frontiers, through the strengthening of economic and social cohesion and through the establishment of economic and monetary union, ultimately including a single currency in accordance with the provisions of this Treaty;
- to assert its identity on the international scene, in particular through the implementation of a common foreign and security policy including the eventual framing of a common defence policy, which might in time lead to a common defence;
- to strengthen the protection of the rights and interests of the nationals of its Member States through the introduction of a citizenship of the Union;
- to develop close cooperation on justice and home affairs;
- to maintain in full the *acquis communautaire* and build on it with a view to considering, through the procedure referred to in Article N(2), to what extent the policies and forms of cooperation introduced by this Treaty may need to be revised with the aim of ensuring the effectiveness of the mechanisms and the institutions of the Community.

The objectives of the Union shall be achieved as provided in this Treaty and in accordance with the conditions and the timetable set out therein while respecting the principle of subsidiarity as defined in Article 3b of the Treaty establishing the European Community.

\*\*\*

## Article F

1. The Union shall respect the national identities of its Member States, whose systems of government are founded on the principles of democracy.

2. The Union shall respect fundamental rights, as guaranteed by the European Convention for the Protection of Human Rights and Fundamental Freedoms signed in Rome on 4 November 1950, and as they result from the constitutional traditions common to the Member States, as general principles of Community law.

3. The Union shall provide itself with the means necessary to attain its objectives and carry through its policies.

# Document no. 29

**Copenhagen European Council Presidency conclusions, 21–22 June 1993[2]**

*Introduction*

The European Council welcomed the outcome of the Danish referendum and the prospect of a rapid completion of ratification procedures on the Maastricht Treaty in all Member States. It is determined that this important step should mark the ending of a prolonged period of uncertainty on the Community's direction and be the occasion for the Union to meet with renewed vigour and determination the many challenges with which it is faced internally and externally, making full use of the possibilities offered by the new Treaty. The principles spelled out by the European Councils in Birmingham and Edinburgh regarding Democracy, subsidiary, and openness will guide the implementation of the new Treaty with a view to bringing the Community closer to its citizens.

The European Council in Copenhagen gave special attention, on the one hand, to action aimed at tackling the economic and social problems faced by the Community and particularly the unacceptably high level of unemployment and, on the other hand, to the wide range of issues relating to peace and security in Europe. It recognises that only by proving that the Community is instrumental in contributing to the security and well-being of all the citizens can the Community count on continued public support for the construction of Europe.

The members of the European Council held an exchange of views with the President of the European Parliament. The discussion took place against the background of the increased political and legislative role which the European Parliament will have under the Treaty of Maastricht. The European Council underlined the importance of making the best possible use of those provisions while fully respecting the institutional balance set out in the Maastricht Treaty.

\*\*\*

## 4. Enlargement

The European Council took note of progress in the enlargement negotiations with Austria, Finland, Sweden, and Norway. It noted that the initial difficulties encountered in launching the negotiations had now been overcome and that the pace of the negotiations was speeding up. It recalled that the negotiations will, to the extent possible, be conducted in parallel, while dealing with each candidate on its own merit.

The European Council invited the Commission, the Council, and the candidate countries to ensure that the negotiations proceed constructively and expeditiously. The European Council is determined that the objective of the first enlargement of the European Union in accordance with the guidelines laid down by the Lisbon and Edinburgh European Councils should become a reality by 1 January 1995.

## 7. Relations with the countries of Central and Eastern Europe

### A. *The associated countries*

i. The European Council held a thorough discussion on the relations between the Community and the countries of Central and Eastern Europe with which the Community has concluded or plans to conclude Europe agreements ("associated countries"), on the basis of the Commission's communication prepared at the invitation of the Edinburgh European Council.

ii. The European Council welcomed the courageous efforts undertaken by the associated countries to modernise their economies, which have been weakened by forty years of central planning, and to ensure a rapid transition to a market economy. The Community and its Member States pledge their support to this reform process. Peace and security in Europe depend on the success of those efforts.

iii. The European Council today agreed that the associated countries in Central and Eastern Europe that so desire shall become members of the European Union. Accession will take place as soon as an associated country is able to assume the obligations of membership by satisfying the economic and political conditions required.

Membership requires that the candidate country has achieved stability of institutions guaranteeing democracy, the rule of law, Human Rights and respect for and protection of minorities, the existence of a functioning market economy as well as the capacity to cope with competitive pressure and market forces within the Union. Membership presupposes the candidate's ability to take on the obligations of membership including adherence to the aims of political, economic, and monetary union.

The Union's capacity to absorb new members, while maintaining the momentum of European integration, is also an important consideration in the general interest of both the Union and the candidate countries.

The European Council will continue to follow closely progress in each associated country towards fulfilling the conditions of accession to the Union and draw the appropriate conclusions.

iv. The European Council agreed that the future cooperation with the associated countries shall be geared to the objective of membership which has now been established.

\*\*\*

# Document no. 30

## European Union agreements with third countries and the Human Rights clause

*Editors' comment:* In addition to internal regulations and decisions expressing the importance of Human Rights, since the early 1990s, the European Community (EC) has included, more or less systematically, a so-called Human Rights clause in its bilateral trade and cooperation agreements with third countries, including association agreements such as the Europe agreements, Mediterranean agreements and the Cotonou Agreement (ex Lomé Convention). A Council decision of May 1995 spells out the basic modalities of this clause, with the aim of ensuring consistency in the text used and its application. Since this Council decision of May 1995, the Human Rights clause has been included in all subsequently negotiated bilateral agreements of a general nature (excluding sectoral agreements on textiles, agricultural products, etc.). More than twenty such agreements have already been signed. These agreements add to the more than thirty agreements negotiated before May 1995 which have a Human Rights clause not necessarily following the model launched in 1995.

## Commission Communication COM (95)216 of 23 May 1995, on the inclusion of respect for democratic principles and Human Rights in agreements between the community and third countries[3]

### Introduction

A commitment to respect, promote, and protect Human Rights and democratic principles is a key element of the European Community's relations with third countries. These issues have been gradually incorporated into the Community's activities over a period of time through a series of commitments culminating in the insertion of explicit references to Human Rights and democratic principles in the body of the Union Treaty. To help it meet those commitments the Community has a broad range of instruments at its disposal, including Union intervention in international forums and specific operations aimed at bolstering the rule of law and respect for Human Rights in the context of the Community's relations with non-member countries. Taking account of Human Rights in contractual relations with third countries is one of those instruments. It is on this latter instrument that the communication focuses.

## A. Foundations and references

References to Human Rights in agreements with third countries are based on the positions the Community has taken by:

- subscribing to universal and regional instruments and assuming responsibility for promoting the principles of democracy, the rule of law, and respect for Human Rights (paragraph 5 of the preamble to the Single European Act);
- making respect for, and promotion of, these principles one of the general objectives of Community development cooperation policy (Union Treaty, Article 130U) and one of the objectives of the common foreign and security policy (Union Treaty, Article J1(2));
- defining the main components of a hands-on strategy through its development cooperation policy and by inserting clauses on Human Rights into economic and cooperation agreements with third countries (Luxembourg European Council's Declaration on Human Rights, June 1991, paragraph 11);
- jointly identifying guidelines appropriate to the different types of agreement:
- in its relations with developing countries, by adopting guidelines, procedures and practical measures and including clauses on Human Rights in its cooperation agreements (paragraph 10 of the resolution on Human Rights, democracy and development of the Council and the Member States meeting within the Council, 28 November 1991);
- in its relations with CSCE [Conference on Security and Cooperation in Europe] countries, by recognising democratic principles and Human Rights as an essential element of its contractual relations with those countries by incorporating the appropriate provisions into the agreements concerned; these provisions allow the Community to take action in cases of special urgency, including any failure to meet the obligations deriving from the agreement (Council Declaration of 11 May 1992).

These commitments as a whole are consistent with the opinions voiced by Parliament in its various Human Rights-related initiatives, including its annual resolutions on the world Human Rights situation.

## B. Evolution

The Community's growing commitment to the promotion of Human Rights and democratic principles is reflected in the evolving nature of the references to these issues in the relevant agreements.

Initially they were mentioned either not at all or only in passing in the preamble of some agreements. The first reference in the body of a contractual document was in Article 5 of the fourth Lomé Convention, concluded in December 1989. In this way the European Community and its Member States tangibly demonstrated their commitment to Human Rights in their relations with third countries. In the ensuing three years, this stance was confirmed as such references gradually began to appear in cooperation agreements, defining respect for democratic principles and Human Rights as one of the foundations of the parties' relations.

However, Article 5 of Lomé IV and similar articles in other agreements do not provide a clear legal basis to suspend or denounce agreements in cases of serious Human Rights violations or interruptions of democratic process.

It is for this reason that a clause defining democratic principles and Human Rights as an "essential element" of the agreements with Brazil, the Andean Pact countries, the Baltic States, and Albania was introduced in 1992 (see Annex 1–1).

This is a substantial innovation, in that:

- it makes Human Rights the subject of common interest, part of the dialogue between the parties and an instrument for the implementation of positive measures, on a par with the other key provisions;
- it enables the parties, where necessary, to take restrictive measures in proportion to the gravity of the offence (see Annex 2). In the spirit of a positive approach, it is important that such measures should not only be based on objective and fair criteria, but they should also be adapted to the variety of situations that can arise, the aim being to keep a dialogue going;

In the selection and implementation of these measures it is crucial that the population should not be penalised for the behaviour of its government;

- it allows the parties to regard serious and persistent Human Rights violations and serious interruptions of democratic process as a "material breach" of the agreement in line with the Vienna Convention, constituting grounds for suspending the application of the agreement in whole or in part in line with the procedural conditions laid down in Article 65. The main condition involves allowing a period of three months between notification and suspension proper, except in "cases of special urgency," plus an additional period of grace if an amicable solution is being sought.

In application of a General Affairs Council declaration, since May 1992 all agreements concluded with CSCE countries include an innovative provision in addition to the "essential element" clause.

This additional clause (see Annex 1–2) provides for an immediate response, diverging from the procedure laid down in Article 65 of the Vienna Convention. It takes one of two forms:

- an explicit suspension clause authorising the suspension of the application of the agreement in whole or in part "with immediate effect" in cases of serious

breach of essential provisions; this, so-called "Baltic clause" was used only in the first agreements with the Baltic States, Albania and Slovenia; or
- a general non-execution clause known as the "Bulgarian clause" which provides for appropriate measures should the parties fail to meet their obligations, following a consultation procedure "except in cases of special urgency"; this clause was used in the agreements with Romania, Bulgaria, the Russian Federation, Ukraine, Kyrgyzstan, Moldavia, the Czech Republic, Slovakia, Kazakhstan, and Belarus.

The difference between the two formulas resides in the degree of sensitivity allowed for. The "Baltic clause" is more severe in that it provides only for extreme cases warranting immediate suspension without consultation of any kind. The "Bulgarian clause" not only provides for a conciliation procedure and a range of different options but is also designed to keep the agreement operational wherever possible. It asserts that immediate suspension should be envisaged only in cases of special urgency.

In January 1993, in response to the disparate nature of the references in the relevant agreements, the Commission, determined to adopt a non-discriminatory approach, drafted guidelines on these issues (decision of 26 January 1993, MIN (93)1137, point XIV), stipulating that draft negotiating directives for association agreements and economic cooperation agreements should incorporate the following:

*a. in the body of the agreement:*

- a clause specifying that relations between the Community and the country concerned and all provisions of the relevant agreement are based on respect for the democratic principles and Human Rights which inspire the domestic and external policies of the Community and the country concerned and which constitute essential elements of the agreement;

*b. in the preamble:*

- general references to respect for Human Rights and democratic values;
- references to the universal and/or regional instruments common to both parties.

An explicit suspension clause or a general non-execution clause may be included in specific cases.

The main points of these guidelines are featured in a letter from Mr Van den Broek to the Council, Parliament and the Member States.

*C. Assessment*

Although the Commission guidelines have been respected, the objective of a systematic approach has not yet been achieved.

As regards the preamble, the practice of using different references depending on the regional location of the party concerned, when not supplemented by universal references, can appear to contradict the principle of universality; references to the market economy in agreements with OSCE [Organization for Security and Cooperation in Europe] countries create a different perspective having no direct connection with Human Rights, a fact that could be prejudicial to the aim of consistency.

References to Human Rights and/or democratic principles as an essential element, although systematically included in all recent agreements of a general nature, have been positioned differently (Article 1, Article 6, etc.) depending on whether or not the agreements in question provide for political dialogue, and also supplemented with other references.

The "Baltic" clause was last used in October 1992, since when the preferred formula has been the "Bulgarian" clause, in some cases supplemented by one of two types of interpretative declaration (see Annex 1–3):

- joint declarations (Annex 1–4.i) in which the parties agree that a "case of special urgency" means a material breach of the agreement, i.e. the breach of an essential element of the agreement or repudiation of the agreement not sanctioned by the general rules of international law;
- unilateral declarations by the Community (e.g. the agreement concluded in July 1993 with the Czech Republic, Annex 1–3.i) that subsequently became bilateral declarations (for the first time in the agreement signed with Russia in June 1994, Annex 1–3.ii); these declarations emphasise the inclusion in the agreement of the "essential element" clause and the reference to "cases of special urgency" resulting from the Council Declaration of 11 May 1992, on the Community's relations with its CSCE partners;
- in the case of the partnership and cooperation agreement with Russia, a joint declaration (Annex 1.4.ii) in which the parties agree that the "appropriate measures" referred to in the non-execution clause mean measures taken in accordance with international law, and that when one party takes measures in cases of special urgency, the other may avail itself of the dispute settlement procedure.

The use of two different formulas (the "Baltic" and "Bulgarian" clauses) in the same part of the world could be interpreted as a discriminatory practice, putting the Commission in a difficult position in its negotiations with third countries. There is also a growing tendency to regain the margin of flexibility lost in the clauses themselves through an increasingly varied range of interpretative declarations.

Nevertheless, the innovative use of specific clauses in the main body of the agreements concluded with third countries places the European Community in the vanguard of the international community's endeavours in this field and highlights the parallel importance of adopting a positive approach.

190   *European Union and human rights*

This impact of this initiative has been positive in a number of ways:

a. the additional clause initially intended for the OSCE countries has, at the Council's behest, gradually been applied to other geographical areas, e.g. the Lomé IV review, Morocco and Tunisia, South Korea and Nepal;
b. enshrining Human Rights as an essential element of the Community's relations with third countries enhances cooperation and improves the visibility of its initiatives, many of which are entrusted to specialist organisations, such as the reinforcement of the rule of law, the consolidation of the legal system, support for freedom of expression, the defence of vulnerable groups, and support for the grassroots;
c. it has introduced a range of restrictive measures (see Annex 2) that is sufficiently broad to enable the parties to respond in a manner appropriate to the gravity of the case in question; to date, none of the agreements with an "essential element" clause, with or without an additional clause, has had to be suspended in any way.

## D. Conclusions

The concern expressed by the European Parliament and the Council with regard to the issue of Human Rights and the Community's contractual relations with third countries and the experience acquired in this area would suggest that there is a need for a number of initiatives to improve the consistency, transparency, and visibility of the Community approach and to make greater allowance for the sensitivity of third countries and the principle of non-discrimination.

The following conclusions set out the basic references to Human Rights and democratic principles. They provide for the following mechanism.

In all new draft negotiating directives for Community agreements with third parties, the following should be included:

*a. in the preamble:*

- general references to Human Rights and democratic values; (the recitals could also mention the rule of law and good governance and the Vienna Human Rights conference of June 1993);
- references to universal and regional instruments common to both parties;

*b. in the body of the agreement:*

1. Insertion of an Article X, defining the essential elements, to be adapted according to circumstances (e.g. OSCE membership, market economic principles, etc.):

> Respect for the democratic principles and fundamental Human Rights established by [the Universal Declaration of Human Rights]/[the Helsinki

Final Act and the Charter of Paris for a New Europe] inspires the domestic and external policies of the Community and of [the country or group of countries concerned] and constitutes an essential element of this agreement.

The same applies to the principles of market economy as they are defined in the CSCE Bonn conference document on economic cooperation.

2. Insertion of an Article Y on non-execution:

If either Party considers that the other Party has failed to fulfil an obligation under this Agreement, it may take appropriate measures. Before so doing, except in cases of special urgency, it shall supply the Association Council with all relevant information required for a thorough examination of the situation with a view to seeking a solution acceptable to the Parties.

In the selection of measures, priority must be given to those which least disturb the functioning of this Agreement. These measures shall be notified immediately to the Association Council and shall be the subject of consultations within the Association Council if the other Party so requests.

3. Insertion of interpretative declarations on Article Y:

"(a) The Parties agree, for the purpose of the correct interpretation and practical application of this Agreement, that the term "cases of special urgency" in Article Y means a case of the material breach of the Agreement by one of the Parties. A material breach of the Agreement consists in:

i. repudiation of the Agreement not sanctioned by the general rules of international law;

or

ii. violation of essential elements of the Agreement, namely its Article X.

(b) The parties agree that the "appropriate measures" referred to in Article Y are measures taken in accordance with international law. If a party takes a measure in a case of special urgency as provided for under Article Y, the other party may avail itself of the procedure relating to settlement of disputes."

In the Commission's opinion the application of this mechanism comes within the ambit of respect for the principle of proportionality between the breach cited and the degree of reaction. Use of the concept "special urgency" opens an option without creating an obligation and it is in this context that it is for the parties to gauge what measures they should take.

This may entail building on the standard provisions on Human Rights and democratic principles to strengthen or clarify the nature of the commitments involved, without altering the legal scope of the text. The wording given for Article X should feature among the first articles of the "General principles" title, and it should not be altered or diluted by inclusion in a more general provision.

This Communication will be addressed to the Council and to Parliament.

## Annex 1

*Standard wording for clauses on Human Rights and the relevant interpretative declarations*

1. Essential element clause
   Article X: [general principles or general/political dialogue]

   > Respect for the democratic principles and Human Rights established by [the Helsinki Final Act and the Charter of Paris for a New Europe] [as well as the principles of market economy] [as defined at the Bonn CSCE conference] inspires the domestic and external policies of the Community and of [third country] and constitute an essential element of this agreement.

2. Complementary clause
   Article Y:
   a. explicit suspension or "Baltic" clause

   > The parties reserve the right to suspend this Agreement in whole or in part with immediate effect if a serious breach of its essential provisions occurs.

   b. general non-execution or "Bulgarian" clause

   > If either Party considers that the other Party has failed to fulfil an obligation under this Agreement, it may take appropriate measures. Before so doing, except in cases of special urgency, it shall supply the Association Council with all relevant information required for a thorough examination of the situation with a view to seeking a solution acceptable to the Parties.
   >
   > In the selection of measures, priority must be given to those which least disturb the functioning of this Agreement. These measures shall be notified immediately to the Association Council and shall be the subject of consultations within the Association Council if the other Party so requests.

3. General interpretative declarations
   i. Unilateral declaration by the European Community (agreement with the Czech Republic, July 1993)

   > The reference to the respect for Human Rights as an essential element of the Agreement and to the cases of special urgency has been included in the Agreement as a result of the policy followed by the Community in the area of Human Rights pursuant to the Council Declaration of 11 May 1992, which foresees such reference in the Cooperation or Association Agreements between the Community and its partners in the Conference on Security and Cooperation in Europe.

ii. Joint declaration (agreement with the Russian Federation, June 1994)

> The Parties declare that the inclusion in the Agreement of the reference to respect for Human Rights constituting an essential element of the Agreement and to the cases of special urgency flows from the Community's policy in the area of Human Rights, in conformity with the Declaration of the Council of 11 May 1992 which provides for the inclusion of this reference in cooperation or association agreements between the Community and its CSCE partners, as well as Russia's policy in this field and the attachment of both Parties to the relevant obligations, arising in particular from the Helsinki Final Act and the Charter of Paris for a New Europe.

4. Interpretative declarations accompanying a general non-execution clause
   i. Standard joint declaration

> The Parties agree, for the purpose of the correct interpretation and practical application of this Agreement, that the term "cases of special urgency" in Article Y means a case of the material breach of the Agreement by one of the Parties. A material breach of the Agreement consists in:
> 
>   i. repudiation of the agreement not sanctioned by the general rules of international law;
>   or
>   ii. violation of essential elements of the Agreement, namely its Article X.

   ii. Joint declaration (agreement with the Russian Federation, June 1994)

> The parties agree that the "appropriate measures" referred to in Article Y are measures taken in accordance with international law. If a party takes a measure in a case of special urgency as provided for under Article Y, the other party may avail itself of the procedure relating to settlement of disputes.

## *Annex 2*

Summary of measures that may be taken in response to serious Human Rights violations or serious interruptions of democratic process:

- alteration of the contents of cooperation programmes or the channels used
- reduction of cultural, scientific and technical cooperation programmes
- postponement of a Joint Committee meeting
- suspension of high-level bilateral contacts
- postponement of new projects
- refusal to follow up partner's initiatives
- trade embargoes
- suspension of arms sales, suspension of military cooperation
- suspension of cooperation.

## References to Human Rights and democratic principles in Community agreements with third countries

### Key

*A. Regional European framework*

1. The provisions and principles of the following should be fully implemented:
   a. the Conference on Security and Cooperation in Europe (CSCE);
   b. the Helsinki Final Act, the concluding documents of the Madrid and Vienna conferences;
   c. the closing document of the Copenhagen meeting;
   d. the Charter of Paris for a New Europe, particularly in respect of the rule of law, democracy and Human Rights (November 1990);
   e. the Bonn CSCE conference document on economic cooperation.
2. Recognising the importance of guaranteeing ethnic and national minority rights:
   a. in line with the commitments entered into in the context of the CSCE;
   b. and of establishing a system based on pluralism and free and democratic elections.
3. Aware of the importance of strengthening their democratic institutions and supporting the economic reform process.
4. Reference to the European Convention on the Protection of Human Rights and Fundamental Freedoms.

*B. Attachment to the principles of the United Nations Charter*

1. to democratic values and respect for Human Rights
2. and wishing to express their mutual desire to maintain and strengthen their friendly relations on the basis of those principles.

*C. Attachment to the principles of equality, freedom and justice*

1. and asserting their shared wish to help initiate a new phase of economic cooperation and to facilitate the development of their respective human and material resources on the basis of those principles
2. and asserting their shared wish to promote the development of their human and physical resources in a context of freedom, equality and justice
3. and emphasising their shared attachment to the promotion of international economic relations based on freedom, equality, justice and progress

*D. Other references*

1. welcoming the transformation of the country into a democratic and multi-racial society and the importance attached to Human Rights

2. recognising that in the wake of recent political developments the country wishes to stabilise and consolidate democracy and promote economic and social progress
3. the importance attached by the parties to respect for the Human Rights, democratic principles and economic freedom that underpin this agreement
4. attachment to democratic values and respect for Human Rights
5. whereas the main beneficiary of cooperation is man, and these rights should therefore be promoted.

# Document no. 31

**Cannes European Council Presidency conclusions, 26 and 27 June 1995**[4]

\*\*\*

*Euro-Mediterranean conference in Barcelona*

*Position of the European Union*

*I. General introduction*

The countries of the European Union and their Mediterranean partners must act together to a greater extent to ensure that the Mediterranean becomes, more so than at present, an area of exchange and dialogue guaranteeing peace, stability and the well-being of those who live around it.

In accordance with the guidelines laid down by the European Councils in Lisbon (June 1992), Corfu (June 1994) and Essen (December 1994), the European Union is resolved to establish a lasting pattern of relations with the other Mediterranean countries in a spirit of partnership. An ambitious policy of cooperation to the south forms a counterpart to the policy of openness to the east and gives the European Union's external action its geopolitical coherence.

The European Union and its Mediterranean partners will have to meet common challenges calling for a coordinated overall approach. That approach must take proper account of the characteristics and distinguishing features of each of the countries on the other side of the Mediterranean. The establishment of a multilateral framework between Europe and the other side of the Mediterranean is the counterpart to a strengthening of the bilateral relations which link the Union and each of its partners. The existing bilateral agreements and the current negotiations for the conclusion of new generation agreements will make it possible to safeguard or even accentuate the specific nature of each of these bilateral relations within the new multilateral framework; these agreements will at the same time constitute one of the main instruments for implementing the provisions contained in this document.

The Euro-Mediterranean Ministerial Conference to be held in Barcelona on 27 and 28 November 1995 will give the countries of the European Union and their eastern and western Mediterranean partners an unprecedented opportunity to decide together what their future relationship is to be.

In its relations with these countries, the European Union's objective is to ensure stability and prosperity in the Mediterranean. To that end, the European Union is prepared to support those countries in their efforts to turn the region progressively into an area of peace, stability, prosperity and cooperation and for that purpose to establish a Euro-Mediterranean partnership. That calls for political dialogue, sustainable and balanced economic and social development, combating poverty and the need for greater understanding between cultures through a reinforcement of the human dimension in exchanges.

This is the spirit in which the European Union has embarked on the present discussion, which seeks to establish an overall partnership based on strengthening democracy and respect for Human Rights, which constitute an essential element in relations between Europe and its Mediterranean neighbours. That partnership comprises the following three main aspects:

*A political and security aspect.* The aim here is to establish a number of common principles and interests, acceptable to all, which the partners would undertake to promote together. It involves a reaffirmation of the importance, within each State, of respect for fundamental freedoms and the establishment of the rule of law, which constitute elements of stability for the whole Mediterranean region. Likewise, relations between States must be guided by certain principles acceptable to all which will ensure the stability of the region. This initiative involves a dialogue with countries in the Arab-Muslim world, and with other countries, and will take into account the specific cultural features of the region.

*An economic and financial aspect.* The aim is to build a zone of shared prosperity. An action plan is put forward, setting out the framework, priorities and arrangements for partnership in order to establish a Euro-Mediterranean economic area based on free trade in accordance with the obligations arising from the WTO [World Trade Organization]. It commits the partners to considering the implications of creating a free-trade area in relations between them as well as in the fields of economic development, resources and infrastructure. Particular importance is attached to regional integration. In this context, it is emphasised that European Union aid to the Mediterranean region cannot be a substitute for major efforts by the countries concerned to improve their own situation and their economic and social development. It is acknowledged that the economic modernisation involved requires a substantial increase in financial cooperation, which must promote above all the mobilisation of local economic forces in order to bring about sustainable, self-engendered development. To that end, particular stress will be placed on private sector investment, a powerful factor for the development of the region.

*A social and human aspect.* The aim here is to encourage exchanges among civil societies. In the context of decentralised cooperation, the emphasis is placed on education, training and young people, culture and the media, migrant population groups and health. Greater cooperation in the field of home affairs and justice is also envisaged, with action in particular against drug trafficking, terrorism and international crime.

Thus defined, the Euro-Mediterranean partnership, with its overall approach focused on the relationship between Europe and the Mediterranean, differs fundamentally from the peace process in the Middle East. The partnership is not a new forum for resolving conflicts and should not be seen as the framework for this process, even if, among other objectives, it can help to promote its success. The same applies with regard to the other disputes that may affect relations between countries in the area.

Nor is the Euro-Mediterranean partnership intended to replace the other activities and initiatives undertaken in the interests of the peace, stability and development of the region, which are aimed at strengthening dialogue and cooperation between Europe and its neighbours in the southern and eastern Mediterranean.

More particularly, the European Union intends to play an active part in the economic summit to be held in Amman in October as a follow-up to the Casablanca economic summit. This is a separate process from the Euro-Mediterranean partnership, both by its composition and by its objectives, even if certain synergies may result from it.

All in all, the sole significance of taking part in the Barcelona Conference is that of adhering to the principles underlying the Euro-Mediterranean partnership.

The European Union hopes that the Euro-Mediterranean Conference will lay the foundations for the Euro-Mediterranean partnership by adopting a joint document on the three main aspects referred to above, which form a whole and must be made to interact positively.

*II. Political and security partnership: establishing a common area of peace and stability*

In this field, the European Union proposes that the Euro-Mediterranean partnership should be put into practice with the adoption of a declaration of principles by all the partners, at the Conference in Barcelona this autumn, setting a number of objectives common to the parties with regard to internal and external security.

A. HUMAN RIGHTS, DEMOCRACY AND THE RULE OF LAW

It should be possible for rules of conduct within each State or political entity, which correspond to those recognised by the international community, to be reaffirmed by all the parties. The internal stability of States must be seen as a medium-term element in the stability of the whole Euro-Mediterranean area.

The Euro-Mediterranean partnership should therefore be based on observance of the following principles:

1. (Respect for the basic texts). Commitment by the partners to act in accordance with the UN Charter and the Universal Declaration of Human

Rights, as well as the obligations arising from the international declarations and agreements in this field by which they are bound.

2. (Rule of law). Each partner should be able to commit itself to the development of the rule of law and of democracy in its internal political system (free and regular elections to governing and representative bodies, independent judiciary, balance of powers and good governance), with the partners recognising at the same time the right of each of them to choose and freely develop its own political, socio-cultural and economic system, provided it complies with commonly agreed international standards concerning Human Rights.

3. (Fundamental freedoms). Commitment by each partner to take practical steps to ensure the effective exercise of fundamental freedoms, on the basis of the undertakings entered into by the partners in the previous two paragraphs, including freedom of expression, freedom of association for peaceful purposes and freedom of thought, conscience and religion.

   Commitment by the partners to give favourable consideration to the possibility of exchanging information and responding to any requests for information made to them by the partners on questions in connection with Human Rights and fundamental freedoms.

4. (Pluralism and tolerance). Commitment by each partner to respect diversity and pluralism in its society. Call for the promotion of tolerance between different groups in society and for resistance to manifestations of intolerance, especially racism and xenophobia. Action against terrorism will be all the more effective if it observes the rules of law and the principles of Human Rights and is coupled in the longer term with policies for specific action to deal with the underlying causes. The partners could thus stress the importance of proper education in the matter of Human Rights and fundamental freedoms.

5. (Human rights). Commitment by the partners to respect Human Rights and fundamental freedoms and the exercise of such rights and freedoms, both individually and together with other members of the same group, without any discrimination on the grounds of race, nationality, language, religion or sex.

# Document no. 32

**European Union briefings on the 1996 Intergovernmental Conference: Fundamental Rights**[5]

*Table of contents*

I. Current state of Community Law
II. Positions with a view to the 1996 IGC

## I. Current state of Community Law

1. The protection of fundamental rights is enshrined in Article F(2) of the Treaty on European Union, which stipulates that:

> The Union shall respect fundamental rights, as guaranteed by the European Convention for the Protection of Human Rights and Fundamental Freedoms signed in Rome on 4 November 1950 and as they result from the constitutional traditions common to the Member States, as general principles of Community law.

As far as the adoption and entry into force of the Maastricht Treaty are concerned, this provision marks the successful conclusion of a long process of strengthening the protection of fundamental rights and fundamental freedoms in the European Community. It gives tangible expression to the work of the Court of Justice in this field[6] by incorporating their substance in the corpus of primary Community law. It should be pointed out that this development in case law was previously consolidated by the adoption by the Council, European Parliament and Commission of the Joint Declaration of 5 April 1977[7] and the reference to fundamental rights incorporated in the preamble to the Single European Act[8].

2. What is the significance of this provision? According to legal commentators, a distinction has to be made. The Union will admittedly be required to respect fundamental rights as defined by this provision, but only "as general principles of Community law". This phrase has double legal significance:

- on the one hand, "the fact that primary law refers to fundamental freedoms does not confer on those rights the same legal value as primary law"[9];
- on the other hand, in terms of legal hierarchy, Article F does not incorporate fundamental rights in a kind of constitutional law of the European Union, "but confirms the status conferred on them by the case law of the Court of Justice, namely as unwritten sources of Community law, occupying an intermediate position between primary and secondary law"[10].

3. Respect for fundamental rights is also an aspect of the provisions relating to the second and third pillars of the TEU. Article J.1(2) includes respect for such rights among the objectives of the CFSP and Article K.2(1) stipulates that "the matters referred to in Article K.1 shall be dealt with in compliance with the European Convention for the Protection of Human Rights and Fundamental Freedoms of 4 November 1950 ... ". However, it is quite clear that the impact of these articles will remain limited so long as the provisions of these two pillars remain outside the judicial control of the Court of Justice.

4. To come back to the "Community pillar", it must be recognised that, although the inclusion of Article F(2) in the Treaty on European Union is a step forward, the provision itself has certain deficiencies, as illustrated by the following two examples:

- the added reference — as a complement to the fundamental rights guaranteed by the European Convention signed in Rome on 4 November 1950 — to fundamental rights "as they result from the constitutional traditions common to the Member States" makes it impossible to identify clearly the substance of the rights in question[11];
- in less technical terms, Article F(2), does not have the same symbolic value as a charter of fundamental rights[12].

5. These criticisms fit in with the remarks already made on the subject of the legal scope of Article F(2). Combined, they lead to the conclusion drawn by commentators that it would, in any case, have been "desirable for the protection of fundamental rights to be the object of a genuine material and/or formal constitutionalisation"[13]. This gives us an idea of the scale of the task still to be performed by those responsible for preparing the 1996 Intergovernmental Conference.

## II. Positions with a view to the 1996 Intergovernmental Conference

### A. *Positions of the institutions*

1. European Parliament

- In the space of two months — January and February 1994 — Parliament adopted its position on the subject:

- in its resolution of 18 January 1994, adopted as part of the Bontempi report (A3-0421/93), it expressed its agreement that "the Commission should receive authorisation from the Council to negotiate with the Council of Europe" on arrangements for accession to the European Convention on Human Rights of 4 November 1950[14];
- Parliament's draft Constitution of the European Union — adopted within its resolution of 10 February 1994 (Doc. A3-0064/94) — included an Article 7 which stipulated that:

   In areas where Union law applies, the Union and the Member States shall ensure respect for the rights set out in Title VIII. The Union shall respect fundamental rights as guaranteed by the European Convention on the Protection of Human Rights and Fundamental Freedoms, by the other applicable international instruments and as they derive from the constitutional principles shared by the Member States.

   Title VIII lists the Human Rights to be guaranteed by the Union.
- The resolution adopted on 17 May 1995 as part of the Bourlanges-Martin report (A4-0102/95) refers in paragraph 7 to the principle of accession to the European Convention for the Protection of Human Rights and Fundamental Freedoms, but also calls for:

   inclusion of an explicit reference in the Treaty to the principle of equal treatment irrespective of race, sex, age, handicap or religion (including mentioning the fundamental social rights of workers set out in the Charter, enlarging upon them and extending them to all citizens of the Union)
   and emphasised that:
   the Treaty should contain a clear rejection of racism, xenophobia, sexism, anti-Semitism and all forms of discrimination and guarantee adequate legal protection against discrimination for all individuals resident within the EU.

2. Commission

The Commission was at the origin of the initiatives aimed at Community accession to the European Convention for the Protection of Human Rights and Fundamental Freedoms[15]. It has always argued in favour of Community accession while considering that this would not be incompatible with the establishment of a specific catalogue of fundamental rights for citizens of the European Union[16]. In its report on the operation of the TEU (SEC(95)0731 of 10 May 1995), the Commission, taking as a basis the present provisions on European citizenship, points to the need for a fundamental text summarising the rights and duties of citizens. The passage in question, which is significant in several respects (e.g. the absence of any specific reference to the European Convention on Human Rights of 4 November 1950) reads:

The Treaty makes citizenship an evolving concept, and the Commission recommends developing it to the full. Moreover, although the task of building Europe is centred on democracy and Human Rights, citizens of the Union have at this stage no fundamental text which they can invoke as a summary of their rights and duties. The Commission thinks this gap should be filled, more especially since such an instrument would constitute a powerful means of promoting equal opportunities and combating racism and xenophobia[17].

3. Court of Justice

The Court of Justice considers the question of inserting a catalogue of fundamental rights into the Treaty as an introduction to the problem which would then arise with regard to the current wording of Article 173 of the EC Treaty:

> 20. ... if a catalogue of fundamental rights were to be introduced into the text of the Treaty, the question would arise as to the mechanism for reviewing observance of those rights in legislative and administrative measures adopted in the framework of Community law.
>
> In the exercise of its present jurisdiction, the Court already examines whether fundamental rights have been respected by the legislative and executive authorities of the Communities and by the Member States when their actions fall within the field of Community law. In doing so, it draws on the constitutional traditions common to the Member States and on the international instruments relating to the protection of Human Rights in which the Member States have cooperated or to which they are parties, in particular the European Convention on Human Rights. The Court would not, therefore, be taking on a new role in reviewing respect for such fundamental rights as might be provided for in the Treaty. It may be asked, however, whether the right to bring an action for annulment under Article 173 of the EC Treaty (and the corresponding provisions of the other treaties) which individuals enjoy only in regard to acts of direct and individual concern to them, is sufficient to guarantee for them effective judicial protection against possible infringements of their fundamental rights arising from the legislative activity of the Institutions.

4. Council

The Council's report on the functioning of the Treaty on European Union remains extremely cautious about "any long-term considerations concerning possible reforms"[18]. The Council states that "care has been taken not to anticipate the discussions of the Reflection Group"[19] and, as a result, "no value judgments are offered other than those arising from a straightforward account of the facts"[20]. It is therefore hardly surprising that no mention is made of the issue of fundamental rights in the report.

*B. Positions of the Member States*

The main feature of the positions expressed by the Member States, insofar as these have been made official, is caution: in fact, five Member States have not yet stated their views. On the other hand, clearly defined positions have been adopted in a few Member States — by governments or political parties — ranging from accession to the European Convention for the Protection of Human Rights and

Fundamental Freedoms to the simple requirement that respect for Human Rights at Union level should comply with European "standards". The positions expressed are set out below under various headings.

1. IN FAVOUR OF ACCESSION TO THE EUROPEAN CONVENTION FOR THE
PROTECTION OF HUMAN RIGHTS AND FUNDAMENTAL FREEDOMS OF
4 NOVEMBER 1950

- This category includes various political bodies in the Federal Republic of Germany and the Belgian Government.
- Discussion paper by the Executive Committee of the CDU/CSU parliamentary group (page 6):

    (...) a people's Europe also requires the greatest possible standardisation in Community law as regards fundamental rights. Although Article F(2) of the TEU guarantees a high level of consistency in the field of fundamental rights, the European Union should formally accede to the European Convention for the Protection of Human Rights and Fundamental Freedoms.

- Belgian Government policy note (August 95): The Government is willing to consider EU accession to the European Convention on Human Rights (ECHR) and other conventions defining fundamental rights and freedoms, including the Social Charter.

2. IN FAVOUR OF ANNEXING A CATALOGUE OF HUMAN RIGHTS AND
FUNDAMENTAL FREEDOMS TO THE TREATY

- This section includes the positions of the Länder of the Federal Republic of Germany, the Bundestag FDP group, Spain, Italy, the Netherlands and Belgium.
- The regional (Länder) ministers and senators responsible for European affairs are proposing in the long term "consideration of the question of including a list of fundamental rights in European law"[21].

Their basic position on this subject is as follows:

"1. Fundamental rights
The Intergovernmental Conference could, in addition to the protection of basic rights at present afforded by the European Court of Justice, combine European citizenship with a few fundamental rights already guaranteed by the EC Treaty and add to it a number of specific rights, such as the right of Union citizens to receive information from the Union Institutions. A provision against racism and xenophobia could also be incorporated in Community law. In the long term, a catalogue of fundamental rights should be incorporated in Community law at an appropriate stage in the process of further European integration."

- The Bundestag FDP Group has called for a commitment to drawing up a European Constitution, with "a list of European civil rights and incorporation of the principle of subsidiarity"[22].
- *Spain*: Spain's position is set out in the document entitled "The 1996 Intergovernmental Conference: bases for discussion". This document emphasises the link between Union citizenship and fundamental rights and mentions two practical alternatives:

    either the catalogue of rights contained in the existing chapter on "Citizenship of the Union" (Articles 8 to 8E) should be substantially extended, to include, inter alia, a specific article condemning racism and xenophobia; or there should be a charter of fundamental rights of the citizens of the Union, including, with a view to future enlargements, all the rights considered as basic in the context of the *acquis communautaire*, which would thus receive protection from both the Union institutions and the Member States. The concept of "democratic principles", referred to in Article F(1) as the foundation of the Union could also be further specified for eventualities such as a change of régime or violation of those principles.[23]

- *Italy*: The position upheld in the Italian Government statement of 23 February 1995 on foreign policy guidelines comes out strongly in favour of a catalogue of fundamental rights, though in more cautious terms. This position is expressed as follows:

    the Italian government proposes ... that Treaty provisions be organised according to a new technical and legal system, in order to make them more readily comprehensible to the public, and that certain essential constitutional principles be spelt out explicitly, one such being the basic rights of European citizens, which must be properly protected and subject to review by the Luxembourg Court of Justice.[24]

    In its statement of 23 May 1995 on the IGC [Intergovernmental Conference], the Italian Government suggests that a full catalogue of fundamental rights and freedoms be drawn up in the context of a people's Europe. It also suggests extending the instruments for the protection and enforcement of rights before the institutions, in particular, the IGC.

- *Netherlands*: The Dutch Government's position can be found in its "Note on the enlargement of the European Union: the opportunities and obstacles", which was sent to both Chambers on 14 November 1994 and was debated in plenary on 15 February 1995. It is a cautious statement, insofar as the subject is discussed as a side issue to the question of enlargement of the European Union and is worded ambiguously. The government's position will apparently be "guided, not only by the objective of safeguarding cultural values, but also by the democratic principles and fundamental rights set out in the Union Treaty", as well as four other aims listed in the note[25].

    It is not clear whether this statement is referring to fundamental rights to be incorporated in the Treaty or simply those fundamental rights already

included in the Treaty. These two alternatives would undoubtedly have fundamentally different implications.
- *Belgium*: The government is willing to consider incorporating a list of fundamental rights and freedoms in the Treaty.

3. A SPECIFIC REFERENCE IN THE PREAMBLE TO THE NEW TREATY

This is the position expressed by the Luxembourg Government, which "would welcome a specific reference in the preamble to the new Treaty, to the protection of Human Rights and fundamental freedoms of European citizens, equality between men and women and the combating of racism and xenophobia" (see page 13 of the document).

4. REFERENCE TO THE PROTECTION OF FUNDAMENTAL RIGHTS, BUT WITHOUT SPECIFYING THE MEANS OF PROTECTION

- *Austria*: The protection of fundamental rights must meet "European standards". However, the means of guaranteeing this protection will need to be defined during the preparatory phase of the Conference. This is the Austrian government's basic position in the document entitled "Leitlinien zu den voraussichtlichen Themen der Regierungskonferenz 1996".
  The document reads:

  The protection of fundamental rights and freedoms should be effectively guaranteed in accordance with European standards. The decision as to the most appropriate method for achieving this will need to be taken during preparations for the Intergovernmental Conference (page 33, paragraph 14, "Grund und Freiheitsrechte").

- *Greece*: As in the Dutch Government's statement, the Greek Government mentions fundamental rights in the context of another chapter, namely the common foreign and security policy. In the memorandum for the 1996 IGC, entitled "Towards a citizens' Europe – Democracy and Development", respect for Human Rights is considered as a vital element of the "multi-dimensional security system which the European Union must set up". That is why any future new Member States must respect Human Rights in a context of constitutional democracy[26]. However, the document fails to specify what exactly is meant by "context of constitutional democracy".
- *Finland:* In its memorandum of 18 September 1995, the Finnish Government calls for protection of fundamental rights in the Union to be strengthened. This could be achieved through accession to the ECHR and the incorporation of certain fundamental rights in the Treaty (e.g. the principle of equality). It would not be necessary to mention all fundamental rights, but simply to set out the principal rights in a clearer and more binding form (including a clause condemning racism and xenophobia).

5. NO CLEAR POSITION

To date, the following Member States have not expressed their views on the issue of protection of fundamental rights[27]. Admittedly a number of these Member States have not yet submitted any official document with a view to the 1996 Intergovernmental Conference. In some cases, statements by political leaders have appeared as "positions with a view to the 1996 IGC". The Member States which have not yet adopted a position on this subject are as follows:

- *France* (statements by political leaders — no official document);
- *Ireland* (White Paper on foreign policy and the 1996 Intergovernmental Conference currently being prepared);
- *Portugal* (no official document);
- *Sweden* (unlikely to adopt a position before the end of 1995);
- *United Kingdom* (the British Government memorandum of 2 March 1995 is limited in scope since it only refers to consideration of matters relating to European security at the 1996 Intergovernmental Conference).

# Document no. 33

**Consolidated version of the Treaty on European Union (as amended by the Treaty of Amsterdam Amending the Treaty on European Union, the Treaties Establishing The European Communities and Related Acts)[28]**

*** [Signatories]

RESOLVED to mark a new stage in the process of European integration undertaken with the establishment of the European Communities;

RECALLING the historic importance of the ending of the division of the European continent and the need to create firm bases for the construction of the future Europe,

CONFIRMING their attachment to the principles of liberty, democracy and respect for Human Rights and fundamental freedoms and of the rule of law,

CONFIRMING their attachment to fundamental social rights as defined in the European Social Charter signed at Turin on 18 October 1961 and in the 1989 Community Charter of the Fundamental Social Rights of Workers,

DESIRING to deepen the solidarity between their peoples while respecting their history, their culture and their traditions,

DESIRING to enhance further the democratic and efficient functioning of the institutions so as to enable them better to carry out, within a single institutional framework, the tasks entrusted to them,

RESOLVED to achieve the strengthening and the convergence of their economies and to establish an economic and monetary union including, in accordance with the provisions of this Treaty, a single and stable currency,

DETERMINED to promote economic and social progress for their peoples, taking into account the principle of sustainable development and within the context of the accomplishment of the internal market and of reinforced cohesion and environmental protection, and to implement policies ensuring that advances in economic integration are accompanied by parallel progress in other fields,

RESOLVED to establish a citizenship common to nationals of their countries,

RESOLVED to implement a common foreign and security policy including the progressive framing of a common defence policy, which might lead to a common defence in accordance with the provisions of Article 17, thereby reinforcing the European identity and its independence in order to promote peace, security and progress in Europe and in the world,

RESOLVED to facilitate the free movement of persons, while ensuring the safety and security of their peoples, by establishing an area of freedom, security and justice, in accordance with the provisions of this Treaty,

RESOLVED to continue the process of creating an ever closer union among the peoples of Europe, in which decisions are taken as closely as possible to the citizen in accordance with the principle of subsidiarity,

IN VIEW of further steps to be taken in order to advance European integration,

HAVE DECIDED to establish a European Union and to this end have designated as their Plenipotentiaries:

\*\*\*

WHO, having exchanged their full powers, found in good and due form, have agreed as follows.

## Title I: Common provisions

*Article 1 (ex Article A)*

By this Treaty, the HIGH CONTRACTING PARTIES establish among themselves a EUROPEAN UNION, hereinafter called "the Union".

This Treaty marks a new stage in the process of creating an ever closer union among the peoples of Europe, in which decisions are taken as openly as possible and as closely as possible to the citizen.

The Union shall be founded on the European Communities, supplemented by the policies and forms of cooperation established by this Treaty. Its task shall be to organise, in a manner demonstrating consistency and solidarity, relations between the Member States and between their peoples.

*Article 2 (ex Article B)*

The Union shall set itself the following objectives:

- to promote economic and social progress and a high level of employment and to achieve balanced and sustainable development, in particular through the creation of an area without internal frontiers, through the strengthening of economic and social cohesion and through the establishment of economic and monetary union, ultimately including a single currency in accordance with the provisions of this Treaty;
- to assert its identity on the international scene, in particular through the implementation of a common foreign and security policy including the

progressive framing of a common defence policy, which might lead to a common defence, in accordance with the provisions of Article 17;
- to strengthen the protection of the rights and interests of the nationals of its Member States through the introduction of a citizenship of the Union;
- to maintain and develop the Union as an area of freedom, security and justice, in which the free movement of persons is assured in conjunction with appropriate measures with respect to external border controls, asylum, immigration and the prevention and combating of crime;
- to maintain in full the *acquis communautaire* and build on it with a view to considering to what extent the policies and forms of cooperation introduced by this Treaty may need to be revised with the aim of ensuring the effectiveness of the mechanisms and the institutions of the Community.

The objectives of the Union shall be achieved as provided in this Treaty and in accordance with the conditions and the timetable set out therein while respecting the principle of subsidiarity as defined in Article 5 of the Treaty establishing the European Community.

\*\*\*

*Article 6 (ex Article F)*

1. The Union is founded on the principles of liberty, democracy, respect for Human Rights and fundamental freedoms, and the rule of law, principles which are common to the Member States.

2. The Union shall respect fundamental rights, as guaranteed by the European Convention for the Protection of Human Rights and Fundamental Freedoms signed in Rome on 4 November 1950 and as they result from the constitutional traditions common to the Member States, as general principles of Community law.[29]

3. The Union shall respect the national identities of its Member States.

4. The Union shall provide itself with the means necessary to attain its objectives and carry through its policies.

*Article 7 (ex Article F.1)*

1. The Council, meeting in the composition of the Heads of State or Government and acting by unanimity on a proposal by one third of the Member States or by the Commission and after obtaining the assent of the European Parliament, may determine the existence of a serious and persistent breach by a Member State of principles mentioned in Article 6(1), after inviting the government of the Member State in question to submit its observations.

2. Where such a determination has been made, the Council, acting by a qualified majority, may decide to suspend certain of the rights deriving from the application of this Treaty to the Member State in question, including the voting

rights of the representative of the government of that Member State in the Council. In doing so, the Council shall take into account the possible consequences of such a suspension on the rights and obligations of natural and legal persons.

The obligations of the Member State in question under this Treaty shall in any case continue to be binding on that State.

3. The Council, acting by a qualified majority, may decide subsequently to vary or revoke measures taken under paragraph 2 in response to changes in the situation which led to their being imposed.

4. For the purposes of this Article, the Council shall act without taking into account the vote of the representative of the government of the Member State in question. Abstentions by members present in person or represented shall not prevent the adoption of decisions referred to in paragraph 1. A qualified majority shall be defined as the same proportion of the weighted votes of the members of the Council concerned as laid down in Article 205(2) of the Treaty establishing the European Community.

This paragraph shall also apply in the event of voting rights being suspended pursuant to paragraph 2.

5. For the purposes of this Article, the European Parliament shall act by a two-thirds majority of the votes cast, representing a majority of its members.

## Consolidated version of the Treaty establishing the European Community[30]

\*\*\*

*Article 12 (ex Article 6)*

Within the scope of application of this Treaty, and without prejudice to any special provisions contained therein, any discrimination on grounds of nationality shall be prohibited.

The Council, acting in accordance with the procedure referred to in Article 251, may adopt rules designed to prohibit such discrimination.

*Article 13 (ex Article 6a)*

Without prejudice to the other provisions of this Treaty and within the limits of the powers conferred by it upon the Community, the Council, acting unanimously on a proposal from the Commission and after consulting the European Parliament, may take appropriate action to combat discrimination based on sex, racial or ethnic origin, religion or belief, disability, age or sexual orientation.

\*\*\*

*Article 309 (ex Article 236)*

1. Where a decision has been taken to suspend the voting rights of the representative of the government of a Member State in accordance with Article 7(2) of the Treaty on European Union, these voting rights shall also be suspended with regard to this Treaty.

2. Moreover, where the existence of a serious and persistent breach by a Member State of principles mentioned in Article 6(1) of the Treaty on European Union has been determined in accordance with Article 7(1) of that Treaty, the Council, acting by a qualified majority, may decide to suspend certain of the rights deriving from the application of this Treaty to the Member State in question. In doing so, the Council shall take into account the possible consequences of such a suspension on the rights and obligations of natural and legal persons.

The obligations of the Member State in question under this Treaty shall in any case continue to be binding on that State.

3. The Council, acting by a qualified majority, may decide subsequently to vary or revoke measures taken in accordance with paragraph 2 in response to changes in the situation which led to their being imposed.

4. When taking decisions referred to in paragraphs 2 and 3, the Council shall act without taking into account the votes of the representative of the government of the Member State in question. By way of derogation from Article 205(2) a qualified majority shall be defined as the same proportion of the weighted votes of the members of the Council concerned as laid down in Article 205(2).

This paragraph shall also apply in the event of voting rights being suspended in accordance with paragraph 1. In such cases, a decision requiring unanimity shall be taken without the vote of the representative of the government of the Member State in question.

\*\*\*

# Document no. 34

**Declaration of the European Union on the occasion of the 50th Anniversary of the Universal Declaration on Human Rights, Vienna, 10 December, 1998**[31]

*A.*

On the occasion of the 50th Anniversary of the adoption of the Universal Declaration of Human Rights, the Union recalls the primary importance that it attaches to this Declaration. It constitutes the foundation for national, regional and global policies to advance and ensure human dignity world-wide.

The universality and indivisibility of Human Rights and the responsibility for their protection and promotion, together with the promotion of pluralistic democracy and effective guarantees for the rule of law, constitute essential objectives for the European Union as a union of shared values and serve as a fundamental basis for our action.

The human being is at the centre of our policies. Ensuring the human dignity of every individual remains our common goal.

The full realisation of the rights of women and children deserve in particular to be highlighted as neglect in this respect remains widespread.

The protection and promotion of Human Rights and fundamental freedoms, for which Governments have responsibility, contributes to prosperity, justice, and peace in the world. However, these goals cannot be realised without the work of international organisations, civil society and individuals.

The Union pledges its continuing support for the further promotion and protection of Human Rights, in fulfilment of the Treaty on the European Union, the European Convention on the Protection of Human Rights and Fundamental Freedoms and the Declarations of the European Council of Luxembourg 1991 and 1997, and adopts the following Declaration

*B.*

**I.** Since the adoption, fifty years ago, of the Universal Declaration of Human Rights, the Union has witnessed progress in the field of Human Rights and the spread of democracy throughout the world. At the same time, however, the Union remains aware of threats to progress and the need to strengthen its determination and efforts for the world-wide realisation of all Human Rights for all.

**II.** The adoption of the Universal Declaration initiated an irreversible process of awareness-building in civil society on Human Rights and fundamental freedoms throughout the world. The Declaration constitutes, in particular, the foundation for the subsequent development of an impressive body of important international legal instruments, including the International Covenants on Civil and Political Rights and on Economic, Social and Cultural Rights. The 1993 Vienna World Conference on Human Rights reconfirmed the universality and indivisibility of all Human Rights. The Union calls upon all countries that have not yet done so to become a party to all major Human Rights treaties.

The implementation of the Universal Declaration and of the other international Human Rights instruments is of paramount importance for the universal character of the rights laid down therein to become a reality. There can be no valid exemption from the principles enshrined in those instruments through special provisions based on national, cultural or religious considerations. The 50th Anniversary of the Universal Declaration is a time to take stock, and a time to redouble efforts to promote the implementation of Human Rights in all countries in the world. The Union seizes this opportunity to reaffirm its commitment to realise all Human Rights for all.

Mindful of the Declaration of the European Council of 28/29 June 1991, in Luxembourg, the Union recognises and welcomes the achievements since the adoption of the Universal Declaration. The Union feels compelled, however, to deplore the persistence of violations of Human Rights throughout the world. The Union reaffirms that it is the legitimate and permanent responsibility of the international community and of all States acting individually or collectively to promote and safeguard Human Rights throughout the world. The Union for its part will continue to take up violations wherever they occur. At the same time the Union welcomes the fact that an increasing number of States work together with the EU on the basis of partnership to promote Human Rights and to ensure their universality.

During the past fifty years, throughout the world, thousands of women and men have fought for the protection of those values, often paying a heavy toll. The Union pays tribute to their courageous actions that shall inspire the EU in its determination to promote the rights enshrined in the Declaration.

The Union welcomes, in this context, the adoption of a Declaration on Human Rights Defenders by the General Assembly of the United Nations. Individuals and non-governmental organisations throughout the world are making indispensable and courageous contributions to safeguarding and promoting Human Rights. They need continuing strong support.

**III.** The European Union, which is founded on the principles of liberty, democracy, respect for Human Rights and fundamental freedoms and the rule of law, shares the values in which the Declaration is rooted. It is conscious of the need to promote Human Rights in its own countries. Both internally and externally, respect for Human Rights as proclaimed in the Universal Declaration is one of the essential components of the activities of the Union. In their activities, the institutions of the Union respect Human Rights as guaranteed by the European Convention on the Protection of Human Rights and Fundamental Freedoms and as resulting from the constitutional traditions common to the Member States, under the control of the Court of Justice of the European Communities. Equally, Member States are bound by the European Convention and their actions are submitted to the supervision of the European Court of Human Rights. With the entry into force of the Treaty of Amsterdam, respect for Human Rights and fundamental freedoms will be a condition for accession to the European Union, and a serious and persistent breach of these rights may lead to the suspension of rights of a Member State.

Moreover, the Amsterdam Treaty will further strengthen the commitment to safeguard and promote Human Rights and fundamental freedoms, especially by measures against discrimination in a wide range of fields including by strengthening the possibilities of ensuring equal opportunities for men and women. Furthermore, aware of the European Social Charter and the Community Charter on Basic Social Rights of Workers, it defines aims in the field of basic social rights. The European Union in its cooperation in the field of justice and security will also be guided by its respect for Human Rights.

Respect for Human Rights and fundamental freedoms is also one of the objectives of the Union's Common Foreign and Security Policy as well as of its development cooperation. The Union pursues this goal both in its bilateral relations with third countries and in the framework of the United Nations and other multilateral fora, in particular the Organisation for Security and Cooperation in Europe, and the Council of Europe.

In pursuit of its policy of promoting Human Rights in all parts of the world, the Union regularly raises Human Rights questions in its dialogue with third countries, as an important and legitimate part of this dialogue, and in demarches as well as declarations.

The European Community has included in the agreements it concludes a clause which makes respect for Human Rights, in particular as contained in the Universal Declaration on Human Rights, an essential element for its agreement to be bound. The Union thus assumes its responsibility for the promotion and protection of Human Rights as a legitimate concern of the international community, while reaffirming that this protection and promotion remain the primary responsibility of each and every government.

The Union expresses its preoccupation about recent incidents of racism and xenophobia, both within the Union and throughout the world, and will work actively towards achieving meaningful results at the World Conference on Racism. A range of practical measures complement the Union's efforts in these fields; the Union wishes to highlight, in this context, notably the activities of the Vienna Monitoring Centre on Racism and Xenophobia.

The Union has decided this year to reinforce its efforts for the universal abolition of the death penalty as a strongly held policy agreed by the EU. Where the death penalty still exists, the Union calls for its use to be restricted, and demands that it be carried out only in accordance with international safeguards. The Union is also pressing, where relevant, for moratoria to be introduced.

The Union accords high importance to supporting efforts for the promotion of democracy, respect for Human Rights, the rule of law, and good governance. The Union therefore provides support for a wide range of projects and programmes in these fields throughout the world.

The Union and its Member States are committed to cooperating with international Human Rights mechanisms at the global and regional levels. The Union actively supports the action of the UN High Commissioner for Human Rights and her activities, especially at the field level. The Union encourages the efforts by the UN Secretary General towards better integrating Human Rights into the broad range of UN activities.

The Union particularly welcomes the adoption of the Statute of a permanent International Criminal Court to try the most serious crimes and violations of humanitarian law of concern to the international community and calls for an early ratification of this statute.

**IV.** These policies must be continued and, where necessary, strengthened and improved. In this regard, it is important that the Union reinforce its capacity to achieve its objectives on the protection and promotion of Human Rights and fundamental freedoms. In this context, the Union is determined to ensure respect for Human Rights in all its actions. In particular the Union will consider concrete measures such as:

1. enhance the capacity to jointly assess the Human Rights situation in the world by closer coordination and otherwise ensure that all pertinent means for action are available within the framework of the Union, including through the possible publication of an annual EU Human Rights report;
2. further develop cooperation in the field of Human Rights, such as education and training activities, in coordination with other relevant organisations, and ensure the continuation of the Human Rights Masters Programme organised by fifteen European universities;
3. reflect on the usefulness of convening a periodic Human Rights discussion forum with the participation of EU institutions as well as representatives of academic institutions and NGOs [non-governmental organizations];
4. strengthen the capacities to respond to international operational requirements in the field of Human Rights and democratisation, such as through the possible establishment of a common roster of European Human Rights and democracy experts, for Human Rights field operations and electoral assistance and monitoring;
5. foster the development and consolidation of democracy and the rule of law and respect for Human Rights and fundamental freedoms in third countries, in particular through working towards the earliest possible adoption of the draft regulations, currently under consideration in the EU framework, on the implementation of cooperation operations;
6. ensure all means to achieve the coherent realisation of these goals, including through the consideration of strengthening relevant EU structures.

# 7 Turkey–EU relations: 1963–94

The Ankara agreement, emergence of Turkey's Human Rights record as a problem

# Document no. 35

**Turkey–EU brief history[1]**

Relations between the European Union (EU) and Turkey began with the agreement establishing an association between the European Economic Community (EEC) and Turkey, the so-called Ankara Agreement. The Ankara Agreement was signed on 12 September 1963, and came into force on 1 December 1964. The cornerstone of this agreement was the establishment of a customs union in three stages. A Financial Protocol accompanied this agreement. The second and third Financial Protocols were signed in 1970 and 1977, respectively. The Ankara Agreement also set up an Association Council that met regularly and discussed the work of the association. This institutional framework was expanded with the implementation of the final phase of the Customs Union.

The Association Agreement was supplemented by an Additional Protocol, which was signed on 23 November 1970 and came into force on 1 January 1973. The Additional Protocol established a timetable of technical measures to be taken to attain the objective of the Customs Union within a period of twenty-two years. On 14 April 1987, Turkey presented its application for membership into the Community. The Commission adopted its opinion on the application on 18 December 1989. It concluded "that it would not be useful to open accession negotiations with Turkey straight away". The Commission gave both economic and political reasons. The Commission also noted "'the negative effects' of the dispute between Greece and Turkey and 'the situation in Cyprus.'"

\*\*\*

On 5 February 1990, the Council adopted the general content of the Commission opinion and asked it to make detailed proposals developing the ideas expressed in the opinion on the need to strengthen EC–Turkey relations.

\*\*\*

On 6 March 1995, the EC–Turkey Association Council decided to move onto the final stage of the Customs Union and resume financial cooperation. The

Council also decided to step up cooperation in several sectors to solidify institutional cooperation and to intensify political dialogue. On 13 December 1995, Parliament gave its assent to the Customs Union. The decision on the final phase of the Customs Union came into force on 31 December 1995, and set up a consultation body, the Customs Union Joint Committee, on the institutional front. On 15 July 1996, the General Affairs Council adopted the Regulation on the MEDA [Euro-Mediterranean Partnership] programme, the principal financial instrument of the EU for the implementation of the Euro-Mediterranean Partnership, for twelve Mediterranean countries, including Turkey.

\*\*\*

In the wake of the informal Foreign Affairs Council in Apeldoorn (16 March 1997), the EU reaffirmed Turkey's eligibility for membership into the EU at the meeting of the EC–Turkey Association Council on 29 April 1997. In correlation, the EU also stated that Turkey's application would be judged on the same criteria as the other applicant countries. The Commission was called on to draw up a communication on the future development of relations between the EU and Turkey, in the context of the Customs Union.

On 15 July 1997, the European Commission adopted Agenda 2000, a strategy paper which set out a project for Europe for the year 2000, which stated that "the European Union should continue to support Turkey's efforts to resolve its problems and to forge closer links with the EU". The Commission expanded on this point with the communication on the further development of relations with Turkey adopted by the Commission on 15 July 1997.

The communication proposed a series of measures designed to consolidate the Customs Union and to extend it to new fields (services and agriculture), such as the establishment of cooperation in several sectors (environment, energy, telecommunications, etc), some of which come under the second and third pillars of the EU. The Commission also proposed helping Turkey in its efforts to improve the Human Rights situation. Accordingly, the Commission prepared a preliminary draft programme proposing cooperation with the Turkish authorities and NGOs [non-governmental organisations] to support the Turkish authorities' efforts to increase respect for Human Rights and the rule of law. As of March 2005, the Turkish authorities had not yet followed up this proposal.

The Luxembourg European Council of December 1997 confirmed at the highest level "Turkey's eligibility for accession to the European Union". The Heads of State and Government also decided to draw up a strategy "to prepare Turkey for accession by bringing it closer to the European Union in every field". This strategy would consist of "development of the possibilities afforded by the Ankara Agreement, intensification of the Customs Union, implementation of financial cooperation, approximation of laws and adoption of the Union *acquis*; participation, to be decided case by case, in certain programmes and certain agencies … " In addition, the European Council listed a number of principles which would allow for the strengthening of ties with Turkey (paragraph 35 of the Conclusions). The European

Council also indicated that Turkey would be invited to participate in the European Conference on the same basis as the other applicant countries.

As requested by the Luxembourg European Council, the Commission adopted on 4 March 1998 the initial operational proposals of the "European Strategy for Turkey".

## Developments in the enlargement process

The European Council in Helsinki (10–11 December 1999) welcomed "recent positive developments in Turkey, as well as its intention to continue its reform towards complying with the Copenhagen criteria". The Council Declaration stated that "Turkey is a candidate State destined to join the Union on the basis of the same criteria as applied to the other candidate States".

The decisions taken at Helsinki were an important watershed in EU–Turkey relations. Turkey, like other candidate countries, would benefit from a pre-accession strategy to stimulate and support its reforms.

The Association Council met in April 2000 for the first time in three years and was chaired by Turkey. It adopted two important political decisions: one on the establishment of eight sub-committees of the Association Committee and the other on the opening of negotiation for an agreement aiming at the liberalisation of services and the mutual opening of procurement markets between the EC and Turkey.

The Accession Partnership was formally adopted by the EU Council on 8 March 2001 as a roadmap of the priorities for Turkey in making progress towards meeting all the criteria for accession to the EU.

The purpose of the Accession Partnership was to set out, in a single framework, the priority areas for further work, as identified in the Commission's 2000 regular report. It addressed the progress made by Turkey towards membership of the European Union, the financial means available to help Turkey implement these priorities, and the conditions which would apply to that assistance.

On the basis of this Accession Partnership, the Turkish government adopted its National Programme for the Adoption of the *Acquis* (NPAA) on 19 March 2001.

The programme, still in force after amendments, provided a wide-ranging agenda of political and economic reform. At the same time, a government decree was adopted on the implementation, coordination and monitoring of the NPAA. The Gothenburg European Council of 15 and 16 June 2001 regarded the National Programme as the cornerstone of the pre-accession strategy, a "welcome[d] development", and "urged Turkey at the same time to take concrete measures to implement the priorities of the Accession Partnership".

On 26 February 2001, the Council adopted a regulation that provided for the coordination of EC pre-accession financial assistance to Turkey.

The Council decided on 5 June 2001 to authorise the Commission to negotiate with Turkey a framework agreement to simplify the legal procedures to permit Turkey's participation in individual Community programmes. Subsequently, negotiations for Turkey's participation in the European Environment Agency and in the European Information and Observation Network (EIONET) were concluded.

In December 2001, the Council adopted a regulation on pre-accession financial assistance to Turkey. This new regulatory framework ensured an accession-driven approach to the EC's financial cooperation with Turkey. As with all candidate countries, financial assistance would focus on the priorities identified in the Accession Partnership.

[Finally, the Brussels European Council in 17 December 2004 decided to open accession negotiations with Turkey.]

# Document no. 36

**Agreement establishing an association between the European Economic Community and Turkey, 12 September 1963**[2]

*Preamble*

[Signatories],

DETERMINED to establish ever closer bonds between the Turkish people and the peoples brought together in the European Economic Community;

RESOLVED to ensure a continuous improvement in living conditions in Turkey and in the European Economic Community through accelerated economic progress and the harmonious expansion of trade, and to reduce the disparity between the Turkish economy and the economies of the Member States of the Community;

MINDFUL both of the special problems presented by the development of the Turkish economy and of the need to grant economic aid to Turkey during a given period;

RECOGNISING that the support given by the European Economic Community to the efforts of the Turkish people to improve their standard of living will facilitate the accession of Turkey to the Community at a later date;

RESOLVED to preserve and strengthen peace and liberty by joint pursuit of the ideals underlying the Treaty establishing the European Economic Community;

HAVE DECIDED to conclude an Agreement establishing an Association between the European Economic Community and Turkey in accordance with Article 238 of the Treaty establishing the European Economic Community, and to this end have designated as their Plenipotentiaries:

\*\*\*

WHO, having exchanged their Full Powers, found in good and due form, HAVE AGREED AS FOLLOWS:

### Title I: Principles

*Article 1*

By this Agreement an Association is established between the European Economic Community and Turkey.

*Article 2*

1. The aim of this Agreement is to promote the continuous and balanced strengthening of trade and economic relations between the Parties, while taking full account of the need to ensure an accelerated development of the Turkish economy and to improve the level of employment and the living conditions of the Turkish people.
2. In order to attain the objectives set out in paragraph 1, a Customs Union shall be progressively established in accordance with Articles 3, 4 and 5.
3. Association shall comprise:
a. a preparatory stage;
b. a transitional stage;
c. a final stage.

\*\*\*

*Article 5*

The final stage shall be based on the Customs Union and shall entail closer coordination of the economic policies of the Contracting Parties.

*Article 6*

To ensure the implementation and the progressive development of the Association, the Contracting Parties shall meet in a Council of Association which shall act within the powers conferred upon it by this Agreement.

*Article 7*

The Contracting Parties shall take all appropriate measures, whether general or particular, to ensure the fulfilment of the obligations arising from this Agreement.

They shall refrain from any measures liable to jeopardise the attainment of the objectives of this Agreement.

### Title II: Implementation of the transitional stage

*Article 8*

In order to attain the objectives set out in Article 4, the Council of Association shall, before the beginning of the transitional stage and in accordance with the procedure laid down in Article 1 of the Provisional Protocol, determine the conditions, rules and timetables for the implementation of the provisions relating to the fields covered by the Treaty establishing the Community which must be considered; this shall apply in particular to such of those fields as are mentioned under this Title and to any protective clause which may prove appropriate.

*Article 9*

The Contracting Parties recognise that, within the scope of this Agreement and without prejudice to any special provisions which may be laid down pursuant to Article 8, any discrimination on grounds of nationality shall be prohibited in accordance with the principle laid down in Article 7 of the Treaty establishing the Community.

CHAPTER 1

The Customs Union

*Article 10*

1. The Customs Union provided for in Article 2 (2) of this Agreement shall cover all trade in goods.
    2. The Customs Union shall involve:

- the prohibition between Member States of the Community and Turkey, of customs duties on imports and exports and of all charges having equivalent effect, quantitative restrictions and all other measures having equivalent effect which are designed to protect national production in a manner contrary to the objectives of this Agreement;
- the adoption by Turkey of the Common Customs Tariff of the Community in its trade with third countries, and an approximation to the other Community rules on external trade.

\*\*\*

## Title III: General and final provisions

*Article 22*

1. In order to attain the objectives of this Agreement the Council of Association shall have the power to take decisions in the cases provided for therein. Each of the Parties shall take the measures necessary to implement the decisions taken. The Council of Association may also make appropriate recommendations.
    2. The Council of Association shall periodically review the functioning of the Association in the light of the objectives of this Agreement. During the preparatory stage, however, such reviews shall be limited to an exchange of views.

3. Once the transitional stage has been embarked on, the Council of Association shall adopt appropriate decisions where, in the course of implementation of the Association arrangements, attainment of an objective of this Agreement calls for joint action by the Contracting Parties but the requisite powers are not granted in this Agreement.

\*\*\*

*Article 25*

1. The Contracting Parties may submit to the Council of Association any dispute relating to the application or interpretation of this Agreement which concerns the Community, a Member State of the Community, or Turkey.

2. The Council of Association may settle the dispute by decision; it may also decide to submit the dispute to the Court of Justice of the European Communities or to any other existing court or tribunal.

3. Each Party shall be required to take the measures necessary to comply with such decisions.

4. Where the dispute cannot be settled in accordance with paragraph 2 of this Article, the Council of Association shall determine, in accordance with Article 8 of this Agreement, the detailed rules for arbitration or for any other judicial procedure to which the Contracting Parties may resort during the transitional and final stages of this Agreement.

*Article 26*

This Agreement shall not apply to products within the province of the European Coal and Steel Community.

*Article 27*

The Council of Association shall take all appropriate steps to promote the necessary cooperation and contacts between the European Parliament, the Economic and Social Committee and other organs of the Community on the one hand and the Turkish Parliament and the corresponding organs in Turkey on the other.

During the preparatory state, however, such contacts shall be limited to relations between the European Parliament and the Turkish Parliament.

*Article 28*

As soon as the operation of this Agreement has advanced far enough to justify envisaging full acceptance by Turkey of the obligations arising out of the Treaty establishing the Community, the Contracting Parties shall examine the possibility of the accession of Turkey to the Community.

\*\*\*

# Document no. 37

**ECtHR: France, Norway, Denmark, Sweden and The Netherlands *v.* Turkey (1982) "friendly settlement" proceedings][3]**

This case, brought by the abovementioned five state parties to the European Convention on Human Rights, alleged that Turkey had violated the following provisions of the Convention between 12 September 1980 and 1 July 1982 when that country was under martial law.

- Article 3 by torturing detainees or subjecting them to inhuman or degrading treatment on a widespread scale;
- Articles 5 and 6 with regard to detention and criminal proceedings under martial law; and
- Articles 9, 10 and 11 with regard to restrictions on political parties, trades unions and the press.

The applicant governments also challenged Turkey's use of the derogation provision (Article 15) of the Convention, arguing that, whatever situation existed prior to 12 September 1980, a public emergency threatening the life of the nation did not exist in the country as of 1 July 1982. They further alleged that, in any case, the legislative and administrative measures and practices complained of went beyond what was strictly required by the exigencies of the situation. The applicants also submitted that, even if the derogation notice filed by Turkey was valid, it could not justify violations of Article 3 of the Convention. Finally, it was alleged that Turkey had not discharged her obligation to keep the Secretary General of the Council of Europe fully informed of the measures taken and the reasons therefore.

The Turkish government denied the allegations and maintained that it had validly exercised its right of derogation as a state of veiled war or public emergency existed which threatened the life of the nation during the period under question. It denied that an administrative practice of torture or ill-treatment of prisoners existed and submitted that the measures taken did not go beyond the exigencies of the situation.

The European Commission on Human Rights declared the complaints admissible on 6 December 1983 and initiated measures to see if a friendly settlement could be arrived at. This included a visit to Turkey by a delegation to gather first-hand information on the prevailing situation as it related to Turkey's obligations under the Convention. After further discussions and meetings between the various parties, a friendly settlement was announced on 5 and 6 December 1985.

The settlement included the following points:

1. A supervisory mechanism was to be set up to monitor progress on Turkey's compliance with Article 3, with the government being obliged to submit periodic reports to the Commission on the measures it had taken in domestic law to ensure such compliance. There would also be a continuing dialogue between the government and the Commission on the question of such compliance. A short final report on the implementation of this mechanism was to be made on or before 1 February 1987 by participants of the dialogue that would be made available to States party to the Convention;

2. The Turkish government was to continue its policy of progressive reduction of the geographic scope of martial law and to use martial law powers with the greatest restraint. Some of the laws restricting personal rights and freedoms had already been amended, having regard to Turkey's obligations under the Convention, and the government was to keep the Commission informed of further changes to be made "in the same spirit".

3. The Turkish government was to undertake a programme of granting amnesty, pardons or similar measures of leniency to those detained under martial law legislation. The Commission was to be kept informed of developments in this regard.

After some clarifications were made to the outline of the settlement submitted by the parties, the Commission approved it as a valid settlement made under Article 28(b) of the Convention.

# Document no. 38

**European Commission's 1989 opinion on Turkey's request for accession to the Community**[4]

*Introduction*

1. On 14 April 1987 the Turkish Government sent to the Community Turkey's application for accession to the Community on the basis of Article 237 of the EEC Treaty, Article 98 of the ECSC Treaty and Article 205 of the EAEC Treaty.

On 27 April of that year the Council took note of Turkey's application and asked the Commission for the Opinion required by the Treaties.

The Commission instructed its departments to gather all the information and documentation needed to assess the consequences and implications of Turkish accession. The results are contained in the report on the structure and development of the Turkish economy, which is annexed to this Opinion.

The conclusions drawn from that report and from an examination of the political situation in Turkey form the basis for the Opinion on Turkey's application for accession to the Community.

2. The implications of any position the Community adopts concerning a further enlargement of the Community of Twelve will be greater than those of the positions adopted with regard to previous applications for accession, on account both of new ambitions of European integration resulting from the Single Act and of the increased rights and obligations which now apply to the status of Member State.

This obliges the Commission to pursue its reflections on Turkey's application for accession in the broader context of a batch of actual or potential applications in respect of which the Community must adopt an overall strategy.

*I. General considerations*

3. Since its third enlargement and the entry into force of the Single Act, the Community has been in a state of flux. It has entered into a new stage in its development which, on account of the importance of the objectives at stake,

requires all its energy. Indeed, the success of this stage will make it possible subsequently to achieve European union, the ultimate objective of the Treaties.

The tasks involved are great and complex, since the completion of the single market must be accompanied by major progress, not only towards economic and monetary union but also towards political union, along the lines of the mission which the Community has given itself of reducing tensions and divisions in Europe.

4. The Community is progressing in accordance with the objectives of the Single Act on the road towards economic and monetary union and European union, is improving the operation of its institutions and is thereby reconciling enlargement and consolidation.

Only when it has carried out an objective assessment of the results achieved in this respect will the Community have at its disposal one component of the data on which it will be required to base its assessment of any further enlargement. There should be reservations about taking any premature step here as the consequences could be very serious for the Community.

This reason alone is sufficient for the Commission to consider that it would be unwise, with regard both to the candidate countries and to the Member States, to envisage the Community becoming involved in new accession negotiations before 1993 at the earliest, except in exceptional circumstances.

5. In order to make an informed decision on the opening of accession negotiations, the Community will have to engage in in-depth political consideration of the implications for the architecture of an enlarged Europe and the functioning of the Community. With the existing institutional mechanisms, such an enlargement would run the risk of weakening the Community's capacity to pursue the internal and external policies required for the very success of the Single Act. Thus the question will be whether the Community can adapt its institutional operation in such a way as to enable it to welcome within its fold new members without running the risk of weakening its management and decision-making capacity.

Thus complex and delicate deliberations will have to take place within the Community institutions. These deliberations would inevitably compete with the pursuit of the priority objectives of the Single Act, if an attempt were made to force the pace and rush matters.

Unless we enter into purely formal negotiations, the fundamental questions being held back for a later stage — an approach which the Commission would not recommend — the interests of all parties require us first to strive towards the implementation of the Single Act and to postpone until later a thoroughgoing debate on the case for the accession of the candidate countries.

The Community cannot, however, limit itself to such an attitude. The fact that negotiations cannot be opened at this stage should be accompanied by a set of proposals which would not mean that our partners must abandon their aim of accession and would offer them the possibility of entering into a new stage along the road of a closer association between their country and the Community.

## II. Opening of accession negotiations

6. The Commission believes that any decision to open negotiations with a particular country must be based on a strong conviction that a positive conclusion is possible, indeed probable, within a reasonable period. This presupposes first that the candidate country is considered capable, at the end of a traditional transitional period, of bearing all the constraints and disciplines now applying to Member States, since otherwise the further progress of the Community would be hampered, and second that the Community is in a position to cope with the problems which the integration, albeit progressive, of the candidate into the Community would raise.

In the particular case of Turkey, these two aspects are all the more significant in that Turkey is a large country — it has a greater geographical area and will eventually have bigger population than any Community Member State — and its general level of development is substantially lower than the European average.

7. Turkey's economic and political situation, as far as the Commission can evaluate it in the last quarter of 1989, does not convince it that the adjustment problems which would confront Turkey if it were to accede to the Community could be overcome in the medium term, despite the positive features of the recent developments in Turkey.

8. Economic context

\*\*\*

In spite of the progress achieved since 1980, there is still a substantial development gap between the Community and Turkey, such that a comparison of GDP [gross domestic product] per head reveals that purchasing power in Turkey is one-third of the Community average.

This gap, which does not seem likely to be reduced rapidly given the rapid population growth in Turkey and in spite of efforts to slow it down, is also reflected in the breakdown of employment — more than 50 per cent of the labour force is employed in agriculture — and the low level of productivity.

\*\*\*

These are the major questions raised by the economic situation and the structural data in connection with the prospect of Turkey acceding to the Community and with its capacity, within a short period, to face up to the constraints of the Community economy, made more severe by the implementation of the Single Act.

As long as these disparities continue to exist, there will be reason to fear that Turkey would experience serious difficulties in taking on the obligations resulting from the Community's economic and social policies.

\*\*\*

9. Political context. Since the military coup in 1980, Turkey has adopted a new constitution. The system set up by a series of reforms and on the occasion of, or following, various elections has resulted in a parliamentary democracy closer to Community models.

Public life is still marked, however, by the weight of legislation which, while containing provisions similar to those which prevail within the Community, has still to become open to the whole range of political forces in Turkey and to the trades unions.

Although there have been developments in recent years in the Human Rights situation and in respect for the identity of minorities, these have not yet reached the level required in a democracy.

Examination of the political aspects of the accession of Turkey would be incomplete if it did not consider the negative effects of the dispute between Turkey and one Member State of the Community, and also the situation in Cyprus, on which the European Council has just expressed its concern once again. At issue are the unity, independence, sovereignty and territorial integrity of Cyprus, in accordance with the relevant resolutions of the United Nations.

*III. Conclusions*

10. As stated in the general considerations, the Commission is of the opinion that it would be inappropriate for the Community — which is itself undergoing major changes while the whole of Europe is in a state of flux — to become involved in new accession negotiations at this stage.

11. Furthermore, the political and economic situation in Turkey leads the Commission to believe that it would not be useful to open accession negotiations with Turkey straight away.

12. The Commission does believe, however, that the Community should pursue its cooperation with Turkey, given that country's general opening towards Europe.

The Community has a fundamental interest in intensifying its relations with Turkey and helping it to complete as soon as possible its process of political and economic modernisation. Turkey, associated with the Community, is a large expanding country; it is also one of the Member States' partners in the Atlantic alliance, occupying a strategically important geopolitical position.

13. To contribute to the success of Turkey's modernisation efforts, the Commission recommends that the Community proposes to Turkey a series of substantial measures which, without casting doubt on its eligibility for membership of the Community, would enable both partners to enter now on the road towards increased interdependence and integration, in accordance with the political will shown at the time of the signing of the Ankara Treaty.

These measures will focus on the following four aspects corresponding to Turkey's aspirations and needs: completion of the Customs Union; the resumption and intensification of financial cooperation; the promotion of industrial and technological cooperation; and the strengthening of political and cultural links.

These measures should be situated in the framework of the Association Agreement which currently governs relations between Turkey and the Community.

13.1. The completion in 1995 of the Customs Union, in accordance with the provisions of the Agreement, would require the Community to review the arrangements for trade in Turkish textiles and agricultural products. It will have to involve the adoption by Turkey of the common policies essential for the proper operation of the Customs Union.

Progressive completion of the Customs Union will give the Community the opportunity to associate Turkey more closely with the operation of the single market, while taking into account the constraints imposed by the economic disparities between Turkey and the Community. This requires a strengthening of the machinery for agreeing concerted economic and social policies between the Turkish Government and the Community institutions.

13.2. Financial cooperation should be revitalised by releasing the resources of the fourth Financial Protocol. The Community should further reflect on the possibility of unilaterally granting loans pursuant to Article 18 of the Statute of the EIB [European Investment Bank] for the financing of infrastructure projects of interest to both Turkey and the Community.

13.3. Using the various means at its disposal, notably risk capital, the Community should encourage closer industrial cooperation and direct investment. Completion of the Customs Union should make an important contribution to the attainment of these goals.

In the same spirit the Community and Turkey should strengthen their cooperation in the field of science and technology. To this end the Community should offer to allow Turkey to participate, in line with its needs and resources, in Community research programmes.

13.4. The intensification of political links between the Community and Turkey, extending beyond the current framework of political dialogue, should be an objective. A further possibility might be ad hoc procedures intended to involve Turkey in discussions on issues which are of particular interest for Turkey and the Community or on which one of the parties has information of interest to the other.

It would also be appropriate to intensify the training and cultural links between the Community and Turkey, with a view to contributing to improved mutual understanding. To this end, Turkey could usefully be associated with certain Community programmes.

Taken together these actions, and the spirit in which they are implemented, will bear witness to the will of the two partners to build their future in common.

# Document no. 39

**The Council of Europe Parliamentary Assembly (PACE) Resolution 985 (1992) on the situation of Human Rights in Turkey[5]**

1. In its Resolution 860 (1986), the Assembly instructed its Political Affairs Committee and its Committee on Legal Affairs and Human Rights to continue following closely the developments in Turkey. They had been doing so since the military intervention of 12 September 1980.

2. As the political situation had stabilised after 1983 when Turkey returned to parliamentary democracy, the Assembly's committees concentrated their work on the Human Rights situation. Thus:

i. the Committee on Legal Affairs and Human Rights held hearings on trades union rights (Istanbul, 1986, and Paris, 1987) and on Human Rights in general (Paris, 1990);
ii. the committee also studied the reservations made by Turkey when accepting the right to individual petition under Article 25 of the European Convention on Human rights (January 1987);
iii. both committees held frequent internal discussions and their Rapporteurs visited Ankara, Diyarbakir and Istanbul in July 1991 and in April–May 1992.

3. On 24 April 1991, the Assembly adopted Recommendation 1151 on the reception and settlement of refugees in Turkey, as well as Recommendation 1150 and Order No. 460 on the situation of the Iraqi Kurdish population and other persecuted minorities. It instructed the Committee on Migration, Refugees and Demography, if necessary in cooperation with other committees concerned, to follow closely developments in the refugees' situation. However, these serious matters fall outside the scope of the present resolution.

4. There is no doubt that Turkey has made progress in improving the protection of fundamental rights and freedoms since the Assembly adopted Resolution 860 (1986). Thus, at an international level, Turkey:

i. has recognised the right to individual petition under Article 25 of the European Convention on Human Rights (declaration of January 1987, renewed in January 1990);
ii. was the first Council of Europe Member State to ratify the European Convention on the Prevention of Torture and Inhuman or Degrading Treatment or Punishment (February 1988);
iii. became a party to the United Nations Convention on Torture and Other Cruel, Inhuman or Degrading Treatment or Punishment (September 1989);
iv. ratified the European Social Charter (June 1989);
v. recognised the compulsory jurisdiction of the European Court of Human Rights (January 1990);
vi. signed the CSCE Paris Charter (November 1990).

5. At national level the Assembly welcomes the following legislative measures and decisions:

i. the abolition of the death penalty for thirteen crimes out of twenty-nine for which this penalty previously existed (November 1990);
ii. the commutation of all 258 death penalties pending into prison sentences of ten to twenty years (April 1991);
iii. the practice, followed since 1984, of not carrying out death penalties;
iv. the abrogation of martial law (1987);
v. the creation of a committee within the Grand National Assembly to examine allegations of Human Rights violations and to make proposals for amending existing legislation (December 1990);
vi. the repeal of Articles 141, 142 and 163 of the Penal Code (April 1991);
vii. the release of approximately 46,000 prisoners, hundreds of whom may be considered "political" (spring 1991);
viii. the abolition of the law restricting the use of languages other than Turkish (April 1991).

6. These international and national measures and decisions constitute substantial progress and the Assembly notes with great satisfaction that a large number of the recommendations it made in its Resolution 860 (1986) were put into effect. Thus the trials against the trade union confederation DISK and against the Turkish Peace Association ended with the acquittal of their leaders and clear court decisions, showing that these organisations were not unconstitutional nor had been engaging in illegal activities.

7. Furthermore, the Assembly welcomes the important reforms made to the code of criminal procedure, and the draft legislation submitted by the Turkish Government to Parliament on 26 April 1992, approved by the Grand National Assembly on 21 May 1992, but not yet signed by the President of the Republic, containing important draft amendments to the law on the establishment and criminal procedure of the State Security Courts, to the law on police duties and powers, as well as to the anti-terrorism legislation.

8. It further welcomes the assurances given by the Turkish Minister for Justice that the reports of the visits to Turkey of the European Committee for the Prevention of Torture and Inhuman or Degrading Treatment or Punishment, in September 1990 and in September–October 1991, will be made public although it is not compulsory.

9. However, despite the government's good intentions, very serious Human Rights violations, including torture and disappearances, continue to occur in Turkey.

10. Although the investments made in the region by the Turkish state have, for some years, been far greater than those made in other regions, the economic situation in southeast Turkey remains precarious. In addition the Assembly is deeply concerned about the escalation of violence in this region. It strongly condemns terrorist attacks, perpetrated mainly by the PKK (Kurdish Workers' Party), as well as certain actions by the security forces and recalls that, in a democratic state, any reply to terrorist provocation must remain within the rule of law.

11. The Assembly welcomes the very positive approach towards fundamental rights and freedoms in the declaration of the Government of Turkey, and encourages the fulfilment of its pledges.

12. Accordingly, the Assembly calls upon the Parliament and Government of Turkey:

i. to do whatever possible to prevent completely the use of torture and force, as the legislation adopted on 21 May 1992 by the Grand National Assembly leads the Assembly to hope;
ii. to amend the anti-terrorism legislation of 12 April 1991;
iii. to give due consideration to reports of Human Rights violations submitted by organisations such as bar associations, Human Rights associations and other national or international non-governmental organisations with recognised competence;
iv. to initiate, as in other democracies, public inquiries when particularly serious facts are alleged, and to accelerate ongoing inquiries and render their conclusions public;
v. to follow the examples of Austria, Denmark and the United Kingdom, in accordance with the statement made by the Ministry of Justice, and to make public, although it is not compulsory, the reports of the visits to Turkey of the European Committee for the Prevention of Torture and Inhuman or Degrading Treatment or Punishment;
vi. to proceed, as a matter of urgency, with the adoption of amendments to the Constitution, in particular those aimed at introducing democratic improvements in accordance with the standards of the Council of Europe;
vii. to accelerate the introduction of new legislation, based on an amended constitution, aimed at lifting existing restrictions on trades unions;
viii. to lift the reservations relating to the right of individual petition under Article 25 of the European Convention of Human Rights;

ix. to continue to improve the training of the police, and to improve the overall control of its activities, in particular at police stations;
x. to improve its control of its security forces.

13. The Assembly also calls upon the Parliament and government of Turkey, with regard to the situation in the southeastern provinces:

i. to lift the state of emergency;
ii. to withdraw the derogation under Article 15 of the European Convention on Human Rights;
iii. to respect fully the identity, freedoms and rights of the Kurdish population, including the use of Kurdish on radio and television;
iv. to initiate genuine political dialogue with those people who, considering themselves Kurds, wish to develop peacefully their ethnic, cultural and linguistic identity and obtain more political rights.

14. Finally, the Assembly appeals to Turkey (and to all those Council of Europe Member States which have not yet done so) to ratify the following protocols to the European Convention on Human Rights:

\*\*\*

# Document no. 40

## Public statement on Turkey by the Council of Europe European Committee for the Prevention of Torture (1992)[6]

### Introduction

1. The European Committee for the Prevention of Torture and Inhuman or Degrading Treatment or Punishment (CPT) has to date organised three visits to Turkey. The first two visits, carried out from 9 to 21 September 1990 and from 29 September to 7 October 1991, were of an ad hoc nature. They were visits which appeared to the Committee "to be required in the circumstances" (Article 7, paragraph 1, of the European Convention for the Prevention of Torture and Inhuman or Degrading Treatment or Punishment). The circumstances in question were essentially the considerable number of reports received by the Committee, from a variety of sources, containing allegations of torture or other forms of ill-treatment of persons deprived of their liberty in Turkey. The reports related in particular to persons held in police custody. The third visit took place from 22 November to 3 December 1992, and formed part of the CPT's programme of periodic visits for that year.

2. Throughout 1991 and 1992 an ongoing dialogue has been maintained between the Turkish authorities and the CPT on matters of concern, based on the reports drawn up by the Committee after its first and second visits and the reports provided by the Turkish authorities in response. This dialogue culminated in a number of meetings between the Turkish authorities and a delegation of the CPT held in Ankara from 22 to 24 September 1992.

Subsequently, at its fourteenth meeting (28 September to 2 October 1992), the CPT reviewed the action taken by the Turkish authorities upon the recommendations made by the Committee in its visit reports. The Committee concluded that the continuing failure of the Turkish authorities to improve the situation in the light of its recommendations concerning (i) the strengthening of legal safeguards against torture and other forms of ill-treatment in police (and gendarmerie) establishments and (ii) the activities of the anti-terror departments of the Ankara and Diyarbakir police, justified resort to Article 10, paragraph 2, of the Convention.

3. The Turkish authorities were informed of the conclusion reached by the CPT and, in accordance with the Convention, invited to make known their views. Those views were received on 16 November 1992. The CPT examined the views presented by the Turkish authorities at its fifteenth meeting, held from 14 to 17 December 1992; on the same occasion, the Committee considered the facts found by the delegation which carried out the periodic visit to Turkey in November/December 1992, in particular insofar as they related to matters of police and gendarmerie custody. By the required majority of two-thirds of its members, the Committee decided to make a public statement.

## *The ad hoc visits*

*a. First visit*

4. In the report drawn up following its first visit to Turkey in 1990, the CPT reached the conclusion that torture and other forms of severe ill-treatment were important characteristics of police custody in that country. More specifically, in the light of all the information gathered concerning the Anti-Terror Departments of the Ankara and Diyarbakir police, the CPT concluded that detectives in those departments frequently resorted to torture and/or other forms of severe ill-treatment, both physical and psychological, when holding and questioning suspects. A variety of elements led the Committee to those conclusions.

5. In the first place, the CPT was struck by the extremely large number of allegations of torture and other forms of ill-treatment by the police received in the course of the visit, the wide range of persons making those allegations, and their consistency as regards the particular types of torture and ill-treatment said to have been inflicted. It should be noted that the allegations emanated from persons suspected or convicted of offences under anti-terrorism provisions and from persons suspected or convicted of ordinary criminal offences. As regards the latter, the number of allegations was especially high among persons detained for drug-related offences, offences against property (burglary, robbery, theft) and sex offences. Concerning the types of ill-treatment involved, the following forms were alleged time and time again: suspension by the arms; suspension by the wrists, which were fastened behind the victim (so-called "Palestinian hanging", a technique apparently employed in particular in anti-terror departments); electric shocks to sensitive parts of the body (including the genitals); squeezing of the testicles; beating of the soles of the feet ("falaka"); hosing with pressurised cold water; incarceration for lengthy periods in very small, dark and unventilated cells; threats of torture or other forms of serious ill-treatment to the person detained or against others; severe psychological humiliation.

6. The CPT's medical findings must also be emphasised. Indeed, a considerable number of persons examined by doctors in the CPT's visiting delegation displayed physical marks or conditions consistent with their allegations of torture or ill-treatment by the police. The delegation also met several persons in police custody who, while not stating openly that they had been ill-treated, displayed

clear medical signs consistent with very recent torture or other severe ill-treatment of both a physical and psychological nature. Some specific cases were described in the Committee's report.

7. Other on-site observations in police establishments visited (relating in particular to the often extremely poor material conditions of detention, the interrogation facilities and the general attitude and demeanour of police officers) did nothing to reassure the CPT's delegation about the fate of persons taken into custody. The same can be said of the circumstances under which certain of the visits took place, in particular at Ankara police headquarters, where the delegation was subjected to a series of delays and diversions (and on several occasions given false information) and a number of detainees were removed in order to prevent the delegation from meeting them.

8. In its report the CPT recommended a series of measures to the Turkish authorities designed to combat the problem of torture and other forms of ill-treatment. These measures related in part to the introduction or reinforcement of formal safeguards against such methods (shortening of the maximum periods of custody by the police or gendarmerie; notification of a person's custody to his next of kin or a third party of his choice; access to a lawyer; medical examination of detained persons; a code of practice for the conduct of interrogations).

The Committee also placed considerable emphasis on the need for a major and sustained effort by the Turkish authorities in the areas of education on Human Rights matters and professional training for law enforcement officials. It is axiomatic that the best possible guarantee against ill-treatment of persons deprived of their liberty is for its use to be unequivocally rejected by such officials.

As for the anti-terror departments of the Ankara and Diyarbakir police, the Committee recommended that appropriate steps be taken immediately to remedy the situation identified in those services.

9. The implementation of these recommendations was the subject of numerous exchanges between the Turkish authorities and the CPT during 1991. However, by the time of the Committee's second visit, few tangible results had been achieved, with the exception of the drawing up and subsequent revision of regulations for the conduct of interrogations.

*b. Second visit*

10. In the course of its second visit to Turkey in the Autumn of 1991, the CPT found that no progress had been made in eliminating torture and ill-treatment by the police. Many persons alleged that they had received such treatment during the previous twelve months. The types of ill-treatment alleged remained much the same; however, an increasing number of allegations were heard of forcible penetration of bodily orifices with a stick or truncheon. Once again, a number of the persons who claimed to have been ill-treated were found, on medical examination, to display marks or conditions consistent with their allegations. The delegation also had access to a considerable number of reports

drawn up during the previous twelve months, at the end of periods of police custody, by doctors belonging to forensic institutes; many of them contained findings consistent with particular forms of torture or severe ill-treatment. As regards more specifically the anti-terror departments of the Ankara and Diyarbakir police, the only conclusion that could be reached in the light of all the information gathered was that torture and other forms of severe ill-treatment continued unabated in those services.

11. In the report on its second visit to Turkey, the CPT reiterated the previously made recommendations designed to prevent torture and other forms of ill-treatment. Further, the Committee recommended that a body composed of independent persons be set up immediately, with terms of reference to carry out a thorough investigation of the methods used by police officers of the anti-terror departments of the Ankara and Diyarbakir police when holding and questioning suspects. In the light of the information gathered in the course of the CPT's second visit, it was also pointed out that it would be appropriate for the terms of reference of that body to include the anti-terror department of the Istanbul police.

## *Review of action taken on the ad hoc visit reports*

12. One year after submission of the CPT's second report, at its meeting of September/October 1992, the Committee reviewed the action taken by the Turkish authorities upon all the recommendations set out in the reports drawn up after its two visits. It was noted that some progress had been made on certain issues. Measures of both a legal and practical nature had been taken in response to the CPT's recommendations on material conditions of detention in police and gendarmerie establishments. The dialogue between the Turkish authorities and the Committee on prison matters also appeared to be bearing fruit. However, implementation of the central recommendations concerning torture and other forms of ill-treatment in police establishments was clearly at a standstill.

13. Legislation going in the direction of the recommendations made by the CPT on the strengthening of legal safeguards against torture and other forms of ill-treatment had been approved by the Turkish Grand National Assembly on 21 May 1992. However, it was subsequently returned by the President of the Republic to the Assembly for reconsideration; and at the time of the Committee's review of the situation, the fate of that legislation was a matter of conjecture.

14. Further, no satisfactory action had been taken on the CPT's recommendation concerning the anti-terror departments of the Ankara and Diyarbakir police. The Human Rights Inquiry Commission of the Grand National Assembly — to which the task of carrying out the investigation recommended by the Committee was entrusted — had failed to act expeditiously. It was only on 29 June 1992 that the relevant Sub-Committee of the Commission visited Ankara police headquarters for the first time (apparently a second visit was carried out on 7 July 1992). Further, at the time of the meetings between the Turkish authorities and a delegation of the CPT held in Ankara towards the end of

September 1992, the Sub-Committee had still not apprised the Human Rights Inquiry Commission of its findings. Nor had the Sub-Committee carried out any visits to the anti-terror department of the Diyarbakir police (or for that matter the anti-terror department of the Istanbul police). Moreover, from the information provided to the CPT's delegation by a member of the Sub-Committee, it was clear that the visits carried out to the Ankara police headquarters had been of a quite perfunctory nature. Furthermore, it was also clear that the Sub-Committee possessed neither the powers nor the relevant professional competence necessary to carry out a "thorough investigation" as envisaged in the recommendation made by the CPT in its second report.

15. It should be added that, in the course of the abovementioned meetings in Ankara in September 1992, information received from officials of the Ministry of the Interior indicated that no credible action had been taken at the internal administrative level in response to the successive recommendations of the CPT concerning the anti-terror departments of the Ankara and Diyarbakir police. The only investigations instigated had been entrusted to the very police forces which the Committee had concluded were resorting to torture. Not surprisingly, they had led nowhere.

16. In short, more than two years after the CPT's first visit, very little had been achieved as regards the strengthening of legal safeguards against torture and ill-treatment and no concrete steps capable of remedying the situation found by the Committee in the anti-terror departments of the Ankara and Diyarbakir police had been taken. At the same time, the Committee continued to receive reports of torture and other forms of severe ill-treatment in those departments, as well as in many other police establishments in Turkey.

It was under those conditions that the CPT decided on 2 October 1992 to set in motion the procedure provided for in Article 10, paragraph 2, of the European Convention for the Prevention of Torture.

## *The periodic visit*

17. The information gathered in the course of the CPT's periodic visit to Turkey, from 22 November to 3 December 1992, shows that the problem of torture and other forms of ill-treatment of persons in police custody has not been resolved, despite the importance which had been attached to this subject by the present government when it came to power at the end of 1991. The Committee's delegation was inundated with allegations of such treatment, from both ordinary criminal suspects and persons detained under anti-terrorism provisions. Further, numerous persons examined by the delegation's doctors displayed marks or conditions consistent with their allegations.

18. By way of illustration, reference might be made to the following cases:

- several prisoners charged with offences against property, encountered in the reception unit of Bayrampasa Prison (Istanbul), who bore fresh haematomas consistent with their allegations that they had recently been subjected

to *falaka* and to beating on the palms of the hands and ventral face of the wrists;
- a prisoner charged with a drug-related offence being held for observation in a forensic section at Bakirköy Hospital (Istanbul) who had a fresh rounded mark on his penis (reddish-brown and slightly swollen edge, whitish centre without induration), consistent with his allegation that an electrode had been placed by the police on that part of his body some five days earlier in order to deliver electric shocks;
- a prisoner charged with smuggling who was examined at Adana prison and who displayed haematomas on the soles of his feet and a series of vertical violet stripes (ten centimetres long by two centimetres wide) across the upper part of his back, consistent with his allegation that he had recently been subjected to *falaka* and beaten on the back with a truncheon while in police custody.

19. Comparable cases in Ankara and Diyarbakir could also have been described, including those of persons who had been held by the anti-terror departments of the Ankara and Diyarbakir police (in particular, cases of motor paralysis of the arms and severe sensory loss consistent with allegations of suspension).

However, the CPT shall instead draw attention to highly incriminating material evidence found in police establishments in those cities.

20. Acting in each case on concordant information independently received from several different sources, the Committee's delegation carried out two impromptu visits to specific rooms situated on the top floors of both the Ankara police headquarters (new building) and the Diyarbakir police headquarters. The rooms in question were located within the areas occupied by the law and order departments, which deal with ordinary criminal suspects. In the room at the Ankara police headquarters, the delegation discovered a low stretcher-type bed equipped with eight straps (four each side), fitting perfectly the description of the item of furniture to which persons had said they were secured when electric shocks were administered to them. No credible explanation could be proffered for the presence of this bed in what was indicated by a sign as being an "interrogation room".

In Diyarbakir, the delegation found the equipment necessary for suspension by the arms in place and ready for use (i.e. a three metre long wooden beam which was mounted on heavily weighted filing cabinets on opposite sides of the room and fitted with a strap made of strong material securely bedded in the middle). On both occasions, the delegation's discoveries caused considerable consternation among police officers present; some expressed regret, others defiance.

### Conclusions based on the ad hoc and periodic visits

21. In the light of all the information at its disposal, the CPT can conclude only that the practice of torture and other forms of severe ill-treatment of persons in

police custody remains widespread in Turkey and that such methods are applied to both ordinary criminal suspects and persons held under anti-terrorism provisions. The words "persons in police custody" should be emphasised.

22. The Committee has heard very few allegations of ill-treatment by prison staff in the different prisons visited over the last two years, and practically none of torture. Certainly, there are problems which need to be addressed in Turkish prisons, but the phenomenon of torture is not one of them. As already indicated, the CPT's dialogue with the Turkish authorities on prison matters is on the whole progressing satisfactorily.

23. Further, in the course of its third visit to Turkey, the CPT visited the largest psychiatric establishment in the country, namely the Bakirköy Mental and Psychological Health Hospital. No allegations of torture or other forms of ill-treatment by hospital staff were heard by the Committee's delegation in the course of that visit; nor was any other evidence of such treatment found. In fact, the delegation was favourably impressed by staff–patient relations.

24. As for the gendarmerie (which is responsible for police functions in rural areas), the CPT has heard allegations that suspects are frequently handled roughly and on occasion even beaten by members of the gendarmerie, in particular when apprehended. Further, the CPT has reason to believe that, from time to time, ill-treatment occurs in the course of the transport of prisoners (which is another task performed by the gendarmerie). However, the CPT has heard fewer allegations — and found less medical evidence — of torture or other forms of premeditated severe ill-treatment by members of the gendarmerie.

25. To sum up, as far as the CPT can judge, the phenomenon of torture and other forms of ill-treatment of persons deprived of their liberty in Turkey concerns at the present time essentially the police (and to a lesser extent the gendarmerie). All the indications are that it is a deep-rooted problem.

## *Action required*

26. Action is required on several fronts if this problem is to be addressed effectively. Legal safeguards against torture and other forms of ill-treatment need to be reinforced and new safeguards introduced. At the same time, education on Human Rights matters and professional training for law enforcement officials must be intensified. In this respect, the recent arrangements to send some twenty Turkish police officers to various other European countries in order to study police methods there are to be welcomed, and the CPT trusts that they represent part of an ongoing process.

Furthermore, public prosecutors must react expeditiously and effectively when confronted with complaints of torture and ill-treatment. On this point, the recent annulment by the Constitutional Court of section 15(3) of the Law to Fight Terrorism of 12 April 1991 (which severely curtailed the possibilities for public prosecutors to proceed against police officers alleged to have ill-treated persons in the performance of duties relating to the suppression of terrorism) is a very positive development. In order to facilitate effective action by public prosecutors, the medical examinations of persons in police and gendarmerie custody carried out by the forensic institutes should be broadened in scope (medical certificates should contain a statement of allegations, a clinical description and the corresponding conclusions). Further, appropriate steps should be taken to guarantee the independence of both forensic institute doctors and other doctors who perform forensic tasks, as well as to provide such doctors with specialised training.

Proper managerial control and supervision of law enforcement officials must also be ensured, including through the institution of effective independent monitoring mechanisms possessing appropriate powers. Neither should the issue of the conditions of service of such officials be overlooked, as satisfactory conditions of service are indispensable to the development of a high-calibre police force.

Application of the recently drawn up custody regulations, which relate inter alia to material conditions of detention, must also be vigorously pursued throughout the whole of Turkey. Considerable progress in this area has been made in Ankara and Diyarbakir, in pursuance of the CPT's recommendations. However, the situation found recently at Adana police headquarters (in particular in the anti-terror department) suggests that, in other parts of the country, persons detained by the police or gendarmerie may still be held under totally unacceptable conditions.

27. Particular reference must be made to the recently adopted law amending some provisions of the Code of Criminal Procedure and of the law relating to the organisation and procedure of State Security Courts, which entered into force on 1 December 1992. This is a revised version of the text returned to the Grand National Assembly earlier in the year by the President of the Republic. The new law inter alia clarifies the existence of certain fundamental safeguards against ill-treatment, such as the right to have a relative notified of one's custody and the right of access to a lawyer (safeguards which had been provided for previously but which had been largely inoperative in practice), regulates in detail the mechanics of the interrogation process, introduces a right to apply to a judge for the immediate release of an apprehended person and shortens the maximum periods of police/gendarmerie custody. The introduction of these provisions is a most welcome step forward. However, it is a matter of great regret to the CPT that their application to offences within the jurisdiction of State Security Courts has been specifically excluded. Admittedly, the number of offences under the jurisdiction of such courts has also been reduced by the new law, but it remains considerable: crimes against the State; terrorist offences; drugs and arms-related offences, etc. ...

28. The CPT wishes to take this opportunity to underline that it abhors terrorism, a crime which is all the more despicable in a democratic country such as Turkey. The Committee also deplores illicit drugs and arms dealing. Further, it is fully conscious of the great difficulties facing security forces in their struggle against these destructive phenomena. Criminal activities of this kind rightly meet with a strong response from state institutions. However, under no circumstances must that response be allowed to degenerate into acts of torture or other

forms of ill-treatment by law enforcement officials. Such acts are both outrageous violations of Human Rights and fundamentally flawed methods of obtaining reliable evidence for combating crime. They are also degrading for the officials who inflict or authorise them. Worse still, they can ultimately undermine the very structure of a democratic State.

29. Unfortunately, Turkish law as it stands today does not offer adequate protection against the application of those methods to persons apprehended on suspicion of offences falling under the jurisdiction of State Security Courts; on the contrary, it facilitates the use of such methods. Suspects in relation to collectively committed crimes may be held for up to fifteen days by the police or gendarmerie (rising to thirty days in regions where a state of emergency has been declared), during which time they are routinely denied any contact with the outside world.

It is true that the provisions of section 13 of the new law, concerning prohibited interrogation procedures, apply also to persons suspected of offences under the jurisdiction of State Security Courts. However, it would be unwise to believe that these provisions alone will be able to stem torture and ill-treatment. The methods described in section 13 have been illegal for many years under Turkish law by virtue of the general prohibition of torture and ill-treatment in Article 17(3) of the Constitution. Further, the stipulation that statements made as a consequence of such methods shall not have the value of evidence is merely a welcome reaffirmation of a principle already recognised by the Turkish legal system.

In reality, the long periods of incommunicado custody allow time for physical marks caused by torture and ill-treatment to heal and fade; countless prisoners have described to CPT delegations the treatment techniques applied by police officers. It should also be noted that certain methods of torture commonly used do not leave physical marks, or will not if carried out expertly. Consequently, it shall often be difficult to demonstrate that a statement has been made as a consequence of ill-treatment. The same point applies to the admissibility of other evidence obtained as a result of ill-treatment (see section 24 of the new law).

30. The CPT does not contest that, exceptionally, specific legal procedures might be required in order to combat certain types of crime, in particular those of a terrorist nature. However, even taking into account the very difficult security conditions prevailing in several areas of Turkey, an incommunicado custody period of up to fifteen days, let alone thirty, is patently excessive; it is clear that a proper balance has not been struck between security considerations and the basic rights of detainees.

The CPT calls upon the Turkish government to take appropriate measures to reduce the maximum periods for which persons suspected of offences falling under the jurisdiction of State Security Courts can be held in police or gendarmerie custody, to clearly define the circumstances under which the right of such persons to notify their next of kin of their detention can be delayed and strictly limit in time the application of such a measure, and to guarantee to such persons, as from the outset of their custody, a right of access to an independent lawyer (though not necessarily their own lawyer) as well as to a doctor, other than one selected by the police.

31. As regards ordinary criminal suspects, the amendments introduced by the abovementioned law could deal a severe blow to the practice of torture and ill-treatment. However, much will depend on how the new provisions are applied in practice. This is a matter that the CPT intends to follow carefully in the coming months, in close cooperation with the Turkish authorities. Nevertheless, a number of points should be raised now.

32. The maximum period of police custody for collective crimes (three or more persons), although reduced, remains quite high — up to eight days at the request of a public prosecutor and by decision of a judge. In this regard, the CPT wishes to emphasise that, in the interests of the prevention of ill-treatment, it is essential that the person in custody be physically brought before the judge to whom the request for an extension of the custody period is submitted. The new law is not clear on this point.

33. Although the precise content of the right of access to a lawyer is impressive (see in particular sections 14, 15 and 20 of the law), a potential flaw lies in the fact that, with the exception of persons who are under the age of 18 or disabled, a lawyer will be appointed only if the person in custody so requests. A failsafe procedure will have to be found that ensures detainees are (as the law requires) informed of their right to appoint a lawyer and not subjected to pressure when considering the exercise of that right. The same point applies as regards the right of persons in custody to make known to a relative of their choice that they have been apprehended. Care will also have to be taken that the possibility offered to take a statement, in certain cases, in the absence of the lawyer appointed by the person detained is not abused.

34. Under the new provisions, public prosecutors are in an even better position to exercise considerable influence over the manner in which police officers perform their duties and, more specifically, treat persons in their custody. The CPT very much hopes that they will make effective use of the possibilities open to them, with a view to the prevention of ill-treatment.

35. The new law is silent on the question of the right of persons in police or gendarmerie custody to have access to a doctor. However, by a circular issued by the Ministry of the Interior on 21 September 1992, a right of access to a doctor in the form previously recommended by the CPT (i.e. a right for the detainee to be examined by a doctor chosen by him — if appropriate from among a list of doctors agreed with the relevant professional body — in addition to any examination carried out by a state-employed doctor) was recognised. The CPT welcomes this development, though the inclusion of this right in a law would be preferable. Previous circulars relating to important safeguards for detained persons have remained a dead letter.

36. Finally, it should be re-emphasised that the phenomenon of torture and other forms of ill-treatment by the police will not be eradicated by legislative fiat alone. It shall always be possible for the impact of legal provisions to be diminished by ever more expertly applied techniques of ill-treatment. Indeed, it can

legitimately be advanced that attacking the root of the problem of torture and ill-treatment involves not so much changing laws as transforming mentalities. This process is required not simply amongst police officers but throughout the criminal justice system.

37. The CPT is convinced that it would have been counterproductive from the standpoint of the protection of Human Rights for it to have refrained — as it was requested to do by the Turkish authorities — from making this public statement. The statement is issued in a constructive spirit. Far from creating an obstacle, it should facilitate the efforts of both parties — acting in cooperation — to strengthen the protection of persons deprived of their liberty from torture and inhuman or degrading treatment or punishment.

# Document no. 41

## [European Parliament] Resolution on the trial of members of the Turkish Grand National Assembly[7]

**The European Parliament**

\*\*\*

A. Whereas on 3 August 1994 the trial started of six Kurdish members of the Turkish Grand National Assembly, belonging to the DEP Party [Party of Democracy],

B. Whereas on 17 June 1994 the Ankara Constitutional Court declared unconstitutional the DEP Party, which has thirteen members in the National Assembly, in addition to the six members already in detention,

C. Whereas the six Members of Parliament, Mr Ahmet Türk, Mrs Leyla Zana, Mr Orhan Dogan, Mr Sirri Sakik, Mr Hatip Dicle and Mr Mahmut Alinak, are being accused of separatism and support for the terrorist organisation PKK; whereas these accusations are based on Article 125 of the Penal Code, for which the death sentence is mandatory,

D. Whereas the main accusation against these Members of Parliament is their defence of the interests of the Kurdish people in Turkey by public statements in the media and by contacts with representatives of international institutions, including the European Parliament and the Council of Europe,

E. Whereas the Constitutional Court decided, on 1 June 1994, the "closure" of the DEP as a party, outlawing by this decision the DEP and its Members of Parliament from that date,

\*\*\*

1. Denounces the whole trial against the six DEP members of the Turkish Grand National Assembly and the outlawing of the DEP Party as an attack on pluralist democracy in this country, and requests the immediate release of these Members of Parliament;

2. Insists that this trial should be seen to be absolutely fair and therefore urges the Turkish authorities to allow international observers to be present, including some appointed by the EU;

3. Resolves to freeze the EU–Turkey joint parliamentary committee pending the outcome of the trial;

4. Welcomes the Turkish Grand National Assembly's initiative to hold partial elections on 4 December 1994 and calls on the government to guarantee free and democratic elections;

5. Instructs its President to forward this resolution to the Council, the Commission, the Turkish Grand National Assembly, the Secretary General of the Council of Europe and the Secretary General of the United Nations.

# Document no. 42

**[European Parliament] Resolution on the trial of Turkish members of Kurdish origin of the Turkish Grand National Assembly**[8]

*The European Parliament*

A. Having regard to its resolutions of 10 March [OJ C 91, 3.28.1994, p. 213], 21 April [OJ C 128, 5.9.1994, p. 313] and 29 September 1994 [OJ C 305, 10.31.1994, p. 95] on the arrest and trial of Turkish MPs of Kurdish origin in Turkey,

B. Whereas Turkey is a member of the Council of Europe and has signed and ratified the European Convention on Human Rights (ECHR),

C. Whereas the eight MPs were arrested, imprisoned and convicted as a consequence of performing their parliamentary duties, representing an act of intimidation against all members of parliament and a flagrant breach of the ECHR,

D. Whereas on 8 December 1994 the State Security Court altered the charges, but nevertheless sentenced Mrs Leyla Zana, Mr Hatip Dicle, Mr Ahmet Turk, Mr Orhan Dogan and Mr Selim Sadak to fifteen years' imprisonment; Mr Sedat Yurtdas to seven years and six months' imprisonment; and Mr Sirri Sakik and Mr Mahmut Alinak to three years and six months' imprisonment,

E. Whereas Mrs Leyla Zana is suffering from a serious illness, and whereas her continued imprisonment, in insanitary conditions and with no medical care, is a major factor in the deterioration of her health and may be regarded as unacceptable treatment within the meaning of the ECHR,

F. Noting with alarm that a prison sentence of four years and a fine of two hundred million Turkish lira has been imposed on Mehdi Zana, apparently in connection with testimony given to the European Parliament's Sub-Committee on Human Rights in 1992, concerning Human Rights issues in southeastern Turkey,

G. Concerned that the chairmen of the Turkish Human Rights Foundation (which is subsidised from the Union's budget) and the Turkish Human Rights Association, who supported the MPs and condemned their trial, have been summoned to appear before the same court on 19 December 1994, charged with involvement in separatist activities,

H. Whereas the number of persons arrested and imprisoned in Turkey for expressing their political beliefs and support for trades unions is continually increasing,

I. Whereas the bomb attacks on the opposition newspaper "Özgür Ülke" killed three people and wounded several others and have made critical reporting extremely dangerous,

J. Whereas, as a result of the arbitrary dismissal of the Turkish MPs of Kurdish origin of the DEP, entire regions of southeastern Turkey are no longer represented in the Turkish Grand National Assembly; whereas the Assembly is therefore no longer representative of the whole country,

## *The European Parliament*

1. Condemns the fact that the parliamentary immunity of the victims of this political trial was withdrawn on the grounds of their opinions;

2. Condemns all the aspects of the trial, the verdict handed down against the eight members of the Turkish Grand National Assembly and the outlawing of their party, the DEP, as a persistent violation of the principles of Turkey's representative and pluralist democracy and of fundamental Human Rights;

3. Expresses its solidarity with the convicted MPs and calls for the verdict to be quashed, for the sentences handed down to be rescinded, for the MPs to be released and restored to their duties and for the decision to dissolve their party to be revoked;

4. Is horrified by the fact that Mr Faik Candan, one of the lawyers defending the Kurdish MPs and who disappeared on 3 December 1994, has been found dead in Ankara, his body riddled with bullets;

5. Resolves to maintain the suspension of the EU–Turkey Joint Parliamentary Committee until Turkey takes note of Parliament's demands; believes, however, that unofficial contacts with Turkish parliamentarians with democratic views should be continued;

6. Decides to submit to the Council a call for the immediate suspension of the talks on the establishment of a customs union between Turkey and the EU and, therefore, the postponement of the meeting scheduled for 19 December 1994;

7. Points out that the agreement on a customs union with Turkey is subject to the assent procedure;

8. Calls on the Council of Europe to urge Turkey to embark on a process of dialogue in order to seek a democratic solution to the legitimate aspirations of its fifteen million citizens of Kurdish origin, thereby removing a source of tension and conflict which is threatening peace and stability in the countries of the region and in Europe;

9. Calls on the Member States not to deport Kurdish refugees who have fled from Turkey;

10. Instructs its President to forward this resolution to the Council, the Commission, the governments of the Member States, the Turkish Grand National Assembly and the Turkish Government, the Council of Europe, the UN Secretary General and the Secretariat of the OSCE.

# 8 Customs Union decision and the first implications of the Human Rights problems

# Document no. 43

**[European Parliament] Resolution on the draft agreement on the conclusion of a customs union between the EU and Turkey**[1]

*The European Parliament*

- having regard to the Council and Commission statements of 14 February 1995 on the conclusion of a customs union between the European Union and Turkey,
- having regard to its resolution of 15 December 1994 on the trial of Turkish Members of Kurdish origin of the Turkish Grand National Assembly, and regretting that the Council has not taken this into account,
- having regard to the final negotiations between the Union and Turkey for the customs union which are supposed to be held at the time of the meeting of the General Affairs Council on 6 and 7 March 1995,

A. whereas the Turkish political parties have agreed to examine the modifications to be made to the Constitution, which may affect the very provisions that led to the trial of the parliamentarians,

B. whereas, however, the latest Amnesty International report, the Turkish Human Rights Association and the Human Rights Foundation all record a serious deterioration in the Human Rights situation in Turkey,

C. whereas, with regard to agreements with third countries, the conditionality clause on Human Rights is deemed important by all EU Institutions,

1. Believes that the Human Rights situation in Turkey is too serious to allow the formation of the proposed customs union at present;

2. Appeals to the Turkish government and to the Turkish Grand National Assembly to undertake a fundamental reform of its Constitution in order better to guarantee the protection of democracy and Human Rights in Turkey, and to contribute to a solution of the Cyprus problem;

3. Calls on the Commission to establish a system of interim reporting on the modifications currently being made to the Turkish Constitution and, more generally, on the measures taken and to be taken to strengthen the rule of law;

reminds the Commission and the Council that the planned agreement establishing a customs union between the European Union and Turkey must be submitted for Parliament's assent, which it intends to make conditional on the interim reports on progress made;

4. Instructs its President to forward this resolution to the Council and Commission and the Government and Grand National Assembly of Turkey.

# Document no. 44

**[European Parliament] Resolution on the visit of the troika to Ankara and the Turkish military intervention in northern Iraq**[2]

*The European Parliament*

- having regard to its previous resolutions on the violations of Human Rights by Turkey and on the condemnation of terrorist attacks by the PKK [Kurdish Workers' Party],
- having regard to its resolution of 16 February 1995 on the draft agreement on the conclusion of a customs union between the EU and Turkey[(1)],

A. gravely disturbed by the spread of the conflict between the Turkish State and the PKK terrorists to northern Iraq,

B. whereas northern Iraq has been declared a UN [United Nations]-protected zone,

C. appalled by the disproportionate size of this action, in which 35,000 Turkish troops, supported by fighter planes, tanks and other heavy weapons, launched an attack on Kurdish villages, killing over several hundred people and wounding and imprisoning innocent civilians,

D. whereas the large-scale nature of this operation and the absence of any time limit indicate that it is more than a simple exercise of the right of hot pursuit,

E. fearing for the safety of the thousands of Kurdish refugees who have sought safety either from the murderous repression of Saddam Hussein or from the savage fighting raging in southeast Turkey, and for the safety of all the inhabitants of the region,

F. noting that the presence of independent journalists and TV crews, which would have provided full, uncensored information for the international public, was prohibited,

G. noting that the operation has been partly carried out with heavy weapons originating from European Union Member States,

H. supporting the French Presidency's warnings to the Turkish government and the German government's decision to suspend financial credits for the purchase of warships by Turkey and further arms deliveries to Turkey,

I. whereas the state of Human Rights in Turkey is too grave to allow the establishment of the proposed customs union at present,

J. whereas the Kurdish problem cannot be solved by military means,

1. Strongly condemns Turkey's military intervention in northern Iraq and the resulting violation of international law and Human Rights;

2. Repeats its condemnation of terrorist acts by the PKK and warns the Turkish government that the continuation of the policy of repression against the reasonable aspirations of Kurds in Turkey is bound to strengthen the appeal of the PKK, whatever the success of Turkish military operations;

3. Urges Turkey to withdraw its troops from northern Iraq immediately and to seek a political solution to the tensions in its eastern provinces, whilst respecting the rules of international law;

4. Calls on the European Union and its Member States to assist the UNHCR [United Nations High Commissioner for Refugees] financially and technically in its efforts to succour the people threatened by this latest outburst of violence;

5. Urges the Member States not to extradite any Kurdish refugees while the present Turkish action against the Kurdish people continues, except for leaders of terrorist movements;

6. Calls on the Member States to follow Germany's example and make future military aid to Turkey conditional on Turkey withdrawing its troops;

7. Urges the Council and the Commission to draw up strict rules on the export of weapons in order to prevent weapons originating in European Union Member States from being used in the settlement of this and similar conflicts;

8. Calls for Red Cross representatives to be allowed to travel to northern Iraq in order to assist the civilian population, especially injured and imprisoned persons;

9. Recalls the terms of its abovementioned resolution of 16 February 1995;

10. Instructs its President to forward this resolution to the Council, the Commission, the Council of Europe, the OSCE [Organization for Security and Cooperation in Europe], the Secretary General of the UN, the UNHCR, the ICRC [International Committee of the Red Cross] and the governments of Turkey and Iraq.

# Document no. 45

**PACE [Council of Europe Parliamentary Assembly] recommendation 1266 (1995) on Turkey's military intervention in northern Iraq and on Turkey's respect of commitments concerning constitutional and legislative reforms[3]**

1. The Assembly is deeply concerned about Human Rights violations in Turkey — notably in the southeast of the country, following armed conflict between central government forces, the PKK and Kurdish nationalists.

2. The Assembly underlines the right of Turkey, as of any other country, to fight — within the limits of international law and in particular the European Convention on Human Rights — against terrorism.

3. The Assembly condemns PKK terrorism, as much within as outside Turkey.

4. The Assembly condemns Turkey's military intervention in northern Iraq, regards it as contrary to international law and expresses its anxiety for the safety of the civilian population, as well as that of the over 15,000 Turkish Kurd refugees who have fled the conflict in southeastern Turkey.

5. The Assembly asks Turkey to guarantee the fundamental rights of civilians, in particular those of the more vulnerable, that is to say children, women and old people.

6. The Assembly considers that Turkey should immediately withdraw its forces from northern Iraq and commit itself to seeking a peaceful solution to the Kurdish problem.

7. The Assembly expects the Turkish authorities to assist in the organisation of an Assembly fact-finding mission to areas of tension in the southeast as part of the effort to find such a solution.

8. The Assembly notes that despite repeated assurances from the Turkish government and despite repeated requests from the Assembly (notably following its delegation's visit from 1 to 3 September 1994), there has been no significant progress in constitutional and legislative reform.

9. In this latter regard, the Assembly strongly condemns the sentencing of several Kurdish parliamentarians to up to fifteen years' imprisonment for their political beliefs.

10. The Assembly considers that Turkey, in the light of the above facts, is in violation of its obligations under the Council of Europe's Statute.

11. Furthermore, the Assembly notes the European Parliament's position that the "state of Human Rights in Turkey is too grave to allow the establishment of a customs union".

12. The Assembly recommends that the Committee of Ministers:

i. call on Turkey to withdraw its forces from northern Iraq;
ii. call on Turkey to seek a peaceful solution to the Kurdish problem on the basis of the principles embodied in the Statute and the relevant conventions of the Council of Europe;
iii. set a specific timetable for Turkey to bring its Constitution and legislation in line with the principles and standards of the Council of Europe;
iv. consider suspending Turkey's rights of representation, unless the Committee of Ministers can report substantial progress on items i–iii above at the Assembly's third part-session (26–30 June 1995).

13. The members of the Parliamentary Assembly of the Council of Europe urgently ask their fellow parliamentarians, members of the Grand National Assembly of Turkey, to do their best by the earliest possible date to bring the Turkish Constitution and legislation into line with the principles and standards of the Council of Europe.

# Document no. 46

### ECtHR-Yagci and Sargin v. Turkey[4]

1. The case was referred to the Court by the European Commission of Human Rights ("the Commission") on 11 March 1994, within the three-month period laid down by Article 32 para. 1 and Article 47 (art. 32-1, art. 47) of the Convention. It originated in two applications (nos 16419/90 and 16426/90) against the Republic of Turkey lodged with the Commission under Article 25 (art. 25) by two Turkish nationals, Mr Nabi Yagci and Mr Nihat Sargin, on 6 February 1990.

The Commission's request referred to Articles 44 and 48 (art. 44, art. 48) and to the declaration whereby Turkey recognised the compulsory jurisdiction of the Court (Article 46) (art. 46). The object of the request was to obtain a decision as to whether the facts of the case disclosed a breach by the respondent State of its obligations under Articles 5 para. 3 and 6 para. 1 (art. 5-3, art. 6-1) of the Convention.

\*\*\*

[Mr Yagci, a journalist, and Mr Sargin, a doctor, were the general secretaries of the Turkish Workers' Party and the Turkish Communist Party, respectively. At a press conference in Brussels in October 1987, they announced their intention of returning to Turkey to found the Turkish United Communist Party (TBKP) and develop its organisation and political action while staying within the law. Upon arrival in Ankara on 16 November 1987, they were arrested as they alighted from the plane and were taken into police custody. On 4 December, the public prosecutor's office applied to the Ankara State Security Court (SSC) to have them placed in detention pending trial. On 5 December, a judge of that court made an order to that effect on the basis of strong evidence of guilt. He charged them with leading an organisation whose aim was to establish the domination of a particular social class, disseminating propaganda to that end, and with the intention of abolishing the rights guaranteed in the Constitution; inciting public hostility and hatred; and harming the reputation of the Republic of Turkey, its President, and its government. These offences also amounted to an attack on the government's authority and could be classified as serious crimes. On 10 December 1987, the applicants' counsel appealed against that decision, which was, however, unanimously upheld by the SSC on 16 December. On 11 March 1988, the public prosecutor's office brought proceedings against Mr Yagci, Mr Sargin and fourteen others. The trial opened on 8 June 1988, and forty-eight hearings were held. The first two hearings were taken up with a reading of the indictment, which ran to 229 pages. The court then devoted six hearings (from 4 July to 24 August 1988) to questioning the applicants and hearing their addresses. This process, taken together with the content of the file and the nature of the offences, was held by the court to justify keeping the defendants in detention. At the hearing on 29 August 1988, one of the counsels for the applicants made the first application for their provisional release. He put forward the following arguments: his clients had been in detention for nine and a half months, including the period spent in police custody, and, although the nature of the offences with which Mr Yagci and Mr Sargin were charged might have given rise to fears that they would abscond if released, that danger was ruled out in their case as they had publicly stated that they would be returning to Turkey to put their party on a lawful footing; and the differences of political opinion between the applicants and the regime in power could not be regarded as an attack on the authority of the government and the State. The court refused the application, holding that the reasons set out in the order of 5 December 1987 remained valid. On 21 September 1988, another of the applicants' representatives renewed the application, which was rejected by the court. On 14 October and 4 November 1988, the SSC ordered that Mr Yagci and Mr Sargin should be kept in detention, again on the basis of the file's contents. A fresh application for provisional release was lodged on 2 December 1988, by one of the applicants' lawyers, which was again dismissed. Identical applications from 30 December 1988, 27 January, 22 February, 24 March, 21 April and 18 May 1989 were similarly dismissed. In a further application for release made on 3 July 1989, relying on the Convention, the court again dismissed the application. Similar subsequent applications on 2 August, 25 August and 18 September 1989 were dismissed as well. On 18 October 1989, one of the applicants' lawyers raised in court the concept of "reasonable time" referred to in Article 5, paras 3 and 6, and Article 6, para. 1, of the Convention and asserted that the length of his clients' detention infringed those provisions. He challenged, in particular, the repetitiveness of the reasons advanced by the court for refusing their applications for release. The court ordered that detention should continue, again relying on the nature of the offences and the content of the file. Consequent applications on 17 November 1989, 15 December 1989 and 6 April 1990 were dismissed. Mr Yagci and Mr Sargin were eventually released provisionally on 4 May 1990, subject to the condition that they must not leave the country. On 11 September 1990, the court dismissed an application to defer judgment on the grounds that it would be advisable to await the outcome of proceedings pending before the Constitutional Court concerning the dissolution of the Turkish Communist Party. On 10 June 1991, following the entry into force of the Antiterrorist Act of 12 April 1991, which changed applicable law, the court decided to interrupt the reading out of the evidence relating to those provisions and to read out the evidence relating to the other charges. This process ended on 10 July during the forty-fifth hearing. On 26 July 1991, the prosecutor made his closing address, and on 9 and 26 August the applicants put forward their defence. On 9 October 1991, the SSC acquitted Mr Yagci and Mr Sargin on all the charges.]

\*\*\*

32. Mr Yagci and Mr Sargin applied to the Commission on 6 February 1990. They complained of the length of their detention pending trial (Article 5 para. 3 of the Convention) (art. 5-3) and of the criminal proceedings brought against them (Article 6 para. 1) (art. 6-1).

33. The Commission declared the applications (nos 16419/90 and 16426/90) admissible on 10 July 1991. In its report of 30 November 1993 (Article 31) (art. 31), it expressed the unanimous opinion that there had been a breach of those two provisions (art. 5-3, art. 6-1). The full text of the Commission's opinion is reproduced as an annex to this judgment.

\*\*\*

34. In their memorial the government asked the Court to "allow [their] preliminary objections both as regards the Court's jurisdiction and as regards the admissibility of the case before the Commission and the Court itself. In the alternative ... to hold that Article 5 para. 3 and Article 6 para. 1 (art. 5-3, art. 6-1) of the Convention ha[d] not been violated".

## AS TO THE LAW

*I. Introductory observation*

35. The government submitted that their arguments in the present case should be considered only if Turkey's recognition of the Court's compulsory jurisdiction were deemed valid in its entirety.

In the case of *Loizidou v. Turkey* the government contended that Turkey's declaration of 22 January 1990 under Article 46 (art. 46) of the Convention would not be valid if the Court held the limitation *ratione loci* it contained to be invalid. The Court, in its judgment of 23 March 1995, while holding the limitation in question invalid, ruled that the said declaration contained a valid acceptance of its competence (Series A no. 310, p. 32, para. 98).

*II. The government's preliminary objections*

36. As their main submission the government raised three objections to admissibility, based on lack of jurisdiction *ratione temporis*, failure to exhaust domestic remedies and loss of victim status.

264  *Customs Union decision*

1. LACK OF JURISDICTION *RATIONE TEMPORIS*

37. The government contended that when, on 22 January 1990, Turkey had recognised the Court's compulsory jurisdiction over "matters raised in respect of facts, including judgments which are based on such facts which have occurred subsequent to" that date, its intention had been to remove from the ambit of the Court's review events that had occurred before the date on which the declaration made under Article 46 (art. 46) of the Convention was deposited. Moreover, in the present case the Court's jurisdiction *ratione temporis* was also excluded in respect of facts subsequent to 22 January 1990, which by their nature were merely "extensions of ones occurring before that date".

38. Mr Yagci and Mr Sargin submitted that the Court, in the same way as the Commission, had jurisdiction to deal with the case from the time it began, namely 16 November 1987, when they were arrested. Any other solution would result in different treatment of the same facts by the two Convention institutions.

39. The Delegate of the Commission argued that, even if the Court held that it had jurisdiction from 22 January 1990, it would have to take into consideration the fact that on that date the applicants had been in detention pending trial, in connection with criminal proceedings, for more than two years and two months.

40. Having regard to the wording of the declaration Turkey made under Article 46 (art. 46) of the Convention, the Court considers that it cannot entertain complaints about events which occurred before 22 January 1990 and that its jurisdiction *ratione temporis* covers only the period after that date. However, when examining the complaints relating to Article 5 para. 3 and Article 6 para. 1 (art. 5-3, art. 6-1) of the Convention, it will take account of the state of the proceedings at the time when the abovementioned declaration was deposited (see, among other authorities and *mutatis mutandis*, the *Neumeister v. Austria* judgment of 27 June 1968, Series A no. 8, p. 38, para. 7, and the *Baggetta v. Italy* judgment of 25 June 1987, Series A no. 119, p. 32, para. 20).

It therefore cannot accept the government's argument that even facts subsequent to 22 January 1990 are excluded from its jurisdiction where they are merely extensions of an already existing situation. From the critical date onwards all the State's acts and omissions not only must conform to the Convention but are also undoubtedly subject to review by the Convention institutions.

\*\*\*

[The ECtHR then found that the non-exhaustion of domestic remedies defence and loss of victim status defence were unfounded and proceeded to discuss the alleged violation of Article 5, para. 3, of the Convention.]

47. Mr Yagci and Mr Sargin complained of the length of their detention pending trial. They considered it contrary to Article 5 para. 3 (art. 5–3) of the Convention, which provides:

Everyone arrested or detained in accordance with the provisions of paragraph 1 (c) of this Article (art. 5-1-c) shall be ... entitled to trial within a reasonable time or to release pending trial. Release may be conditioned by guarantees to appear for trial.

48. The government contested this view, in the alternative, whereas the Commission accepted it.

A. Period to be taken into consideration

49. [T]he Court can only consider the period of three months and twelve days which elapsed between 22 January 1990, when the declaration whereby Turkey recognised the Court's compulsory jurisdiction was deposited, and 4 May 1990, when the applicants were provisionally released (see paragraph 23 above). However, when determining whether the applicants' continued detention after 22 January 1990 was justified under Article 5 para. 3 (art. 5-3) of the Convention, it must take into account the fact that by that date the applicants, having been placed in detention on 16 November 1987 (see paragraph 8 above), had already been in custody for two years and two months.

B. Reasonableness of the length of detention

50. It falls in the first place to the national judicial authorities to ensure that, in a given case, the detention of an accused person pending trial does not exceed a reasonable time. To this end they must examine all the facts arguing for or against the existence of a genuine requirement of public interest justifying, with due regard to the principle of presumption of innocence, a departure from the rule of respect for individual liberty and set them out in their decisions on the applications for release. It is essentially on the basis of the reasons given in these decisions and of the true facts mentioned by the applicant in his appeals, that the Court is called upon to decide whether or not there has been a violation of Article 5 para. 3 (art. 5-3) of the Convention (see, among other authorities, the *Letellier v. France* judgment of 26 June 1991, Series A no. 207, p. 18, para. 35).

The persistence of reasonable suspicion that the person arrested has committed an offence is a condition *sine qua non* for the validity of the continued detention, but, after a certain lapse of time, it no longer suffices; the Court must then establish whether the other grounds cited by the judicial authorities continue to justify the deprivation of liberty (ibid. and see the *Wemhoff v. Germany* judgment of 27 June 1968, Series A no. 7, pp. 24–25, para. 12, and the *Ringeisen v. Austria* judgment of 16 July 1971, Series A no. 13, p. 42, para. 104).

Where such grounds are "relevant" and "sufficient", the Court must also ascertain whether the competent national authorities displayed "special diligence" in the conduct of the proceedings (see the *Matznetter v. Austria* judgment of 10 November 1969, Series A no. 10, p. 34, para. 12; the *B. v. Austria* judgment of 28 March 1990, Series A no. 175, p. 16, para. 42; and the Letellier judgment previously cited, p. 18, para. 35).

51. During the period covered by the Court's jurisdiction *ratione temporis* the Ankara National Security Court (SSC) considered the question of the

applicants' continued detention on three occasions — on 8 February and 9 March 1990 of its own motion and on 6 April on an application by the applicants . . . .

As grounds for refusing to release Mr Yagci and Mr Sargin it cited the nature of the offences (classified as serious crimes, they gave rise in law to a presumption that there was a risk that the accused would abscond), "the state of the evidence" and the date of arrest, namely 16 November 1987 . . . .

In the government's submission, the applicants were kept in detention for as long as was necessary to prevent them from absconding.

52. The Court points out that the danger of an accused's absconding cannot be gauged solely on the basis of the severity of the sentence risked. It must be assessed with reference to a number of other relevant factors which may either confirm the existence of a danger of absconding or make it appear so slight that it cannot justify detention pending trial (see, *mutates mutandis*, the Letellier judgment previously cited, p. 19, para. 43).

Mr Yagci and Mr Sargin had returned to Turkey of their own accord and with the specific aim of founding the Turkish United Communist Party (see paragraphs 7 and 13 above) and they could not be unaware that they would be prosecuted for this.

The SSC's orders confirming detention nearly always used an identical, not to say stereotyped, form of words, without in any way explaining why there was a danger of absconding.

53. The expression "the state of the evidence" could be understood to mean the existence and persistence of serious indications of guilt. Although in general these may be relevant factors, in the present case they cannot on their own justify the continuation of the detention complained of (see the *Kemmache v. France* (nos 1 and 2) judgment of 27 November 1991, Series A no. 218, p. 24, para. 50).

54. The third reason put forward by the SSC, namely the date of the applicants' arrest, does not stand up to scrutiny either, since no total period of detention is justified in itself, without there being relevant grounds under the Convention.

55. In the light of these considerations, the Court holds that the applicants' continued detention during the period in question contravened Article 5 para. 3 (art. 5–3).

That conclusion makes it unnecessary to look at the way in which the judicial authorities conducted the case.

[The ECtHR then found that the length of the criminal proceedings in question contravened Article 6, para. 1, and obliged Turkey to pay each of the applicants non-pecuniary damages and costs.]

*Editors' comment*: In 1995, the ECtHR decided in a similar case, *Mansur v. Turkey*,[5] that the detention period had breached Article 5, para. 3, and Article 6, para. 1, of the European Convention and obliged Turkey to pay non-pecuniary damages and costs. In *Mansur*, Mr Mansur, who was of Iranian origin, had acquired

Turkish nationality by naturalisation on 5 May 1989. He was sentenced to four years' imprisonment for drug trafficking between Greece and Turkey on 12 June 1981, by a court in Greece. Three years later, in respect of the same facts, two sets of criminal proceedings were brought against the applicant in the First and Second Assize Courts at Edirne (Turkey). He was arrested on 1 November 1984 in Istanbul and was placed in detention pending trial. The trials were conducted concurrently until 6 May 1987, when the Second Assize Court realised that the subject matter of the two cases was identical and relinquished jurisdiction in favour of the First Assize Court. His detention, which started on 5 November 1984, finally ended on 1 July 1991. During the trial, Turkish courts continuously rejected his applications for release and held him in detention pending trial.

# Document no. 47

**The Bill pertaining to amending the Preamble and some of the Articles of the Constitution of the Republic of Turkey, 23 July 1995[6]**

*Article 1:* The PREAMBLE of the Constitution of the Republic of Turkey dated 7.11.1982 No. 2709 has been amended as follows:

## Preamble

In parallel with the concept of nationalism and the reforms and principles set forth by the founder of the Republic of Turkey Atatürk, the immortal leader and the unrivalled hero, this Constitution, which determines the everlasting existence of the Turkish nation and country and the indivisible unity of the Turkish State, embodies;

The determination to ensure the everlasting existence, welfare, material and spiritual well-being of the Republic of Turkey as an honourable member with equal rights of the family of world nations and to attain the standards of contemporary civilisation for the Republic of Turkey;

The understanding of the absolute supremacy of national will and of the full and unconditional vestiture of sovereignty in the Turkish Nation and that no person or institution vested with the power of exercising this sovereignty in the name of the Nation shall exceed the boundaries of liberal democracy and the legal system determined by its requirements;

The principle of the separation of powers, which does not mean a hierarchical ordering of the state organs but refers solely to the exercising of certain State authorities and duties, which is limited to cooperation and the division of functions, and which accepts the supremacy of the Constitution and the law;

The principle that no idea or opinion contrary to Turkish national interests, the principle of the indivisibility of the Turkish entity with its State and country, the Turkish historical and spiritual values, nationalism, the principles and reforms and modernisation concepts set forth by Atatürk shall be supported, and that, as it is required by the principle of secularism, the sacred tenets of religion shall in no way be involved in the affairs of the State and in politics;

The birthright of every Turkish citizen to exercise the fundamental rights and freedoms set forth by this Constitution according to the requirements of equality and social justice, in order to lead a dignified life in a civilised and legal system as well as the right and authority to develop one's material and spiritual being towards this end;

The principle of sharing by Turkish citizens as a whole of national pride and honour, of national joy and grief of rights and duties concerning national entity, of benefits and burdens and of all of the manifestations of living as a nation, and the right to demand a peaceful life with absolute respect for each other's rights and duties, with mutual feelings of affection and fraternity, and with the wish and belief in "peace at home, peace in the world."

This Constitution which contains the abovementioned IDEAS, BELIEFS, AND DETERMINATION and which is to be interpreted and implemented accordingly with respect for and absolute loyalty to its letter and spirit, is entrusted BY THE TURKISH NATION to the patriotism and nationalism of its democracy-loving sons and daughters.

*Article 2:* The fourth and fifth paragraphs of Article 33 of the Constitution of the Republic of Turkey dated 7.11.1982, No. 2709, have been repealed; the sixth, seventh and eighth paragraphs have been amended as follows:

> Associations may be dissolved or hindered from executing their activities by a decision of a judge in cases prescribed by law. In cases where any delay may endanger national security or public order and in cases where it is necessary to prevent the continuation of a crime or to stop a crime, an authority may be vested with the power of the law to suspend the association from its activity. The decision of the said authority shall be presented for approval to the judge in charge within twenty-four hours. Unless the judge declares a decision within seven days, this administrative decision shall be annulled automatically.

Provisions of the first paragraph shall not prevent the imposition of legal restrictions on the rights of the Armed Forces and Security Forces and on civil servants as required by their duties.

The provisions of this Article are also applicable to foundations.

*Article 3:* Article 52 of the Constitution of the Republic of Turkey dated 7.11.1982, No. 2709, has been repealed.

*Article 4:* The following paragraph is included between the second and third paragraphs of Article 53 of the Constitution of the Republic of Turkey dated 7.11.1982, No. 2709:

> The unions and their higher organizations, which will be established by the public employees mentioned in the first paragraph of Article 128 and which do not fall under the scope of the first and second paragraphs of Article 53 and also Article 54 overall, may appeal to judicial authorities on behalf of their members and may hold collective bargaining meetings with the

Administration in accordance with their aims. If an agreement is reached as to the result of the collective bargaining, a text of the agreement will be signed by the parties. Such a text will be presented to the Council of Ministers in order to make administrative or judicial alignments. If such a text is not signed as a result of the collective bargaining, the points of agreement and disagreement will also be presented for evaluation to the Council of Ministers by the relative parties. The regulations for the execution of this article is stipulated by law.

*Article 5:* 1. Paragraphs 2 and 3 of Article 67 of the Constitution of the Republic of Turkey dated 7.11.1982, No. 2709, have been amended as follows:

Elections and referenda shall be held under the direction and supervision of the judiciary, in accordance with the principles of free, equal, secret, and direct voting, universal suffrage, public counting and tally of the votes. However, special legal arrangements will determine the provisions to enable those Turkish citizens who are abroad to exercise their right to vote.

All Turkish citizens over the age of eighteen shall have the right to vote in elections and to take part in referenda.

2. The fifth paragraph of the same Article has been amended as follows:

Privates and corporals serving in the Armed Services, students in military schools, and convicts in penal execution institutions cannot vote. The Supreme Election Board shall determine the measures to be taken to ensure the security of the counting and tallying of votes when detainees in penal execution institutions or prisons exercise their right to vote; such voting is done under the on-site direction and supervision of an authorised judge.

3. The following paragraph has been added as paragraph 6 to the same Article:

The laws about elections shall be drawn in accordance with the principles of fair representation and consistency in administration.

*Article 6:* Article 68 of the Constitution of the Republic of Turkey dated 7.11.1982, No. 2709, has been amended as follows:
A. Forming parties, becoming a member in and resignation from membership in a party

*Article 68*: Citizens are free to form political parties in accordance with the law and become a member of and withdraw from a party. One must be over eighteen years of age to become a member of a party.

Political parties are an inevitable element of political life.

Political parties are formed without prior permission and continue their activities in accordance with the Constitution and legal provisions.

The statutes and programmes, as well as the activities of political parties shall not be in conflict with the independence of the State, its indivisible integrity with its country and Nation, Human Rights, the principles of equality and rule of law of the State, sovereignty of the nation, the principles of a democratic and secular Republic; they shall not aim to protect nor establish any class or group dictatorship or any kind of dictatorship; they shall not encourage committing a crime.

Judges and prosecutors, members of higher judicial organs including the Court of Accounts employees in public institutions and organisations who have civil servant status, other public employees who are not considered to be labourers by virtue of the services they perform, members of the armed forces and students who are not yet in higher education institutions, cannot become members of political parties.

The membership of the members of the Higher Education Institutions in political parties is regulated by law. The said law does not allow those members to assume responsibilities outside of the central organs of the political parties and sets the regulations by which those members of the Higher Education Institutions must abide as members of political parties.

The principles and limitations concerning the membership of students at higher education institutions are regulated by law.

The State gives financial support to political parties in sufficient amounts and in an equitable manner. The aid given to political parties, monthly dues collected from members and donations are regulated by law.

*Article 7:* Article 69 of the Constitution of the Republic of Turkey dated 7.11.1982 No. 2709, has been amended as follows:

B. Principles to be observed by political parties

*Article 69:* The activities, internal regulations and operation of political parties shall be in accordance with democratic principles. The application of these principles is regulated by law.

Political parties shall not engage in commercial activities.

The incomes and expenditures of political parties shall be in accordance with their objectives. The application of this rule is regulated by law. Laws regulate the supervision of the receipts and acquisitions of political parties, the establishment of the legality of their incomes and expenditures by the Constitutional Court, the supervision methods of compliance to these principles and the sanctions to be enforced in case of infractions. The Constitutional Court may work in cooperation with the Court of Accounts in carrying out this supervisory duty. The decisions taken by the Constitutional Court as a result of the said supervision shall be final.

The decisions concerning the dissolution of political parties shall be taken by the Constitutional Court in the form of final decisions, as a result of lawsuits initiated by the Attorney-General of the Supreme Court of Appeals.

The decision to dissolve a political party permanently shall be taken when it is established that the statutes and programme of the political party violate the provisions of the fourth paragraph of Article 68.

The decision to dissolve a political party permanently due to activities violating the provisions of the fourth paragraph of Article 68 may be taken only when the Constitutional Court determines that the party in question has become a centre for the execution of such activities.

A party which has been dissolved permanently cannot be founded under another name. The members, including the founders, of a political party whose acts or statements have caused the party to be dissolved permanently cannot be founders, members, directors or supervisors in any other party for a period of five years starting on the date of publication in the Official Gazette of the Constitutional Court's final decision and its justification for permanently dissolving the party. Political parties which take financial aid from Foreign States, international institutions and persons and corporate bodies shall be dissolved permanently.

The foundation and activities of political parties, their supervision and dissolution, as well as the election expenditures and election methods of political parties and candidates, are regulated by law in accordance with the above mentioned principles. ***

*Article 9:* Article 84 of the Constitution of the Republic of Turkey dated 7.11.1982, No. 2709, has been amended as follows:

5. Loss of membership

*Article 84:* The loss of membership of a deputy who has resigned shall be decided upon by the General Council of the Turkish Grand National Assembly after the Council of the Chairman of the Turkish Grand National Assembly determines the validity of the resignation.

The loss of membership caused by a final judicial sentence or deprivation of legal capacity shall be realised after the final court decision on this issue is communicated to the General Council.

The loss of membership of a deputy who insists on holding a position or continues an activity incompatible with membership according to Article 82 shall be decided by secret voting by the General Council, upon the submission of a report drawn by the authorised commission which determines the said situation.

The loss of membership of a deputy who fails to attend, without an excuse or permission, five meetings in a period of one month shall be decided by the absolute majority of the full members of the General Council after the Council of the Chairman of the Assembly determines the said situation.

The membership of deputies who, according to the final decision of the Constitutional Court concerning the permanent dissolution of a political party, have caused the permanent dissolution of their party by their acts and statements shall terminate on the day the said decision and its justifications are published in the Official Gazette. The Presidency of the Turkish Grand National Assembly shall immediately take the necessary actions concerning such a decision and shall inform the General Council.

*Article 10:* Article 85 of the Constitution of the Republic of Turkey dated 7.11.1982, No. 2709, has been amended as follows:

6. Annulment procedures

*Article 85:* If the parliamentary immunity of a deputy has been waived or if the loss of membership has been decided according to the first, third or fourth paragraph of Article 84, the deputy in question or another deputy may appeal to the Constitutional Court within seven days, starting on the day the General Council of the Assembly took the decision, for the decision to be annulled on the grounds that it is contrary to the Constitution, law or the rules of procedure of the Assembly. Unless the Constitutional Court takes a final decision on the appeal within fifteen days, the decision of the Assembly does not come into force.

\*\*\*

*Article 14:* The following sentence has been added to the last paragraph of Article 149 of the Constitution of the Republic of Turkey dated 7.11.1982, No. 2709:

> ... and, in lawsuits on whether to permanently dissolve a political party or not, the Constitutional Court shall hear the defence of the head of the party the dissolution of which is in question or of a proxy appointed by the head, after the Attorney-General of the Supreme Court of Appeals.

\*\*\*

# Document no. 48

### Amendment to Article 8 of the Turkish Anti-Terrorism Law[7]

*Article 1:* Article 8 of the Anti-Terrorism Law, No: 3713, has been amended as follows:

No one shall make written and oral propaganda or hold assemblies, demonstrations and manifestations against the indivisible integrity of the State of the Turkish republic with its land and nation. Those carrying out such an activity shall be sentenced to imprisonment from one to three years and to heavy fine from one hundred to three hundred million Turkish lira. In case of re-occurrence of this offence, sentences shall not be commuted to fines.

If such propaganda stated in the first paragraph is carried out by means of publications specified in Article 3 of Press Law No. 5680 which are issued more often than monthly period, owners of such publications in question shall be sentenced to heavy fine of an amount equivalent to 90 per cent of the amount of the average sale of the said publication in one month before the occurrence of the crime. However, this fine shall not be less than one hundred million Turkish lira. The legally responsible directors of these publications shall be fined half of the amount which the owner is fined and sentenced to imprisonment from six months to two years.

If such propaganda stated in the first paragraph is carried out through written publications and mass media organs other than the publications specified in the second paragraph, the legally responsibles [editors] [sic] and the owners of the mass media organs concerned shall be sentenced to imprisonment from six months to two years and fined from one hundred to three hundred million Turkish lira. Furthermore, in case such an act of propaganda is carried out via radio and TV channels transmission of the channel in question shall be suspended from one to fifteen days.

If acts specified in the first paragraph are carried out through mass media organs specified in the second and third paragraphs, the sentence shall be increased by between one third and a half.

*Article 2:* The following paragraph has been added to Article 13 of the Anti-Terrorism Law [non-commutability and non-convertibility of sentences to a fine or other measures, and non-suspension of the punishment given], No: 3713:

However, this article does not apply to sentences given under Article 8.
Article 13.

*Temporary Article:* Within a month after this law enters into force, files of those sentenced according to Article 8 of the Anti-Terrorism Law, No: 3713, shall be re-examined by the court which initially decided on the case. The re-examining court shall make the appropriate re-determination on the sentencing periods and whether Articles 4 and 5 of Law No. 647 of 13 July 1965 [commuting or converting sentences to fines or other measures and suspension of sentences] apply.

\*\*\*

*Grounds for the article* (summary from the Ministry of Foreign Affairs web page)

Restrictions on basic rights and freedoms in the 1982 Constitution were derived from the European Convention on Human Rights.

The restrictions on freedom of expression and dissemination of thought with a view to protecting the indivisible integrity of the State together with the country and the nation are set out in our Penal Code.

This code describes those forms of expression of thought which are forbidden as "incitements to crime". Actually, what is prohibited is the expression of thought favouring to commit acts which constitute offences under the law and which could severely damage the social order in various ways.

The basic provision to this effect is contained in Article 311 of the Penal Code, which says: "Anyone who openly incites the commission of a crime ... shall be punished." Article 312 provides that "Anyone who provokes the public into disobedience against law or openly praises or affirms an act that is stipulated as offence by law" will be punished. Paragraph 2 of Article 312 points out that anyone who provokes by way of inciting the public and foments social hatred and enmity between "classes, races, religions, sects, or regions" will be subject to punishment.

In these paragraphs, incitement means the possibility of causing others to commit an act. If the idea expressed or words spoken are incitement to or encouragement of the commission of crime, then this constitutes "provocation", and as such lies outside the limits of freedom of expression.

Undoubtedly, the expression of thought is not a crime. It would be contrary to the freedom of thought, thus to the whole idea of liberal democracy, to consider the expression of an idea, thought or opinion as an offence. But if an idea has the characteristic, because of the fashion in which it is expressed, of inciting people to act against the existence of the State and to endanger the social order, then that idea, because of the fashion in which it is expressed, is accepted as amounting to a crime. In fact, inherent to this conclusion is the general recognition that democracies have the right to defend themselves against threats to their existence and that this constitutes legitimate self-defence.

Propaganda, as referred to in the article, needs to be assessed in this context.

Democratic States regard the freedom of propaganda as legitimate, so long as this freedom is not used for incitement, provocation, encouragement of the commission of crime, overthrowing the liberal political order; destroying the rights and freedoms of others; handing over part of the territory of the State to foreign rule, or dividing the nation.

Whether or not the way of expression of thought or opinion creates a clear and immediate threat to the society, State, regime and social order and whether or not it orientates persons towards acts against laws are important points in evaluating propaganda as a crime in this context.

Therefore, the prohibition of propaganda, which aims at the disruption of indivisible integrity of the State together with the homeland and the nation as mentioned in Article 8, does not vitiate by itself the democratic characteristics of our State.

On the other hand, the first paragraph of Article 8 as currently in force has been responsible for a good deal of debate and criticism nationally and internationally. This paragraph states that "irrespective of the method, objective or thought behind it, any form of written and oral propaganda aimed at disrupting the indivisible integrity of the Republic of Turkey" is ambiguous. In fact the wording of the Article is so general that it makes it possible for the Article to include anything as propaganda. Thus it permits excessive restrictions on freedom of expression which are incompatible with the requirements of a democratic society.

In view of the practical problems currently experienced in connection with freedom of thought and expression and the international agreements to which our State is a party, it is necessary to revise the existing Article 8.

The revision made in the article removes the wording in the first paragraph which created the ambiguity: "Whatever method, objective and thought". .... In making this revision, we aim to create the circumstances which will be conducive to the free expression of thought, thus meeting the standards of western democracies. In addition, lowering the minimum prison term from two years to one enables the courts to suspend sentences or commute them to fines, by virtue of a new clause added to Article 13.

In Article 13 of Law No. 3713, it was stated that all offences contained in the aforementioned law may not be commuted to fines or other measures.

The seriousness of terrorist crimes for the society as a whole was considered not to justify the conversion of sentences of imprisonment into fines or other penalties.

However, as a result of the amendment to Article 8, this prohibition is to be lifted as far as propaganda crimes are concerned. This will be in line with trends in modern enforcement and penal laws which take account of the character of the person who committed the offence. In line with this trend, a light sentence should not be served in prison. Thus it is appropriate to commute prison sentences given for separatist propaganda to fines or to convert into another measure or to suspend them.

To this end a temporary article is introduced into the amendment in order to enable the application of the provisions of Articles 4 and 6 of Law No. 647, when conditions are met.

## *Summary analysis of the amendment*

The revision comprises the following points:

1. The phrase in the old Article 8 "irrespective of means, objective and thought" practically deprived this article of the slightest notion of intent. Consequently the court had to judge exclusively the meaning of the words expressed in a speech, while supposing that they automatically contained intent to disrupt the territorial integrity. As a result of this broad and unclear focus, the freedom of expression has been restricted in Turkey beyond "what is necessary in a democratic society" (Article 10, European Convention on Human Rights).

2. The law introduces the concept of intent (or aim to disrupt the territorial integrity and political unity) in written or oral propaganda. This will focus the statute on those whose "intent to destroy" can be considered serious or effective. In a country where there is separatist terrorist violence, this aim or intention should be manifested in written or oral propaganda which encourages violence, terrorism, and related crimes for the purpose of separatism.

3. Prison sentences of two to five years in the previous version of Article 8 are lowered in the law to one to three years. Thus the penalty ceases to be "criminal imprisonment" and becomes simple "imprisonment" in the Turkish legal system, the revision in Article 13 enables the courts to suspend the execution of punishment or to commute them to fines.

4. New amendments therefore introduce the possibility of commuting punishments to fines as well.

5. Consequently, the Article helps release those serving prison sentences under the previous Articles 8 and 13, through:

- reducing the upper and lower limits of imprisonment;
- converting prison terms into fines or suspending future prison terms;
- requiring "aim or intent" to disrupt the integrity of the country.

6. Article 8 stipulates that the courts have to re-examine the cases of those in prison within a month of the effective date of the law. In line with the new spirit of this article, the courts quickly and benevolently reviewed the cases and began releasing those in prison even before the end of one month.

7. People, especially journalists and academicians, now enjoy much broader freedom of expression, since "they do not aim or intend to break up the territorial integrity and political unity of the country."

8. The courts take into account in their decisions the grounds for the article which is adopted together with the article itself by the Parliament.

There are three main points in the text of the grounds as follows:

1. The concept of intent must be clarified.

2. The new article introduces the possibility of commuting prison sentences to fines.

3. The amendment has been inspired by and complies with articles of the European Human Rights Convention, especially Article 10 of the Convention.

Impact of the amendment

As a result of the amendment, the courts ruled 141 release decisions and seven acquittals as of 8 January 1996.

# Document no. 49

**[European Parliament] Decision on the unblocking of the EU–Turkey Joint Parliamentary Committee[8]**

*The European Parliament,*

A. whereas the operation of the EU–Turkey Joint Parliamentary Committee was frozen at the request of its European members on 29 September 1994 [OJ C 305, 10.31.1994, p. 95]; whereas this freezing was reconfirmed on 15 December 1994 [OJ C 18, 1.23.1.1995, p. 177],

B. recalling its demands for democratisation in Turkey,

C. whereas the Customs Union agreement with Turkey should be subject to the assent procedure,

D. having regard to the unanimous request of its Foreign Affairs Committee to unfreeze the operation of the EU–Turkey Joint Committee,

*The European Parliament,*

1. Considers that recent events in Turkey demonstrate the need for a dialogue with that country regarding Parliament's demands for democratisation;

2. Decides to unblock the operation of its joint committee, and instructs it to resume its work forthwith.

# Document no. 50

[European Parliament] Legislative resolution on the proposal for a council decision relating to a common position by the community in the EC–Turkey association council on implementing the final phase of the Customs Union[9]

(Assent procedure)

### *The European Parliament,*

- having regard to the proposal for a Council Decision, 7092/95-95/0813 (AVC),
- having regard to the Council's request for Parliament's assent pursuant to Articles 238 and 228(3), second subparagraph, of the EC Treaty (C4-0241/95),
- having regard to the corrigendum by the Council of 6 December 1995 (7092/95/COR2-C4-0563/95),
- having regard to Rule 90(7) of its Rules of Procedure,
- having regard to the report of the Committee on Foreign Affairs, Security and Defence Policy and the opinions of the Committee on External Economic Relations and the Committee on Civil Liberties and Internal Affairs (A4-0322/1995),
1. Gives its assent to the common position of the Community;
2. Instructs its President to forward this resolution to the Council and Commission, and the governments and parliaments of the Member States and of the Republic of Turkey.

# Document no. 51

**[European Parliament] Resolution on the Human Rights situation in Turkey**[10]

*The European Parliament,*

A. having given its assent on 13 December 1995 to a common position by the Community in the EC–Turkey Association Council on implementing the final phase of the Customs Union,

B. whereas Turkey should respect the rules of international organisations it has joined and agreements it has signed, notably those of the UN, the Council of Europe, the OSCE, the European Convention of Human Rights and the International Convention Against Torture,

C. whereas the Heads of State of the EU Member States, when deciding upon the creation of the Union, confirmed their commitment to the principles of freedom, democracy and respect for Human Rights and fundamental freedoms and the rule of law,

D. convinced that the implementation of the final phase of the Customs Union constitutes a decisive step towards the development of Turkey's relationship with Europe; whereas therefore the European Union, its Member States and Turkey must ensure through dialogue that these shared values are being implemented ever more effectively,

E. convinced that this relationship and dialogue will benefit both sides by strengthening Turkey as a secular democracy at the crossroads of Central Asia and the Middle East,

F. whereas at the same time reports keep coming in which show that Human Rights violations are still being committed; whereas although certain improvements have been made, the situation of Human Rights and democracy in Turkey still leaves much to be desired,

G. whereas recently the Turkish government and Grand National Assembly started bringing about positive changes in constitutional and other laws regarding Human Rights and fundamental freedoms,

H. whereas terrorist actions by the PKK are still continuing, especially but not only, in the southeastern region of Turkey,

I. whereas in that same region the Turkish government continues to take repressive military measures, such as the evacuation of Kurdish villages,

J. whereas no concrete steps have been taken to solve the conflict in Cyprus and to end the Turkish occupation of part of this country,

## *The European Parliament,*

1. Calls upon the European Union, its Member States and Turkey to give their full backing to a continuous and broad dialogue to promote respect for Human Rights and freedoms and calls on the Turkish government and the Grand National Assembly to continue the necessary process of reform of the Constitution and the criminal laws in order to guarantee an ongoing improvement of the Human Rights situation and democratic reform in Turkey;

2. Calls upon the European Union, its Member States and Turkey to use every available mechanism to translate this dialogue into practice, including the Association Council and the Joint Parliamentary Committee and the Euro-Mediterranean Partnership agreed at the Conference in Barcelona;

3. Appeals to the Turkish government, the PKK and other Kurdish organisations to do all in their power to find a non-violent and political solution to the Kurdish issue, calls upon the PKK to refrain from violence and calls upon the Turkish government and Grand National Assembly to lift the curfew operating in the southeastern region and to consider ways and means of allowing citizens of Kurdish origin to express their cultural identity while ensuring that the territorial unity of Turkey is guaranteed and respected;

4. Calls upon the Turkish government and Grand National Assembly to review the case of the four members of the Grand National Assembly and others still in prison by considering a new amnesty bill;

5. Calls on the Council, the Commission, the United Nations and the Cyprus government to do all in their power to bring the partition of Cyprus to an end and urges the Turkish government to undertake concrete steps in that direction by implementing the UN Security Council Resolution on this issue;

6. Calls on the Commission and the Council to monitor permanently Human Rights and democratic development in Turkey and requests the Commission to present a report on the situation to the European Parliament at least once a year;

7. Calls on the Turkish government to be rigorous in applying the law against torture and maltreatment of prisoners; points out that torture is a particularly serious problem in police stations and calls on the Turkish government not to shelter behind any Article of the International Convention Against Torture, which allows it to refuse the publication of reports on torture in Turkey;

8. Will remain vigilant regarding developments in Turkey in order to react immediately if the government of Turkey or the Grand National Assembly were to backtrack on moves towards strengthening democracy and guaranteeing full respect for Human Rights, principles which characterise Western European democracy to which Turkey aspires; reminds Turkey that its assent is to be

considered as an encouragement to the Turkish government's commitment to continue the process of democratisation and improvement of the Human Rights situation;

9. Instructs its President to forward this resolution to the Council, the Commission, the governments of the Member States, the Government and the Grand National Assembly of Turkey, the government of Cyprus and the UN Secretary General.

# Document no. 52

**Decision No. 1/95 of the EC–Turkey Association Council of 22 December 1995 on implementing the final phase of the Customs Union**[11]

*THE EC-TURKEY ASSOCIATION COUNCIL,*

Having regard to the Agreement establishing an Association between the European Economic Community and Turkey, hereinafter referred to as the "Ankara Agreement",

Considering that the objectives set out by the Ankara Agreement, and in particular by its Article 28, which established the Association between Turkey and the Community maintain their significance at this time of great political and economic transformation on the European scene;

Recalling its resolution of 8 November 1993 in which it reaffirmed the will of the Parties to enter into the Customs Union according to the calendar and modalities set out in the Ankara Agreement and its Additional Protocol;

Considering that the Association relations as provided for in Article 5 of the Ankara Agreement are entering into their final phase based on the Customs Union, which will complete the transitional phase through the fulfilment by the two parties of their reciprocal obligations and which leads to the elaboration of the modalities for the effective functioning of the Customs Union within the framework of the Ankara Agreement and Additional Protocol;

Considering that the Customs Union represents an important qualitative step, in political and economic terms, within the Association relations between the Parties;

Having met in Brussels on 6 March 1995,

*HAS DECIDED AS FOLLOWS:*

*Article 1:* Without prejudice to the provisions of the Ankara Agreement, its Additional and Supplementary Protocols, the Association Council hereby lays down the rules for implementing the final phase of the Customs Union, laid down in Articles 2 and 5 of the abovementioned Agreement.

[Chapter I: Free movement of goods and commercial policy
Section I: Elimination of customs duties and charges having equivalent effect
Section II: Elimination of quantitative restrictions or measures having equivalent effect
Section III: Commercial policy
Section IV: Common customs tariff and preferential tariff policies
Section V: Processed agricultural products not covered by Annex II to the Treaty establishing the European Community
Chapter II: Agricultural products
Chapter III: Customs provisions
Chapter IV: Approximation of laws
Section I: Protection of intellectual, industrial and commercial property
Section II: Competition
A. Competition rules of the Customs Union
B. Approximation of legislation
Section III: Trade defence instruments
Section IV: Government procurement
Section V: Direct taxation
Chapter V: Institutional provisions
Section I: The EC–Turkey Customs Union Joint Committee
Section II: Consultation and decision procedures
Section III: Settlement of disputes
Section IV: Safeguard measures
Chapter VI: General and final provisions
Statements
Annexes]

*Editors' comment:* As the table of contents of the Decision No. 1/95 demonstrates, the agreement signifying the final phase of the Customs Union did not contain any explicit referrals to Human Rights. Only the preamble contained subtle references to Human Rights. However, this should not lead one to the conclusion that Human Rights concerns were not an important consideration. Indeed, Human Rights concerns underlined the negotiation process for entry into the final phase of the Customs Union process.

# 9 After the Customs Union decision: problems persist: 1996–98

# 1996
# Document no. 53

**PACE [Council of Europe Parliamentary Assembly] Recommendation 1298 (1996) on Turkey's respect of commitments to constitutional and legislative reforms (follow-up to Recommendation 1266 (1995))**[1]

1. The Turkish Grand National Assembly has accomplished several constitutional and legal reforms since April 1995. The Assembly regards these reforms as progress towards the aims of Recommendation 1266 (1995).

2. In its interim reply of 23 June 1995 to Recommendation 1266 (1995), the Committee of Ministers informed the Assembly that it had opened dialogue with the Turkish government. The Assembly regrets the fact that it has not been informed of the progress of this dialogue and expects the Committee of Ministers to provide urgently such information together with a full and final reply to the present recommendation.

3. In July 1995, several articles of the 1982 Constitution were amended. These amendments covered questions relating to political parties, the status of members of parliament and parliamentary immunity, general and local elections, and trade union freedom.

4. In October 1995, Article 8 of the 1991 Anti-Terrorism Law was amended. Previously, it had given rise to serious Human Rights violations.

5. The Assembly welcomes these developments. However, revised Article 8 of the Anti-Terrorism Law still raises serious Human Rights issues. The Assembly therefore repeats its call for the abolition of Article 8 and of any similar provisions in other laws.

6. The Assembly invites the Turkish authorities — and in particular the newly elected parliament — to pursue reform in order to bring the constitution and laws of Turkey in line with the principles and standards of the Council of Europe.

7. The Assembly notes that Turkish forces have been withdrawn from the territory of Iraq. The Assembly still awaits, however, a statement from the Turkish authorities that among their highest political priorities is the search for a peaceful resolution of the Kurdish question.

8. By decision of the Turkish Supreme Court on 26 October 1995, two of the six parliamentarians from the DEP party [Party of Democracy], who were

sentenced in 1994, were released. However, the continuing imprisonment of the other four remains a serious violation of Human Rights and negates the very essence of parliamentary democracy. A presidential pardon or a new amnesty law would confirm Turkey's commitment to democracy.

9. From now on, in the light of these developments, the Assembly considers that Recommendation 1266 (1995) can be followed up within the framework of its monitoring procedure under Order no. 508 (1995) on the honouring of obligations and commitments by Member States of the Council of Europe, instructs its committees concerned to open the procedure under this order, and invites them to nominate their rapporteurs as soon as possible.

10. The Assembly recommends the Committee of Ministers:

i. to urge Turkey to pursue reform in order to bring legislation and practice into line with the Council of Europe's standards and principles;
ii. to appraise developments in Turkey under its own procedure for monitoring the compliance of Member States of the Council of Europe with their obligations and commitments.

# Document no. 54

**EP [European Parliament] resolution on Human Rights and the situation in Turkey[2]**

*The European Parliament,*

- having regard to the Human Rights clause included in the proposal for a Council Regulation regarding the implementation of a special financial cooperation measure for Turkey (COM(95)0389 - C4-) [OJ C 271, 17.10.1995, p. 12],
- having regard to the Barcelona Declaration of which Turkey is a signatory,

A. anxious to achieve good relations with Turkey, but recalling its numerous previous resolutions on Human Rights and statements made by the Turkish authorities prior to the approval of the Customs Union, promising improvements,

B. deeply concerned at the recent military operations undertaken by the Turkish armed forces in Eastern Turkey and the refusal to attempt to achieve a peaceful settlement despite the declaration of a ceasefire by the PKK on 15 December 1995,

C. whereas Kurdish prisoners in many Turkish prisons have been on hunger strike in protest against repressive measures introduced by Mr Mehmet Agar, formerly Chief of Security and subsequently Minister of Justice,

D. concerned by reports that medical treatment is being obstructed and that the health of various prisoners participating in the prison hunger strike is now in grave danger,

E. deeply concerned by reports of ill-treatment against prisoners which, inter alia, has resulted in four deaths in January 1996 in Istanbul's prison,

F. deeply disturbed by the fact that the former Members of Parliament of Kurdish origin, Leyla Zana, Hatip Dicle, Selim Sadak and Orhan Dogan, have still not been released from prison, and have joined the hunger strike by other political prisoners,

G. unable to accept that the prosecutions of the writer Yasar Kamal and the sociologist Ismail Besikci and the treatment of political prisoners in general are compatible with internationally accepted standards of Human Rights,

H. condemning the bans on assembly and demonstration, the violence, the arrests and baton charges by the police during the HABITAT II conference,

I. concerned that the president of the Diyarbakir medical association and committed Human Rights activist, Seyfettin Kizilkan, has been sentenced to over three years' imprisonment by a state security court, although observers assume that the charges were fabricated,

J. taking fully into account the uncertainty prevailing on the Turkish political scene following the fall of the present government and the resignation of the Prime Minister, Mr Mesut Yilmaz,

1. Appeals to the incoming government to commit itself to recognise and uphold Human Rights in Turkey, in accordance with the European Convention on Human Rights of which Turkey is a signatory, and to undertake further and substantial legislative reforms required to prevent their infringement;

2. Requests the new government to declare a general amnesty designed to secure the release of prisoners convicted of offences under laws in conflict with the principles of free speech and Human Rights and to terminate court actions against those still on trial, and in particular renews its call for the immediate release of Mrs Leyla Zana and the three other members of the DEP;

3. Calls on the Turkish government to end its military operations in the southeast of the country and to open negotiations with all Kurdish organisations in order to overcome the deadlock and move towards a peaceful political settlement of the problem;

4. Asks the Turkish authorities to recognise the rights of all Kurds within Turkey and to facilitate the return of all displaced Kurds to their homes;

5. Presses the Council to put the Kurdish issue in Turkey on the agenda of the OSCE [Organization for Security and Cooperation in Europe] and to seek other ways to promote initiatives designed to assist in resolving the problems of Human Rights and the Kurds in Turkey;

6. Calls on the new government to take firm steps to end the practice of torture and to make provision for the International Red Cross to visit prisons and political prisoners;

7. Considers that such disregard of obligations with regard to both international law and Human Rights instruments, is seriously inconsistent with the spirit of the EU/Turkey Customs Union, and therefore calls on the Council and the Commission to urge the Turkish Authorities to take steps to ensure that ill-treatment of prisoners and the obstruction of medical treatment stops;

8. Calls on the Commission to meet its commitments as regards monitoring the Human Rights situation in Turkey and asks it to forward the second interim report on Human Rights in Turkey to Parliament as soon as possible;

9. Instructs its President to forward this resolution to the Council and the Commission, the government of Turkey, and to all Member State governments.

# Document no. 55

**Editors' comment on other EP resolutions in 1996**

In 1996, the European Parliament criticized Turkey in other resolutions as well. In a Resolution dated January 18, 1996 (Resolution on the situation in Turkey and the offer of a ceasefire made by the PKK),[3] the EP referred to its December 13, 1995, resolution on the Human Rights situation in Turkey. It recalled its appeal to the PKK and other Turkish organizations to do all in their power to find a non-violent and political solution to the Kurdish issue respecting territorial integrity and unity of Turkey, while acknowledging the right of Turkish citizens to strive for a form of cultural autonomy within Turkey by peaceful means. In conclusion of the Resolution, the EP "[C]all[ed] on the new Turkish Government which will be formed as a result of the recent elections to continue and reinforce its policies for further democratic reforms and for respect of Human Rights; in particular reiterate[d] its appeal to find ways and means of allowing citizens of Kurdish origin to express their rights to cultural identity while ensuring that the territorial unity of Turkey is guaranteed and respected." It furthermore "[w]elcome[d] the announcement of a unilateral ceasefire made by the President of the PKK and consider[ed] it a first positive response to its appeal of 13 December 1995; expresse[d] its hope that the Turkish Government will view this gesture as a positive contribution to finding a peaceful solution to the problem and call[ed] upon all concerned in Turkey to seize the present opportunity to consider ways and means to start a national dialogue, with the objective of finding a political and non-violent solution to the problems in the southeastern region."

In a Resolution on September 9, 1996 (Resolution on the political situation in Turkey),[4] the EP referred again to its resolution of December 13, 1995, and, noting recent judgments of the European Court on Human Rights on the Human Rights situation in Turkey, "expressed its deep concerns of the military operations recently conducted by the Turkish armed forces in eastern Turkey and their refusal to seek ways of reaching a peaceful settlement of the conflict in Kurdistan." In conclusion, the EP declared that it "[d]emands that the Turkish Government explain clearly its position to the European Union in the four areas — Human Rights, democratisation, the Cyprus question, and the Kurdish problem — raised in Parliament's abovementioned resolution of 13 December 1995, which was the basis for its assent to the Customs Union; expects the Turkish government to confirm the obligations ensuing from its signing of the agreement on the Customs Union; declares that the continuing Human Rights violations in Turkey are in conflict with the letter and spirit of the agreement and irreconcilable with the specific financial aid instruments and the MEDA programme; and decides, therefore, to begin the procedure for entering in the reserve the appropriations relating to the EC–Turkey agreement." To this end, the EP called on the Commission, to block, with immediate effect, all appropriations set aside under the MEDA program for projects in Turkey, except those concerning the promotion of democracy, Human Rights and civil society, pending clarification of unresolved questions and improvements in the abovementioned areas.

In a Resolution on October 24, 1996 (Resolution on violations of religious freedom in Turkey),[5] the EP expressed its concern with some attacks on religious institutions. Finally in a Resolution on December 12, 1996 (Resolution on freedom of the press and Human Rights in Turkey),[6] the EP stated its grave concerns about the continuing deterioration of the Human Rights situation in Turkey, and affirmed that "Turkey's anti-terrorist legislation lends itself to unacceptable violations of freedom of expression, contrary to international Human Rights conventions signed by Turkey." Stressing that a "significant improvement in the Human Rights situation is one of the indispensable conditions for the development of future relations between the European Union and Turkey," and reaffirming "its commitment to freedom of expression," the EP "expresse[d] its firm opposition to attempts to restrict freedom of the press in Turkey and call[ed] on the Turkish government to abandon its plans to adopt a new law to restrict this freedom, which would damage relations between the EU and Turkey."

# Document no. 56

**ECtHR — *Aksoy v. Turkey*[7]**

\*\*\*

AS TO THE FACTS

I. Circumstances of the case
A. \*\*\* The applicant
7. The applicant, Mr Zeki Aksoy, was a Turkish citizen who, at the time of the events in question, lived in Mardin, Kiziltepe, in southeast Turkey, where he was a metal worker. He was born in 1963 and was shot and killed on 16 April 1994. Since then, his father has indicated that he wishes to pursue the case.
B. The situation in the southeast of Turkey
8. Since approximately 1985, serious disturbances have raged in the southeast of Turkey between the security forces and the members of the PKK (Workers' Party of Kurdistan). This confrontation has so far, according to the government, claimed the lives of 4,036 civilians and 3,884 members of the security forces.
9. At the time of the Court's consideration of the case, ten of the eleven provinces of southeastern Turkey had since 1987 been subjected to emergency rule.
C. The detention of the applicant
10. The facts in the case are in dispute.
11. According to the applicant, he was taken into custody on 24 November 1992, between 11 p.m. and midnight. Approximately twenty policemen had come to his home, accompanied by a detainee called Metin who, allegedly, had identified the applicant as a member of the PKK, although Mr Aksoy told the police that he did not know Metin.
12. The government submitted that the applicant was arrested and taken into custody on 26 November 1992 at around 8.30 a.m., together with thirteen others, on suspicion of aiding and abetting PKK terrorists, being a member of the Kiziltepe branch of the PKK and distributing PKK tracts.
13. The applicant stated that he was taken to Kiziltepe Security Headquarters. After one night, he was transferred to Mardin Antiterrorist Headquarters.

He was allegedly detained, with two others, in a cell measuring approximately 1.5 by 3 metres, with one bed and a blanket, but no pillow. He was provided with two meals a day.

14. He was interrogated about whether he knew Metin (the man who had identified him). He claimed to have been told: "If you don't know him now, you will know him under torture."

According to the applicant, on the second day of his detention he was stripped naked, his hands were tied behind his back and he was strung up by his arms in the form of torture known as "Palestinian hanging". While he was hanging, the police connected electrodes to his genitals and threw water over him while they electrocuted him. He was kept blindfolded during this torture, which continued for approximately thirty-five minutes.

During the next two days, he was allegedly beaten repeatedly at intervals of two hours or half an hour, without being suspended. The torture continued for four days, the first two being very intensive.

15. He claimed that, as a result of the torture, he lost the movement of his arms and hands. His interrogators ordered him to make movements to restore the control of his hands. He asked to see a doctor, but was refused permission.

16. On 8 December 1992 the applicant was seen by a doctor in the medical service of the sub-prefecture. A medical report was prepared, stating in a single sentence that the applicant bore no traces of blows or violence. According to Mr Aksoy, the doctor asked how his arms had been injured and was told by a police officer that he had had an accident. The doctor then commented, mockingly, that everyone who came there seemed to have an accident.

17. The government submitted that there were fundamental doubts as to whether the applicant had been ill-treated while in police custody.

18. On 10 December 1992, immediately before his release, Mr Aksoy was brought before the Mardin public prosecutor.

According to the government, he was able to sign a statement denying any involvement with the PKK and made no complaint about having been tortured.

The applicant, however, submitted that he was shown a statement for signature, but said that its contents were untrue. The prosecutor insisted he sign it but Mr Aksoy told him that he could not because he could not move his hands.

D. Events on the applicant's release

19. Mr Aksoy was released on 10 December 1992. He was admitted to Dicle University Medical Faculty Hospital on 15 December 1992, where he was diagnosed as suffering from bilateral radial paralysis (that is, paralysis of both arms caused by nerve damage in the upper arms). He told the doctor who treated him that he had been in custody and strung up with his arms tied behind his back.

He remained at the hospital until 31 December 1992 when, according to the government, he left without having been properly discharged, taking his medical file with him.

20. On 21 December 1992, the public prosecutor decided that there were no grounds to institute criminal proceedings against the applicant, although eleven of the others detained with him were charged.

21. No criminal or civil proceedings have been brought in the Turkish courts in relation to the alleged ill-treatment of the applicant.

E. The death of the applicant

22. Mr Aksoy was shot dead on 16 April 1994.

According to his representatives, he had been threatened with death in order to make him withdraw his application to the Commission, the last threat being made by telephone on 14 April 1994, and his murder was a direct result of his persisting with the application.

The government, however, submitted that his killing was a settling of scores between quarrelling PKK factions. A suspect, allegedly a member of the PKK, has been charged with the murder.

6. The Commission's findings of fact

23. Delegates of the Commission heard evidence from witnesses in the case in Diyarbakir between 13 and 14 March 1995 and in Ankara between 12 and 14 April 1995, in the presence of representatives from both sides who were able to cross-examine the witnesses. In addition, the Commission heard oral submissions on admissibility and the merits at hearings in Strasbourg on 18 October 1994 and 3 July 1995.

After evaluating the oral and documentary evidence, the Commission came to the following conclusions with regard to the facts:

a. It was not possible to make a definite finding as to the date on which Mr Aksoy was arrested, although this clearly took place no later than 26 November 1992. He was released on 10 December 1992, therefore he was detained for at least fourteen days.
b. On 15 December 1992 he was admitted to hospital and was diagnosed with bilateral radial paralysis. He left hospital on 31 December 1992; on his own initiative, without having been properly discharged.
c. There was no evidence that he had suffered any disability prior to his arrest, nor any evidence of any untoward incident during the five days between his release from police custody and his admission to hospital.
d. The Commission noted that the medical evidence indicated that the applicant's injuries could have had various causes, but one of these could have been the trauma suffered by a person who had been strung up by his arms. Moreover, radial paralysis affecting both arms was apparently not a common condition, although it was consistent with the form of ill-treatment known as "Palestinian hanging".
e. The delegates heard evidence from one of the policemen who had interrogated Mr Aksoy and from the public prosecutor who saw him prior to his release; both claimed that it was inconceivable that he could have been ill-treated in any way. The Commission found this evidence unconvincing, since it gave the impression that the two public officers were not prepared even to consider the possibility of ill-treatment occurring at the hands of the police.
f. The government offered no alternative explanation for Mr Aksoy's injuries.

g. There was insufficient evidence to enable any conclusions to be drawn with regard to the applicant's other allegations of ill-treatment by electric shocks and beatings. However, it did seem clear that he had been detained in a small cell with two other people, all of whom had had to share a single bed and blanket, and that he had been kept blindfolded during interrogation.

II. Relevant domestic law and practice
A. Criminal-law provisions against torture

24. The Turkish Criminal Code makes it an offence for a government employee to subject someone to torture or ill-treatment (Article 243 in respect of torture, and Article 245 in respect of ill-treatment).

25. Article 8 of Decree no. 430 of 16 December 1990 provides as follows:

> No criminal, financial or legal responsibility may be claimed against the State of Emergency Regional Governor or a Provincial Governor within a state of emergency region in respect of their decisions or acts connected with the exercise of the powers entrusted to them by this decree, and no application shall be made to any judicial authority to this end. This is without prejudice to the rights of an individual to claim indemnity from the State for damage suffered by them without justification.

26. Prosecutors are under a duty to investigate allegations of serious offences which come to their attention, even if no complaint is made. However, in the state of emergency region, the investigation of criminal offences by members of the administration is taken up by local administrative councils, composed of civil servants. These councils are also empowered to decide whether or not to bring a prosecution, subject to an automatic judicial review before the Supreme Administrative Court in cases where they decide not to prosecute (Legislative Decree no. 285).

B. Administrative law remedies

27. Article 125 of the Turkish Constitution provides as follows:

> All acts or decisions of the administration are subject to judicial review ... The administration shall be liable to indemnify any damage caused by its own acts and measures.

By virtue of this provision, the State is liable to indemnify any person who can prove that he has suffered damage in circumstances where the State has failed in its duty to safeguard individual life and property.

C. Civil proceedings

28. Any illegal act which causes damage committed by a civil servant (except the regional or district prefects in the state of emergency region) may be the subject of a claim for compensation before the ordinary civil courts.

D. The law relating to detention in police custody

29. Pursuant to Article 128 of the Code of Criminal Procedure, a person arrested and detained shall be brought before a justice of the peace within twenty-four hours. This period may be extended to four days when the individual is detained in connection with a collective offence.

The permissible periods of detention without judicial control are longer in relation to proceedings before the State security courts. In such a case, it is possible to detain a suspect for a period of forty-eight hours in connection with an individual offence, and fifteen days in connection with a collective offence (citations omitted).

In the region under emergency rule, however, a person arrested in connection with proceedings before the State security courts may be detained for four days in the case of individual offences and thirty days in the case of collective offences before being brought before a magistrate (citations omitted).

30. Article 19 of the Turkish Constitution gives to a detained person the right to have the lawfulness of his detention reviewed, on application to the court with jurisdiction over his case.

E. The Turkish derogation from Article 5 of the Convention (art. 5)

[The court then provided the text of Turkey's Derogation Letter of August 6, 1990 (see Document no. 14 in Chapter 3).]

\*\*\*

Attached to this letter was a "descriptive summary of the content of the Decrees which have the force of law nos. 424 and 425".

The only measure therein described relating to Article 5 of the Convention (art. 5) was as follows:

> The Governor of the state of emergency region can order persons who continuously violate the general security and public order, to settle at a place to be specified by the Minister of the Interior outside the state of emergency region for a period which shall not exceed the duration of the state of emergency . . . .

32. By a letter of 3 January 1991 the Permanent Representative of Turkey informed the Secretary General that Decree no. 430 had been enacted, which limited the powers previously afforded to the Governor of the state of emergency region under Decrees nos. 424 and 425.

33. On 5 May 1992 the Permanent Representative wrote to the Secretary General that:

> As most of the measures described in the decrees which have the force of Law nos. 425 and 430 that might result in derogating from rights guaranteed by Articles 5, 6, 8, 10, 11 and 13 of the Convention are no longer being implemented, I hereby inform you that the Republic of Turkey limits henceforward the scope of its Notice of Derogation with respect to Article 5 of the Convention only. The Derogation with respect to Articles 6, 8, 10, 11 and 13 of the Convention is no longer in effect; consequently, the corresponding reference to these Articles is hereby deleted from the said Notice of Derogation.

## PROCEEDINGS BEFORE THE COMMISSION

34. In his application of 20 May 1993 (no. 21987/93) to the Commission, Mr Aksoy complained that he had been subjected to treatment contrary to Article 3 of the Convention (art. 3) during his detention in police custody in November/December 1992; that, during the course of his detention, he was not brought before a judge or other authorised officer in violation of Article 5 para. 3 (art. 5-3); and that he was not provided with the opportunity to bring proceedings against those responsible for his ill-treatment, in violation of Articles 6 para. 1 and 13 (art. 6-1, art. 13).

Following Mr Aksoy's death on 16 April 1994, his representatives alleged that the killing was a direct result of his application to the Commission and was an interference with his right of individual petition under Article 25 of the Convention (art. 25).

35. The Commission declared the application admissible on 19 October 1994. In its report of 23 October 1995 (Article 31) (art. 31), it expressed the opinion, by fifteen votes to one, that there had been a violation of Article 3 (art. 3) and that there had been a violation of Article 5 para. 3 (art. 5-3); by thirteen votes to three, that there had been a violation of Article 6 para. 1 (art. 6-1) and that no separate issue arose under Article 13 (art. 13); and, unanimously, that no further action need be taken in respect of the alleged interference with the effective exercise of the right of individual petition under Article 25 (art. 25).

\*\*\*

## FINAL SUBMISSIONS TO THE COURT

36. At the hearing, the government invited the Court to reject the application on the ground that the available domestic remedies had not been exhausted or, in the alternative, to find that there had been no violation of the Convention.

37. On the same occasion, the applicant asked the Court to find violations of Articles 3, 5, 6, 13 and 25 of the Convention (art. 3, art. 5, art. 6, art. 13, art. 25), and to rule that these breaches had been aggravated because the measures complained of formed part of an administrative practice. He also requested just satisfaction pursuant to Article 50 of the Convention (art. 50).

## AS TO THE LAW

I. The Court's assessment of the facts

38. The Court recalls its constant case-law that under the Convention system the establishment and verification of the facts is primarily a matter for the Commission (Articles 28 para. 1 and 31) (art. 28-1, art. 31). While the Court is not bound by the Commission's findings of fact and remains free to make its own appreciation in the light of all the material before it, it is only in exceptional circumstances that it will exercise its powers in this area (see the *Akdivar and Others v. Turkey* judgment of 16 September 1996, Reports of Judgments and Decisions 1996-IV, p. 1214, para. 78).

39. In the instant case, it must be recalled that the Commission reached its findings of fact after a delegation had heard evidence in Turkey on two separate

occasions, in addition to hearings in Strasbourg (see paragraph 23 above). In these circumstances, the Court considers that it should accept the facts as established by the Commission (see, *mutatis mutandis*, the abovementioned Akdivar and Others judgment, p. 1214, para. 81).

40. It is thus against the background of the facts as found by the Commission (see paragraph 23 above) that the Court must examine the government's preliminary objection and the applicant's complaints under the Convention.

II. The government's preliminary objection

A. The arguments of those appearing before the Court

41. The government asked the Court to reject the applicant's complaint under Article 3 of the Convention (art. 3) on the grounds that, contrary to Article 26 of the Convention (art. 26), he had failed to exhaust the domestic remedies available to him. Article 26 (art. 26) provides:

> The Commission may only deal with the matter after all domestic remedies have been exhausted, according to the generally recognised rules of international law, and within a period of six months from the date on which the final decision was taken.

The applicant (see paragraph 3 above), with whom the Commission agreed, argued that he had done all that could be expected of him to exhaust domestic remedies.

42. The government contended that the rule relating to the exhaustion of domestic remedies was clearly established in international law and in the case-law of the Convention organs, and required the applicant to avail himself of all national remedies unless these clearly offered him no chance of success. In fact, Mr Aksoy could have had recourse to three different types of domestic remedy: a criminal prosecution, a civil action and/or administrative proceedings (see paragraphs 24–28 above).

43. With regard to the first of these options, they submitted that he could have complained about the alleged ill-treatment to the public prosecutor who saw him on 10 December 1992 (see paragraph 18 above). However, according to the government, Mr Aksoy gave no indication on that occasion or at any time subsequently that he had been ill-treated during his time in police custody.

Articles 243 and 245 of the Criminal Code, which were in force throughout Turkey, penalised the use of torture and ill-treatment for the extraction of confessions (see paragraph 24 above). Legislative Decree no. 285 on the state of emergency region transferred the power to carry out investigations into criminal acts allegedly committed by civil servants from the public prosecutors to the administrative councils (see paragraph 26 above). However, decisions by the administrative councils not to prosecute were always reviewed by the Supreme Administrative Court. In this connection, the government submitted a number of judgments reversing orders made by administrative councils in the state of emergency region and ordering criminal proceedings to be brought against members of the gendarmerie and security police in respect of allegations of ill-treatment of detainees, and other rulings on sentencing for similar forms of misconduct.

44. Nonetheless, the government reasoned that criminal proceedings were perhaps not the most appropriate remedy in this type of case, because of the emphasis placed on the rights of the accused as opposed to those of the complainant. They therefore drew the Court's attention to the existence of an administrative remedy under Article 125 of the Turkish Constitution (see paragraph 27 above). In order to receive compensation under this provision, an individual needed only to show that there was a causal link between the acts committed by the administration and the wrong suffered; there was no requirement to prove serious misconduct on the part of a government agent. In this connection, the government submitted examples of administrative decisions in which compensation had been awarded in respect of death caused by torture in police custody.

45. In addition, the government argued that Mr Aksoy could have brought a civil action for damages. Again, they referred to a number of decisions of the domestic courts, including a judgment of the Court of Cassation in a case concerning a claim for damages for torture, where it was held that offences committed by members of the security forces were governed by the Code of Obligations and that, under Article 53 of that Code, an acquittal for lack of evidence in criminal proceedings was not binding on the civil courts.

46. While the applicant did not deny that the remedies identified by the government were formally part of the Turkish legal system, he claimed that, in the region under emergency rule, they were illusory, inadequate and ineffective because both torture and the denial of effective remedies were carried out as a matter of administrative practice.

In particular, he argued that reports by a number of international bodies showing that the torture of detainees continued to be systematic and widespread in Turkey raised questions about the commitment of the State to bringing an end to this practice. In this respect he referred to the European Committee for the Prevention of Torture's Public Statement on Turkey (15 December 1992); the United Nations Committee against Torture's Summary Account of the Results of the Proceedings Concerning the Inquiry on Turkey (9 November 1993); and the United Nations Special Rapporteur on Torture's Report of 1995 (E/CN.4/1995/34).

47. He stated that there was a policy on the part of the State authorities of denying that torture ever took place, which made it extremely difficult for victims to succeed in receiving compensation and in having those responsible brought to justice. For example, it was now impossible for individuals alleging torture to obtain medical reports proving the extent of their injuries, because the forensic medical service had been reorganised and doctors who issued such reports were either threatened or moved to a different area. Prosecutors in the state of emergency region routinely failed to open investigations into alleged abuses of Human Rights and frequently refused even to acknowledge complaints. Such investigations as were carried out were biased and inadequate. Furthermore, lawyers and others who acted for the

victims of Human Rights violations were subjected to threats, intimidation and abusive prosecutions and individuals were afraid to pursue domestic remedies because reprisals against complainants were so common.

In these circumstances, the applicant claimed that he should not be required to pursue domestic remedies before making a complaint to Strasbourg.

48. In any case, he maintained that he had informed the public prosecutor on 10 December 1992 that he had been tortured (see paragraph 18 above) and asserted that, even if he had not, the prosecutor could plainly have observed that he did not have the proper use of his hands.

The failure of the prosecutor to start a criminal investigation made it extremely difficult for the applicant to avail himself of any domestic remedy. It was not possible for him to take steps to ensure that a criminal prosecution was brought, for example by challenging a decision not to bring a prosecution in the administrative courts (see paragraph 26 above), because the lack of investigation meant that no formal decision not to prosecute was ever made. In addition, this failure prejudiced his chances of victory in civil or administrative proceedings, because in order to succeed with either type of claim it would have been necessary to prove that he had suffered torture, and in practice a ruling to that effect by a judge in criminal proceedings would have been required.

49. Finally, he reminded the Court that no remedy was available even in theory in relation to his complaint regarding the length of time he was detained without judicial control, since this was perfectly lawful under the domestic legislation (see paragraph 29 above).

50. The Commission was of the opinion that the applicant had been injured during his time in police custody (see paragraph 23 above). It followed that, although it was not possible to establish exactly what happened during his meeting with the public prosecutor on 10 December 1992, there must undoubtedly have been elements which should have prompted the latter to open an investigation or, at the very least, try to obtain further information about the applicant's state of health and the treatment to which he had been subjected. The applicant had done all that could be expected of him in the circumstances, particularly in view of the facts that he must have felt vulnerable as a result of his detention and ill-treatment and that he suffered health problems requiring hospitalisation following his release. The threats which he claimed to have received after making his application to the Commission and his death in circumstances which had not been fully clarified, were further elements which supported the view that the pursuance of remedies might have been attended by risks.

In view of its finding that the applicant had done all that could be required of him to exhaust domestic remedies, the Commission decided that it was not necessary to determine whether there was an administrative practice on the part of the Turkish authorities of tolerating Human Rights abuses.

B. The Court's assessment

51. The Court recalls that the rule of exhaustion of domestic remedies referred to in Article 26 of the Convention (art. 26) obliges those seeking to bring

their case against the State before an international judicial or arbitral organ to use first the remedies provided by the national legal system. Consequently, States are dispensed from answering before an international body for their acts before they have had an opportunity to put matters right through their own legal systems. The rule is based on the assumption, reflected in Article 13 of the Convention (art. 13) — with which it has close affinity — that there is an effective remedy available in respect of the alleged breach in the domestic system whether or not the provisions of the Convention are incorporated in national law. In this way, it is an important aspect of the principle that the machinery of protection established by the Convention is subsidiary to the national systems safeguarding Human Rights (see the Akdivar and Others judgment cited at paragraph 38 above, p. 1210, para. 65).

52. Under Article 26 (art. 26), normal recourse should be had by an applicant to remedies which are available and sufficient to afford redress in respect of the breaches alleged. The existence of the remedies in question must be sufficiently certain not only in theory but in practice, failing which they will lack the requisite accessibility and effectiveness.

However, there is no obligation to have recourse to remedies which are inadequate or ineffective. In addition, according to the "generally recognised rules of international law" to which Article 26 (art. 26) makes reference, there may be special circumstances which absolve the applicant from the obligation to exhaust the domestic remedies at his disposal. The rule is also inapplicable where an administrative practice consisting of a repetition of acts incompatible with the Convention and official tolerance by the State authorities has been shown to exist, and is of such a nature as to make proceedings futile or ineffective (see the abovementioned Akdivar and Others judgment, p. 1210, paras 66 and 67).

53. The Court emphasises that its approach to the application of the rule must make due allowance for the fact that it is being applied in the context of machinery for the protection of Human Rights that the Contracting Parties have agreed to set up.

Accordingly, it has recognised that Article 26 (art. 26) must be applied with some degree of flexibility and without excessive formalism. It has further recognised that the rule of exhaustion is neither absolute nor capable of being applied automatically; in reviewing whether it has been observed it is essential to have regard to the particular circumstances of each individual case. This means amongst other things that it must take realistic account not only of the existence of formal remedies in the legal system of the Contracting Party concerned but also of the general legal and political context in which they operate, as well as the personal circumstances of the applicant (see the abovementioned Akdivar and Others judgment, p. 1211, para. 69).

54. The Court notes the provision under Turkish law of criminal, civil and administrative remedies against the ill-treatment of detainees by the agents of the State and it has studied with interest the summaries of judgments dealing with similar matters provided by the government (see paragraphs 43–45 above).

However, as previously mentioned (paragraph 53), it is not here solely concerned with the question whether the domestic remedies were in general effective or adequate; it must also examine whether, in all the circumstances of the case, the applicant did everything that could reasonably be expected of him to exhaust the national channels of redress.

55. For the purposes of this examination, the Court reiterates that it has decided to accept the Commission's findings of fact in the present case (see paragraphs 39–40 above). The Commission, as has been seen (in paragraph 50 above), was of the view that the applicant was suffering from bilateral radial paralysis at the time of his interview with the public prosecutor.

56. The Court considers that, even if it were accepted that the applicant made no complaint to the public prosecutor of ill-treatment in police custody, the injuries he had sustained must have been clearly visible during their meeting. However, the prosecutor chose to make no enquiry as to the nature, extent and cause of these injuries, despite the fact that in Turkish law he was under a duty to investigate (see paragraph 26 above).

It must be recalled that this omission on the part of the prosecutor took place after Mr Aksoy had been detained in police custody for at least fourteen days without access to legal or medical assistance or support. During this time he had sustained severe injuries requiring hospital treatment (see paragraph 23 above). These circumstances alone would have given him cause to feel vulnerable, powerless and apprehensive of the representatives of the State. Having seen that the public prosecutor was aware of his injuries but had taken no action, it is understandable if the applicant formed the belief that he could not hope to secure concern and satisfaction through national legal channels.

57. The Court therefore concludes that there existed special circumstances which absolved the applicant from his obligation to exhaust domestic remedies. Having reached this conclusion it does not consider it necessary to examine the applicant's claim that there exists an administrative practice of withholding remedies in breach of the Convention.

III. The merits

A. Alleged violation of Article 3 of the Convention (art. 3)

58. The applicant alleged that he was subjected to treatment contrary to Article 3 of the Convention (art. 3), which states:

> No one shall be subjected to torture or to inhuman or degrading treatment or punishment.

The government considered the allegations of ill-treatment to be unfounded. The Commission, however, found that the applicant had been tortured.

59. The government raised various objections to the way in which the Commission had evaluated the evidence. They pointed to a number of factors which, in their view, should have given rise to serious doubt as to whether Mr Aksoy had been ill-treated as he claimed.

For example, they questioned why the applicant had made no complaint to the public prosecutor about having been tortured (see paragraph 18 above) and found it difficult to understand why, if he had indeed been subjected to torture, he had not made any incriminating confession. They also found it suspicious that he had waited for five days between being released from police custody and contacting the hospital (see paragraph 19 above) and observed that it could not be assumed that nothing untoward had occurred in the meantime. Finally, they raised a number of points relating to the medical evidence, including the facts that the applicant took his medical records with him when he left hospital and that there was no medical evidence of burns or other marks left by the application of electric shocks.

60. The applicant complained of having been ill-treated in different ways. He claimed to have been kept blindfolded during interrogation, which caused disorientation; to have been suspended from his arms, which were tied together behind his back ("Palestinian hanging"); to have been given electric shocks, which were exacerbated by throwing water over him; and to have been subjected to beatings, slapping and verbal abuse. He referred to medical evidence from Dicle University Medical Faculty which showed that he was suffering from a bilateral brachial plexus injury at the time of his admission to hospital (see paragraph 19 above). This injury was consistent with Palestinian hanging.

He submitted that the treatment complained of was sufficiently severe as to amount to torture; it was inflicted with the purpose of inducing him to admit that he knew the man who had identified him.

In addition, he contended that the conditions in which he was detained (see paragraph 13 above) and the constant fear of torture which he suffered while in custody amounted to inhuman treatment.

61. The Court, having decided to accept the Commission's findings of fact (see paragraphs 39–40 above), considers that, where an individual is taken into police custody in good health but is found to be injured at the time of release, it is incumbent on the State to provide a plausible explanation as to the causing of the injury, failing which a clear issue arises under Article 3 of the Convention (art. 3) (see the *Tomasi v. France* judgment of 27 August 1992, Series A no. 241-A, pp. 40–41, paras 108–11, and the *Ribitsch v. Austria* judgment of 4 December 1995, Series A no. 336, p. 26, para. 34).

62. Article 3 (art. 3), as the Court has observed on many occasions, enshrines one of the fundamental values of democratic society. Even in the most difficult of circumstances, such as the fight against organised terrorism and crime, the Convention prohibits in absolute terms torture or inhuman or degrading treatment or punishment. Unlike most of the substantive clauses of the Convention and of Protocol nos 1 and 4 (P1, P4), Article 3 (art. 3) makes no provision for exceptions and no derogation from it is permissible under Article 15 (art. 15) even in the event of a public emergency threatening the life of the nation (see the *Ireland v. the United Kingdom* judgment of 18 January 1978, Series A no. 25, p. 65, para. 163, the *Soering v. the United Kingdom* judgment of 7 July 1989, Series A

no. 161, p. 34, para. 88, and the *Chahal v. the United Kingdom* judgment of 15 November 1996, Reports 1996–V, p. 1855, para. 79).

63. In order to determine whether any particular form of ill-treatment should be qualified as torture, the Court must have regard to the distinction drawn in Article 3 (art. 3) between this notion and that of inhuman or degrading treatment. As it has remarked before, this distinction would appear to have been embodied in the Convention to allow the special stigma of "torture" to attach only to deliberate inhuman treatment causing very serious and cruel suffering (see the *Ireland v. United Kingdom* judgment previously cited, p. 66, para. 167).

64. The Court recalls that the Commission found, inter alia, that the applicant was subjected to "Palestinian hanging", in other words, that he was stripped naked, with his arms tied together behind his back, and suspended by his arms (see paragraph 23 above).

In the view of the Court this treatment could only have been deliberately inflicted; indeed, a certain amount of preparation and exertion would have been required to carry it out. It would appear to have been administered with the aim of obtaining admissions or information from the applicant. In addition to the severe pain which it must have caused at the time, the medical evidence shows that it led to a paralysis of both arms which lasted for some time (see paragraph 23 above). The Court considers that this treatment was of such a serious and cruel nature that it can only be described as torture.

In view of the gravity of this conclusion, it is not necessary for the Court to examine the applicant's complaints of other forms of ill-treatment.

In conclusion, there has been a violation of Article 3 of the Convention (art. 3).

B. Alleged violation of Article 5 para. 3 of the Convention (art. 5-3)

65. The applicant, with whom the Commission agreed, claimed that his detention violated Article 5 para. 3 of the Convention (art. 5-3). The relevant parts of Article 5 (art. 5) state:

> 1. Everyone has the right to liberty and security of person. No one shall be deprived of his liberty save in the following cases and in accordance with a procedure prescribed by law: ...
> (c) the lawful arrest or detention of a person effected for the purpose of bringing him before the competent legal authority on reasonable suspicion of having committed an offence ....
> 3. Everyone arrested or detained in accordance with the provisions of paragraph 1 (c) of this Article (art. 5-1-c) shall be brought promptly before a judge or other officer authorised by law to exercise judicial power ....

66. The Court recalls its decision in the case of *Brogan and Others v. the United Kingdom* (judgment of 29 November 1988, Series A no. 145–B, p. 33, para. 62), that a period of detention without judicial control of four days and six hours fell outside the strict constraints as to time permitted by Article 5 para. 3 (art. 5-3). It clearly follows that the period of fourteen or more days during which

Mr Aksoy was detained without being brought before a judge or other judicial officer did not satisfy the requirement of "promptness".

67. However, the government submitted that, despite these considerations, there had been no violation of Article 5 para. 3 (art. 5-3), in view of Turkey's derogation under Article 15 of the Convention (art. 15), which states:

> 1. In time of war or other public emergency threatening the life of the nation any High Contracting Party may take measures derogating from its obligations under [the] Convention to the extent strictly required by the exigencies of the situation, provided that such measures are not inconsistent with its other obligations under international law.
>
> 2. No derogation from Article 2 (art. 2), except in respect of deaths resulting from lawful acts of war, or from Articles 3, 4 (paragraph 1) and 7 (art. 3, art. 4-1, art. 7) shall be made under this provision (art. 15-1).
>
> 3. Any High Contracting Party availing itself of this right of derogation shall keep the Secretary General of the Council of Europe fully informed of the measures which it has taken and the reasons therefor. It shall also inform the Secretary General of the Council of Europe when such measures have ceased to operate and the provisions of the Convention are again being fully executed.

The government reminded the Court that Turkey had derogated from its obligations under Article 5 of the Convention (art. 5) on 5 May 1992 (see paragraph 33 above).

1. The Court's approach

68. The Court recalls that it falls to each Contracting State, with its responsibility for "the life of [its] nation", to determine whether that life is threatened by a "public emergency" and, if so, how far it is necessary to go in attempting to overcome the emergency. By reason of their direct and continuous contact with the pressing needs of the moment, the national authorities are in principle better placed than the international judge to decide both on the presence of such an emergency and on the nature and scope of the derogations necessary to avert it. Accordingly, in this matter a wide margin of appreciation should be left to the national authorities.

Nonetheless, Contracting Parties do not enjoy an unlimited discretion. It is for the Court to rule whether, inter alia, the States have gone beyond the "extent strictly required by the exigencies" of the crisis. The domestic margin of appreciation is thus accompanied by a European supervision. In exercising this supervision, the Court must give appropriate weight to such relevant factors as the nature of the rights affected by the derogation and the circumstances leading to, and the duration of, the emergency situation (see the *Brannigan and McBride v. the United Kingdom* judgment of 26 May 1993, Series A no. 258-B, pp. 49–50, para. 43).

2. Existence of a public emergency threatening the life of the nation

69. The government, with whom the Commission agreed on this point, maintained that there was a public emergency "threatening the life of the

nation" in southeast Turkey. The applicant did not contest the issue, although he submitted that, essentially, it was a matter for the Convention organs to decide.

70. The Court considers, in the light of all the material before it, that the particular extent and impact of PKK terrorist activity in southeast Turkey has undoubtedly created, in the region concerned, a "public emergency threatening the life of the nation" (see, *mutatis mutandis*, the *Lawless v. Ireland* judgment of 1 July 1961, Series A no. 3, p. 56, para. 28, the abovementioned *Ireland v. United Kingdom* judgment, p. 78, para. 205, and the abovementioned *Brannigan and McBride* judgment, p. 50, para. 47).

3. Whether the measures were strictly required by the exigencies of the situation

*a. The length of the unsupervised detention*

71. The government asserted that the applicant had been arrested on 26 November 1992 along with thirteen others on suspicion of aiding and abetting PKK terrorists, being a member of the Kiziltepe branch of the PKK and distributing PKK tracts (see paragraph 12 above). He was held in custody for fourteen days, in accordance with Turkish law, which allows a person detained in connection with a collective offence to be held for up to thirty days in the state of emergency region (see paragraph 29 above).

72. They explained that the place in which the applicant was arrested and detained fell within the area covered by the Turkish derogation (see paragraphs 31–33 above). This derogation was necessary and justified, in view of the extent and gravity of PKK terrorism in Turkey, particularly in the southeast. The investigation of terrorist offences presented the authorities with special problems, as the Court had recognised in the past, because the members of terrorist organisations were expert in withstanding interrogation, had secret support networks and access to substantial resources. A great deal of time and effort was required to secure and verify evidence in a large region confronted with a terrorist organisation that had strategic and technical support from neighbouring countries. These difficulties meant that it was impossible to provide judicial supervision during a suspect's detention in police custody.

73. The applicant submitted that he was detained on 24 November 1992 and released on 10 December 1992. He alleged that the post-dating of arrests was a common practice in the state of emergency region.

74. While he did not present detailed arguments against the validity of the Turkish derogation as a whole, he questioned whether the situation in southeast Turkey necessitated the holding of suspects for fourteen days or more without judicial supervision. He submitted that judges in southeast Turkey would not be put at risk if they were permitted and required to review the legality of detention at shorter intervals.

75. The Commission could not establish with any certainty whether the applicant was first detained on 24 November 1992, as he claimed, or on 26 November 1992, as alleged by the government, and it therefore proceeded on the basis that he was held for at least fourteen days without being brought before a judge or other officer authorised by law to exercise judicial power.

76. The Court would stress the importance of Article 5 (art. 5) in the Convention system: it enshrines a fundamental human right, namely the protection of the individual against arbitrary interference by the State with his or her right to liberty. Judicial control of interferences by the executive with the individual's right to liberty is an essential feature of the guarantee embodied in Article 5 para. 3 (art. 5-3), which is intended to minimise the risk of arbitrariness and to ensure the rule of law (see the abovementioned *Brogan and Others* judgment, p. 32, para. 58). Furthermore, prompt judicial intervention may lead to the detection and prevention of serious ill-treatment, which, as stated above (paragraph 62), is prohibited by the Convention in absolute and non-derogable terms.

77. In the *Brannigan and McBride* judgment (cited at paragraph 68 above), the Court held that the United Kingdom government had not exceeded their margin of appreciation by derogating from their obligations under Article 5 of the Convention (art. 5) to the extent that individuals suspected of terrorist offences were allowed to be held for up to seven days without judicial control.

In the instant case, the applicant was detained for at least fourteen days without being brought before a judge or other officer. The government sought to justify this measure by reference to the particular demands of police investigations in a geographically vast area faced with a terrorist organisation receiving outside support (see paragraph 72 above).

78. Although the Court is of the view — which it has expressed on several occasions in the past (see, for example, the abovementioned *Brogan and Others* judgment) — that the investigation of terrorist offences undoubtedly presents the authorities with special problems, it cannot accept that it is necessary to hold a suspect for fourteen days without judicial intervention. This period is exceptionally long, and left the applicant vulnerable not only to arbitrary interference with his right to liberty but also to torture (see paragraph 64 above). Moreover, the government had not adduced any detailed reasons before the Court as to why the fight against terrorism in southeast Turkey rendered judicial intervention impracticable.

*b. Safeguards*

79. The government emphasised that both the derogation and the national legal system provided sufficient safeguards to protect Human Rights. Thus, the derogation itself was limited to the strict minimum required for the fight against terrorism; the permissible length of detention was prescribed by law and the consent of a public prosecutor was necessary if the police wished to remand a suspect in custody beyond these periods. Torture was prohibited by Article 243 of the Criminal Code (see paragraph 24 above) and Article 135 (a) stipulated that any statement made in consequence of the administration of torture or any other form of ill-treatment would have no evidential weight.

80. The applicant pointed out that long periods of unsupervised detention, together with the lack of safeguards provided for the protection of prisoners, facilitated the practice of torture. Thus, he was tortured with particular intensity on his third and fourth days in detention, and was held thereafter to allow his

injuries to heal; throughout this time he was denied access to either a lawyer or a doctor. Moreover, he was kept blindfolded during interrogation, which meant that he could not identify those who mistreated him. The reports of Amnesty International ("Turkey: a Policy of Denial", February 1995), the European Committee for the Prevention of Torture and the United Nations Committee against Torture (cited at paragraph 46 above) showed that the safeguards contained in the Turkish Criminal Code, which were in any case inadequate, were routinely ignored in the state of emergency region.

81. The Commission considered that the Turkish system offered insufficient safeguards to detainees; for example there appeared to be no speedy remedy of *habeas corpus* and no legally enforceable rights of access to a lawyer, doctor, friend or relative. In these circumstances, despite the serious terrorist threat in southeast Turkey, the measure which allowed the applicant to be detained for at least fourteen days without being brought before a judge or other officer exercising judicial functions exceeded the government's margin of appreciation and could not be said to be strictly required by the exigencies of the situation.

82. In its abovementioned *Brannigan and McBride* judgment (cited at paragraph 68), the Court was satisfied that there were effective safeguards in operation in Northern Ireland which provided an important measure of protection against arbitrary behaviour and incommunicado detention. For example, the remedy of habeas corpus was available to test the lawfulness of the original arrest and detention. There was an absolute and legally enforceable right to consult a solicitor forty-eight hours after the time of arrest and detainees were entitled to inform a relative or friend about their detention and to have access to a doctor (op. cit., pp. 55–56, paras 62–63).

83. In contrast, however, the Court considers that in this case insufficient safeguards were available to the applicant, who was detained over a long period of time. In particular, the denial of access to a lawyer, doctor, relative or friend and the absence of any realistic possibility of being brought before a court to test the legality of the detention meant that he was left completely at the mercy of those holding him.

84. The Court has taken account of the unquestionably serious problem of terrorism in southeast Turkey and the difficulties faced by the State in taking effective measures against it. However, it is not persuaded that the exigencies of the situation necessitated the holding of the applicant on suspicion of involvement in terrorist offences for fourteen days or more in incommunicado detention without access to a judge or other judicial officer.

4. Whether the Turkish derogation met the formal requirements of Article 15 para. 3 (art. 15-3)

\*\*\*

[After stating that the Court can raise the issue *sua sponte*, it decided that in view of its finding that the impugned measure was not strictly required by the exigencies of the situation, it was unnecessary to rule on this matter.]

## 5. Conclusion

87. In conclusion, the Court finds that there has been a violation of Article 5 para. 3 of the Convention (art. 5-3).

### C. Alleged lack of remedy

88. The applicant complained that he was denied access to a court, in violation of Article 6 para. 1 of the Convention (art. 6-1), which provides, so far as is relevant:

> In the determination of his civil rights ... , everyone is entitled to a fair and public hearing within a reasonable time by an independent and impartial tribunal established by law ... .

In addition, he claimed that there was no effective domestic remedy available to him, contrary to Article 13 of the Convention (art. 13), which states:

> Everyone whose rights and freedoms as set forth in [the] Convention are violated shall have an effective remedy before a national authority notwithstanding that the violation has been committed by persons acting in an official capacity.

89. The government contended that, since the applicant had never even attempted to bring proceedings, it was not open to him to complain that he had been denied access to a court. They further argued, as they had in connection with their preliminary objection (see paragraphs 41–45 above) that there were a number of effective remedies available.

90. For the applicant, the prosecutor's decision not to open an investigation had effectively rendered it impossible for him to enforce his civil right to compensation (see paragraph 48 above). He submitted that, under Turkish law, civil proceedings could not be contemplated until the facts concerning the events had been established and the perpetrators identified by a criminal prosecution. Without this, civil proceedings had no prospect of success. In addition, he stated that the ability to seek compensation for torture would represent only one part of the measures necessary to provide redress; it would be unacceptable for a State to claim that it fulfilled its obligation simply by providing compensation, since this would in effect be to allow States to pay for the right to torture. He claimed that the remedies necessary to meet his Convention claims either did not exist, even in theory, or did not operate effectively in practice (see paragraphs 46–47 above).

91. The Commission found a violation of Article 6 para. 1 (art. 6-1), for the same reasons that it found in the applicant's favour under Article 26 of the Convention (art. 26) (see paragraph 50 above). In view of this finding, it did not consider it necessary to examine the complaint under Article 13 (art. 13).

### 1. Article 6 para. 1 of the Convention (art. 6-1)

92. The Court recalls that Article 6 para. 1 (art. 6-1) embodies the "right to a court", of which the right of access, that is, the right to institute proceedings

before a court in civil matters, constitutes one aspect (see, for example, the *Holy Monasteries v. Greece* judgment of 9 December 1994, Series A no. 301–A, pp. 36–37, para. 80). There can be no doubt that Article 6 para. 1 (art. 6-1) applies to a civil claim for compensation in respect of ill-treatment allegedly committed by agents of the State (see, for example, the Tomasi judgment cited at paragraph 61 above, p. 43, paras 121–22).

93. The Court notes that it was not disputed by the applicant that he could in theory have brought civil proceedings for damages in respect of his ill-treatment. He did claim that the failure of the prosecutor to mount a criminal investigation in practice meant that he would have had no chance of success in civil proceedings (see paragraph 90 above). The Court recalls, however, that because of the special circumstances which existed in his case (see paragraph 57 above), Mr Aksoy did not even attempt to make an application before the civil courts. Given these facts, it is not possible for the Court to determine whether or not the Turkish civil courts would have been able to deal with Mr Aksoy's claim, had he brought it before them.

In any event, the Court observes that the crux of the applicant's complaint concerned the prosecutor's failure to mount a criminal investigation (see paragraph 90 above). It further notes the applicant's argument that the possibility of seeking compensation for torture would represent only one part of the measures necessary to provide redress (also in paragraph 90 above).

94. In the Court's view, against this background, it is more appropriate to consider this complaint in relation to the more general obligation on States under Article 13 (art. 13) to provide an effective remedy in respect of violations of the Convention.

2. Article 13 of the Convention (art. 13)

95. The Court observes that Article 13 (art. 13) guarantees the availability at a national level of a remedy to enforce the substance of the Convention rights and freedoms in whatever form they might happen to be secured in the domestic legal order. The effect of this Article (art. 13) is thus to require the provision of a domestic remedy allowing the competent national authority both to deal with the substance of the relevant Convention complaint and to grant appropriate relief, although Contracting States are afforded some discretion as to the manner in which they conform to their obligations under this provision (art. 13) (see the Chahal judgment cited at paragraph 62 above, pp. 1869–70, para. 145). The scope of the obligation under Article 13 (art. 13) varies depending on the nature of the applicant's complaint under the Convention (see the abovementioned Chahal judgment, pp. 1870–71, paras 150–51). Nevertheless, the remedy required by Article 13 (art. 13) must be "effective" in practice as well as in law, in particular in the sense that its exercise must not be unjustifiably hindered by the acts or omissions of the authorities of the respondent State.

96. The Court would first make it clear that its finding (in paragraph 57 above) that there existed special circumstances which absolved the applicant from his obligation to exhaust domestic remedies should not be taken as

meaning that remedies are ineffective in southeast Turkey (see, *mutatis mutandis*, the *Akdivar and Others* judgment cited at paragraph 38 above, pp. 1213–14, para. 77).

97. Secondly, the Court, like the Commission, would take judicial notice of the fact that allegations of torture in police custody are extremely difficult for the victim to substantiate if he has been isolated from the outside world, without access to doctors, lawyers, family or friends who could provide support and assemble the necessary evidence. Furthermore, having been ill-treated in this way, an individual will often have had his capacity or will to pursue a complaint impaired.

98. The nature of the right safeguarded under Article 3 of the Convention (art. 3) has implications for Article 13 (art. 13). Given the fundamental importance of the prohibition of torture (see paragraph 62 above) and the especially vulnerable position of torture victims, Article 13 (art. 13) imposes, without prejudice to any other remedy available under the domestic system, an obligation on States to carry out a thorough and effective investigation of incidents of torture.

Accordingly, as regards Article 13 (art. 13), where an individual has an arguable claim that he has been tortured by agents of the State, the notion of an "effective remedy" entails, in addition to the payment of compensation where appropriate, a thorough and effective investigation capable of leading to the identification and punishment of those responsible and including effective access for the complainant to the investigatory procedure. It is true that no express provision exists in the Convention such as can be found in Article 12 of the 1984 United Nations Convention against Torture and Other Cruel, Inhuman or Degrading Treatment or Punishment, which imposes a duty to proceed to a "prompt and impartial" investigation whenever there is a reasonable ground to believe that an act of torture has been committed. However, in the Court's view, such a requirement is implicit in the notion of an "effective remedy" under Article 13 (art. 13) (see, *mutatis mutandis*, the Soering judgment cited at paragraph 62 above, pp. 34–35, para. 88).

99. Indeed, under Turkish law the prosecutor was under a duty to carry out an investigation. However, and whether or not Mr Aksoy made an explicit complaint to him, he ignored the visible evidence before him that the latter had been tortured (see paragraph 56 above) and no investigation took place. No evidence has been adduced before the Court to show that any other action was taken, despite the prosecutor's awareness of the applicant's injuries.

Moreover, in the Court's view, in the circumstances of Mr Aksoy's case, such an attitude from a State official under a duty to investigate criminal offences was tantamount to undermining the effectiveness of any other remedies that may have existed.

100. Accordingly, in view in particular of the lack of any investigation, the Court finds that the applicant was denied an effective remedy in respect of his allegation of torture.

In conclusion, there has been a violation of Article 13 of the Convention (art. 13).

[After stating that the Commission was unable to find any evidence to show that Mr Aksoy's death was connected with his application, or that the State authorities had been responsible for any interference, in the form of threats or intimidation, with his rights under Article 25 para. 1, and because no new evidence in this connection was presented to the Court, it could not find that there has been a violation of Article 25 para. 1 of the Convention.]

E. Alleged administrative practice of violating the Convention

\*\*\*

109. The Court is of the view that the evidence established by the Commission is insufficient to allow it to reach a conclusion concerning the existence of any administrative practice of the violation of the above Articles of the Convention (art. 3, art. 5-3, art. 6-1, art. 13, art. 25-1).

\*\*\*

[The Court granted compensation for pecuniary and non-pecuniary damages and obliged Turkey to pay costs and expenses with interest.]

# Document no. 57

### Editors' comment on other ECtHR cases in 1996

In 1996, the ECtHR decided on three other applications regarding Human Rights abuses in Turkey. In one of these cases, *Yagiz v. Turkey*,[8] the Court concluded that it could not deal with the merits of the case, as the detention in police custody during which Mrs Yagiz had allegedly suffered ill-treatment had taken place on December 15 and 16, 1989, more than a month before Turkey's recognition of the Court's compulsory jurisdiction.

However, in another case, *Mitap and Muftuoglu v. Turkey*,[9] the Court found Turkey in violation of Article 6(1) of the Convention. In that case, the applicants complained of the length of detention pending trial and of the length of the criminal proceedings. The Court decided that it lacked jurisdiction *ratione temporis*, except with regard to the complaint concerning length of the criminal proceedings. With respect to the reasonableness of the length of the proceedings, the Court noted that the proceedings before the Court of Cassation had lasted more than six years. According to the Court, even though the case was complex, it had not been informed of any circumstance justifying such a lengthy period, especially as proceedings at first instance had lasted approximately eight years and six months.

Furthermore, in the case of *Akdivar and Others v. Turkey*,[10] the Court found Turkey in violation of Articles P1(1), 8, 25(1) of the Convention. That case originated in an application lodged by eight Turkish citizens, who were former residents of the village of Keleki in the Dicle District of the Province of Diyarbakir. In July 1992, the applicants' village was attacked by the PKK. Three people died and three were injured. On the night of November 1, 1992, between 100 and 150 PKK terrorists attacked the gendarmerie station at Bogazkoy, a neighboring village, killing a soldier and injuring eight others. In the following days, the security forces searched the surrounding area in an attempt to find the terrorists. The sequence of events after that was disputed. According to the applicants, during the evening of November 10, 1992, the soldiers entered the village and instructed the mayor to evacuate all the inhabitants immediately. In the meantime, the soldiers set fire to nine houses, including those belonging to some of the applicants. On April 6, 1993, the security forces returned to the village and set fire to the rest of the houses. According to the government, after the PKK attack in July 1992, the villagers began to evacuate their homes voluntarily as they felt insecure there; the abandoned houses collapsed. After the attack on the Bogazkoy gendarmerie station, the security forces searched the area, found several deserted terrorist shelters, but caused no damage in Keleki. In April 1993, the security forces searched the village once more without causing any damage. After the soldiers left, PKK terrorists came to the village and set fire to the remaining houses. The government claimed that the applicants' failure to avail themselves of remedies in southeast Turkey was part of the general policy of the PKK to denigrate Turkey and its judicial institutions and to promote the idea of the legitimacy of their terrorist activities. As part of this strategy, it was necessary to prove that the Turkish judicial system was ineffective in general and unable to cope with such complaints and to distance the population in southeast Turkey from the institutions of the Republic and, in particular, the courts. The applicants' failure to exhaust remedies in this case had thus a political objective. According to the government, there was an abuse of process. The Court recalled that the Commission's findings of fact had substantially upheld the applicants' allegations concerning the destruction of their property. Under these circumstances, it rejected the government's plea. In response to the government's motion to reject the application for failure to exhaust domestic remedies, the Court recalled the general principles concerning the exhaustion of domestic remedies and rejected the motion. However, the Court emphasized that this ruling was confined to the particular circumstances of the present case and it could not be interpreted as a general statement that the remedies are ineffective in this area of Turkey. With respect to the merits of the case, the Court found that "the security forces were responsible for burning of the applicants' houses." Stating that the deliberate burning of houses and contents constituted a serious interference with rights under Article 8 and Article 1 of Protocol no. 1 and finding no justification for these interferences, the Court concluded that there had been a violation of both Article 8 and Article 1 of Protocol no. 1. With respect to Article 25(1) of the Convention, the Court found that applicant's right to free communication with the Commission without being subjected to any form of pressure from the authorities to withdraw or modify their complaints was not respected.

# 1997
# Document no. 58

### Editors' comment on relevant 1997 ECtHR cases in which Turkey was a party

In 1997, the ECtHR decided eight complaints brought against Turkey. In two of these eight cases, the Court did not find a breach of the Convention (*Kalac v. Turkey*,[11] a case regarding religious freedom; and *Erdagoz v. Turkey*,[12] torture). One case was resolved by a friendly settlement (*Sur v. Turkey*).[13] In the remaining five cases the Court found breaches of several articles of the Convention.

In *Akkus v. Turkey*,[14] the applicant complained that, at a time when the annual rate of inflation in Turkey had been 70 per cent, she had been paid insufficient interest on additional compensation received following the expropriation of her land and the authorities had delayed in paying her. She complained that the authorities had calculated her compensation on the basis of the value her land had when it was expropriated, or when the Court proceedings were commenced. Finding that the deferral of the payment of the compensation for seventeen months rendered the compensation inadequate, the Court decided that there was a violation of Article 1 of Protocol no. 1.

In *Aydin v. Turkey*,[15] the applicant complained that she has been tortured and raped while in the custody of the State security forces. According to the applicant, she was arrested together with her father and her sister-in-law. Village guards and gendarmerie officers took them to the gendarmerie headquarters. During her detention the applicant was blindfolded. She was beaten, stripped naked, placed in a tyre and hosed with pressurised water. She was then taken to another room where she was stripped and raped by a member of the security forces. She and the other members of her family were released after three days. According to the government, the applicant and the other members of her family were never held in custody. Furthermore, intelligence reports and other evidence revealed that the applicant had had intimate relations with two members of the PKK. The applicant, her father and her sister-in-law complained about their treatment in custody. The Public Prosecutor took their statements and sent them to the State hospital for a medical examination. A report on each person was issued on the same day. Two further reports were issued on the applicant and stated that the applicant and the other members of her family had never been in custody. Thereupon, the Public Prosecutor reported to the Principal State Counsel that there was no evidence to support the applicant's complaints but the investigation was continuing. The Court found that the evidence proved beyond reasonable doubt that the applicant was detained by the security forces and had been raped and ill-treated while in detention. Stating that the rape of a detainee by an official of the State is an especially grave and abhorrent form of ill-treatment, the Court found a violation of Article 3 of the Convention. Furthermore, the Court found that the official investigation regarding the allegations was inadequate and found a violation of Article 13 of the Convention.

In *Zana v. Turkey*,[16] the applicant, while serving several sentences in the Diyarbakir military prison, had said in an interview with journalists that he supported the PKK national liberation movement, but on the other hand that he was not in favour of massacres by the PKK. That statement was published in the national daily newspaper. The "press offences" department of the Istanbul public prosecutor's office began a preliminary investigation in respect of the applicant, among others, on the ground that he had "defended an act punishable by law as a serious crime". The applicant was charged with supporting the activities of an armed organisation, the PKK, whose aim was to break up Turkey's national territory. The court sentenced him to imprisonment and noted that because he had refused to speak Turkish he had waived his right of defending himself. The applicant maintained that his conviction by the Diyarbakir National Security Court on account of his statement to journalists had infringed his right to freedom of expression. With respect to the merits of the case, the Court observed that the applicant's conviction and sentence had amounted to an interference with his freedom of expression, but nevertheless under the totality of circumstances held that the penalty imposed could reasonably have been regarded as answering a pressing social need, and the reasons adduced by the national authorities were relevant and sufficient. However, on the questions of "an infringement of the principle of a fair trial" and "the length of the criminal proceedings against the applicant," the Court found a breach of Article 6(1) and (3)(c).

In *Sakik and Others v. Turkey*,[17] the issue was the arrest and detention in police custody of six former members of the National Assembly who were prosecuted in a State Security Court (SSC). The six applicants were formerly members of the Turkish parliament, where they sat as members of the People's Labour Party (HEP). On 2 March 1994 their parliamentary immunity was lifted. By order of the public prosecutor of the SSC they were taken into police custody on suspicion of undermining the territorial integrity of the State. Their detention in police custody was then extended until 16 March 1994 after the public prosecutor's department at the SSC refused applications to be brought before a judge lodged by the applicants on 3 and 11 March. On 16 March 1994 the applicants were brought before a single judge of the Ankara National Security Court, who remanded them in custody. Finally on 8 December 1994 the SSC sentenced the applicants to imprisonment. It dismissed the charge of high treason — a capital offence — brought under Article 125 of the Criminal Code. Before the ECtHR, the applicants complained of breaches of Article 5(1), (3), (4) and (5). Before proceeding to the merits of the case, the Court considered Turkey's derogation from Article 5 in accordance with Article 15 of the Convention. It noted that Legislative Decrees nos 424, 425 and 430, which are referred to in the derogation of 6 August 1990 and the letter of 3 January 1991, apply, according to the descriptive summary of their content, only to the region where a state of emergency has been proclaimed, which, according to the derogation, does not include the city of Ankara. The Court then noted that in the present case it would be working against the object and purpose of that provision if, when assessing the territorial scope of the derogation concerned, it were to extend its effects to a part of Turkish territory not explicitly named in the notice of derogation. It followed that the derogation in question is inapplicable rations loci to the facts of the case. Consequently, it was not necessary to determine whether it satisfies the requirements of Article 15. On the merits of the case, the Court decided that there had been a breach of Article 5(3) due to the lengthy detention. The Court also found violations of Articles 5(4) and 5(5) of the Convention.

In *Mentes and Others v. Turkey*,[18] the question before the Court was alleged burning of houses by security forces and lack of remedies in southeast Turkey. Stating that the facts of the case were more or less the same as those in the Akdivar and Others judgment, the Court declared that "despite the extent of the problem of village destruction, there appears to be no example of compensation being awarded in respect of allegations that property has been purposely destroyed by members of the security forces or of prosecutions having been brought against them in respect of such allegations." Therefore, the Court, affirming its judgment in Akdivar, found a violation of Article 8 of the Convention. Furthermore, the Court found a violation of Article 13 due to the fact that no thorough and effective investigation had been conducted into the applicants' allegations and this had resulted in undermining the exercise of any remedies at their disposal, including the pursuit of compensation before the courts.

# Document no. 59

**Law of March 1997 amending the Code of Criminal Procedure (CMUK)[19]**

Law concerning amending the Code of Criminal Procedure, the Law on the Creation of State Security Courts and their Judicial Procedures and Law no. 3842 of 18 November 1992, which amended the aforementioned laws [passed by the Parliament of Turkey on 6 March 1997].

*Article 1*: The first sentence of the first paragraph and the second sentence of the second paragraph of Article 128 of Code of Criminal Procedure, Law no. 1412 of 4 April 4 1929 will be amended in the manner below.

> If the detained suspect is not released, within twenty four hours he will be brought before a magistrate and questioned (excluding time necessary in reaching the magistrate nearest the point of detention).
>
> If the investigation is not completed within this period of time, it can be extended to seven days by request of a state prosecutor and the decision of a magistrate.

*Article 2*: The phrase, "in the 384th and 385th articles" will be removed from the text of sub-paragraph (a) of the first paragraph of Article 9 of the Law on the Creation of State Security Courts and their Judicial Procedures, Law no. 2845 of 18 June 1983.

*Article 3*: Article 31 of Law no. 3842 of 18 November 1992 and annulled Article 16 of Law no. 2854, together with its heading, shall be amended in the manner below:

> Detention, Arrest, and Conferring with Legal Counsel Article 16:
>
> An individual detained or arrested for crimes under the jurisdiction of State Security Courts shall be brought before a magistrate no later than within forty-eight hours and questioned (excluding time necessary in reaching the magistrate nearest the point of detention or arrest).
>
> In crimes committed collectively by three or more persons, or where there are difficulties in gathering evidence, or where there are numerous

suspects, or for similar reasons, the state prosecutor can give a written order to extend this period to four days. If the investigation is not completed within this time, the detention period can be extended to seven days by the request of a state prosecutor and the order of a judge.

With respect to persons detained or arrested in areas where a State of Emergency has been declared according to Article 120 of the Constitution, the seven day period indicated in the second paragraph [of Article 3 of this law] may be extended to ten days by request of a state prosecutor and decision of a judge.

An arrested suspect can meet with his lawyer at all times. The same right applies to an individual in detention after a judge has given his decision to extend the period of detention.

Until a public trial has been opened, a judge may withhold from the suspect information which he [the judge] feels inappropriate for the suspect to know. Where the reason for the arrest so requires, a judge in person, or his deputy, or a judge appointed as a proxy may be present when the defendant confers with legal counsel.

*Article 4*: Articles numbered "7," "9", and "20" shall be removed from the text of Article 31 of the Law no. 3842 of 18 November 1992, concerning amending several articles of the Code of Criminal Procedure and the Law on the Creation of State Security Courts and their Judicial Procedures.

*Article 5*: Article 30 of Law no. 3842 shall be abolished.

\*\*\*

# Document no. 60

**Luxembourg European Council Presidency Conclusions (12–13 December 1997)[20] and its aftermath**

\*\*\*

6. The States which accept these criteria [a common commitment to peace, security and good neighbourliness, respect for other countries' sovereignty, the principles upon which the European Union is founded, the integrity and inviolability of external borders and the principles of international law and a commitment to the settlement of territorial disputes by peaceful means, in particular through the jurisdiction of the International Court of Justice in the Hague] and subscribe to the above principles will be invited to take part in the Conference. Initially, the EU offer will be addressed to Cyprus, the applicant States of Central and Eastern Europe and Turkey.

\*\*\*

### A European strategy for Turkey

31. The Council confirms Turkey's eligibility for accession to the European Union. Turkey will be judged on the basis of the same criteria as the other applicant States. While the political and economic conditions allowing accession negotiations to be envisaged are not satisfied, the European Council considers that it is nevertheless important for a strategy to be drawn up to prepare Turkey for accession by bringing it closer to the European Union in every field.

32. This strategy should consist in:

- development of the possibilities afforded by the Ankara Agreement;
- intensification of the Customs Union;
- implementation of financial cooperation;
- approximation of laws and adoption of the Union *acquis*.
- participation, to be decided case by case, in certain programmes and in certain agencies provided for in paragraphs 19 and 21.

33. The strategy will be reviewed by the Association Council in particular on the basis of Article 28 of the Association Agreement in the light of the Copenhagen criteria and the Council's position of 29 April 1997.

34. In addition, participation in the European Conference will enable the Member States of the European Union and Turkey to step up their dialogue and cooperation in areas of common interest.

35. The European Council recalls that strengthening Turkey's links with the European Union also depends on that country's pursuit of the political and economic reforms on which it has embarked, including the alignment of Human Rights standards and practices on those in force in the European Union; respect for and protection of minorities; the establishment of satisfactory and stable relations between Greece and Turkey; the settlement of disputes, in particular by legal process, including the International Court of Justice; and support for negotiations under the aegis of the UN on a political settlement in Cyprus on the basis of the relevant UN Security Council Resolutions.

36. The European Council endorses the guidelines that emerged from the General Affairs Council of 24 November 1997 on future relations between the Union and Turkey and asks the Commission to submit suitable proposals.

\*\*\*

*Editors' comment*: The issue of relations with Turkey has been predominantly limited to economic matters in the past, at least in the European Council Conclusions. For example, the Corfu European Council of June 14–15, 1994, only stated "[c]oncerning Turkey, the European Council notes the convening of the EC–Turkey Association Council to deal in particular with the achievement of the Customs Union foreseen in the Association Agreement of 1964."

Similarly, the Essen European Council of December 9–10, 1994, mainly considered Turkey within the framework of its Mediterranean policy and stated that "[t]he Mediterranean represents a priority area of strategic importance for the European Union." Reiterating the European Union's "willingness to support the Mediterranean countries in their efforts progressively to transform their region into a zone of peace, stability, prosperity and cooperation, and to this end its willingness to establish a Euro-Mediterranean partnership, develop appropriate agreements, progressively strengthen trade relations between the parties on the basis, inter alia, of the results of the Uruguay Round, and in the light of the Community's changing priorities maintain an appropriate balance in the geographical allocation of Community expenditure and commitments," the Council confirmed the importance it attached "to concluding the negotiations with Turkey on the completion and unrestricted implementation of the customs union and to reinforcing relations with this partner." The only reference to the Human Rights situation in Turkey was the declaration that "[t]he European Council [has] made a statement to the press expressing its concern that freely elected Members of Parliament had been sentenced to imprisonment in Turkey and urging respect for Human Rights."

In the Cannes European Council of June 26–27, 1995, the Council referred to Turkey only in the context of its intention "to strengthen relations in all spheres with the Mediterranean countries, and to implement the customs union with Turkey as part of a developing relationship with that country" and stated that "[i]t welcome[d] the closer ties between the European Union and Turkey."

The Florence European Council of June 21–22, 1996, reference only addressed the Customs Union as well. In that Council, the EU declared that " [t]he European Council, recalling the decisions of 6 March 1995, stresses the priority it attaches to the strengthening and deepening of relations with Turkey and looks forward to the early creation of the appropriate conditions for successfully holding the Association Council." It was only in the Dublin European Council of December 13–14, 1996, that the EU mentioned political issues. In its conclusions, the Council "reaffirm[ed] the importance it attaches to the further development of the EU's relations with Turkey in both the economic and political fields." However, "[i]t note[d] with regret ... that certain serious issues remain to be resolved in the relationship." Following these statements, the European Council stated that it welcomed the Turkish government's stated intention to take measures to improve the Human Rights situation and emphasized the need for the observance of the highest standards of Human Rights in the context of a closer partnership with the European Union. Also mentioned in the Council were the promotion of an "acceptable solution to the situation in the Aegean area in accordance with established international norms and to pursue contacts with the Turkish Government with a view to an early Association Council," and Cyprus.

The conclusions of the Dublin European Council were of extreme importance particularly because they marked the beginning of a low ebb in EU–Turkey relations. Even though the Customs Union had entered into force in January 1996, only six months later a dispute over an islet in the Aegean Sea which almost resulted in a war between Greece and Turkey. This development led the EU to express serious concern and make clear that its natural solidarity is with Greece as a Member State.

"Five months later, the Luxembourg summit of the European Council left Turkey outside the enlargement towards Central and Eastern Europe. The summit declaration confirmed Turkey's eligibility for EU membership. Yet it made it clear that Turkey's eligibility did not merit any EU commitment with respect to Turkey's accession. What was on offer was a 'European strategy for Turkey', which would involve 'enhanced co-operation' and would be reviewed by the Association Council — a body that had failed graphically to resolve contentious issues in the past. In addition, paragraph 35 of the Luxembourg declaration made it clear that strengthening Turkey's relations with the EU would be conditional on the 'establishment of stable and satisfactory relations' with Greece; settlement of disputes by legal rules, including the International Court of Justice (ICJ); and support for a political settlement in Cyprus.

Turkey reacted very strongly to the Luxembourg summit declaration. The then Prime Minister, Mesut Yilmaz, stated that Turkey will 'freeze' its relations with the EU — i.e., Turkey would not treat the EU as an interlocutor with respect to 'political issues concerning Turkey' but bilateral relations with the Member States would continue. Mr Yilmaz also stated that Turkey would go ahead with its policy of integrating Northern Cyprus. Integration of Northern Cyprus was a policy decision taken previously in close consultations with the military. The decision was ratified by the Turkish Parliament in 1995, when it became evident that the EU would start accession negotiations with the Cypriot government."[21]

# 1998
# Document no. 61

### Cardiff European Council Presidency Conclusions (15–16 June 1998)[22]

\*\*\*

62. Noting that the Luxembourg European Council assessed the candidatures addressed in Agenda 2000 and took the decisions necessary to launch the overall enlargement process, the European Council welcomes the substantial progress made since Luxembourg in preparing for enlargement.

63. The Union's priority is to maintain the enlargement process for the countries covered in the Luxembourg European Council conclusions, within which they can actively pursue their candidatures and make progress towards taking on the obligations of membership, including the Copenhagen criteria. Each of these candidate countries will be judged on the basis of the same criteria and will proceed in its candidature at its own rate, depending on its degree of preparedness. Much will depend on the efforts made by the candidate countries themselves to meet the criteria. All will benefit from strengthened relations with the EU including through political dialogue and tailored strategies to help them prepare for accession.

64. The European Council welcomes the Commission's confirmation that it will submit at the end of 1998 its first regular reports on each candidate's progress towards accession. In the case of Turkey, reports will be based on Article 28 of the Association Agreement and the conclusions of the Luxembourg European Council.

65. The European Council welcomes the launch of the Accession Process in Brussels on 30 March. It is an evolutionary and inclusive process. A productive further meeting of the Ministers for Justice and Home Affairs of the fifteen Members of the European Union with their opposite numbers from the ten Central and East European applicant states and Cyprus was held on 28–29 May. Further Ministerial meetings will take place as the need arises.

\*\*\*

68. The European Council also welcomes the Commission's communication of 4 March 1998 on taking forward the European Strategy to prepare Turkey for membership. It agrees that, taken as a package, this provides the platform for developing our relationship on a sound and evolutionary basis. The European Council invites the Commission to carry forward this strategy, including the tabling of any proposals necessary for its effective implementation. The Strategy can be enriched over time, taking into account Turkey's own ideas. The European Council further invites the Presidency and the Commission and the appropriate Turkish authorities to pursue the objective of harmonising Turkey's legislation and practice with the *acquis*, and asks the Commission to report to an early Association Council on progress made. Recalling the need for financial support for the European Strategy, the European Council notes the Commission's intention to reflect on ways and means of underpinning the implementation of the European strategy, and to table appropriate proposals to this effect.

# Document no. 62

**ECtHR — *Incal v. Turkey*[23]**

\*\*\*

AS TO THE FACTS

## *I. The circumstances of the case*

9. Mr Ibrahim Incal, a Turkish national born in 1953, lives in Izmir. A lawyer by profession, he was at the material time a member of the executive committee of the Izmir section of the People's Labour Party ("the HEP"). That party, which was represented in the National Assembly, was dissolved by the Constitutional Court on 14 July 1993.

10. On 1 July 1992 the executive committee decided to distribute in the Izmir constituency a leaflet criticising the measures taken by the local authorities, in particular against small-scale illegal trading and the sprawl of squatters' camps around the city.

The title of the leaflet, of which ten thousand copies were printed, was "To all democratic patriots!" and the text read as follows:

> In the last few days a campaign aimed at "DRIVING THE KURDS OUT OF THE CITIES" has been launched in Izmir against the Kurdish population by a combination of prefecture, security police and town hall. In this campaign Izmir has been designated a pilot-city. The first stage was the operation [against] street traders, stall keepers and mussel sellers, whom they tried to hide away on the grounds that it was necessary to smarten up the city and ease traffic congestion. The purpose of this operation was to impose an "economic blockade" on our, mainly Kurdish, fellow citizens who make their living through these activities, condemning them to destitution and starvation. In this way the masses were to be frightened, oppressed and compelled to return to their province of origin.
>
> Before the "DRIVING THE KURDS OUT" campaign began the organisational and psychological ground had already been prepared by

leaflets signed by "Patriotic inhabitants of Izmir" and handed out in large numbers for weeks by "obscure forces". These leaflets incited hostility against the Kurdish population in particular and stirred up anti-Kurdish feelings. This led to racist and chauvinistic anti-Kurdish attitudes through propaganda saying: "Don't give employment or housing to the Kurds. Don't speak to them, don't let your daughters marry them and don't marry one yourself. Smash the Kurds." That is how the psychological foundations were laid down, the preparations for the future offensives. Although these leaflets were handed out in broad daylight, those responsible — and nobody knows why — were never arrested.

But the campaign was by no means limited to the operation against street traders, stall keepers and mussel sellers. The second prong was "Operation shantytown". The same combination of prefecture, security police and town hall launched the demolition of the squatters' camps. It began in Yamanlar and Semikler and continued in Gaziemir, [all] shantytown districts inhabited mainly by Kurds, who, before the elections, were regarded by the parties in favour of the status quo as a source of votes. Those who had encouraged the mushrooming of the shantytowns by dishonestly promising freedom to build in exchange for votes and those who, with the local mafia, had appropriated public land this time set about the ferocious destruction of these huts to oppress and intimidate the Kurds and force them to go back home.

The Kurdish and Turkish proletarian people suddenly and without any warning saw the huts they had run into debt to build, with so many sacrifices made by cutting down on their children's food, collapsing about their ears. That is how they are trying to oppress the Kurdish and Turkish people and drive them into distress and despair.

**IT'S STATE TERROR AGAINST TURKISH AND KURDISH PROLETARIANS!**

It is certain that these demolitions, which began in Yamanlar and are still continuing in Gaziemir, will soon spread to Izmir's other shantytowns. The State is testing the people's reactions and will to resist by causing various kinds of destruction. Passivity as a form of defence against this devastation has encouraged the State to commit further kinds of destruction.

In conclusion: The "Driving-the-Kurds-Out policy" forms part of the SPECIAL WAR being conducted in the country at present against the Kurdish people. It is one of the mechanisms of that war, the way it impinges on the cities. Because the methods used are the same, namely enslavement, violence, terror and oppression through compulsion. It is a psychological war.

While, in the country, they are trying to oppress and silence the people through counter-insurgency tactics, special patrols, village guards, the SS [initials of the words "*sansur* (censorship) and "*surgun* (banishment); an allusion to the terms used by the media when referring to the legislative decrees declaring a state of emergency in certain regions of Turkey] decree and

every [other] form of State terror, in Izmir they want to achieve the same aim by depriving our fellow citizens of their means of subsistence and in the end by knocking their houses down about their ears. The methods used, although different in form, are in the final analysis mechanisms serving the purposes of the special war. It is the urban form of the special war.
TO ALL DEMOCRATIC PATRIOTS!
The way to nullify these insults to the cities is to set up NEIGHBOURHOOD COMMITTEES BASED ON THE PEOPLE'S OWN STRENGTH.
We call on all Kurdish and Turkish democratic patriots to assume their responsibilities and oppose this special war being waged against the proletarian people.
LONG LIVE THE BROTHERHOOD OF NATIONS!
STOP THE SPECIAL WAR BEING SPREAD INTO THE CITIES!

11. By a letter of 2 July 1992, accompanied by a copy of the leaflet in question, the president of the HEP informed the Izmir prefecture of the executive committee's decision (see paragraph 10 above) and asked for permission to implement it.

12. The Izmir security police, to whom this request had been referred, considered that the leaflet contained separatist propaganda capable of inciting the people to resist the government and commit criminal offences.

On 3 July 1992 they asked the Principal Public Prosecutor attached to the Izmir National Security Court ("the public prosecutor", "the National Security Court") to state his opinion as to whether the contents of the leaflet contravened the law.

13. On the same day, at the request of the public prosecutor's office, a substitute judge of the National Security Court issued an injunction ordering the seizure of the leaflets and prohibiting their distribution.

The police searched the HEP's premises in Izmir, first at the headquarters, where the party leaders handed over, without demur, nine thousand copies of the leaflet which were still parcelled up, and then at the Buca district office, where the thousand remaining copies were seized.

14. Still on 3 July 1992 the public prosecutor's office opened a criminal investigation against the HEP's local leaders and the members of its executive committee, including the applicant.

15. On 27 July 1992 the public prosecutor instituted criminal proceedings in the National Security Court against the applicant and the other eight members of the HEP committee who had taken part in the decision of 1 July 1992 (see paragraph 10 above). Citing the text of the leaflet, he accused them of attempting to incite hatred and hostility through racist words and asked the court to apply Articles 312 §§ 2 and 3 of the Criminal Code, section 5 of the Prevention of Terrorism Act (Law no. 3713) and additional section 4 of the Press Act (Law no. 5680) (see paragraphs 21, 23 and 24 below). He also asked the court to order confiscation of the leaflets.

16. On 9 February 1993 the National Security Court, composed of three judges, one of whom was a member of the Military Legal Service, found the applicant guilty of the offences charged and sentenced him to six months and twenty days' imprisonment and a fine of 55,555 Turkish liras. It also ordered the confiscation of the leaflets and disqualified him from driving for fifteen days.

In its interpretation of the wording of the leaflet, the National Security Court accepted the public prosecutor's oral submissions entirely, except for that part which related to the applicability of the Prevention of Terrorism Act (Law no. 3713). It noted in particular that the leaflet suggested recourse to resistance against the police and the establishment of "neighbourhood committees", which it held to be illegal forms of protest. It further held that the offence had been intentionally committed, since the accused had not contested either the existence or wording of the text on which the charge was based.

With regard to the severity of the sentence, it observed that although commission of the offence through the medium of print was an aggravating circumstance, it was necessary to take into account the accused's good faith and the fact that the authorities had been able to lay hands on the leaflets before they had been distributed.

17. On 9 March 1993 the applicant and the other convicted persons appealed to the Court of Cassation. In their notice of appeal they asked for a public hearing to be held and challenged the National Security Court's interpretation of the leaflet and its refusal to commute the prison sentence to a fine.

18. On 20 May the Principal Public Prosecutor attached to the Court of Cassation forwarded the case file together with an opinion couched in a standard form of words — which was not communicated to Mr Incal — asking the court to uphold the judgment.

19. In a judgment of 6 July 1993 the Court of Cassation upheld all the operative provisions of the impugned judgment, after observing that, regard being had to the nature and length of the sentence imposed at first instance, it was not necessary to hold a hearing.

20. On 23 August 1993 the prosecuting authorities decided, at the applicant's request, to stay execution of the prison sentence for four months.

## II. Relevant domestic law and practice

A. *Criminal law*

1. THE CRIMINAL CODE

21. The relevant provisions of the Criminal Code read as follows:

*Article 311 § 2*

> Public incitement to commit an offence
> Where the incitement [to commit an offence] is done by means of mass communication, of whatever type, by tape recordings, gramophone records,

newspapers, press publications or other published material, by the circulation or distribution of printed papers or by the placing of placards or posters in public places, the terms of imprisonment to which convicted persons are liable shall be doubled ... .

*Article 312*

Non-public incitement to commit an offence

Whosoever expressly praises or condones an act punishable by law as an offence or incites the population to break the law shall be sentenced to between six months' and two years' imprisonment and a ... fine of between six thousand and thirty thousand liras.

Whosoever expressly arouses hatred and hostility in society on the basis of a distinction between social classes, races or religions, or one based on allegiance to a particular denomination or region, shall be sentenced to between one and three years' imprisonment and a fine of between nine thousand and thirty-six thousand liras. If this incitement is done in a manner likely to endanger public safety, the sentence shall be increased [by one third to one half].

The penalties to be imposed on those who have committed the abovementioned offences by the means listed in Article 311 § 2 shall be doubled.

22. A conviction under Article 312 § 2 entails further consequences, particularly with regard to the exercise of certain activities governed by special legislation. For example, persons convicted of an offence under that section may not found associations (Law no. 2908, section 4(2)(b)) or trades unions, nor may they be members of the executive committee of a trade union (Law no. 2929, section 5). They are also forbidden to found or join political parties (Law no. 2820, section 11(5)) and may not stand for election to Parliament (Law no. 2839, section 11(f3)). In addition, if the sentence imposed exceeds six months' imprisonment, the convicted person is debarred from entering the civil service, provided that the offence has been committed intentionally (Law no. 657, section 48(5)).

2. THE PRESS ACT (LAW NO. 5680)

23. Additional section 4(1) of the Press Act (Law no. 5680) provides:

Where distribution [of the printed matter whose distribution constitutes the offence] is prevented ... by a court injunction or, in an emergency, by order of the Principal Public Prosecutor, to be confirmed by a court, ... the penalty imposed shall be one-third of that laid down by law for the offence concerned.

### 3. THE PREVENTION OF TERRORISM ACT (LAW NO. 3713)

24. Law no. 3713 of 12 April 1991, promulgated with a view to preventing acts of terrorism, refers to a number of offences defined in the Criminal Code which it describes as "acts of terrorism" or "acts perpetrated for the purposes of terrorism" (sections 3 and 4) and to which it applies. However, the act punishable pursuant to Article 312 of the Criminal Code (see paragraph 21 above) is not among them.

### 4. THE CODE OF CRIMINAL PROCEDURE

25. Article 318 of the Code of Criminal Procedure provides for the holding of a public hearing in proceedings before the Court of Cassation only where the impugned judgment concerns offences classified as "serious", such as those punishable by the death penalty or a term of imprisonment of more than ten years. The Court of Cassation's jurisdiction, according to Article 307 of the Code, is limited to questions concerning the lawfulness and procedural regularity of the first-instance judgment.

## B. *The National Security Courts*

26. The National Security Courts were created by Law no. 1773 of 11 July 1973, in accordance with Article 136 of the 1961 Constitution. That Law was annulled by the Constitutional Court on 15 June 1976. The courts in question were later reintroduced into the Turkish judicial system by the 1982 Constitution. The relevant part of the statement of reasons contains the following passage:

> There may be acts affecting the existence and stability of a State such that when they are committed special jurisdiction is required in order to give judgment expeditiously and appropriately. For such cases it is necessary to set up National Security Courts. According to a principle inherent in our Constitution, it is forbidden to create a special court to [give judgment on] a specific act after it has been committed. For that reason the National Security Courts have been provided for in our Constitution to try cases involving the abovementioned offences. Given that the special provisions laying down their powers have [thus] been enacted in advance and that the courts have been created before the commission of any offence ... , they may not be described as courts set up to deal with this or that offence after the commission of such an offence.

The composition and functioning of the National Security Courts are subject to the following rules.

### 1. THE CONSTITUTION

27. The constitutional provisions governing judicial organisation are worded as follows:

*Article 138 §§ 1 and 2*

> In the performance of their duties, judges shall be independent; they shall give judgment, according to their personal conviction, in accordance with the Constitution, statute and the law.
>
> No organ, authority, officer or other person may give orders or instructions to courts or judges in the exercise of their judicial powers, or send them circulars or make recommendations or suggestions to them.

*Article 139 § 1*

> Judges ... shall not be removed from office or compelled to retire without their consent before the age prescribed by the Constitution ... .

*Article 143 § 4*

> Presidents, regular members and substitute judges of the National Security Courts shall be appointed for a renewable period of four years.

*Article 145 § 4*

> The personal rights and obligations of military judges ... shall be regulated by law in accordance with the principles of the independence of the courts, the safeguards enjoyed by the judiciary and the requirements of military service. Relations between military judges and the commanders under whom they serve as regards their non-judicial duties shall also be regulated by law ... .

2. LAW NO. 2845 ON THE CREATION AND RULES OF PROCEDURE OF THE NATIONAL SECURITY COURTS

28. Based on Article 143 of the Constitution, the relevant provisions of Law no. 2845 on the National Security Courts, provide as follows:

*Section 1*

> In the capitals of the provinces of ... National Security Courts shall be established to try persons accused of offences against the Republic — whose constituent qualities are enunciated in the Constitution — against the indivisible unity of the State — meaning both the national territory and its people — or against the free, democratic system of government and offences directly affecting the State's internal or external security.

*Section 3*

> The National Security Courts shall be composed of a president and two other regular members. In addition, there shall sit at each National Security Court two substitute members.

*Section 5*

The president of a National Security Court, one of the other regular members and one of the substitutes shall be civilian ... judges, the other members, whether full or substitute, military judges of the first rank ....

*Section 6(2), (3) and (6)*

The appointment of military judges to sit as regular members and substitutes shall be carried out according to the procedure laid down for that purpose in the special legislation [concerning those posts].

Except as provided in the present Law or other legislation, the president and the regular or substitute members of the National Security Courts ... may not be appointed to another post or place, without their consent, within four years ... .

If, after an investigation concerning the presidents and regular or substitute members of the National Security Courts conducted according to the legislation concerning them, competent committees or authorities decide to change the duty station of a military judge, the duty station of that judge or his duties [themselves] ... may be changed in accordance with the procedure laid down in that legislation.

*Section 9(1)(a)*

The National Security Courts shall try persons accused of the offences defined in

(a) [Article] 312 § 2 ... of the Turkish Criminal Code ....

*Section 27(1)*

The Court of Cassation shall hear appeals from the judgments of the National Security Courts.

*Section 34(1) and (2)*

The rules governing the rights and obligations of ... military judges appointed to the National Security Courts and their supervision ... , the institution of disciplinary proceedings against them, the imposition of disciplinary penalties on them and the investigation and prosecution of any offences ... they may commit in the performance of their duties shall be as laid down in the relevant provisions of the laws governing their professions ....

The observations of the Court of Cassation and the assessment reports drawn up by Ministry of Justice assessors on judges of the Military Legal Service ... and the files on any investigations conducted against them ... shall be transmitted to the Ministry of Justice.

*Section 38*

A National Security Court may be transformed into a Martial-Law Court, under the conditions set forth below, where a state of emergency has been declared in all or part of the territory in respect of which the National Security Court concerned has jurisdiction, provided that within that territory there is more than one National Security Court ... .

3. THE MILITARY LEGAL SERVICE ACT (LAW NO. 357)

29. The relevant provisions of the Military Legal Service Act are worded as follows:

*Additional section 7*

The aptitude of military judges ... appointed as regular or substitute members of the National Security Courts that is required for promotion or advancement in salary step, rank or seniority shall be determined on the basis of assessment reports drawn up according to the procedure laid down below, subject to the provisions of the present Act and the Turkish Armed Forces Personnel Act (Law no. 926).

(a) The immediate superior competent to carry out assessment and draw up assessment reports for military judges, whether full or substitute members ... shall be the Minister of State in the Ministry of Defence, followed by the Minister of Defence ... .

*Additional section 8*

Members ... of the National Security Courts belonging to the Military Legal Service ... shall be appointed by a committee composed of the personnel director and legal advisor of the General Staff, the personnel director and legal adviser attached to the staff of the arm in which the person concerned is serving and the Director of Military Judicial Affairs at the Ministry of Defence ... .

*Section 16(1) and (3)*

Military judges ... shall be appointed by a decree issued jointly by the Minister of Defence and the Prime Minister and submitted to the President of the Republic for approval, in accordance with the provisions on the appointment and transfer of members of the armed forces ...

The procedure for appointment as a military judge shall take into account the opinion of the Court of Cassation, the reports by Ministry of Justice assessors and the assessment reports drawn up by the immediate superiors ... .

*Section 18(1)*

> The rules governing the salary scales, salary increases and various personal rights of military judges ... shall be as laid down in the provisions relating to officers.

*Section 29*

> The Minister of Defence may apply to military judges, after considering their defence submissions, the following disciplinary sanctions:
> A. A warning, which consists in giving the person concerned notice in writing that he must exercise more care in the performance of his duties ....
> B. A reprimand, which consists in giving the person concerned notice in writing that a particular act or a particular attitude has been found to be blameworthy ....
> The said sanctions shall be final, mentioned in the assessment record of the person concerned and entered in his personal file ....

*Section 38*

> When military judges ... sit in court they shall wear the special dress of their civilian counterparts ....

4. ARTICLE 112 OF THE MILITARY CRIMINAL CODE

30. Article 112 of the Military Criminal Code of 22 May 1930 provides:

> It shall be an offence, punishable by up to five years' imprisonment, to abuse one's authority as a [public] official in order to influence the military courts.

5. LAW NO. 1602 OF 4 JULY 1972 ON THE SUPREME MILITARY ADMINISTRATIVE COURT

31. Under section 22 of Law no. 1602 the First Division of the Supreme Military Administrative Court has jurisdiction to hear applications for judicial review and claims for damages based on disputes relating to the personal status of officers, particularly those concerning their promotion and professional advancement.

*C. Case law*

1. THE SUPREME MILITARY ADMINISTRATIVE COURT

32. The government produced several judgments of the First Division of the Supreme Military Administrative Court setting aside decisions concerning the

appointment and promotion of military judges or disciplinary sanctions applied to them. These were the judgments of 31 May 1988 (no. 1988/185), 14 December 1993 (no. 1993/1116), 22 December 1993 (no. 1993/1119), 19 November 1996 (no. 1996/950), 1 April 1997 (no. 1997/262), 27 May 1997 (no. 1997/405) and 3 July 1997 (no. 1997/62).

It appears from these judgments that in setting aside the transfer decisions concerned, the First Division gave as its grounds either lack of consent on the part of the person concerned or abuse of the military authorities' discretionary power. In connection with assessment reports, failure to state reasons or a lack of objectivity on the part of the immediate superior was taken into account. Lastly, in connection with a disciplinary sanction, against which in principle no appeal lies, the First Division held that the acts of which the person concerned stood accused had been incorrectly established and that the sanction was accordingly null and void.

2. THE NATIONAL SECURITY COURTS

33. The government also submitted a number of judgments rendered by National Security Courts relevant to the impartiality of military judges sitting as members of such courts. These were the judgments of 12 September 1995 (no. 1995/171), 27 February 1996 (no. 1996/38), 7 March 1996 (no. 1996/55), 21 March 1996 (no. 1996/70), 2 April 1996 (no. 1996/102), 9 April 1996 (no. 1996/112), 2 May 1996 (no. 1996/141), 9 May 1996 (no. 1996/150), 19 August 1996 (no. 1996/250), 12 September 1996 (no. 1996/258), 19 September 1996 (no. 1996/263), 1 October 1996 (no. 1996/270), 3 October 1996 (no. 1996/273), 8 October 1996 (no. 1996/278), 12 June 1997 (no. 1997/128) and 15 July 1997 (no. 1997/393).

Most of these decisions declared the accused guilty but also contained separate opinions by military judges adopting a dissenting opinion with regard to the establishment and classification of the facts, the way sentence was determined or the finding of guilt itself.

PROCEEDINGS BEFORE THE COMMISSION

34. Mr Incal applied to the Commission on 7 September 1993. He asserted that he had not had a fair trial in the National Security Court, firstly because it could not be regarded as an independent tribunal, and secondly because it had refused to commute his sentence of imprisonment into a fine on account of his political opinions (Article 6 § 1 of the Convention taken separately and in conjunction with Article 14). He also submitted that by rejecting his request for leave to appear and by omitting to send him a copy of the Principal Public Prosecutor's opinion on his appeal on points of law the Court of Cassation had breached Article 6 §§ 1 and 3 (b). He further alleged that his conviction for helping to prepare a political leaflet constituted a breach of Articles 9 and 10 and that his temporary disqualification from driving was a degrading punishment contrary to Article 3.

35. On 16 October 1995 the Commission declared inadmissible the complaint relating to the applicant's disqualification from driving and declared the remainder of the application (no. ) admissible. In its report of 25 February 1997 (Article 31), it expressed the opinion:

a. that there had been a violation of Article 10 (unanimously);
b. that, contrary to Article 6 § 1, the applicant had not had a fair hearing by an independent and impartial tribunal (unanimously);
c. that there had been no violation of Article 6 § 1 taken in conjunction with Article 14 (unanimously);
d. that the fact that the applicant had been unable to reply to the public prosecutor's opinion had breached Article 6 § 1 (twenty-six votes to five); and
e. that there had been no violation of Article 6 § 1 on account of the fact that the applicant had not appeared in the Court of Cassation (twenty-six votes to five).
f. The full text of the Commission's opinion and of the partly dissenting opinion contained in the report is reproduced as an annex to this judgment.

## FINAL SUBMISSIONS TO THE COURT

36. In their memorial, and later at the hearing, the government asked the Court to hold that the proceedings complained of had not infringed the rights secured to the applicant by Articles 6, 10 and 14 of the Convention.

37. The applicant asked the Court to hold that Article 6 § 1, Article 9 and Article 10 of the Convention had been breached and to award him just satisfaction under Article 50.

## AS TO THE LAW

### *I. Alleged violation of Article 10 of the Convention*

38. Mr Incal submitted that his criminal conviction on account of his contribution to preparation of the leaflet in issue had infringed his right to freedom of expression guaranteed by Article 10 of the Convention, which provides:

> 1. Everyone has the right to freedom of expression. This right shall include freedom to hold opinions and to receive and impart information and ideas without interference by public authority and regardless of frontiers. This Article shall not prevent States from requiring the licensing of broadcasting, television or cinema enterprises.
>
> 2. The exercise of these freedoms, since it carries with it duties and responsibilities, may be subject to such formalities, conditions, restrictions or penalties as are prescribed by law and are necessary in a democratic society, in the interests of national security, territorial integrity or public safety, for the prevention of disorder or crime, for the protection of health or morals, for the protection of the reputation or rights of others, for

preventing the disclosure of information received in confidence, or for maintaining the authority and impartiality of the judiciary.

The Commission accepted this argument, which the government contested.

### A. Existence of an interference

39. The participants in the proceedings agreed that the applicant's conviction amounted to an interference with the exercise of his right to freedom of expression. That is also the Court's opinion.

### B. Justification of the interference

40. Such interference breaches Article 10 except where it is "prescribed by law", is directed towards one or more of the legitimate aims set out in Article 10 § 2 and is "necessary in a democratic society" to achieve the aim or aims concerned.

#### 1. "PRESCRIBED BY LAW"

41. The participants in the proceedings all accepted that the interference was "prescribed by law", as the applicant's conviction had been based on Article 312 §§ 2 and 3 of the Criminal Code and additional section 4(1) of the Press Act (Law no. 5680) (see paragraphs 21 and 23 above).

#### 2. LEGITIMATE AIM

42. The Court notes that no argument was presented on this point by the parties to the case. The Commission took the view that in applying Article 312 of the Criminal Code the Turkish courts' aim in the present case had been to prevent disorder.

The Court considers that Mr Incal's conviction pursued at least one of the legitimate aims set out in Article 10, namely "the prevention of disorder".

#### 3. "NECESSARY IN A DEMOCRATIC SOCIETY"

##### a. **Arguments of the participants**
###### i. *The applicant*

43. The applicant submitted that in a pluralist democratic system political parties such as his ought to be able to express their views on the country's social and political problems. The opinions expressed in the leaflet in issue were based on actual events and were limited to criticism of the discriminatory administrative and economic pressure brought to bear on citizens of Kurdish origin. The authors of the leaflet, of whom he was one, had never intended to advocate separatism and did not seek to foment disorder.

Contrary to the findings of the judges at his trial, it was not a factual description of the situation in a country which provoked hatred and hostility but the fact that it was not possible for reactions to problems of general interest to be submitted to the public by the political parties.

Mr Incal challenged the necessity of the interference and emphasised the fact that the leaflets in question had not been distributed. In any event, the penalty had been completely disproportionate, especially as his conviction had led to his being permanently debarred from the civil service and from certain activities within associations, trade unions or political organisations, in the latter case in the capacity of leader, founder member, parliamentary candidate, mayor or town councillor.

ii. *The government*

44. The government asserted that, despite the anger expressed in the leaflet concerned, the operations aimed at closing down booths unlawfully erected on land belonging to others and driving out street traders met the requirements of the relevant legislation and regulations, which had no other purpose than the prevention of disorder and the protection of the rights of others. However, in the racial perspective of the leaflet prepared by the applicant, who was then a member of the HEP, a party working in favour of Kurdish separatism, the measures thus taken were presented as the destruction of Kurdish citizens' houses with a view to depriving them of all means of subsistence.

Through its aggressive and provocative language the leaflet in question had been likely to incite citizens of "Kurdish" origin to believe that they suffered from discrimination and that, as victims of a "special war", they were justified in acting in self-defence against the authorities by setting up "neighbourhood committees". In addition, the population of Izmir in general, and its shopkeepers in particular might have been tempted to think that those who were truly responsible for their social and economic troubles were their "Kurdish" fellow citizens and that the street traders — all "Kurdish" according to the leaflet — might endanger their well-being. Such a message was not consistent with the calls to "brotherhood", which were designed only to enable the leaflet's authors to evade their criminal responsibility.

With reference to the analysis of the situation in Turkey made by the Court in the *Zana v. Turkey* judgment of 25 November 1997 (*Reports of Judgments and Decisions* 1997-VII), the government observed that in the present case the National Security Court had noted a dangerous tendency in İzmir, which had the potential to create an explosive situation, as in southeastern Turkey, where there had been an intolerable increase in terrorism in the years 1992 and 1993. In such a case the wide limits of criticism acceptable in political debate and the high level of protection enshrined by the Court's case-law on the question were completely without relevance.

In that context, Mr Incal, who was a lawyer by profession, had overstepped the normal limits of political controversy by disregarding his "duties" and "responsibilities". He had tried to incite an ethnic group to rise against the officials and authorities of the State at a time when the PKK, a terrorist separatist organisation, had intensified its atrocities prompted by racial hatred. In such a social climate, which made it extremely easy to stir up internal dissent, or even civil strife, the Turkish authorities had had no other choice than to seize the leaflets in issue and to punish the applicant as one of those responsible.

iii. *The Commission*

45. The Commission agreed for the most part with the applicant's arguments. It emphasised that the leaflet in issue only drew attention in general terms to the existence of a "Kurdish problem" and did not contain any element of incitement to violence. Considering that an opponent of official ideas and positions must be able to find a place in the political arena, it expressed the opinion that Mr Incal's conviction had not been necessary in a democratic society.

b. **The Court's assessment**

46. As the Court has often observed, the freedom of expression enshrined in Article 10 constitutes one of the essential foundations of a democratic society and one of the basic conditions for its progress and each individual's self-fulfilment. Subject to paragraph 2, it is applicable not only to "information" or "ideas" that are favourably received or regarded as inoffensive or as a matter of indifference, but also to those that offend, shock or disturb; such are the demands of that pluralism, tolerance and broadmindedness without which there is no "democratic society" (see, among many other authorities, the *Castells v. Spain* judgment of 23 April 1992, Series A no. 236, p. 22, § 42, and the *Vogt v. Germany* judgment of 26 September 1995, Series A no. 323, p. 25, § 52).

While precious to all, freedom of expression is particularly important for political parties and their active members (see, *mutatis mutandis*, the *United Communist Party of Turkey and Others v. Turkey* judgment of 30 January 1998, *Reports* 1998-I, p. 22, § 46). They represent their electorate, draw attention to their preoccupations and defend their interests. Accordingly, interferences with the freedom of expression of a politician who is a member of an opposition party, like the applicant, call for the closest scrutiny on the Court's part (see the Castells judgment cited above, ibid.)

47. In the present case the Izmir National Security Court based its decision to convict Mr Incal on a leaflet which it held to make out the offence defined in Article 312 of the Criminal Code, namely non-public incitement to commit an offence (see paragraph 21 above).

48. In the light of the above considerations, the Court must now consider the leaflet's content in order to determine whether it justified Mr Incal's conviction.

In that connection, the Court reiterates that its task, in exercising its supervisory jurisdiction, is not to take the place of the competent domestic courts but rather to review under Article 10 the decisions they delivered pursuant to their power of appreciation. In so doing, it must satisfy itself that the national authorities based their decisions on an acceptable assessment of the relevant facts (see, *mutatis mutandis*, the Vogt judgment cited above, p. 26, § 52).

49. The National Security Court held that, by describing the State as terrorist, by drawing a distinction between citizens even though all of them were of Turkish nationality and by criticising certain municipal measures as operations

in a special war, the authors of the leaflet had knowingly incited the people to hatred and hostility and, to that end, had urged them to have recourse to illegal methods.

50. The Court notes that the relevant passages in the leaflet criticised certain administrative and municipal measures taken by the authorities, in particular against street traders. They thus reported actual events which were of some interest to the people of Izmir.

The leaflet began by complaining of an atmosphere of hostility towards citizens of Kurdish origin in Izmir and suggested that the measures concerned were directed against them in particular, to force them to leave the city. The text contained a number of virulent remarks about the policy of the Turkish government and made serious accusations, holding them responsible for the situation. Appealing to "all democratic patriots", it described the authorities' actions as "terror" and as part of a "special war" being conducted "in the country" against "the Kurdish people". It called on citizens to "oppose" this situation, in particular by means of "neighbourhood committees" (see paragraph 10 above).

The Court certainly sees in these phrases appeals to, among others, the population of Kurdish origin, urging them to band together to raise certain political demands. Although the reference to "neighbourhood committees" appears unclear, those appeals cannot, however, if read in context, be taken as incitement to the use of violence, hostility or hatred between citizens.

51. Admittedly, as the Court has already noted in other circumstances (see, *mutatis mutandis*, the United Communist Party of Turkey and Others judgment cited above, p. 27, § 58), it cannot be ruled out that such a text may conceal objectives and intentions different from the ones it proclaims. However, as there is no evidence of any concrete action which might belie the sincerity of the aim declared by the leaflet's authors, the Court sees no reason to doubt it.

52. There remains, therefore, the question whether, in the light of the foregoing considerations, the applicant's criminal conviction can be regarded as necessary in a democratic society, that is to say whether it met a "pressing social need" and was "proportionate to the legitimate aim pursued".

53. The freedom of political debate is undoubtedly not absolute in nature. A Contracting State may make it subject to certain "restrictions" or "penalties", but it is for the Court to give a final ruling on the compatibility of such measures with the freedom of expression enshrined in the Convention (see the Castells judgment cited above, p. 23, § 46).

In the present case the government pleaded the "duties" and "responsibilities" with which Article 10 links exercise of the freedom of expression (see paragraph 44 above). However, these do not dispense with the obligation to ensure that an interference satisfies the requirements of paragraph 2 (see, *mutatis mutandis*, the *Thorgeir Thorgeirson v. Iceland* judgment of 25 June 1992, Series A no. 239, p. 27, § 64).

54. The limits of permissible criticism are wider with regard to the government than in relation to a private citizen, or even a politician. In a democratic system the actions or omissions of the government must be subject to the close

scrutiny not only of the legislative and judicial authorities but also of public opinion. Furthermore, the dominant position which the government occupies makes it necessary for it to display restraint in resorting to criminal proceedings, particularly where other means are available for replying to the unjustified attacks and criticisms of its adversaries. Nevertheless it remains open to the competent State authorities to adopt, in their capacity as guarantors of public order, measures, even of a criminal-law nature, intended to react appropriately and without excess to such remarks (see the Castells judgment cited above, p. 23, § 46).

55. In the present case the Izmir executive committee of the HEP submitted one copy of the leaflet to the Izmir prefecture on 2 July 1992 with an application for permission to distribute it (see paragraph 11 above). The security police, who were then asked to study its content, considered that the leaflet could be regarded as separatist propaganda (see paragraph 12 above). At that stage the authorities were accordingly in a position to require changes to the text. However, the day after this application was lodged at the prefecture the leaflets were seized and prosecutions brought against its authors, including Mr Incal, under Article 312 of the Criminal Code, among other provisions (see paragraph 21 above).

56. The Court notes the radical nature of the interference in question. Its preventive aspect by itself raises problems under Article 10 (see, among other authorities, the *Vereniging Weekblad* Bluf! *v. the Netherlands* judgment of 9 February 1995, Series A no. 306-A, p. 16, §§ 45 and 46, and, *mutatis mutandis*, the *Vereinigung demokratischer Soldaten Österreichs and Gubi v. Austria* judgment of 19 December 1994, Series A no. 302, pp. 18–19, § 40).

In addition, the Izmir National Security Court sentenced the applicant to six months and twenty days' imprisonment and a fine of 55,555 Turkish liras and disqualified him from driving for fifteen days (see paragraph 16 above).

Furthermore, as a result of his conviction of a "public order" offence, Mr Incal was debarred from the civil service and forbidden to take part in a number of activities within political organisations, associations or trades unions (see paragraph 22 above).

57. In order to demonstrate the existence of a "pressing social need" which would justify the finding that the interference complained of was "proportionate to the legitimate aim pursued", the representative of the government asserted at the hearing before the Court that "it was apparent from the wording of the leaflets ... that they were intended to foment an insurrection by one ethnic group against the State authorities". It had therefore been the State's "duty to forestall any attempt to promote terrorist activities by means of incitement to hatred", given that "the interest in combating and crushing terrorism takes precedence in a democratic society". Certain armed groups such as the PKK increased their effectiveness by putting out propaganda cloaked by the freedom of expression.

58. The Court is prepared to take into account the background to the cases submitted to it, particularly problems linked to the prevention of terrorism (see, among other authorities, the *Ireland v. the United Kingdom* judgment of 18 January

1978, Series A no. 25, pp. 9 et seq., §§ 11 et seq.; the *Aksoy v. Turkey* judgment of 18 December 1996, *Reports* 1996-VI, pp. 2281 and 2284, §§ 70 and 84; the Zana judgment cited above, p. 2549, §§ 59 and 60; and, most recently, the United Communist Party of Turkey and Others judgment cited above, p. 27, § 59). It observes, however, that the circumstances of the present case are not comparable to those found in the Zana case (ibid.). Here the Court does not discern anything which would warrant the conclusion that Mr Incal was in any way responsible for the problems of terrorism in Turkey, and more specifically in Izmir. It should be pointed out in that connection that not even the National Security Court upheld the public prosecutor's submission that the Prevention of Terrorism Act (Law no. 3713) should be applied to the applicant (see paragraphs 15, 16 and 24 above).

59. In conclusion, Mr Incal's conviction was disproportionate to the aim pursued, and therefore unnecessary in a democratic society. There has accordingly been a breach of Article 10 of the Convention.

60. The applicant further complained of an infringement of his right to freedom of thought, guaranteed by Article 9 of the Convention. Like the Commission, the Court considers that this complaint is subsumed by the complaint under Article 10 and that it is not necessary to examine it separately.

## *II. Alleged violation of Article 6 § 1 of the Convention*

61. Mr Incal further argued that neither his trial in the Izmir National Security Court nor the proceedings before the Criminal Division of the Court of Cassation had satisfied the requirements of Article 6 § 1 of the Convention, the relevant part of which provides:

> In the determination of ... any criminal charge against him, everyone is entitled to a fair and public hearing ... by an independent and impartial tribunal ... .

He submitted that the National Security Court was not an "independent and impartial tribunal"; as to the Court of Cassation, it had not respected the principle of adversarial procedure or equality of arms and had not held a hearing.

The government rejected this argument, whereas the Commission accepted it, except for that part which related to the lack of a public hearing.

*A. The proceedings in the National Security Court*

1. ARGUMENTS OF THE PARTICIPANTS

a. **The applicant**

62. Mr Incal submitted that the Izmir National Security Court could not be regarded as an "independent and impartial tribunal" within the meaning of Article 6 § 1. The military judge who sat in it was dependent on the executive

and, more specifically, on the military authorities, because while performing his judicial duties he remained an officer and maintained his links with the armed forces and his hierarchical superiors. The latter retained the power to influence his career by means of the assessment reports they drew up on him.

Mr Incal maintained that the National Security Courts were special courts set up to protect the State's interests rather than to do justice as such; in that respect their function was similar to that of the executive. The presence of a military judge in the court's composition only served to confirm the army's authority and its intimidating influence over both the defendant and public opinion in general. The fact that a military judge was able to pass judgment on a civilian, and a politician at that, in connection with an offence that had nothing to do with military justice, evidenced the armed forces' influence over the handling of Turkey's political problems.

b. **The government**

63. The government submitted that the procedure for the appointment of the military judges sitting as members of the National Security Courts and the safeguards they enjoyed in the performance of their judicial duties perfectly satisfied the criteria laid down by the Court's case-law on the subject.

The arguments concerning these judges' responsibility towards their commanding officers and the rules governing their professional assessment were overstated; their duties as officers were limited to obeying military regulations and observing military courtesies. They were safe from any pressure from their hierarchical superiors, as such an attempt was punishable under the Military Criminal Code. The assessment system applied only to military judges' non-judicial duties. In addition, they had access to their assessment reports and could even challenge their content in the Supreme Military Administrative Court.

In the present case, neither the colleagues or hierarchical or disciplinary superiors of the military judge in question nor the public authorities who had appointed him had any connection with the parties to Mr Incal's trial or any interest whatsoever in the judgment to be delivered.

c. **The Commission**

64. In the Commission's submission, the legal rules governing the composition and functioning of the National Security Courts raised a number of questions about their independence, particularly as regards the system for the appointment and assessment of the military judges who sat in them. It took the view that the participation of a military judge in criminal proceedings against a civilian showed the exceptional nature of such proceedings and could be interpreted as an intervention by the armed forces in the field of civil justice. The applicant's concerns about the National Security Court's lack of impartiality could therefore be regarded as objectively justified.

2. THE COURT'S ASSESSMENT

65. The Court reiterates that in order to establish whether a tribunal can be considered "independent" for the purposes of Article 6 § 1, regard must be had,

inter alia, to the manner of appointment of its members and their term of office, the existence of safeguards against outside pressures and the question whether it presents an appearance of independence (see, among many other authorities, the *Findlay v. the United Kingdom* judgment of 25 February 1997, *Reports* 1997-I, p. 281, § 73).

As to the condition of "impartiality" within the meaning of that provision, there are two tests to be applied: the first consists in trying to determine the personal conviction of a particular judge in a given case and the second in ascertaining whether the judge offered guarantees sufficient to exclude any legitimate doubt in this respect. It was not contested before the Court that only the second of these tests was relevant in the instant case (see, *mutatis mutandis*, the *Gautrin and Others v. France* judgment of 20 May 1998, *Reports* 1998-III, pp. 1030–31, § 58).

In the instant case, however, the Court will consider both issues — independence and impartiality — together.

66. Law no. 2845, promulgated on 16 June 1983, pursuant to Article 143 of the Constitution, governs the composition and functioning of the National Security Courts (see paragraph 28 above). Under the provisions of section 5, these courts are composed of three judges, one of whom is a regular officer and member of the Military Legal Service.

As the independence and impartiality of the two civilian judges is not disputed, the Court must determine what the position was with regard to the military judge.

67. The Court notes that the status of military judges sitting as members of National Security Courts provides certain guarantees of independence and impartiality. For example, military judges undergo the same professional training as their civilian counterparts, which gives them the status of career members of the Military Legal Service. When sitting as members of National Security Courts, military judges enjoy constitutional safeguards identical to those of civilian judges; in addition, with certain exceptions, they may not be removed from office or made to retire early without their consent (see paragraphs 27 and 28 above); as regular members of a National Security Court they sit as individuals; according to the Constitution, they must be independent and no public authority may give them instructions concerning their judicial activities or influence them in the performance of their duties (see paragraphs 27 and 30 above and, *mutatis mutandis*, the *Ettl and Others v. Austria* judgment of 23 April 1987, Series A no. 117, p. 18, § 38).

68. On the other hand, other aspects of these judges' status make it questionable. Firstly, they are servicemen who still belong to the army, which in turn takes its orders from the executive. Secondly, they remain subject to military discipline and assessment reports are compiled on them by the army for that purpose (see paragraphs 28 and 29 above). Decisions pertaining to their appointment are to a great extent taken by the administrative authorities and the army (see paragraph 29 above). Lastly, their term of office as National Security Court judges is only four years and can be renewed.

69. The Court notes that the National Security Courts were set up pursuant to the Constitution to deal with offences affecting Turkey's territorial integrity and national unity, its democratic regime and its State security (see paragraphs 26 and 28 above). Their main distinguishing feature is that, although they are non-military courts, one of their judges is always a member of the Military Legal Service.

70. At the hearing before the Court the government submitted that the only justification for the presence of military judges in the National Security Courts was their undoubted competence and experience in the battle against organised crime, including that committed by illegal armed groups. For years the armed forces and the military judges — in whom, moreover, the people placed great trust — had acted, partly under martial law, as the guarantors of the democratic and secular Republic of Turkey, while assuming their social, cultural and moral responsibilities. For as long as the terrorist threat persisted, military judges would have to continue to lend their full support to these special courts, whose task was extremely difficult.

It is not for the Court — which is aware of the problems caused by terrorism (see, *mutatis mutandis*, the judgments cited in paragraph 58 above) — to pass judgment on these assertions. Its task is not to determine *in abstracto* whether it was necessary to set up such courts in a Contracting State or to review the relevant practice, but to ascertain whether the manner in which one of them functioned infringed the applicant's right to a fair trial (see, among many other authorities, *mutatis mutandis*, the *Fey v. Austria judgment* of 24 February 1993, Series A no. 255-A, p. 12, § 27).

71. In this respect even appearances may be of a certain importance. What is at stake is the confidence which the courts in a democratic society must inspire in the public and above all, as far as criminal proceedings are concerned, in the accused (see, among other authorities, the *Hauschildt v. Denmark* judgment of 24 May 1989, Series A no. 154, p. 21, § 48, the Thorgeir Thorgeirson judgment cited above, p. 23, § 51, and the *Pullar v. the United Kingdom* judgment of 10 June 1996, *Reports* 1996-III, p. 794, § 38). In deciding whether there is a legitimate reason to fear that a particular court lacks independence or impartiality, the standpoint of the accused is important without being decisive. What is decisive is whether his doubts can be held to be objectively justified (see, *mutatis mutandis*, the Hauschildt judgment cited above, p. 21, § 48, and the Gautrin and Others judgment cited above, pp. 1030–31, § 58).

72. Mr Incal was convicted of disseminating separatist propaganda capable of inciting the people to resist the government and commit criminal offences, for participating in the decision to distribute the leaflet in issue, taken on 1 July 1992 by the executive committee of the İzmir section of the HEP (see paragraphs 15 and 16 above). As the acts which gave rise to the case were considered likely to endanger the founding principles of the Republic of Turkey, or to affect its security, they came *ipso jure* under the jurisdiction of the National Security Courts (see paragraph 28 above).

The Court notes, however, that in considering the question of compliance with Article 10 it did not discern anything in the leaflet which might be regarded as incitement of part of the population to violence, hostility or hatred between citizens (see paragraph 50 above). Moreover, the National Security Court refused to apply the Prevention of Terrorism Act (Law no. 3713) (see paragraph 16 above). In addition, the Court attaches great importance to the fact that a civilian had to appear before a court composed, even if only in part, of members of the armed forces.

It follows that the applicant could legitimately fear that because one of the judges of the İzmir National Security Court was a military judge it might allow itself to be unduly influenced by considerations which had nothing to do with the nature of the case. The Court of Cassation was not able to dispel these concerns, as it did not have full jurisdiction (see paragraph 25 above and, among other authorities, *mutatis mutandis*, the *Helle v. Finland* judgment of 19 December 1997, *Reports* 1997-VIII, p. 2926, § 46).

73. In conclusion, the applicant had legitimate cause to doubt the independence and impartiality of the İzmir National Security Court. There has accordingly been a breach of Article 6 § 1.

## B. *The proceedings in the Court of Cassation*

74. Having regard to the above conclusion (see paragraph 73 above), the Court considers that it is not necessary to consider the other complaints under Article 6 relating to the proceedings in the Court of Cassation (see, *mutatis mutandis*, the Findlay judgment cited above, pp. 282–83, § 80).

\*\*\*

[Then the Court ordered Turkey to pay non-pecuniary damages and costs.]

# Document no. 63

**List of some decisions rendered by the ECtHR in 1998 in which Turkey was a party[24]**

| Application no. | Case name | Issue | Decision date | Decision |
|---|---|---|---|---|
| 19392/92 | United Communist Party of Turkey | Freedom of association and expression | 28 October 1996 | Violation of Article 11 |
| 22729/93 | Mehmet, Kaya | Killing | 19 February 1998 | Violation of Articles 2 and 13 |
| 23184–5/94 | Selcuk and Asker | Village destruction | 24 April 1998 | Violation of Articles 3, 8, P1(1) and 13 |
| 22275/93 | Gundem | Inhumane treatment | 25 May 1998 | No violation |
| 24276/94 | Kurt | Disappearances | 25 May 1998 | Violation of Articles 5, 3, 13 and 25(1) |
| 21237/93 | Socialist Party and Others | Freedom of association and expression | 25 May 1998 | Violation of Article 11 |
| 22496/93 | Tekin, Salih | Torture and ill-treatment | 9 June 1998 | Violation of Article 3 and 13 |
| 22678/93 | Incal | Independent judiciary | 9 June 1998 | Violation of Articles 6 and 10 |
| 21593/93 | Gulec | Killing | 27 July 1998 | Violation of Article 2 |
| 23818/94 | Ergi | Killing | 28 July 1998 | Violation of Articles 2, 13 and 25(1) |
| 22495/93 | Yasa | Killing | 2 September 1998 | Violation of Article 13 |
| 22880/93 | Aytekin | Killing | 23 September 1998 | Objection withheld |
| 19639/92 | Aka | Delay in payment | 23 September 1998 | Violation of Article p1(1) |
| 21380/93, 21381/93, 21383/93 | Demir and Others | Length of custody | 23 September 1998 | Violation of Article 5(3) |
| 19601/92 | Ciraklar | Independent judiciary | 28 October 1998 | Violation of Article 6 |

# Document no. 64

**[European Parliament] Resolution on the commission reports on developments in relations with Turkey since the entry into force of the Customs Union[25]**

*The European Parliament,*

- having regard to the Commission reports (COM(96)0491 - C4-0605/96 and COM(98)0147 - C4-0217/98),
- having regard to its assent of 13 December 1995 to the common position of the Community in the EC–Turkey Association Council on implementing the final phase of the Customs Union, its opinion of 13 December 1995 on the proposal for a Council Regulation regarding the implementation of a special financial cooperation measure for Turkey and its resolution on the Human Rights situation in Turkey of the same date,
- having regard to its resolution of 18 January 1996 on the situation in Turkey and the offer of a ceasefire made by the PKK,
- having regard to its resolution of 15 February 1996 on the outcome of the conciliation procedure provided for in the Joint Declaration of 4 March 1975 by the European Parliament, the Council and the Commission on the common position adopted by the Council with a view to adopting a Council Regulation regarding the implementation of a special financial cooperation measure for Turkey,
- having regard to its resolution of 15 February 1996 on the provocative actions and contestation of sovereign rights by Turkey against a Member State of the Union,
- having regard to its resolution of 20 June 1996 on Human Rights and the situation in Turkey,
- having regard to its opinion of 18 July 1996 on the proposal for a Council Decision laying down the procedure for adopting the Community's position in the Customs Union Joint Committee set up by Decision no. 1/95 of the EC–Turkey Association Council on the implementation of the final phase of the Customs Union,
- having regard to its resolutions of 19 September 1996 on the political situation in Turkey and on the situation in the Kurdish security zone in northern Iraq,

- having regard to its resolution of 24 October 1996 on violations of religious freedom in Turkey,
- having regard to its resolution of 12 December 1996 on freedom of the press and Human Rights in Turkey,
- having regard to its resolution of 13 March 1997 on the release of Leyla Zana,
- having regard to its resolution of 15 May 1997 on freedom of the media in Turkey,
- having regard to its resolution of 12 June 1997 on the abolition of the death penalty,
- having regard to its resolution of 17 July 1997 on the situation in Turkey and northern Iraq,
- having regard to its opinion of 18 November 1997 on the proposal for a Council Decision laying down the procedure for adopting the Community's position in the Customs Union Joint Committee set up by Decision no. 1/95 of the EC–Turkey Association Council on the implementation of the final phase of the Customs Union (reconsultation),
- having regard to its resolution of 15 January 1998 on Kurdish refugees and on the position of the European Union,
- having regard to its resolution of 14 May 1998 on Turkey, in which it expressed its abhorrence at the attack on Akin Birdal, President of the Turkish Human Rights Association,
- having regard to the conclusions of the EU–Turkey Association Council of 29 April 1997,
- having regard to the report of the Committee on Foreign Affairs, Security and Defence Policy and the opinions of the Committee on Budgets and the Committee on External Economic Relations and the Committee on Civil Liberties and Internal Affairs (A4-0251/1998),

A. whereas its assent to the Customs Union was given on the understanding that Turkey would introduce political reforms that would bring it closer to fulfilling the criteria for accession to the European Union,

B. whereas the Commission's conclusion is that "no substantial progress has been achieved as regards Human Rights and the democratic reform process in Turkey",

\*\*\*

E. having regard to the conclusions of the European Council of 12 and 13 December 1997, which reaffirm Turkey's eligibility to become a member of the European Union, and having regard also to the conditions which Turkey must satisfy in order to obtain such membership,

F. whereas relations between the European Union and Turkey must develop with due respect for the mutual undertakings they have given in the context of different agreements,

G. whereas the development of a democratic state subject to the rule of law in Turkey is impeded by severe structural problems,

\*\*\*

I. having regard to the various specific measures proposed by the Commission, which could constitute a basis for a new beginning in long-term relations with Turkey provided that the country demonstrates in practical terms that it is ready to adjust to European standards in respect of Human Rights, minorities and the development of good relations with its neighbouring countries,

1. Agrees with the Commission that the Customs Union is, in general, working satisfactorily and welcomes the latest trends towards a rebalancing of the increased trade between the EU and Turkey which is one of its consequences;

\*\*\*

3. Reiterates its support for proposals from Turkish civil society aimed at achieving improvements in Turkish democracy and in Human Rights which would bring it into line with EU standards and fulfil promises made by the Turkish authorities when the Customs Union agreement was signed, including constitutional guarantees of Human Rights, minority rights, respect for fundamental freedoms, the right of freedom of expression for all and the accountability of the military to the country's political authorities, on the basis of international pacts and the European Convention on Human Rights to which Turkey is a signatory;

4. Wishes to make it clear that it will examine Turkey, like all other applicant countries, in the light of the Copenhagen criteria;

\*\*\*

9. Acknowledges the structural problems that Turkey has in establishing a well-functioning constitutional state and in adapting and creating the institutions forming part thereof and, in this connection, calls on the Commission to consider whether a specific budgetary item for Turkey should be included in the MEDA programme on democracy;

10. Calls on the Commission to continue with its annual examination of relations with Turkey, with all due attention and in a spirit of refusal of compromise, since it is essential that it should be possible to apply the Customs Union agreement with Turkey in all its provisions, including the financial ones; insists that the Commission should publish its annual report in time for it to be available during the consideration, in Parliament, of the following year's budget;

\*\*\*

13. Takes note of the considerable development in economic relations within the Customs Union with Turkey and the progressive alignment of Turkish

legislation and tariff schemes with EU measures; considers, however, that the customs law should be improved and implemented as soon as possible in order to ensure the existence of legislation covering all administrative procedures; stresses the need for a commitment by the Turkish government to strengthen legislation on intellectual property so as to combat counterfeiting;

\*\*\*

16. Calls on the Commission to rule out any measures which would isolate Turkey and thus prevent any improvement in its political system, the living conditions of the population and the Human Rights situation;

17. Notes the Commission's desire, as reflected in the strategy for Turkey it has submitted, to extend the Customs Union in specific sectors (transit, public contracts, harmonisation of laws);

18. Recalls the proposals made at the fourth meeting of the Joint Consultative Committee (Gaziantep, 12 June 1997), with particular regard to the priorities for aid for "civil society" and participation by Turkey in Community programmes;

\*\*\*

20. Fully agrees with the Commission on the importance of the following points: continuing democratisation, safeguarding Human Rights and establishing political control of the armed forces;

\*\*\*

21. Reaffirms its view that a solution of the conflict in the southeast can only by achieved politically and supports proposals aimed at providing legal recognition of Kurdish identity and national and international initiatives which could promote dialogue and negotiation between the parties; points to the need for a ceasefire and calls on the Turkish authorities to seek a peaceful negotiated political solution to the Kurdish question;

22. Condemns the invasion of northern Iraq and considers that the need to deal with PKK terrorism does not justify the violation of international borders; the problem should be dealt with on the basis of respect for the rule of law and the international conventions to which Turkey is a party;

23. Calls for the immediate release of Leyla Zana, to whom Parliament has already awarded its Sakharov Prize, and the other political prisoners;

\*\*\*

25. Insists on the need for the renewal of political dialogue;

\*\*\*

# Document no. 65

[European Parliament] Resolution on the communication from the Commission to the Council and the European Parliament on the further development of relations with Turkey and on the communication from the Commission to the Council: European Strategy for Turkey — The Commission's initial operational proposals[26]

\*\*\*

A. whereas Turkey has been associated with the European Community since the entry into force of the Ankara Agreement on 1 December 1964,

B. whereas Article 28 of the Association Agreement affirms Turkey's eligibility for membership of the European Union, an eligibility confirmed most recently in the Luxembourg European Council,

C. whereas all applicant countries to the Union have to fulfil a number of economic and political criteria, laid down at the Copenhagen European Council, before they can accede to the Union,

D. whereas despite repeated assurances by the government, the democratic deficit in Turkey has still not been eliminated and the need for lasting reform persists;

E. noting that the relations between the EU and Turkey, from the Association Agreement and via the implementation of the final phase of the Customs Union on 13 December 1995, constitute a longer and economically closer relationship than with the applicant countries from Central and Eastern Europe, thus requiring a different strategy from those countries for preparing accession,

\*\*\*

G. whereas the Luxembourg European Council called for a strategy to be drawn up to prepare Turkey for accession by bringing it closer to the European Union in every field,

H. whereas the Commission's initial operational proposals on taking forward this strategy, published in March 1998 in its communication to the Council

COM(98)0124 mentioned above, were welcomed by the Cardiff European Council, which also asked the Commission to table financial proposals to underpin its implementation, and invited Turkey to provide its own proposals to enrich the strategy,

I. whereas the Council to date has failed to agree on a legal basis for a financial protocol with Turkey,

J. noting that the report on Turkey's progress towards accession, based on Article 28 of the Association Agreement, referred to hereafter as the progress report, was adopted by the Commission on 4 November 1998 and will be submitted by the Commission to the European Council at the end of 1998,

K. noting, however, the negative position adopted by Turkey after the decision of the Luxembourg European Council and the absence of Turkey from the European Conference convened in London for all the candidate countries,

1. Reaffirms Turkey's eligibility to apply for membership of the EU, and believes that its membership could be an important contribution to peace and security in Europe;

2. Regrets that Turkey has so far not agreed to take part in the European Conference;

3. Rejects any reference to religious beliefs as a reason for rejecting Turkey's (or any other nation's) eligibility;

*Economic aspects*

\*\*\*

*Political aspects*

13. Notes that the criteria agreed at the Copenhagen European Council require that all applicant countries must achieve "stability of institutions guaranteeing democracy, the rule of law, Human Rights and respect for and protection of minorities";

14. Agrees with the view of significant sections of Turkish civil society, and of the Commission, that Turkey is far from achieving these criteria;

15. Calls on the Turkish government to fulfil the promises made to Parliament concerning Human Rights and democratic reform at the time when Parliament gave its assent to the Customs Union;

16. Calls on Turkey to fulfil its obligations concerning democracy, Human Rights and freedom of expression under the Customs Union agreement with the EU and to put an end to persecution, imprisonment and torture, to which Kurds in particular are subjected;

17. Agrees with the Commission that no substantial progress has been achieved as regards Human Rights and the democratic reform process in Turkey since the Customs Union entered into force and that it is "the sole responsibility of Turkey to improve the situation with regard to the pressing need to reinforce democracy and to protect human and minority rights";

18. Is disturbed by reports in the Turkish press concerning the close links between state representatives and illegal economic and paramilitary activities;

19. Believes that a resolution of the Kurdish question in Turkey would have important implications for democracy, Human Rights and minority rights in Turkey and would bring Turkey significantly closer to fulfilling the Copenhagen criteria; considers in this regard that the cessation of terrorist activities by certain Kurdish organisations as declared in a ceasefire would be an undoubted step forward;

20. Calls for the release of Leyla Zana, the European Parliament's Sakharov Prize Laureate, and the release of all political prisoners;

21. Believes that the following would contribute substantially to a solution, one which respects Turkey's territorial integrity and which could be achieved through a dialogue between all the relevant forces of society, including the representatives of the Kurdish population:

- constitutionally guaranteed cultural rights including freedom of expression and publication in the Kurdish language as well as rights to mother tongue education in all parts of Turkey;
- democratic reforms which would allow the participation and fair representation of all interests in the Grand National Assembly including reform of the Law of Political Parties, the Law of Elections, and, in particular, the lowering of the 10 per cent threshold for representation and the repeal of "anti-terror legislation", especially the infamous Article 8 under which intellectuals, writers and political figures are still held in prison;
- reinforcement of the leadership and control of elected and democratic institutions over civilian and military administration including the removal of the military from their current constitutional role in the political system as steps towards the demilitarisation of Turkish society;
- the lifting of the State of Emergency in the east and southeast provinces and the dismantling of the system of village guards in these areas;
- social and economic development for the benefit of the local population in those areas devastated by the violent conflict and which have suffered the long-term effects of lack of investment and destruction of infrastructure;

22. Welcomes the unilateral ceasefire by the PKK and calls on Turkey to put an immediate stop to attacks on Kurdish targets;

\*\*\*

27. Welcomes the opening of negotiations on the implementation of the Commission's European Strategy and calls for the resumption of political dialogue between the EU and Turkey and the strengthening of political dialogue between political forces in European and Turkish society, including with the Turkish armed forces;

## Proposals

28. Considers that the main obstacles for Turkey's application to the European Union are political ones, as is also underlined in the Commission's progress report;

29. Asks the Turkish authorities, therefore, to make concrete proposals for action within a clear timeframe to bring Turkey closer to fulfilling the Copenhagen criteria, especially the political criteria, and to include a detailed timetable; urges the Commission and Council to draw up, in conjunction with the Turkish authorities, a joint programme for Turkey's accession to the Union;

30. Calls for an international conference to be held on the Kurdish problem with a view to finding a political and peaceful solution acceptable to all parties involved;

31. Considers that the participation of Turkey in the European Conference has the potential to positively influence the integration of Turkey and the accession procedure and calls on Turkey to take part in the next meeting of the Conference;

32. Believes that the Commission's European strategy for Turkey, combined with adequate financing, could constitute an appropriate pre-accession strategy for Turkey.

\*\*\*

# 10 1999 Helsinki European Council and European Union membership perspective for Turkey

# Document no. 66

**Council of Europe Committee on the Honouring of Obligations and Commitments by Member States of the Council of Europe. Honouring of Obligations and Commitments by Turkey, 15 January 1999**[1]

\*\*\*

*Foreword*

1. Over the years, Turkey has, more than any other member State, been the subject of recommendations, resolutions and orders of the Parliamentary Assembly; your co-rapporteurs have reproduced a list in Appendix 1 to this information report. And yet, we are all impressed by the efforts made by the respective governments, by the many activities and unconditioned cooperation of the Turkish Parliamentary Delegation, by the number of Conventions signed and ratified and, in general, by progress made towards full implementation of the obligations and commitments under the Council of Europe membership.

2. In this information report, the co-rapporteurs will try and analyse the present situation in the country. They will report on the areas where they have seen progress and they will identify the problems which warrant further action and assistance. But they will also endeavour to create understanding for the reasons why in some respects this important and devoted member State takes a specific position in the Council of Europe and define guidelines for further development. In doing so, they have no pretension to give an authoritative interpretation of the history of Turkey; they merely wish to explain the background against which they view the developments in Turkey and they would be grateful for any complementary remarks by their Turkish colleagues.

\*\*\*

5. Since the instalment of democracy in Turkey, the country is characterised by some traditions which have gradually disappeared elsewhere: the nearly untouchable position of the military and the police forces, the extensive powers

of the public prosecution, the respect for, in particular, the senior civil service and the influence of university professors. The co-rapporteurs have gained the impression that today, contrary to the reformist intentions of the founder of the Republic of Turkey, in certain circles in Turkey these principles in their original, petrified form of 1923 are being considered and applied as still valid doctrines to solve the topical problems of modern Turkey.

6. There can be no doubt that Turkey is a democracy — with a multi-party system, free elections and an active and independent legislature. However, in general the Turkish nation is more patriotic, more disciplined and more obedient to authority; it is more easily ready to accept the limitations of fundamental freedoms and Human Rights when the integrity and the independence of the Turkish State so requires. This respect of the heritage of Kemalism causes clashes when individuals or groups of individuals want to implement norms and standards which are applied in other member States where the supremacy of the State is less evident.

7. When they take into account the above conception of Human Rights and individual freedoms, the co-rapporteurs can more easily understand why in Turkey, notwithstanding the efforts made and progress achieved, there are still some areas where there is room for improvement in the fulfilment of obligations and commitments. These areas are set out in the following report.

*A. Introduction*

8. Following visits in November 1996 and March 1997 within the framework of the former monitoring process of Order 508 the Rapporteurs visited Turkey from 23 to 26 November 1997 and from 6 to 9 September 1998. The purpose was to extend and deepen dialogue with the Turkish authorities, in cooperation with the Turkish Parliamentary Delegation, on a certain number of issues which the Committee had determined as "priority" following an exchange of views with the Delegation at the Committee's meeting in Strasbourg on 25 September 1997. The programmes are contained in Appendices 2 and 3.

9. For many observers outside Turkey the country has a negative Human Rights image, which seems justified by a number of facts, and it is important to take action. This image reflects negatively on the Council of Europe and on Turkey, notably as regards its aspirations for membership of the European Union. There is therefore a common interest in seeking to determine whether the dynamics exist in Turkey for improving the Human Rights situation, taking into account mainly the obligations and commitments entered into by Turkey with respect to the Council of Europe but also to the history and the geopolitics of the region.

*B. Main issues*

I. TORTURE AND INHUMAN OR DEGRADING TREATMENT OR PUNISHMENT

10. The most damaging criticism of Turkey is recourse to torture and to inhuman or degrading treatment of detainees as part of its administrative culture. In

this respect, the co-rapporteurs refer, inter alia, to the 1996 Declaration made by the European Committee for the Prevention of Torture and Inhuman or Degrading Treatment or Punishment.

11. However, times have changed since 1995 when the Assembly expressed its deep concern about Human Rights violations in Turkey in Recommendation 1266. Human rights in general, and these aspects in particular, have become a persistent theme of domestic political debate. Moreover, they have now become a part of Government policy, including in its foreign relations dimension, as shown by the Prime Minister's circular of 3 December 1997. It contains the following passage:

> ... bearing in mind that the violation of Human Rights is a disgrace for humanity, that it adversely affects public opinion in our country and in the civilised world and that it can cause damage for our country which is difficult to remedy, the measures set out below shall be implemented without fail and their implementation shall be monitored by the authorities responsible.

12. The co-rapporteurs were impressed by the activity of the High Coordinating Committee for Human Rights which has now met fifty-two times, to propose new laws or amendments to existing legislation, promote deregularisation and improve training and education. They regret, however, that the Parliament has not yet started to discuss these proposals, mainly because of the lack of strength of the ruling coalition.

13. The co-rapporteurs also noted that the Parliamentary Inquiry Committee on Human Rights had toured the country and was preparing a report on the respect of Human Rights in Turkey. They express the hope that this report will be finalised as quickly as possible and given due publicity.

14. This growing awareness of the need to put an end to degrading treatment and torture of detainees in particular has resulted in a number of practical measures, both preventive and repressive, such as training and education of police officers, the distribution in police stations of rules for correct interrogation and of the texts of the related Conventions, medical checks before and after interrogation and investigation and punishment in cases of torture. In this respect, the co-rapporteurs refer to the following initiatives which have been taken:

- a draft law amending articles 243, 245 and 354 of the Turkish Penal Code and redefining torture, ill-treatment and abuse of power and introducing or increasing penalties, has been approved by the TGNA [Turkish Grand National Assembly] Justice Commission;
- a "Regulation on Apprehension, Detention and Release Procedure", which constitutes a reform in this field and improves the current practice, has entered into force on 1 October 1998;
- a draft law on the prosecution of civil servants and other public officers has been approved by the TGNA Justice Commission;

- a draft Criminal Code, lifting death penalty, defining torture and imposing penalties has been presented to the TGNA Justice Commission;
- a Circular has been issued by the General Directorate of Security in June 1998 which states that "until it is proven by law that a person is guilty, he is presumed innocent".

15. The co-rapporteurs welcome these initiatives as important steps forward but are not yet convinced that they are or will be systematically implemented in practice. One reason for the continuing torture might be the importance which is attached to the confession in Turkish criminal law, which in itself is sufficient for conviction of the suspect. Another difficulty lies in the fear of suspects to report on torture which they have undergone; here measures should be taken to establish formal and safe procedures for such complaints to be investigated objectively. Furthermore, the co-rapporteurs recommend that the initial period of detention for persons accused of "political offences" (e.g. terrorism, narcotics) should be the same as for ordinary suspects and thus be reduced from four days to forty-eight hours; similarly, detainees brought before the State Security Court should be provided with the same rights as "normal" suspects in police custody, in particular the right to consult a lawyer without delay.

16. Concern about still ongoing torture and inhuman or degrading treatment seems justified in the light of information supplied by the Diyarbakir Bar Association and non-governmental Human Rights organisations in Turkey, such as the Human Rights Association, the Human Rights Foundation, the Mazlem Der Organisation of Human Rights and Solidarity for Oppressed People and the Turkish Medical Association, who can play a very important role in this context. The co-rapporteurs firmly recommend that these organisations, which are now tolerated by the authorities, will in the near future be assisted in their work, in particular by facilitating their access to detainees.

II. THE RULE OF LAW

17. The co-rapporteurs noted that a number of important amendments to existing laws, including the Penal Code and the Prevention of Terrorism Act, have been prepared which, if enacted, would improve the respect of Human Rights in Turkey. The text of these amendments was, however, not yet available in English and it was said that these amendments might still be modified. The co-rapporteurs have asked to be kept informed about developments in this respect.

18. The co-rapporteurs welcomed improvements already made in existing legislation, such as certain rules on the treatment of detainees. However, after their visit to the Aksaray Security Headquarters in Istanbul, they wish to express their concern that some changes made in the relevant laws should be strictly implemented, in particular respect for the right of the detainee to consult a lawyer, medical examination and the duration of detention.

19. Another aspect of the rule of law in Turkey is the existence of emergency rule in certain parts of the country, justified by the Turkish authorities as

necessary to fight terrorism perpetrated by the PKK (Workers' Party of Kurdistan). While Turkey has the right, like any other state, to combat terrorism and preserve its territorial integrity, in the medium and long-term such emergency rule is incompatible with the rule of law. Since 1987, emergency rule has been imposed in a number of provinces of Turkey. After the number of provinces subject to such rule had decreased, it was again extended, by a decision of the National Security Council on 29 June 1998, for four months in the provinces of Diyarbakir, Hakkari, Siirt, Sirnak, Tunceli and Van.

20. Under these emergency rules a number of villages have been evacuated and even destroyed. The fact that such dramatic actions are being taken can only underline the immediate need for peace to be established in the region. In that context, an accompanying feature of emergency rule in these provinces is the existence of a village guard system. The village guards are a force of approximately 50,000 ethnic Kurdish villagers armed and paid by the Government to fight the PKK. Pressure to join the village guards and reprisals by the security forces against those who refuse, or retaliation by the PKK against those who consent, puts the local population in an impossible situation. In two cases by the European Court of Human Rights, Turkish security forces were found guilty of burning houses to force the evacuation of villages in the southeast which refused to join the village guard system. In the most recent case also linked to the village guard system, the Turkish authorities failed to protect a Turkish citizen's right to life on account of the defects in the planning and conduct of a security forces' operation and the lack of an adequate and effective investigation. The co-rapporteurs therefore recall the appeal to abolish the village guard system contained in Assembly Recommendation 1377 (1998) on the humanitarian situation of the Kurdish refugees and displaced persons in southeast Turkey and north Iraq.

21. The co-rapporteurs furthermore consider that it is incompatible with the rule of law for military staff to participate as judges in State Security Courts and thus sit in judgment over civilians.

22. Although there are no more executions in Turkey, the co-rapporteurs observe that the death penalty still exists in Turkish law and that death sentences are still pronounced by the courts. After their visit to Turkey, they have been informed that a Draft Turkish Criminal Code has been presented to the TGNA Justice Commission, providing inter alia for the abolishment of the death penalty. Pending the adoption of this Code and its enactment, the co-rapporteurs recommend that Turkey sign and ratify Protocol no. 6 to the Convention for the Protection of Human Rights and Fundamental Freedoms concerning the Abolition of the Death Penalty.

III. FREEDOM OF EXPRESSION AND ARTICLE 8 OF THE PREVENTION OF TERRORISM ACT

23. The right of freedom of expression is one of the pre-conditions for democracy and as such confirmed by Article 10 of the Human Rights Convention. The exercise of this freedom may be restricted by law on very precise conditions,

as indeed most Member States have done. The criticism of Article 8 of Turkey's Prevention of Terrorism Act is that it sanctions but does not clearly and sufficiently define "offences of opinion". This opens the door to arbitrary action by the State against individuals for "crimes of thought", not only in violation of the right to freedom of expression but also of the rights to freedom of thought and conscience and to freedom of peaceful assembly and association (Articles 9, 10 and 11 of the European Convention on Human Rights).

24. The recent prosecution and imprisonment of some journalists for terms of ten to forty months is but one example of the different interpretation by the Turkish authorities of Article 10 of the Human Rights Convention. The co-rapporteurs are concerned about many other incidents, not only involving journalists but also elected officials, particularly from the Virtue party and HADEP [People's Democratic Party], which have been reported to them and which would seem to indicate that freedom of expression is excessively restricted on matters considered to be sensitive. The co-rapporteurs recommend that Article 8 in the Prevention of Terrorism Act should be adapted to prevent any interpretation contrary to the Human Rights Convention.

IV. IMPRISONED FORMER DEP PARLIAMENTARIANS

25. Four former DEP parliamentarians continue to serve a fifteen-year sentence. Convicted under Article 168 of the Criminal Code for "membership of and assistance to separatist gangs", they claim they are being punished for their political views. This claim is rejected by the Turkish authorities, which shows, once again, how extremely narrow the margin is in Turkey between freedom of expression and prohibited propaganda. Their application to the European Commission on Human Rights was declared admissible in October 1997. In discussions with the co-rapporteurs on 24 November 1997, they affirmed their commitment to work for constitutional reform through Turkey's democratic institutions and without challenge to Turkey's territorial integrity. The Council of Europe and the OSCE [Organization for Security and Cooperation in Europe] Parliamentary Assemblies as well as the European Parliament and NATO [North Atlantic Treaty Organization] have all made appeals for their release.

26. For their visit on 6–9 September, the co-rapporteurs had asked to be enabled to visit again the former DEP parliamentarians, and this visit had been arranged for 7 September at 09:45. When the co-rapporteurs arrived at Ankara central prison at 09:45, they were kept waiting for fifteen minutes in front of the gates, with press and public watching, before being told that the prison administration could not ensure their safety and therefore could not let them enter. According to an article in the *Turkish Daily News*, riot teams from the gendarmerie and the police had carried out on the preceding Sunday morning a search for prohibited objects and had transferred more than one hundred inmates to other prisons. According to the article, police and gendarmerie officials had said that all necessary security measures had been taken inside and outside the

prison. The co-rapporteurs regret that they were thus prevented from meeting the former DEP parliamentarians and, in particular, that they had not been informed of this before their trip to the prison.

V. CONSTITUTIONAL REFORM

27. In Article 2 of its Constitution Turkey is affirmed to be a democratic State, committed to respect for Human Rights. This affirmation was challenged by Assembly Recommendations 1266 (1995) and 1298 (1996). Some Articles of the Constitution and Article 8 of the Prevention of Terrorism Act were amended in 1995. Other Articles of the Constitution (on freedom of thought and expression, on freedom of science and the arts, and on rights and freedoms of the press) are now being examined, with a view to amendment, by the Turkish High Co-ordinating Committee for Human Rights. The co-rapporteurs welcome the pledge made on 7 August 1998 by the Human Rights Minister that he would push through legal measures to ease restrictions on freedom of expression and shorten jail sentences for "separatist propaganda". It will be important to act on this pledge before the parliamentary elections set for 18 April 1999; during the visit on 6 September the Minister voiced, however, some doubts about this possibility.

28. A basic concern of the Assembly, however, is still not being addressed. The Turkish Constitution, adopted under military rule in 1982, leaves room for (although it does not necessarily entail) conceptions of the relationship of the State to the individual which are authoritarian and not compatible with the Council of Europe's Statute and the European Convention on Human Rights.

29. A recent report by the Civilian Affairs Committee of the North Atlantic Assembly referred to the general weakness of political forces vis-à-vis the military establishment. The most important aspect in this context is the existence of the National Security Council (NSC). The NSC was set up during military rule and given constitutional status in 1982 (see Article 118 of the Constitution). It has been described as a "State within the State" because the scope of its activities has extended beyond security to cover the economy, foreign policy, education, Human Rights and religion. The co-rapporteurs therefore share the conclusion by the North Atlantic Assembly's report that, if Turkey wishes to move in the direction of a modern democracy, the issues of domestic and foreign security and national defence must be differentiated, and the Turkish Armed Forces' sphere of interest must be restricted to national defence. In line with one of the points made in Recommendation 1377, this entails that civilian control must be established over all military activity in Turkey.

30. A democratic state is characterised, among others, by a multi-party system. In this respect, the co-rapporteurs wish to voice their concern about the issue of the ban in Turkey of certain political parties.

31. Radical changes of a Constitution are not easy to envisage. However, adjustment to the Preamble might suffice, since it governs interpretation of the General Principles (set forth in Part one). The co-rapporteurs suggest that the

opinion of the European Commission for Democracy through Law (the "Venice Commission") be sought on these constitutional issues.

## VI. RESPECT FOR THE RIGHTS OF TURKISH CITIZENS OF KURDISH ORIGIN

32. From the very beginning of the monitoring procedure, the co-rapporteurs have paid special attention to the Kurdish question. In addition, Order no. 545 (1998) instructed the Monitoring Committee to study the issue of the Kurdish minority in the framework of the monitoring procedure concerning Turkey.

33. Turkish citizens of Kurdish origin, notably in the southeastern part of the country, who wish to maintain their languages and traditional cultural identities should be able to do so. The Turkish authorities, in their observations on this report, have argued that thirty local radio and television stations broadcast in Turkish and Kurdish, that there is no restriction on the sale of magazines and music cassettes in Kurdish and that fifteen newspapers and periodicals are printed in Kurdish. However, several interlocutors told the co-rapporteurs in the course of their visit to Turkey that the freedom of expression of Kurdish media is severely limited, that many Kurdish publications have been banned and that access to the remaining publications is difficult.

34. The co-rapporteurs do not consider it useful to exchange arguments as to whether there is an obligation on the Turkish State to regard any groups of citizens as "national minorities". They merely wish to underline that here is clearly a case of an ethnic group with a cultural identity and common traditions which in accordance with the principles and norms of the Council of Europe should be preserved and protected and that such protection is not in contradiction with the Turkish Constitution nor with the Treaty of Lausanne. The essential point is that any such group should have the opportunities and material resources to use and sustain its natural languages and cultural traditions in circumstances and under conditions now clearly and reasonably defined by two important Council of Europe Conventions: the Framework Convention on Protection of National Minorities and the European Charter for Regional or Minority Languages, as well as by Assembly Recommendation 1201 (1993) on an additional protocol on the rights of national minorities to the European Convention on Human Rights. The argument that this would threaten the unity of the Turkish State is unconvincing. The effect is more likely to be the contrary, as terrorism is progressively brought under control.

35. Since the Treaty of Lausanne which established Turkey's borders in 1923, conceptions of international law and of obligations of States vis-à-vis their citizens have considerably evolved. States with a unitary structure which are reluctant to sign and ratify certain Council of Europe texts are nonetheless ready to accept these texts as enlightened statements of principle and to translate these principles into policy. As political, economic, social and cultural conditions improve in the southeast, the Turkish authorities, including the military, should accept the concepts and principles of the rest of Europe, and act accordingly. Many examples in Europe show that the implementation of cultural

rights for ethnic groups that are different from the majority of the population do not harm the territorial integrity of the State.

36. In this respect, the co-rapporteurs discussed with the Turkish authorities the "cease fire" offer by the leader of the PKK as from 1 September 1998. The authorities considered that this was a political manoeuvre and would not be respected. In fact, it was withdrawn less than two weeks later.

37. One important aspect of the restoration of peace and prosperity in the southeast are measures to reconstruct and revive the economy. The co-rapporteurs refer in this respect to Recommendation 1377 (1998), in which the Parliamentary Assembly asks the Committee of Ministers to use its influence with the European Union to resume promised financial cooperation with a view to fostering economic development in Turkey, particularly in its southeastern provinces. The co-rapporteurs therefore also support all efforts by the Turkish authorities which go in that direction so long as they are also accompanied by confidence-building measures in favour of the Kurdish population in the cultural and social fields. Altogether, these measures would encourage those members of the Kurdish population who desire to return to do so, thus also supporting the activities of the United Nations High Commissioner for Refugees.

*C. Concluding remarks*

38. In summary, the co-rapporteurs wish to draw the attention of the Turkish authorities to the following important steps to be taken:

- legislative changes to improve freedom of expression, freedom of association and the rights of detainees;
- improvements in the implementation of legislative changes already enacted, especially as regards torture and the treatment of detainees;
- readiness to engage in a dialogue on cultural rights of Turkish citizens of Kurdish origin and, together with the European Union, to foster the economic development of the southeastern provinces of Turkey;
- continuing willingness to engage in constitutional reform, and as a Party to the Partial Agreement on the European Commission for Democracy through Law to use the possibility of consulting this Commission.

39. The co-rapporteurs submit these considerations to the Assembly so that it can take stock of the situation on the honouring of obligations and commitments of Turkey. Thereafter they expect to return to the country to verify whether progress has been made with regard to the aforementioned steps to be taken and, if appropriate, submit a final report to the Assembly within the next twelve months.

# Document no. 67

## ECtHR Judgments in Thirteen Cases against Turkey[2]

On 8 July 1999 at Strasbourg the European Court of Human Rights delivered judgment in the following thirteen cases: *Ceylan v. Turkey, Arslan v. Turkey, Gerger v. Turkey, Polat v. Turkey, Karatas v. Turkey, Erdogdu and Ince v. Turkey, Baskaya and Okçuoglu v. Turkey, Okçuoglu v. Turkey, Sürek and Özdemir v. Turkey, Sürek v. Turkey* (no. 1), *Sürek v. Turkey* (no. 2), *Sürek v. Turkey* (no. 3) and *Sürek v. Turkey* (no. 4).

The Court held that there had been a violation of freedom of expression, as guaranteed by Article 10 of the European Convention on Human Rights, in the cases of Ceylan v. Turkey (16 votes to 1), Arslan v. Turkey (unanimously), Gerger v. Turkey (16 votes to 1), Polat v. Turkey (unanimously), Karatas v. Turkey (12 votes to 5), Erdogdu and Ince v. Turkey (unanimously), Baskaya and Okçuoglu v. Turkey (unanimously), Okçuoglu v. Turkey (unanimously), Sürek and Özdemir v. Turkey (11 votes to 6), Sürek v. Turkey (no. 2) (16 votes to 1) and Sürek v. Turkey (no. 4) (16 votes to 1). It found no violation of Article 10 in the cases of Sürek v. Turkey (no. 1) (11 votes to 6) and Sürek v. Turkey (no. 3) (10 votes to 7).

Further, in the cases of Gerger v. Turkey, Karatas v. Turkey, Baskaya and Okçuoglu v. Turkey, Okçuoglu v. Turkey, Sürek and Özdemir v. Turkey, Sürek v. Turkey (no. 1), Sürek v. Turkey (no. 2), Sürek v. Turkey (no. 3) and Sürek v. Turkey (no. 4), the Court held, by sixteen votes to one, that the applicants had been denied the right to have their cases heard by an "independent and impartial tribunal" within the meaning of Article 6 § 1 of the Convention because they had been tried by National Security Courts, in which one of the bench of three judges was a military judge.

In the case of Baskaya and Okçuoglu v. Turkey, it held, unanimously, that there had been a breach of Article 7 of the Convention (no punishment without law) as regards the second applicant.

\*\*\*

### A. Principal facts

*1. Case of Ceylan v. Turkey*

The applicant, Münir Ceylan, is a Turkish national. He was born in 1951 and lives in Istanbul.

While president of the petroleum workers' union (*Petrol-Is Sendikasi*), Mr Ceylan wrote an article entitled "The time has come for the workers to speak out — tomorrow it will be too late" in the 21–28 July 1991 issue of *Yeni Ülke* (*New Land*), a weekly newspaper published in Istanbul. Criminal proceedings were brought against him in the Istanbul National Security Court as a result and on 3 May 1993 he was convicted under Article 312 §§ 2 and 3 of the Turkish Criminal Code of inciting the people to hostility and hatred by making distinctions based on ethnic or regional origin or social class. He was sentenced to one year and eight months' imprisonment and a fine of 100,000 Turkish liras (TRL).

## 2. Case of Arslan v. Turkey

The applicant, Günay Arslan, is a Turkish national. He was born in 1960 and lives in Istanbul.

He is the author of the book *Yas Tutan Tarih, 33 Kursun* (*History in Mourning, 33 Bullets*). A first edition was published in December 1989. On 29 March 1991 the Istanbul National Security Court sentenced Mr Arslan to six years and three months' imprisonment for making separatist propaganda contrary to Article 142 §§ 3 and 6 of the Criminal Code. However, as that provision was repealed by the Prevention of Terrorism Act 1991 (Law no. 3713 of 12 April 1991), the National Security Court declared his conviction null and void in a supplementary judgment of 3 May 1991.

A second edition of the book was published on 21 July 1991. In a judgment of 28 January 1993 the National Security Court convicted Mr Arslan of making propaganda against the "indivisibility of the State" contrary to section 8 of Law no. 3713 and sentenced him to one year and eight months' imprisonment and a fine of TRL 41,666,666.

## 3. Case of Gerger v. Turkey

The applicant, Haluk Gerger, is a Turkish national. He was born in 1950 and is a journalist living in Ankara.

On 23 May 1993 a memorial ceremony was held in Ankara for Denis Gezmis, Yusuf Aslan and Hüseyin Inan, the founders of an extreme left-wing movement among university students at the end of the 1960s. They had been sentenced to death for seeking to destroy the constitutional order by violence and had been executed in May 1972. The applicant had been invited to speak at the ceremony but was unable to attend and sent the organising committee a message that was read out in public.

Holding that the message contained separatist propaganda against the unity of the Turkish nation and the territorial integrity of the State, the Ankara National Security Court found Mr Gerger guilty of an offence under section 8 of the Prevention of Terrorism Act 1991 (Law no. 3713) and sentenced him to one year and eight months' imprisonment and a fine of TRL 203,333,333.

### 4. Case of Polat v. Turkey

The applicant, Edip Polat, is a Turkish national. He was born in 1962 and lives in Diyarbakir.

In 1991 a book of his entitled *Nevrozladik Safaklari (We Made Each Dawn a Spring Festival)* was published. In a judgment of 23 December 1992 the Ankara National Security Court held that the work contained propaganda against the territorial integrity of the State and the indivisible unity of the nation, contrary to section 8 of the Prevention of Terrorism Act 1991 (Law no. 3713). It sentenced the applicant to two years' imprisonment and a fine of TRL 50,000,000.

### 5. Case of Karatas v. Turkey

The applicant, Hüseyin Karatas, is a Turkish national. He was born in 1963 and lives in Istanbul.

In November 1991 his anthology of poems entitled *Dersim — Bir Isyanin Türküsü (The Song of a Rebellion — Dersim)* was published. In a judgment of 22 February 1993 the Istanbul National Security Court held that the work contained propaganda against the indivisible unity of the State, contrary to section 8 of the Prevention of Terrorism Act 1991 (Law no. 3713) and sentenced the applicant to one year and eight months' imprisonment and a fine of 41,666,666 Turkish liras. After Law no. 4126 of 27 October 1995 came into force the sentence was reviewed, the term of imprisonment being reduced to one year, one month and ten days and the fine increased to TRL 111,111,110.

### 6. Case of Erdogdu and Ince v. Turkey

Ümit Erdogdu and Selami Ince are Turkish nationals. Mr Erdogdu was born in 1970 and lives in Istanbul. Mr Ince was born in 1966 and lives in Ankara.

At the material time, Mr Erdogdu was the editor of the monthly review *Demokrat Muhalefet! (Democratic Opposition!)*. The January 1992 issue of the review included an interview with a Turkish sociologist conducted by the second applicant, Mr Ince. The Istanbul National Security Court held that, by publishing the interview, the applicants had committed the offence of disseminating propaganda against the indivisibility of the State contrary to section 8 of the Prevention of Terrorism Act 1991 (Law no. 3713). In a judgment of 12 August 1993 the first applicant was sentenced to five months' imprisonment and a fine of TRL 41,666,666 and the second applicant to one year and eight months' imprisonment and a fine of TRL 41,666,666. After Law no. 4126 of 27 October 1995 and Law no. 4304 of 14 August 1997 came into force, the Istanbul National Security Court decided to defer passing a final sentence upon Mr Erdogdu and to suspend execution of Mr Ince's sentence.

### 7. Baskaya and Okçuoglu v. Turkey

Fikret Baskaya and Mehemet Selim Okçuoglu are Turkish nationals. They were born in 1940 and 1964 respectively. Mr Baskaya is a professor of economics and a journalist and lives in Ankara; Mr Okçuoglu is the owner of a publishing house, *Doz Basin Yayin Ltd Sti,* and lives in Istanbul.

In April 1991, *Doz Basin Yayin Ltd Sti* published a book written by the first applicant entitled *Batililasma, Çagdaslasma, Kalkinma — Paradigmanin Iflasi: Resmi Ideolojinin Elestirisine Giris* (*Westernisation, Modernisation, Development — Collapse of a Paradigm: An Introduction to the Critique of the Official Ideology*).

The Public Prosecutor at the Istanbul National Security Court brought criminal proceedings against the applicants on the grounds that, through the book, they had disseminated propaganda against the indivisibility of the State contrary to section 8 of the Prevention of Terrorism Act 1991 (Law no. 3713 of 12 April 1991). On 14 October 1992 the National Security Court acquitted the applicants, holding that the book as a whole was an academic work containing no elements of propaganda. The Public Prosecutor appealed to the Court of Cassation, which quashed the decision of the trial court and remitted the case back to it for retrial. In a judgment of 5 August 1993 the Istanbul National Security Court convicted the applicants, sentencing the first applicant to one year and eight months' imprisonment and a fine of TRL 41,666,666 and the second applicant to five months' imprisonment and a fine of the same amount.

## 8. Okçuoglu v. Turkey

The applicant, Ahmet Zeki Okçuoglu, is a Turkish national. He was born in 1950 and lives in Istanbul.

In May 1991, issue no. 12 of a magazine called *Demokrat (Democrat)* included an article on a round-table debate organised by the magazine and in which the applicant had taken part. The article was entitled "Kürt Sorununun Dünü ve Bugünü" ("The past and present of the Kurdish problem").

On 11 March 1993 the Istanbul National Security Court held that the views expressed by the applicant as reproduced in the article amounted to propaganda against the indivisibility of the State contrary to section 8 of the Prevention of Terrorism Act 1991 (Law no. 3713). It sentenced him to one year and eight months' imprisonment and a fine of 41,666,666 Turkish liras. After Law no. 4126 of 27 October 1995 came into force, the National Security Court reviewed the applicant's case on the merits and reduced his prison sentence to one year, one month and ten days but increased the fine to TRL 111,111,110.

## 9. Case of Sürek and Özdemir v. Turkey

Kamil Tekin Sürek and Yücel Özdemir are Turkish nationals. Mr Sürek was born in 1957 and lives in Istanbul. Mr Özdemir was born in 1968 and lives in Cologne, in Germany.

At the material time, Mr Sürek was the majority shareholder in *Deniz Basin Yayin Sanayi ve Ticaret Organizasyon,* a Turkish company which owns a weekly review entitled *Haberde Yorumda Gerçek* (*The Truth of News and Comments*), published in Istanbul. Mr Özdemir was the editor-in-chief of the review.

In the 31 May 1992 and 7 June 1992 issues of the review, an interview with a leader of the Kurdistan Workers' Party ("the PKK"), an illegal organisation, was published in two parts. The edition of 31 May 1992 also contained a joint declaration by four socialist organisations.

On 27 May 1993, the Istanbul National Security Court found the applicants guilty of disseminating propaganda against the indivisibility of the State in the form of the above publications, contrary to sections 6 and 8 of the Prevention of Terrorism Act 1991 (Law no. 3713). The first applicant was sentenced to two fines totalling TRL 300,000,000. The second applicant was sentenced to six months' imprisonment and two fines totalling TRL 150,000,000.

*10. Case of Sürek v. Turkey (no. 1)*

Issue no. 23 of *Haberde Yorumda Gerçek*, dated 30 August 1992, contained two readers' articles entitled "Silahlar Özgürlügü Engelleyemez" ("Weapons cannot win against freedom") and "Suç Bizim" ("It is our fault").

On 12 April 1992 the Istanbul National Security Court held that the applicant, in his capacity as the owner of the review in which the articles had been published, was guilty of disseminating propaganda against the indivisibility of the State contrary to section 8 of the Prevention of Terrorism Act 1991 (Law no. 3713) and sentenced him to a fine of TRL 166,666,666. The applicant appealed to the Court of Cassation, which quashed the judgment and remitted the case to the Istanbul National Security Court for retrial. On 12 April 1994 the court sentenced the applicant to a reduced fine of TRL 83,333,333.

*11. Case of Sürek v. Turkey (no. 2)*

The 26 April 1992 issue of *Haberde Yorumda Gerçek* contained coverage of a press conference given by a delegation visiting Sirnak village in the wake of tensions in the area. The delegation comprised two former members of the Turkish Parliament, Leyla Zana and Orhan Dogan, together with Lord Avebury and a member of the Anglican Church. The coverage included an article reporting the Governor of Sirnak as having told the delegation that the Sirnak Chief of Police had ordered his men to open fire on the local population. It also reproduced a dialogue between Leyla Zana, Orhan Dogan and Ismet Yediyildiz, a Gendarme Commander.

On 2 September 1993, the Istanbul National Security Court found the applicant, in his capacity as the owner of the review, guilty of revealing the identity of officials responsible for combating terrorism and thus making them terrorist targets. It sentenced him to pay a fine of TRL 54,000,000 under section 6 of the Prevention of Terrorism Act 1991 (Law no. 3713).

*12. Case of Sürek v. Turkey (no. 3)*

Issue no. 42 of the review *Haberde Yorumda Gerçek*, dated 9 January 1993, contained an article entitled "In Botan the poor peasants are expropriating the landlords!".

On 27 September 1993 the Istanbul National Security Court found the applicant, in his capacity as the owner of the review in which the article had been published, guilty of disseminating propaganda against the indivisibility of the State contrary to section 8 of the Prevention of Terrorism Act (Law no. 3713) and sentenced him to a fine of TRL 83,333,333.

*13. Case of Sürek v. Turkey (no. 4)*

Issue no. 51 of the review *Haberde Yorumda Gerçek*, dated 13 March 1993, included an article entitled "Kawa and Dehak once again". The article discussed what might occur during the forthcoming *Newroz* (spring festival) celebrations. The same issue also contained an interview by the Kurdish News Agency with a representative of the National Liberation Front of Kurdistan, the political wing of the PKK, an illegal organisation.

On 27 September 1993 the Istanbul National Security Court found the applicant, in his capacity as the owner of the review in which the article and the interview had been published, guilty of disseminating propaganda against the indivisibility of the State contrary to sections 6 and 8 of the Prevention of Terrorism Act 1991 (Law no. 3713) and sentenced him to a fine of TRL 83,333,333.

## B. Procedure and composition of the Court

The applications were lodged with the European Commission of Human Rights in 1994–95. Having found the applications admissible or partly admissible (as the case might be), the Commission adopted thirteen separate reports, eight on 11 December 1997 and five on 13 January 1998. The Commission expressed the opinion that there had been a violation of Article 10 of the Convention in ten of the cases (Ceylan v. Turkey, Arslan v. Turkey, Gerger v. Turkey, Polat v. Turkey, Karatas v. Turkey, Erdogdu and Ince v. Turkey, Baskaya and Okçuoglu v. Turkey, Okçuoglu v. Turkey, Sürek and Özdemir v. Turkey and Sürek v. Turkey (no. 4)). It further expressed the opinion that there had been a violation of Article 6 § 1 of the Convention in nine of the cases (Gerger v. Turkey, Karatas v. Turkey, Baskaya and Okçuoglu v. Turkey, Okçuoglu v. Turkey, Sürek and Özdemir v. Turkey, Sürek v. Turkey (no. 1), Sürek v. Turkey (no. 2), Sürek v. Turkey (no. 3), and Sürek v. Turkey (no. 4)). Lastly, it expressed the opinion that there had been a violation of Article 7 of the Convention with regard to the second applicant in the Baskaya and Okçuoglu v. Turkey case.

\*\*\*

*3. Summary of the judgment*

### a. Article 10 of the Convention

The applicants all complained that their convictions amounted to an infringement of their right to freedom of expression, as guaranteed by Article 10 of the Convention.

The Court found that in each case the convictions amounted to an "interference" in the applicant's right to freedom of expression. Accepting that the interference was "prescribed by law" within the meaning of the second paragraph of Article 10 and pursued at least one of the "legitimate aims" set out in that provision, the Court went on to examine whether the interference was "necessary in a democratic society" for those aims to be achieved. It concluded that there had been a violation of Article 10 in eleven of the thirteen cases.

In the cases of Erdogdu and Ince v. Turkey, Okçuoglu v. Turkey, Sürek and Özdemir v. Turkey, Sürek v. Turkey (no. 1), Sürek v. Turkey (no. 2), Sürek v. Turkey (no. 3) and Sürek v. Turkey (no. 4), it referred in particular to the essential role of the press in ensuring the proper functioning of political democracy. While the press had not to overstep the bounds set, among other things, for the protection of vital interests of the State such as national security or territorial integrity against the threat of violence or the prevention of disorder or crime, it was nevertheless incumbent on it to impart information and ideas on political issues, including divisive ones. Not only had the press the task of imparting such information and ideas; the public had a right to receive them. Freedom of the press afforded the public one of the best means of discovering and forming an opinion of the ideas and attitudes of political leaders.

Lastly, in the case of Karatas v. Turkey the Court observed that Article 10 included freedom of artistic expression, which afforded the opportunity to take part in the public exchange of cultural, political and social information and ideas of all kinds. Those who created, performed, distributed or exhibited works of art contributed to the exchange of ideas and opinions which was essential for a democratic society. Hence the obligation on the State not to encroach unduly on their freedom of expression.

The Court went to say in each of the judgments that, in line with its case-law, there was little scope under Article 10 § 2 of the Convention for restrictions on political speech or on debate on matters of public interest. Furthermore, the limits of permissible criticism were wider with regard to the government than in relation to a private citizen, or even a politician. In a democratic system the actions or omissions of the government had to be subject to the close scrutiny not only of the legislative and judicial authorities but also of public opinion. Moreover, the dominant position which the government occupied made it necessary for it to display restraint in resorting to criminal proceedings, particularly where other means were available for replying to the unjustified attacks and criticisms of its adversaries. Nevertheless, it certainly remained open to the competent State authorities to adopt, in their capacity as guarantors of public order, measures, even of a criminal-law nature, intended to react appropriately and without excess to such remarks. Finally, where such remarks constituted an incitement to violence against an individual or a public official or a sector of the population, the State authorities enjoyed a wider margin of appreciation when examining the need for an interference with freedom of expression.

The Court reached its decision in each case in the light of the foregoing principles and having regard to the offending passages — the Court verifying in every case whether they constituted an incitement to violence, armed resistance or an uprising — the context in which they were made and the type and severity of the sentence imposed.

b. **Article 6 § 1 of the Convention**

In the nine cases in which it had jurisdiction to hear the complaint, the Court held that the applicants had been denied the right to have their cases heard by an "independent and impartial tribunal" within the meaning of Article 6 § 1 of the Convention, as they had been tried by the National Security Courts, in which three judges sat, one of whom was a military judge.

The Court pointed out in that connection that in its Incal v. Turkey judgment of 9 June 1998 and its Çiraklar v. Turkey judgment of 28 October 1998 it had noted that, although the status of military judges sitting as members of National Security Courts did provide some guarantees of independence and impartiality, certain aspects of these judges' status made their independence and impartiality questionable: for example, the fact that they were servicemen who still belonged to the army, which in turn took its orders from the executive; the fact that they remained subject to military discipline; and the fact that decisions pertaining to their appointment were to a great extent taken by the administrative authorities and the army. The Court saw no reason to reach a conclusion different from its decision in those cases and held that there had also been a breach of Article 6 § 1 in the nine cases before it.

c. **Article 7 of the Convention**

In the case of Baskaya and Okçuoglu v. Turkey, the Court reiterated that, according to its case-law, Article 7 embodied, among other things, the principle that only the law could define a crime and prescribe a penalty (*nullum crimen, nulla poena sine lege*) and the principle that the criminal law had not to be extensively construed to an accused's detriment, for instance by analogy.

The Court considered that in the case before it the applicants' conviction as such under section 8 of the Prevention of Terrorism Act 1991 had not contravened the "*nulla poena sine lege*" principle embodied in Article 7. On the other hand, it held that the fact that the second applicant had been given a prison sentence was incompatible with that Article as the sentence had been imposed under section 8(2), which expressly applies to editors, while publishers were liable only to a fine. The Court considered that section 8(2) was a *lex specialis* on the sentencing of editors and publishers and that the sentencing of the second applicant, who was in fact a publisher, had in that instance been based on an extensive construction, by analogy, of the rule in the same sub-section on the sentencing of editors.

\*\*\*

# Document no. 68

## 1999 Regular Report from the European Commission on Turkey's progress towards accession[3]

\*\*\*

### A. Introduction

*a. Preface*

The European Council in Cardiff, which took place in June 1998, welcomed the Commission's confirmation that it will submit at the end of 1998 its first regular reports on each candidate's progress towards accession. In the case of Turkey, the European Council noted that "the report would be based on Article 28 of the Association Agreement and the conclusions of the Luxembourg European Council".

The European Council in Vienna invited the Commission to present its further progress reports with a view to the Helsinki European Council.

Like the previous one, this Regular Report takes account of the conclusions of the European Council in Copenhagen. It:

- describes the relations between Turkey and the Union, particularly in the framework of the Association Agreement;
- analyses the situation in respect of the political conditions set by the European Council (democracy, rule of law, Human Rights, protection of minorities);
- assesses Turkey's situation and prospects in respect of the economic conditions mentioned by the European Council (functioning market economy, capacity to cope with competitive pressures and market forces within the Union);
- addresses the question of Turkey's capacity to adopt the obligations of membership, that is, the *acquis* of the Union as expressed in the Treaty, the secondary legislation and the policies of the Union;
- gives a general evaluation of Turkey's situation and prospects on the road to accession with particular reference to the European strategy set out in the Commission communication of 4 March 1998.

It also covers judicial and administrative capacity as requested by the Madrid European Council which underlined the necessity for the candidate countries to adapt their administrative structures so as to guarantee the harmonious implementation of Community policies after membership. However, the examination of judicial and administrative capacity is limited to areas covered by the Customs union.

The report takes into consideration progress since the last Regular Report. It looks at whether intended reforms referred to in the 1998 Regular Report have been carried out and examines new initiatives.

While the assessment of progress in meeting the political and *acquis* criteria focuses on that which has been accomplished since the last Regular Report, the economic assessment is based on a longer term evaluation of Turkey's economic performance. The assessment of progress made in adopting the *acquis* has been made on the basis of adopted legislation rather than legislation which is in various stages of either preparation or Parliamentary approval. This approach ensures equal treatment for all the candidate countries and permits objective assessment and comparison between countries in terms of concrete progress in preparation for accession.

The report draws on numerous sources of information. The candidate countries were invited to provide information on progress made in preparations for membership since the publication of the last Regular Report. Council deliberations and European Parliament reports and resolutions have been taken into account in the preparations. The Commission also drew on assessments made by various international organisations and in particular on contributions from the Council of Europe, the OSCE and the international financial institutions as well as non-governmental organisations.

*b. Relations between the European Union and Turkey*

RECENT DEVELOPMENTS

Since the adoption of the last Regular Report on Turkey, bilateral relations have developed without any major change. Although the political dialogue which Turkey brought to a halt after the Luxembourg European Council has not been re-established, regular meetings take place on the implementation of the European Strategy (see below). Given the deadlock at the political level, the Association Council has not been able to hold a meeting since April 1997.

In its conclusions, the European Council of Vienna of 11 and 12 December 1998 underlined "the great importance it attaches to the further development of relations between the EU and Turkey taking forward the European strategy to prepare Turkey for membership". It also recognised "the central role of the further implementation of the European Strategy in line with its conclusions in Luxembourg and Cardiff".

Despite efforts by the EU Presidency, the European Council of Cologne has not been able to adopt any agreed conclusions on Turkey.

EU–Turkey relations have also been marked by the arrest and trial of PKK leader Abdullah Öcalan, as well as the death sentence pronounced by the Ankara State Security Court against him on 29 June 1999.

After his capture in Kenya in February 1999, Öcalan was brought to the Imrali prison-island in the Sea of Marmara. The Öcalan operation triggered violent PKK demonstrations in some EU Member States and terrorist acts in Turkey for a short period. In this context, the European Union made the following declaration at the General Affairs Council of 22 February 1999:

> The European Union reiterates its condemnation of all forms of terrorism. The legitimate fight against terrorism must be conducted in full respect of Human Rights, the rule of law and democratic norms. Legitimate interests must be expressed through a political process, not through violence.
>
> The EU strongly deplores the fact that the arrest of Abdullah Öcalan has sparked massive unrest and violent acts which have resulted in death, hostage-taking, intimidation and extensive destruction. It reaffirms its position that such acts of violence are inadmissible and under no circumstance tolerable.
>
> The European Union takes note of the assurance of the Turkish Government that Abdullah Öcalan will have a fair trial. It expects this to mean fair and correct treatment and an open trial according to the rule of law before an independent court, with access to legal counsel of his choice and with international observers admitted to the trial. It underlines once more its strict opposition to the death penalty.
>
> The EU fully upholds the territorial integrity of Turkey. At the same time, the EU expects Turkey to resolve its problems by political means with full respect for Human Rights, the rule of law in a democratic society and in full accordance with Turkey's commitments as a member of the Council of Europe. In this context it welcomes all genuine efforts to separate the fight against terrorism from the search for political solutions and to promote conciliation. In support of this the EU stands ready to contribute, including through continued financial assistance.
>
> Turkey's efforts in dealing with these problems in this spirit cannot but affect EU–Turkey relations positively.

On 23 February 1999, the Turkish Ministry of Foreign Affairs stated that:

> Questioning the independence of courts in Turkey is unacceptable. The intention of the EU to send observers to the hearings is tantamount to accepting and encouraging the efforts to intervene in and influence the independent judiciary. This attitude which is against the principle of the rule of law is also unacceptable.

The trial of Abdullah Öcalan started on 31 May 1999 before the Ankara State Security Court in the presence of certain foreign representatives as well as the press. According to the Council of Europe's Ad hoc Committee to ensure the presence of the Assembly at the trial of Abdullah Öcalan, the procedure of the trial "seems to have been largely correct and in accordance with the applicable Turkish law ... ". On the other hand, Amnesty International considered that standards for fair trials had been violated throughout the pre-trial detention period and the trial.

The passing of the death sentence against Öcalan on 29 June 1999 by the State Security Court was followed by EU reactions. In its declaration of 29 June 1999, the EU Presidency expressed "the hope that Turkey will follow what has invariably been the practice for the last fifteen years and not carry out the death sentence passed on Mr Öcalan." In a Resolution on 22 July 1999, the newly elected EP also called on the Turkish authorities not to carry out the sentence.

The death sentence against Öcalan has been appealed before the Turkish Supreme Court and would also have to be confirmed by Parliament before it could be executed. If confirmed by the Supreme Court, the sentence could also be appealed to the European Court of Human Rights.

The catastrophic earthquake of 17 August 1999 has also influenced to a large extent relations between the European Union and Turkey. The response of the international community to the disaster relief was immediate, involving provision of rescue teams, medical assistance, firefighting equipment as well as financial aid. The Commission immediately released four million euros for emergency assistance and prepared a thirty-million euro support package in order to help Turkey in the rehabilitation phase. Further support measures to help in the reconstruction phase are being examined. The General Affairs Council of 13 September 1999 adopted conclusions on Turkey, welcoming in particular the Commission's intention concerning further aid to Turkey ... The same day, the Turkish Minister of Foreign Affairs Mr Cem participated in the General Affairs Council luncheon.

Noteworthy is the recent positive development in relations between Turkey and Greece. Ministers of Foreign Affairs from both countries agreed on exploring possibilities of promoting cooperation between the two countries in fields such as tourism, culture, environment and combating organised crime (including illegal immigration, drug trafficking and terrorism). Talks at high official level have already been held and are reported to have taken place in a positive atmosphere.

THE EUROPEAN STRATEGY

As stated in the last Regular Report, the first discussions on the implementation of the European strategy took place in September 1998. After this inaugural meeting, the contact group established between the Commission and the Turkish authorities to ensure the implementation of the strategy, met three times, either in Ankara or in Brussels. It also met under an ad hoc form, on 30 April 1999 in Brussels, to discuss the possibility of an agreement on the liberalisation of services and public procurement markets. Through these regular meetings, some progress has been made. Another meeting will be held before the Helsinki summit.

\*\*\*

## B. Criteria for membership

*1. Political criteria*

INTRODUCTION

In its 1998 Regular Report on Turkey's progress towards accession, the Commission concluded that:

> On the political side, the evaluation highlights certain anomalies in the functioning of the public authorities, persistent Human Rights violations and major shortcomings in the treatment of minorities. The lack of civilian control of the army gives cause for concern. This is reflected by the major role played by the army in political life through the National Security Council. A civil, non-military solution must be found to the situation in southeastern Turkey, particularly since many of the violations of civil and political rights observed in the country are connected in one way or another with this issue. The Commission acknowledges the Turkish government's commitment to combat Human Rights violations in the country but this has not so far had any significant effect in practice. The process of democratic reform on which Turkey embarked in 1995 must continue.
>
> In addition to resolving these problems, Turkey must make a constructive contribution to the settlement of all disputes with various neighbouring countries by peaceful means in accordance with international law.

The present analysis examines the progress that has been made since the 1998 Regular Report.

RECENT DEVELOPMENTS

In November 1998, the minority government fell. After having been assigned by President Demirel in December 1998 to form a new government, DSP [Democratic Left Party] leader Ecevit took office in January 1999 to be in charge until the general elections of April 1999. As a result of these elections, the DSP and the centre-right party MHP [Nationalist Action Party] became the two biggest parties of the country. These two parties together with the centre-right party ANAP [Motherland Party] formed a coalition, led by Mr Ecevit and received a large vote of confidence by the Parliament in June. The ruling coalition now has a solid majority in the Parliament (354 seats out of 550). Since the start of the new Parliament, there has been intense legislative activity which has led to the adoption of important laws in areas crucial for democratisation. Together with the general elections, local government elections were held. On this occasion, the pro-Kurdish HADEP party won a majority in seven provincial capitals in the southeast, including Diyarbakir.

After the closure of the Refah Party in January 1998, the Turkish Constitutional Court ordered in February 1999 the closure of the pro-Kurdish Democratic

Mass Party (DKP) on grounds of promotion of separatism. In April 1999, the Constitutional Court rejected an application from the Chief Prosecutor to suspend the HADEP party. In May 1999, an application was also made to the Constitutional Court against the islamist Fazilet Party, which presented its defence in September 1999.

The Öcalan case and the August earthquake have been the two major events in Turkey. The earthquake led to substantial public debate as to the effectiveness of the Turkish authorities in organising disaster relief and indicates that civil society is increasingly present in Turkish politics.

*1.1. Democracy and the rule of law*

As far as the political party system is concerned, the Turkish Grand National Assembly (TGNA) adopted in August 1999 amendments to the Political Parties Law, which in particular makes it more difficult for the authorities to close a political party and ban its members from subsequent participation in political life.

THE PARLIAMENT

There has been no change in the parliamentary structure. The establishment of the new TGNA in April 1999 took place in accordance with the constitutional provisions. Its powers are respected and the opposition plays a full part in its activities.

The national threshold of 10 per cent for political party representation in the TGNA led to the non-representation of about five million votes out of thirty-one million valid votes cast.

THE EXECUTIVE

No particular development has been noted in the executive.

The new government has taken a positive step by establishing a system for the recruitment of civil servants via a centralised examination supervised by the Student Selection and Placement Centre (OSYM), in order to prevent corruption in recruitment. Applications were submitted in July 1999, and the examination will take place in autumn 1999.

THE JUDICIARY

The main legislative change in the judicial system concerns the reform of the State Security Courts (SSCs), which deal with overtly political crimes. In 1998, the European Court of Human Rights stated that the presence of a military judge in the SCC panel violated the European Convention of Human Rights. More recently, in July 1999, the European Court delivered judgment in thirteen cases lodged by individuals in 1994–95. In nine of these cases, the Court concluded that the applicants had been denied the right to have their cases heard by an "independent and impartial tribunal" because they had been tried by a SSC.

Constitutional and legal amendments removing the military judge in the SSCs were adopted by the TGNA and entered into force on 22 June 1999. As a direct effect of this reform, the military judge of the Ankara SSC in charge of the trial against Öcalan was replaced by a civilian judge on 23 June 1999.

Such a reform should clearly improve the functioning of the SSC, even if there are still some doubts about the full rights offered to the defendants in these courts. According to Justice Ministry sources, more than 7000 cases are awaiting trial by SSCs.

A number of proposals made by the current government and the previous ones and currently in the Parliament could have a positive effect on the functioning of the judicial system. They include:

- a draft of the Penal Code which in particular lifts the death penalty;
- a draft law entitled "Law on the Prosecution of Civil Servants and other Public Officers", which facilitates the prosecution of public officers;
- a draft law amending the Code of Criminal Procedure regarding new arrangements on witness protection, payment of compensation to witnesses, physical examination and genetic analyses.

Finally it has to be noted that the government announced its intention to develop existing training programmes for judges and prosecutors. These initiatives aiming at raising awareness and improving training in the Human Rights field are of great importance.

\*\*\*

THE NATIONAL SECURITY COUNCIL

Through the National Security Council, the Military continues to have an important influence in many areas of political life.

The National Security Council continues to play a major role in political life. While the emergency courts system remains in place, the replacement of the military judge by a civilian one in State Security Courts represents a clear improvement in terms of independence of the judiciary.

*1.2. Human rights and the protection of minorities*

The Human Rights situation in Turkey is still under the monitoring procedures opened in 1996 by the Council of Europe. An information report on "Honouring of Obligations and Commitments by Turkey" has been published in January 1999, taking into account a visit in Turkey by the rapporteurs in September 1998.

The information report contains an analysis of the present situation in the country, focusing on the following areas: practices of torture and ill-treatment, rule of law, freedom of expression, imprisoned former DEP parliamentarians, constitutional reform and respect for the rights of Turkish citizens of Kurdish origin. The rapporteurs make also recommendations to the Turkish authorities to improve the situation.

Since the last Regular Report, Turkey signed in June 1999 the European Convention on the Exercise of Children's Rights, aiming at the protection of the best interests of children. However a number of important Human Rights Conventions have not yet been ratified by Turkey (see annex).

CIVIL AND POLITICAL RIGHTS

Even if certain positive steps have been made since October 1998, there are still problems in Turkey that give cause for concern.

Recent information from international organisations confirm that, even if torture, disappearances and extra-judicial executions are not systematic, they still exist. Precise cases of torture and ill-treatment have been recently registered by a delegation of the "European Committee for the Prevention of Torture and Inhuman or Degrading Treatment or Punishment (CPT)" from the Council of Europe, during their last visit to Turkey in February 1999. Most international sources indicate also that systematic judicial prosecution of law enforcement officials for misdemeanours is still not ensured. On this question, the report of the UN "Working Group on Enforced or Involuntary Disappearances" published in December 1998 recalls that impunity for law enforcement officials is one of the root causes of enforced disappearance and Human Rights violations. Policemen who had been previously acquitted from charges of torture in the Manisa case, will be re-tried following a verdict from the Penal Board of the Supreme Court of Appeals.

In a judgment in July 1999, the European Court of Human Rights underlined once again the existence of extra-judicial executions and torture.

The situation described in the last Regular Report has therefore not substantially changed. Nevertheless, Turkey has taken some steps that clearly go in the right direction.

As far as extra-judicial executions are concerned, the Constitutional Court annulled in January 1999 a legal provision that entitled security officers to "fire directly and without hesitation at persons who do not stop when warned." The government has been given one year to prepare a new legal provision to replace the old one.

Concerning detention procedures, as underlined in the previous Regular Report, an important move was made in March 1997 by reducing the duration of police custody. Many cases of torture happen during incommunicado detention in police stations. The entry into force of a "Regulation on Apprehension, Detention and Release Procedures" in October 1998 which aims at improving the current practice is another important step forward. Even if a detainee may still be held incommunicado for up to four days, the systematic implementation of this Regulation will probably allow for some progress. A circular issued by the Prime Ministry in June 1999 aims also at the effective implementation and stringent verification of the implementation of the October 1998 Regulation. As stated by Turkey in its opinion on the report by the "Committee on Honouring of Obligations and Commitments by Member States of the Council of Europe" dated January 1999, training courses for the police authorities began in November 1998.

These measures against the practice of torture have also recently been supplemented by the adoption by the Parliament in August 1999 of a law amending articles 243, 245 and 354 of the Penal Code. This law redefines torture, ill-treatment and abuse of power against individuals by public officials and foresees higher penalties for public officials who commit such offences, or medical personnel who draft fake reports on torture.

It is also important to note that Turkey finally authorised in February 1999 the publication of the report of the Council of Europe CPT delegation after its visit to Turkey in October 1997.

Despite recent positive gestures made by the authorities, the situation regarding freedom of expression remains worrying.

In the aftermath of the Öcalan capture, the situation has actually slightly worsened. In March 1999, the Minister of Justice issued a communiqué to Governors to be zealous in identifying associations, foundations, publications, individuals and organisations that are likely to take initiatives in favour of PKK leader Öcalan. In April 1999, the Public Relations Department of the Ministry of Interior issued a circular forbidding the use of certain terminology in relation to the Kurdish question in press releases and publications by public institutions and organisations ... At the end of May 1999, the General Penal Board of the Supreme Court of Appeals increased the sentences in relation to abuse of freedom of expression.

An encouraging measure should however be noted, albeit one of limited scope. In September 1999, President Demirel approved a law postponing prosecutions and punishment for offences committed through the press and broadcasting. This law foresees that sentences can be suspended for a three-year parole period and that, if offences are repeated during this time, the original sentence comes back into effect. According to the Justice Ministry, twenty-one persons including the Turkish writer Ismail Besikci had already been released before mid-September 1999. [According to the Turkish Human Rights Association Report of May 1999, there were at that time 134 persons in prison for offences in the general sense of freedom of expression and thought. Out of these, 84 were journalists]. However, the situation of journalists in prison for offences falling outside the scope of the law (i.e. those charged with being members of illegal organisations) will remain unchanged.

Among others, the case of Mr Akin Birdal, former Chairman of the Turkish Human Rights Association, remains a matter of concern. Although he was released in September 1999 on medical grounds after nearly four months in prison, his case is to be reviewed in six months' time.

Another reason for concern is the case brought against the board members of the non-governmental organisation TOSAV [Centre for the Research of Societal Problems] in May 1999. They are prosecuted for "separatist propaganda" on the basis of a document which is the output of a project co-financed by the EU in 1997. This project intended to strengthen civil society, Human Rights and democracy in Turkey through the organisation of education programmes and workshops and the publication of newsletters. Though the incriminated document is moderate in tone and appears to provide a useful contribution to debate and consensus building in Turkey, its dissemination has been prohibited.

In its July 1999 judgment, the European Court of Human Rights concluded in eleven cases that there had been a violation of the freedom of expression as guaranteed by the European Convention of Human Rights. In some of these cases the Court referred to the essential role of the press in ensuring the proper functioning of political democracy, as well as to the freedom of artistic expression.

Regarding the freedom of the press, the situation has not substantially changed. Cases of harassment and police violence against individual journalists have still been reported by domestic and international Human Rights organisations.

The conditions in Turkish prisons do not seem to have improved. Overpopulation and lack of adequate medical care remain major problems, to which hunger strikes and revolts often relate. In September 1999, a major prisoner revolt was severely repressed.

The situation regarding freedom of association and freedom of assembly has not changed. These freedoms continue to be subject to the limitations raised in the last Regular Report. Since October 1998, several branches of the Turkish Human Rights Association have been closed by the authorities either temporarily or for an indefinite period.

As far as freedom of religion is concerned, there still exists a difference of treatment between those religious minorities recognised by the Lausanne Treaty and other religious minorities.

Regarding the status of women, a positive development is the lifting in July 1999 of Turkey's reservations against the UN Convention for the Elimination of All Forms of Discrimination Against Women. The reservations were made fourteen years ago on grounds that it contradicted the provisions of the Turkish Civil Code that govern marriage and family relations.

The question of capital punishment has recently been a major subject of debate in Turkey as well as outside Turkey in connection with the Öcalan trial. As mentioned above, on 29 June 1999, Öcalan was convicted of treason and the intention to separate part of the territory of the Turkish Republic, and sentenced to the death penalty. It is clear that the application of such a sentence would nullify the important effort made for the abolition of the death penalty in Turkey. In this context, it has to be recalled that the draft Turkish Penal Code bill which is on the agenda of the Parliament provides for the abolition of the death penalty.

## HUMAN RIGHTS PROTECTION INSTRUMENTS

As mentioned above, new rulings against Turkey have been adopted by the European Court of Human Rights since the last Regular report. The case of Mrs Loizidou which is developed under part 1.3 is still pending.

Generally speaking, since the last report, the situation concerning civil and political rights in Turkey has not evolved significantly. Several sources continue to underline the existence of torture, disappearances and extra-judicial executions. Moreover, certain administrative measures taken in the aftermath of the Öcalan affair show a more restrictive attitude by the Turkish authorities as regards freedom of expression. Nevertheless, there have been some concrete improvements reflecting the intention of the authorities to end Human Rights abuses by law enforcement officials. Several legislative and administrative measures adopted since October 1998 in order to fight against torture practices are important in this context. The recent adoption of a law postponing prosecution and punishment for some offences committed by journalists appear as a goodwill gesture from the authorities. Its implementation will be followed carefully.

## ECONOMIC, SOCIAL AND CULTURAL RIGHTS

There has been no particular development concerning these rights.

## MINORITY RIGHTS AND PROTECTION OF MINORITIES

Contrary to certain hopes expressed notably by some Member States in the context of the Öcalan trial, progress on the Kurdish question has not been made. These hopes were mainly based on the expectations that the arrest of Öcalan as well as other key PKK figures would help bring terrorism under control and increase the prospects of a civil solution to the problems of the South east. As stated in the last Regular Report, "a civil solution could include recognition of certain forms of Kurdish cultural identity and greater tolerance of the ways of expressing that identity, provided it does not advocate separatism or terrorism". For instance, TV broadcasting in Kurdish, while apparently tolerated for non-political programmes, is still officially not allowed.

The "Committee on the Honouring of Obligations and Commitments by Member States of the Council of Europe" indicated in its January 1999 report that "the essential point is that any such group [Turkish citizens of Kurdish origin] should have the opportunity and material resources to use and sustain its natural languages and cultural traditions in circumstances and under conditions now clearly and reasonably defined by two important Council of Europe Conventions: the Framework Convention on Protection of National Minorities and the European Charter for Regional or Minority Languages, as well as by Assembly Recommendation 1201 (1993) on an additional protocol on the rights of national minorities to the European Convention on Human Rights."

Emergency legislation remains in force in six provinces. Certain developments are however likely to have a positive impact on the situation in the region. Firstly, the Repentance Law (no. 4450), applicable for a six-month period and granting an amnesty notably to PKK members who surrender and disclose information on their organisation, has been adopted by the Parliament in August 1999. This law excludes from its application the PKK command structure and those PKK members who have killed members of the security forces. Secondly, PKK leader Öcalan called in August 1999 the members of its organisation to end attacks on Turkish targets and to withdraw from Turkish territory. He asked the PKK to end its struggle as of 1 September 1999. It is difficult at this stage to evaluate to what extent the withdrawal has been implemented. Thirdly, last August, President Demirel met with representatives of the HADEP party apparently to discuss the problems of the South east.

On the economic side, it is worth noting that, in March 1999, Prime Minister Ecevit announced that the Government will support the socio-economic development of the southeast Anatolia region with an additional US$100m over the next two years.

Concerning the right of asylum, some positive changes have been made in January 1999 to the existing legislation. The period of requesting residence permission of an asylum seeker is extended to ten days from the previously recognised five days. Also for those aliens whose applications are refused, the time for appealing has been extended from ten days to fifteen days.

*1.3. The Cyprus issue*

Since the last Regular Report, the UN Secretary General and his representative in Cyprus have continued the process of separate meetings with the two Cypriot leaders aimed at finding a basis for a resumption of direct talks.

In order to reinforce the UN efforts the G8 Summit of Head of States decided on 21 June 1999 to "urge the UN Secretary-General in accordance with relevant UN Security Council resolutions to invite the leaders of the two parties to negotiations in the fall of 1999". In the conclusions it was further stated that both parties should commit to set no pre-conditions, put all issues on the table, negotiate in good faith until a settlement is reached, and to take full consideration of relevant UN resolutions and treaties.

With resolution 1250 on 29 June, the Security Council requested the UN Secretary General to invite the Greek and Turkish Cypriot leaders to hold negotiations in the autumn. It also called on the two sides on Cyprus, including military authorities, to work constructively with the Secretary General and his special representative to create a positive climate on the island that will pave the way for these negotiations.

As evidenced by the Joint Declaration of 20 July 1999 issued by Messrs. Denktash and Ecevit, Turkey and the north of Cyprus still envisage to develop their relations "in line with the target of integration set at the highest level."

Turkey as a guarantor country should show strong commitment to bring the two sides together under the UN process launched at the invitation of the G8.

Turkey could have an active and constructive role in this framework in order to reach a comprehensive solution that addresses the legitimate concerns of all parties.

In 1996, the European Court of Human Rights delivered a ruling against Turkey in the case of a Greek-Cypriot woman (Mrs Loizidou), who was deprived of access to her property in northern Cyprus. In a second judgment in July 1998, the Court decided on pecuniary compensation for the claimant and gave Turkey until October 1998 to pay the compensation. Till now, arguing that the land in question is not Turkish but part of the TRNC [Turkish Republic of Northern Cyprus], Turkey has not complied with the Court judgment. In April 1999, the President of the Committee of Ministers of the Council of Europe recalled the obligation of Turkey to pay the compensation awarded by the Court.

Other questions related to the situation in the north of Cyprus have been referred to the European Court of Human Rights since the last Regular Report, in particular within the context of the interstate complaint Cyprus against Turkey (application no. 25781/94).

*1.4 General evaluation*

Recent developments confirm that, although the basic features of a democratic system exist in Turkey, it still does not meet the Copenhagen political criteria. There are serious shortcomings in terms of Human Rights and protection of minorities. Torture is not systematic but is still widespread and freedom of expression is regularly restricted by the authorities. The National Security Council continues to play a major role in political life. Although there have been some improvements in terms of the independence of the judiciary the emergency courts system remains in place. In recent months there have been some more encouraging signs of democratisation. The government and Parliament have worked to adopt some keys [sic] laws regulating political life, the justice system and protection of Human Rights. It is too early to assess the impact of these measures but these efforts should be pursued and extended to all citizens, including those of Kurdish origin. The Commission hopes that the positive impact of these measures will not be undone by the carrying out of the death sentence passed on Mr Abdullah Öcalan.

*2. Economic criteria*

\*\*\*

*2.4 General evaluation*

Turkey has many of the characteristics of a market economy. It should be able to cope, albeit with difficulties, with competitive pressure and market forces within the Union, provided sustainable macroeconomic stability is attained and there is further progress towards the implementation of legal and structural reform programmes.

Turkey has continued its consolidation policy and economic imbalances have been reduced. The public deficit and inflation have been reduced, the latter through a change in wage and price indexation. Pension reform has been approved by parliament. The efficiency of revenue collection procedures has been improved. The constitution has been changed to permit international arbitration. This should facilitate privatisation of the electricity sector and investment in infrastructure and remove an important impediment for foreign direct investments.

Priority should be given to reduce inflationary pressures and fiscal deficits in order to reduce real interest rates and high financing needs of the public sector, which are crowding out private sector investment. In view of the financing needs for the repair of earthquake damage, special attention should be paid to the overall fiscal discipline and to the swift implementation of further structural reforms. Privatisation needs to be continued and the promotion of SMEs [small- and medium-sized enterprises] has to be enhanced. The uneven distribution of income and the huge regional disparities impede sound economic development. Attention should be paid to education as an element of an overall socio-economic development strategy.

*3. Ability to assume the obligation of membership*

\*\*\*

*3.4. General evaluation*

Turkey continues to make most progress in alignment in the areas covered by the Customs Union and, to a lesser extent, in areas covered by the European strategy. In general terms the situation with regard to free movement of goods is satisfactory and Turkey has reached a high level of adoption of European standards even if it has still not adopted a framework law. Despite the high degree of alignment in the customs area there is still a need for a new customs code. The Customs Union was further developed in the last year through the establishment of a common system of outward processing for textiles. There is a need for early progress in the area of copyright law. Although there has been no recent progress in the area of capital movements the general situation is good and the recent adoption of a new Banking Act has brought further alignment.

In competition there has been progress in the area of anti-trust although the Commission remains concerned about the operation of the TEKEL [Turkish Alcohol and Tobacco Company] monopoly. Turkey has notified its state aid schemes to the Commission and these are under examination. Agriculture is still characterised by high levels of support and protection and there has been no progress in legislative alignment since the last Report.

In public procurement and in some other parts of the internal market *acquis* the Commission does not have sufficient information available to be able to assess progress.

The administrative capacity to apply the *acquis* in the context of the Customs Union remains very satisfactory. However, Turkey needs to further modernise its administrative structures and to increase staff training.

*4. Administrative capacity to apply the* acquis.

\*\*\*

CONCLUSION

Turkey's administrative capacity to apply the *acquis* in the context of the Customs union remains very satisfactory. However further efforts are needed in terms of modernisation of the structures and staff training.

\*\*\*

# Document no. 69

**Helsinki European Council Presidency Conclusions (10–11 December 1999)**[4]

\*\*\*

4. The European Council reaffirms the inclusive nature of the accession process, which now comprises thirteen candidate States within a single framework. The candidate States are participating in the accession process on an equal footing. They must share the values and objectives of the European Union as set out in the Treaties. In this respect the European Council stresses the principle of peaceful settlement of disputes in accordance with the United Nations Charter and urges candidate States to make every effort to resolve any outstanding border disputes and other related issues. Failing this they should within a reasonable time bring the dispute to the International Court of Justice. The European Council will review the situation relating to any outstanding disputes, in particular concerning the repercussions on the accession process and in order to promote their settlement through the International Court of Justice, at the latest by the end of 2004. Moreover, the European Council recalls that compliance with the political criteria laid down at the Copenhagen European Council is a prerequisite for the opening of accession negotiations and that compliance with all the Copenhagen criteria is the basis for accession to the Union.

\*\*\*

9. (a) The European Council welcomes the launch of the talks aiming at a comprehensive settlement of the Cyprus problem on 3 December in New York and expresses its strong support for the UN Secretary General's efforts to bring the process to a successful conclusion.

(b) The European Council underlines that a political settlement will facilitate the accession of Cyprus to the European Union. If no settlement has been reached by the completion of accession negotiations, the Council's decision on accession will be made without the above being a precondition. In this the Council will take account of all relevant factors.

\*\*\*

12. The European Council welcomes recent positive developments in Turkey as noted in the Commission's progress report, as well as its intention to continue its reforms towards complying with the Copenhagen criteria. Turkey is a candidate State destined to join the Union on the basis of the same criteria as applied to the other candidate States. Building on the existing European strategy, Turkey, like other candidate States, will benefit from a pre-accession strategy to stimulate and support its reforms. This will include enhanced political dialogue, with emphasis on progressing towards fulfilling the political criteria for accession with particular reference to the issue of Human Rights, as well as on the issues referred to in paragraphs 4 and 9(a). Turkey will also have the opportunity to participate in Community programmes and agencies and in meetings between candidate States and the Union in the context of the accession process. An accession partnership will be drawn up on the basis of previous European Council conclusions while containing priorities on which accession preparations must concentrate in the light of the political and economic criteria and the obligations of a Member State, combined with a national programme for the adoption of the *acquis*. Appropriate monitoring mechanisms will be established. With a view to intensifying the harmonisation of Turkey's legislation and practice with the *acquis*, the Commission is invited to prepare a process of analytical examination of the *acquis*. The European Council asks the Commission to present a single framework for coordinating all sources of European Union financial assistance for pre-accession.

\*\*\*

# 11 After Helsinki: initial developments — 2000

# Document no. 70

**Editors' comment on capture of Abdullah Öcalan, the leader of the PKK**

In February 1999, the leader of the PKK, Abdullah Öcalan, was captured in Nairobi, Kenya, and was brought to Turkey by Turkish security forces. Following his trial, in summing up the accusations against Mr. Öcalan, the prosecutors of the Ankara State Security Court no. 2 asked for the capital punishment of Öcalan under Article 125 of the Turkish Penal Code. Article 125 of the Turkish Penal Code titled "Treason and Crimes Against the State's Country and Sovereignty" states that "[t]he person who commits crimes aiming at putting the whole or a part of the state's territories under a foreign state's sovereignty, diminishing the state's independence, or separating a part of territories which are under the state's sovereignty from the state's administration, will be sentenced to death." The court sentenced Abdullah Öcalan to death on June 29, 1999. Kurds around the world objected to the decision; several European nations voiced their concerns about the penalty and expressed their desire that the penalty not be imposed. On July 2, 1999, Mr. Öcalan's lawyers asked the European Court of Human Rights (ECtHR) to request the Turkish government to stay the decision to impose the death penalty until the Court could decide the merits of their complaints. The ECtHR, on July 6, 1999, asked Turkey "to take all necessary steps to ensure that the death penalty is not carried out so as to enable the Court to proceed effectively with the examination of the admissibility and merits of the applicant's complaints under the Convention."

After stating that the presence of a military judge in the State Security Court resulted in a violation of the right to a fair trial, the European Parliament (EP) expressed in a resolution on July 22, 1999,[1] that all States applying to join the EU "must fulfil the Copenhagen Criteria, which require achievement of 'stability of institutions guaranteeing democracy, the rule of law, Human Rights, respect for and promotion of minorities.'" It concluded that the fundamental rights of the Kurdish minority in Turkey are not respected and condemned Mr. Öcalan's sentence, reiterating its firm opposition to the use of the death penalty. Furthermore, the EP called on the Turkish authorities to not carry out the death sentence, stated its expectation that the Supreme Court of Appeal will reverse the verdict against Mr. Öcalan "as a violation of Turkey's international legal commitments under the European Convention on Human Rights," and "urge[d] the Turkish Grand National Assembly to transform the current *de facto* moratorium on executions into a formal abolition of the death penalty in Turkey." Finally, the EP "[c]alled on the Turkish government to address the causes of the conflict in Turkey by finding a solution which recognises the political, social and cultural rights of the Kurdish people and takes the view that, in this connection, the requisite democratic reforms must be carried out."

On January 12, 2000, the Turkish Prime Minister announced that Turkey would respect the request from the ECtHR.

# Document no. 71

**[European Parliament] Briefing no. 7: Turkey and relations with the European Union**[2]

On 13 December 1999 the Helsinki European Council adopted the Commission proposal to grant Turkey the status of an applicant for EU membership.

There is, however, still much ground to be covered on the road to membership. As the second regular Commission report (October 1999) indicates, Turkey needs to make substantial progress on the Copenhagen political criteria ... "There are serious shortcomings in terms of Human Rights and protection of minorities".

\*\*\*

Parliament, in its resolution on preparations for the Helsinki European Council, points out that "negotiations cannot be opened because Turkey is still nowhere near meeting the political criteria of Copenhagen". Parliament insists that "as a candidate country, Turkey must make clear and verifiable progress in meeting those criteria".

\*\*\*

## 2. *The constitutional situation*

Since the April 1999 elections, the government coalition with its large majority has pushed through a number of legislative measures.

In particular, the State Security Courts have been reformed. Since 1998, the European Court of Human Rights has held the view that these courts could not be considered impartial and independent as they were presided over by a military judge, and were thus in violation of the European Convention of Human Rights (to which Turkey is a signatory).

On 22 June 1999 the constitutional review demilitarising the State Security Courts came into force (Art. 143 of the Constitution). This has enabled the military judge in the øcalan trial to be replaced immediately by a civilian judge.

Since April 1999, following a revision of the law, the government has been able to impose long prison sentences and demotion on police officers and civil servants found guilty of torture or cruel, inhuman or degrading treatment. This is in line with the recommendations of the European Committee against Torture (President Demirel admitted that torture existed in Turkey, but said it was not State policy (cf. Milliyet, 22.11.1999) [sic.].

In August 1999 the GANT (Grand Assembly) adopted changes to the party political system, liberalising it to a certain extent. Nevertheless, in February 1999 the Constitutional Court banned the pro-Kurd DKP party (the Islamist Refah party had been banned in January 1998).

Although there are calls from some quarters for abolition of the National Security Council, the prime minister, Bulent Ecevit, supports it and does not consider its existence incompatible with a democratic system (cf. the Turkish press of 13.12.1999). The prime minister has, however, expressed himself in favour of abolishing the death penalty.

Article 8 of the Anti-Terrorism Law is still in existence. Although it was slightly amended in 1995 it still allows imprisonment — on the pretext of having spread separatist propaganda — of journalists in particular. The Council of Europe and the European Parliament had called for this article to be entirely abolished.

The joint parliamentary committee responsible for harmonising the constitution is said to have started work in December 1999 on bringing the constitution into line with EU standards and on "drafting a civil constitution"; among the changes to be made, the media list the following:

- abolition of the death penalty;
- freedom of opinion;
- prevention of torture;
- granting of cultural rights (radio, television, education) to the Kurds;
- abolition of the National Security Council;
- abolition of emergency laws;
- civil solution to the problem of the southeast;
- military chiefs of staff to be attached to the National Defence Ministry;
- settlement of the Aegean Sea dispute and the Cyprus problem.

## 3. *Human rights*

The second regular Commission report (13 October 1999) considers that the situation has changed little since the 1998 report, and, despite a few steps in the right direction, it still gives cause for concern. The report cites a number of particular sectors where there has been no progress at all: freedom of expression, press freedom, prison conditions, freedom of association and assembly, the problem of minorities.

> Generally speaking, since the last report, the situation concerning civil and political rights in Turkey has not evolved significantly.
> (Second Regular Commission Report)

## 4. The Kurdish question

*Reminder:* Parliament has always encouraged the Turkish government to tackle the problem of terrorism by democratic means, respecting the rule of law. Parliament called on the EU (resolution of 15 January 1998) to take action internationally to resolve this problem [influx of Kurdish refugees to Europe] and called on the Council and the Member States to raise the question of Human Rights violations against the Kurds with the United Nations Commission on Human Rights.

\*\*\*

In its resolution of 17 September 1998 on the Commission report on developments in relations with Turkey, Parliament advocated a political solution to the conflict and supported proposals aiming at legal recognition of Kurdish identity, even if only certain elements of its cultural identity, and all initiatives which could promote dialogue between the parties. But in its 1999 Regular Report on Turkey's progress towards accession, the Commission deplored the fact that no progress had been observed in this area.

\*\*\*

# Document no. 72

### ECtHR — *Kilic v. Turkey*[3]

\*\*\*

[The applicant complained under Article 2 to the ECtHR that his brother was killed by or with the connivance of the security forces because he was a journalist working for the newspaper *Ozgur Gundem*. He also complained of the lack of a proper and effective investigation into the death of his brother, in breach of the procedural aspects of Article 2 and also in violation of Article 13. He further complained that the killing of his brother, who was targeted as a journalist, constituted interference with the freedom of expression, guaranteed under Article 10, and discrimination, contrary to Article 14. The facts of the case were as follows.

Following a search and arrest operation at the *Ozgur Gundem* office (a daily newspaper, which sought to reflect the opinions of Turkish Kurds) in Istanbul on December 10, 1993, charges were brought against, inter alia, the editor, manager and owner of the newspaper, alleging that they were members of the Kurdistan Workers' Party (PKK) and had rendered the PKK assistance and published propaganda. On December 23, 1992, Kemal Kilic sent a press release to the Sanlıurfa governor requesting protection. The letter stated that death threats had been made against the United Press Distribution representative carrying out the distribution of *Ozgur Gundem*, and against the driver and owner of the taxi used for distribution. By a letter dated December 30, 1992, the governor's office refused the request. On January 11, 1993, Kemal Kilic issued a press release stating that attacks against persons involved in the sale and distribution of *Ozgur Gundem* in Sanlıurfa were continuing, despite urgent requests for protective measures. Details were given of an arson attack on a news-stand on January 5, 1993, and on another news-stand on January 10, 1993. The press release criticized the governor for not ensuring the safe distribution of the newspaper and called on him and the police to fulfill their responsibilities. Following a complaint by the governor, Kemal Kilic was charged with insulting the governor through the publication and broadcasting of the press release. He was taken into detention at the Sanlıurfa Security Directorate on January 18, 1993, and released the same day. Later that day, Kemal Kilic was shot dead by four men who had waited for him on his route home from work. The incident was reported to the gendarmerie that rapidly arrived on the scene and took charge of the investigation at the scene. An autopsy of the body revealed that Kemal Kilic had died due to destruction of brain tissue and brain hemorrhage. On February 26, 1993, the gendarmerie carried out a search, with a warrant, of Kemal Kilic's house. The gendarmerie seized books, newspaper cuttings, a photograph, and two cassettes for further examination. Following the seizure, the public prosecutor issued a decision to continue the investigation, which stated that "it had not been possible to identify or apprehend the perpetrators of the killing and that the search should continue until the expiry of the twenty-year limitation period." The gun used in Kemal Kilic's shooting matched the gun used in another case. In an indictment on February 3, 1994, Huseyin Guney was charged with the offense of membership in the outlawed Hezbollah organization and carrying out activities with the intention of removing part of the country from the sovereignty of the State with the intent of forming a Kurdish state based on Islamic principles. These activities were said to include the attack on Kemal Kilic. In a judgment on March 23, 1999, the court convicted Huseyin Guney of being a member of Hezbollah. However, the court noted that different individuals could have used the gun in different attacks. Following the court's decision, the Diyarbakır State Security Court chief public prosecutor opened an investigation into the killing of Kemal Kilic. In a letter dated December 20, 1999, the prosecutor instructed the Sanlıurfa gendarmerie command to report to him every three months concerning any evidence obtained about the Kilic murder.]

\*\*\*

## II. Material before the convention organs

### B. *The Susurluk report*

[Susurluk was the scene of a road accident in November 1996 involving a car in which a member of parliament, a former deputy director of the Istanbul security services, a notorious far-right extremist, a drug trafficker wanted by Interpol and his girlfriend had been travelling. The last three were killed. The fact that they had all been travelling in the same car had so shocked public opinion that it had been necessary to start more than sixteen judicial investigations at different levels and a parliamentary inquiry.]

29. The applicant provided the Commission with a copy of the so-called "Susurluk report", produced at the request of the Prime Minister by Mr Kutlu Savaş, Vice-President of the Board of Inspectors within the Prime Minister's Office. After receiving the report in January 1998, the Prime Minister made it available to the public, although eleven pages and certain annexes were withheld.

30. The introduction states that the report was not based on a judicial investigation and did not constitute a formal investigative report. It was intended for

information purposes and purported to do no more than describe certain events which had occurred mainly in southeast Turkey and which tended to confirm the existence of unlawful dealings between political figures, government institutions and clandestine groups.

31. The report analyses a series of events, such as murders carried out under orders, the killings of well-known figures or supporters of the Kurds and deliberate acts by a group of "informants" supposedly serving the State, and concludes that there is a connection between the fight to eradicate terrorism in the region and the underground relations that have been formed as a result, particularly in the drug-trafficking sphere. The passages from the report that concern certain matters affecting radical periodicals distributed in the region are reproduced below.

> ... In his confession to the Diyarbakır Crime Squad, ... Mr G. ... had stated that Ahmet Demir [p. 35] would say from time to time that he had planned and procured the murder of Behçet Cantürk and other partisans from the mafia and the PKK who had been killed in the same way ... The murder of ... Musa Anter had also been planned and carried out by A. Demir [p. 37] ...
>
> Summary information on the antecedents of Behçet Cantürk, who was of Armenian origin, are set out below [p. 72] ...
>
> As of 1992 he was one of the financiers of the newspaper Özgür Gündem. ... Although it was obvious who Cantürk was and what he did, the State was unable to cope with him. Because legal remedies were inadequate Özgür Gündem was blown up with plastic explosives and when Cantürk started to set up a new undertaking, when he was expected to submit to the State, the Turkish Security Organization decided that he should be killed and that decision was carried out [p. 73] ...
>
> All the relevant State bodies were aware of these activities and operations. ... When the characteristics of the individuals killed in the operations in question are examined, the difference between those Kurdish supporters who were killed in the region in which a state of emergency had been declared and those who were not lay in the financial strength the latter presented in economic terms. ... The sole disagreement we have with what was done relates to the form of the procedure and its results. It has been established that there was regret at the murder of Musa Anter, even among those who approved of all the incidents. It is said that Musa Anter was not involved in any armed action, that he was more concerned with the philosophy of the matter and that the effect created by his murder exceeded his own real influence and that the decision to murder him was a mistake. (Information about these people is to be found in Appendix 9). Other journalists have also been murdered [p. 74].

32. The report concludes with numerous recommendations, such as improving coordination and communication between the different branches of the

security, police and intelligence departments; identifying and dismissing security-force personnel implicated in illegal activities; limiting the use of "confessors"; reducing the number of village guards; terminating the use of the Special Operations Bureau outside the southeast region and incorporating it into the police outside that area; opening investigations into various incidents; taking steps to suppress gang and drug-smuggling activities; and recommending that the results of the Grand National Assembly Susurluk inquiry be forwarded to the appropriate authorities for the relevant proceedings to be undertaken.

*C. The 1993 report of the Parliamentary Investigation Commission (10/90 no. A.01.1. GEC)*

33. The applicant provided this 1993 report into extra-judicial or "unknown perpetrator" killings by a Parliamentary Investigation Commission of the Turkish Grand National Assembly. The report referred to 908 unsolved killings, of which nine involved journalists. It commented on the public lack of confidence in the authorities in southeast Turkey on and referred to information that the Hezbollah had a camp in the Batman region where they received political and military training and assistance from the security forces. It concluded that there was a lack of accountability in the region and that some groups with official roles might be implicated in the killings.

*D. Evidence given before the Commission's delegates*

\*\*\* [A delegation from the Commission heard evidence from four witnesses. Three other witnesses did not appear.]

35. Mr Ziyaeddin Akbulut, the governor of Sanlıurfa at the material time, was asked to attend the hearings on 4 February and 4 July 1997 but did not appear. After the first hearing, the Agent of the government provided the explanation that Mr Akbulut had been taking his annual leave. Regarding the second hearing, the Agent submitted a letter from Mr Akbulut which stated that he could not remember being petitioned by Kemal Kilic, that the allegations made were false and that he could not attend due to his annual leave.

### III. Relevant domestic law and practice

36. The principles and procedures relating to liability for acts against the law may be summarised as follows.

*A. Criminal prosecutions*

37. Under the Criminal Code all forms of homicide (Articles 448 to 455) and attempted homicide (Articles 61 and 62) constitute criminal offences. The authorities' obligations in respect of conducting a preliminary investigation into acts or omissions capable of constituting such offences that have been brought to

their attention are governed by Articles 151 to 153 of the Code of Criminal Procedure. Offences may be reported to the authorities or the security forces as well as to public prosecutors' offices. The complaint may be made in writing or orally. If it is made orally, the authority must make a record of it (Article 151).

If there is evidence to suggest that a death is not due to natural causes, members of the security forces who have been informed of that fact are required to advise the public prosecutor or a criminal court judge (Article 152). By Article 235 of the Criminal Code, any public official who fails to report to the police or a public prosecutor's office an offence of which he has become aware in the exercise of his duty is liable to imprisonment.

A public prosecutor who is informed by any means whatsoever of a situation that gives rise to the suspicion that an offence has been committed is obliged to investigate the facts in order to decide whether or not there should be a prosecution (Article 153 of the Code of Criminal Procedure).

38. In the case of alleged terrorist offences, the public prosecutor is deprived of jurisdiction in favour of a separate system of national security prosecutors and courts established throughout Turkey.

39. If the suspected offender is a civil servant and if the offence was committed during the performance of his duties, the preliminary investigation of the case is governed by the Law of 1914 on the prosecution of civil servants, which restricts the public prosecutor's jurisdiction *ratione personae* at that stage of the proceedings. In such cases it is for the relevant local administrative council (for the district or province, depending on the suspect's status) to conduct the preliminary investigation and, consequently, to decide whether to prosecute. Once a decision to prosecute has been taken, it is for the public prosecutor to investigate the case.

An appeal to the Supreme Administrative Court lies against a decision of the council. If a decision not to prosecute is taken, the case is automatically referred to that court.

40. By virtue of Article 4, paragraph (i), of Decree no. 285 of 10 July 1987 on the authority of the governor of a state of emergency region, the 1914 Law (see paragraph 39 above) also applies to members of the security forces who come under the governor's authority.

41. If the suspect is a member of the armed forces, the applicable law is determined by the nature of the offence. Thus, if it is a "military offence" under the Military Criminal Code (Law no. 1632), the criminal proceedings are in principle conducted in accordance with Law no. 353 on the establishment of courts martial and their rules of procedure. Where a member of the armed forces has been accused of an ordinary offence, it is normally the provisions of the Code of Criminal Procedure which apply (see Article 145 § 1 of the Constitution and sections 9 to 14 of Law no. 353).

The Military Criminal Code makes it a military offence for a member of the armed forces to endanger a person's life by disobeying an order (Article 89). In such cases civilian complainants may lodge their complaints with the authorities referred to in the Code of Criminal Procedure (see paragraph 37 above) or with the offender's superior.

## B. Civil and administrative liability arising out of criminal offences

42. Under section 13 of Law no. 2577 on administrative procedure, anyone who sustains damage as a result of an act by the authorities may, within one year after the alleged act was committed, claim compensation from them. If the claim is rejected in whole or in part or if no reply is received within sixty days, the victim may bring administrative proceedings.

43. Article 125 §§ 1 and 7 of the Constitution provides:

> All acts or decisions of the authorities are subject to judicial review ...
>
> The authorities shall be liable to make reparation for all damage caused by their acts or measures.

That provision establishes the State's strict liability, which comes into play if it is shown that in the circumstances of a particular case the State has failed in its obligation to maintain public order, ensure public safety or protect people's lives or property, without it being necessary to show a tortious act attributable to the authorities. Under these rules, the authorities may therefore be held liable to compensate anyone who has sustained loss as a result of acts committed by unidentified persons.

44. Article 8 of Decree no. 430 of 16 December 1990, the last sentence of which was inspired by the provision mentioned above (see paragraph 43 above), provides:

> No criminal, financial or legal liability may be asserted against ... the governor of a state of emergency region or by provincial governors in that region in respect of decisions taken, or acts performed, by them in the exercise of the powers conferred on them by this decree, and no application shall be made to any judicial authority to that end. This is without prejudice to the rights of individuals to claim reparation from the State for damage which they have been caused without justification.

45. Under the Code of Obligations, anyone who suffers damage as a result of an illegal or tortious act may bring an action for damages (Articles 41 to 46) and non-pecuniary loss (Article 47). The civil courts are not bound by either the findings or the verdict of the criminal court on the issue of the defendant's guilt (Article 53).

However, under section 13 of Law no. 657 on State employees, anyone who has sustained loss as a result of an act done in the performance of duties governed by public law may, in principle, only bring an action against the authority by whom the civil servant concerned is employed and not directly against the civil servant (see Article 129 § 5 of the Constitution and Articles 55 and 100 of the Code of Obligations). That is not, however, an absolute rule. When an act is found to be illegal or tortious and, consequently, is no longer an "administrative" act or deed, the civil courts may allow a claim for damages to be made against the official concerned, without prejudice to the victim's right to bring an action against the authority on the basis of its joint liability as the official's employer (Article 50 of the Code of Obligations).

## THE LAW

*I. The Court's assessment of the facts*

[The Court accepting a Commission delegations findings concluded that "it was unable to determine who had killed Kemal Kilic. There was insufficient evidence to establish beyond reasonable doubt that State agents or persons acting on their behalf had carried out the murder. It also found that there was no direct evidence linking the suspect Huseyin Guney to that incident. However noting the "lack of any satisfactory or convincing explanation by the government as to the non-attendance of an important witness, who was a State official, at the hearings before the Commission's delegates," it confirmed that in this case the government fell short of their obligations under former Article 8 § 1 (a) of the Convention to furnish all necessary facilities to the Commission in its task of establishing the facts.]

\*\*\*

*II. Alleged violations of Article 2 of the Convention*

54. The applicant alleged that the State was responsible for the death of his brother Kemal Kilic through the lack of protection and for the failure to provide an effective investigation into his death. He invoked Article 2 of the Convention, which provides:

> 1. Everyone's right to life shall be protected by law. No one shall be deprived of his life intentionally save in the execution of a sentence of a court following his conviction of a crime for which this penalty is provided by law.
> 2. Deprivation of life shall not be regarded as inflicted in contravention of this Article when it results from the use of force which is no more than absolutely necessary:
> (a) in defence of any person from unlawful violence;
> (b) in order to effect a lawful arrest or to prevent the escape of a person lawfully detained;
> (c) in action lawfully taken for the purpose of quelling a riot or insurrection.

55. The government disputed those allegations. The Commission expressed the opinion that, on the facts of the case, which disclosed a lack of effective guarantees against unlawful conduct by State agents, the State, through their failure to take investigative measures or otherwise respond to the concerns of Kemal Kilic about the pattern of attacks on persons connected with *Ozgur*

*Gundem* and through the defects in the investigative and judicial procedures carried out after his death, did not comply with their positive obligation to protect Kemal Kilic's right to life.

A. SUBMISSIONS OF THOSE WHO APPEARED BEFORE THE COURT

[The applicant submitted, agreeing with the Commission's report that the authorities had failed to ensure the effective implementation and enforcement of law in the southeast region in or about 1993. He also referred to the Susurluk report as strongly supporting the allegations that unlawful attacks were being carried out with the support and knowledge of the authorities. Relying on the defects in investigations into unlawful killings found by the Convention organs as showing that public prosecutors were unlikely to carry out effective inquiries into allegations against the security forces, and pointing to the way in which the jurisdiction to investigate complaints against the security forces was transferred from the public prosecutors to administrative councils, which were not independent, and to the use of SSCs, which were also lacking in independence due to the presence of a military judge, to deal with alleged terrorist crime, he argued that these facts disclosed a lack of accountability on the part of the security forces or those acting under their control or with their acquiescence and this was incompatible with the rule of law. He argued that, in the particular circumstances of this case where Kemal Kilic, as a journalist for *Ozgur Gundem*, was at risk of being targeted, the authorities, in failing to take adequate measures following his request for protection, had failed to protect his life as required by law. He further argued that the investigation into Kemal Kilic's death was fundamentally flawed.

The government rejected the Commission's approach as general and imprecise. It argued strongly that the Susurluk report had no evidential or probative value and could not be taken into account in assessing the situation in southeast Turkey. As regards the applicant's and the Commission's assertions that Kemal Kilic had been at risk from unlawful violence, the government pointed out that the State had been dealing with a high level of terrorist violence since 1984 which reached its peak between 1993 and 1994, causing the death of more than 30,000 Turkish citizens. According to the government, the situation in the southeast was exploited by many armed terrorist groups, including the PKK and the Hezbollah, who were involved in a struggle for power in that region in 1993/94, and while "the security forces did their utmost to establish law and order, they faced immense obstacles and, as in other parts of the world, terrorist attacks and killings could not be prevented." As regards the investigation into the death of Kemal Kilic, the government asserted that "this was carried out with utmost precision and professionalism. All necessary steps were taken promptly and efficiently, including an investigation at the scene, an autopsy, a ballistics examination and the taking of statements from witnesses."]

\*\*\*

B. THE COURT'S ASSESSMENT

Alleged failure to protect the right to life

*a. Alleged failure to take protective measures*   62. The Court recalls that the first sentence of Article 2 § 1 enjoins the State not only to refrain from the intentional and unlawful taking of life, but also to take appropriate steps to safeguard the lives of those within its jurisdiction [citation omitted]. This involves a primary duty on the State to secure the right to life by putting in place effective criminal-law provisions to deter the commission of offences against the person, backed up by law-enforcement machinery for the prevention, suppression and punishment of breaches of such provisions. It also extends in appropriate circumstances to a positive obligation on the authorities to take preventive operational measures to protect an individual or individuals whose life is at risk from the criminal acts of another individual [citation omitted].

63. Bearing in mind the difficulties in policing modern societies, the unpredictability of human conduct and the operational choices which must be made in terms of priorities and resources, the positive obligation must be interpreted in a way which does not impose an impossible or disproportionate burden on the authorities. Accordingly, not every claimed risk to life can entail for the authorities a Convention requirement to take operational measures to prevent that risk from materialising. For a positive obligation to arise, it must be established that the authorities knew or ought to have known at the time of the existence of a real and immediate risk to the life of an identified individual or individuals from the criminal acts of a third party and that they failed to take measures within the scope of their powers which, judged reasonably, might have been expected to avoid that risk [citation omitted].

64. In the present case, it has not been established beyond reasonable doubt that any State agent or person acting on behalf of the State authorities was involved in the killing of Kemal Kilic (see paragraphs 48 and 50 above). The question to be determined is whether the authorities failed to comply with their positive obligation to protect him from a known risk to his life.

65. The Court notes that Kemal Kilic made a request for protection to the governor of Sanlıurfa on 23 December 1992, just under two months before he was shot dead by unknown gunmen. His petition shows that he considered himself and others to be at risk because they worked for *Ozgur Gundem*. He claimed that distributors and sellers of the newspaper had been threatened and attacked in Sanlıurfa and in other towns in the southeast region. In his press release of 11 January 1993, he detailed specific attacks on two news-stands in Sanlıurfa.

66. The government have claimed that Kemal Kilic was no more at risk than any other person or journalist in the southeast, referring to the tragic number of victims to the conflict in that region. The Court has previously found, however, that in early 1993 the authorities were aware that those involved in the publication and distribution of *Ozgur Gundem* feared that they were falling victim to a

concerted campaign tolerated, if not approved, by State officials [citation omitted]. It is undisputed that a significant number of serious incidents occurred involving killings of journalists, attacks on newspaper kiosks and distributors of the newspaper (citations omitted). The Court is satisfied that Kemal Kilic, as a journalist for *Ozgur Gundem*, was at this time at particular risk of falling victim to an unlawful attack. Moreover, this risk could in the circumstances be regarded as real and immediate.

67. The authorities were aware of this risk. The governor of Sanlıurfa had been petitioned by Kemal Kilic who had requested protective measures. In Diyarbakır, the police were in consultation with the *Ozgur Gundem* office there about protective measures.

68. Furthermore, the authorities were aware, or ought to have been aware, of the possibility that this risk derived from the activities of persons or groups acting with the knowledge or acquiescence of elements in the security forces. A 1993 report by a Parliamentary Investigation Commission (see paragraph 33 above) stated that it had received information that a Hezbollah training camp was receiving aid and training from the security forces and concluded that some officials might be implicated in the 908 unsolved killings in the southeast region. The Susurluk report, published in January 1998, informed the Prime Minister's Office that the authorities were aware of killings being carried out to eliminate alleged supporters of the PKK, including the murders of Musa Anter and other journalists during this period. The government insisted that this report did not have any judicial or evidential value. However, even the government described the report as providing information on the basis of which the Prime Minister was to take further appropriate measures. It may therefore be regarded as a significant document.

The Court does not rely on the report as establishing that any State official was implicated in any particular killing. The report does, however, provide further strong substantiation for allegations, current at the time and since, that "contra-guerrilla" groups or terrorist groups were targeting individuals perceived to be acting against State interests, with the acquiescence, and possible assistance, of members of the security forces.

69. The Court has considered whether the authorities did all that could reasonably be expected of them to avoid the risk to Kemal Kilic.

70. It recalls that, as the government submits, there were large numbers of security forces in the southeast region pursuing the aim of establishing public order. They faced the difficult task of countering the violent armed attacks of the PKK and other groups. There was a framework of law in place with the aim of protecting life. The Turkish Criminal Code prohibited murder and there were police and gendarmerie forces with the role of preventing and investigating crime, under the supervision of the judicial branch of public prosecutors. There were also courts applying the provisions of the criminal law in trying, convicting and sentencing offenders.

71. The Court observes, however, that the implementation of the criminal law in respect of unlawful acts allegedly carried out with the involvement of the

security forces discloses particular characteristics in the southeast region in this period.

72. Firstly, where offences were committed by State officials in certain circumstances, the competence to investigate was removed from the public prosecutor in favour of administrative councils which took the decision whether to prosecute. These councils were made up of civil servants, under the orders of the governor, who was himself responsible for the security forces whose conduct was in issue. The investigations which they instigated were often carried out by gendarmes linked hierarchically to the units concerned in the incident. The Court accordingly found in two cases that the administrative councils did not provide an independent or effective procedure for investigating deaths involving members of the security forces (citations omitted).

73. Secondly, the cases examined by the Convention organs concerning the region at this time have produced a series of findings of failure by the authorities to investigate allegations of wrongdoing by the security forces, both in the context of the procedural obligations under Article 2 of the Convention and the requirement for effective remedies imposed by Article 13 (citations omitted).

A common feature of these cases is a finding that the public prosecutor has failed to pursue complaints by individuals claiming that the security forces were involved in an unlawful act, for example not interviewing or taking statements from implicated members of the security forces, accepting at face value the reports of incidents submitted by members of the security forces and attributing incidents to the PKK on the basis of minimal or no evidence.

74. Thirdly, the attribution of responsibility for incidents to the PKK had particular significance as regards the investigation and judicial procedures which ensue since jurisdiction for terrorist crimes has been given to the State Security Courts. In a series of cases, the Court has found that the State Security Courts do not fulfil the requirement of independence imposed by Article 6 of the Convention, due to the presence of a military judge whose participation gives rise to legitimate fears that the court may be unduly influenced by considerations which had nothing to do with the nature of the case [citation omitted].

75. The Court finds that these defects undermined the effectiveness of the protection afforded by the criminal law in the southeast region during the period relevant to this case. It considers that this permitted or fostered a lack of accountability of members of the security forces for their actions which, as the Commission stated in its report, was not compatible with the rule of law in a democratic society respecting the fundamental rights and freedoms guaranteed under the Convention.

76. In addition to these defects which removed the protection which Kemal Kilic should have received by law, there was an absence of any operational measures of protection. The government have disputed that they could have effectively provided protection against attacks. The Court is not convinced by this argument. A wide range of preventive measures were available which would have assisted in minimising the risk to Kemal Kilic's life and which would not have involved an impractical diversion of resources. On the contrary, however,

the authorities denied that there was any risk. There is no evidence that they took any steps in response to Kemal Kilic's request for protection either by applying reasonable measures of protection or by investigating the extent of the alleged risk to *Ozgur Gundem* employees in Sanlıurfa with a view to taking appropriate measures of prevention.

77. The Court concludes that in the circumstances of this case the authorities failed to take reasonable measures available to them to prevent a real and immediate risk to the life of Kemal Kilic. There has, accordingly, been a violation of Article 2 of the Convention.

*b. Alleged inadequacy of the investigation* 78. The Court reiterates that the obligation to protect life under Article 2 of the Convention, read in conjunction with the State's general duty under Article 1 of the Convention "to secure to everyone within [its] jurisdiction the rights and freedoms defined in [the] Convention", requires by implication that there should be some form of effective official investigation when individuals have been killed as a result of the use of force (citations omitted).

79. The Court recalls that in the present case an investigation was carried out at the scene of the killing by the gendarmerie captain Kargılı, who also took steps to identify and interview potential witnesses and to obtain a ballistics examination of the cartridges found at the scene.

80. However, no investigative step was taken by Captain Kargılı after his letter of 15 March 1993 transmitting information and documents to the Sanlıurfa public prosecutor. Furthermore, although the indictment lodged against the suspect Huseyin Guney arrested in Diyarbakır on 24 December 1993 listed the killing of Kemal Kilic as one of the separatist offences committed by him as a Hezbollah member, there was no direct evidence linking him with that particular crime [citation omitted]. The Diyarbakır National Security Court did not hear any witnesses concerning the Kilic incident nor had Huseyin Guney made any admissions as to his involvement. No steps had been taken to link Huseyin Guney, who had previously lived in Batman, to the killing of Kemal Kilic in Sanlıurfa. While the prosecution relied on a ballistics examination which showed that the gun allegedly used by Huseyin Guney in an attack on a shop in Diyarbakır had also been used in fifteen other incidents, including the shooting of Kemal Kilic, there was no evidence to show that it had been in his possession before the attack on the shop. This finding is confirmed by the decision of 29 March 1999 of the Diyarbakır State Security Court, which found that it was not proved that Huseyin Guney had used the gun in any other incident [citation omitted].

81. The government contested the applicant's and the Commission's view that the misconceived inclusion of the murder of Kemal Kilic in the prosecution of Huseyin Guney had the practical effect of closing the investigation. However, the Court notes that on 16 February 1994 the Sanlıurfa public prosecutor issued a decision of non-jurisdiction in respect of the incident, stating that the incident fell within the jurisdiction of the State Security Court to which he therefore transferred the file. It is not apparent that any steps were taken by the Diyarbakır

National Security Court prosecution with a view to continuing the investigation in any concrete form. The inactive status of the file is also supported by the government's information that following the National Security Court decision of 29 March 1999 a new file has been opened into the matter by its public prosecutor, who has sent out a general request for information to be forwarded to him concerning the incident.

82. The Court observes that the investigation by the gendarmes and the Sanliurfa public prosecutor after the incident did not include any inquiries as to the possible targeting of Kemal Kilic due to his job as an *Ozgur Gundem* journalist. The fact that the case was transferred to the National Security Court prosecutor indicates that it was regarded as a separatist crime. There is no indication that any steps have been taken to investigate any collusion by security forces in the incident.

83. Having regard therefore to the limited scope and short duration of the investigation in this case, the Court finds that the authorities have failed to carry out an effective investigation into the circumstances surrounding Kemal Kilic's death. It concludes that there has in this respect been a violation of Article 2 of the Convention.

## III. Alleged violation of Article 10 of the Convention

\*\*\* [The Court rejected the applicant's complaint that the killing of his brother Kemal Kilic was a violation of Article 10 of the Convention (freedom of expression)].

## IV. Alleged violation of Article 13 of the Convention

[The applicant complained that he had not had an effective remedy within the meaning of Article 13 of the Convention (the requirement of effective remedies for violations of rights and freedoms). The Court reiterated that Article 13 of the Convention "guarantees the availability at the national level of a remedy to enforce the substance of the Convention rights and freedoms in whatever form they might happen to be secured in the domestic legal order." The Court thus held that Article 13 requires the existence of an "in practice and in law" effective domestic remedy provision even for a merely "arguable complaint," the exercise of which must not be unjustifiably hindered by the acts or omissions of the authorities of the respondent State. Even though stating that, in the present case, "the Court has not found it proved beyond reasonable doubt that agents of the State carried out, or were otherwise implicated in, the killing of the applicant's brother," the Court concluded that the authorities "had an obligation to carry out an effective investigation into the circumstances of the killing of the applicant's brother" and in this case "no effective criminal investigation can be considered to have been conducted in accordance with Article 13."]

\*\*\*

[In the following parts the Court declined to determine whether "the failings identified in this case are part of a practice adopted by the authorities." The Court also rejected to consider the argument that the killing was an example "of discrimination on grounds of presumed political or other opinion and of national origin," and was thus contrary to Article 14. Finally, the Court granted non-pecuniary damages and costs and expenses, with interest.]

*Editors' comment on other ECtHR cases in 2000.*[4]  In 2000, Turkey lost twenty-three of the twenty-eight cases to which it was a party and was fined US$1.2 million. In nine cases, the ECtHR ruled against Turkey for death of persons who had been killed in detention or taken into custody and then disappeared. In all of these cases, the court noted that domestic legal remedies were insufficient. In two cases, Turkey was found in violation of the freedom of expression. Three decisions against Turkey concerned destruction of villages. In nine torture cases, the ECtHR ruled against Turkey. In eleven additional cases, mostly relating to failure to ensure due process of law, Turkey accepted friendly settlements.

# Document no. 73

[European Parliament] Resolution on the 1999 Regular Report from the Commission on Turkey's Progress Towards Accession[5]

*The European Parliament,*

\*\*\*

A. recalling the decision taken on 13 December 1999 by the European Council meeting in Helsinki to grant Turkey the status of candidate country for accession to the European Union and to establish an accession partnership and a single financial framework with a view to helping Turkey's application to progress in accordance with the Copenhagen Criteria,

B. whereas, following the granting to Turkey of candidate country status, the Union must now, by common agreement with the Turkish government, devise and implement in an appropriate manner a credible comprehensive strategy with a view to accession,

C. whereas accession negotiations cannot begin until Turkey complies with the Copenhagen criteria,

\*\*\*

E. whereas a clear and detailed programme will be an effective encouragement to accelerate reform in favour of protection of Human Rights and democracy, and will greatly strengthen the hand of those in the Turkish government, parliament, and civil society institutions who are keen to establish full respect for basic rights in their country,

F. noting the legislative changes carried out along the path towards democratisation since the 1995 constitutional reform and the establishment in the Turkish Grand National Assembly of the Conciliation Committee, which is responsible for reforming the constitution,

G. welcoming the signature by Turkey on 15 August and 8 September 2000 of four important UN conventions, on political, civil, social and cultural rights respectively, which must be ratified as soon as possible so that Human Rights and democratic pluralism may be guaranteed in that country,

H. emphasising that, despite the progress already achieved along the path towards democratisation, Human Rights and the situation of minorities must continue to be improved by the implementation of those conventions,

\*\*\*

1. Welcomes the resumption of institutional activities and political dialogue in the Association Council, which met on 11 April 2000 after being suspended for three years, and welcomes in particular the recent implementation of the Association Council's conclusions with the initiation of an analytical review of the *acquis communautaire* through the establishment of eight subcommittees entrusted with the task of setting priorities for incorporation of the *acquis*; notes with satisfaction that the first meetings of three of those subcommittees have been successful and trusts that the remaining subcommittees' meetings will be held by the end of this year;

2. Encourages the Turkish government to step up its efforts to achieve democratisation, with particular regard to reform of the Penal Code, independence of the judiciary, freedom of expression, the rights of minorities and the separation of powers, and especially the impact of the role of the army on Turkish political life;

3. Calls on the Turkish government and Parliament to ratify and implement the UN conventions on political, civil, social and cultural rights which it signed recently;

4. Encourages in this respect the Turkish Parliament and government to incorporate in the government programme the report drawn up by the Secretariat of the Turkish Supreme Coordination Council for Human Rights; welcomes the Turkish Council of Ministers' adoption of this report on 21 September 2000 as a "reference and working document"; and calls for the section on cultural rights to be reinserted into the report, with specific measures to protect the rights of minorities being added thereto;

5. Looks forward to the early abolition of the State Security Courts and welcomes the adoption of the law suspending the prosecution of, and penalties imposed on, press and broadcasting offences;

6. Calls, initially, for an amnesty with a view to achieving a reform of the Penal Code in the medium term so that it complies with the universal principle of freedom of expression;

7. Views the recent decision by the Constitutional Court on the law offering a reprieve to those who have committed press offences as a step that reinforces the rule of law; encourages the competent authorities to take this opportunity to continue their reforms in this direction, knowing that this process will logically lead them to a fundamental reconsideration of Article 312 of the Penal Code;

8. Calls, after the many promises made to this effect, for the death penalty to be abolished as soon as possible as part of the reform of the Penal Code and, pending such abolition, for the current moratorium on executions to be maintained;

9. Recalls the importance it attaches to recognition of the basic rights of the cultural, linguistic and religious groups in Turkey, who make up the country's multifaceted population;

\*\*\*

11. Notes the decisions taken on 30 November 1999 to lift the state of emergency in the Province of Siirt and on 26 June 2000 in the Province of Van, and calls on the Turkish government to lift the state of emergency in the other provinces of the southeastern region as well; calls for a specific solution to be found for the Kurdish people, encompassing the requisite political, economic and social responses;

12. Urges the Turkish government genuinely to redirect its policy with a view to improving the Human Rights situation of all its citizens, including those belonging to groups whose roots go back deep into the country's past, by putting an end to the political, social and cultural discrimination which they suffer, and in order to find, for those of Kurdish origin, a political solution which respects the territorial integrity of Turkey; calls also on the Turkish authorities to engage in a dialogue with the political representatives of the Kurdish community, especially the mayors of towns in the southeast of the country;

13. Demands the release of Leyla Zana, winner of the European Parliament Sakharov Prize, and of the former MPs of Kurdish origin imprisoned because of the views they hold;

14. Welcomes the Turkish government's adoption in September 2000 of an action plan which aims to restore economic balance with a view to resolving regional disparities by committing appropriate resources, and to promote the reopening of hamlets and the reconstruction of villages so that their inhabitants may return to them, together with other measures aimed at boosting investment in the southeast;

\*\*\*

24. Calls on the Turkish government to comply with previous and future decisions of the European Court of Human Rights and to consider the proposals made by the Council of Europe with regard to the training of judges and police officers;

25. Reminds Turkey also of the commitments it has given within the Council of Europe and calls on it to transpose Council of Europe instruments in particular so as to permit more effective monitoring of the application of political measures that are part of the accession partnership;

26. Takes the view that Turkey does not currently meet all the Copenhagen political criteria and reiterates its proposal for the setting up of discussion forums, consisting of eminent politicians from the European Union and Turkey as well as representatives of civil society, in order to promote political dialogue and help Turkey progress along the path towards accession; welcomes the

initiative taken by the former President of Turkey, Mr Demirel, to establish a Europe–Turkey Foundation, which might also be involved in those forums;

\*\*\*

*Editors' comment on European Council Decisions of 2000.* In the Feira European Council in June 2000, the initiatives of Turkey as a candidate country to meet accession criteria were noted. In that Council meeting, the EU went on to say that it looked forward to concrete progress, in particular on Human Rights, the rule of law, and the judiciary. In the Nice European Council in December 2000, the EU welcomed "the progress made in implementing the pre-accession strategy for Turkey" and stressed the importance of the Accession Partnership.

# 12 Turkish reforms on Civil Rights begin — 2001

# Document no. 74

**European Council Regulation (EC) no. 390/2001 of 26 February 2001 on Assistance to Turkey in the Framework of the Pre-Accession Strategy, and in Particular on the Establishment of an Accession Partnership[1]**

*The Council of the European Union*

- Having regard to the Treaty establishing the European Community, and in particular Article 308 thereof,
- Having regard to the proposal from the Commission,
- Having regard to the opinion of the European Parliament,

*Whereas:*

1. The conditions to be fulfilled by applicant States wishing to join the European Union were set out at the European Council meeting in Copenhagen in June 1993.

2. The Heads of State and government meeting at the European Council in Helsinki from 10 to 11 December 1999 reaffirmed the inclusive nature of the accession process, which now comprises thirteen candidate States within a single framework.

3. The European Council in Helsinki stated that Turkey is a candidate State destined to join the Union on the basis of the same criteria applied to other candidate States and that building on the existing European strategy, Turkey, like other candidate States, will benefit from a pre-accession strategy to stimulate and support its reforms.

4. The European Council in Helsinki stated that an Accession Partnership will be drawn up for Turkey on the basis of previous European Council conclusions while containing priorities on which accession preparations must concentrate in the light of the political and economic criteria and the obligations of a Member State.

5. It would be appropriate for European Community assistance within the framework of the Accession Partnership to focus on the aforementioned political

and economic criteria and be guided by defined principles, priorities, intermediate objectives and conditions.

6. The Heads of State and government meeting at the European Council in Feira from 19 to 20 June 2000 invited the Commission to present as soon as possible proposals for a single financial framework for assistance to Turkey, as well as for an Accession Partnership.

7. The Partnership, and in particular its intermediate objectives, should assist Turkey in preparing for membership within a framework of economic and social convergence and in developing its national programme for the taking up of the *acquis* as well as a relevant timetable for its implementation.

8. \*\*\*

9. Community assistance under the pre-accession strategy should be provided by applying to Turkey the aid programmes adopted in accordance with the provisions of the Treaties and therefore this Regulation will have no financial implications.

10. Community assistance is conditional upon respect of the commitments contained in the EC–Turkey Agreements, the Accession Partnership and upon progress towards fulfilment of the Copenhagen criteria.

11. \*\*\*

12. The role played by the bodies set up under the EC–Turkey Agreements is central to ensuring the proper implementation and follow-up of this Accession Partnership.

13. Establishing the Accession Partnership is likely to help achieve the Community's objectives. The Treaty does not provide, for the adoption of this Regulation, powers other than those of Article 308,

## *HAS ADOPTED THIS REGULATION:*

*Article 1*

As part of the European Union's pre-accession strategy for Turkey, an Accession Partnership shall be established for Turkey. The Accession Partnership shall provide a single framework covering:

- the priorities, as defined in the analysis of the situation in Turkey, on which preparations for accession must concentrate in view of the political and economic criteria and the obligations incumbent upon a Member State of the European Union as defined by the European Council,

\*\*\*

*Article 4*

Where an element that is essential for continuing to grant pre-accession assistance is lacking, in particular when the commitments contained in the

EC–Turkey Agreements are not respected and/or progress towards fulfilment of the Copenhagen criteria is insufficient, the Council, acting by a qualified majority on a proposal from the Commission, may take appropriate steps with regard to pre-accession assistance granted to Turkey.

\*\*\*

# Document no. 75

**Turkey–EU Association Council Decision of 8 March 2001 on the Principles, Priorities, Intermediate Objectives and Conditions Contained in the Accession Partnership with the Republic of Turkey[2]**

*The Council of the European Union*

- Having regard to the Treaty establishing the European Community,
- Having regard to Council Regulation (EC) no. 390/2001 of 26 February 2001 on assistance to Turkey in the framework of the pre-accession strategy, and in particular on the establishment of an Accession Partnership (1), and in particular to Article 2 thereof,
- Having regard to the proposal from the Commission,

*Whereas:*

1. The Helsinki European Council stated: "Turkey is a candidate State destined to join the Union on the basis of the same criteria as applied to the other candidate States. Building on the existing European strategy, Turkey, like other candidate States, will benefit from a pre-accession strategy to stimulate and support its reforms." As a key feature of such a strategy, an Accession Partnership will be drawn up on the basis of previous European Council conclusions.

2. Regulation (EC) no. 390/2001 provides that the Council is to decide, by a qualified majority and following a proposal from the Commission, on the principles, priorities, intermediate objectives and conditions contained in the individual Accession Partnership, as it will be submitted to Turkey, as well as on subsequent significant adjustments applicable to it.

3. Community assistance is conditional on the fulfilment of essential elements, and in particular on progress towards fulfilment of the Copenhagen criteria. Where an essential element is lacking, the Council, acting by a qualified majority on a proposal from the Commission, may take appropriate steps with regard to any pre-accession assistance.

4. The EC–Turkey Association Council decided that the implementation of the Accession Partnership for Turkey will be monitored by the Association Agreement bodies as appropriate.

5. The Commission's 2000 regular report presented an objective analysis on Turkey's preparations for membership and identified a number of priority areas for further work.

6. In order to prepare for membership, Turkey should prepare a national programme for the adoption of the *acquis*. This programme should set out a timetable for achieving the priorities and intermediate objectives established in the Accession Partnership,

## HAS DECIDED AS FOLLOWS:

*Article 1*

In accordance with Article 2 of Regulation (EC) no. 390/2001, the principles, priorities, intermediate objectives and conditions contained in the Accession Partnership for Turkey are set out in the annex hereto, which forms an integral part of this Decision.

*Article 2*

The implementation of the Accession Partnership shall be monitored in the Association Agreement bodies as appropriate and through the competent Council bodies to which the Commission shall report regularly.

\*\*\*

## Annex: Turkey—2000 Accession Partnership

*1. Introduction*

\*\*\*

At its meeting in Helsinki, the European Council decided that an Accession Partnership will be drawn up "on the basis of previous European Council conclusions". It shall contain priorities on which accession preparations must concentrate in the light of the political and economic criteria and the obligations of a Member State combined with a national programme for the adoption of the *acquis*.

At its meeting in Luxembourg in December 1997, the European Council had decided that the Accession Partnership would be the key feature of the enhanced pre-accession strategy, mobilising all forms of assistance to the candidate countries within a single framework.

\*\*\*

## 2. Objectives

The purpose of the Accession Partnership is to set out in a single framework the priority areas for further work identified in the Commission's 2000 regular report on the progress made by Turkey towards membership of the European Union, the financial means available to help Turkey implement these priorities and the conditions which will apply to that assistance. This Accession Partnership provides the basis for a number of policy instruments, which will be used to help the candidate States in their preparations for membership. It is expected that Turkey on the basis of this Accession Partnership adopts before the end of the year a national programme for the adoption of the *acquis*.

This is not an integral part of this Partnership but the priorities it contains should be compatible with it.

## 3. Principles

The main priority areas identified for each candidate State relate to its ability to take on the obligations of meeting the Copenhagen criteria which state that membership requires:

- that the candidate State has achieved stability of institutions guaranteeing democracy, the rule of law, Human Rights and respect for and protection of minorities,
- the existence of a functioning market economy, as well as the capacity to cope with competitive pressure and market forces within the Union,
- the ability to take on the obligations of membership, including adherence to the aims of political, economic and monetary union.

\*\*\*

Furthermore, the European Council emphasised that Turkey will benefit from a pre-accession strategy to stimulate and support its reforms including an enhanced political dialogue, with emphasis on progressing towards fulfilling the political criteria for accession with particular reference to Human Rights, as well as the issues referred to in paragraphs 4 and 9(a) of the Helsinki conclusions; in this spirit, the European Union encourages Turkey, together with all parties, to continue to support the UN Secretary General's efforts to bring the process, aiming at a comprehensive settlement of the Cyprus problem, to a successful conclusion.

## 4. Priorities and intermediate objectives

The Commission's regular reports have highlighted the extent of the efforts which still have to be made in certain areas by the candidate States to prepare for accession. This situation requires the definition of intermediate stages in terms of priorities, each to be accompanied by precise objectives to be set in collaboration with the States concerned, the achievement of which will condition the degree of assistance granted and the progress of the negotiations under way with some countries and the opening of new negotiations with the others. The priorities and intermediate objectives in the Accession Partnership are divided into two groups — short and medium term. Those listed under the short term have been selected on the basis that it is realistic to expect that Turkey can complete or take them substantially forward by the end of 2001. The priorities listed under the medium term are expected to take more than one year to complete although work should, wherever possible, also begin on them during 2001.

The Accession Partnership indicates the priority areas for Turkey's membership preparations. Turkey will nevertheless have to address all issues identified in the regular report. It is also important that Turkey fulfils the commitments of legislative approximation and implementation of the *acquis* in accordance with the commitments made under the Association Agreement, Customs Union and related decisions of the EC–Turkey Association Council for example on the trade regime for agricultural products. It should be recalled that incorporation of the *acquis* into legislation is not in itself sufficient; it will also be necessary to ensure that it is actually applied to the same standards as those which apply within the Union. In all of the areas listed below there is a need for credible and effective implementation and enforcement of the *acquis*.

Drawing on the analysis of the Commission's Regular Report, the following short- and medium-term priorities and intermediate objectives have been identified for Turkey:

4.1. SHORT-TERM (2001)

*Enhanced political dialogue and political criteria*

- In accordance with the Helsinki conclusions, in the context of the political dialogue, strongly support the UN Secretary General's efforts to bring to a successful conclusion the process of finding a comprehensive settlement of the Cyprus problem, as referred to in point 9(a) of the Helsinki conclusions.
- Strengthen legal and constitutional guarantees for the right to freedom of expression in line with Article 10 of the European Convention of Human Rights. Address in that context the situation of those persons in prison sentenced for expressing non-violent opinions.
- Strengthen legal and constitutional guarantees of the right to freedom of association and peaceful assembly and encourage development of civil society.
- Strengthen legal provisions and undertake all necessary measures to reinforce the fight against torture practices, and ensure compliance with the European Convention for the Prevention of Torture.
- Further align legal procedures concerning pre-trial detention with the provisions of the European Convention on Human Rights and with recommendations of the Committee for the Prevention of Torture.
- Strengthen opportunities for legal redress against all violations of Human Rights.

- Intensify training on Human Rights issues for law enforcement officials in mutual cooperation with individual countries and international organisations.
- Improve the functioning and efficiency of the judiciary, including the State security court in line with international standards. Strengthen in particular training of judges and prosecutors on European Union legislation, including in the field of Human Rights.
- Maintain the de facto moratorium on capital punishment.
- Remove any legal provisions forbidding the use by Turkish citizens of their mother tongue in TV/radio broadcasting.
- Develop a comprehensive approach to reduce regional disparities, and in particular to improve the situation in the southeast, with a view to enhancing economic, social and cultural opportunities for all citizens.

*Economic criteria*

4.2. MEDIUM-TERM

*Enhanced political dialogue and political criteria*

- In accordance with the Helsinki conclusions, in the context of the political dialogue, under the principle of peaceful settlement of disputes in accordance with the UN Charter, make every effort to resolve any outstanding border disputes and other related issues, as referred to in point 4 of the Helsinki conclusions.
- Guarantee full enjoyment by all individuals without any discrimination and irrespective of their language, race, colour, sex, political opinion, philosophical belief or religion of all Human Rights and fundamental freedoms.
- Further develop conditions for the enjoyment of freedom of thought, conscience and religion.
- Review of the Turkish Constitution and other relevant legislation with a view to guaranteeing rights and freedoms of all Turkish citizens as set forth in the European Convention for the Protection of Human Rights; ensure the implementation of such legal reforms and conformity with practices in EU Member States.
- Abolish the death penalty, sign and ratify Protocol 6 of the European Convention of Human Rights.
- Ratify the International Covenant on Civil and Political Rights and its optional Protocol and the International Covenant on Economic, Social and Cultural Rights.
- Adjust detention conditions in prisons to bring them into line with the UN Standard Minimum Rules for the Treatment of Prisoners and other international norms.
- Align the constitutional role of the National Security Council as an advisory body to the government in accordance with the practice of EU Member States.
- Lift the remaining state of emergency in the southeast.

- Ensure cultural diversity and guarantee cultural rights for all citizens irrespective of their origin. Any legal provisions preventing the enjoyment of these rights should be abolished, including in the field of education.

*Economic criteria*

\*\*\*

## 6. Conditionality

Community assistance for financing projects through the pre-accession instruments for Turkey is conditional on respect by Turkey of its commitments under the Association Agreement, Customs Union and related decisions of the EC–Turkey Association Council, for example on the trade regime for agricultural products. Further steps towards satisfying the Copenhagen criteria and in particular progress in meeting the specific priorities of this Accession Partnership in 2001 need to be taken. Failure to respect these general conditions could lead to a decision by the Council on the suspension of financial assistance on the basis of Article 4 of the proposed single-framework Regulation.

## 7. Monitoring

The implementation of the Accession Partnership will be monitored in the framework of the Association Agreement.

As underlined by the European Council in Helsinki, for Turkey it is important that the institutions of the Association Agreement continue to be the framework within which the adoption of the *acquis* can be examined, in accordance with the same arrangements, irrespective of whether or not negotiations have been opened.

The relevant sections of the Accession Partnership will be discussed in the appropriate subcommittee. The Association Committee discusses overall developments, progress and problems in meeting its priorities and intermediate objectives as well as more specific issues referred to it from the subcommittees.

# Document no. 76

## Turkish National Programme for the Adoption of the *Acquis*[3]

[Following the Accession Partnership Decision of 8 March, 2001, Turkey adopted its National Programme for the Adoption of the *Acquis* (NPAA) on 24 March, 2001. Following the table of contents of the NPAA is the edited text relevant to political criteria.]

### *Table of contents*

|  |  |  |
|---|---|---|
|  | Executive summary | 5 |
|  | Executive summary of the Turkish National Programme for the Adoption of the Aquis | 5 |
| 1. | Introduction | 19 |
| 1.1. | Introduction | 19 |
| 2. | Political criteria | 21 |
| 2.1. | Political criteria | 21 |
| 2.1.1. | Freedom of thought and expression | 21 |
| 2.1.2. | Freedom of association and peaceful assembly, and the civil society |  |
| 2.1.3. | Fight against torture | 22 |
| 2.1.4. | Pre-trial detention | 23 |
| 2.1.5. | Strengthening opportunities to redress the consequences of Human Rights violations | 23 |
| 2.1.6. | Training of law enforcement personnel and other civil servants on Human Rights issues | 24 |
| 2.1.7. | Improving the functioning and effectiveness of the judiciary, including the State Security Courts | 24 |
| 2.1.8. | Abolition of the death penalty | 25 |
| 2.1.9. | Cultural life and individual freedoms | 25 |
| 2.1.10. | Alleviating regional disparities to increase economic, social and cultural opportunities for all citizens | 25 |

| | | |
|---|---|---|
| 2.1.11. | Full enjoyment by all individuals without any discrimination and irrespective of their language, race, colour, sex, political opinion, philosophical belief or religion of all Human Rights and fundamental freedoms; freedom of thought, conscience and religion | 25 |
| 2.1.12. | Alignment of the Turkish Constitution and other relevant legislation with the EU *acquis* | 26 |
| 2.1.13. | International Covenant on Civil and Political Rights and its Optional Protocol, and International Covenant on Economic, Social and Cultural Rights | 26 |
| 2.1.14. | Detention conditions in prisons | 27 |
| 2.1.15. | The National Security Council | 27 |
| 2.1.16. | State of emergency | 27 |
| 3. | Economic criteria | 29 |
| 3.1. | Economic criteria | 29 |
| 3.1.1. | Liberalisation process in the economy | 29 |
| 3.1.2. | Disinflation and economic restructuring programme | 29 |
| 3.1.3. | Economic developments in 2000 and 2001 | 31 |
| 3.1.4. | Structural reforms | 33 |
| 4. | Capacity to undertake the membership obligations | 39 |
| 4.1. | Customs Union (within the framework of the Association relations) | |
| 4.2. | Free movement of goods | 47 |
| 4.2.1. | General | 47 |
| 4.2.2. | Market surveillance | 52 |
| 4.2.3. | Motor vehicles | 54 |
| 4.2.4. | Foodstuff industry | 58 |
| 4.2.5. | Chemicals | 75 |
| 4.2.6. | Pharmaceuticals | 79 |
| 4.2.7. | Cosmetics | 92 |
| 4.2.8. | Legal metrology and pre-packaging | 96 |
| 4.2.9. | Electrical risk and electrical equipment | 98 |
| 4.2.10. | Telecommunications | 100 |
| 4.2.11. | Toys | 101 |
| 4.2.12. | Other product groups | 103 |
| 4.2.13. | Free movement of the goods — miscellaneous | 109 |
| 4.3. | Free movement of persons | 115 |
| 4.3.1. | Right of residence | 115 |
| 4.3.2. | Free movement of workers | 117 |
| 4.3.3. | Coordination of social security | 120 |
| 4.3.4. | Medical and paramedical activities | 123 |
| 4.3.5. | Visas | 125 |
| 4.3.6. | Immigration | 126 |
| 4.4. | Freedom to provide services | 129 |
| 4.4.1. | Sectoral practice | 129 |
| 4.5. | Free movement of capital | 149 |

| | | |
|---|---|---|
| 4.6. | Company law | 157 |
| 4.6.1. | Company law | 157 |
| 4.6.2. | Industrial property rights | 165 |
| 4.6.3. | Intellectual property rights | 169 |
| 4.7. | Competition and state aid | 173 |
| 4.7.1. | Competition policy | 173 |
| 4.7.2. | State aid | 177 |
| 4.8. | Common agricultural policy | 185 |
| 4.8.1. | General | 185 |
| 4.8.2. | Agricultural products | 195 |
| 4.8.3. | Plant health | 204 |
| 4.8.4. | Animal health | 206 |
| 4.8.5. | Animal identification system | 212 |
| 4.8.6. | Land registration system | 214 |
| 4.8.7. | Rural development policies | 219 |
| 4.9. | Common fisheries policy | 223 |
| 4.10. | Common transport policy | 229 |
| 4.10.1. | Navigation (general — infrastructure) | 229 |
| 4.10.2. | Inland transport | 230 |
| 4.10.3. | Waterway navigation | 237 |
| 4.10.4. | Air transport | 243 |
| 4.11. | Taxation | 251 |
| 4.12. | Economic and monetary union | 257 |
| 4.12.1. | Monetary policy | 259 |
| 4.12.2. | Economic policy | 263 |
| 4.13. | Statistics | 267 |
| 4.13.1. | Statistics | 267 |
| 4.13.2. | Classifications | 268 |
| 4.13.3. | Statistical coordination | 271 |
| 4.13.4. | Registers | 272 |
| 4.13.5. | Data security and statistical confidentiality | 274 |
| 4.13.6. | Population | 275 |
| 4.13.7. | Labour market (labour statistics) | 276 |
| 4.13.8. | Statistics related to the labour force, wages, labour costs and earnings | ??? |
| 4.13.9. | Health, safety and protection of consumers | 282 |
| 4.13.10. | Annual economic accounts | 283 |
| 4.13.11. | Quarterly accounts and environment accounts | 285 |
| 4.13.12. | Financial accounts | 286 |
| 4.13.13. | Monitoring and resources | 287 |
| 4.13.14. | Prices | 288 |
| 4.13.15. | Industry | 291 |
| 4.13.16. | Construction statistics | 292 |
| 4.13.17. | Energy and raw materials | 294 |
| 4.13.18. | Transport | 296 |

| | | |
|---|---|---|
| 4.13.19. | Tourism | 298 |
| 4.13.20. | Trade of goods | 300 |
| 4.13.21. | Land use and landscape | 303 |
| 4.13.22. | Agricultural structures | 305 |
| 4.13.23. | Crop production | 305 |
| 4.13.24. | Animal production | 306 |
| 4.13.25. | Other agricultural statistics | 307 |
| 4.13.26. | Forestry statistics | 308 |
| 4.13.27. | Fisheries statistics | 309 |
| 4.13.28. | Regional and geographical information | 310 |
| 4.13.29. | Committees in the field of statistics | 311 |
| 4.13.30. | Balance of payments | 312 |
| 4.13.31. | Money and banking statistics | 314 |
| 4.14. | Social policy and employment | 317 |
| 4.14.1. | Labour law | 317 |
| 4.14.2. | Social dialogue | 325 |
| 4.14.3. | Equal treatment of men and women | 328 |
| 4.14.4. | Fight against racism | 331 |
| 4.14.5. | Employment | 333 |
| 4.14.6. | European social fund | 337 |
| 4.14.7. | Social assistance and services, elderly people and exclusion | 339 |
| 4.14.8. | Dublin Foundation (European Foundation for the Improvement of Living and Working Conditions) | 341 |
| 4.14.9. | Public health | 342 |
| 4.14.10. | Health and safety at work | 346 |
| 4.15. | Energy | 351 |
| 4.16. | Industrial policy | 361 |
| 4.17. | SMEs | 369 |
| 4.18. | Science and research | 375 |
| 4.19. | Education, training and youth | 379 |
| 4.20. | Telecommunications | 385 |
| 4.21. | Culture and audio-visual policy | 389 |
| 4.21.1. | Culture | 389 |
| 4.21.2. | Audio-visual | 391 |
| 4.22. | Regional policy | 393 |
| 4.23. | Environment | 403 |
| 4.23.1. | Horizontal | 403 |
| 4.23.2. | Air quality | 407 |
| 4.23.3. | Waste management | 410 |
| 4.23.4. | Water quality | 415 |
| 4.23.5. | Nature protection | 421 |
| 4.23.6. | Chemicals and genetically modified organisms | 424 |
| 4.23.7. | Noise from vehicles and machinery | 430 |
| 4.23.8. | Nuclear safety and protection from radiation | 432 |
| 4.23.9. | Climate change | 433 |

| 4.24. | Consumer protection and health | 435 |
| 4.25. | Justice and home affairs | 443 |
| 4.25.1. | General | 443 |
| 4.25.2. | Asylum | 446 |
| 4.25.3. | External borders | 448 |
| 4.25.4. | Migration | 450 |
| 4.25.5. | Organised crime, fraud and corruption | 452 |
| 4.25.6. | Police cooperation | 458 |
| 4.25.7. | Customs cooperation | 464 |
| 4.25.8. | Judicial cooperation in legal and criminal matters | 465 |
| 4.25.9. | Matters related to Human Rights | 470 |
| 4.26. | Customs Union | 473 |
| 4.27. | External relations | 481 |
| 4.28. | Common foreign and security policy | 489 |
| 4.29. | Financial control | 491 |
| 5. | Administrative Capacity | 503 |
| 5.1. | Administrative capacity | 503 |
| 5.1.1. | Coordination | 503 |
| 5.1.2. | Administrative capacity for the adoption of the *acquis* | 503 |
| 5.1.3. | Training of public officers | 511 |
| 6. | Global financial assessment of the reforms | 513 |
| 6.1. | Global financial assessment of reforms | 513 |
| 6.1.1. | Free movement of goods | 514 |
| 6.1.2. | Free movement of capital | 514 |
| 6.1.3. | Common agricultural policy | 514 |
| 6.1.4. | Common fisheries policy | 515 |
| 6.1.5. | Common transportation policy | 515 |
| 6.1.6. | Statistics | 516 |
| 6.1.7. | Social policy and employment | 517 |
| 6.1.8. | Energy | 517 |
| 6.1.9. | SMEs | 517 |
| 6.1.10. | Science and research | 518 |
| 6.1.11. | Culture and audio-visual policies | 518 |
| 6.1.12. | Regional policies | 518 |
| 6.1.13. | Environment | 518 |
| 6.1.14. | Justice and home affairs | 519 |
|  | Abbreviations | 521 |

\*\*\*

## Introduction

The modern Turkish Republic is founded on the principles of peaceful foreign policy, secularism, the rule of law, a pluralistic and participatory democratic system, and fundamental Human Rights and freedoms.

Founded under the leadership of Atatürk, the Turkish Republic undertook rapidly sweeping reforms based on the contemporary system of values in all spheres of social life. These reforms enabled the Turkish nation to participate in the value system shared by the European family of nations with whom Turkey has a common history and geography.

Since the proclamation of the Republic, Turkey has developed her legal and social order in accordance with Western norms; multi-party politics was introduced in 1946 and major strides were taken towards an open and participatory social order, first and foremost in areas of the freedom of the press and labour union rights. Turkey placed the individual and the inalienable Human Rights and freedoms of the individual at the very core of her efforts. Thus, a dynamic evolution of democracy and the legal order was set in motion in Turkey.

Since 1984 Turkey has been fighting against separatist terrorism, which enjoys considerable external support. This phenomenon has adversely affected the environment of democracy and Human Rights, as well as the social and economic progress of Turkey. Despite this threat the Turkish Republic has maintained her national integrity and unity based on the equality of her citizens.

\*\*\*

The Republic of Turkey would like to share in, and is resolved to contribute to, a peaceful and prosperous future with the Member States of the EU on the basis of universal values.

The Turkish government regards EU membership as a new step forward, a milestone confirming the founding philosophy of, and Atatürk's vision for, the Republic.

For the Turkish nation, conforming to contemporary values is a way of life and an ideal to be pursued. Therefore, the Turkish nation is able and willing to assume the significant duties and responsibilities entailed by the ideal of European unification, drawing upon its centuries-old historical heritage and respect for civilisation. In this context, Turkey is fully resolved to adopt and implement the EU *acquis*.

Turkey intends to fulfil the Copenhagen criteria and complete the accession process on the basis of the fundamental principles of the Republic as articulated in the Turkish Constitution. The basic ideals of EU membership are one and the same as the ideals inherent in Turkey's national identity. Therefore, membership in the EU is a conscious choice for Turkey, promising new horizons in the nation's progress towards the highest standards of contemporary life. In this context, raising the standards of education for all citizens, both in terms of quality and quantity, will further align Turkey with EU norms and facilitate the achievement of the objectives set out in the National Programme.

Turkey will accede to all relevant international conventions and take the necessary measures for their effective implementation in order to ensure alignment with the universal norms manifest in the EU *acquis* and with practices in

EU Member States, particularly in the areas of democracy and Human Rights. In fact, Turkey has already acceded to a majority of the international conventions in these areas.

Turkey's membership in the EU will be a symbol of the convergence of dynamic trends, embracing aspirations for the harmonious co-existence of cultures, and enriching the spiritual fabric of the EU. In this context, a process that sustains continuous cultural interaction between Turkey and the EU may well pave the way for the common achievement of a higher moral and philosophical synthesis. This process will enable both parties to help shape a brighter future within a more stable and secure environment by encouraging positive developments in the political, economic and social spheres.

Turkey can assume an important role in the process of European unification through concrete and distinct contributions that she can offer. The combined experiences and contributions of Turkey and the EU will be a major advantage in meeting the promising, but also challenging prospects of our era. It would thus be possible to reap long-term benefits more fully by seizing the opportunities that the spiritual and material wealth of the contemporary world offers today. Hence, through a mutually beneficial partnership, Turkey and the European Union would be better prepared for and capable of shaping the dynamics of the twenty-first century, and will continue to work together in cooperation and solidarity for the advancement and the development of their peoples and the international community.

\*\*\*

### *Political criteria*

In 2001, the Turkish government will speed up the ongoing work on political, administrative and judicial reforms and will duly convey its legislative proposals to the Turkish Grand National Assembly. The goal is to further develop, on the basis of Turkey's international commitments and EU standards, the provisions of the Constitution and other legislation to promote freedom; provide for a more participatory democracy with additional safeguards; reinforce the balance of powers and competences between State organs; and enhance the rule of law. In the context of the reform process regarding democracy and Human Rights, the review of the Constitution will have priority. The constitutional amendments will also establish the framework for the review of other legislation.

The Turkish government will closely monitor progress in the areas of Human Rights, democracy and the rule of law, regularly evaluate the work under way for harmonisation with the EU *acquis* and will take all necessary measures to speed up ongoing work.

The Turkish Grand National Assembly has already undertaken a substantial amount of work on reforms and the Inter-Party Constitutional Harmonisation Commission is currently working on amendments to the Constitution.

*Freedom of thought and expression*

Further development of the freedom of thought and expression in line with the EU *acquis* and practices in EU Member States is a priority for the Turkish government. The Turkish Constitution and relevant provisions in other legislation will be reviewed in order to enhance the freedom of thought and expression, in the light of the criteria referred to in Article 10 of the European Convention on Human Rights and Fundamental Freedoms, including those concerning territorial integrity and national security. This review will be undertaken on the basis of the fundamental principles of the Turkish Constitution, particularly those concerning the secular and democratic character of the Republic, national unity and the unitary state model.

With a view to enhancing the constitutional and legal guarantees concerning freedom of expression, in the short term, the Turkish government plans to:

- review the provisions of the Constitution on Human Rights and freedoms, in particular those concerning the expression and the dissemination of ideas, the freedom of science, the arts, and the press;
- review Article 312 of the Turkish Penal Code, without prejudice to values protected therein;
- review Articles 7 and 8 of the Anti-Terrorism Act, with the same understanding;
- review the Act on the Establishment of Radio and Television Enterprises and Their Broadcasts;
- review the Act on Press, in relation to the scope of the offences and penalties.

And in the medium term, the Turkish government plans to:

- review the Political Parties Act;
- review the Act on the Duties and Competences of the Police, and the relevant regulation; the Act on the Organisation, Duties and Competences of the Gendarmerie, and the relevant bylaw; and the Act on the Coast Guard Command, and the relevant regulation;
- review the Act on Cinema, Video and Musical Works and other relevant legislation;
- enact the new Turkish Penal Code;
- undertake work concerning reimbursement of payments of reparations from public officials who are found at fault, in light of the decisions taken by the European Court of Human Rights.

*Freedom of association and peaceful assembly, and the civil society*

Encouraging the further development of the civil society is a priority for the Turkish government. Strengthening the civil society will contribute to the development of democracy in Turkey. Enhancement of freedom of association and peaceful assembly is expected to encourage individuals to become more actively involved in social issues.

In this context, in the short term, the Turkish government plans to:

- enact the Draft Act on the Establishment and Working Principles and Procedures of the Economic and Social Council;
- enhance constitutional safeguards for non-governmental organisations and the institutions for social and economic democracy;
- enact the Draft Act on Job Security.

And in the medium term, the Turkish government plans to:

- review any restrictions there may be on rights of labour unions and employers' associations, and the relevant articles of the Constitution regarding the right to go on strike on justifiable grounds;
- review rights of labour unions and employers' associations on the basis of ILO Conventions Nos 87 and 98 and of the European Social Charter;
- review the legislation on the freedom of association and holding meetings and demonstration marches.

A circular issued by the Prime Ministry in August 1999 cautions against undue restrictions on public employees who may wish to organise trades unions and confederations and the activities thereof, pending the enactment of the Draft Act on Public Employees' Trade Unions.

*Fight against torture*

The Turkish government is determined to fight against torture. To this end, the government has strengthened legal and administrative measures ranging from enhanced training programmes on Human Rights to the thorough and timely investigation of incidents of torture and prosecution of those responsible.

Recent measures introduced in this context are as follows:

- A circular was issued by the Prime Ministry in June 1999 on the effective implementation of the Bylaw on Apprehension, Custody and Interrogation, and on the strict supervision of the implementation of this bylaw.
- In August 1999, provisions in the Turkish Penal Code on torture and inhuman or degrading treatment were amended so as to align the definitions thereof with those in international conventions. Moreover, sanctions were increased in general and criminal penalties were introduced for health services personnel issuing falsified reports on incidents of torture.
- The Act on the Prosecution of Civil Servants and other Public Employees was enacted on 2 December 1999, thereby speeding up the investigation and prosecution of public personnel.
- In addition to the ministries concerned, the Human Rights Directorate of the Prime Ministry has been authorised to undertake measures necessary for the prevention of incidents of torture and inhuman or degrading treatment

that may arise despite measures already in force. Such incidents will not be tolerated by the government under any circumstances.

A series of laws and amendments are planned in order to enhance the fight against torture and inhuman or degrading treatment. In this context, in the short term, the Turkish government plans to:

- review the Act on the Duties and Competences of the Police, and the relevant regulation; the Act on the Organisation, Duties and Competences of the Gendarmerie, and the relevant bylaw; and the Act on the Coast Guard Command, and the relevant regulation;
- undertake arrangements to modernise the Forensic Medicine Institution.

And in the medium term, the Turkish government plans to:

- enact the new Turkish Penal Code;
- enact the new Code of Penal Procedure;
- explore the availability of financial resources for training law enforcement personnel for the prevention of Human Rights violations and increase the use of technology to effectively monitor places where incidents of Human Rights violations continue to occur;
- introduce legal provisions on the joint and several liability of perpetrators of torture.

*Pre-trial detention*

In order to align legal practices and procedures related to pre-trial detention with the provisions of the Convention for the Protection of Human Rights and Fundamental Freedoms, the decisions of the European Court of Human Rights, the recommendations of the European Committee for the Prevention of Torture and Inhuman or Degrading Treatment or Punishment, and to attain uniformity throughout the relevant Turkish legislation, the Turkish government, in the medium term, plans to:

- review Article 19/6 of the Constitution;
- enact the new Code of Penal Procedure;
- amend the Act on the Establishment and Procedure of the State Security Courts.

*Strengthening opportunities to redress the consequences of Human Rights violations*
The Turkish government, in the medium term, plans to:

- enact the new Code of Penal Procedure;
- enact the Draft Act on the Indemnification of Losses Resulting from Terrorism and the Fight Against Terrorism.

*Training of law enforcement personnel and other civil servants on Human Rights issues*

Work to intensify training of law enforcement personnel and other civil servants on Human Rights issues is currently under way at all relevant institutions. The Turkish government will seek to intensify international cooperation in this area both on a bilateral and multilateral basis.

To this end, in the short term, the Turkish government plans to:

- undertake legal arrangements to extend the duration of education at Police Academies from nine months to two years;
- put into action, within the framework of the UN Decade of Human Rights Education, the Human Rights Education Project of the Ministry of the Interior and Its Affiliated Agencies (2000–2007);
- train law enforcement personnel on Human Rights over a period of seven years, within the framework of a project developed in light of the 1997–2000 Police and Human Rights Programme of the Directorate of Human Rights of the Council of Europe.

Other measures in this area are covered in the section on Justice and home affairs.

*Improving the functioning and effectiveness of the Judiciary, including the State Security Courts*

The Turkish government accords particular importance to the improved functioning and effectiveness of the Judiciary. The government, in the short term, plans to:

- review the constitutional provisions on the State Security Courts and the Act on the Establishment and Procedures of the State Security Courts;
- strengthen legal defence by introducing a constitutional provision that will establish this as one of the fundamental elements of the judicial process, and enact the Draft Advocacy Act;
- review provisions which may infringe upon the independence of the Judiciary, and restructure the Supreme Council for Judges and Public Prosecutors;
- undertake legal arrangements to modernise the Forensic Medicine Institution;
- step up activities for the UN Decade of Human Rights Education and seek further opportunities for the education and training of Turkish judges and prosecutors in Member States of the European Union and the Council of Europe;
- provide regular in-service training on Human Rights and the decisions of the European Court of Human Rights for Turkish judges and prosecutors.

And the Turkish government, in the medium term, plans to:

- review Act no. 4483 on the Prosecution of Civil Servants and other Public Employees, in light of the experience gained since its implementation;

- review the Military Penal Code, the Act no. 353 on the Establishment and Procedure of Military Courts, and the Act no. 1602 on Military Administrative High Courts;
- review the Act on the State of Emergency, in the light of the relevant amendments to be made in the Constitution and other legislation.

Other measures in this area are covered in the section on Justice and home affairs.

*Abolition of the death penalty*

According to the Constitution of the Republic of Turkey only the Turkish Grand National Assembly is authorised to take the decision to enforce a sentence of capital punishment. The Turkish government respects the practice of not infringing upon the essence of the right to life, upheld by the Turkish Grand National Assembly since 1984.

The abolition of the death penalty in Turkish criminal law, its form and its scope, will be considered by the Turkish Grand National Assembly in the medium term.

*Cultural life and individual freedoms*

The official language and the formal educational language of the Republic of Turkey is Turkish.

This, however, does not prohibit the free usage of different languages, dialects and tongues by Turkish citizens in their daily lives. This freedom may not be abused for the purposes of separatism and division.

*Alleviating regional disparities to increase economic, social and cultural opportunities for all citizens*

The government has adopted a comprehensive strategy to alleviate regional disparities and increase cultural and social opportunities for all citizens.

Since separatist terrorist activities ongoing since 1984 were effectively curbed, the Turkish government has undertaken a series of measures for economic and social development. The implementation of this strategy is planned for the medium term.

*Full enjoyment by all individuals without any discrimination and irrespective of their language, race, colour, sex, political opinion, philosophical belief or religion of all Human Rights and fundamental freedoms; freedom of thought, conscience and religion*

Article 10 of the Constitution prohibits discrimination on any grounds, and adopts the principle of the equality of all citizens before the law.

In the short term, in accordance with this principle, the Turkish government plans to:

- conclude the UN Convention on the Elimination of All Forms of Racial Discrimination;
- reinforce in the Constitution the principle that men and women have equal rights;
- enact the Draft Turkish Civil Code embodying improvements in gender equality;
- enact the Draft Act on the Organisation of the Directorate General for the Status and Problems of Women, and the Draft Act on the Organisation of the Family Research Institution;
- conclude the ILO [International Labour Organization] Convention Concerning the Prohibition and Immediate Action for the Elimination of Worst Forms of Child Labour (no. 182) and put into effect the National Action Plan prepared in cooperation with ILO on this subject.

In the medium term, the Turkish government plans to:

- conclude the Optional Protocol to the UN Convention on the Elimination of All Forms of Discrimination against Women;
- conclude Protocol no. 4 to the Council of Europe Convention for the Protection of Human Rights and Fundamental Freedoms, securing certain rights and freedoms other than those already included in the Convention and in Protocol no. 1;
- conclude Protocol no. 7 to the Council of Europe Convention for the Protection of Human Rights and Fundamental Freedoms;
- conclude the European Social Charter (Revised) and the Additional Protocol to the European Social Charter Providing for a System of Collective Complaints;
- conclude Protocol no. 12 of the Council of Europe Convention for the Protection of Human Rights and Fundamental Freedoms, which extends the scope of Article 14 of the Convention to prohibit discrimination on any grounds;
- take further practical measures, within the framework of the legislation on the protection of the public order, to facilitate religious practice for non-Muslim foreign nationals residing in Turkey and practices in other areas pertaining to these persons;
- take measures in accordance with the ILO Convention (no. 159) Concerning Vocational Rehabilitation and Employment (Disabled Persons).

*Alignment of the Turkish Constitution and other relevant legislation with the EU* acquis

In the short term the Turkish government plans to review the Constitution in the light of the European Convention on Human Rights and Fundamental Freedoms, and to undertake, in the medium term, necessary amendments to other legislation.

*International Covenant on Civil and Political Rights and its Optional Protocol, and International Covenant on Economic, Social and Cultural Rights*

The fact that Turkey has signed these conventions demonstrates the government's political will and resolve in this regard. Legislation initiating the process of ratification will be submitted to the Turkish Grand National Assembly along with any reservations there may be.

*Detention conditions in prisons*

The Turkish government is resolved to eliminate any unfavourable conditions that may exist in prisons and has undertaken intensive efforts to this end.

The dormitory system, which was discontinued in Europe in the 1960s and 1970s, is also being phased out in Turkey. In accordance with the recommendations of the Council of Europe and the European Committee for the Prevention of Torture and Inhuman or Degrading Treatment or Punishment, prison rules and standards are being aligned with the United Nations Standard Minimum Rules for the Treatment of Prisoners and the European Prison Rules of the Council of Europe.

In the short term:

- the Ministry of Justice will render more effective the supervision and control over prisons by public administrators and chief public prosecutors;
- the Draft Act Amending the Anti-Terrorism Act will be enacted, and in the course of this process, matters related to open visits and workshop activities for prisoners convicted of such crimes will be reviewed.

Other measures in this area are covered in the section on Justice and home affairs.

*The National Security Council*

The National Security Council, which is a constitutional body, has the status of a consultative body in areas of national security. Relevant articles of the Constitution and other legislation will be reviewed in the medium term to define more clearly the structure and the functions of this Council.

*State of emergency*

The state of emergency was introduced to fight terrorism and it was lifted in six provinces out of a total of ten. The lifting of the state of emergency in the remaining four provinces is an integral part of the comprehensive strategy for economic, social and cultural development in the area. The state of emergency will be lifted with due regard to threat assessment and developments on the ground with respect to security.

\*\*\*

## Justice and home affairs

*General*

I. PRIORITY DESCRIPTION

The following are the main objectives on which work is being initiated in 2001 to be completed by the medium term:

- Work on administrative reform in the field of justice and home affairs will be accelerated.
- Coordination between competent ministries and other public institutions will be enhanced.
- Existing accommodation facilities and social support mechanisms for refugees will be further developed.

\*\*\*

The following are the subject headings of the *acquis* on justice and home affairs:

- Organised crime, fraud and corruption
- Terrorism
- Police cooperation
- Human rights-related issues

# Document no. 77

## 3 October 2001 Amendments to the Constitution of the Republic of Turkey[4]

*Preamble*

In line with the concept of nationalism and the reforms and principles introduced by the founder of the Republic of Turkey, Atatürk, the immortal leader and the unrivalled hero, this Constitution, which affirms the eternal existence of the Turkish nation and motherland and the indivisible unity of the Turkish state, embodies;

The determination to safeguard the everlasting existence, prosperity and material and spiritual well-being of the Republic of Turkey, and to attain the standards of contemporary civilisation as an honourable member with equal rights of the family of world nations;

The understanding of the absolute supremacy of the will of the nation and of the fact that sovereignty is vested fully and unconditionally in the Turkish nation and that no individual or body empowered to exercise this sovereignty in the name of the nation shall deviate from liberal democracy and the legal system instituted according to its requirements;

The principle of the separation of powers, which does not imply an order of precedence among the organs of state, but refers solely to the exercising of certain state powers and discharging of duties which are limited to cooperation and division of functions, and which accepts the supremacy of the Constitution and the law;

The recognition that no protection shall be accorded to an activity contrary to Turkish national interests, the principle of the indivisibility of the existence of Turkey with its state and territory, Turkish historical and moral values or the nationalism, principles, reforms and modernism of Atatürk and that, as required by the principle of secularism, there shall be no interference whatsoever by sacred religious feelings in state affairs and politics; the acknowledgment that it is the birthright of every Turkish citizen to lead an honourable life and to develop his or her material and spiritual assets under the aegis of national culture, civilisation and the rule of law, through the exercise of the fundamental rights and freedoms set forth in this Constitution in conformity with the requirements of equality and social justice;

The recognition that all Turkish citizens are united in national honour and pride, in national joy and grief, in their rights and duties regarding national existence, in blessings and in burdens, and in every manifestation of national life, and that they have the right to demand a peaceful life based on absolute respect for one another's rights and freedoms, mutual love and fellowship and the desire for and belief in "Peace at home, peace in the world".

This Constitution, which is to be embraced with the ideas, beliefs, and resolutions it embodies below should be interpreted and implemented accordingly, thus commanding respect for, and absolute loyalty to, its letter and spirit.

Is entrusted by the Turkish nation to the patriotism and nationalism of its democracy-loving sons and daughters.

## Article 13

Fundamental rights and freedoms may be restricted only by law and in conformity with the reasons mentioned in the relevant articles of the Constitution without infringing upon their essence. These restrictions shall not be in conflict with the letter and spirit of the Constitution and the requirements of the democratic order of the society and the secular Republic and the principle of proportionality.

## Article 14

None of the rights and freedoms embodied in the Constitution shall be exercised with the aim of violating the indivisible integrity of the state with its territory and nation, and endangering the existence of the democratic and secular order of the Turkish Republic based upon Human Rights.

No provision of this Constitution shall be interpreted in a manner that enables the State or individuals to destroy the fundamental rights and freedoms embodied in the Constitution or to stage an activity with the aim of restricting them more extensively than stated in the Constitution.

The sanctions to be applied against those who perpetrate these activities in conflict with these provisions shall be determined by law.

## Article 19

Everyone has the right to liberty and security of person. No one shall be deprived of his or her liberty except in the following cases where procedure and conditions are prescribed by law: execution of sentences restricting liberty and the implementation of security measures decided by court order; apprehension or detention of an individual in line with a court ruling or an obligation upon him designated by law; execution of an order for the purpose of the educational supervision of a minor or for bringing him or her before the competent authority; execution of measures taken in conformity with the relevant legal provision for the treatment, education or correction in institutions of a person of unsound mind, an alcoholic or drug addict or vagrant or a person spreading contagious diseases, when such persons constitute a danger to the public, apprehension or detention of a person who enters or attempts to enter illegally into the country or for whom a deportation or extradition order has been issued.

Individuals against whom there is strong evidence of having committed an offence can be arrested by decision of a judge solely for the purposes of preventing escape, or preventing the destruction or alteration of evidence as well as in similar other circumstances which necessitate detention and are prescribed by law. Apprehension of a person without a decision by a judge shall be resorted to only in cases when a person is caught in the act of committing an offence or in cases where delay is likely to thwart the course of justice; the conditions for such acts shall be defined by law. Individuals arrested or detained shall be promptly notified, and in all cases in writing, or orally, when the former is not possible, of the grounds for their arrest or detention and the charges against them; in cases of offences committed collectively this notification shall be made, at the latest, before the individual is brought before a judge.

The person arrested or detained shall be brought before a judge within forty-eight hours and in the case of offences committed collectively within fifteen days, excluding the time taken to send the individual to the court nearest to the place of arrest. No one can be deprived of his or her liberty without the decision of a judge after the expiry of the above-specified periods. These periods may be extended during a state of emergency, under martial law or in time of war.

Notification of the situation of the person arrested or detained shall be made to the next of kin, except in cases of definite necessity pertaining to the risks of revealing the scope and subject of investigation compelling otherwise.

An individual detained or arrested shall be brought before a judge within, at latest, forty-eight hours and in the case of offences committed collectively within at most four days, excluding the time required to be sent to the nearest Court to the place of arrest. Release may be made conditional to the presentation of an appropriate guarantee with a view to securing the presence of the person at the trial proceedings and the execution of the court sentence.

The arrest or detention of a person shall be notified to next of kin immediately.

Damage suffered by persons subjected to treatment contrary to the above provisions shall be compensated by the State with respect to the general principles of the law on compensation.

## *Article 20*

Everyone has the right to demand respect for his or her private and family life. Privacy of an individual or family life cannot be violated.

Unless there exists a decision duly passed by a judge on one or several of the grounds of national security, public order, prevention of crime commitment, protection of public health and public morals, or protection of the rights and freedoms of others, or unless there exists a written order of an agency authorised by law in cases where delay is prejudicial, again on the abovementioned grounds, neither the person nor the private papers, nor belongings, of an individual shall be searched nor shall they be seized. The decision of the authorised agency shall be submitted for the approval of the judge having jurisdiction within twenty-four hours. The judge shall announce his decision within forty-eight hours from the time of seizure; otherwise, seizure shall automatically be lifted.

## Article 21

The domicile of an individual shall not be violated.

Unless there exists a decision duly passed by a judge on one or several of the grounds of national security, public order, prevention of crime commitment, protection of public health and public morals, or protection of the rights and freedoms of others, or unless there exists a written order of an agency authorised by law in cases where delay is prejudicial, again on the abovementioned grounds, no domicile may be entered or searched or the property therein seized. The decision of the authorised agency shall be submitted for the approval of the judge having jurisdiction within twenty-four hours. The judge shall announce his decision within forty-eight hours from the time of seizure; otherwise, seizure shall automatically be lifted.

## Article 22

Everyone has the right to freedom of communication.

Secrecy of communication is fundamental.

Unless there exists a decision duly passed by a judge on one or several of the grounds of national security, public order, prevention of crime commitment, protection of public health and public morals, or protection of the rights and freedoms of others, or unless there exists a written order of an agency authorised by law in cases where delay is prejudicial, again on the abovementioned grounds, communication shall not be impeded nor its secrecy be violated. The decision of the authorised agency shall be submitted for the approval of the judge having jurisdiction within twenty-four hours. The judge shall announce his decision within forty-eight hours from the time of seizure; otherwise, seizure shall automatically be lifted.

Public establishments or institutions where exceptions to the above may be applied are defined by law.

## Article 23

Everyone has the right to freedom of residence and movement.

Freedom of residence may be restricted by law for the purpose of preventing offences, promoting social and economic development, ensuring sound and orderly urban growth, and protecting public property; freedom of movement may be restricted by law for the purpose of investigation and prosecution of an offence, and prevention of offences. A citizen's freedom to leave the country may be restricted on account of civic obligations, or criminal investigation or prosecution.

Citizens may not be deported, or deprived of their right of entry to their homeland.

## Article 26

Everyone has the right to express and disseminate his thoughts and opinion by speech, in writing or in pictures or through other media, individually or collectively. This right includes the freedom to receive and impart information and ideas without interference from official authorities. This provision shall not preclude subjecting transmission by radio, television, cinema, and similar means to a system of licensing.

The exercise of these freedoms may be restricted for the purposes of protecting national security, public order and public safety, the basic characteristics of the Republic and safeguarding the indivisible integrity of the State with its territory and nation, preventing crime, punishing offenders, withholding information duly classified as a state secret, protecting the reputation and rights and private and family life of others, or protecting professional secrets as prescribed by law, or ensuring the proper functioning of the judiciary.

The formalities, conditions and procedures to be applied in exercising the right to expression and dissemination of thought shall be prescribed by law.

## Article 28

The press is free, and shall not be censored. The establishment of a printing house shall not be subject to prior permission or the deposit of a financial guarantee.

The state shall take the necessary measures to ensure freedom of the press and freedom of information.

In the limitation of freedom of the press, Articles 26 and 27 of the Constitution are applicable.

Anyone who writes or prints any news or articles which threaten the internal or external security of the state or the indivisible integrity of the state with its territory and nation, which tend to incite offence, riot or insurrection, or which refer to classified state secrets and anyone who prints or transmits such news or articles to others for the above purposes, shall be held responsible under the law relevant to these offences. Distribution may be suspended as a preventive measure by the decision of a judge, or in the event delay is deemed prejudicial, by the competent authority designated by law. The authority suspending distribution shall notify a competent judge of its decision within twenty-four hours at the latest. The order suspending distribution shall become null and void unless upheld by a competent judge within forty-eight hours at the latest.

No ban shall be placed on the reporting of events, except by the decision of judge issued to ensure proper functioning of the judiciary, within the limits specified by law.

Periodical and non-periodical publications may be seized by a decision of a judge in cases of ongoing investigation or prosecution of offences prescribed by law, and, in situations where delay could endanger the indivisible integrity of the state with its territory and nation, national security, public order or public morals and for the prevention of offence by order of the competent authority designated by law. The authority issuing the order to confiscate shall notify a competent judge of its decision within twenty-four hours at the latest. The order to confiscate shall become null and void unless upheld by the competent court within forty-eight hours at the latest.

The general common provisions shall apply when seizure and confiscation of periodicals and non-periodicals for reasons of criminal investigation and prosecution takes place.

Periodicals published in Turkey may be temporarily suspended by court sentence if found to contain material which contravenes the indivisible integrity of the state with its territory and nation, the fundamental principles of the Republic, national security and public morals. Any publication which clearly bears the characteristics of being a continuation of a suspended periodical is prohibited; and shall be seized following a decision by a competent judge.

## Article 31

Individuals and political parties have the right to use mass media and means of communication other than the press owned by public corporations. The conditions and procedures for such use shall be regulated by law.

The law shall not impose restrictions preventing the public from receiving information or forming ideas and opinions through these media, or preventing public opinion from being freely formed, on the grounds other than national security, public order, public morals, or the protection of public health.

## Article 33

Everyone has the right to form associations, or become a member of an association, or withdraw from membership without prior permission.

No one shall be compelled to become or remain a member of an association.

Freedom of association may only be restricted by law on the grounds of protecting national security and public order, or prevention of crime commitment, or protecting public morals, public health.

The formalities, conditions, and procedures governing the exercise of freedom of association shall be prescribed by law.

Associations may be dissolved or suspended from activity by the decision of a judge in cases prescribed by law. In cases where delay endangers national security or public order and in cases where it is necessary to prevent the perpetration or the continuation of a crime or to effect apprehension, an authority designated by law may be vested with power to suspend the association from activity. The decision of this authority shall be submitted for the approval of the judge in charge within twenty-four hours. The judge shall announce his decision within forty-eight hours, otherwise this administrative decision shall be annulled automatically.

Provisions of the first paragraph shall not prevent imposition of restrictions on the rights of armed forces and security forces officials and civil servants to the extent that the duties of civil servants so require.

The provisions of this article are also applicable to foundations.

## *Article 34*

Everyone has the right to hold unarmed and peaceful meetings and demonstration marches without prior permission.

The right to hold meetings and demonstration marches shall only be restricted by law on the grounds of national security, and public order, or prevention of crime commitment, public health and public morals or for the protection of the rights and freedoms of others.

The formalities, conditions and procedures governing the exercise of the right to hold meetings and demonstration marches shall be prescribed by law.

## *Article 36*

Everyone has the right of litigation either as plaintiff or defendant and the right to a fair trial before the courts through lawful means and procedures.

No court shall refuse to hear a case within its jurisdiction.

## *Article 38*

No one shall be punished for any act which does not constitute a criminal offence under the law in force at the time committed; no one shall be given a heavier penalty for an offence other than the penalty applicable at the time when the offence was committed.

The provisions of the above paragraph shall also apply to the statute of limitations on offences and penalties and on the results of conviction.

Penalties, and security measures in lieu of penalties, shall be prescribed only by law.

No one shall be held guilty until proven guilty in a court of law.

No one shall be compelled to make a statement that would incriminate himself or his legal next of kin, or to present such incriminating evidence. Criminal responsibility shall be personal.

General confiscation shall not be imposed as a penalty.

The death penalty shall not be imposed excluding the cases in time of war, imminent threat of war and terrorist crimes.

Findings obtained through illegal methods shall not be considered as evidence.

No one shall be deprived of his liberty merely on the ground of inability to fulfil a contractual obligation.

## Article 40

Everyone whose constitutional rights and freedoms have been violated has the right to request prompt access to the competent authorities.

The State is obliged to indicate, in its transactions, the legal remedies and authorities the persons concerned should apply and their time limits.

Damages incurred by any person through unlawful treatment by holders of public office shall be compensated for by the state. The state reserves the right of recourse to the official responsible.

## Article 41

The family is the foundation of the Turkish society and based on the equality between the spouses.

The state shall take the necessary measures and establish the necessary organisation to ensure the peace and welfare of the family, especially where the protection of the mother and children is involved, and recognising the need for education in the practical application of family planning.

## Article 46

The State and public corporations shall be entitled, where the public interest requires it, to expropriate privately owned real estate wholly or in part and impose administrative servitude on it, in accordance with the principles and procedures prescribed by law, provided that the actual compensation is paid in advance.

The compensation for expropriation and the amount regarding its increase rendered by a final judgement shall be paid in cash and in advance. However, the procedure to be applied for compensation for expropriated land in order to carry out land reform, major energy and irrigation projects, and housing and resettlement schemes and afforestation, and to protect the coasts and to build tourist facilities shall be regulated by law. In the cases where the law may allow payment in instalments, the payment period shall not exceed five years, whence payments shall be made in equal instalments.

Compensation for the land expropriated from the small farmer who cultivates his own land shall in all cases be paid in advance.

An interest equivalent to the highest interest paid on public claims shall be implemented in the instalments envisaged in the second paragraph.

## Article 49

Everyone has the right and duty to work.

The State shall take the necessary measures to raise the standard of living of workers, and to protect workers and the unemployed in order to improve the general conditions of labour, to promote labour, to create suitable economic conditions for prevention of unemployment and to secure labour peace.

## Article 51

Employees and employers have the right to form labour unions, employers' associations and higher organisations, without obtaining permission, and they also possess the right to become a member of a union and to freely withdraw from membership, in order to safeguard and develop their economic and social rights and the interests of their members in their labour relations. No one shall be forced to become a member of a union or to withdraw from membership.

The right to form a union shall be solely restricted by law and with the purposes of safeguarding national security and public order and to prevention of crime commitment, protection of public health and public morals and the rights and freedoms of others.

The formalities, conditions and procedures to be applied in exercising the right to form a union shall be prescribed by law.

Membership in more than one labour union cannot be obtained at the same time and in the same work branch.

The scope, exceptions and limits of the rights of civil servants who do not have a worker status are prescribed by law in line with the characteristics of their job.

The regulations, administration and functioning of labour unions and their higher bodies should not be inconsistent with the fundamental characteristics of the Republic and principles of democracy.

## Article 55

Wages shall be paid in return for work.

The state shall take the necessary measures to ensure that workers earn a fair wage commensurate with the work they perform and that they enjoy other social benefits.

In determining the minimum wage, the living conditions of the workers and the economic situation of the country shall be taken into account.

## Article 65

The State shall fulfil its duties as laid down in the Constitution in the social and economic fields within the capacity of its financial resources, taking into consideration the priorities appropriate with the aims of these duties.

## Article 66

Everyone bound to the Turkish state through the bond of citizenship is a Turk.
The child of a Turkish father or a Turkish mother is a Turk.

Citizenship can be acquired under the conditions stipulated by law, and shall be forfeited only in cases determined by law.

No Turk shall be deprived of citizenship, unless he commits an act incompatible with loyalty to the motherland.

Recourse to the courts in appeal against the decisions and proceedings related to the deprivation of citizenship, shall not be denied.

## Article 67

In conformity with the conditions set forth in the law, citizens have the right to vote, to be elected, and to engage in political activities independently or in a political party, and to take part in a referendum.

Elections and referenda shall be held under the direction and supervision of the judiciary, in accordance with the principles of free, equal, secret and direct, universal suffrage, and public counting of the votes. However, the conditions under which the Turkish citizens who are abroad shall be able to exercise their right to vote are regulated by law.

All Turkish citizens over eighteen years of age shall have the right to vote in elections and to take part in referenda.

The exercise of these rights shall be regulated by law.

Privates and corporals serving in the armed services, students in military schools, and convicts in penal execution excluding those convicted of negligent offences cannot vote. The Supreme Election Council shall determine the measures to be taken to ensure the safety of the counting of votes when detainees in penal institutions or prisons vote; such voting is done under the on-site direction and supervision of an authorised judge. The electoral laws shall be drawn up in such a way as to reconcile the principles of fair representation and consistency in administration.

The amendments made in the electoral laws shall not be applied to the elections to be held within the year from when the amendments go into force.

## Article 69

The activities, internal regulations and operation of political parties shall be in line with democratic principles. The application of these principles is regulated by law.

Political parties shall not engage in commercial activities.

The income and expenditure of political parties shall be consistent with their objectives. The application of this rule is regulated by law. The auditing of the income, expenditure and acquisitions of political parties as well as the establishment of the conformity to law of their revenue and expenses, methods of auditing and sanctions to be applied in the event of unconformity shall also be regulated by law. The Constitutional Court shall be assisted in performing its task of auditing by the Court of Accounts. The judgments rendered by the Constitutional Court as a result of the auditing shall be final.

The dissolution of political parties shall be decided finally by the Constitutional Court after the filing of a suit by the office of the Chief Public Prosecutor of the Republic.

The permanent dissolution of a political party shall be decided when it is established that the statute and programme of the political party violate the provisions of the fourth paragraph of Article 68.

A political party shall be deemed to become the centre of such actions only when such actions are carried out intensively by the members of that party or the situation is shared implicitly or explicitly by the grand congress, general chairmanship or the central decision-making or administrative organs of that party or by the group's general meeting or group executive board at the Turkish Grand National Assembly or when these activities are carried out in determination by the abovementioned party organs directly.

Instead of dissolving them permanently in accordance with the abovementioned paragraphs, the Constitutional Court may rule the concerned party to be deprived of State aid wholly or in part with respect to intensity of the actions brought before the court.

The foundation and activities of political parties, their supervision and dissolution, or their deprival of State aid wholly or in part as well as the election expenditures and procedures of the political parties and candidates, are regulated by law in accordance with the abovementioned principles.

## Article 74

Citizens and foreigners resident considering the principle of reciprocity have the right to apply in writing to the competent authorities and to the Turkish Grand National Assembly with regard to the requests and complaints concerning themselves or the public.

The result of the application concerning himself shall be made known to the petitioner in writing without delay.

The way of exercising this right shall be determined by law.

## Article 86

The salaries, allowances and retirement arrangements of the members of the Turkish Grand National Assembly shall be regulated by law. The monthly amount of the salary shall not exceed the salary of the most senior civil servant; the travel allowance shall not exceed half of that salary. The members of the Turkish Grand National Assembly and its retirees are affiliated with the Pension Fund of the Turkish Republic, and the affiliation of those continue upon their will in case of their membership expires.

The salaries and allowances paid to the members of the Turkish Grand National Assembly shall not necessitate the suspension of payments of pensions and similar benefits by the Pension Fund of the Turkish Republic.

A maximum of three months' salaries and allowances may be paid in advance.

### Article 87

The functions and powers of the Turkish Grand National Assembly comprise the enactment, amendment, and repeal of laws; the supervision of the Council of Ministers and the Ministers; authorisation of the Council of Ministers to issue governmental decrees having the force of law on certain matters; debating and approval of the budget draft and the draft law of the final accounts, making decisions regarding the printing of currency and declaration of war; ratifying international agreements, deciding with the three-fifth's of the Turkish Grand National Assembly on the proclamation of amnesties and pardons of the Constitution; confirming death sentences passed down by the courts; and exercising the powers and executing the functions envisaged in the other articles of the Constitution.

### Article 89

The President of the Republic shall promulgate the laws adopted by the Turkish Grand National Assembly within fifteen days.

He shall, within the same period, refer to the Turkish Grand National Assembly for further consideration, laws which he deems wholly or in part unsuitable for promulgation, together with a statement of his reasons. In the event of being deemed unsuitable by the President, the Turkish Grand National Assembly may only discuss those articles deemed to be unsuitable. Budget laws shall not be subjected to this provision.

Provisions relating to Constitutional amendments are reserved.

### Article 94

The Bureau of the Assembly of the Turkish Grand National Assembly shall be composed of the Speaker, the Deputy Speaker, Secretary Members and Administrative Members elected from among the Assembly members.

The Bureau of the Assembly shall be so composed as to ensure proportionate representation to the number of members of each political party group in the Assembly. Political party groups shall not nominate candidates for the Office of the Speaker.

Two elections to the Bureau of the Turkish Grand National Assembly shall be held in the course of one legislative term. The term of office of those elected in the first round is two years and the term of office of those elected in the second round is three years.

The candidates from among the members of the Assembly for the Office of the Speaker of the Turkish Grand National Assembly shall be announced, within five days of the convening of the Assembly, to the Bureau of the Assembly. Election of the Speaker shall be held by secret ballot. In the first two ballots, a two-thirds majority of the total number of members, and in the third ballot an absolute majority of the total number of members, is required. If an absolute majority cannot be obtained in the third ballot a fourth ballot shall be held between the two candidates who have received the highest number of votes in the third ballot; the member who receives the greatest number of votes in the fourth ballot shall be elected Speaker. The election of the Speaker shall be completed within five days of the expiry of the period for the nomination of candidates.

The quorum required for election, the number of ballots and its procedure, the number of Deputy Speakers, Secretary Members and Administrative Members, shall be stipulated by the Assembly Rules of Procedure.

The Speaker and Deputy Speaker of the Turkish Grand National Assembly cannot participate in the activities of the political party or party group in which they are a member, nor in debates, within or outside the Assembly, except in cases required by their functions; the Speaker and the Deputy Speaker who is presiding over the session shall not vote.

## Article 100

Parliamentary investigation concerning the Prime Minister or other ministers may be requested through a motion tabled by at least one-tenth of the total number of members of the Turkish Grand National Assembly. The Assembly shall consider and decide on this request with a secret ballot within one month at the latest.

In the event of a decision to initiate an investigation, this investigation shall be conducted by a commission of fifteen members chosen by lot on behalf of each party from among three times the number of members the party is entitled to have on the commission, representation being proportional to the parliamentary membership of the party. The commission shall submit its report on the result of the investigation to the Assembly within two months. If the investigation is not completed within the time allotted, the commission shall be granted a further and final period of two months. At the end of this period, the report shall be submitted to the Office of the Speaker of the Turkish Grand National Assembly.

Following its submission to the Office of the Speaker of the Turkish Grand National Assembly, the report shall be distributed to the members within ten days and debated within ten days after its distribution and, if necessary, a decision may be taken to bring the person involved before the Supreme Court. The decision to bring a person before the Supreme Court shall be taken by a secret ballot only by an absolute majority of the total number of members.

Political party groups in the Assembly shall not hold discussions or take decisions regarding parliamentary investigations.

## Article 118

The National Security Council shall be composed of the Prime Minister, the Chief of the General Staff, Deputy Prime Ministers, Ministers of Justice, National Defence, Internal Affairs, and Foreign Affairs, the Commanders of the Army, Navy and Air Forces and the General Commander of the Gendarmerie, under the chairmanship of the President of the Republic.

Depending on the particulars of the agenda, Ministers and other persons concerned may be invited to meetings of the Council and their views heard.

The National Security Council shall submit to the Council of the Ministers its views on the advisory decisions that are taken and ensuring the necessary condition with regard to the formulation, establishment and implementation of the national security policy of the state. The Council of Ministers shall evaluate decisions of the National Security Council concerning the measures that it deems necessary for the preservation of the existence and independence of the state, the integrity and indivisibility of the country and the peace and security of society.

The agenda of the National Security Council shall be drawn up by the President of the Republic taking into account the proposals of the Prime Minister and the Chief of the General Staff.

In the absence of the President of the Republic, the National Security Council shall meet under the chairmanship of the Prime Minister.

The organisation and duties of the General Secretariat of the National Security Council shall be regulated by law.

## Article 149

The Constitutional Court shall convene with its president and ten members, and shall take decisions by absolute majority. Decision of annulment of Constitutional amendments and closure in the cases of the political parties shall be taken by three-fifths majority.

The Constitutional Court shall give priority to the consideration of, and to decisions on, applications for annulment on the grounds of defect in form.

The organisation and trial procedures of the Constitutional Court shall be determined by law; its method of work and the division of labour among its members shall be regulated by the Rules of Procedure made by the Court.

The Constitutional Court shall examine cases on the basis of written evidence, except where it acts as the Supreme Court. However, when it deems necessary, it may call on those concerned and those having knowledge relevant to the case, to present oral explanations (Annexed sentence: 23.7.1995 — 4121/14 Article) and in lawsuits on whether to permanently dissolve a political party or not, the Constitutional Court shall hear the defence of the chairman of the party whose dissolution is in process or of a proxy appointed by the chairman, after the Chief Public Prosecutor of the Republic.

*Editors' Comment.* The 2001 bill also amended certain other articles of the Constitution. These amendments affected Art. 41 (the Protection of the Family), Art. 46 (Expropriation), Art. 49 (Right and Duty to Work), Art. 55 (Guarantee of a Fair Wage), Art. 65 (The Extent of Social and Economic Duties of the State, Art. 74 (Right of Petition [to the GNA and competent authorities]), Art. 86 (Salaries and Allowances of the GNA), Art. 94 (Bureau of the Assembly [of the TGNA]), and Art. 100 (Parliamentary Investigation [Procedure]).

# Document no. 78

**Editors' comment on developments related to the European Court of Human Rights (ECtHR) in 2001[5]**

In January, the Ministry of Foreign Affairs issued a letter to the judiciary noting the large number of cases at the ECtHR involving free expression, and urged that judges take the country's international obligations into account. Additionally, another circular issued by the Ministry of Interior noted the ECtHR decisions against the country and warned officials to comply with existing regulations against torture, particularly those regulating detention registration, timing and conditions, and those relating to access to an attorney. Probably as a result of the ruling, the armed forces emphasized Human Rights in training for officers and non-commissioned officers throughout the year.

However, during the year, the government lost 154 cases to which it was a party, most of which pertained to dispossession of property (from villages in the southeast), due process, torture, deaths, and past disappearances. In fifty-seven additional cases, the government accepted a friendly settlement and paid US$2 million. In eight cases, in which eighteen persons had been killed in detention or taken into custody and then disappeared, the ECtHR decided against Turkey. In all these cases, the court reiterated that most domestic legal remedies were insufficient and citizens could pursue a case in the ECtHR before all domestic legal remedies have been exhausted. Furthermore, the ECtHR ruled against Turkey in several cases of torture from previous years. Even though government officials admitted that torture occurs, they denied that it was systematic and stated that the government investigates "all claims of torture" and "punish[es] those personnel who are accused of torture"; the ECtHR did not agree with the government. The ECtHR noted that, in torture cases, domestic legal remedies were insufficient because prosecutors had not taken adequate steps to investigate the torture claims. During 2001, there were also unsubstantiated claims that persons applying to the ECtHR for decisions had been harassed by the police.

In 2001, the ECtHR dismissed three cases. In one very important decision in July, the ECtHR upheld the government's 1998 closure of the Islamic Refah (Welfare) Party, on the grounds that the closure did not violate the European Human Rights Convention. The Court held that the sanctions imposed on the

Welfare Party could "reasonably be considered to meet a pressing social need for the protection of democratic society, since, on the pretext of giving a different meaning to the principle of secularism, the leaders of the party had declared their intention to establish a plurality of legal systems based on differences in religious belief, to institute Islamic law (the *Sharia*), a system of law that was in marked contrast to the values embodied in the Convention." Important in the Court's decision was the fact that the Welfare Party had also "left in doubt [its] position regarding recourse to force in order to come to power and, more particularly, to retain power."

# Document no. 79

**PACE [Council of Europe Parliamentary Assembly] Resolution no: 1256 (2001): Honouring of Obligations and Commitments by Turkey**[6]

1. The Assembly recalls firstly its Recommendation 1298 (1996) on Turkey's respect of commitments to constitutional and legislative reforms, in which it instructed its committees concerned to open the monitoring procedure in respect of Turkey under Order no. 508 (1995), and secondly Order no. 545 (1998) on the humanitarian situation of the Kurdish refugees and displaced persons in southeastern Turkey and northern Iraq, in which it instructed its Monitoring Committee to study the issue of the Kurdish minority in the framework of the monitoring procedure concerning Turkey.

2. The Assembly is aware of the importance of Turkey — one of the oldest Member States of the Council of Europe — for the organisation, because of Turkey's choice in favour of Europe, its contribution to Europe's social and cultural heritage and basic values, as well as the geopolitical significance of Turkey.

3. The Assembly is pleased with the increased mutual understanding of each other's concerns: in the other Council of Europe Member States comprehension of the difficulties met by Turkey in its efforts to solve the conflict in southeastern Turkey and, within Turkey, understanding of the criticism from other Member States on the country's Human Rights record.

4. The Assembly commends the Turkish authorities on the establishment — notwithstanding an economic crisis without precedent throughout the country — of the National Programme for the Adoption of the *Acquis Communautaire*, approved in March 2001 by the Turkish government in the framework of the accession process to the European Union, and out of which Chapters 1.1 (Introduction) and 1.2 (Political criteria) have been presented by the government as a programme for honouring the obligations and commitments of Turkey as a Member State of the Council of Europe.

5. The Assembly recognises that Turkey is a functioning democracy with a multi-party system, free elections and an active and independent legislature, based on a constitution approved by referendum in 1982.

6. However, the Assembly recalls also that this constitution was drafted when Turkey was under military rule and that it is partly based on principles which are no longer in line with present-day criteria in force in the Council of Europe.

7. The Assembly welcomes, therefore, the amendments which have since been made to the constitution, in particular regarding the replacement of the military judges in each of the Turkish State Security Courts. It also notes with satisfaction that in the National Programme the review of the constitution will have priority and trusts that the amendments will include the changes which the Assembly suggests in paragraph 16 of this resolution.

8. With regard to the rule of law, the Assembly welcomes the measures taken by the Turkish authorities to improve the conditions of police custody, to eradicate torture and ill-treatment and to identify and efficiently sanction those who have committed such acts.

9. In particular, the Assembly commends the Turkish authorities on their recent decision to authorise publication of the reports drawn up by the European Committee for the Prevention of Torture and Inhuman or Degrading Treatment or Punishment (CPT) after its visits to Turkey in 1999, 2000 and January 2001.

10. The Assembly welcomes also the adoption of laws amending the Penal Code, the Law on Penal Procedures against Civil Servants and the Law on the Fight against Organised Crime, and encourages the authorities concerned to accelerate work on the new Code of Criminal Procedure, the new Penal Code, amendments to the Civil Code, the draft bill on the creation of the institute of ombudsman and the draft bill on local authorities.

11. The Assembly notes with satisfaction that the Turkish authorities have accepted the need to reform their penitentiary institutions and that Article 16 of the Prevention of Terrorism Act has been amended to allow prisoners to take part in communal activities.

12. Turkey is to be commended on progress made in creating awareness of the need for the respect for Human Rights and fundamental freedoms, as well as on the measures taken by the Turkish authorities to improve or complement legislation in this field.

13. Above all, the Assembly welcomes the return of tranquillity in south-eastern Turkey, the cease-fire announced by the PKK [Kurdish Workers' Party] and the reduction of action by the Turkish armed forces to some occasional security operations; it also notes that the Turkish authorities have embarked on a relief programme for people who have left their homes and returnees, and that they are determined to develop the economy in the region.

14. The Assembly acknowledges the increased freedom of association in Turkey, which enables a growing number of associations, foundations and trades unions to state their opinions and views, and thus to influence public opinion. However, there are concerns that defenders of Human Rights and Human Rights organisations are still under pressure.

15. The Assembly welcomes the extension of freedom of expression following the adoption of the Law on the Postponement of Sentences and Trials in

respect of Crimes Committed through the Press and Broadcasting and the ongoing amendment of the Penal Code, including the debate on modifying Article 312, which provides for sentences of up to three years and exclusion for life from public functions for incitement to hatred on grounds of race or religion.

16. However, the Assembly is concerned about a number of obligations where progress made cannot yet be considered to be substantial and the honouring of which requires further action by the Turkish authorities in charge:

- the Assembly trusts that the revision of the constitution announced in the National Programme will lead also to the establishment of a certain parliamentary control over the Turkish National Security Council, revision and completion of the system of protection of Human Rights and fundamental freedoms, abolition of the death penalty, confirmation of the pre-eminence of law and reinforcement of the judiciary's control over all administrative acts:
- whilst recognising fully the independence of Turkey in constitutional matters, its experience and its expertise, the Assembly nevertheless recommends that in any amendment of the Turkish Constitution account be taken of the experience and work of the European Commission for Democracy through Law (Venice Commission) in constitutional revisions;
- the Assembly recommends that the Turkish authorities ensure that the relevant constitutional provisions and other legal rules cannot be interpreted in a way which prevents political parties from carrying out their normal functions and elected representatives from expressing freely their political opinions, with due respect to the principle of refraining from engaging in any activity or performing any act aimed at inciting violence or discrimination, at undermining parliamentary democracy or at destroying any of the rights and freedoms set forth in the European Convention on Human Rights;
- pending a judgment of the European Court of Human Rights in the case of Mrs Leyla Zana and others, the legal possibilities should be examined or, if necessary, be created to revise prosecution procedures and subsequent sentences in respect of the former DEP [Party of Democracy] parliamentarians imprisoned since that time;
- the Assembly encourages the Turkish authorities to ensure implementation of the measures taken to improve the conditions of police custody, to eradicate torture and ill-treatment and to identify and efficiently sanction those who have committed such acts; they should also continue their cooperation with the European Committee for the Prevention of Torture and Inhuman or Degrading Treatment or Punishment (CPT);
- with regard to prison reform which has converted the large dormitory system to cells for one to three prisoners, the Assembly regrets that hunger strikes have caused to date the loss of twenty-three lives and urges the fasting prisoners and the Turkish authorities to end this human drama. The Turkish government should follow the advice of the CPT and take immediately the necessary measures to ensure that, in particular, prisoners in the F-type

prisons spend a reasonable part of the day engaged in a programme of communal activities outside their cells;
- with regard to the right to life, the Assembly encourages Turkish society to continue and conclude the ongoing debate: no death sentences must be executed; the death penalty must be abolished *de jure* and Protocol no. 6 to the European Convention on Human Rights must be signed and ratified;
- full enjoyment of the freedom of association should also be guaranteed in respect of organisations, and in particular organisations working legally for the protection of Human Rights in southeastern Turkey; investigations should be conducted by the competent authorities into their complaints that these organisations are being prosecuted for exercising their legal activities, their offices being closed, their members being arrested and their telephone lines being tapped. The Assembly also urges the Turkish authorities to again grant Human Rights organisations access to prisoners;
- the Assembly urges the Turkish authorities to accelerate modification of Article 312 of the Turkish Penal Code and to revise Article 8 of the Prevention of Terrorism Act, which in its present unclear wording opens the door to arbitrary action by the state against individuals for "crimes of expression of thought", in particular journalists and politicians for having expressed opinions which, under the existing rules, could be interpreted as incitement to separatism, and to avoid further contravention of the European Convention on Human Rights;
- although the Turkish authorities have executed most of the judgments of the European Court of Human Rights in which Turkey has been condemned, the Assembly encourages these authorities to accelerate procedures for adequate follow-up to those judgments which have not yet been completely implemented. In particular, the Assembly refers to the Loizidou case and takes full note of the third interim resolution of the Committee of Ministers (DH (2001) 80), adopted on 26 June 2001, whereby the Committee of Ministers declares its resolve to ensure, with all means available to the organisation, Turkey's compliance with its obligations under the judgment;
- the Assembly recommends that the Turkish authorities lift the state of emergency in the four remaining southeastern provinces and replace it with an economic state of emergency, and that they take the necessary legislative and administrative measures to guarantee full respect of the Human Rights of the Kurdish people in Turkey and enable them to live their Kurdish cultural identity (including teaching of the Kurdish language in schools in the Kurdish regions and authorisation of Kurdish language audiovisual media);
- the Assembly also recommends that the Turkish authorities examine the principles laid down in the Framework Convention for the Protection of National Minorities (ETS no. 157) and in the European Charter for Regional or Minority Languages (ETS no. 148), with a view to signing and ratifying these instruments and applying the principles in respect of the different ethnic groups which live in Turkey;

- in order to identify the various questions raised by the cohabitation of different ethnic groups, to exchange experiences and to define appropriate solutions, the Assembly invites the Turkish authorities to consider the opportunity of organising with the Parliamentary Assembly a seminar on multi-ethnic societies, to be held in Turkey.

17. The Assembly is aware that most of its concerns, expressed in paragraph 16 above, have been taken into account by the drafters of Chapters 1.1 and 1.2 of the National Programme for the Adoption of the *Acquis Communautaire*. It realises also that these chapters, ambitious and far-reaching as they may seem, reflect a delicate compromise between the ruling political forces in Turkey and are therefore worded in a cautious way, as good intentions, with long and flexible deadlines for their implementation.

18. The decision of the Turkish Constitutional Court of 22 June 2001 to ban the Virtue Party (the country's main opposition party with 102 seats out of 550 in the Turkish Grand National Assembly) for activities contrary to the principle of a secular republic, to expel two of its members from parliament and to impose political bans on five more members, although it may be in accordance with the Turkish law, is in contradiction with the principles of pluralist democracy. The Assembly regrets this decision, which would contribute to political instability at a time when Turkey is engaging in important reforms.

19. In conclusion, the Assembly welcomes the progress Turkey has made in the honouring of its obligations as a Member State of the Council of Europe since the start of the monitoring procedure, and in particular the open and sincere dialogue that has developed on still outstanding issues. The Assembly therefore encourages the Turkish authorities to implement the National Programme and to continue taking the legislative and administrative measures necessary to comply with the outstanding obligations listed in paragraph 16 above.

20. Whilst thus recognising that progress has been made in the honouring of certain aspects of Turkey's obligations, but that other aspects still warrant further action, the Assembly resolves to pursue, in close cooperation with the Turkish delegation, the monitoring procedure in respect of Turkey, with a view to advising and assisting the Turkish authorities concerned in their policy towards complying with Turkey's obligations as a Member State and to assess further progress until the Assembly decides to close the monitoring procedure.

# Document no. 80

Republic of Turkey Secretariat General of European Affairs Studies within the framework of National Programme: Comparison Chart between the Accession Partnership, NPAA, and the 2001 Regular Report[7]

| Accession partnership | NPAA | Progress accomplished (2001 Progress Report) |
|---|---|---|
| Enhanced political dialogue and political criteria | | |
| *Short term* | | |
| • In the context of the political dialogue, strongly support the UN Secretary General's efforts to bring to a successful conclusion the process of finding a comprehensive settlement of the Cyprus problem, as referred to in point 9(a) of the Helsinki conclusions<br>• Strengthen legal and constitutional guarantees of the right to freedom of association and peaceful assembly and encourage development of civil society<br>• Strengthen legal provisions and undertake all necessary measures to reinforce the fight against torture practices, and ensure compliance with the European Convention for the Prevention of Torture | • Strengthen legal and constitutional guarantees for the right to freedom of expression in line with Article 10 of the European Convention of Human Rights. Address in that context the situation of those persons in prison sentenced for expressing non-violent opinions<br>• Turkey will continue to undertake initiatives and efforts towards the settlement of bilateral problems through dialogue with Greece. Turkey will continue to support the efforts of the UN Secretary General in the context of his good-offices mission aiming at a mutually acceptable settlement with a view to establishing a new partnership in Cyprus based on the sovereign equality of the two parties and the realities on the island | • The issue of enhanced political dialogue has been taken up on the occasion of the Turkish–EU Association Meeting in Luxemburg on 26 June 2001 |

*continued*

| Accession partnership | NPAA | Progress accomplished (2001 Progress Report) |
|---|---|---|
| Enhanced political dialogue and political criteria | | |

*Short term*

| | | |
|---|---|---|
| • Further align legal procedures concerning pre-trial detention with the provisions of the European Convention on Human Rights and with recommendations of the Committee for the Prevention of Torture<br>• Strengthen opportunities for legal redress against all violations of Human Rights<br>• Intensify training on Human Rights issues for law enforcement officials in mutual cooperation with individual countries and international organisations<br>• Improve the functioning and efficiency of the judiciary, including the State Security Court in line with international standards. Strengthen in particular training of judges and prosecutors on European Union legislation, including in the field of Human Rights<br>• Maintain the de facto moratorium on capital punishment. EN Official Journal of the European Communities 24.3.2001 L 85/17<br>• Remove any legal provisions forbidding the use by Turkish citizens of their mother tongue in TV/radio broadcasting | • Review the provisions of the Constitution on Human Rights and freedoms, in particular those concerning the expression and the dissemination of ideas, the freedom of science, the arts and the press<br>• Review Article 312 of the Turkish Penal Code, without prejudice to values protected therein<br>• Review Articles 7 and 8 of the Anti-Terrorism Act, with the same understanding<br>• Review the Act on the Establishment of Radio and Television Enterprises and Their Broadcasts<br>• Review the Act on Press, in relation to the scope of the offences and penalties<br>• Enact the Draft Act on the Establishment and Working Principles and Procedures of the Economic and Social Council<br>• Enhance constitutional safeguards for non-governmental organisations and the institutions for social and economic democracy<br>• Enact the Draft Act on Job Security<br>• Review the Act on the Duties and Competences of the Police, and the relevant regulation; the Act on the Organisation, Duties and Competences of the Gendarmerie, and the relevant bylaw; and the Act on the Coast Guard Command, and the relevant regulation<br>• Undertake arrangements to modernise the Forensic Medicine Institution<br>• Undertake legal arrangements to extend the duration of education at Police Academies from nine months to two years | |

*continued*

| Accession partnership | NPAA | Progress accomplished (2001 Progress Report) |
|---|---|---|
| Enhanced political dialogue and political criteria *Short term* • Develop a comprehensive approach to reduce regional disparities, and in particular to improve the situation in the southeast, with a view to enhancing economic, social and cultural opportunities for all citizens | • Put into action, within the framework of the UN Decade of Human Rights Education, the Human Rights Education Project of the Ministry of the Interior and Its Affiliated Agencies (2000–2007)<br>• Train law enforcement personnel on Human Rights over a period of seven years, within the framework of a project developed in light of the 1997–2000 Police and Human Rights Programme of the Directorate of Human Rights of the Council of Europe<br>• Procedures of the State Security Courts<br>• Strengthen legal defence by introducing a constitutional provision that will establish this as one of the fundamental elements of the judicial process, and enact the Draft Advocacy Act<br>• Review provisions which may infringe upon the independence of the Judiciary, and restructure the Supreme Council for Judges and Public Prosecutors<br>• Undertake legal arrangements to modernise the Forensic Medicine Institution<br>• Step up activities for the UN Decade of Human Rights Education and seek further opportunities for the education and training of Turkish judges and prosecutors in Member States of the European Union and the Council of Europe<br>• Provide regular in-service training on Human Rights and the decisions of the European Court of Human Rights for Turkish judges and prosecutors<br>• Conclude the UN Convention on the Elimination of All Forms of Racial Discrimination<br>• Reinforce in the Constitution the principle that men and women have equal rights | |

*continued*

| Accession partnership | NPAA | Progress accomplished (2001 Progress Report) |
|---|---|---|
| Enhanced political dialogue and political criteria | | |
| *Short term* | • Enact the Draft Turkish Civil Code embodying improvements in gender equality<br>• Enact the Draft Act on the Organisation of the Directorate General for the Status and Problems of Women, and the Draft Act on the Organisation of the Family Research Institution<br>• Conclude the ILO Convention Concerning the Prohibition and Immediate Action for the Elimination of Worst Forms of Child Labour (no. 182) and put into effect the National Action Plan prepared in cooperation with ILO on this subject<br>• The Ministry of Justice will render more effective the supervision and control over prisons by public administrators and chief public prosecutors<br>• The Draft Act Amending the Anti-Terrorism Act will be enacted, and, in the course of this process, matters related to open visits and workshop activities for prisoners convicted of such crimes will be reviewed | |
| *Medium term*<br>• In accordance with Helsinki conclusions, in the context of the political dialogue, under the principle of peaceful settlement of disputes in accordance with the UN Charter, make every effort to resolve any outstanding border disputes and other related issues, as referred to in point 4 of the Helsinki conclusions | • Review the Political Parties Act<br>• Review the Act on the Duties and Competences of the Police, and the relevant regulation; the Act on the Organisation, Duties and Competences of the Gendarmerie, and the relevant bylaw; and the Act on the Coast Guard Command, and the relevant regulation<br>• Review the Act on Cinema, Video and Musical Works and other relevant legislation<br>• Enact the new Turkish Penal Code | |

*continued*

| Accession partnership | NPAA | Progress accomplished (2001 Progress Report) |
|---|---|---|
| Enhanced political dialogue and political criteria | | |

*Medium term*

| | | |
|---|---|---|
| • Guarantee full enjoyment by all individuals without any discrimination and irrespective of their language race, colour, sex, political opinion, philosophical belief or religion of all Human Rights and fundamental freedoms. Further develop conditions for the enjoyment of freedom of thought, conscience and religion<br>• Review of the Turkish Constitution and other relevant legislation with a view to guaranteeing rights and freedoms of all Turkish citizens as set forth in the European Convention for the Protection of Human Rights; ensure the implementation of such legal reforms and conformity with practices in EU Member States<br>• Abolish the death penalty, sign and ratify Protocol no. 6 of the European Convention of Human Rights<br>• Ratify the International Covenant on Civil and Political Rights and its optional Protocol and the International Covenant on Economic, Social and Cultural Rights<br>• Adjust detention conditions in prisons to bring them into line with the UN Standard Minimum Rules for the Treatment of Prisoners and other international norms | • Undertake work concerning reimbursement of payments of reparations from public officials who are found at fault, in light of the decisions taken by the European Court of Human Rights<br>• Review any restrictions there may be on rights of labour unions and employers' associations, and the relevant articles of the Constitution regarding the right to go on strike on justifiable grounds<br>• Review rights of labour unions and employers' associations on the basis of ILO Conventions nos 87 and 98 and of the European Social Charter<br>• Review the legislation on the freedom of association and holding meetings and demonstration marches<br>• Enact the new Turkish Penal Code<br>• Enact the new Code of Penal Procedure<br>• Explore the availability of financial resources for training law enforcement personnel<br>• Conclude the Optional Protocol to the UN Convention on the Elimination of All Forms of Discrimination against Women<br>• Conclude Protocol no. 4 to the Council of Europe Convention for the Protection of Human Rights and Fundamental Freedoms, securing certain rights and freedoms other than those already included in the Convention and in Protocol no. 1<br>• Conclude Protocol no. 7 to the Council of Europe Convention for the Protection of Human Rights and Fundamental Freedoms<br>• Conclude the European Social Charter (Revised) and the Additional Protocol to the European Social Charter Providing for a System of Collective Complaints | |

*continued*

| Accession partnership | NPAA | Progress accomplished (2001 Progress Report) |
|---|---|---|
| Enhanced political dialogue and political criteria | | |
| *Medium term* | | |
| • Align the constitutional role of the National Security Council as an advisory body to the Government in accordance with the practice of EU Member States
• Lift the remaining state of emergency in the southeast
• Ensure cultural diversity and guarantee cultural rights for all citizens irrespective of their origin. Any legal provisions preventing the enjoyment of these rights should be abolished, including in the field of education | • Conclude Protocol no. 12 of the Council of Europe Convention for the Protection of Human Rights and Fundamental Freedoms, which extends the scope of Article 14 of the Convention to prohibit discrimination on any grounds
• Take further practical measures, within the framework of the legislation on the protection of the public order, to facilitate religious practice for non-Muslim foreign nationals residing in Turkey and practices in other areas pertaining to these persons
• Take measures in accordance with the ILO Convention (no. 159) Concerning Vocational Rehabilitation and Employment (Disabled Persons)
• Prevention of Human Rights violations and increase the use of technology to effectively monitor places where incidents of Human Rights violations continue to occur
• Introduce legal provisions on the joint and several liability of perpetrators of torture
• Review Article 19/6 of the Constitution
• Enact the new Code of Penal Procedure
• Amend the Act on the Establishment and Procedure of the State Security Courts
• Enact the new Code of Penal Procedure
• Enact the Draft Act on the Indemnification of Losses Resulting from Terrorism and the Fight Against Terrorism
• Review Act no. 4483 on the Prosecution of Civil Servants and other Public Employees, in light of the experience gained since its implementation | |

*continued*

| Accession partnership | NPAA | Progress accomplished (2001 Progress Report) |
|---|---|---|
| Enhanced political dialogue and political criteria<br>*Medium term* | • Review the Military Penal Code, the Act no. 353 on the Establishment and Procedure of Military Courts, and the Act no. 1602 on Military Administrative High Courts<br>• Review the Act on the State of Emergency, in the light of the relevant amendments to be made<br>• The National Security Council, which is a constitutional body, has the status of a consultative body in areas of national security. Relevant articles of the Constitution and other legislation will be reviewed in the medium term to define more clearly the structure and the functions of this Council<br>• Constitution and other legislation<br>• The abolition of the death penalty in Turkish criminal law; its form and its scope will be considered by the Turkish Grand National Assembly in the medium term | |

# Document no. 81

**Editors' additional comment**

*Comment on European Council Decisions of 2001.*[8] In the Gothenburg European Council of June 15 and 16, 2001, the EU concluded that: "The decisions in Helsinki have brought Turkey closer to the EU and opened up new prospects for her European aspirations. Good progress has been made in implementing the pre-accession strategy for Turkey, including an enhanced political dialogue." In the Laeken European Council of December 14 and 15, 2001, the EU declared that "Turkey has made progress towards complying with the political criteria established for accession, in particular through the recent amendment of its constitution. This has brought forward the prospect of the opening of accession negotiations with Turkey. Turkey is encouraged to continue its progress towards complying with both economic and political criteria, notably with regard to Human Rights. The pre-accession strategy for Turkey should mark a new stage in analysing its preparedness for alignment on the *acquis.*"

*Comment on some additional issues.* On December 8, 2001, the Turkish Civil Code was substantially modified. The changes in the law constituted an important recognition of fundamental social change. Amendments included provisions establishing equality of spouses in the family, removal of the designation of the husband as the head of the household, recognition of equal inheritance rights to children born out of wedlock, and recognition of adopted children as equal family members. Ardently defended by nationalists and religious conservatives, the previous separation of property regime for marital assets (strengthened in its effects by the practice of putting title to all property in the husband's name), was replaced as a default regime with one which accords the spouses equal shares in property acquired during the marriage (in effect for property acquired after January 1, 2003). However, such changes affect only those marriages entered into after the law entered into force. Rules regarding foreign-currency mortgages were also made less restrictive. For the changes in the New Civil Code and its relation to Copenhagen Criteria see Turkey's European Communication Group, *Highlights of the New Turkish Civil Code with Regard to the Copenhagen Political Criteria,* at http://www.abig.org.tr/en (last visited March 10, 2005).

# Document no. 82

**Measures taken by the Republic of Turkey against terrorism — 2001 Report to the United Nations Security Council[9]**

*Introduction*

The terrorist attacks that took place in New York, Washington DC and Pennsylvania on 11 September 2001 have been a major shock for the international community. While causing unprecedented condemnation and unwavering determination of the international community to bring their perpetrators to justice, these heinous attacks showed once again the dimensions of terrorism and the need for international solidarity and common effort to combat it.

As a country that has long suffered from terrorism and is still a major target, Turkey has condemned in the strongest terms the culprits and instigators of those attacks and called for intensified international cooperation for the prevention of this scourge. Turkey has therefore welcomed the adoption of Security Council Resolution 1373, which constitutes a solid and comprehensive instrument for combating terrorism on a universal scale. The resolution provides a clear road map for the steps that need to be taken in this regard. We hope that all Member States will fully comply with this groundbreaking resolution. Turkey is for its part determined to continue to actively contribute to the enhancement of international cooperation in fighting terrorism.

It should be noted that, in the aftermath of the 11 September attacks, Turkey expressed its unequivocal solidarity with the United States of America and responded favourably to its call to join in an international coalition aiming at bringing to justice the perpetrators and organisers of those attacks. In this context, Turkey opened its airspace to US military transport aircraft participating in operation "Enduring Freedom" and issued a blanket clearance for landing to and take off from a number of Turkish airfields.

Having had to cope with terrorism for more than two decades, Turkey is well equipped with internal legal instruments required for the struggle against that evil. It is also party to a number of bilateral and multilateral agreements on cooperation in the prevention of terrorism, organised crime and drugs trafficking.

International efforts to combat terrorism cannot be fully effective in the absence of a global instrument completing the existing UN Conventions in this field. The draft Comprehensive Convention on International Terrorism, under discussion at the Working Group established by the Sixth Committee, aims at addressing this shortcoming. Turkey calls upon all Member States to make additional efforts towards finalising that Convention.

Note: the numbers of the following paragraphs and sub-paragraphs correspond to those of the relevant paragraphs and sub-paragraphs of UNSC Resolution 1373.

## Operative paragraph 1

*Legal provisions for the prevention of the financing of terrorist activity*

Turkey has various pieces of legislation that contain provisions which may apply to prevent and suppress the financing of terrorist acts. The Law on the Fight Against Terrorism no. 3713, the Penal Code, the Law on the Prevention of Money Laundering and the Law on the Prevention of Benefit-Oriented Criminal Organisations no. 4422, in particular, are basic instruments prohibiting the financing of terrorist acts:

- Article 7, paragraph 4, of the Law on the Fight Against Terrorism: "The activities of associations, foundations, unions ( ... ) which are found to have lent support to terror movements will be prohibited and they will be dissolved by the decision of the concerned court. The assets of such institutions will be confiscated".
- Article 4 of the Law on the Fight Against Terrorism stipulates that the crimes referred to in Article 169 (among others) of the Penal Code are terrorist crimes. According to Article 169 of the Penal Code, assistance in any form to a criminal organisation is a punishable crime.
- Article 7 of the Law on the Prevention of Money Laundering no. 4208: "Whoever commits the offence of money laundering shall be sentenced to imprisonment for two to five years and to a heavy fine equal to the amount of the money laundered and all the property and assets in the scope of dirty money, including the returns thereof, and in case the property and assets cannot be seized, the corresponding value shall be subject to confiscation.
 If dirty money is derived from offences of terrorism or from smuggling of substances or materials whose export or import is prohibited or if the offence is committed in order to obtain financial sources for the commission of terrorist offences, the term of imprisonment referred to in the paragraph above shall not be less than four years."
- Article 9 of the Law on the Prevention of Money Laundering no. 4208 reads: "When there is serious circumstantial evidence of money laundering, the authority entitled to order the freezing of claims and rights in banks, non-banking financial institutions, as well as in real and other legal persons,

including the values in deposit boxes; the total or partial annulment of the right of disposition; the seizure of property, negotiable instruments, cash and other valuables; the holding of the assets in custody and the taking of other precautionary measures on claims and rights, is the Criminal Court of Peace Magistrate during the preliminary investigation and the Court during the trial. Requests for precautionary measures are concluded immediately as a result of evaluation of documents and at latest within twenty-four hours. Public prosecutors may also decide to freeze claims and rights in cases where it is necessary to avoid delay. The Office of the Public Prosecutor notifies the Criminal Court of Peace Magistrate about the decision at latest within twenty-four hours. The Peace Court Magistrate decides at most within twenty-four hours whether to approve the decision or not; in case of non-approval, the decision of the Public Prosecutor becomes void."

- Article 6 of the Law on the Prevention of Benefit-Oriented Criminal Organisations, no. 4422:

"Without prejudice to the provisions of the Law 4208 dated 13.11.1996, a decision may be taken during investigations to confiscate all movable or immovable assets of persons who are strongly suspected of having committed crimes mentioned under Article 1 of the present law and to prohibit totally or partially their exercise over rights and claims, including rented vaults, in banks or non-banking institutions and other real or corporate bodies; to invest such assets a depository location; and to take additional measures for the administration of property, commercial papers, cash or other values.

Upon demand of the Public Prosecutor, the Financial Crimes Investigation Board of the Ministry of Finance carries out the investigation, examination, identification and evaluation of the assets mentioned in the paragraph above, be they within the country or abroad.

When it becomes apparent that the assets mentioned in Paragraph 1 are legitimate, no confiscation order shall be given and prior confiscation orders shall be annulled.

Should the accused be found guilty, the assets in question shall become State property."

- According to Article 16 of the abovementioned law this measure is also applied for offences falling within the scope of the Law on the Fight Against Terrorism.

Regulatory provisions barring the financing of terrorist activity

- Regulations which require minimum qualifications and the endorsement of the Capital Market Board (Board; CMB) for founders, shareholders and holders of managerial posts of capital market institutions.
- The oversight and control of the Board, in transfers of shares of capital market institutions over a certain percentage.
- Customer name-based custody system used in Istanbul Stock Exchange (ISE) Settlement and Custody Bank Inc. This method enables to determine the identity of the securities investors.

- "Know your customer rule" applied for the intermediary institutions. This method provides the determination of the identities of securities investors who effect trades.
- Memoranda of understanding concluded between the Board and equivalent foreign authorities, providing for international cooperation in cases of securities fraud
- Regulations on suspicious transactions that apply also to transactions carried out by terrorists. (Type 2 transactions have to be reported to the Financial Crimes Investigation Board of the Ministry for Finance (FCIB). Type 2 transactions are transfers of large amounts of money from or to countries in which there are illegal activities regarding narcotic substances, smuggling or in which there are terrorist organisations and transfers of large amounts of money from or to offshore centres.)

*Action taken in the aftermath of the 11 September attacks against the financing of terrorism*

Pursuant to the request by the government of the United States of America concerning the blocking of the assets of persons, companies and organisations connected with Osama ben-Laden and the Al-Qaida terror organisation, the government of Turkey has launched an official investigation which resulted in the identification of one individual of foreign nationality having assets in Turkey. The assets of this individual have been blocked through an administrative decision taken by the Investigation Board of the Ministry of Finance.

## Operative paragraph 2

a. There are two principal laws that regulate terrorist offences and their punishments, namely the Turkish Penal Code (TPC) and the Law on the Fight Against Terrorism (LFAT).

- According to Article 7 (paras 2 and 5) of LFAT, assistance to members of terrorist organisations and propaganda of such organisations are terrorist crimes punishable under that law. Propaganda with the purpose of recruitment to terrorist groups and the expression of sympathy for such groups are offences falling within the scope of this Article. In case such propaganda is made in periodical publications, their owners and responsible editor-in-chiefs are also punished.
- Article 314 of the TPC provides for prison sentences of up to one year for supplying food and shelter, weapons or ammunition to organisations established with the purpose of committing crimes.
- Article 169 of the TPC: "Whoever, in circumstances other than prescribed in Articles 64 and 65, knowingly gives shelter, assistance, provisions, arms or ammunition to such a society or a band, or facilitates their actions, shall be punished by heavy imprisonment for three to five years."
- According to Article 2 (para. 2) of LFAT, those who commit crimes for and on behalf of a terrorist organisation are also considered terrorists even

if they do not take part therein and are punished as members of that organisation.
- As already stated, According to Article 7 (para. 4) of LFAT, "The activities of associations, foundations, unions ( … ) which are found to have lent support to terror movements will be prohibited and they will be dissolved by the decision of the concerned court. The assets of such institutions will be confiscated."

b. For an effective, reliable and speedy exchange of information on terrorist activity, liaison officers are being reciprocally appointed with a number of counties (USA, Germany, Belgium, Denmark, France, Holland, UK, Spain, Italy and Saudi Arabia). There are also Turkish contact persons at expert level in Germany, Austria, Holland, Italy and Romania. Furthermore, within a well-established cooperation and information-exchange mechanism, all information regarding persons for whom there are grounds to believe that they have been or will be involved in terrorist activities is immediately conveyed by the Turkish Ministry of Interior to its counterparts.

c, d, e. Financing, planning, preparing, perpetrating and supporting terrorist acts are established as serious criminal offences for which numerous articles of the Turkish Penal Code and the Law on the Fight Against Terrorism provide for heavy punishments:

- Legal persons involved in terrorism are also subject to prosecution. The activities of associations, foundations, trades unions or other similar institutions who support terrorist groups are being prohibited and their assets confiscated.
- According to Article 168 of the Turkish Penal Code; "Whoever establishes armed societies and bands or undertakes the duty of chieftain or command or any particular duty in such societies or bands, with the purpose of committing the crimes defined in Articles 125, 131, 146, 147, 149 and 156, shall be punished by heavy imprisonment for not less then fifteen years. Other members of such society or band shall be punished by heavy imprisonment for ten to fifteen years."
- According to the LFAT those establishing, organising and directing the organisations covered by Section 1 of that law are sentenced to heavy imprisonment from five to ten years and to heavy fine. Those joining such organisations are sentenced to heavy imprisonment from three to five years and to heavy fine.
- According to LFAT Article 7, those who help the adherents of the organisations referred to above or are involved in propaganda activities for the said organisations are sentenced to imprisonment from one to five years and to heavy fine, even if their acts constitute different crimes under other laws.
- According to LFAT Article 5, sentences pronounced for those who commit the crimes mentioned in various articles of the Turkish Penal Code are aggravated by one-half for both the freedom-restricting and monetary sanctions, when those crimes are committed for terrorist purposes.

- Terrorist offences are tried in specialised State Security Courts.
- Sentences for terrorist offences cannot be commuted nor deferred.

f. Through the liaison officers appointed by or to Turkey and through bilateral Security Cooperation Agreements with some forty countries, Turkey enjoys an effective information flow and mutual assistance in criminal matters. Joint Committee Meetings based on those agreements are being held periodically to discuss and exchange information related to security and criminal matters including terrorist ones.

g. Passport applicants in Turkey are subject to thorough investigation. Entries and exits of persons are recorded in the computer network and checked with criminal information. A draft Passport Law is in process, which foresees heavier sentences for illegal border crossings and a new type of Turkish passports more difficult to forge.

## *Operative paragraph 3*

a. The existing exchange of operational intelligence with regard to the activities of terrorist groups within the cooperation between the relevant security authorities of Turkey and their foreign counterparts greatly intensified after the terrorist attacks of 11 September 2001.

b. Relevant bodies exchange intelligence and cooperate on administrative and judicial matters with their foreign counterparts with a view to preventing terrorist activities.

With a circular dated 25.10.2001, the Ministry of Justice has forwarded UNSC Resolution 1373 (2001) to all public prosecutors, with the instruction that the resolution be meticulously implemented and be taken into consideration with respect to requests for judicial assistance received in accordance with agreements to which Turkey is party.

c. In addition to its multilateral commitments, Turkey is also party to forty-nine bilateral agreements with some forty countries on cooperation in combating terrorism, organised crime and drugs trafficking.

d. Turkey has ratified ten out of the twelve UN conventions relating to terrorism. The remaining two conventions, namely the "International Convention for the Suppression of Terrorist Bombings" and the "International Convention for the Suppression of the Financing of Terrorism" are expected to be ratified by the Turkish Grand National Assembly soon.

e. As a country which has been a victim of terrorism for almost three decades, Turkey condemned the perpetrators and sponsors of the murderous attacks of 11 September officially and called upon the international community to make every effort to enhance and contribute to international cooperation. Turkey strongly condemns all acts, methods and practices of terrorism regardless of their motivation, in all their forms and manifestations, wherever and by whomever they are committed. Turkey endorses and fully abides by the provisions of all relevant UNSC Resolutions including 1269 (1999) and 1368 (2001).

Immediately after President George W. Bush's Executive Order was released on 23 September 2001, Turkey formed a committee to investigate whether the persons and companies in that list, suspected to have relations with Osama ben-Laden and Al-Qaida, are present and active in Turkey. After thorough investigation by relevant authorities it appeared that one person on the list had lucrative activities in Turkey, following which all his assets were frozen.

It should be noted that Turkey has so far played an active role in drafting and adopting various international documents, thus contributing to codification efforts in this field. The 1977 European Convention on the Suppression of Terrorism is an example to these instruments.

f. In accordance with the reservation it has put to the Geneva Convention on the Legal Status of Refugees, Turkey accepts refugees from only European countries. Non-European asylum seekers are temporarily hosted in Turkey until a safe third country is prepared to receive them. In both cases applications for asylum are carefully examined so as to ensure that the applicants are not involved in any terrorist activity.

g. Turkey does not extradite persons whose offences are of a political nature in accordance with Article 3 of the "European Convention on the Extradition of Convicts". However, this principle does not apply in case of terrorist offences, in conformity with Turkey's commitments under UN conventions on terrorism.

*Turkey's efforts in international fora in view of securing enhanced cooperation in the fight against terrorism*

Turkey fully supports all efforts by the international community aimed at combating terrorism. In this context, it has substantially contributed to the drafting and adoption of resolutions and agreements in various international organisations.

At NATO [North Atlantic Treaty Organization], Turkey has consistently maintained the view that terrorism should be accepted as a new threat to the Alliance within the new Strategic Concept. After the horrendous attacks against the United States of America on 11 September 2001, a NATO ally, Turkey strongly supported the invoking of Article 5 of the North Atlantic Treaty. As before, Turkey will be actively supporting all efforts within NATO with regard to combating terrorism.

Furthermore, Turkey contributed intensely to all efforts within the Organization for Security and Cooperation in Europe for fighting against terrorism. In this context, Turkey has actively participated in and contributed to the recent international conference entitled "Enhancing Security and Stability in Central Asia; Strengthening Comprehensive Efforts to Counter Terrorism" held on 13–14 December 2001 in Bishkek, Krgyzystan.

Turkey also supports the regional initiatives on combating transnational crime and terrorism within the Southeastern European Cooperation Initiative (SECI) and the Black Sea Economic Cooperation (BSEC).

Turkey has ratified the Agreement on Cooperation to Prevent and Combat Trans-Border Crime (SECI Agreement) and appointed two liaison officers to the

SECI Centre on Combating Trans-Border Crime in Bucharest that was established in accordance with the SECI Agreement.

Turkey also ratified the Agreement Among the Governments of the Black Sea Economic Cooperation Participating States on Cooperation in Combating Crime, in Particular in its Organized Forms (BSEC Agreement). Turkey is actively participating in the meetings of the BSEC Working Group on Combating Crime and has contributed to the elaboration and finalisation of the Draft Additional Protocol to the BSEC Agreement that concerns the establishment of a BSEC Network of Liaison Officers.

Furthermore, as a member of the Organization of the Islamic Conference, Turkey has actively participated in the drafting and conclusion of the Convention of the Organization of the Islamic Conference on combating international terrorism.

*The Council of Europe Context*

Turkey has undertaken a number of commitments as a member of the Council of Europe, which specialises in Human Rights protection and legal cooperation on a pan-European scale, in the field of combating terrorism and related areas.

First of all, Turkey has signed and ratified the 1977 European Convention on the Suppression of Terrorism (see para. c under Operative paragraph 3).

The fact that the Convention is far from being satisfactory with regard to the current needs in the field has become evident in time. The very concept of "political crimes" contained in the text and the possibility of making reservations in matters of extradition has seriously flawed the mechanism stipulated by the Convention. Turkey has long been stressing the need to update and if necessary revise the instrument. Turkey is of the opinion that should the work to update and/or revise the Convention fail, a new legal instrument which will be compatible with today's needs must be drafted.

Turkey is also party to the following Council of Europe Conventions covering directly or indirectly the fields of terror and organised crime:

- European Convention on Extradition (ETS 24)
- Second Additional Protocol to the European Convention on Extradition (ETS 98)
- European Convention on Mutual Assistance in Criminal Matters (ETS 30)
- Additional Protocol to the European Convention on Mutual Assistance in Criminal Matters (ETS 99)
- European Convention on the Transfer of Proceedings in Criminal Matters (ETS 73)
- Convention on the Transfer of Sentenced Persons (ETS 112)

Turkey has signed and initiated formalities on ratification for the following Council of Europe instruments:

- Convention on Laundering, Search, Seizure and Confiscation of the Proceeds from Crime (ETS 141)

- Criminal Law Convention on Corruption (ETS 173)
- European Convention on the Supervision of Conditionally Sentenced or Conditionally Released Offenders (ETS 51)
- European Convention on the Control of the Acquisition and Possession of Firearms by Individuals (ETS 101)
- European Convention on the Compensation of Victims of Violent Crimes (ETS 116)
- Civil Law Convention on Corruption (ETS 174)

Finally, the following instruments are under study with a view to being signed and ratified:

- Additional Protocol to the European Convention on Extradition (ETS 86)
- Additional Protocol to the Convention on the Transfer of Sentenced Persons (ETS 167)
- Agreement on Illicit Traffic by Sea, implementing Article 17 of the United Nations Convention against illicit traffic in narcotic drugs and psychotropic substances (ETS 156)

Turkey has always taken part actively in all efforts to increase the level of cooperation in the field at all Council of Europe fora, including the Parliamentary Assembly.

Just after the 11 September events, the Committee of Ministers of the Council of Europe has adopted, on 12 September, a declaration condemning the attacks in the strongest terms. Turkey has energetically supported the initiative.

Turkey also supported the 21 September decision of the Committee of Ministers to establish special institutions to work on the legal aspects of European cooperation in the fight against terrorism. With this understanding in mind, it has participated in the first meetings of the newly established "Committee of Experts on Combating Terrorism and Human Rights" and "Multi Disciplinary Group on Terrorism".

Turkey extended its unreserved support to the initiatives of the Secretary General of the Council of Europe in the field of combating terrorism.

Furthermore, Turkish members of the Parliamentary Assembly of the Council of Europe have worked vigorously for the adoption of the Resolution (1258(2001)) and Recommendation (1534(2001)) "Democracies facing terrorism". They have exerted specific efforts to have a reference to the principle of "either try or extradite" (*aut dedere aut judicare*) in terror crimes in the aforementioned texts.

Finally, Turkey has supported the Declaration adopted by the 109th Ministerial Session of the Committee of Ministers, which defines terrorism as a crime against humanity.

## Conclusion

Whatever its strength, no country can defeat terrorism without close international cooperation. Recent events have demonstrated it. Hence, the international community must exert every effort to contribute to the fight against this scourge. UNSC Resolution 1373 sets valuable guidelines for Member States to adopt a common approach in identifying, defining, condemning, isolating and bringing before justice the perpetrators of terrorists acts.

Turkey also welcomes initiatives within regional organisations in view of combating terrorism. However, as terrorism has no particular geography, these initiatives must complement universal cooperation in this regard, rather than having an exclusionist nature. The fight against terrorism must be a common one and Turkey is firmly committed to work hand in hand with every State or international organisation for its success.

Selective attitudes based on political motivations and assessments are the main obstacles before an efficient international cooperation against terrorism. Illusionary distinctions, tolerance for or condoning of certain terrorist movements are approaches which cannot but impair labours aiming at eradicating this evil from the surface of our planet.

Many of Turkey's extradition demands have been refused in the past on various grounds and perpetrators of most wicked crimes have found safe havens in third countries. We have renewed our extradition requests hoping that they would be re-evaluated in the wake of the 11 September events. In the same vein, we recently provided the names of terrorist organisations of separatist, extreme leftist and fundamentalist nature that pose a major threat to Turkey, to be included in a list that the EU will prepare, as a contribution to the efforts in progress in the Union. Turkey is of the opinion that the response of its partners in the EU will constitute a test of their solidarity in our struggle against terrorism.

# 13 Turkey's progress on Human Rights: changes in anti-terrorism-related laws: 2002–2003

# Document no. 83

## Harmonisation package (1)[1]

[*Introductory comment.* On January 22, 2002, the Council of Europe Parliamentary Assembly agreed on a new resolution, Resolution 1268, on the Implementation of Decisions of the European Court of Human Rights.[2] In the part of the resolution pertaining to Turkey, the Assembly declared that: "[c]onsidering the high number of decisions against Turkey that have not been implemented, the Assembly instructs its Committee on Legal Affairs and Human Rights to confer with the national delegation of Turkey and with the Turkish government and to report to the Assembly, by June 2002 at the latest, on the progress made. The Assembly envisages inviting the Turkish Minister for Justice to the June part-session to confer on this matter."

On February 1, 2002, Turkey withdrew the derogation it had made in 1992, concerning Article 5 of the European Convention on Human Rights (right to liberty and security) with respect to provinces under emergency rule. The step was welcomed by the Council of Europe. During the remainder of the year, Turkey enacted laws for bringing Turkish Laws in compliance with the Copenhagen Criteria. The so-called "Harmonisation packages" amended numerous laws in different areas. The text provided below is a translated and edited Harmonization Package (P). The new wording in various laws is indicated in bold and deletions are indicated by brackets.]

### Article 1

The first and third paragraphs of Article 159 of the Turkish Penal Code no. 765, dated 01.03.1926, are amended as follows:

Paragraph 1. Those who overtly insult and deride Turkishness, the Republic, the Grand National Assembly, the moral personality of the government, the Ministers, the military or security forces of the State or the moral personality of the judiciary shall be sentenced to from one year up to **three** [six] years of [heavy] imprisonment.

Paragraph 3. Those who overtly curse the Laws of the Turkish Republic or the Decisions of the Grand National Assembly shall be sentenced from fifteen days up to six months of imprisonment [and a heavy fine from 100 Turkish lira (TRL) to 500 TRL].

## Article 2

Article 312 of the Turkish Penal Code is amended as follows:

Anyone who overtly praises or speaks favourably **of a crime** [an action which is openly defined as a criminal offence by the law] or incites the public **not to abide by** [to disobedience to] the law is sentenced from six months to two years of imprisonment [and to a heavy fine from 2,000 to 10,000 TL].

Anyone who **overtly** incites the public to hostility or **to harbour resentments against one another in a manner that may be dangerous to public order** on the basis of [with consideration to] **social** class, race, religion, sect or regional difference shall be sentenced from one to three years of imprisonment [and to a heavy fine from 3,000 TL up to 12,000 TL]. [If this incitement is undertaken in a manner that may be dangerous to the general security, the penalty of the perpetrator shall be increased by one third to one half.]

Anyone who insults a section of the public in a denigrating and degrading manner shall also be sentenced to the penalty *(stipulated)* in the first paragraph.

**If the criminal offences written *(stipulated)* in the preceding paragraphs are** committed with the means or in the ways indicated [**by those using the ways listed] in Article 311/2, the penalties shall be doubled.**

## Article 3

Article 7/2 of the Anti-Terror Act no. 3713, dated 12.04.1991, is amended as follows:

Paragraph 2. Those who assist members of organisations established as defined in the preceding paragraph or those who carry out propaganda on behalf of the organisation **in a manner that encourages resorting to terrorist methods**, even if these acts constitute another criminal offence, shall also be sentenced from one year to five years of imprisonment and to a heavy fine from **500** [50] million TL up to **1,000,000,000** [100,000,000] TL.

## Article 4

Article 8 of the Anti-Terror Act no. 3713 is amended to read as follows:

**Those who carry out** written, oral **or visual** propaganda or hold meetings, demonstrations or marches with **the aim of disrupting** [in order to disrupt] the indivisible integrity of the State of the Turkish Republic with its territory and nation [may not be undertaken. Those who do so] shall be sentenced from one to three years of imprisonment and to a heavy fine from **1,000,000,000** [100,000,000] TL to **3,000,000,000** [300,000,000] TL, **unless these actions require a greater penalty**. If this criminal offence **is committed in a way that encourages resorting to terrorist methods, the penalty is increased by one-third**; if the criminal offence is repeated, the prison sentences may not be converted to fines.

In case the criminal offence of carrying out propaganda indicated in the first paragraph is committed by way of **a** publication [publications] as referred to in Article 3 of the Press Act no. 5680, the owners of the **relevant** publication [if published more frequently that once a month] shall also be sentenced to a heavy fine of **three-fourths** of the average **value** of sales in the previous month, **if applicable**. However, this fine may not be **under any circumstances less than 3,000,000,000 TL.** The editors in charge of these publications shall be sentenced to pay a fine half the amount of the fine to which the owners are sentenced and to imprisonment from six months up to two years.

If the criminal offence of carrying out propaganda is committed by way of published work and other means of mass media, apart from those written *(stipulated)* in the second paragraph, those in charge and [in addition] the owners of the means of mass media shall be sentenced to imprisonment from six months up to two years and to a heavy fine from **1,000,000,000 TL** [100,000,000 TL] to **3,000,000,000 TL** [300,000,000 TL]. In addition, [in case that this act is committed by way of radio and televisions] the court shall decide to ban the relevant radio and television agency from broadcasting from one day up to **seven** days [fifteen] days.

In case the **criminal offence of propaganda indicated** [acts written] in the first paragraph is committed through means of mass media written *(stipulated)* in the second and third paragraphs, the penalty to be **given** [identified] shall be increased by **one-third** [from one-third to one-half].

## Article 5

Article 16 of the Act no. 2845 on the Establishment of and Proceedings at State Security Courts, dated 16.06.1983, is amended. The second sentence in the second paragraph is deleted from the text of the Article and the third and fourth paragraphs are amended. Even though there are no amendments to the first paragraph, it has been included for ease of reference.

Paragraph 1. The person who has been apprehended or arrested for crimes coming under the competence of the State Security Courts will be brought before a judge and questioned within forty-eight hours at the latest, excluding the time necessary to transfer him/her to the court nearest to the place of apprehension or arrest.

Paragraph 2. In crimes committed collectively by the participation of three or more persons, the Public Prosecutor may issue a written order extending this period to up to four days, for reasons of difficulty encountered in the collection of evidence or a high number of perpetrators and for other similar reasons. [If the investigation is not concluded during this period of time, then this period may be extended to up to seven days on the request of the Public Prosecutor and the decision of the judge].

Paragraph 3. The *(detention)* period for persons who are apprehended or arrested in regions declared to be under a State of Emergency in accordance with Article 120 of the Constitution, which is established as **four** [seven] days in the second paragraph, may be extended to **seven** [ten] days on the request of the Public Prosecutor and the decision of the judge. **The judge shall listen to the person who is apprehended or arrested before taking a decision.**

Paragraph 4. The suspect under arrest may always see his or her lawyer. The same provision is applied also to the person under detention, after **a written order is issued** [a decision is taken] by the **Public Prosecutor** [judge] to extend the detention period.

## Article 6

Article 107 of the Code of Penal Procedure no. 1412, dated 04.04.1929, is amended to read as follows:

*New version*

The arrest, and any decision to extend the period of arrest, shall be notified without any delay to a relative of or to a person designated by the person under arrest, with the decision of the judge.

Furthermore, the arrested person is allowed to notify in person a relative or a person he or she designates of the arrest, provided that this does not jeopardize the purpose of the investigation.

*Former version*

[Under the condition that the purpose of the arrest is not violated, the suspect under arrest is allowed to notify of the detention his or her relatives and other persons with whom he or she enjoys substantive relations. If the arrested person requests, these persons will be notified officially as well.]

[When the suspect under arrest is brought before the judge, the relatives are notified of the situation immediately with the decision of this judge.]

## Article 7

Article 128 of the Code of Penal Procedure is amended. The second sentence of the second paragraph of this Article is deleted and the third paragraph is amended. Even though there are no amendments to the first paragraph, it has been included for ease of reference.

Paragraph 1. If the person apprehended is not released, he or she will be brought before the justice of peace and questioned within twenty-fours hours, excluding the time necessary to transfer him/her to the justice of peace nearest to the place of apprehension. The lawyer may be present at the questioning upon the request of the apprehended person.

Paragraph 2. In crimes committed collectively by the participation of three or more persons, the Public Prosecutor may issue a written order to extend this period to up to four days, for reasons of difficulty encountered in the collection of evidence or a high number of perpetrators and for other similar reasons. [If the investigation is not concluded during this period of time, then this period may be extended to up to seven days on the request of the Public Prosecutor and the decision of the justice of peace].

Paragraph 3. **The apprehension, and the order to extend the period of apprehension, shall be notified without any delay to a relative of or a person designated by the person apprehended, with the decision of the Public Prosecutor.** [If the justice of peace sees no reason for apprehension or if the reasons for apprehension no longer prevail, he shall decide to release the person.]

## Article 8

This Act shall enter into force on the date of its publication.

## Article 9

The provisions of this Act shall be enforced by the Council of Ministers.

*General reasoning[3]*

**Modern democracies, which develop in a climate of tolerance, are systems based on pluralism, participation, and *(free)* thought, which aim to guarantee fundamental rights and freedoms. The recognition of fundamental rights and freedoms in our era is not solely an issue of universal concern; certain international organisations have been created and various international instruments have been adopted at these organisations in order to protect these *(fundamental rights and freedoms)* from controversial practices and to carry them forward to a more advanced level. The leading organisations amongst these are the United Nations Organization, which covers nearly all countries in the world, and the Council of Europe, which is the political union of democratic European countries. The most important documents related to this matter are the Universal Declaration of Human Rights, adopted on 10 December 1948, and the Council of Europe Convention on the Protection of Human Rights and Fundamental Freedoms and its additional protocols. Freedom of thought and expression is guaranteed by Articles 18 and 19 of the Universal Declaration of Human Rights and Article 10 of the Convention for the Protection of Human Rights and Fundamental Freedoms, also referred to as the "European Convention on Human Rights".**

There are detailed provisions on fundamental rights and freedoms also in our Constitution. Among these, the freedom of thought and expression is especially important in terms of the development of the democratic regime.

**Needs that have arisen and views that have evolved over time have made it necessary to amend the Constitution. As a new step forward in democratisation, Act no. 4709 Amending Some Articles of the Constitution of the Republic of Turkey, dated 03.10.2001, entered**

into force following its publication in the Official Gazette, no. 24556, dated 17.10.2001 (repeat issue).

With the amendment of the Constitution by Act no. 4709, a new system was adopted in which fundamental rights and freedoms may be restricted, without infringing upon their essence, only for reasons indicated in the relevant Articles of the Constitution and only by law. With this amendment, *(the scope of the)* fundamental rights and freedoms have been extended, including *(that of)* the freedom of thought and expression.

In order to implement the constitutional amendments, it is necessary to amend the relevant laws as well. With the *(current)* act, which has been drafted for this purpose, *(constituent)* elements of crimes contained in Articles 159 and 312 of the Turkish Penal Code and Articles 7 and 8 of the Anti-Terror Act have been revised so as to ensure proportionality with the aims of the penal sanctions; thus, the scope of the freedom of thought and expression has been extended.

Furthermore, the reduction of detention periods envisaged for crimes committed collectively to four days and the immediate notification of a relative of the person apprehended or arrested are amongst the recent important amendments introduced by Act no. 4709. In this context, detention periods in the Code of Penal Procedure and the Act on the Establishment of and Proceedings at State Security Courts have been revised in accordance with the *(respective)* amendment to the Constitution; the principle in the Constitution on the immediate notification of a relative has *(thus)* been put into force with the Code of Penal Procedure.

The draft act has been prepared to realise the changes indicated above.

### *Reasoning for Articles*

*Article 1*

The first and the third paragraphs of Article 159 of the Turkish Penal Code are amended so as to reduce the upper limit for imprisonment from six years to three years, to change the condition of imprisonment from heavy to standard, and to revoke the clauses on the heavy fine.

In Article 1 of the Constitution, there is the provision that "the Turkish State is a Republic", and, in Article 3, there is the provision that "The Turkish State, with its territory and nation is an indivisible entity". The Turkish nation that exercises its sovereignty through authorised organs in accordance with the principles of the Constitution is a legal concept that encompasses all people who are within the definition "Everyone bound to the Turkish State through the bond of citizenship is a Turk" in Article 66 of the Constitution.

*Article 2*

**Article 312 of the Turkish Penal Code, as amended, incorporates the clause "in a manner that may be dangerous to public order", which was previously provided as an aggravating clause, into the constituent elements of the crime. Heavy fines stipulated in the previous text have been abolished.**

With this amendment, the freedom of expression, along with social protection, has been strengthened through the clarification of the definition of criminal offences stipulated in Article 312.

Four criminal offences, which are closely related in terms of their qualifications, have been indicated:

1. overtly praises or speaks favourably of a crime;
2. incites the public not to abide by the law;
3. overtly incites the public to hostility or to harbour resentments against one another in a manner that may be dangerous to public order on the basis of social class, race, religion, sect or regional difference;
4. insults a section of the public in a denigrating and degrading manner.

For the first criminal offence to be considered to have been committed, the perpetrator has to overtly praise or speak favourably of a crime already committed. Praising or speaking favourably in abstraction of crimes that have not yet been committed indicates either the crime of incitement to not abide by the law or the incitement to commit a crime as stipulated in Article 311.

In terms of the second criminal offence, all kinds of legal arrangements are covered by the term "law". Thus, incitement not to abide by legislative acts as well as regulations, by-laws and other arrangements issued by the administration in the framework of its competence to undertake legal arrangements also constitutes a criminal offence. Actions that may incite the public not to abide by the law have not been identified and enumerated in the Article. Therefore, concrete elements of the crime may be realised in different ways.

In cases where the perpetrator of the crime or the personality of the perpetrator that does not abide by the law is praised just for committing the crime, the criminal offence of praising the crime is considered to have taken place.

For both acts to be considered as crimes, the concrete elements must be performed overtly.

The act defined above by the clause "overtly incites the public to hostility or to harbour resentments against one another in a manner that may be dangerous to public order on the basis of social class, race, religion, sect or regional difference" is actually a "danger" crime.

"Danger" crimes create an area conducive to hesitations and misunderstandings in terms of the exercise of the right to the freedom of expression. Therefore, danger crimes are to be guarded against to the extent possible in democratic legal systems; however, individuals must take into account danger crimes as they live in an era where technology dominates to this extent.

Modern democratic societies are pluralist. This means that the society is made up of people with religious, sectoral, racial, social class and regional differences, political views and ideals, and people with different mentalities and views on ways and means to serve people in society. The democratic principle in such a social structure makes it necessary to live together in peace, continuing to integrate while being different; structural elements forming the social architecture need to continue to create a harmonious whole. If the level of integration is high, then the exercise of democratic freedom may be as high. The main basic condition of integration is to agree to treat people of different temperament, ideas, convictions and beliefs with full tolerance. Therefore, it is necessary and imperative for the legal system to bring to bear defensive measures against the danger arising from the incitement of the public to hostility or to harbour resentments against one another on the basis of social class, race, religion, sect or regional difference. This necessity is even more important for countries whose social structure is an expansive mosaic.

However, the fundamental problem is to meet this need without harming the freedom of expression and the right to propaganda.

In this respect, the modern democratic penal law implements the following method or strategy. Concrete dangers, not abstract ones, are considered to constitute danger crimes, and declarations made for various purposes are punishable only if they lead to crimes identifiable in terms of their real elements. In other words, it is necessary to look into the incitement in order to determine whether this may lead to a concrete danger. This approach — with the criteria developed by the United States Supreme Court — is in accordance with the concept of the "clear and present danger".

While this aim may be achieved with the decisions and interpretations of higher judicial organs competent to interpret in practice texts of legislation on danger crimes, that is through the interpretations of these higher institutions of texts of legislation on the basis of the probability that a concrete danger may arise, this aim may also be achieved by placing the terms and concepts indicating the concrete danger into the text of the laws. Thus, social protection and freedoms may be ensured and protected at the same time.

The criteria, which have finally been recognised by jurists, and identified and established by the United States Supreme Court and the European Court of Human Rights, are considered to be sound principles, remedies and practices to achieve, by way of interpretations, the prevention of social dangers and to ensure the freedom to criticise and the freedoms of expression and political propaganda simultaneously.

Some countries, on the other hand, which have preferred the second alternative as a strategy to eliminate the danger and at the same time ensure freedoms, have considered it appropriate to adapt texts of laws regarding this matter and to clarify them. Article 238 of the Austrian Penal Code, Article 130 of the German Penal Code and Article 24 of the 1881 French Press Code are cases in point in this regard.

Apparently, provisions similar to the provision in the second paragraph of Article 312 are also enforced in some democratic countries to reconcile the need for social peace and the freedom of criticism and expression and political propaganda.

The second paragraph of the Article has made the act a concrete danger crime in order to protect the public order and social integrity in line with the principle and strategy explicated above. The outline of the crime may be identified as such:

1. The public will be incited to hostility and to harbour resentments against one another.
2. This incitement will be by way of a dependent act that is on the basis of social class, race, religion, sect or regional difference in that the hostility or resentment is to be sown on the basis of this difference.
3. The act, statement or expressions will be undertaken in a manner that may be dangerous to public order. The decision on whether these actions demonstrate the indicated intention is to be taken by the judge, who shall keep in mind that the act must constitute a concrete danger crime. Naturally, when this decision is taken, the criteria continuously repeated by the European Court of Human Rights on this matter should be borne in mind.
4. The existence of criminal intent related to the conditions and actions indicated above will be determined.

The third paragraph of the Article defines a special type of slander or libel. For an act to constitute a crime of slander or libel, the victim must be named, or it must be possible to identify the victim. However, in foreign legislation, the insulting of groups has also been established as a crime, also known as "group libel". In this Article, in order to preserve social peace, provisions have been made for a kind of group slander or libel. In order to indicate concrete danger, the slander or libel directed to a section of the public must be undertaken in "a denigrating and degrading manner".

The last paragraph of the article stipulates that the penalties are to be doubled if the crimes are committed in the ways and means indicated in the second paragraph of Article 311.

*Article 3*

With the amendment to the second paragraph of Article 7 of the Anti-Terror Act, provisions have been made for punishment of actions of those who assist members of organisations established as defined in the first paragraph of the same Article or those who carry out propaganda on behalf of the organisation in a manner that encourages resorting to terrorist methods.

With the insertion of the clause "in a manner that encourages resorting to terrorist methods" after the clause "those who carry out propaganda on behalf of the organisation", it has been envisaged that not all propaganda, but only propaganda that encourages resorting to terrorist methods, is to be considered a crime. Thus, by extending the boundaries of the freedom of thought, an arrangement that has been sought by the European Court of Human Rights in this area has been realised.

## Article 4

With the amendments made to Article 8 of the Anti-Terror Act, the upper limit of bans on broadcasting by TV and radio institutions for offences under the third paragraph is reduced from fifteen days to seven days, and, in the aggravating situation clause in the last paragraph, the upper limit of the increase in the penalty is changed from "from one-third to half" to "one-third".

With the amendment to the first paragraph of Article 8, the specific intent to disrupt the indivisible integrity of the State of the Turkish Republic with its territory and nation has been explicitly indicated as the element of the crime. In accordance with Article 13 of the Constitution as amended by Act no. 4709, this amendment has been made as a necessary precaution in a democratic society and in proportion to the cherished aim. In addition, if the propaganda crime indicated in Article 8 is carried out in a manner that encourages resorting to terrorist methods, this has been indicated as a reason for increasing penalties in relation to the crime. Furthermore, the phrase "written and oral propaganda" in the first paragraph has been extended to cover "visual propaganda" as well, in keeping with the conditions of the times.

## Article 5

With the amendment, the second sentence of the second paragraph of Article 16 of the Act on the Establishment of and Proceedings at State Security Courts has been deleted from the text of the Article, and the third and fourth paragraphs have been revised.

With the deletion of the second sentence of the second paragraph of Article 16 of the Act, the procedure for the extension of the detention periods to up to seven days at the request of the Public Prosecutor and the decision of the judge for crimes committed collectively by the participation of three or more persons is no longer in force, and, to ensure alignment with investigations of criminal offences under the competence of other courts, the detention period has been reduced to up to four days in accordance with the amendment to Article 19 of the Constitution with Act no. 4709.

With the amendment to the third paragraph of the Article, the detention period in the state of emergency regions may be extended to up to seven days on the request of the Public Prosecutor and the decision of the judge, instead of up to ten days. Furthermore, the judge shall listen to the person who is apprehended or arrested before taking a decision.

With the amendment to the fourth paragraph of the Article, it is envisaged that the detainee may always see his or her lawyer following a written order by the Public prosecutor for the extension of the detention period.

## Article 6

In alignment with the amendment to Article 19 of the Constitution by Act no. 4709, Article 107 of the Code of Penal Procedure on "Persons to be notified of the arrest of the suspect" has been revised.

With the amendment, the two paragraphs of this Article have been revised fully. According to the new first paragraph, a relative of or a person designated by the person under arrest is to be notified without any delay of the arrest and of any decision to extend the period of arrest, with the decision of the judge. According to the new second paragraph, it is now possible for the person under arrest to notify in person a relative or a person that he or she designates, provided that this does not jeopardise the purpose of the investigation.

## Article 7

With the amendment, the second sentence of the second paragraph of Article 128 of the Code of Penal Procedure and the third paragraph have been deleted from the text of the Article. The procedure for the extension of detention periods up to seven days at the request of the Public Prosecutor and the decision of the Judge of Peace for crimes committed collectively by the participation of three or more persons are no longer in force. In accordance with the amendment to Article 19 of the Constitution with Act no. 4709, the maximum detention period for these kinds of crimes is envisaged to be up to four days. Thus, alignment with the decisions of the European Court of Human Rights and with legislation in the Member States of the European Council has been attained.

On the other hand, in accordance with the amendment to Article 19 of the Constitution, a provision has been introduced on the notification without any delay of the apprehension or the decision to extend the period of apprehension to a relative of or a person designated by the person apprehended with the decision of the Public Prosecutor.

\*\*\*

# Document no. 84

## Harmonisation package (2)[4]

### Article 1

The following clause is added to Article 29 of the Provincial Administration Act no. 5442, dated 10 June 1949.

"Only persons of the civil administrative service category may act as sub-governors."

[The amendment removed the possibility of gendarmerie commanders to act temporarily in place of governors in provinces or sub-governors in sub-governorates.]

### Article 2

**A**. The first and second paragraphs of the Supplementary Article 1 of the Act on the Press no. 5680, dated 15 July 1950, are amended as given below, and the third paragraph is repealed.

"The justice of the criminal court of peace at the investigation stage, and the competent court at the prosecution stage, on the request of the public prosecutor, may order confiscation or ban distribution of all types of printed material as a precautionary measure for the protection of the indivisible integrity of the State with its nation and territory, for national security, public order, public morals and for prevention of crime. In situations where delay may be detrimental, the public prosecutor may order confiscation or ban distribution, on his own authority, with a written decision. In such cases, the public prosecutor shall submit [his/her] decision to the approval of the competent justice of the peace within twenty-four hours. The justice of the peace shall give [his/her] judgment within forty-eight hours; otherwise the decision of the public prosecutor shall become, by default, invalid.

Machines and other printing devices, belonging to one or more offenders convicted of a crime against the indivisible integrity of the State with its nation and territory, the fundamental principles of the Republic or national security and which have been used to print periodical publications, or printed material not defined as periodicals, containing the offending material, shall also be ruled confiscated."

[The amendment removed some of the activities in the context of offences relating to the press out of the scope of the Article.]

**B.** The first and third paragraphs of the Supplementary Article 2 of the Act on the Press are amended as follows:

"In cases of conviction of the offences in the Supplementary Article 1 which are committed through the press, courts may sentence the periodical publication in which the offending Article is published to one to fifteen days stoppage."

"Those who continue to publish a periodical during the period of its stoppage, or those who publish a periodical publication clearly a continuation of the stopped periodical publication, are punished with one to three months imprisonment."

[The amendment reduced the applicable penalty limits.]

## Article 3

The following paragraph is added to the Article 13 of the Civil Servants Law no. 657, dated 14 July 1965, after the first paragraph:

"The provision in the above paragraph also applies to cases where the compensation for cruel, inhuman or degrading treatment paid by the State in compliance with the judgments of the European Court of Human Rights are recovered from the personnel responsible."

[The amendment provided for potential recourse to the personnel responsible for the cruel, inhuman, or degrading treatment for the compensation paid by the State in compliance with the judgments of the European Court of Human Rights.]

## Article 4

**A.** The following paragraph is added to the Article 101 of the Political Parties Act no. 2820, dated 22 April 1983.

"The Constitutional Court may decide, instead of permanent closure in cases described in items (a) and (b) of the above provision, to deprive the political party concerned from state aid in part or in full, according to the gravity of the offence. This may not be less than half of the latest annual assistance received by that party. If the state aid has been paid in full, it may be ruled that the said amount be returned to the Treasury."

**B.** The first and third paragraphs of the Article 102 of the Political Parties Act is amended as given below; the expressions "Chief Public Prosecutor" in the second paragraph is changed to "Chief Public Prosecutor of the Court of Cassation."

"A second writ is served to the political party which fails to submit information and documentation, requested by the Chief Public Prosecutor of the Court of Cassation for the purpose of following the activities of political parties, within the set time limit. This writ shall state that the political party concerned may be prosecuted to closure or deprivation, in part or in full, of state aid if it has not responded to and met the request within the set time limit. If the request is not met or responded to within the time stated in the writ, the Chief Public Prosecutor of the Court of Cassation may directly apply to the Constitutional Court to close the concerned political party or to deprive it, in part or in full, of state aid."

"If the political party does not meet the request in the writ within thirty days of it being served, the Chief Public Prosecutor of the Court of Cassation applies to the Constitutional Court for the closure of the concerned political party or its deprivation, in part or in full, of state aid. If the concerned political party dismisses the relevant party organ authority or committee and expels absolutely the party member or members within thirty days of the indictment being served, the case for the closure or deprivation, in part or in full, of state aid is struck off. Otherwise, the Constitutional Court, after examining the file, listening to the oral explanations of the Chief Public Prosecutor of the Court of Cassation and the representatives of the political party, and, if deemed necessary, other relevant persons and those with information on the affair, passes judgement on the case."

[With the amendments in the Articles 101–2, "deprival of the concerned political parties from state aid, in part or in full" was introduced as an alternative to permanent closure of political parties.]

**C**. The following paragraph is added to the Article 103 of the Political Parties Act.

"If acts of this nature are committed with an intense frequency by the members of a party and this circumstance is secretly or overtly accepted by the grand convention or the general chairman or the central decision-making or executive bodies or the general council of the party group in the Turkish Grand National Assembly or the group executive board or if these acts are committed directly by the said party organs in determination, the said party is said to have become the centre of execution of such acts."

[With the amendment, "the centre of execution" criteria were introduced regarding the closure of political parties. This is in line with the latest Constitutional changes.]

## Article 5

**A**. Article 4 of the Act on Associations no. 2908 of 6 October 1983 is amended as follows:

"Article 4. All legally competent persons have the right to form associations without prior permission.

However,

1. Members of the Turkish Armed Forces and general and specific security forces and public personnel with the status of civil servants who are not permitted by special laws to form associations;

2. Those, even if pardoned;

a. convicted of crimes defined in the first chapter of the second volume of the Turkish Criminal Code,

b. convicted of such offences as simple or qualified embezzlement, corruption, bribery, theft, fraud, forgery, abuse of trust, fraudulent bankruptcy, smuggling with the exception of for consumption and use, and conspiracy against official tenders, purchases and sales,

c. convicted of one of the offences set in the Articles 316, 317 and 318 of the Turkish Penal Code,

can never,

3. a. Those convicted of the offence set in the second paragraph of the Article 312 of the Turkish Penal Code, from the date on which their sentence is finalized,

b. Those who form and run banned associations and officers of associations closed by courts for banned activities, from the date on which the closure decision is finalised,

cannot for five years,

form associations."

[With the amendment, freedom of association was expanded and some prohibitions regarding the founders of associations were removed (i.e. in addition to the lifting of some other restrictions, the permanent prohibition of the convicted people under Article 312 to found associations was limited to five years).]

**B**. Item 6 of Article 5 of the Act on Associations is amended as follows:

"6. To create racial, religious, sectarian, cultural or linguistic differences within the territory of the Republic of Turkey, or to create a minority based on these, or to achieve that people of a region or race or class or a particular religion or sect be dominant over or be more privileged than others."

[The amendment removed the prohibition for founding an association "to protect, develop or expand languages or cultures other than the Turkish language or culture or to claim that they are minorities (based on racial, religious, sectarian, cultural or linguistic differences)."]

**C**. Article 6 of the Act on Associations, along with its title, is amended as follows:

"Ban on use of certain names and symbols

Article 6. Associations are banned from using the name, logo, code [acronym], badge and similar symbols of a political party extant or closed, a trade union or higher organisation, or an association or higher organisation banned under the provisions of this act or publicly recognisable flags, logos or banners of Turkish states established in the past.

Associations use Turkish in their official affairs."

[With the amendment, the freedoms of associations were expanded (i.e. while Turkish had to be used in the official affairs of associations, the prohibition that the associations cannot use languages prohibited by law was removed).]

**D**. First, second and third paragraphs of Article 34 of the Act on Associations are amended as follows:

"Federations are formed by the union of at least five associations with a common founding aim, and confederations are formed by the union of at least three federations with a common founding aim, through the bond of membership, to realise their aims.

On other matters concerning federations and confederations, the provisions of this act are applicable.

If the numbers of members of federations fall below five and if the numbers of members of confederations fall below three, and this situation is not rectified within three months, provisions of Article 51 on auto-disbandment are applied against them."

[With the amendment, the freedom of associations to establish federations was expanded.]

**E**. Article 38 of the Act on Associations is amended as follows:

"Article 38. Students registered in higher education institutions may form student associations only for the purposes of meeting training, educational, study, moral, nutritional, recreational needs, development of physical and spiritual health and representing students before the institutional authority or other institutions for these purposes."

[With the amendment, the freedoms of student associations were expanded.]

**F**. Article 43 of the Act on Associations is amended as given below.

"Article 43. Associations may invite members of associations or institutions in foreign countries to Turkey or may send abroad their members, or third parties qualified to be members in the associations, in acceptance of invitations from foreign associations or institutions, provided that the governorates of the provinces where their centres are and the activity is to take place are informed at least seven days in advance. The information given must include the purpose of the invitation, date, place, the name and address of the relevant association or institution as well as the details of the participating members or representatives."

[With the amendment, freedoms of associations were expanded by the replacement of the "permission" requirement for international activities with the "advance notice" requirement.]

## *Article 6*

**A**. Article 9 of the Law on Meetings and Demonstration Marches no. 2911, dated 6 October 1983, is amended as follows:

"Article 9. Meetings to be held in accordance with this Act are to be organised by an organising committee formed of at least seven persons who are over the age of eighteen and legally competent. This committee elects one of its members as chairperson. Persons with diplomatic immunity may not be members or chairpersons of organising committees.

Organisation of meetings and demonstration marches by legal persons depends on the decision of their competent authorities."

With the amendments, the freedoms of holding meetings and demonstration marches were expanded. [The age limit was reduced to eighteen, the requirements for membership in the organising committees were reduced and legal persons were allowed to organise meetings and demonstration marches with the consent of their competent bodies.]

**B**. Article 17 of the Law on Meetings and Demonstration Marches is amended as follows:

"Article 17. The regional governor, governor or district commissioner may ban a specific meeting or postpone it for up to a maximum of two months for reasons of national security, public order, prevention of crime, public health and public morals or protection of rights and freedoms of others."

[The freedoms of holding meetings and demonstration marches were expanded with the amendment through a reduction in the reasons allowing the local authorities to prohibit or postpone them.]

**C**. The first sentence of Article 19 of the Law on Meetings and Demonstration Marches is amended as follows:

"The regional governor may postpone all meetings in one or more provinces or in one or more districts of a province in the region, for a maximum of three months for reasons of national security, public order, prevention of crime, public health and public morals or for the protection of rights and freedoms of others."

[The amendment introduced a system of "postponement" rather than "prohibition" of meetings and reduced the reasons for postponement.]

## Article 7

The following provisions of the law are repealed.

A. Paragraph 5 of Article 16 of the Act on Press. [removing the paragraph on "publishing in a language prohibited by law".]

B. Second sentence of the first paragraph of Article 9 of the Act on Organisation, Duties and Competences of the Gendarmerie.

C. Last paragraph of Article 16 of the Act no. 2845 on the Establishment of and Proceedings of the State Security Courts, dated 16 June 1983. [The access of a person detained or taken into custody for offences under the jurisdiction of the State Security Courts to their legal counsel was guaranteed and right of defence was reinforced.]

D. Articles 7, 11 and 12 of the Law on Associations [The Articles titled "The prohibition of international activities", "The activities abroad of associations established in Turkey" and "The activities in Turkey of associations established abroad" were repealed. Provisions of Turkish Civil Code would be applied on these issues.]

E. Article 21 of the Law on Meetings and Demonstration Marches. [The Article titled "Meetings and demonstration marches not within the purpose" was repealed expanding the freedom in this area.]

***

# Document no. 85

**Council of Europe Guidelines on Human Rights and the Fight Against Terrorism**[5]

\*\*\*

*Preamble*

The Committee of Ministers,

a. Considering that terrorism seriously jeopardises Human Rights, threatens democracy, and aims notably to destabilise legitimately constituted governments and to undermine pluralistic civil society;

b. Unequivocally condemning all acts, methods and practices of terrorism as criminal and unjustifiable, wherever and by whomever committed;

c. Recalling that a terrorist act can never be excused or justified by citing motives such as Human Rights and that the abuse of rights is never protected;

d. Recalling that it is not only possible, but also absolutely necessary, to fight terrorism while respecting Human Rights, the rule of law and, where applicable, international humanitarian law;

e. Recalling the need for States to do everything possible, and notably to cooperate, so that the suspected perpetrators, organisers and sponsors of terrorist acts are brought to justice to answer for all the consequences, in particular criminal and civil, of their acts;

f. Reaffirming the imperative duty of States to protect their populations against possible terrorist acts;

g. Recalling the necessity for States, notably for reasons of equity and social solidarity, to ensure that victims of terrorist acts can obtain compensation;

h. Keeping in mind that the fight against terrorism implies long-term measures with a view to preventing the causes of terrorism, by promoting, in particular, cohesion in our societies and a multicultural and inter-religious dialogue;

i. Reaffirming States' obligation to respect, in their fight against terrorism, the international instruments for the protection of Human Rights and, for the Member States in particular, the Convention for the Protection of Human

Rights and Fundamental Freedoms and the case-law of the European Court of Human Rights; adopts the following guidelines and invites Member States to ensure that they are widely disseminated among all authorities responsible for the fight against terrorism.

## *I. States' obligation to protect everyone against terrorism*

States are under the obligation to take the measures needed to protect the fundamental rights of everyone within their jurisdiction against terrorist acts, especially the right to life. This positive obligation fully justifies States' fight against terrorism in accordance with the present guidelines.

## *II. Prohibition of arbitrariness*

All measures taken by States to fight terrorism must respect Human Rights and the principle of the rule of law, while excluding any form of arbitrariness, as well as any discriminatory or racist treatment, and must be subject to appropriate supervision.

## *III. Lawfulness of anti-terrorist measures*

1. All measures taken by States to combat terrorism must be lawful.
2. When a measure restricts Human Rights, restrictions must be defined as precisely as possible and be necessary and proportionate to the aim pursued.

## *IV. Absolute prohibition of torture*

The use of torture or of inhuman or degrading treatment or punishment is absolutely prohibited, in all circumstances, and in particular during the arrest, questioning and detention of a person suspected of or convicted of terrorist activities, irrespective of the nature of the acts that the person is suspected of or for which he/she was convicted.

## *V. Collection and processing of personal data by any competent authority in the field of State security*

Within the context of the fight against terrorism, the collection and the processing of personal data by any competent authority in the field of State security may interfere with the respect for private life only if such collection and processing, in particular:

i. are governed by appropriate provisions of domestic law;
ii. are proportionate to the aim for which the collection and the processing were foreseen;
iii. may be subject to supervision by an external independent authority.

## VI. Measures which interfere with privacy

1. Measures used in the fight against terrorism that interfere with privacy (in particular body searches, house searches, bugging, telephone tapping, surveillance of correspondence and use of undercover agents) must be provided for by law. It must be possible to challenge the lawfulness of these measures before a court.

2. Measures taken to fight terrorism must be planned and controlled by the authorities so as to minimise, to the greatest extent possible, recourse to lethal force and, within this framework, the use of arms by the security forces must be strictly proportionate to the aim of protecting persons against unlawful violence or to the necessity of carrying out a lawful arrest.

## VII. Arrest and police custody

1. A person suspected of terrorist activities may only be arrested if there are reasonable suspicions. He/she must be informed of the reasons for the arrest.

2. A person arrested or detained for terrorist activities shall be brought promptly before a judge. Police custody shall be of a reasonable period of time, the length of which must be provided for by law.

3. A person arrested or detained for terrorist activities must be able to challenge the lawfulness of his/her arrest and of his/her police custody before a court.

## VIII. Regular supervision of pre-trial detention

A person suspected of terrorist activities and detained pending trial is entitled to regular supervision of the lawfulness of his or her detention by a court.

## IX. Legal proceedings

1. A person accused of terrorist activities has the right to a fair hearing, within a reasonable time, by an independent, impartial tribunal established by law.

2. A person accused of terrorist activities benefits from the presumption of innocence.

3. The imperatives of the fight against terrorism may nevertheless justify certain restrictions to the right of defence, in particular with regard to:

i. the arrangements for access to and contacts with counsel;
ii. the arrangements for access to the case-file;
iii. the use of anonymous testimony.

4. Such restrictions to the right of defence must be strictly proportionate to their purpose, and compensatory measures to protect the interests of the accused must be taken so as to maintain the fairness of the proceedings and to ensure that procedural rights are not drained of their substance.

## X. Penalties incurred

1. The penalties incurred by a person accused of terrorist activities must be provided for by law for any action or omission which constituted a criminal offence at the time when it was committed; no heavier penalty may be imposed than the one that was applicable at the time when the criminal offence was committed.

2. Under no circumstances may a person convicted of terrorist activities be sentenced to the death penalty; in the event of such a sentence being imposed, it may not be carried out.

## XI. Detention

1. A person deprived of his/her liberty for terrorist activities must in all circumstances be treated with due respect for human dignity.

2. The imperatives of the fight against terrorism may nevertheless require that a person deprived of his/her liberty for terrorist activities be submitted to more severe restrictions than those applied to other prisoners, in particular with regard to:

i. the regulations concerning communications and surveillance of correspondence, including that between counsel and his/her client;
ii. placing persons deprived of their liberty for terrorist activities in specially secured quarters;
iii. the separation of such persons within a prison or among different prisons, on condition that the measure taken is proportionate to the aim to be achieved.

\*\*\* [Asylum, return ("refoulement") and expulsion; and Extradition]

## XIV. Right to property

The use of the property of persons or organisations suspected of terrorist activities may be suspended or limited, notably by such measures as freezing orders or seizures, by the relevant authorities. The owners of the property have the possibility to challenge the lawfulness of such a decision before a court.

## XV. Possible derogations

1. When the fight against terrorism takes place in a situation of war or public emergency which threatens the life of the nation, a State may adopt measures temporarily derogating from certain obligations ensuing from the international instruments of protection of Human Rights, to the extent strictly required by the exigencies of the situation, as well as within the limits and under the conditions fixed by international law. The State must notify the competent authorities of the adoption of such measures in accordance with the relevant international instruments.

2. States may never, however, and whatever the acts of the person suspected of terrorist activities, or convicted of such activities, derogate from the right to life as guaranteed by these international instruments, from the prohibition against torture or inhuman or degrading treatment or punishment, from the principle of legality of sentences and of measures, nor from the ban on the retrospective effect of criminal law.

3. The circumstances that led to the adoption of such derogations need to be reassessed on a regular basis with the purpose of lifting these derogations as soon as these circumstances no longer exist.

## *XVI. Respect for peremptory norms of international law and for international humanitarian law*

In their fight against terrorism, States may never act in breach of peremptory norms of international law nor in breach of international humanitarian law, where applicable.

## *XVII. Compensation for victims of terrorist acts*

When compensation is not fully available from other sources, in particular through the confiscation of the property of the perpetrators, organisers and sponsors of terrorist acts, the State must contribute to the compensation of the victims of attacks that took place on its territory, as far as their person or their health is concerned.

# Document no. 86

**Editors' comment on ECtHR decisions in 2002[6] and PACE [Council of Europe Parliamentary Assembly] Resolution no. 1297 (2002): Implementation of Decisions of the European Court of Human Rights by Turkey[7]**

During 2002, the ECtHR ruled against the Republic of Turkey in fifty-four cases. Twenty-two of these cases involved the right to a fair trial, twenty-one cases involved dispossession of property (from villages in the southeast), six cases involved freedom of expression, five cases involved the unlawful deprivation of life, six cases involved unlawful arrest and detention, and three cases involved torture. The government accepted a friendly settlement in forty-three cases, and the ECtHR dismissed one case.

In two cases the ECtHR ruled in favor of the government. Between October 2001 and July 2002, 1,874 applications regarding Turkey were made to the ECtHR. The majority of these, 1,125 cases, involved the right to a fair trial, 304 concerned the right to liberty and security, 246 concerned the prohibition of torture, 104 concerned the freedom of assembly and association, and ninety-five concerned freedom of expression.

According to the Parliamentary Assembly of the Council of Europe and the Council of Europe Commission, the government's failure to execute ECtHR judgments remained a serious problem. In a resolution dated September 23, 2002, Resolution 1297 (2002): Implementation of Decisions of the European Court of Human Rights by Turkey, the PACE listed the oldest and/or most important cases still unresolved. These cases "notably raised issues relating to respect for life (Article 2 of the European Convention on Human Rights) and the prohibition of torture (Article 3), freedom of expression (Article 10) and the right to a fair trial (Article 6)."

After welcoming "the constitutional and legal changes which have taken place in Turkey ... which will contribute to preventing the repetition of violations of the Convention in the future," and "the progress made with the reform aimed at ensuring that the security forces and other law enforcement authorities respect the Convention in all circumstances," the Resolution noted that "despite the progress recently achieved, the Assembly cannot but regret that a number of important problems remain outstanding."

Accordingly, the Assembly "reiterate[d] its calls upon the Turkish authorities to ensure rapidly that: the modalities of payment of just satisfaction respect the judgments of the Court (ninety cases); the recently adopted legislation on the reopening of judicial proceedings is given immediate effect and made applicable to all cases pending before the Committee of Ministers for control of execution, so as to enable the consequences of the violations found to be remedied; legislation be adopted to allow the consequences of the violations of the Convention to be immediately erased, including by restoring the applicants' civil and political rights (eighteen cases of freedom of expression); further legislative action is rapidly taken to ensure respect for freedom of expression, notably in application of the anti-terror legislation; further progress is made in preventing, through development of the training of the security forces and the development of effective criminal and civil remedies, new violations notably of Articles 2 and 3 of the Convention (thirty-eight cases concerning actions by the security forces); ... the necessary legislative amendments in the Zana case are adopted without further delay."

# Document no. 87

## Harmonisation package (3)[8]

### Article 1

A. Excluding death penalties envisaged for crimes committed in the time of war or during the imminent threat of war, the death penalties foreseen in the Turkish Penal Code no. 765 dated 1.3.1926, Law no. 1918 on the Interdiction and Pursuit of Smuggling dated 7.1.1932 and Forests Law no. 6831 dated 31.8.1956 shall be converted into heavy life imprisonment.

In so far as,

a. The provisions of Articles 47, 50, 51, 55, 58, 59, 61, 62, 64, 65, 66, 102, 112, 451, 452, 462 and 463 of the Turkish Penal Code and Article 12 of Law no. 2253 on the Establishment, Duties and Trial Procedures of Juvenile Courts dated 7.11.1979 relating to the death penalty and,

b. Provisions on individuals who have received death sentences on the basis of Article 17 of the Turkish Penal Code and Article 19 and Additional Article 2 of the Law on the Execution of Penalties dated 13.7.1965, and whose death sentences have been commuted by the Turkish Grand National Assembly, are legally guaranteed.

B. According to the provisions of this Law, the time periods envisaged in Articles 70, 73 and 82 of the Turkish Penal Code for those individuals whose death sentences have been converted into heavy life imprisonment shall be doubled for ordinary and tripled for terror-related criminals.

According to the provisions of this Law, the provisions of the Law on the Execution of Penalties and the Anti-Terror Law no. 3713 dated 12.4.1991 relating to conditional release shall not be applied to individuals whose death sentences have been converted to heavy life imprisonment. The heavy life imprisonment of such individuals shall continue until their death.

### Article 2

A. The following paragraph has been added to Article 159 of the Turkish Penal Code:

"Written, oral or visual expressions of thought made only for criticism, without the intention to insult or deride the bodies or institutions listed in the first paragraph, do not require a penalty."

\*\*\* [With another amendment to the TPC 201(a)–(b), new definitions and measures were introduced to remedy the lack of a special provision in the Turkish Penal Code against trafficking of migrants and especially the forced labor or conditions akin to slavery, of foreigners arriving from other countries as economic refugees. This issue has recently become prominent in both Europe's and Turkey's agenda.]

## Article 3

A. The Article 11 of Law no. 2908 on Associations dated 6.10.1983, which is no longer in force, has been amended along with its title to read as follows:

*"The activities undertaken abroad by associations established in Turkey"*

*Article 11.* — In cases where international cooperation is deemed to be useful, the establishment of associations that will be active internationally, the establishment of branches abroad by these associations, their membership to or cooperation with associations or organisations established abroad for similar purposes or holding international activities is contingent upon the permission of the Council of Ministers upon the proposal of the Ministry of Interior, in consultation with the Ministry of Foreign Affairs.

The association or supra-organisation that wishes to become a member of or cooperate with an association or organisation abroad shall be obliged to provide the Ministry of Interior with two copies of a document detailing the status of that association or organisation, translated into Turkish and approved by a notary.

If the foreign associations or organisations in which associations in Turkey are members or cooperate with in activities that are against our laws or our national interests, the relations of the association established in Turkey with these associations or organisations shall be terminated by a decision of the Council of Ministers upon a proposal submitted by the Ministry of Interior in consultation with Ministry of Foreign Affairs.

B. The repealed Article 12 of the Law on Associations, together with its title is amended as follows:

*"The activities in Turkey of associations established abroad"*

*Article 12.*—In cases where international cooperation is deemed to be useful and reciprocal, in order to benefit from their knowledge and technologies in the fields of culture, economics, technical matters, sports and science, associations established abroad can be permitted by a decision of the Council of Ministers, upon the proposal of the Ministry of Interior in consultation with the Ministry of Foreign Affairs, to establish branches in Turkey, to become members of or cooperate with associations established in Turkey and to undertake activities in Turkey.

In cases where the abovementioned associations are involved in activities that are against our laws or national interests, the permission can be revoked by a decision of the Council of Ministers acting on the proposal of the Ministry of Interior in consultation with the Ministry of Foreign Affairs.

C. The first and second paragraphs of Article 15 of the Law on Associations have been amended to read as follows:

"An Associations Register shall be created at the Department of Associations in the Ministry of Interior and at the governorates of the provinces for the registration of associations.

All confederations, federations and associations, in addition to their branches and headquarters, and the branches in Turkey of associations whose headquarters are abroad, shall be registered in the Associations Register at the Department of Associations."

D. The title and paragraph 1 of Article 40 of the Law on Associations are changed in the following manner:

"*Prohibition on activities preparing individuals for National Defence and police services*

Associations cannot undertake educational or training activities for preparation for military, national defence and police services. They cannot create camps or training grounds for these purposes."

E. Article 45 of the Law on Associations together with its title is changed in the following manner:

"*The obligation to submit a declaration and inspection*

Article 45.—At the end of each year, associations are required to submit a declaration to the highest ranking gubernatorial administrator in their area regarding their activities, revenues and expenses prepared according to the regulation to be issued by the Ministry of Interior.

When deemed necessary, the administrative centres, facilities and all annexed buildings, books, accounts and transactions of associations may always be inspected/audited by the Ministry of Interior or the highest gubernatorial authority of their location. The Ministry of Interior shall carry out the audit through the staff of its Department of Associations or through the Prime Ministry Inspection Board or the highest ranking gubernatorial administrators themselves or through officials they designate.

The Ministries relevant to their aims and activities can also inspect associations. The results of these audits are forwarded to the Ministry of Interior for information.

All information, documents and records that may be requested by the officials in charge during the audit must be shown or provided by the association staff and all requests by the officials of entering administrative centres, facilities and annexes must be met.

If acts that constitute a crime are encountered during the inspection, the relevant gubernatorial authority immediately notifies the Public Prosecutor."

F. Article 46 of the Law on Associations and its title have been changed as follows:

"*The Department of Associations*

Article 46. — A Department of Associations shall be established within the Ministry of Interior to carry out services related to associations, to inspect if their operations are in line with the objectives specified in their statutes and if activities are undertaken to achieve those objectives, and whether they keep their books and accounts according to the regulations and their statutes. The establishment, operation and auditing principles and procedures of this unit shall be determined by a regulation to be prepared by the Ministry of Interior."

G. Article 62 of the Law on Associations is changed as follows:

"*Article 62.* — The principles and procedures relating to books to be kept by associations shall be determined by a regulation to be prepared jointly by the Ministries of Interior and Finance. These books must be approved by a notary."

H. Article 73 of the Law on Associations is changed in the following manner:

"*Article 73.* — A unit shall be established by the Ministry of Interior within the governorates in the provinces and within the prefectures in the districts to carry out the procedures and services relating to associations.

The organisation, duties and responsibilities of this unit in the provinces and the form, organisation and registration procedures of the Associations Register to be established under Article 15 shall be elaborated in a regulation to be prepared by the Ministry of Interior."

## Article 4

[With an amendment of Article 1 of the Law on Foundations, foundations, regardless of whether or not they have a "charter of foundation," could acquire and dispose of real property with the permission of the Council of Ministers. With another amendment, the activities of foundations established abroad that may wish to establish branches or already have established branches in Turkey were regulated.]

## Article 5

A. The second paragraph of Article 3 of Law no. 2911 dated 6.10.1983 on Meetings and Demonstrations is changed as follows:

"The organisation of meetings and demonstrations by foreigners in accordance with the provisions of this Law requires the permission of the Ministry of Interior. Foreigners can address a crowd and carry posters, placards, pictures, flags, inscriptions and equipment as long as the highest gubernatorial authority of the meeting's location [is not fixed] at least forty-eight hours before the meeting."

B. The first paragraph of Article 10 of the Law on Meetings and Demonstrations is changed in the following manner:

"In order for a meeting to be held, a notice to be signed by all members of the organisational committee must be submitted to the governorate or the prefect with jurisdiction over the locale of the meeting at least forty-eight hours before the meeting and within working hours."

## Article 6

A. The following Article 445/A is added to come after Article 445 of Law no. 1086 on Legal Procedures, dated 18.6.1927:

"Article 445/A. — If a final or finalised decision is found by the European Court of Human Rights to be in violation of the Convention on the Protection of Human Rights and Fundamental Freedoms or its annexed protocols and if the results of this violation cannot be compensated for as provided for in Article 41 of the Convention due to the character or significance of the particular violation; the Minister of Justice, the Chief Public Prosecutor at the Court of Appeals, the individual who has applied to the European Court of Human Rights or his/her legal representative can apply for a retrial to First Presidency of the Court of Appeals within a year of the finalisation of the decision of the European Court of Human Rights.

This request is to be reviewed in the General Legal Council of the Court of Appeals. If the results of the violation confirmed by the European Court of Human Rights are compensated or if the request has not been filed within the specified period, it is rejected. Otherwise, the file will be forwarded without a hearing to the court that has made the decision."

B. The following provision is added as the last paragraph to Article 448 of the Law on Legal Procedures:

"The provisions of Article 445/A are exceptions."

## Article 7

A. The following Article 327/a has been inserted after Article 327 of the Code of Criminal Procedure no. 1412 dated 4.4.1929:

"Article 327/a. — If a finalised judgment is found by the European Court of Human Rights to be in violation of the Convention on the Protection of Human Rights and Fundamental Freedoms or its annexed protocols and if the results of this violation cannot be compensated for as provided for in Article 41 of the Convention due to the character or significance of the particular violation; the Minister of Justice, the Chief Public Prosecutor of the Court of Appeals, the applicant to the European Court of Human Rights or his/her legal representative can apply for a retrial to First Presidency of the Court of Appeals within a year of the finalisation of the decision of the European Court of Human Rights.

This request is to be reviewed in the General Legal Council of the Court of Appeals. If the results of the violation confirmed by the European Court of Human Rights have been compensated for or if the request has not been filed within the specified period, the application is rejected. Otherwise, the file will be sent without a hearing to the court that has made the decision for re-examination."

B. The following provision is added as a last paragraph to Article 335 of the Code of Criminal Procedures:

The provisions of Article 327/a are exceptions.

## Article 8

A. The following provisions have been added to the first paragraph of Article 4 of the Law no. 3984 on the Establishment and Broadcasting of Radio Stations and Television Channels, dated 13.4.1994:

"Furthermore, there may be broadcasts in the different languages and dialects used traditionally by Turkish citizens in their daily lives. Such broadcasts shall not contradict the fundamental principles of the Turkish Republic enshrined in the Constitution and the indivisible integrity of the state with its territory and nation. The principles and procedures for these broadcasts and the supervision of these broadcasts shall be determined through a regulation to be issued by the Supreme Board."

B. The sub-paragraphs (f) and (v) of the second paragraph of Article 4 of the Law on the Establishment and Broadcasting of Radio Stations and Television Channels have been amended as to read as follows:

"f. The privacy of private life shall be respected.

v. The broadcasts shall not encourage the use of violence or incite feelings of racial hatred."

C. The first paragraph of Article 26 of the Law on the Establishment and Broadcasting of Radio Stations and Television Channels has been amended to read as follows:

"The re-transmission of the broadcasts shall be allowed provided that it does not contradict with this Law. The principles and procedures relating to re-transmission shall be by a regulation to be issued by the Supreme Board."

## Article 9

\*\*\* [The scope of freedom of the press was expanded by the amendments to the Press Act removing the then applicable prison sentences for offenses related to the press. Furthermore, Article 31 and the Supplementary Article 3 were removed to expand the scope of the freedom of thought and the press and to ensure alignment with international conventions in which Turkey participates.]

## Article 10

\*\*\*

B. Article 9 of the Law no. 2559 on the Duties and Competences of the Police has been amended to read as follows:

"Article 9.—In order to protect the national security, public order, public health and morality, or the rights and freedoms of others, to prevent crime and to identify any type of arms, explosive substances or object whose possession, or carrying of, is prohibited, the police may undertake searches on individuals, their vehicles, personal documents and belongings with a decision taken through appropriate procedures by the judge or the written instruction of the highest ranking gubernatorial administrator in the locale in cases where a delay may be detrimental, in the following places:

A. The places of meetings and demonstrations which come under the scope of the Law no. 2911 on Meetings and Demonstrations or areas adjacent to these places,

B. Areas adjacent to places where the board meetings of private legal entities, and professional associations and trades unions with the status of a public institutions are held,
C. In places where the public may assemble or are present in groups,
D. In order to ensure freedom of education, educational institutions at all levels, the universities, independent faculties or affiliated institutions to be attended in line with Article 20 paragraph 2 sub-paragraph (A), areas adjacent to, and the entrances and exits of, such places,
E. Public places, places open to the public, student dormitories and annexed buildings,
F. The entrances and exits of settlements,
G. In all kinds of public transportation or moving vehicles.

Following the search, the police shall confiscate any criminal object and shall refer it to the office of the public prosecutor, along together with the documents.

For any search to be conducted by the police in order to identify the clues, indications, circumstantial evidence or proof of a crime or to apprehend its perpetrators in accordance with the Law on Criminal Procedure and other laws, the appropriate decision of the judge or where a delay may cause harmful effects, the written order of the competent body authorised by other laws, shall be necessary.

The search and seizure of published works in the scope of Press Act no. 5680 shall be subject to the general provisions."

C. Article 11 paragraph (C) of the Law on the Duties and Competences of the Police has been amended to read as follows:

"Those who produce and sell any kind of audio-visual work against general morality and decency, regardless of the type of material used for recording,"

D. Article 12 of the Law on the Duties and Competences of the Police has been amended to read as follows:

"Article 12—Persons under 18 cannot be employed in establishments serving alcohol, providing entertainment and gaming and similar establishments that are open to the public and whose establishment requires prior permission, with the exceptions provided for by law being reserved. The police shall prohibit the entry of those under eighteen to places serving alcohol, such as bars, nightclubs, casinos, taverns and traditional coffee houses and gaming establishments even if they are accompanied by their parents or legal guardians. For individuals and workplaces who breach the provisions of this Article, necessary action shall be carried out in accordance with the provisions of Article 17 for individuals and Article 8 for workplaces."

E. Article 13 of the Law on the Duties and Competences of the Police has been amended to read as follows:

"Article 13—The police shall apprehend and carry out the necessary procedures on the below:

A. Those caught in flagrante delicto or where a delay may cause harmful effect, the suspects for whom there are significant signs, indications, circumstantial evidence or proof that a crime has been committed or there has been an attempt to commit a crime,

B. Those for whom there is an apprehension or arrest warrant issued by the competent authorities,

\*\*\*

Any measure that does not harm the detainees' health can be taken in order to prevent them from escaping or attacking.

The detainees shall be notified of the apprehension reasons in writing; if this is not possible then they shall immediately be informed of the reasons verbally; in cases of collective crimes they shall be informed at the latest prior to being taken to the presence of the judge.

The apprehension of the person shall immediately be reported to those legally defined relations to be specified by the detainee.

Upon apprehension, the health situation of the below shall be determined with a physician's report:

A. Those who are drunk or have used drugs,
B. Those who have been apprehended through the use of force,
C. Suspects and accused against whom a criminal investigation is to be conducted.

The detainees who are suspected of committing a crime shall be referred to the judicial authorities. Those for whom rehabilitation or treatment is necessary shall be referred to authorities of the relevant institutions. Those for whom the apprehension reason ceases to exist shall immediately be released."

F. Additional Article 1 of the Law on the Duties and Competences of the Police has been amended to read as follows:

"Additional Article 1.—Natural persons or communities may stage plays or performances or organise various types of shows in public places, places that are open to the public or on public transport, provided that they notify in writing the highest ranking gubernatorial administrator in the locale at least forty-eight hours in advance.

The highest ranking gubernatorial administrator of the locale shall immediately lodge a complaint to the public prosecutor about those who are found to be against the indivisible integrity of the state with its territory and nation, the Constitutional order or public morality.

The notification made pursuant to paragraph 1 shall indicate the identity, residential address and nationality of the managers and other persons who have participated in the play or performance."

### *Article 11*

A. The name of the "Foreign Language Education and Teaching Law" no. 2923, dated 14.10.1983, has been changed to the "Law on Foreign Language

Education and Teaching, and the Learning of Different Languages and Dialects by Turkish Citizens".

B. Article 1 of the Law on Foreign Language Education and Teaching has been amended to read as follows:

"Article 1.—The purpose of this law is to regulate the procedures pertaining to the teaching of foreign languages in educational institutes, schools instructing in a foreign language and the learning of different languages and dialects traditionally used by Turkish citizens in their daily lives."

C. The following provisions have been added to Article 2 paragraph (a) of the Law on Foreign Language Education and Teaching:

"Private courses subject to the provisions of the Law on Private Educational Institutions no. 625, dated 8.6.1965, can be opened to enable the learning of the different languages and dialects used traditionally by Turkish citizens in their daily lives. Such courses cannot be against the fundamental principles of the Turkish Republic enshrined in the Constitution and the indivisible integrity of the state with its territory and nation. The procedures and principles related to the opening and regulation of these courses shall be undertaken through a regulation to be issued by the Ministry of National Education."

## *Article 12*

The following provisions have been repealed:

A. Articles 39, 47 and 56 of the Law on Associations,
B. Additional Article 1 and Article 31 of the Press Act,
C. The final paragraph of Article 11 of the Law the Duties and Competences of the Police,
D. Provisional Article 1 of the Law no. 3218 on Free Zones, dated 6.6.1985.

## *Provisional Article 1*

The following cases of persons who have been sentenced to capital punishment due to having committed a crime within the scope of Article 1 paragraph (A) before this code comes into force, shall be considered to be priority cases and shall be decided on by the bodies referred to below with consideration to Article 2 of the Turkish Penal Code:

a. The files that have not yet been sent to the Court of Appeals or that are presently in the Office of the Chief Public Prosecutor of the Court of Appeals and the ones which have already been sent to the Turkish Grand National Assembly by the court which decided the case,

b. The cases which are already in the Court of Appeals, by the relevant criminal chamber.

The cases at the Office of the Chief Public Prosecutor of the Court of Appeals or the Turkish Grand National Assembly shall be sent back to the court that has decided on the case within one month after the entry into force of this law, in accordance with the procedures by which it was sent.

The provisions of this Article shall be applied by means of comparison to the cases at Military Courts, Office of the Chief Public Prosecutor of the Military Court of Appeals and the Military Court of Appeals.

## *Provisional Article 2*

Articles 6 and 7 of this law shall be applicable to decisions taken pursuant to applications lodged at the European Court of Human Rights after the entry into force of these Articles.

\*\*\*

## *General reasoning*

With the amendment of the Constitution on 3.10.2001 through the adoption of Law no. 4709, a new system was put in place, which guarantees that fundamental rights and freedoms can be restricted only by law and only based on reasons stated in the relevant Articles of the Constitution. This expands the scope of basic rights and liberties.

The EU–Turkey relations, which acquired a new dimension with the acceptance of Turkey's candidacy for full membership at the European Union Summit in Helsinki on 10–11 December 1999, have been intensifying with time. In the process for full membership, both Turkey and the EU have reciprocal obligations. Within this context, an "Accession Partnership" Document for Turkey was approved on 4 December 2000 and "The National Programme of Turkey for the Harmonisation of the European Union *Acquis Communitaire*" was adopted by the Decision no. 2001/2129 of the Council of Ministers on 19 March 2001 and the Programme entered into force after its publication in the Official Gazette no. 24352 on 24 March 2001.

Modern democracies are pluralist systems based on participation and tolerance that aim to guarantee basic rights and liberties. The recognition of Human Rights and basic liberties has not only has become a matter of universal interest in our time but international organisations have also been formed to guarantee these rights, to prevent their violation and to promote them further, and various international documents have been adopted by these organisations. Some of the most prominent of these organisations are the United Nations, which covers nearly all the world's countries, and the Council of Europe, which is a political union of democratic states in Europe. The most important of the related international documents is the Universal Declaration of Human Rights adopted by the General Assembly of the United Nations on 10 December 1948 and the Convention on the Protection of Human Rights and Fundamental Freedoms, and its annexed protocols, signed within the Council of Europe and is known as the "European Convention on Human Rights".

The Turkish Civil Code no. 4721, dated 22.11.2001, and Law no. 4722, on the Entry into Force and Implementation of the Turkish Civil Code, dated

3.12.2001, were published in the Official Gazette no. 24607 on 8.12.2001 and entered into force on 1.1.2002.

This proposal has been prepared, on the one hand, with the intention of ensuring harmonisation with the changes made in the Constitution and the provisions of the Turkish Civil Code and amending, on the other hand, various laws in line with the obligations under the National Programme of Turkey for the Adoption of the European Union *Acquis Communitaire*.

## Article justifications

*Article 1.* Paragraph (A) of the Article converts the death penalties stipulated in the Turkish Penal Code, the Law on the Prevention and Monitoring of Smuggling and Forests Law into heavy life imprisonment. However, crimes committed in time of war or during an imminent threat of war have been excluded from the provisions of this Article, as provided for Article 38 of the Constitution, as amended by Law no. 4709.

With this Article, according to the provisions of this Law, Articles 47, 50, 51, 55, 58, 59, 61, 62, 64, 65, 66, 102, 112, 451, 452, 462 and 463 of the Turkish Penal Code and Article 12 of Law no. 2253 on the Establishment, Duties and Trial Procedures of Juvenile Courts relating to the death penalty are reserved, and these provisions will continue to apply to those whose death sentences have been converted into heavy life imprisonment. According to the Article, for instance, the reduction foreseen in the first paragraph of Article 61 of Law no. 765, for sentences given to an individual who partially attempts a crime that requires the death penalty in the relevant Articles of the law, shall be applied to the sentences of heavy life imprisonment which are converted from a death sentence as well, and the perpetrator shall be sentenced to fifteen to twenty years of heavy imprisonment.

Sub-paragraph (b) of the paragraph states that the provisions for those individuals who have received death sentences based on Article 17 of the Turkish Penal Code and Article 19 of Law 647 on the Execution of Penalties and whose death sentences have been overturned by the Turkish Grand National Assembly have been reserved and these provisions shall continue to be applied to sentences of heavy life imprisonment converted from death sentences. The provision in Additional Article 2 of Law no. 647 that stipulates no reduction of the sentences of those individuals whose death sentences have been overturned by the Turkish Grand National Assembly shall continue to be applied to sentences of heavy life imprisonment converted from death sentences.

Paragraph (B) of the Article states that the time periods stipulated in Articles 70, 73 and 82 of the Turkish Penal Code for those individuals whose death sentences have been converted into heavy life imprisonment shall be doubled for ordinary and tripled for terror-related criminals, that the provisions of the Law on the Execution of Penalties and the Anti-Terror Law relating to conditional release shall not be implemented for those individuals whose death sentences have been converted into heavy life imprisonments and that the heavy life imprisonment of such individuals shall continue until their death.

*Article 2.* With paragraph (A) of the Article, a last paragraph is being added to Article 159 of the Turkish Penal Code. The Article states that written, oral or visual expressions of thought made with the intention of criticism without a deliberate attempt to insult or deride the bodies and institutions listed in paragraph 1 do not require a penalty. In this way, no penalties have been stipulated for expressions of thought that remain within the scope of the freedom of thought and expression and are aimed at criticism.

\*\*\*

*Article 3.* Paragraph (A) of the Article amends the abolished Article 11 of Law no. 2908. With this amendment, the principles and procedures relating to the activities abroad of associations established in Turkey are regulated.

Paragraph (B) of the Article amends the abolished Article 12 of the Law and specifies the principles and procedures relating to the activities in Turkey of associations established abroad.

Paragraph (C) of the Article amends Article 15 of the Law and states that that the Associations Register shall be kept and the registration procedures shall be carried out by the Department of Associations within the Ministry of Interior and the governorates.

Paragraph (D) of the Article amends Article 40 of the Law and removes the prohibitions on civil defence activities from the Article. The useful activities of search and rescue associations set up by Turkish citizens after the earthquake of 17 August 1999 has led to the need for this new arrangement.

Paragraph (E) of the Article amends Article 45 of the Law and introduces the declaration procedure in the inspection of associations, replacing the existing practice of inspection on location. However, in cases where it is deemed necessary, the inspection of associations by the staff of the Department of Associations or the Inspection Board of the Ministry of Interior, by the highest gubernatorial authorities and by relevant ministries, public bodies and institutions is also provided. The results of these inspections are to be forwarded to the Ministry of Interior to ensure the collection of the information on associations in a single archive.

In addition, the following provision has been included in the Article: "If actions that constitute a crime are encountered during the inspection/audit, the relevant gubernatorial authority shall notify the Public Prosecutor immediately."

Paragraph (F) of the Article amends Article 46 of the Law and aims for the institution of a "Department of Associations" within the central structure of the Ministry of Interior to carry out the services related to associations and their inspection in a more effective and coordinated manner.

Paragraph (G) of the Article amends Article 62 of the Law and states that the principles and procedures relating to the keeping of books, which have to be approved by a notary, by associations shall be determined through a regulation to be prepared by the Ministries of Interior and Finance; thereby aiming to ensure compliance with the rapid economic and technological developments of our time and to prevent too detailed an elaboration in the law itself.

Paragraph (H) of the Article amends Article 73 of the Law and specifies the organisation of central and provincial units that will be responsible for the effective provision of services to associations and their inspection/auditing in their respective areas.

*Article 4.* With the amendment made to paragraph (A) of the Article, harmonisation has been achieved with the principles of the prohibition of discrimination in the European Convention on Human Rights and the protection of property rights guaranteed in Annexed Protocol 1 of the Convention. In this way, community foundations are provided with the possibility of acquiring and disposing of immovables.

\*\*\*

*Article 5.* Paragraph (A) of the Article amends the second paragraph of Article 3 of the Law and, while retaining the existing system where foreigners have to obtain permission from the Ministry of Interior to organise meetings and demonstrations, it abolishes the permission system for foreigners addressing a crowd at a meeting or demonstration or carrying posters, placards, pictures, flags, inscriptions and equipment, replacing it with the notification system.

With the amendment made to paragraph (B) of the Article, the notification period stipulated in Article 10 of the law has been reduced from seventy-two hours to forty-eight hours.

*Article 6.* By adding 445/A to Article 445 of the Law on Legal Procedures, the final decisions of our national courts which were found by the European Court of Human Rights to have violated the Convention on the Protection of Human Rights and Fundamental Freedoms or its additional protocols and which were understood to have caused results that could not be compensated under Article 41 of the Convention due to the nature or gravity of the violation, are now being considered as reasons for retrial.

On the other hand, this Article further defines those who may apply for retrial upon ECtHR judgments of violation and the procedures regarding how the application will be processed.

Following the violation judgments of the European Court of Human Rights, due to the importance of the issue, the processing of the retrial applications was transferred to the Court of Appeals (CoA) General Legal Council by the first Presidency of the CoA. Furthermore, the retrial application period, which shall commence once the judgment of the ECtHR becomes final, shall be limited to one year. Applications lodged after one year shall be refused. The abovementioned application period shall start after the judgment becomes final in accordance with Article 44 of the European Convention on Human Rights.

If the CoA General Legal Council finds that for the consequences of the violation determined by the ECtHR has been compensated or if the retrial application has not been filed during the course of the application period, then the retrial application shall be rejected. If the consequences of the violation determined by the ECtHR have not been compensated, then the case shall be sent to the court responsible for the decision. In the Article it is also stated that the decisions of the CoA General Legal Council as regards retrial shall be given without a hearing and these decisions shall be final.

With paragraph (B) of the Article, a paragraph has been added to Article 448 of the Law on Legal Procedures in order to ensure its conformity with the added Article of 445/A of the Law, thus the said provision has been preserved.

*Article 7.* With paragraph (A) of the Article, a final decision which was found to have violated the Convention on the Protection of Human Rights and Fundamental Freedoms or its additional protocols by the European Court of Human Rights and which was understood to have created irreparable damage (that cannot be compensated) according to Article 41 of the Convention due to the nature and gravity of the violation, is now being considered as a reason for the reinstitution of the proceedings in favour of the convict.

On the other hand, this Article further regulates who can apply for the reinstitution of the proceedings upon ECtHR judgment confirming violation and the procedures regarding how the application will be processed.

Following the judgments of the European Court of Human Rights, the processing of the applications for the reinstitution of the proceedings were transferred to the Court of Appeals (CoA) General Legal Council by the first Presidency of the CoA, due to the importance of the issue. Furthermore, the application period for the reinstitution of the proceedings, which shall commence once the judgment of the ECtHR becomes final, shall be limited to one year. The abovementioned application period shall start after the judgment becomes final in accordance with Article 44 of the European Convention on Human Rights.

If the consequences of the violation determined by the ECtHR have been compensated or the application for the reinstitution of the proceedings has not been filed during the application period, then application for the reinstitution of the proceedings shall be rejected by CoA General Criminal Council; otherwise the case shall be sent to the court which has judged the case. The Article also states that the decisions of the CoA General Criminal Council as regards reinstitution of the proceedings shall be taken without a hearing and that these decisions shall be final.

With paragraph (B) of the Article, a paragraph has been added to Article 335 of the Law on Criminal Procedures in order to ensure its conformity with the added Article of 327/a of the Law, and the said provision in the Article has been preserved.

*Article 8.* By amending Article 4 of the Law no. 3984 with paragraph (A) of the Article, it has aimed to enhance cultural life within the scope of individual rights and freedoms, in line with the objectives of the Accession Partnership document and the NPAA [National Programme for the Adoption of the *Acquis*] of Turkey. This arrangement has secured conformity with the amendments made to Articles 26 and 28 of the Constitution with Law no. 4709. This amendment is also in line with the international conventions of the Council of Europe where Turkey is a founding member and the Copenhagen political criteria. With the amendment made to the "Law on the Establishment and Broadcasting of Radio Stations and Television Channels" by Law no. 4756, although Turkish will be the basis of TV and radio broadcasts, broadcasts in different languages and dialects used by Turkish citizens in their daily lives is made possible. Furthermore, it has been emphasised that such broadcasts cannot be against the fundamental principles of the Republic enshrined in the Constitution and the indivisible integrity of the state with its territory and nation.

With paragraph (B) of the Article, paragraph (v), one of the broadcasting principles which may lead to vague interpretations; the phrase that "broadcasts, which provoke pessimism, desperation, disorder and violence" has been removed from the Article and this paragraph has been re-written.

Another amendment made with Article (C) has clarified the issue of re-transmission and has provided that the principles and procedures governing re-transmission shall be regulated with a regulation to be prepared by the Supreme Board.

*Article 9.* With paragraph (A) of the Article, the phrase which reads as "the crimes listed under additional Article 1 paragraph 2 of this law" in Article 5 paragraph 3 sub-paragraph (6) of the Press Act has been amended as "the crimes listed under additional Article 1 paragraph 1 of this law".

Furthermore, with the amendments made to paragraphs (B), (C), (D), (E), (F), (G) and (H) of the Article, the fines in Articles 21, 22, 24, 25, 30 and 34 of the Act no. 5680 have been updated to ensure deterrence, and the penalties restricting freedom have been removed from the text.

*Article 10.* With paragraph (A) of this Article, paragraph (D) of Article 8 of Law no. 2559 has been amended, and the principles regarding places open to public and their closure by the police have been revised.

Following the amendments made with Law no. 4709 on Article 19 of the Constitution on individual freedom and security and Articles 20 and 21 on privacy of private life and immunity of domicile, Article 9 of the Law has been amended with paragraph (A) of this Article in order to ensure its conformity.

With paragraph (C) of this Article, Article 11 paragraph (C) of this Law has been rearranged and new provisions have been foreseen to expand its scope due to the changing nature of audio-visual devices with advance of technology.

With paragraph (D) of this Article, Article 12 of the law about persons who may enter or work at entertainment places has been changed, the phrase about places open to public has been updated. In addition, as individuals under eighteen are considered as minors in accordance with the United Nations Convention on the Protection of the Child, to which Turkey is also a signatory, a provision has been added to prevent children being employed in recreational and entertainment facilities by setting the age limit as eighteen. Moreover, the provision, which requires women to get permission from the gubernatorial authority in order to be employed in such places has also been lifted, thus eliminating gender discrimination. Furthermore, eighteen, which is the age of majority in our law, has been taken as the basis, meaning that every male or female who has completed the age of eighteen may be able to work in any area.

With paragraph (E) of this Article, Article 13 of the law about apprehension authority has been revised and paragraph 1 of this Article has specified the situations whereby the law enforcement forces would have the power to apprehend an individual.

Paragraphs 2 and 3 of this Article have been preserved, paragraph 4 has been changed. According to this change, a physician's report will be required not only in the case of apprehended drug addicts and drunk persons, but also for those who have been apprehended by the use of force and those for whom a criminal investigation is to be conducted.

Paragraph 5 of the Article has introduced the obligation of notifying the apprehension reason to the apprehended person.

Paragraph 6 of the Article has been rearranged in line with the amended Article 19 of the Constitution. According to this amendment, the situation of a person apprehended for a judicial proceeding shall immediately be reported to the legally defined relations to be specified by the apprehended person.

Paragraphs 7, 8 and 9 of the Article have been incorporated and rearranged as the seventh and last paragraph of the Article. The word "suspect" has been replaced by "those suspected of having committed a crime"; and the phrase "those for whom rehabilitation or treatment measures have to be taken shall be sent to the relevant institution" has been changed to "those for whom rehabilitation or treatment measures are necessary shall be received by the authorities of the relevant institutions."

With paragraph (F) additional Article 1 of the Law has been amended to regulate the staging of plays or performances or various types of shows in public places, places open to the public or on public transport by natural persons or groups, provided that they notify, in writing, the highest gubernatorial authority of the locale at least forty-eight hours in advance.

Furthermore, it is indicated that "the highest gubernatorial authority of the locality shall immediately notify the public prosecutor about circumstances found to be against the indivisible integrity of the state with its territory and nation, the Constitutional order or public morality. The notification made pursuant to paragraph 1 shall indicate the identity, residential address and nationality of the managers and other persons who have participated in the play or performance."

*Article 11.* With the amendment made to the Law no. 2923 with paragraph (A) of this Article, the legal obstacle preventing the learning of the different languages and dialects used traditionally by Turkish citizens in their daily lives has been removed. In that respect, the name of the law has been changed to "Law on Foreign Language Education and Teaching, and the Learning of Different Languages and Dialects of Turkish Citizens".

Paragraph (B) of the Article has made a parallel change in the Article about the purpose of the Law.

Paragraph (C) of this Article has allowed for private courses, subject to the provisions of the Law on Private Educational Institutions no. 625 and the inspection of the Ministry of National Education, to be opened for the abovementioned languages and dialects. Furthermore, it has been emphasised that these courses cannot be against the fundamental principles of the Republic enshrined in the Constitution and the indivisible integrity of the state with its territory and nation.

*Article 12.* Paragraph (A) of this Article has abrogated the following provision in Article 39 of the Law on Associations no. 2908, "Associations can be established by public servants with a certain profession only to meet the common social, economic, recreational, cultural and vocational needs of its members and only in provinces and districts, even if they are employed in the same institution. Associations cannot engage in activities other than the ones specified above."

The following provision in Article 47 of the same Law, which reads as "Where necessary the Ministry of Finance may also audit the accounts, the related documents and books of an Association working for public benefit" has been abrogated as it has been concluded that, due to Article 45 which already states that associations may be inspected by ministries on issues relating to their purpose and activities, the above provision was deemed to be unnecessary.

The following part in Article 56 of this law has been abrogated: "Students who fail classes for two years and, in higher education institutions where the semester system is applied, students who fail semesters corresponding to this period or students who have not graduated from their educational institutes two years after the normal graduation period cannot be the head of a students' association or take responsibility in the management and inspection boards or other organs of the association, and they cannot be elected to represent students on behalf of the association. If, after having been elected they fall into one of the circumstances indicated above, then they shall lose the titles/posts they have previously acquired." Thus, with regard to associations the restrictions imposed on persons considered students have been eliminated.

Paragraph (B) of the Article abolishes Article 31 and additional Article 3 of the Press Law.

Paragraph (C) of the Article abolishes the provision in the final paragraph of Article 11 of the Law on the Duties and Competences of the Police that requires that those who commercially record video or audiotapes submit a copy of each video or audio recording to the highest gubernatorial authority of their location before the commercial release. This responsibility now rests with the Directorate General of Copyrights within the Ministry of Culture.

Paragraph (D) of the Article abolishes provisional Article 1 of Law no. 3218 on Free Zones relating to the non-implementation of the provisions of Law no. 2822, dated 5.5.1983, on strikes, lockouts and mediation for a period of ten years after the date of establishment of the free zones.

\*\*\*

# Document no. 88

**Editors' comment on European Council Declarations of 2002 and the Copenhagen European Council Presidency Conclusions[9]**

In the Seville European Council of June 21 and 22, 2002, the EU welcomed the reforms recently adopted in Turkey and encouraged Turkey to fulfill the priorities defined in its Accession Partnership. The EU stated that "the implementation of the required political and economic reforms [would] bring forward Turkey's prospects of accession in accordance with the same principles and criteria as are applied to the other candidate countries." The EU further acknowledged that "new decisions could be taken in Copenhagen on the next stage of Turkey's candidature in the light of developments in the situation between the Seville and Copenhagen European Councils, on the basis of the regular report to be submitted by the Commission in October 2002 and in accordance with the Helsinki and Laeken conclusions."

In the Brussels European Council of October 24 and 25, 2002, the EU again welcomed "the important steps taken by Turkey towards meeting the Copenhagen political criteria and the fact that Turkey has moved forward on the economic criteria and alignment with the *acquis*, as registered in the Commission's Regular Report." The EU stated that the developments had "brought forward the opening of accession negotiations with Turkey." In Brussels, the EU encouraging "Turkey to pursue its reform process and to take further concrete steps in the direction of implementation," declared that reforms would "advance Turkey's accession in accordance with the same principles and criteria as are applied to the other candidate States." The EU also invited the Council "to prepare in time for the Copenhagen European Council the elements for deciding on the next stage of Turkey's candidature, on the basis of the Commission's Strategy Paper and in accordance with the conclusions of the European Council in Helsinki, Laeken and Seville."

***Copenhagen European Council Presidency Conclusions (December 12–13, 2002)[10]***

\*\*\*

## I. Enlargement

3. The European Council in Copenhagen in 1993 launched an ambitious process to overcome the legacy of conflict and division in Europe. Today marks an unprecedented and historic milestone in completing this process with the conclusion of accession negotiations with Cyprus, the Czech Republic, Estonia, Hungary, Latvia, Lithuania, Malta, Poland, the Slovak Republic and Slovenia. The Union now looks forward to welcoming these States as members from 1 May 2004. This achievement testifies to the common determination of the peoples of Europe to come together in a Union that has become the driving force for peace, democracy, stability and prosperity on our continent. As fully fledged members of a Union based on solidarity, these States will play a full role in shaping the further development of the European project.

\*\*\*

### Turkey

18. The European Council recalls its decision in 1999 in Helsinki that Turkey is a candidate State destined to join the Union on the basis of the same criteria as applied to the other candidate States. It strongly welcomes the important steps taken by Turkey towards meeting the Copenhagen criteria, in particular through the recent legislative packages and the subsequent implementation measures which cover a large number of key priorities specified in the Accession Partnership. The Union acknowledges the determination of the new Turkish government to take further steps on the path of reform and urges in particular the government to address swiftly all remaining shortcomings in the field of the political criteria, not only with regard to legislation but also in particular with regard to implementation. The Union recalls that, according to the political criteria decided in Copenhagen in 1993, membership requires that a candidate country has achieved stability of institutions guaranteeing democracy, the rule of law, Human Rights and respect for and protection of minorities.

19. The Union encourages Turkey to pursue energetically its reform process. If the European Council in December 2004, on the basis of a report and a recommendation from the Commission, decides that Turkey fulfils the Copenhagen political criteria, the European Union will open accession negotiations with Turkey without delay.

20. In order to assist Turkey towards EU membership, the accession strategy for Turkey shall be strengthened. The Commission is invited to submit a proposal for a revised Accession Partnership and to intensify the process of legislative scrutiny. In parallel, the EC–Turkey Customs Union should be extended and deepened. The Union will significantly increase its pre-accession financial assistance for Turkey. This assistance will from 2004 be financed under the budget heading "pre-accession expenditure".

\*\*\*

# 2003
# Document no. 89

### Harmonisation package (4)[11]

*Article 1.* The heading of Article 316 of the Code of Criminal Procedure, no. 1412, dated 4.4.1929, has been changed to "The application for appeal and the appellate brief and the reply to these, the duty of the Chief Public Prosecutor of the Court of Appeals" and the following paragraph has been added to the Article:

"The recommendation prepared by the Chief Public Prosecutor of the Court of Appeals is communicated to the parties."

*Article 2.* The seventh paragraph of Article 1 of the Act no. 2762 on Foundations, dated 5.6.1935, has been amended to read as follows:

"Community foundations, regardless of whether they have a charter, may acquire immovable properties and dispose of these immovable properties, with the permission of the Directorate General for Foundations, in order to meet their needs in religious, charitable, social, educational, health and cultural areas."

*Article 3.* The following paragraph has been added to Article 15 of the Press Act no. 5690, dated 15.7.1950:

"The owner of the publication may not be forced to reveal his or her sources."

*Article 4.* The following Additional Article has been added to Article 31 of Act no. 488 on Stamp Duties, dated 1.7.1964:

"Additional Article 1. Compensation to be paid in accordance with the decisions of the European Court of Human Rights and sums for friendly settlement (settlement out of court) are exempt from stamp duties."

*Article 5.* The following provisional Article has been added to Act no. 2547 on Higher Education, dated 4.11.1981:

"Provisional Article 50. Disciplinary penalties incurred, and any consequences of these, in accordance with the provisions of Act no. 2547 on Higher Education and the Disciplinary By-law for Students of Institutions of Higher Education referring to this Act, by students registered for preparatory classes, associate degrees and undergraduate education-training programmes at institutions for higher education and students of any grade at two-year higher education institutions from the beginning of the 2001–2 school year to the date of entry into force of this Law, have been repealed. The records of these penalties shall be removed, with no requirement for application by these students, from their files."

*Article 6.* The first paragraph of Article 8 of the Act no. 2820 on Political Parties, dated 22.4.1983, has been amended to read as follows:

"Political parties are established by at least thirty Turkish citizens who are eligible to be members of parties."

*Article 7.* Sentences (3) and (5) of sub-paragraph (b) of the second paragraph of Article 11 of the Act on Political Parties have been amended to read as follows:

"3. Persons sentenced to five or more years of prison, with the exception of crimes of negligence."

"5. Persons convicted of acts of terrorism."

*Article 8.* The second and third paragraphs of Article 66 of the Act on Political Parties has been amended to read as follows:

"It is prohibited for any real or corporate persons other than those referred to in the above paragraph to donate a value of more than two billion in cash or in kind within the same year to a political party or to allow the political party to use its media. It must be clearly designated in the receipt issued by the party that the donation or donations are made to the one donated to or to his or her representative or attorney. Donations may not be accepted by parties in the absence of such a document."

"Political parties may not receive assistance and donations in cash or in kind from foreign states, international organisations and real or corporate persons not of Turkish nationality, from groups and institutions under any circumstances."

*Article 9.* The following sentence has been added to the first paragraph of Article 98 of the Act on Political Parties:

"A three-fifths majority is required for a decision to be taken regarding cases for the dissolution of political parties."

*Article 10.* The following sentence has been added to the first paragraph of Article 102 of the Act on Political Parties:

"The political party may appeal to the Constitutional Court against the request of the Chief Public Prosecutor."

*Article 11.* The second paragraph of Article 104 of the Act on Political Parties has been amended to read as follows:

"If the Constitutional Court sees a violation of these provisions, it may take the decision to warn the relevant political party to remedy this violation. If the violation is not remedied within six months of the notification of the warning, the Chief Public Prosecutor may *ex officio* file a case at the Constitutional Court to have the political party deprived partially or fully of State assistance."

*Article 12.* The following sub-paragraph (d) has been added to follow after sub-paragraph (c) of Article 111 of the Act on Political Parties:

"d. Persons responsible for the deprivation of the political party partially or fully of State assistance by not complying with the requirements of the warning issued in accordance with Article 104 are to be sentenced to three to six months' imprisonment; persons responsible for political parties which do not received State assistance are to be sentenced to six months' to one year's imprisonment."

*Article 13.* Sub-paragraph (3) of paragraph (f) of Article 11 of Act no. 2839 on the Election of Members of Parliament, dated 10.6.1083, has been amended to read as follows:

"3. Persons convicted of acts of terrorism."

*Article 14.* The second paragraph of Article 5 of the Act no. 2908 on Associations, dated 10.6.1983, has been amended to read as follows:

"Article 5. Associations that are in violation of the basic features of the Republic as enshrined in the Constitution and the provisions on the protection of reform laws referred to in Article 174 of the Constitution; national security and public order; general health and general morality or have the purpose of restricting the freedom of others may not be established."

*Article 15.* The second paragraph of Article 6 of the Act on Associations has been amended to read as follows:

"Associations use Turkish in their official correspondence undertaken with the public institutions of the Turkish Republic."

*Article 16.* The first paragraph of Article 16 of the Act on Associations has been amended to read as follows:

"Real and corporate persons with legal capacity may become members of associations."

*Article 17.* The following provision has been added to the fifth paragraph of Article 18 of the Act on Associations:

"In cases where corporate persons are members, the chairman of the board of administrators or the person who will be appointed as representative shall vote. When the period of appointment of this person as chairman or representative ends, the person who will vote on behalf of the corporate person will be designated again."

*Article 18.* Article 44 of the Act on Associations has been amended to read as follows:

"Announcements, statements and other similar publications by associations may be confiscated on the order of the highest gubernatorial administrator of the locality if these publications endanger the internal and external security of the State, are of a nature that are in violation of the fundamental features of the Republic enshrined in the Constitution, disrupt the unity of the State with its territory and nation or encourage the commitment of criminal offences, incite uprisings or rebellions, or make public classified State documents, or violate the reputations or rights, private and family lives of others. The highest gubernatorial administrator shall notify the judge of the criminal court of first instance of his decision within twenty-four hours. The judge shall review the decision of the gubernatorial administrator and take a decision within forty-eight hours at the latest. The decision of the gubernatorial administrator will be considered to be void if a decision cannot be taken in this period of time.

This provision will not be applied to political parties."

*Article 19.* Article 1 of the Act no. 3071 on Exercise of the Right of Petition, dated 1.11.1984, has been amended to read as follows:

"Article 1. The purpose of this law is to regulate the exercise of the right of Turkish citizens and foreigners residing in Turkey to apply in writing regarding requests and complaints relating to themselves or to the public to the Turkish Grand National Assembly and the competent authorities."

*Article 20.* Article 2 of the Act on Exercise of the Right of Petition has been amended to read as follows:

"Article 2. The scope of this law is applications made to the Turkish Grand National Assembly and administrative authorities by Turkish citizens and foreigners residing in Turkey."

*Article 21.* Article 3 of the Act on Exercise of the Right of Petition has been amended to read as follows:

"Foreigners residing in Turkey may exercise the right to petition provided that the principle of reciprocity is observed and the petitions are written in Turkish."

*Article 22.* Article 4 of the Act on Exercise of the Right of Petition has been amended to read as follows:

"Article 4. The name–surname, signature and work or home addresses of those petitioning must be written on the petitions given or sent to the Turkish Grand National Assembly or the competent authorities."

*Article 23.* Article 7 of the Act on Exercise of the Right of Petition has been amended to read as follows:

"Article 7. A reply shall be made on the result or the progress of the processing of petitions made by Turkish citizens or foreigners residing in Turkey on requests and complaints relating to themselves or to the public to the competent authorities within sixty days at the latest. Even if the progress of the process has been notified, the results also will be notified."

*Article 24.* Article 8 of the Act on Exercise of the Right of Petition has been amended to read as follows:

"Article 8. The review of the petitions sent to the Turkish Grand National Assembly and the decisions taken on these petitions shall be concluded within sixty days. The rules and procedures for decisions are indicated in the Internal Regulation of the Turkish Grand National Assembly."

*Article 25.* The heading of Article 5 of the Act on Judicial Records, no. 3682, dated 22.11.1990, has been changed to "Authorities that are competent to provide judicial records information and rules to be applied to children" and the following paragraph has been added to the Article:

"Information recorded in judicial records on children under eighteen years of age may be provided only when requested by Public Prosecutors and courts for matters related to investigations and inquiries or to the competent election councils in relation to elections for membership in the legislative council. This information may not be used for any other transactions or matters."

*Article 26.* The first paragraph and the final paragraph of the Act on Judicial Records have been amended to read as follows:

"Beginning with the date at which the sentence is completed, repealed or no longer to be enforced;

a. In case of conviction of a misdemeanour, within one year for another offence or misdemeanour,

b. For convictions for simple and qualified embezzlement, misappropriation, peculation, bribery, robbery, fraud, forgery, abuse of trust and bankruptcy fraud and for heavy prison sentences and prison sentences exceeding five years, within ten years,

c. In case of convictions for heavy prison sentences or prison sentences of five years or less or for heavy fines, within five years for another offence,

d. In cases where convictions under paragraph (b) for children under the age of eighteen at the time the offence was committed, within five years for another offence,

e. In cases where convictions under paragraph (c) for children under the age of eighteen at the time the offence was committed, within two for another offence,

A decision will be taken by the Public Prosecutor or by the court that has taken the verdict or by the criminal court in the locality where the request has been made, on the request of the Directorate General for Judicial Records and Statistics at the Ministry of Justice, without a hearing, to delete the records of the convict from judicial records, if he or she is not sentenced to a penalty similar to the earlier one or to a heavier penalty. In cases where a postponed conviction is not enforced, this date shall be the basis. One copy of these decisions shall be sent to the Directorate General for Judicial Records and Statistics at the Ministry of Justice.

Information in the judicial records of convicts convicted of offences that have been deleted from the laws through amendments or made into administrative offences, or who have died or who have turned eighty years of age are removed from judicial records by the Directorate General for Judicial Records and Statistics at the Ministry of Justice acting on its own initiative."

*Article 27.* The first paragraph of sub-paragraph (c) of Article 3 of the Decree Law no. 403 on the Governorates of State of Emergency Regions and Additional Measures to be taken for the Duration of the State of Emergency, dated 15.12.1990, has been amended to read as follows:

"Convicts and prisoners whose statements are needed for the investigations of criminal offences that have resulted in the declaration of a state of emergency, in cases where these statements cannot be effectively taken in prisons, may be taken out of the prison or detention house, each time not to exceed seven days, by a decision taken by the judge on the request of the competent Chief Public Prosecutor and the proposal of the governor of the State of Emergency region. This period of time will be considered to be served as a convict or prisoner. The judge shall hear the convict or prisoner prior to taking a decision. The convict or prisoner shall continue to enjoy the rights relating to his or her legal status after being taken out of the prison or detention house. A medical certificate shall be issued on the health of the prisoner or convict each time he or she is taken out of the prison or detention house and returned."

*Article 28.* The following paragraph has been added to Article 2 of the Act no. 4483 on the Prosecution of Civil Servants and other Public Employees, dated 2.12.1999:

"The provisions of this Law are not to be applied to investigations and inquiries undertaken within the scope of Articles 243 and 245 of the Turkish Penal Code, no. 765, dated 1.3.1926."

*Article 29.* Article 91 of the Turkish Civil Code, no. 4721, dated 22.11.2001, has been amended to read as follows:

"Article 91. Associations may undertake international activities and cooperation, establish branches abroad and participate as members in associations or organisations established abroad in order to fulfil the aims indicated in their charters."

*Article 30.* Article 92 of the Turkish Civil Code has been amended to read as follows:

"Article 92. Foreign associations may, in cases where international cooperation is deemed to be beneficial, and provided that this is reciprocal, undertake activities, establish branches, establish higher bodies and participate in higher bodies already established in Turkey, with the permission of the Ministry of the Interior, after obtaining the comments of the Ministry of Foreign Affairs."

*Article 31.* Article 34 of the Act on the Establishment, Duties and Trial Procedures of Child Courts, no. 2353, dated 7.11.1979, the fourth paragraph of Article 16 of the Act no. 2845 on the Establishment and Trial Procedures at State Security Courts, dated 16.6.1983, Articles 11 and 12 of the Act on Associations and Article 9 of the Act on Judicial Records are no longer in force.

\*\*\*

# Document no. 90

## Harmonisation package (5)[12]

*Article 1.* The following sub-paragraph 11 has been added to the first paragraph of Article 445 of the Code of Civil Procedure, no. 1086, dated 18.6.1927:

11. The determination by a finalised decision of the European Court of Human Rights that the judgment was taken for a violation of the Convention of the Protection of Human Rights and Fundamental Freedoms.

*Article 2.* The following third paragraph has been added to Article 447 of the Code of Civil Procedure:

The time period for retrial, for the reason written in sub-paragraph 11 of the first paragraph of Article 445, is one year from the date of the finalisation of the decision of the European Court of Human Rights.

*Article 3.* The following sixth paragraph has been added to Article 327 of the Code of Penal Procedure, no. 1412, dated 4.4.1929:

6. The determination by a finalised decision of the European Court of Human Rights that the judgment for a penalty was taken for a violation of the Convention of the Protection of Human Rights and Fundamental Freedoms. In this case, retrial may be requested within one year of the date of the finalisation of the decision of the European Court of Human Rights.

*Article 4.* Article 82 of the Act no. 2908 on Associations, dated 6.10.1983, has been amended as follows:

Article 82. Persons that do not comply with the requirements of Article 43 or the first and fourth paragraphs of Article 45 of this Act, persons that do not complete the declaration indicated in the second paragraph of Article 64 or persons who do not convert immovable properties into cash within the time period indicated by the Ministry are sentenced to a heavy fine from 1,000,000,000 liras to 3,000,000,000 liras.

*Article 5.* Article 445/A of the Code of Civil Procedure, no. 1086, dated 18.6.1927, the final paragraph of Article 448 of the same Act, Article 327/a of the Code of Penal Procedure, no. 1412, dated 4.4.1929, the final paragraph of Article 335 of the same Act and the provisional Article 2 of Act no. 3771 Amending Various Acts, dated 3.8.2002, have been repealed.

*Provisional Article 1.* Article 1 and 3 of this Act are to be applied to decisions of the European Court of Human Rights that have been finalised by the date of entry into force of this Act and decisions taken on applications to the European Court of Human Rights after the entry into force of this Act. Applications for retrial upon the decisions of the European Court of Human Rights that have been finalised after the date of entry into force of this Act are to be made within one year of the date of entry into force of this Act.

# Document no. 91

### ECtHR — *Ocalan v. Turkey*[13]

\*\*\*

[Abdullah Ocalan, a Turkish national born in 1949 and former leader of the Kurdistan Workers' Party (PKK), is currently incarcerated in Imralı Prison (Bursa, Turkey). At the time of the events in question, the Turkish courts had issued seven warrants for Mr Ocalan's arrest and a wanted notice (red notice) had been circulated by Interpol. He was accused of founding an armed gang in order to destroy the integrity of the Turkish State and of instigating terrorist acts resulting in loss of life. On 9 October 1998, he was expelled from Syria, where he had been living for many years. From there he went to Greece, Russia, Italy and then again Russia and Greece before going to Kenya, where, on the evening of 15 February 1999, in disputed circumstances he was taken on board an aircraft at Nairobi airport and arrested by Turkish officials. He was then flown to Turkey, being kept blindfolded for most of the flight. On arrival in Turkey, a hood was placed over his head while he was taken to Imralı Prison, where he was held in police custody from 16 to 23 February 1999, and questioned by the security forces. He received no legal assistance during that period and made several self-incriminating statements which contributed to his conviction. His lawyer in Turkey was prevented from travelling to visit him by members of the security forces. Sixteen other lawyers were also refused permission to visit on 23 February 1999.

On 23 February 1999, the applicant appeared before an Ankara State Security Court judge, who ordered him to be placed in pre-trial detention. The first visit from his lawyers was restricted to twenty minutes and took place with members of the security forces and a judge present in the same room. Subsequent meetings between the applicant and his lawyers took place within the hearing of members of the security forces. After the first two visits from his lawyers, the applicant's contact with them was restricted to two one-hour visits a week. The prison authorities did not authorize the applicant's lawyers to provide him with a copy of the documents in the case file, other than the indictment. It was not until the hearing on 2 June 1999, that the State Security Court gave the applicant permission to consult the case file under the supervision of two registrars and his lawyers permission to provide him with a copy of certain documents. In an indictment filed on 24 April 1999, the Public Prosecutor at Ankara State Security Court accused the applicant of carrying out actions calculated to bring about the separation of a part of Turkish territory and of forming and leading an armed gang to achieve that end. The Public Prosecutor asked the court to sentence the applicant to death under Article 125 of the Criminal Code. On 29 June 1999, the applicant was found guilty as charged and sentenced to death under Article 125. The Court of Cassation upheld the judgment.

On 30 November 1999, the European Court of Human Rights, applying Rule 39 of the Rules of Court (interim measures), requested the Turkish authorities "to take all necessary steps to ensure that the death penalty [was] not carried out so as to enable the Court to proceed effectively with the examination of the admissibility and merits of the applicant's complaints under the Convention". In October 2001, Article 38 of the Turkish Constitution was amended, abolishing the death penalty except in time of war or of imminent threat of war or for acts of terrorism. Under Law no. 4771, published on 9 August 2002, the Turkish Assembly resolved to abolish the death penalty in peacetime. On 3 October 2002, Ankara State Security Court commuted the applicant's death sentence to life imprisonment. An application to set aside the provision abolishing the death penalty in peacetime for persons convicted of terrorist offences was dismissed by the Constitutional Court on 27 December 2002 ... .]"[14]

## *II. Relevant domestic and international law and practice*

### *A. Provisions on State Security Courts*

48. Before the Constitution was amended on 18 June 1999, Article 143 provided that State Security Courts were composed of a president, two other regular members and two substitute members. The President of the State Security Court, one of the regular members and one of the substitute members were appointed from among civilian judges, and the other regular member and substitute member were appointed from among military judges.

49. As amended by Law no. 4388 of 18 June 1999, Article 143 of the Constitution provides:

" ... State Security Courts shall be composed of a president, two other regular members, a substitute member, a Principal Public Prosecutor and a sufficient number of Public Prosecutors.

The president, two regular members, a substitute member and the Principal Public Prosecutor shall be appointed from among judges and public prosecutors of the first rank and public prosecutors from among public prosecutors of other ranks. Appointments shall be made for four years by the National Legal Service Council, in accordance with procedures laid down in special legislation. Their terms of office shall be renewable ... ."

50. The necessary amendments concerning the appointment of the judges and prosecutors were made to Law no. 2845 on the State Security Courts by Law no. 4390 of 22 June 1999. By the terms of provisional section 1 of Law no. 4390, the terms of office of the military judges and military prosecutors in service in the State Security Courts were to end on the date of publication of that Law (22 June 1999). By provisional section 3 of the same Law, proceedings pending in the State Security Courts on the date of publication of the Law were to continue from the stage they had reached by that date.

## B. Article 125 of the Turkish Criminal Code

51. Article 125 of the Turkish Criminal Code provides:

"Anyone committing an act designed to subject the State or a part of the State to the domination of a foreign State, to diminish its independence or to impair its unity or which is designed to remove from the administration of the State a part of the territory under its control shall be liable to the death penalty."

## C. Review of the lawfulness of detention

52. The fourth paragraph of Article 128 of the Code of Criminal Procedure (as amended by Law no. 3842/9 of 18 November 1992) provides that any person who has been arrested or in respect of whom a prosecutor has made an order for him or her to remain in police custody may challenge the measure in question before the appropriate district judge and, if successful, be released. In proceedings in State Security Courts (governed by Law no. 2845 of 16 June 1983) Article 128 of the Code of Criminal Procedure applies only as it was worded before the amendments of 18 November 1992, when it did not provide any right of appeal to persons arrested or held in police custody on the orders of a prosecutor.

53. Section 1 of Law no. 466 on the Award of Compensation to Persons Arrested Unlawfully or Held in Detention without Due Cause provides:

"Compensation shall be paid by the State in respect of all damage sustained by persons:

1. who have been arrested, or detained under conditions or in circumstances incompatible with the Constitution or statute law;

2. who have not been immediately informed of the reasons for their arrest or detention;

3. who have not been brought before a judicial officer after being arrested or detained within the time-limit laid down by statute for that purpose;

4. who have been deprived of their liberty without a court order after the statutory time-limit for being brought before a judicial officer has expired;

5. whose close family have not been immediately informed of their arrest or detention;

6. who, after being arrested or detained in accordance with the law, are not subsequently committed for trial ... , or are acquitted or discharged after standing trial; or

7. who have been sentenced to a period of imprisonment shorter than the period spent in detention or ordered to pay a pecuniary penalty only ....

54. Article 144 of the Code of Criminal Procedure provides that, in principle, anyone arrested or detained pending trial may speak with his legal representative in private, without any need for the latter to have an authority to act. As regards the procedure in proceedings before the State Security Courts, Article 144 of the Code of Criminal Procedure is applicable only as worded prior to the amendments made on 18 November 1992. That version provides that a member of the state legal service may be present at meetings between the accused and his or her lawyer before the criminal proceedings have commenced.

*D. Council of Europe and the death penalty*

55. Protocol no. 6 to the Convention provides (Article 1):

"The death penalty shall be abolished. No one shall be condemned to such penalty or executed."

Article 2 of Protocol no. 6 provides:

"A State may make provision in its law for the death penalty in respect of acts committed in time of war or of imminent threat of war; such penalty shall be applied only in the instances laid down in the law and in accordance with its provisions. The State shall communicate to the Secretary General of the Council of Europe the relevant provisions of that law."

Protocol no. 6 has been ratified by forty-one of the forty-four Member States of the Council of Europe and signed by all States, most recently on 15 January 2003 by Turkey. Only Turkey, Armenia and Russia have not yet ratified the Protocol.

56. Protocol no. 13 to the Convention, which provides for the abolition of the death penalty in all circumstances, was opened for signature on 3 May 2002. The Preamble to Protocol no. 13 reads:

"The Member States of the Council of Europe signatory hereto,

Convinced that everyone's right to life is a basic value in a democratic society and that the abolition of the death penalty is essential for the protection of this right and for the full recognition of the inherent dignity of all human beings;

Wishing to strengthen the protection of the right to life guaranteed by the Convention for the Protection of Human Rights and Fundamental Freedoms signed at Rome on 4 November 1950 (hereinafter referred to as "the Convention");

Noting that Protocol no. 6 to the Convention, concerning the Abolition of the Death Penalty, signed at Strasbourg on 28 April 1983, does not exclude the death penalty in respect of acts committed in time of war or of imminent threat of war;

Being resolved to take the final step in order to abolish the death penalty in all circumstances,

Have agreed as follows ..."

Article 1 of Protocol no. 13 states:

"The death penalty shall be abolished. No one shall be condemned to such penalty or executed."

In accordance with Article 7 of the Protocol it shall "enter into force on the first day of the month following the expiration of a period of three months after the date on which ten Member States of the Council of Europe have expressed their consent to be bound by the Protocol."

57. In Opinion no. 233 (2002) of the Parliamentary Assembly of the Council of Europe on the *Draft Protocol to the European Convention on Human Rights Concerning the Abolition of the Death Penalty in all Circumstances* the Assembly recalled:

" ... its most recent resolutions on the subject (Resolution 1187 (1999) on *Europe: a death penalty free continent*, and Resolution 1253 (2001) on the *Abolition of the death penalty in Council of Europe Observer states)*, in which it reaffirmed its beliefs that the application of the death penalty constitutes inhuman and degrading punishment and a violation of the most fundamental right, that to life itself, and that capital punishment has no place in civilised, democratic societies governed by the rule of law. (paragraph 2)"

The Assembly further noted:

The second sentence of Article 2 of the European Convention on Human Rights still provides for the death penalty. It has long been in the interest of the Assembly to delete this sentence, thus matching theory with reality. This interest is strengthened by the fact that more modern national constitutional documents and international treaties no longer include such provisions. (paragraph 5)

58. Article X § 2 of the "Guidelines on Human Rights and the Fight Against Terrorism" issued by the Committee of Ministers of the Council of Europe on 15 July 2002 reads:

"Under no circumstances may a person convicted of terrorist activities be sentenced to the death penalty; in the event of such a sentence being imposed, it may not be carried out."

*E. Other international developments concerning the death penalty*

59. By its Resolution 1984/50 of 25 May 1984 on *Safeguards Guaranteeing Protection of the Rights of those Facing the Death Penalty*, the Economic and Social Council of the United Nations set out a series of standards to be observed by States which retained capital punishment.

Article 5 of the Resolution provides as follows:

"Capital punishment may only be carried out pursuant to a final judgment rendered by a competent court after legal process which gives all possible safeguards to ensure a fair trial, at least equal to those contained in Article 14 of the International Covenant on Civil and Political Rights, including the right of anyone suspected of or charged with a crime for which capital punishment may be imposed to adequate legal assistance at all stages of the proceedings."

60. In a number of cases involving application of the death penalty, the United Nations Human Rights Committee observed that, if the due process guarantees in Article 14 of the International Covenant on Civil and Political

Rights were violated, a sentence of death which was carried out would not be in conformity with Article 6 § 2 of the Covenant which delineates the circumstances when it is permissible to give effect to the death penalty.

61. In the case of *Reid v. Jamaica* (no. 250/1987), the Committee stated as follows:

"[T]he imposition of a sentence of death upon the conclusion of a trial in which the provisions of the Covenant have not been respected constitutes ... a violation of Article 6 of the Covenant. As the Committee noted in its general comment 6(7), the provision that a sentence of death may be imposed only in accordance with the law and not contrary to the provisions of the Covenant implies that 'the procedural guarantees therein prescribed must be observed, including the right to a fair hearing by an independent tribunal, the presumption of innocence, the minimum guarantees for the defence, and the right to review by a higher tribunal'."

62. Similar observations were made by the Committee in the case of *Daniel Mbenge v. Zaire* (Communication no. 16/1977, 8 September 1977, UN Doc. Supp. no. 40, [A/38/40], at 134 [1983]) and *Wright v. Jamaica* (Communication no. 349/1989, UN Doc. CCPR/C/45/D/349/1989 [1992]).

63. In an Advisory Opinion on "The right to information on consular assistance in the framework of the guarantees of due process of law" (Advisory Opinion OC-16/99 of 1 October 1999) the Inter-American Court of Human Rights examined the implication of the guarantees of a fair procedure with Article 4 of the American Convention on Human Rights, which permitted the death penalty in certain circumstances. It stated:

"134. It might be useful to recall that in a previous examination of Article 4 of the American Convention (Restrictions to the Death Penalty, Advisory Opinion OC-3/83 of 8 September, 1983, Series A no. 3) the Court observed that the application and imposition of capital punishment are governed by the principle that "[n]o one shall be arbitrarily deprived of his life". Both Article 6 of the International Covenant on Civil and Political Rights and Article 4 of the Convention require strict observance of legal procedure and limit application of this penalty to "the most serious crimes". In both instruments, therefore, there is a marked tendency toward restricting application of the death penalty and ultimately abolishing it.

135. This tendency, evident in other inter-American and universal instruments, translates into the internationally recognised principle whereby those States that still have the death penalty must, without exception, exercise the most rigorous control for observance of judicial guarantees in these cases. It is obvious that the obligation to observe the right to information becomes all the more imperative here, given the exceptionally grave and irreparable nature of the penalty that one sentenced to death could receive. If the due process of law, with all its rights and guarantees, must be respected regardless of the circumstances, then its observance becomes all the more important when that supreme entitlement that every Human Rights treaty and declaration recognises and protects is at stake: human life.

136. Because execution of the death penalty is irreversible, the strictest and most rigorous enforcement of judicial guarantees is required of the State so that those guarantees are not violated and a human life not arbitrarily taken as a result."

64. In its *Hilaire, Constantine and Benjamin et al v. Trinidad and Tobago* judgment of 21 June 2002, the Inter-American Court stated:

"Taking into account the exceptionally serious and irreparable nature of the death penalty, the observance of due process, with its bundle of rights and guarantees, becomes all the more important when human life is at stake (at § 148)."

## The Law

### I. Alleged violation of Article 5 of the Convention

65. The applicant complained of violations of Article 5 §§ 1, 3 and 4 of the Convention, the relevant provisions of which read as follows:

"1. Everyone has the right to liberty and security of person. No one shall be deprived of his liberty save in the following cases and in accordance with a procedure prescribed by law:

...

c. the lawful arrest or detention of a person effected for the purpose of bringing him before the competent legal authority on reasonable suspicion of having committed an offence or when it is reasonably considered necessary to prevent his committing an offence or fleeing after having done so;

...

3. Everyone arrested or detained in accordance with the provisions of paragraph 1 (c) of this Article shall be brought promptly before a judge or other officer authorised by law to exercise judicial power and shall be entitled to trial within a reasonable time or to release pending trial. Release may be conditioned by guarantees to appear for trial.

4. Everyone who is deprived of his liberty by arrest or detention shall be entitled to take proceedings by which the lawfulness of his detention shall be decided speedily by a court and his release ordered if the detention is not lawful."

The government, by way of preliminary objection, have argued that the applicant's complaints under Article 5 §§ 1, 3 and 4 should be rejected for failure to exhaust domestic remedies. In its admissibility decision of 14 December 2000, the Court had noted that this question was so closely related to the merits of the complaint under Article 5 § 4 that it could not be detached from it. Accordingly, the Court will examine the government's preliminary objection in the context of the applicant's claim under Article 5 § 4 and will address that complaint first.

A. ARTICLE 5 § 4 OF THE CONVENTION

66. The applicant complained that, contrary to Article 5 § 4 of the Convention, he had not had an opportunity to take proceedings by which the lawfulness of his detention in police custody could be decided.

He said that during the first ten days of his detention he had been held incommunicado and had been unable to contact his lawyers. He had no legal training that would have enabled him to lodge an appeal without assistance from his lawyers. Nor had he been given access to the documents concerning his arrest that would have enabled him to prepare such an appeal. The applicant noted in that connection that the procedural guarantees provided by Article 6 of the Convention applied by analogy to proceedings for a review of the lawfulness of the detention within the meaning of Article 5 § 4. He added that persons who were detained had to be given access to documents in the possession of the authorities concerning their arrest in order to prepare an application for release and that they required assistance from a lawyer if they were to prepare their application efficiently. The applicant maintained that in his case an application to a district judge or a judge of the State Security Court would have been inadequate, illusory and bound to fail.

67. The government, however, raised a preliminary objection of failure to exhaust domestic remedies. The objection had two limbs and also included the government's observations on the merits of the complaints under Article 5 § 4. Firstly, it was submitted that neither the applicant's lawyers nor his close relatives had lodged an application with the Mudanya Court of First Instance or a judge of the Ankara State Security Court to challenge the arrest, the fact that the applicant had been taken into police custody, the length of that custody or the order for his pre-trial detention. The government referred to Article 128 § 4 of the Code of Criminal Procedure, which entitled suspects to apply to the district judge to have the lawfulness of their detention decided or to challenge an order by the public prosecutor's office that they should remain in custody. If the district judge considered the application well-founded, he could order the police not to question the suspect further and to bring him or her before the public prosecutor forthwith. The government added that by virtue of Article 144 of the Code of Criminal Procedure, the applicant's representatives did not require a written authority to make such an application. Secondly, the government referred to Law no. 466 of 15 May 1964 on the Award of Compensation to Persons Arrested Unlawfully or Held in Detention without Due Cause. They said that the applicant could have made the allegations that he had been detained unlawfully to the appropriate assize court.

68. The Court notes that in its decision of 14 December 2000 regarding the admissibility of the application, the government's preliminary objection concerning, inter alia, this complaint was joined to the merits of the complaint under Article 5 § 4.

69. In that connection, the Court reiterates that the existence of a remedy must be sufficiently certain, not only in theory but also in practice, failing which it will lack the accessibility and effectiveness required for the purposes of Article 5 § 4. There is no requirement that remedies that are neither adequate nor effective should be used (citations omitted). Furthermore, the remedy required by Article 5 § 4 must be of a judicial nature, which implies that "the person concerned should have access to a court and the opportunity to be heard either

in person or, where necessary, through some form of representation, failing which he will not have been afforded the fundamental guarantees of procedure applied in matters of deprivation of liberty" [citation omitted]. In addition, in accordance with generally recognised rules of international law, there may be special grounds for releasing the applicant from the obligation to exhaust the available domestic remedies [citation omitted].

70. The Court refers also to its finding in the *Sakık and Others v. Turkey* judgment (cited above, § 53) that there was "no example of any person detained in police custody having successfully ... appl[ied] to a judge for a ruling on the lawfulness of his detention or for his release" in proceedings before the State Security Courts. However, it also observes that, as the government have argued, a 1997 amendment to Article 128 of the Turkish Code of Criminal Procedure clearly establishes a right under Turkish law to challenge in the courts decisions to hold a suspect in police custody. It follows that such a remedy exists in theory. As to how the remedy operates in practice, the Court notes that the government have not furnished any example of a judicial decision in which an order by the public prosecutor's office at a State Security Court for a suspect to be held in police custody has been quashed before the end of the fourth day (the statutory maximum period for which the public prosecutor's office may order suspects to be held).

71. The Court considers that it is not required to rule on that issue for present purposes as, in any event, the special circumstances of the case made it impossible for the applicant to have effective recourse to the remedy.

72. Firstly, the conditions in which the applicant was held and notably the fact that he was kept in total isolation prevented his using the remedy personally. He possessed no legal training and had no possibility of consulting a lawyer while in police custody. Yet, as the Court has noted above (see paragraph 69 above), the proceedings referred to in Article 5 § 4 must be judicial in nature. The applicant could not reasonably be expected under such conditions to be able to challenge the lawfulness and length of his detention without the assistance of his lawyer.

73. Secondly, as regards the suggestion that the lawyers instructed by the applicant or by his close relatives could have challenged his detention without consulting him, the Court observes that the movements of the sole member of the applicant's legal team to possess an authority to represent him were obstructed by the police (see paragraph 21 above). The other lawyers, who had been retained by the applicant's family, found it impossible to contact him while he was in police custody. Moreover, in view of the unusual circumstances of his arrest, the applicant was the principal source of direct information on events in Nairobi that would have been relevant, at that point in the proceedings, for the purposes of challenging the lawfulness of his arrest.

74. Lastly, solely with regard to the length of time the applicant was held in police custody, the Court takes into account the seriousness of the charges against him and the fact that the period spent in police custody did not exceed that permitted by the domestic legislation. It considers that, in those circumstances,

an application on that issue to a district judge would have had little prospect of success.

75. As to the government's assertion that a claim for compensation could have been made under Law no. 466, the Court considers that that remedy cannot satisfy the requirements of Article 5 § 4 for two reasons: firstly, Law no. 466 merely provides prisoners who have been detained unlawfully or without due cause with an action in damages against the State. It will be noted that the right not to be deprived of one's liberty "save in accordance with a procedure prescribed by law" and the right to "be brought promptly before a judge" after arrest is not the same as the right to receive compensation for detention. Paragraphs 1 and 3 of Article 5 of the Convention cover the former and paragraph 5 of Article 5 the latter [citation omitted]. The court invited to rule on the lawfulness of the detention under Law no. 466 examines the case after the event and therefore does not have jurisdiction to order release if the detention is unlawful, as Article 5 § 4 requires it should [citation omitted].

Secondly, the Court notes that, with the exception of the situation — which did not obtain in the instant case — where a person is not committed for trial, or is acquitted or discharged after standing trial, all the cases in which compensation is payable under the provision concerned require the deprivation of liberty to have been unlawful. However, the detention in issue in the present case was lawful under Turkish law, as indeed the government have conceded.

76. In conclusion, the Court dismisses the government's preliminary objection in respect of Article 5 § 4 and holds that there has been a violation of that provision.

For the same reasons, it rejects the preliminary objection in respect of the complaints under Article 5 §§ 1 and 3 (see paragraph 65 *in fine* above).

B. ARTICLE 5 § 1 OF THE CONVENTION

77. The applicant complained that he had been deprived of his liberty unlawfully, without the procedure applicable on extradition being followed. He alleged a violation of Article 5 § 1 of the Convention.

\*\*\*

[The Court found that the applicant's arrest and detention had complied with orders that had been issued by the Turkish courts "for the purpose of bringing him before the competent legal authority on reasonable suspicion of having committed an offence" within the meaning of Article 5 § 1 (c). Moreover, according to the Court, it had not been established beyond all reasonable doubt that the operation carried out in the instant case partly by Turkish officials and partly by Kenyan officials amounted to a violation by Turkey of Kenyan sovereignty and, consequently, of international law. Then the Court concluded that the applicant's arrest on 15 February 1999 and his detention were to be regarded as having been in accordance with "a procedure prescribed by law" for the purposes of Article 5 § 1 of the Convention. Consequently, there had been no violation of that provision.]

C. ARTICLE 5 § 3 OF THE CONVENTION

104. The applicant alleged that, contrary to, Article 5 § 3 of the Convention, he had not been brought "promptly" before a judge or other officer authorised by law to exercise judicial power.

He said that he had been arrested before 11 p.m. on 15 February 1999 and brought before the judge on 23 February 1999. The government had not provided any plausible explanation for that gap between his arrest and his first appearance before a judge. The weather report which the government had produced on the bad weather conditions that had prevented access to the island of İmralı concerned only the afternoon of 23 February 1999, whereas the public prosecutor and the judge had been on the island since 22 February 1999. The applicant said that he had been held incommunicado in the meantime and that his lawyers' request to visit him on 22 February 1999 had been turned down not by the judicial authorities but by the "crisis desk", an entity which possessed no judicial powers. The applicant went on to say that he had not been assisted by counsel when he appeared before the judge on 23 February 1999. He added that the judge could not be regarded as "a judge or other officer" within the meaning of Article 5 § 3, since he was a member of the State Security Court, whose independence and impartiality were contested.

105. The government observed that, under Turkish rules of criminal procedure, the length of police custody could be extended to seven days where the person detained was suspected of crimes connected with terrorism. In the instant case the applicant had been arrested on 16 February 1999 and taken into police custody for an initial period of four days ending on 20 February 1999. On the latter date a judicial order had been made extending the period to be spent in police custody by three days, that is to say until 23 February 1999. Owing to adverse weather conditions (there was a storm in the region), the representatives of members of the public prosecutor's office and the judge of the State Security Court had been unable to reach the island of İmralı until 22 February 1999. The public prosecutor had questioned the applicant that same day. The applicant had appeared before the judge the following day (23 February 1999). After hearing the applicant, the judge had ordered his detention pending trial on the basis of three warrants that had already been issued for his arrest.

106. The Court has already noted on a number of occasions that the investigation of terrorist offences undoubtedly presents the authorities with special problems (citations omitted). This does not mean, however, that the investigating authorities have carte blanche under Article 5 to arrest suspects for questioning, free from effective control by the domestic courts and, ultimately, by the Convention supervisory institutions, whenever they choose to assert that terrorism is involved [citation omitted].

107. The Court notes that the police custody in issue commenced with the applicant's arrest either very late on 15 February 1999 or very early on 16 February 1999. The applicant was held in police custody for four days until 20 February 1999. On that date a judicial order was made extending the period by three days, that is to say until 23 February 1999. The public prosecutor questioned the applicant on 22 February 1999. The applicant appeared before a judge for the first time on 23 February 1999 and the judge, who was without any doubt an "officer" within the meaning of Article 5 § 3 (see, among other authorities, *Sakık and Others v. Turkey* cited above, §§ 12 and 45), ordered his detention pending trial. The total period thus spent by the applicant in police custody before being brought before a judge came to a minimum of seven days.

108. The Court notes that in the case of *Brogan* it held that a period of four days and six hours in police custody without judicial supervision fell outside the strict constraints as to time permitted by Article 5 § 3, even when the aim was to protect the community as a whole from terrorism [citation omitted].

109. The Court cannot accept the government's argument that adverse weather conditions were largely responsible for the period of seven days it took for the applicant to be brought before a judge. No evidence has been adduced to the Court that establishes that the judge attempted to reach the island on which the applicant was being held so that the latter could be brought before him within the total statutory period of seven days allowed for police custody. The Court observes in that connection that the police custody ran its ordinary course under the domestic rules. In addition to the four days ordered by the public prosecutor's office itself, the judge granted an additional period of three days after examining the case on the basis of the file. It seems unlikely that the judge would have granted the additional time had he intended to have the applicant brought before him before it expired.

110. The Court cannot, therefore, accept that it was necessary for the applicant to be detained for seven days without being brought before a judge.

Consequently, there has been a violation of Article 5 § 3.

## II. *Alleged violation of Article 6 of the Convention*

### A. WHETHER THE ANKARA STATE SECURITY COURT, WHICH CONVICTED THE APPLICANT, WAS INDEPENDENT AND IMPARTIAL

111. The applicant alleged that since a military judge had sat on the bench of the State Security Court that had convicted him, he had not been tried by an independent and impartial tribunal. He relied on Article 6 § 1 of the Convention, the relevant part of which provides:

"In the determination of ... any criminal charge against him, everyone is entitled to a fair ... hearing ... by an independent and impartial tribunal."

112. He pointed out that the independence and impartiality of a court was measured by reference to both subjective and objective tests. A military judge with the rank of colonel had sat on the bench of the State Security Court for

part of the proceedings. The military judge had been replaced by a civilian judge just a week before the applicant's conviction and two months after the hearings before the State Security Court had started. In the meantime, in a case that concerned a conflict between the organisation led by the applicant and the army in which the military judge was an officer, the military judge had heard the evidence and the oral submissions, contributed to important interlocutory rulings and discussed the case with the other judges, thereby potentially influencing the conduct and outcome of the proceedings. The military judge had sat in all the hearings in which interlocutory rulings had been made, including the hearing at which the applicant's application to have additional witnesses examined had been refused. The applicant added that the substitute judge who had replaced the military judge had earlier acted in the case and had ordered the applicant's pre-trial detention.

113. The government, on the other hand, said that the military judge had left the State Security Court following legislative amendments. The substitute judge (a civilian) had been following the proceedings from the start and had attended the hearings, although he had not been entitled to vote. The substitute judge had replaced the military judge before the stage in the proceedings in which evidence was gathered had ended. Had he considered that the State Security Court needed to pursue its investigations, he could have voted against making an order to close that stage of the proceedings before additional investigative measures were ordered. The government said that the attendance of substitute judges at hearings was not a special measure confined to the Öcalan case. Provision for their attendance was made in the rules of criminal procedure.

114. The Court points out that in its judgments in [several] cases [against Turkey], it noted that certain aspects of the status of military judges sitting in the State Security Courts that had convicted the applicants in those cases raised doubts as to the independence and impartiality of the courts concerned. The applicants in those cases had had legitimate cause to fear that the presence of a military judge on the bench might have resulted in the courts allowing themselves to be unduly influenced by considerations that were not relevant to the nature of the case.

What is at stake is the confidence which the courts in a democratic society must inspire in the public and above all, as far as criminal proceedings are concerned, in the accused. In deciding whether there is a legitimate reason to fear that a particular court lacks independence and impartiality, the standpoint of the accused is important without being decisive. What is decisive is whether his doubts can be held to be objectively justified.

115. The applicant appears to have indicated that he accepted the jurisdiction of the State Security Court (see paragraph 34 above). He must, therefore, according to the respondent government, be taken to have waived his right to an independent and impartial tribunal.

116. It is recalled that a waiver — in so far as such a waiver is permissible — must be established in an unequivocal manner [citation omitted]. However, the

applicant's statement cannot be interpreted as an unequivocal waiver of his right to an independent and impartial tribunal since his lawyers actually challenged the independence and impartiality of the court on account of the presence of a military judge. In addition, accepting that a court has "jurisdiction" to conduct a trial refers to its legal competence to try a person and does not necessarily — if at all — involve an acceptance of the independence and impartiality of that court. The Court does not consider, therefore, that the applicant can be said to have waived his right.

117. The Court notes that when the applicant was convicted the State Security Court was composed of three civilian judges. Following a constitutional amendment (see paragraphs 39 and 40 above), the military judge had been replaced by a civilian judge before the defendant's lawyers made their submissions on the merits of the case. Moreover, the civilian judge had sat as a substitute judge and had followed the trial proceedings from the beginning.

118. However, in the Court's view the last-minute replacement of the military judge was not capable of curing the defect in the composition of the court which had led it to find a violation on this point in the abovementioned *İncal* and *Çıraklar* judgments. In the first place, the replacement had occurred only one week before the applicant's conviction and two months after the trial had begun. Moreover, two preliminary hearings and six main hearings had already taken place prior to the replacement on 23 June 1999 and the entire prosecution case against the applicant had already been presented by that stage. In short, most of the trial had already taken place before the military judge ceased to be a member of the court. The Court need not speculate on the question whether the military judge had actually influenced the other judges in the court during the course of the trial since, as in the *İncal* and *Çıraklar* cases, it was his very presence prior to replacement which was the source of the problem.

119. It is true that a change in the composition of a trial court in the course of the proceedings need not necessarily give rise to an issue under Article 6 § 1. However, in the present case it is the presence of the military judge for most of the trial proceedings that gives rise to the problem and not the change in the composition that had taken place.

120. Moreover, the exceptional nature of the trial itself concerning a high-profile accused who had been engaged in a lengthy armed conflict with the Turkish military authorities and who faced the death penalty are factors which cannot be overlooked in this assessment. The presence of a military judge — undoubtedly considered necessary because of his competence and experience in military matters — can only have served to raise doubts in the accused's mind as to the independence and impartiality of the court.

121. Against the above background, the Court concludes that the Ankara State Security Court, which convicted the applicant, was not an independent and impartial tribunal within the meaning of Article 6 § 1 of the Convention. Consequently, there has been a violation of this provision on this point.

## B. WHETHER THE PROCEEDINGS BEFORE THE STATE SECURITY COURT WERE FAIR

122. The applicant complained that the provisions of Article 6 §§ 1, 2 and 3 of the Convention had been infringed owing to the restrictions and difficulties he had encountered in: securing assistance from his lawyers; gaining access for him and his lawyers to the case file; calling defence witnesses; and securing access for his lawyers to the full prosecution file. He also alleged that the judges had been influenced against him by a hostile media.

\*\*\*

## C. THE COURT'S CONCLUSION REGARDING ARTICLE 6

169. The Court consequently notes that the applicant was not tried by an independent and impartial tribunal, was not assisted by his lawyers when questioned in police custody, was unable to communicate with them out of hearing of third parties and was unable to gain direct access to the case file until a very late stage in the proceedings. Furthermore, restrictions were imposed on the number and length of his lawyers' visits and his lawyers were not given proper access to the case file until late in the day. The Court finds that the overall effect of these difficulties taken as a whole so restricted the rights of the defence that the principle of a fair trial, as set out in Article 6, was contravened. There has therefore been a violation of Article 6 § 1, taken together with Article 6 § 3 (b) and (c).

170. As regards the other complaints under Article 6 of the Convention, the Court considers that it has already dealt with the applicant's main grievances arising out of the proceedings against him in the domestic courts. It therefore holds that it is unnecessary to examine the other complaints under Article 6 relating to the fairness of the proceedings.

## III. Death penalty: alleged violation of Articles 2, 3 and 14 of the Convention

171. The applicant maintained that the imposition and/or execution of the death penalty constituted a violation of Article 2 — which should be interpreted as no longer permitting capital punishment — as well as an inhuman and degrading punishment in violation of Article 3 of the Convention. He also claimed that his execution would be discriminatory in breach of Article 14. The relevant part of these provisions provide:

*Article 2*

"1. Everyone's right to life shall be protected by law. No one shall be deprived of his life intentionally save in the execution of a sentence of a court following his conviction of a crime for which this penalty is provided by law."

*Article 3*

"No one shall be subjected to torture or to inhuman or degrading treatment or punishment."

*Article 14*

"The enjoyment of the rights and freedoms set forth in [the] Convention shall be secured without discrimination on any ground such as sex, race, colour, language, religion, political or other opinion, national or social origin, association with a national minority, property, birth or other status."

A. PRELIMINARY ISSUE

172. In further submissions of 19 September 2002, the government informed the Court that the Constitution had been amended so that the death penalty could no longer be ordered or implemented other than in time of war or of imminent threat of war or for acts of terrorism and that the Turkish Grand National Assembly had abolished the death penalty by enacting Law no. 4771 which entered into effect on 9 August 2002. This law provided for the abolition of the death penalty in peacetime by amending, inter alia, the Criminal Code (see paragraphs 7 and 47 above). Moreover, Mr Ocalan's sentence was subsequently commuted to life imprisonment by the Ankara State Security Court, which ruled that the offences under Article 125 of the Criminal Code for which the applicant had been convicted had been committed in peacetime and constituted terrorist acts. In the government's submission, the allegations raised by the applicant under Article 2 of the Convention should now be rejected as inadmissible on the grounds that the death penalty has now been abolished in Turkey.

173. The applicant submitted in reply that the Court should nevertheless continue its examination of the issues raised under Article 2 as the risk that the applicant might be subjected to the death penalty had not been completely removed since, inter alia, an appeal had been lodged against the commutation of his sentence (see paragraph 47 above).

174. It is true that the Court could declare an application inadmissible at any stage of the proceedings in accordance with Article 35 § 4 of the Convention. However, in the present case the applicant had been sentenced to death and had spent more than three years detained in isolation awaiting a determination of his fate. Up until recently (see paragraphs 5 and 47 above) there was reason to fear that the death sentence would be implemented. In addition, his complaint relates not only to the question of the implementation of the sentence but also to that of its imposition. Accordingly, the Court considers it more appropriate to examine the issues raised by the death penalty on the merits.

The Court therefore rejects the government's plea.

B. MERITS

*1. Original submissions of those appearing before the Court*

*a. The applicant*  175. For the applicant any recourse to the death penalty violated both Articles 2 and 3 of the Convention. By their practices over the last fifty-two years the Contracting States should be taken to have abrogated the exception provided in the second sentence of Article 2 § 1 of the Convention. When the Convention was signed in 1950, the death penalty was not perceived as a degrading and inhuman penalty in Europe and was provided for in the legislation of a number of States. Since that time European States have reached a consensus that the death penalty is an inhuman and degrading penalty within the meaning of Article 3 of the Convention. There has been a de facto abolition throughout Europe. Such developments should be seen as an agreement by Contracting States to amend Article 2 § 1.

176. No construction of Article 2 should permit a State to inflict inhuman and degrading treatment since the death penalty per se constitutes such treatment in breach of Article 3 of the Convention. In this latter respect the following submissions were made.

177. Developments in international and comparative law showed that the death penalty could also be seen to be contrary to international law. In this respect reference was made, inter alia, to a judgment of the South African Constitutional Court in which it was held that the death penalty was contrary to the South African Constitution's prohibition on cruel, inhuman or degrading treatment [citation omitted]. and to the judgment of the Canadian Supreme Court in *US v. Burns* (2001) SCC 7, where that Court, in a case concerning the extradition of a fugitive to the United States of America, considered capital punishment to amount to cruel and unusual punishment. The United Nations Human Rights Committee had also held that execution of a death sentence constituted cruel and inhuman treatment contrary to Article 6 of the International Covenant on Civil and Political Rights (see paragraph 60 above). Reference was also made to similar statements by the Hungarian Constitutional Court and the Constitutional Courts of Ukraine, Albania, Lithuania and the Republic of Srpska [Serbian Republic within Bosnia-Herzegovina].

178. The applicant further maintained (1) that it would infringe Article 2 to implement a death sentence which had been imposed following a procedure which did not conform with Articles 5 and 6 of the Convention and (2) that the enforcement of the death penalty imposed on him would be discriminatory given that since 1984 the government had been following a clearly stated policy of no longer carrying out such executions.

179. Finally the applicant maintained that the imposition of the death penalty by a Court which failed to satisfy the requisite standards of the Convention and which permitted violations of the applicant's rights under Article 6 also violated Articles 2 and 3.

*b. The government* 180. The government pointed out that Turkey had not been under any Convention obligation to abolish the death penalty. The text of the Convention could not be changed or corrected by an agreement among States that the death penalty was incompatible with Human Rights standards. It was not open to the Court to substitute such developments in values and standards which had taken place in other societies for the text of the Convention.

181. It was stressed that the death penalty was clearly provided for in Article 2 of the Convention. Irrespective of whether capital punishment ought to be abolished, Article 3 of the Convention could not be interpreted to include a prohibition of that penalty. That provision did not admit of any derogation, whereas Article 2 of Protocol no. 6 made provision for the death penalty to be retained in time of war or of imminent threat of war. It was obvious that the signatories to this Protocol did not consider the death penalty to be a degrading or inhuman punishment, since if they did such an exception would not have been made. The existence of a war could not make a punishment less inhuman or degrading.

182. The government further maintained that the applicant's trial had been conducted fairly by an independent and impartial tribunal within the meaning of Article 6 and that his arrest in Kenya had been lawful.

183. They also rejected any allegation of discrimination against the applicant, arguing that he had not been convicted either because of his ethnic origin or on account of his political opinions but because he had been the instigator of a large number of murders and bomb attacks carried out by the armed organisation that he led.

## 2. The Court's assessment

*a. As regards the implementation of the death penalty*   184. The Court refers to the government's argument that the applicant no longer risks execution. In a letter to the Court of 19 September 2002, the government declared that Abdullah Öcalan no longer faced the execution of the death penalty as finalised on 22 November 1999 by the judgment of the Turkish Court of Cassation (see paragraph 47 above). The Court notes that the death penalty has been abolished in Turkey (ibid.). Furthermore the applicant's sentence has been commuted to a period of life imprisonment (ibid.). In addition the constitutional action challenging the compatibility with the Constitution of the legislation abolishing the death penalty has failed (ibid.). Against this background the Court considers that the threat of implementation of the death sentence has been effectively removed.

185. It is true that a further legal action against the commutation of his sentence is still pending before the Turkish courts. The judgment of the Ankara State Security Court of 3 October 2002 has been appealed against by two trades unions who argue that the PKK's activities in southeast Turkey are akin to war (see paragraph 47 above). However, having regard to the developments described above as well as to the government's declaration to the Court in their letter of 19 September 2002, it can no longer be said that there are substantial grounds for fearing that the applicant will be executed, notwithstanding the abovementioned appeal. It must also be borne in mind in this context that Turkey has now signed Protocol no. 6 (see paragraph 55 above) and that the non-implementation of the capital sentence is in keeping with Turkey's obligations as a signatory State to this Protocol, in accordance with Article 18 of the

Vienna Convention of 23 May 1969 on the Law of Treaties, to "refrain from acts which would defeat the object and purpose" of the Protocol.

186. In these circumstances, the applicant's complaints under Articles 2, 3 and 14 based on the implementation of the death penalty must be rejected. Accordingly there has been no violation of these provisions on this basis.

*b. As regards the imposition of the death penalty* 187. It remains to be determined whether the imposition of the death penalty, in itself, gave rise to a breach of the Convention.

i. *Article 2*

188. At the outset the Court considers that no separate issue arises under the present head as regards Article 2 and prefers to examine this question under Article 3.

ii. *Article 3 read against the background of Article 2*

a. *Legal significance of the practice of the Contracting States as regards the death penalty*

189. The Court reiterates that the Convention is to be read as a whole and that Article 3 must be construed in harmony with the provisions of Article 2. If Article 2 is to be read as permitting capital punishment, notwithstanding the almost universal abolition of the death penalty in Europe, Article 3 cannot be interpreted as prohibiting the death penalty since that would nullify the clear wording of Article 2 § 1 [citation omitted].

Accordingly, the Court must first address the applicant's submission that the practice of the Contracting States in this area can be taken as establishing an agreement to abrogate the exception provided for in the second sentence of Article 2 § 1, which explicitly permits capital punishment under certain conditions.

190. The Court reiterates that it must be mindful of the Convention's special character as a Human Rights treaty and that the Convention cannot be interpreted in a vacuum. It should so far as possible be interpreted in harmony with other rules of public international law of which it forms part (citations omitted). It must, however, confine its primary attention to the issues of interpretation and application of the provisions of the Convention which arise in the present case.

191. It is recalled that the Court accepted in its *Soering v. the United Kingdom* judgment that an established practice within the Member States could give rise to an amendment of the Convention. In that case the Court accepted that subsequent practice in national penal policy, in the form of a generalised abolition of capital punishment, could be taken as establishing the agreement of the Contracting States to abrogate the exception provided for under Article 2 § 1 and hence remove a textual limit on the scope for evolutive [sic] interpretation of Article 3 (see the above-cited judgment, § 103). It was found, however, that Protocol no. 6 showed that the intention of the States was to adopt the normal method of amendment of the text in order to introduce a new obligation to abolish capital punishment in time of peace and to do so by an optional instrument allowing each State to choose the moment when to undertake such an engagement. The Court accordingly concluded that Article 3 could not be interpreted as generally prohibiting the death penalty (ibid. §§ 103–4).

192. The applicant takes issue with the Court's approach in the *Soering* judgment. His principal submission was that the reasoning is flawed since Protocol no. 6 represents merely one yardstick by which the practice of the States may be measured and that the evidence shows that all members of the Council of Europe have, either de facto or *de jure*, effected total abolition of the death penalty for all crimes and in all circumstances. He contended that as a matter of legal theory there was no reason why the States should not be capable of abolishing the death penalty both by abrogating the right to rely on the second sentence of Article 2 § 1 through their practice and by formal recognition of that process in the ratification of Protocol no. 6.

193. The Court reiterates that the Convention is a living instrument which must be interpreted in the light of present-day conditions and that the increasingly high standard being required in the area of the protection of Human Rights and fundamental liberties correspondingly and inevitably requires greater firmness in assessing breaches of the fundamental values of democratic societies [citation omitted].

194. It reiterates that in assessing whether a given treatment or punishment is to be regarded as inhuman or degrading for the purposes of Article 3 it cannot but be influenced by the developments and commonly accepted standards in the penal policy of the Member States of the Council of Europe in this field (see the above-cited *Soering* judgment, p. 40, § 102). Moreover, the concepts of inhuman and degrading treatment and punishment have evolved considerably since the Convention came into force in 1950 and indeed since the Court's *Soering v. the United Kingdom* judgment in 1989.

195. Equally the Court observes that the legal position as regards the death penalty has undergone a considerable evolution since the *Soering* case was decided. The de facto abolition noted in that case in respect of twenty-two Contracting States in 1989 has developed into a *de jure* abolition in forty-three of the forty-four Contracting States — most recently in the respondent State — and a moratorium in the remaining State which has not yet abolished the penalty, namely Russia. This almost complete abandonment of the death penalty in times of peace in Europe is reflected in the fact that all the Contracting States have signed Protocol no. 6 and forty-one States have ratified it, that is to say, all except Turkey, Armenia and Russia. It is further reflected in the policy of the Council of Europe which requires that new Member States undertake to abolish capital punishment as a condition of their admission into the organisation. As a result of these developments the territories encompassed by the Member States of the Council of Europe have become a zone free of capital punishment.

196. Such a marked development could now be taken as signalling the agreement of the Contracting States to abrogate, or at the very least to modify, the second sentence of Article 2 § 1, particularly when regard is had to the fact that all Contracting States have now signed Protocol no. 6 and that it has been ratified by forty-one States. It may be questioned whether it is necessary to await ratification of Protocol no. 6 by the three remaining States before concluding that the death penalty exception in Article 2 has been significantly modified. Against such a consistent background, it can be said that capital

punishment in peacetime has come to be regarded as an unacceptable, if not inhuman, form of punishment which is no longer permissible under Article 2.

197. In expressing this view, the Court is aware of the opening for signature of Protocol no. 13 which provides an indication that the Contracting States have chosen the traditional method of amendment of the text of the Convention in pursuit of their policy of abolition. However this Protocol seeks to extend the prohibition by providing for the abolition of the death penalty in all circumstances — that is to say both in times of peace and in times of war. This final step towards complete abolition of the death penalty can be seen as a confirmation of the abolitionist trend established by the practice of the Contracting States. It does not necessarily run counter to the view that Article 2 has been amended in so far as it permits the death penalty in times of peace.

198. In the Court's view, it cannot now be excluded, in the light of the developments that have taken place in this area, that the States have agreed through their practice to modify the second sentence in Article 2 § 1 in so far as it permits capital punishment in peacetime. Against this background it can also be argued that the implementation of the death penalty can be regarded as inhuman and degrading treatment contrary to Article 3. However it is not necessary for the Court to reach any firm conclusion on this point since for the following reasons it would run counter to the Convention, even if Article 2 were to be construed as still permitting the death penalty, to implement a death sentence following an unfair trial.

b. *Unfair proceedings and the death penalty*

199. In the Court's view, present-day attitudes in the Contracting States towards the abolition of the death penalty, as reflected in the above analysis, must be taken into account when examining the compatibility with Articles 2 and 3 of any death sentence. As noted above, the Court will postulate that the death penalty is permissible in certain circumstances.

200. As already highlighted by the Court in the context of Article 3, the manner in which the death penalty is imposed or executed, the personal circumstances of the condemned person and [the proportionality of the sentence] to the gravity of the crime committed, as well as the conditions of detention while awaiting execution, are examples of factors capable of bringing the treatment or punishment received by the condemned person within the proscription under Article 3 (see *Soering* cited above, p. 41, § 104).

201. Since the right to life in Article 2 of the Convention ranks as one of the most fundamental provisions of the Convention — one from which there can be no derogation in peacetime under Article 15 — and enshrines one of the basic values of the democratic societies making up the Council of Europe, its provisions must be strictly construed (citations omitted).

202. Even if the death penalty were still permissible under Article 2, the Court considers that an arbitrary deprivation of life pursuant to capital punishment is prohibited. This flows from the requirement that "Everyone's right to life shall be protected by law". An arbitrary act cannot be lawful under the Convention [citation omitted].

203. It also follows from the requirement in Article 2 § 1 that the deprivation of life be pursuant to the "execution of a sentence of a court", that the "court" which imposes the penalty be an independent and impartial tribunal within the meaning of the Court's case-law (citations omitted) and that the most rigorous standards of fairness are observed in the criminal proceedings both at first instance and on appeal. Since the execution of the death penalty is irreversible, it can only be through the application of such standards that an arbitrary and unlawful taking of life can be avoided (citations omitted). Lastly, the requirement in Article 2 § 1 that the penalty be "provided by law" means not only that there must exist a basis for the penalty in domestic law but that the requirement of the quality of the law be fully respected, namely that the legal basis be "accessible" and "foreseeable" as those terms are understood in the case-law of the Court (citations omitted).

204. It follows from the above construction of Article 2 that the implementation of the death penalty in respect of a person who has not had a fair trial would not be permissible.

205. It remains for the Court to examine the implications of the above inter pretation for the issue under Article 3 concerning the imposition of the death penalty.

206. The above conclusion concerning the interpretation of Article 2 where there has been an unfair trial must inform the opinion of the Court when it considers the question of the imposition of the death penalty in such circumstances.

207. In the Court's view, to impose a death sentence on a person after an unfair trial is to subject that person wrongfully to the fear that he will be executed. The fear and uncertainty as to the future generated by a sentence of death, in circumstances where there exists a real possibility that the sentence will be enforced, must give rise to a significant degree of human anguish. Such anguish cannot be dissociated from the unfairness of the proceedings underlying the sentence which, given that human life is at stake, becomes unlawful under the Convention. Having regard to the rejection by the Contracting Parties of capital punishment, which is no longer seen as having any legitimate place in a democratic society, the imposition of a capital sentence in such circumstances must be considered, in itself, to amount to a form of inhuman treatment.

iii. *Conclusion*

208. The Court notes that there has been a moratorium on the implementation of the death penalty in Turkey since 1984 and that the Turkish government in the present case complied with the Court's interim measure pursuant to Rule 39 to stay the execution (see paragraph 5 above). It is further noted that the applicant's file was not sent to Parliament for approval of the death sentence as was then required by the Turkish Constitution.

209. The Court has also had regard, in this context, to the case of *Çinar v. Turkey* (no. 17864/91, dec. 5.9.94, D.R. 79, p. 5) in which the Commission rejected a claim that Article 3 had been violated in the case of an applicant who had also been sentenced to death in Turkey. In its reasoning, the Commission took into account the long-standing moratorium on the death penalty and concluded in the circumstances of that case that the risk of the penalty being implemented was illusory.

210. The Court is not persuaded that the same can be said in the case of Mr Öcalan whose political background as leader and founder of the PKK, which had been engaged in a sustained campaign of violence causing many thousands of casualties, had made him Turkey's most wanted person. His singularity as a person convicted of a capital offence is evident from the conditions of strict isolation in which he has been detained. Given the applicant's high profile, the fact that he had been convicted of the most serious crimes under the Turkish Criminal Code and the general political controversy in Turkey — prior to the decision to abolish the death penalty — surrounding the question of whether he should be executed, it cannot be open to doubt that the risk that the sentence would be implemented was a real one. Indeed, the present proceedings have been predicated upon that risk up until the present judgment, as reflected in the Court's interim measure under Rule 39 (see paragraph 5 above). The risk remained in existence for more than three years during the applicant's detention in İmralı from the date of the Court of Cassation's judgment of 25 November 1999 affirming the applicant's conviction until the recent judgment of the Constitutional Court of 27 December 2002 upholding the validity of the law abolishing the death penalty. Thereafter, as the Court has found (see paragraph 184 above) the risk had essentially disappeared.

211. The Court refers to its conclusions concerning the applicant's complaints under Article 6 of the Convention. It has found that he was not tried by an independent and impartial tribunal and that there was a breach of the rights of the defence under Article 6 § 1, taken together with Article 6 § 3 (b) and (c), having regard to the fact that the applicant had no access to a lawyer during police detention, that he was unable to communicate with his lawyers out of the hearing of officials, that restrictions had been imposed on the number and length of his lawyers' visits to him, that he was unable to consult the case-file until a late stage in the procedure and that his lawyers did not have sufficient time to consult the file properly (see paragraph 169 above).

212. The death penalty has thus been imposed on the applicant following an unfair procedure which could not be considered compatible with the strict standards of fairness required in cases involving a capital sentence. Moreover he has had to suffer the consequences of such imposition for more than three years.

213. Having regard to the above, the Court concludes that the imposition of the death sentence on the applicant following an unfair trial amounted to inhuman treatment in violation of Article 3.

*IV. Alleged violation of Article 3 of the Convention: conditions of detention*

214. The applicant further complained that the conditions in which he had been transferred from Kenya to Turkey and detained on the island of İmralı amounted to treatment that infringed Article 3 of the Convention . . . .

\*\*\*

[The Court, regarding the conditions in which the applicant was transferred from Kenya to Turkey, considered that it had not been established "beyond all reasonable doubt" that the applicant's arrest and the conditions in which he was transferred from Kenya to Turkey exceeded the usual degree of humiliation that was inherent in every arrest and detention or attained the minimum level of severity required for Article 3 of the Convention to apply. Consequently, there had been no violation of that provision on this point. With regards to conditions of detention on the island of İmralı, the Court found that the general conditions in which the applicant was being detained at İmralı prison had not reached the minimum level of severity necessary to constitute inhuman or degrading treatment within the meaning of Article 3 of the Convention. Consequently, there had been no violation of that provision on that account.]

## V. Article 34 of the Convention

237. The applicant complained of being hindered in the exercise of his right of individual application in that his legal representatives in Amsterdam had not been permitted to contact him after his arrest and/or the government had failed to reply to the Court's request for them to supply information. He alleged a violation of Article 34 of the Convention . . . .

\*\*\*

[The Court found that as regards the applicant's inability to communicate with his lawyers in Amsterdam following his arrest, there was nothing to indicate that the exercise of the applicant's right to individual application was impeded to any significant extent.

Moreover the Court found, without prejudice to its views on the binding nature of interim measures under Rule 39, that in the special circumstances of the case the refusal of the Turkish government to provide certain information did not amount to a violation of the applicant's right of individual application.]

## VI. Other complaints

\*\*\*

[The Court considered that no separate examination of the complaints under Articles 7, 8, 9, 10, 13, 14 and 18 of the Convention, taken alone or together, was inconsistent with the aforementioned provisions of the Convention.]

[In awarding damages, the Court took the view that any pecuniary or non-pecuniary damage that the applicant might have sustained had been sufficiently compensated by its findings of a violation of Articles 3, 5 and 6 of the Convention. As regards costs and expenses, the Court considered it reasonable to award the applicant a total of EUR 100,000 in respect of the claims made by all his legal representatives.]

# Document no. 92

**Council of Europe: the Committee of Ministers Response to PACE Recommendation no. 1576 and other ECtHR developments in 2003**

*Introductory comment.* In a Recommendation dated September 23, 2002, Recommendation 1576 (2002): Implementation of Decisions of the European Court of Human Rights by Turkey,[15] the PACE recommended to the Committee of Ministers that "the Committee ... consider taking all the necessary measures in the event that Turkey refuses or continues to delay payment of the just satisfaction, including the seizure of the corresponding sum from Turkey's contribution to the Council of Europe, and the application of a daily fine ... on execution of judgments of the European Court of Human Rights." The Committee of Ministers replied to the recommendation on March 31, 2003. The following is an edited version of the reply.

*Reply from the Committee of Ministers to the Recommendation 1576 (2002): Implementation of Decisions of the European Court of Human Rights by Turkey[16]*

1. The Committee can assure the Parliamentary Assembly that supervision of the execution of judgments of the European Court of Human Rights is one of the Committee's main priorities. Speedy and efficient execution is essential for the credibility and efficiency of the European Convention on Human Rights (ECHR) as a constitutional instrument of European public order on which the democratic stability of the Continent depends.

2. The Committee welcomes the recent enhancement of Turkey's political determination to comply with the Court's judgments and, more generally, to meet the requirements of the ECHR and other Council of Europe's standards, as reflected in Prime Minister Gül's statement to the Assembly at the January 2003 part-session. In this context, the Committee welcomes in particular the wide-ranging reforms which have been accomplished within a short time-frame on such matters as the abolition of the death penalty, the lifting of certain restrictions on non-violent speech, the increased efforts to fight torture and ill-treatment not least

through improved investigative procedures and more severe sanctions against members of the security forces responsible for abuses. The Committee also welcomes the programme recently agreed upon by Council of Europe experts and the Turkish authorities, within the framework of a Joint European Union/ Council of Europe Initiative, providing for in-depth training of Turkish judges and prosecutors on the Convention and the Court's case-law, with a view to ensuring their effective implementation in day-to-day practice.

3. The recent constitutional and legislative reforms, the ensuing evolution of domestic case-law, as well as the training and awareness measures represent important developments which will undoubtedly contribute significantly to the execution of a number of judgments concerning Turkey.

4. In addition to the measures already adopted, the Committee has recently received assurances from the Turkish authorities that they intend rapidly to settle, in particular, the problems concerning the remaining restrictions on the applicants' civil and political rights in some twenty cases relating to violations of freedom of expression, and concerning shortfalls in payment of just satisfaction in some forty cases. The Committee will continue its supervision of these matters, and indeed of all other outstanding issues.

\*\*\*

8. The Committee, referring also to Prime Minister Gül's recent expression of the Turkish authorities' determination to comply with the judgments of the Court, expects that the momentum, as illustrated above, will be maintained so that all outstanding issues will be settled rapidly and all judgments complied with fully.

9. On a more general level, the Committee would like to inform the Assembly that reflections are under way, both within the Committee itself and in the context, of the work on reinforcing the ECtHR control system, designed to improve and speed up the execution of judgments. In this context, particular focus is being given to possible measures in the event of slow or negligent execution or non-execution of judgments. Relevant recommendations of the Assembly are being borne in mind in this regard. The Committee will keep the Assembly informed of progress in the reflections.

*Editors' comment on 2003 developments related to the ECtHR.* During 2003, the ECtHR ruled against the Republic of Turkey in seventy-six cases. Of these, fifty-six involved the right to a fair trial, one case involved torture and eight cases involved inhuman or degrading treatment, one case involved the unlawful deprivation of life, nine cases involved unlawful arrest and detention, and six cases involved freedom of expression. In forty-five cases, the government accepted a friendly settlement and the ECtHR ruled in favor of Turkey in one case.

Of particular importance, Leyla Zana, Hatip Dicle, Orhan Dogan and Selim Sadak — former members of Parliament from the pro-Kurdish independence Democracy Party — were granted a retrial in February under legal reforms allowing for a retrial for convicts who win their appeals to the ECtHR. They remained in prison during the trial, which continued at year's end. Attorneys for the defendants and the Geneva-based International Commission of Jurists accused the court of trying the case with pro-prosecution bias. In addition, the Council of Europe in October informed the government of its concern that the conduct of the trial was not consistent with the fair trial provisions of the European Convention on Human Rights.

# Document no. 93

**EU–TR Association Council Decision of 19 May 2003 on the Principles, Priorities, Intermediate Objectives and Conditions Contained in the Accession Partnership with Turkey**[17]

*The Council of the European Union,*

\*\*\*

has decided as follows:

*Article 1*

In accordance with Article 2 of Regulation (EC) no. 390/2001, the principles, priorities, intermediate objectives and conditions in the Accession Partnership for Turkey are set out in the Annex hereto, which forms an integral part of this decision.

*Article 2*

The implementation of the Accession Partnership shall be examined and monitored in the Association Agreement bodies and by the appropriate Council bodies on the basis of the regular report by the Commission to the Council.

\*\*\*

**Turkey: 2003 accession partnership**

\*\*\*

*3. Principles*

The main priority areas identified for each candidate State relate to their ability to take on the obligations of meeting the Copenhagen criteria which state that membership requires:

- that the candidate State has achieved stability of institutions guaranteeing democracy, the rule of law, Human Rights and respect for and protection of minorities,
- the existence of a functioning market economy, as well as the capacity to cope with competitive pressure and market forces within the Union,
- the ability to take on the obligations of membership, including adherence to the aims of political, economic and monetary union.

At its meeting in Madrid in 1995, the European Council stressed the need for the candidate States to adjust their administrative structures to ensure harmonious operation of Community policies after accession and at Luxembourg, in 1997, it stressed that incorporation of the *acquis* into legislation is necessary, but not in itself sufficient; it is necessary to ensure that it is actually applied. The Feira and Gothenburg European Councils in 2000 and 2001 respectively confirmed the vital importance of the applicant countries' capacity to implement and enforce the *acquis*, and added that this required important efforts by the applicants in strengthening and reforming their administrative and judicial structures.

*4. Priorities*

The Commission's regular reports have highlighted, besides the progress already made, the extent of the efforts that still have to be made in certain areas by the candidate States to prepare for accession. This situation requires the definition of intermediate stages in terms of priorities, each to be accompanied by precise objectives to be set in collaboration with the States concerned, the achievement of which will condition the degree of assistance granted and the progress of the negotiations under way with some countries and the opening of new negotiations with the others.

The priorities in the Accession Partnership are divided into two groups — short and medium term. Those under the short term have been selected on the basis that it is realistic to expect that Turkey can fulfil them in 2003/2004. The priorities listed under the medium term are expected to take more than one year to complete although work should be taken forward substantially in 2003/2004.

The Accession Partnership indicates the priority areas for Turkey's membership preparations. Turkey will nevertheless have to address all issues identified in the regular report. It is also important that Turkey fulfils the commitments of legislative approximation and implementation of the *acquis* in accordance with the commitments made under the Association Agreement, Customs Union and related decisions of the EC–Turkey Association Council . . . .

Drawing on the analysis of the Commission's regular report, the following priorities have been identified for Turkey.

**Enhanced political dialogue and political criteria**

*Priorities (2003/2004)*

- In accordance with the Helsinki Conclusions, in the context of the political dialogue, strongly support efforts to find a comprehensive settlement of the

Cyprus problem, through the continuation of the United Nations Secretary General's mission of good offices and of negotiations on the basis of his proposals.
- In accordance with the Helsinki Conclusions, in the context of the political dialogue, under the principle of peaceful settlement of disputes in accordance with the UN Charter, make every effort to resolve any outstanding border disputes and other related issues, as referred to in point 4 of the Helsinki Conclusions.
- Ratify the International Covenant on Civil and Political Rights and its optional Protocol and the International Covenant on Economic, Social and Cultural Rights. Ratify Protocol no. 6 of the European Convention on Human Rights. Comply with the European Convention for the Protection of Human Rights and Fundamental Freedoms, including respect of the judgments of the European Court of Human Rights (section II of the Convention).
- Implement measures to fight against torture and ill-treatment by law enforcement officials, in line with Article 3 of the European Convention on Human Rights and the recommendations of the European Committee for the Prevention of Torture. Adopt further measures to ensure that prosecutors conduct timely and effective investigations of alleged cases and that courts impose adequate punishments on those convicted of abuses.
- Guarantee in practice the right for detained and imprisoned persons to have access in private to a lawyer and to have relatives notified, from the outset of their custody, in line with the European Convention on Human Rights.
- Guarantee in law and in practice the full enjoyment of Human Rights and fundamental freedoms by all individuals without discrimination and irrespective of language, race, colour, sex, political opinion, religion or belief in line with relevant international and European instruments to which Turkey is a party.
- Pursue and implement reforms concerning freedom of expression including freedom of the press. Lift legal restrictions in line with the European Convention on Human Rights (Articles 10, 17 and 18). Remedy the situation of those persons prosecuted or sentenced for non-violent expression of opinion. Implement legal provisions on the right to re-trial following the relevant judgment of the European Court of Human Rights.
- Pursue and implement reforms concerning freedom of association and peaceful assembly. Lift legal restrictions in line with the European Convention on Human Rights, in particular on both foreign and national associations, including trades unions (Articles 11, 17 and 18). Encourage the development of civil society.
- Adapt and implement provisions concerning the exercise of freedom of thought, conscience and religion by all individuals and religious communities in line with Article 9 of the European Convention on Human Rights.
- Establish conditions for the functioning of these communities, in line with the practice of EU Member States.
- This includes legal and judicial protection of the communities, their members and their assets, teaching, appointing and training of clergy, and the

enjoyment of property rights in line with Protocol 1 of the European Convention on Human Rights.
- Ensure cultural diversity and guarantee cultural rights for all citizens irrespective of their origin. Ensure effective access to radio/TV broadcasting and education in languages other than Turkish through implementation of existing measures and the removal of remaining restrictions that impede this access.
- Adapt the functioning of the National Security Council in order to align civilian control of the military with practice in EU Member States.
- Strengthen the independence and efficiency of the judiciary and promote consistent interpretation of legal provisions related to Human Rights and fundamental freedoms in line with the European Convention on Human Rights. Take measures with a view to ensuring that the obligation for all judicial authorities to take into account the case-law of the European Court of Human Rights is respected. Align the functioning of State security courts with European standards. Prepare the establishment of intermediate courts of appeal.
- Continue to bring conditions in prisons into line with standards in EU Member States.
- Extend the training of law enforcement officials on Human Rights issues and modern investigation techniques, in particular as regards the fight against torture and ill-treatment, in order to prevent Human Rights violations.
- Extend the training of judges and prosecutors on the application of the European Convention on Human Rights and the case-law of the European Court of Human Rights.
- Intensify efforts to develop a comprehensive approach to reduce regional disparities, and in particular to improve the situation in the southeast, with a view to enhancing economic, social and cultural opportunities for all citizens. In this context, the return of internally displaced persons to their original settlements should be supported and speeded up.

\*\*\*

# Document no. 94

## Harmonisation package (6)[18]

*Article 1.* The phrase "from four years to eight years" in Article 453 of the Turkish Penal Code, no. 765, dated 1.3.1926, has been amended as "from eight years to twelve years".

*Article 2.* The following provisional Article has been added to Law on Foundations, no. 2762, dated 5.6.1935:

Provisional Article 2. Community Foundations may apply for registration within eighteen months from the date of entry into force of this Law in accordance with the Article 1, sub-paragraph 7.

*Article 3.* Article 55/A of the Law on the Basic Provisions on Elections and Voter Registers, no. 298, dated 26.4.1961, has been regulated to state as follows:

*Broadcast by private televisions and radio channels*

Article 55/A. Private radio and television corporations are subject to Articles 5, 20, 22, 23 and sub-paragraph 2 of the Article 31 of the Law on Turkish Radio and Television, no. 2954, in their broadcast, from the starting date of the elections until the end of the voting day.

The Supreme Board of Elections is in charge of and authorised to lay down the principles of broadcasting for private radio and television channels in line with the above sub-paragraph.

For nationwide radio and television channels, the Supreme Board of Elections, and for the other radio and television channels, the county election boards where these television and radio channels broadcast are in charge of and authorised to monitor, supervise and assess the compatibility of the broadcast with the above principles.

An appeal may be lodged to provincial election boards against the decisions taken by the county election boards within twenty-four hours. The decisions of the provincial election boards are final.

The Supreme Board of Elections has the authority to specify which radio and television channels broadcast nationwide. The decision taken by the Supreme Board of Elections is published in the Official Gazette.

*Article 4.* Article 149/A of Act no. 298 has been regulated to state as follows:

*The crimes related to the broadcasts by private radio and television channels*

Article 149/A. In the event of a broadcast that is in violation of Article 55/A of this Law as well as the principles laid down by the Supreme Board of Elections, private radio and television corporations broadcasting nationwide is warned by the Supreme Board of Elections and other private radio and television corporations broadcasting locally is warned by the county election boards or will be requested by them to unequivocally apologise in the same broadcasting slot. In case of non-compliance with this request or repetition of the violation, the broadcasting of the programme in question shall be stopped from one to twelve times by the Supreme Board of Elections or county election boards. If the violation is repeated, the Supreme Board of Elections shall stop the broadcast by the nationwide private radio and television channels from five days to fifteen days. As for the local private radio and television channels, the broadcast of the channel in question will be stopped from three days to seven days by the decision of the relevant county election board.

These decisions are immediately implemented by the highest public officials in charge.

The responsible members of the private radio and television corporations facing a decision to stop broadcasting taken in line with the first sub-paragraph will be sentenced to a heavy fine ranging from 10,000,000,000 liras to 85,000,000,000 liras, and the responsible members of the local private radio and television channels will be sentenced to a heavy fine ranging from 350,000,000 liras to 4,000,000,000 liras by the competent court. In the event of a repetition of the offence, these sentences are applied three times of the amount indicated. Article 119 of the Turkish Penal Code does not apply to the sentences to be delivered in line with this sub-paragraph.

\*\*\*

*Article 6.* Subdivision (i) has been added to the first sub-paragraph to the Article 53 of the Law on Administrative Procedures, No. 2577, dated 6.1.1982, and the first sentence of sub-paragraph 3 has been amended to read as follows:

Confirmation, by a final judgement of the European Court of Human Rights, that the judgement is reached due to a violation of the Convention on the Protection of Human Rights and Fundamental Freedoms or its annexed protocols.

The period for re-trial is ten years for the reason stated in subdivision (h) of sub-paragraph (1); one year for the reason stated in subdivision (i) of sub-paragraph (1) as of the date of the finalisation of the judgement by the European Court of Human Rights; and sixty days for other reasons.

*Article 7.* The following provisional Article has been added to the Act no. 2577:

Provisional Article 5. Subdivision (i) of sub-paragraph (1) of Article 53 will be applicable to judgements of the European Court of Human Rights finalised at the time of entry into force of this law and the decisions on the applications made by the European Court of Human Rights after the entering into force of this Law. Applications for re-trial upon the decisions of the European Court of

Human Rights that have been finalised at the date of entry into force of this Law are to be made within one year of the date of entry into force of this Law.

*Article 8.* The title of Article 16 of the Law on the Establishment and Proceedings of State Security Courts, no. 2845, dated 16.6.1883, has been amended as "apprehension and arrest".

\*\*\*

*Article 11.* The phrase "General Secretariat of the National Security Council" in the first sentence of sub-paragraph 6 of Article 6 of the Law no. 3257 has been deleted from the text of the Article.

*Article 12.* Sub-paragraph 3 of Article 9 of the Law no. 3257 has been amended and a sub-paragraph has been added as follows:

The work may be deemed unlawful and legal procedures will be launched by a decision of a judge when the inspection carried out by the Ministry or head of the local public authority finds the work in question to be in contradiction with the fundamental principles of the Republic as stated in the constitution, indivisibility of the State with its territory and nation, public morals, and public health and public order. In cases where the delay thereby caused will be detrimental, a written order of the Ministry or the local public authority would be sufficient to start the procedure.

Decisions by the competent authorities based on the above sub-paragraphs will be submitted to the approval of the authorised minor offences judge within twenty-four hours. The judge will announce his decision within forty-eight hours, otherwise the decision will be retracted.

\*\*\*

*Article 14.* The fourth sentence of the first sub-paragraph of the Article 4 of the Law on the Establishment of and Broadcasting by the Radio and Television Channels, no. 3984, dated 13.04.1994, has been amended as follows:

In addition, public and private radio and television corporations may broadcast in different languages and dialects used traditionally by Turkish citizens in their daily lives.

*Article 15.* The second sentence of the fourth sub-paragraph of the Article 15 of the Law no. 3984 has been amended as follows:

Regional offices utilising the existing personnel, may be established where deemed necessary to monitor the local broadcasts.

*Article 16.* The phrase "from the seventh day onwards" in the third sub-paragraph of the Article 32 of the Law no. 3984 has been amended as "within twenty-four hours".

*Article 17* The following Provisional Article has been added to the Law no. 3984:

Provisional Article 10. The regulation prescribed in the first sub-paragraph of Article 4 shall be prepared and put into effect by the Supreme Board of Radio and Television within four months of the promulgation of this Law.

*Article 18.* The first paragraph of the sub-paragraph (A) of the Article 1 of the Law Amending Various Laws, no. 4771, dated 03.08.2002, has been amended as follows:

Apart from the capital punishment prescribed for the crimes committed at times of war and imminent threat of war, capital punishments prescribed in the Turkish Penal Code, dated 01.03.1926, no. 765, the Law on the Prohibition and Prosecution of Smuggling, dated 07.01.1932, no. 1918, the Forest Act, dated 31.08.1956, no. 6831 and the Gallipoli Peninsula Historical National Park Law, dated 17.02.2000, no. 4533 have been converted into heavy lifetime imprisonment.

*Article 19.* The following provisions have been annulled:

a. Article 462 of the Turkish Penal Code no. 756, dated 01.03.1926.
b. Article 8 of the Anti-Terror Law no. 3713, dated 12.04.1991.
c. The first sub-paragraph of the Article 31 of the Law Amending to Some Articles of the Law on Criminal Procedure and the Law on the Establishment and Proceedings of the State Security Courts.

*Article 20.* The title of Article 1 of the Anti-Terror Law, dated 12.04.1991, has been amended as "Definition of terror and organisation", and its first and second sub-paragraphs have been amended as follows:

Terror is the criminal acts committed by a person or persons as members of an organisation by using force and violence; by method of oppressing, scaring, deterring, suppressing or threatening, in order to change the features of the Republic as prescribed in the Constitution, the political, legal, social, secular, economic order, to dismantle the indivisible unity of the State with its territory and nation, to endanger the existence of the Turkish State and the Republic, to weaken or destroy or take over the State authority, to destroy fundamental rights and freedoms, to harm the internal and external security of the State, the public order or the public health.

Should two or more persons get together with an aim to commit the terrorist crime prescribed in the first paragraph, an organisation prescribed in this Law will be deemed to have been formed.

*Article 21.* The following Provisional Article has been added to the Act no. 3713:

Provisional Article 10. For the crimes committed prior to the promulgation of this Law, which are prescribed in the Article 8 of the Law no. 3713, are annulled by this Law:

1. The Public Prosecutors shall give the decision of non-prosecution at the stage of preliminary prosecution.

2. a. Those arrested but not sued against on behalf of the public, shall be released by the Prosecutor,

b. Those arrested and sued against on behalf of the public, shall be released by the competent court.

3. In the circumstances where:

a. the court which had decided on the case thereof, on cases not referred to the Court of Cassation up until that date or those with the Prosecutor of the Court of Cassation,

b. the relevant penal chamber, on cases already referred to the Court of Cassation,

c. the court which had decided on the case thereof, on the cases of the convicts whose sentences are being executed.

The cases shall be considered as urgent and shall be decided upon, with due consideration given to the Article 2 of the Turkish Penal Code.

# Document no. 95

**Turkey's 2003 Revised National Programme for the Adoption of the *Acquis*[19]**

*Preamble*

Forging a strong and prosperous modern state for the information age, united as a nation based on the principles of the rule of law, democracy and secularism, and firmly founded upon the basic tenets of the Republic, is a historic responsibility towards future generations.

Turkey has always regarded progress as its fundamental principle. Since the foundation of the Republic, Turkey has always been a part of renewal movements in politics, economics and law. This inclination has been given substance through progress and visionary reforms, and has been driven by the principle of secularism based on freedom of conscience, and a compact of citizenship that transcends language, religion, race or gender, in such a way as to reinforce the territorial integrity and political unity of the Turkish Republic.

Turkey is determined to continue its development until it reaches the ultimate stage of civilisation. Turkey is making efforts to become a capable and creative twenty-first century state, with world class production, a just distribution of wealth, Human Rights guarantees, the rule of law, participatory democracy, secularism, and the freedom of religion and conscience.

Accession to the European Union is the principal project that will carry Turkey to its goal of prosperity. Turkey's aim of integration with the European Union is a social reform project that will affect both the present and the future of every citizen. It is a great reform movement that will bring universal standards and practices to all areas of daily life, from production to consumption, from health to education, from agriculture to industry, from energy to environment, from justice to security. Every political, legal, economic or social reform on the path to membership, whilst increasing the living standards of the individual, also increases international economic influence, democratic respectability, and the security of the country, in line with international standards.

Accession to the European Union is a national target, which is supported by and reflects the common purpose of the vast majority of the people. This aim, which is also an integral part of Turkey's strategic vision, fully corresponds to the founding philosophy of the Republic and Atatürk's vision for the nation's integration with contemporary civilisation.

Turkey has been a fundamental component of European political, economic and cultural geography throughout history. The confirmation of Turkey's candidacy by the Helsinki European Council in 1999 has ushered in a new era of relations after forty years of association with the European Union. The developments since the Helsinki Council have brought Turkey closer than ever to membership. The European Union, at the Copenhagen Council of 12–13 December 2002, committed itself to starting accession negotiations without delay if it determines, on the basis of European Commission's reports and recommendations, that Turkey has fulfilled the Copenhagen political criteria by December 2004.

Turkey is going through a dynamic process of legal, political and economic reforms on the road to European Union membership. The purpose of this process is to guarantee the functioning of the democratic system with all its rules and institutions. Participatory democracy, the rule of law, Human Rights and fundamental freedoms are not only universal values, but are also the most reliable bases for political and economic stability and development. Turkey has adopted the Copenhagen value system and proven through the reforms and alignment work made to date that it has the will to achieve a more liberal, more participatory, more modern democracy.

In addition, Turkey has a stable functioning market economy, which is reinforced by the economic programme under implementation. The Customs Union has demonstrated Turkey's capacity to cope with the competitive pressures and market forces within the European Union.

A Turkey that has completed its grand social project and is a focus of democratic power in the twenty-first century offers a priceless opportunity for the establishment of regional and international peace and stability, as well as a singular source of inspiration for those who, in our turbulent region and beyond, seek progress.

In international relations, Turkey's EU candidacy advances its position in strategic, security and political terms. Turkey shall continue to develop its relations with its neighbours and adjacent regions in accordance with its peace-loving foreign policy objectives. In the same vein, Turkey will continue to undertake initiatives and efforts for the settlement of bilateral problems with Greece through dialogue. As a part of the enhanced political dialogue, Turkey will continue to support the efforts of the United Nations Secretary General in his good offices mission aimed at a mutually acceptable settlement, with a view to establishing a new partnership in Cyprus, based on the sovereign equality of the two parties and the realities on the island. Turkey supports the steps taken by the Turkish Cypriot side, which will foster an environment of confidence and pave the way for a comprehensive settlement.

The steps taken by Turkey on the path to European Union membership are measures that directly accelerate the raising of economic and social standards and ensure a society with high democratic and legal norms. For this purpose, with an approach that preserves the founding principals of the Republic and Atatürk's legacy, Turkey has the resolution and determination to rapidly fulfil its obligations in order to start accession negotiations at the earliest time and participate in the European Union's enlargement dynamics. The responsibilities set out in the National Programme reflect the stance of the Turkish nation.

## Political criteria

Turkey has completed comprehensive constitutional and legislative reforms that reinforce and safeguard fundamental rights and freedoms, democracy, the rule of law, and the protection of and respect for minorities, as set out in the Turkey National Programme for the Adoption of the European Union Acquis of 24 March 2001.

In this context, the death penalty has been abolished. Comprehensive legislative and administrative measures against torture and maltreatment have been put into force. The right to retrial in the light of the decisions of the European Court of Human Rights (ECtHR) has been introduced. Rules concerning conditions in prisons and detention houses have been brought in line with the norms of the European Convention of Human Rights (ECHR), and the recommendations of the European Committee for the Prevention of Torture (CPT). The state of emergency has been lifted in all provinces. Freedom of thought and expression, and the freedom of the press have been expanded. Provisions concerning associations, foundations and the right to assembly and peaceful demonstration have been advanced. Legislation has been amended to reinforce gender equality, and to protect cultural diversity and guarantee cultural rights, and to enhance the right to learn and broadcast in different languages and dialects. Legislation concerning non-Muslim communities and foreigners have been improved. The Human Rights Advisory Board, which constitutes an effective platform for dialogue between state and civil society in the area of Human Rights, has become operational. The advisory role of the National Security Council has been redefined.

In addition, several conventions relating to the political criteria have been signed or ratified, among which Additional Protocol no. 6 to the ECHR Concerning the Abolishing of the Death Penalty, the UN Convention on the Elimination of All Forms of Racial Discrimination, the UN Covenant on Civil and Political Rights, the UN Covenant on Economic, Social and Cultural Rights, the ILO [International Labour Organization] Convention Concerning the Prohibition and Immediate Action for the Elimination of Worst Forms of Child Labour (no. 182), and the UN Convention on Prevention of All Types of Discrimination Against Women and its Optional Protocol, can be cited.

Efforts to implement the reforms effectively and simultaneously continue. Numerous administrative measures have been put into effect in order to reflect fully the spirit of the reforms in practice. In this respect, by-laws on broadcasting in and teaching of different languages and dialects have been adopted and put into practice. By-laws on the acquisition and disposal of real estate by community foundations, and on associations, have entered into force, and the administrative restructuring has been completed. Circulars have been issued to raise the awareness of civil servants on the prevention of torture and maltreatment. Human rights training programmes for civil servants, particularly law enforcement officers, have been intensified and broadened. Comprehensive training programmes for judges and prosecutors, especially on ECHR provisions and ECtHR case-law, continue in collaboration with the Council of Europe and the European Union. Solid progress in practice, parallel to the reforms, has been registered in all these areas. The EU Harmonisation Commission was created in the Turkish Grand National Assembly in order to increase the efficiency of the process of legislative harmonisation.

The complete redrafting of all basic legislation is a long-term legislative process which will also continue during the accession negotiations. The government has opted to harmonise various laws in order to fulfil the political criteria, the prerequisite to the opening of accession negotiations, through "harmonisation legislation packages" to accelerate the process. However, the ultimate aim is to renew basic legislation in the long term through an integrated approach.

The government is resolved to complete legislation referred to under the various headings below during the first legislative year of the twenty-second legislative session of the Turkish Grand National Assembly. The government is determined, in principle, that the impact of all concluded reforms will be observed simultaneously, in letter and spirit, by June 2004.

*1. Freedom of thought and expression*

The government attaches importance and priority to both the continuation and the expansion of freedom of expression, in line with the EU *acquis* based on universal values, and with the practice in EU Member States, within the framework of Article 10 of the ECHR, which specifies the protection of territorial integrity and national security; and on the basis of safeguarding the secular and democratic nature of the Republic, the unitary structure of the state, and national integrity. Consequently,

- Legislation delineating freedom of expression will be reviewed in the light of the ECHR, especially with regard to the letter and spirit of Articles 10, 17 and 18 of the said Convention.
- Legislative and administrative measures expanding freedom of expression will be implemented effectively.
- Measures will be taken to ensure that the freedom of the press will be applied according to universal norms.
- The provisions on broadcasting in, and learning of, different languages and dialects used by Turkish citizens in daily life will be implemented.
- Training of members of the judiciary on Human Rights, the European Convention on Human Rights and the jurisprudence of the European Court

of Human Rights will be continued and expanded to ensure consistency in implementation.

## 2. Freedom of association, right to peaceful assembly, and civil society

The government will continue to support the development of the civil society and its participation in democratic life. In this vein, the relevant legislation will continue to be reviewed in the light of the European Convention on Human Rights and Fundamental Freedoms, especially with regard to compliance with the letter and spirit of Articles 11, 17 and 18.

In this respect,

- Legislation concerning associations as well as meetings and demonstrations will be reviewed. Provisions in various legislation will be collected into as few laws as possible to provide consistency.
- The legislative and administrative reforms concerning associations, foundations, meetings, and demonstration marches will be implemented effectively.

## 3. Prevention of torture and maltreatment

The government is determined to prevent torture and maltreatment and to allow zero tolerance in this regard. The legislative and administrative measures for the swift execution of justice will be implemented fully. All envisaged legislative and administrative measures, including legal and penal reforms, will be taken with sensitivity to the prevention of torture and maltreatment. During the implementation of the measures special account will be taken of Article 3 of the ECHR and the recommendations of the CPT. Added emphasis will be given to mechanisms for monitoring, supervision, and reporting.

In this connection,

- Allegations of torture and maltreatment will be investigated immediately and thoroughly, and the offenders will be punished rapidly.
- Provisions on the rights of persons arrested, detained or charged to communicate with their lawyers and inform their relatives will be fully implemented.
- Modern investigation techniques and medical monitoring systems to prevent maltreatment and Human Rights violations will be implemented effectively.
- Human rights training for law enforcement officials will be intensified and expanded.
- Implementation of the measures in the Code of Penal Procedure and the by-law on Arrests, Detentions and Interviews will be monitored effectively and immediate legal action will be taken against those failing to comply with their provisions.
- The recourse mechanism against responsible personnel for the compensations paid in compliance with the decisions of the ECtHR on cases of torture or inhumane or degrading treatment will be applied effectively.

- Public awareness will be raised on the rights of individuals during arrest, detention, and custody and the procedures for complaint if these rights are denied.

*4. Human rights training of public officials*

The ongoing Human Rights training of public officials, especially members of the judiciary and law enforcement officials, will be expanded, and training programmes designed to raise awareness on ECHR and ECtHR case-law, as well as EC law, will be developed further.

*5. Functioning and efficiency of the Judiciary*

In this area, the overriding goal of the government is the entrenchment of the principle of the rule of law in Turkey, as it exists in modern nations that embrace such universal values, and which constitutes a leading pillar of the State. Furthermore, the provision of effective justice required by modern society is also a priority. Legal reforms that will take place within this scope will constitute the basis of the democratisation process. In this regard, as a matter of priority, ongoing training programmes on Human Rights and ECHR and ECtHR case-law, designed to provide conformity in implementation, will continue in a broadened manner encompassing members of high courts.

*6. Prison, detention and custody standards*

The government will ensure the effective implementation of the measures adopted for the improvement of conditions in prisons and detention houses. In light of the recommendations of the Council of Europe and the Committee for the Prevention of Torture, the aligning of prisons with international standards and the effective functioning of the Judges of Enforcement and Prison Monitoring Boards will continue. Furthermore, legislation on the execution of sentences will continue to be reviewed.

*7. Full enjoyment of all fundamental rights and freedoms by all individuals without discrimination*

The government is convinced that ensuring the full and equal enjoyment of all fundamental rights and freedoms and cultural rights by all individuals without discrimination is its fundamental duty. In this context, it will continue to fulfil its obligations stemming from all international agreements to which Turkey is a party. The freedoms of thought, conscience, religion and belief will be strictly safeguarded in accordance with Article 9 of the ECHR. Ensuring gender equality in practice will be a particular priority. Consequently,

- The legislation concerning freedom of worship will be simplified in implementation in light of the ECHR and its Additional Protocol no. 1, with a view to addressing the needs of different religions and faiths.

- The provisions on the learning of and the broadcasting in different languages and dialects used by Turkish citizens in their daily lives will be implemented.
- Appropriate measures will be taken in line with the ILO Convention no. 159 for the Vocational Rehabilitation and Employment for Disabled Persons.
- Emphasis will be given to the application of the ILO Convention for Prevention of the Worst Cases of Child Labour.

*8. Functioning of the Executive*

The consultative status of the National Security Council (NSC) was redefined through constitutional and legislative amendments. The functions of the NSC and the Secretariat General of the NSC shall be harmonised with this definition.

*9. Agreements*

The procedures for the signing of Additional Protocol no. 13 to the European Convention on Human Rights and the Optional Protocol of the International Covenant on Civil and Political Rights shall be initiated.

\*\*\*

# Document no. 96

## Harmonisation package (7)[20]

*Article 1.* The expression "from one year" in the first sub-paragraph of Article 159 of the Turkish Penal Code no. 765, dated 1.3.1926, has been amended to read "from 6 months" and its last sub-paragraph has been amended as follows:

"Expressions of thought made only for the purpose of criticism without an intention to insult, deride or abuse do not require punishment."

*Article 2.* The expression "facilitates their actions in any manner whatsoever" has been removed from the Article text.

*Article 3.* The following sub-paragraph has been added to Article 426 of the Law no. 765:

"Scientific and artistic works along with works of literary value shall not be included in the scope of this Article."

*Article 4.* The expression "and destroyed" in sub-paragraph 2 of Article 427 of the Law no. 765 has been deleted from the Article text.

*Article 5.* The following Article has been added to the Code of Criminal Procedures no. 1412, dated 4.4.1929:

"Additional Article 7. The investigation and prosecution concerning those who commit the criminal offences specified in Article 243 and 245 of the Turkish Penal Code no. 765, dated 1.3.1926, shall be considered urgent cases and will be treated without delay as priority cases. Hearings of cases relating to these offences cannot be adjourned for more than thirty days, unless there are compelling reasons, and these hearings will also be held during judicial recess."

*Article 6.* The following sub-paragraph has been added to Article 11 of Law no. 353 on the Establishment and Trial Procedures of Military Courts, dated 25.10.1963:

"If the criminal offences that are specified in Article 58 of the Military Penal Code are committed by non-military individuals during peace time, the trials relating to these offences shall not be held at military courts."

\*\*\*

*Article 8.* The expression "15" in sub-paragraph one of Article 6 of Law no. 2253, dated 7.11.1979, on the Establishment, Duties and Trial Procedures of Juvenile Courts has been amended to read "18".

*Article 9.* The expression "Secretary General of the National Security Council" has been removed from table no. (1) annexed to Law no. 2451, dated 23.4.1981, on the Appointment Procedures in Ministries and Affiliated Institutions.

*Article 10.* The expression "of at least seven natural persons" in Article 1 of the Associations Law no. 2908, dated 6.10.1983, has been amended to read "of at least seven natural or legal persons".

*Article 11.* Article 4 of the Law no. 2908 has been amended to read as follows:

"Article 4. Natural persons, who are legally responsible for their actions and have completed eighteen years of age, and legal persons have the right to establish associations without need for prior permission.

However, the following groups of individuals cannot establish Associations (for specified periods):

1. Members of the Turkish Armed Forces and general and special law enforcement forces and public employees with civil servant status who are subject to special laws preventing them from establishing associations, at all times,

2. a. Those who have been convicted of crimes specified in Part 2 of Chapter 1 of the Turkish Penal Code,

b. Those who have been convicted of simple or qualified embezzlement, malversation, bribery, stealing, looting, fraud, forgery, abuse of trust, fraudulent bankruptcy, smuggling, corruption in official tenders and procurements, disclosure of state secrets, participation in and provoking and encouraging terrorist acts,

c. Those who have been convicted of crimes specified in Articles 316, 317 and 318 of the Turkish Penal Code,

for a period of two years.

3. Those who have established and administered associations whose establishment is prohibited and the executives of associations that have been closed down by a court decision due to engaging in activities which have been prohibited for associations shall not be allowed to establish associations for a period of one year following finalization of the said court decision."

*Article 12.* Subdivision (3) of Article 8 of the Law no. 2908 has been amended to read as follows:

"3. Names and surnames or titles, profession or trade, or area of activity, address and nationality of the founders of associations."

*Article 13.* The expressions "thirty" and "ninety" in sub-paragraph one of Article 10 of the Law no. 2908 have been amended as "sixty".

*Article 14.* Sub-paragraph 3 of Article 16 of the Law no. 2908 has been amended to read as follows and the expression "to the associations specified in Article 39 of this Law" in sub-paragraph 5 has been omitted from the Article text:

"Individuals who are prohibited by other laws from becoming members of associations and primary and secondary education students cannot become members of associations."

*Article 15.* The expression "according to Article 39" in sub-paragraph 1 of Article 17 of the Law no. 2908 has been deleted from the Article text.

*Article 16.* The second sentence of sub-paragraph 1 of Article 31 of Law no. 2908 has been deleted from the Article text and the second sentence of sub-paragraph 2 has been amended to read as follows:

"This written notification shall include the name, surname, father's name, title or trade, area of activity, date and place of birth, profession or trade, nationality and address of the founders, the address of the branch centre, and will also include, as attached, the authorisation document and two copies of the statute of the association."

*Article 17.* The expression "art, culture, science" has been added to follow the word "recreation" in Article 38 of the Law no. 2908.

*Article 18.* The expression "thirty" in Article 15 of the Law no. 2911, dated 6.10.1983, on Meetings and Demonstrations has been amended to read "ten".

*Article 19.* The expressions "thirty" in Article 16 of the Law no. 2911 has been amended to read "ten".

*Article 20.* The title of Article 17 of Law no. 2911 has been amended to read "The postponement and in some cases banning of meetings" and the expression "may ban or postpone for a period not more than two months" in the Article text has been amended to read "may postpone it for a period not more than one month or ban it if there is clear and present danger that criminal offences will be committed".

*Article 21.* The title of Article 18 of Law no. 2911 has been amended to read "the notification of the postponement or banning decision" and in sub-paragraph 1 of the Article the expression "banned or postponed" has been amended to read "postponed or banned", the expression "banning or postponement" has been amended to read "postponement or banning"; and in sub-paragraph 2 the expression "can be banned or postponed" has been amended to read "can be postponed or banned".

*Article 22.* The title of Article 19 of Law no. 2911 has been amended to read "The postponement or banning of all meetings in provinces or districts", the expression "three" in the first sentence of sub-paragraph 1 of the Article has been amended to read "one", and the second sentence of sub-paragraph 1 has been amended to read as follows:

"Based on the same reasons and in cases where there is a clear and present danger that criminal offences will be committed, governors may also ban all meetings in one or several of the districts of the province for a period not exceeding one month."

*Article 23.* Subdivisions (a) and (c) of Article 2 of the Law on the Teaching of Foreign Languages and the Learning of the Different Languages and Dialects of Turkish Citizens no. 2923, dated 14.10.1983, has been amended to read as follows:

"a. In training and educational institutions Turkish citizens cannot be taught any language other than Turkish as their mother tongues. However, private courses can be established to be subject to the provisions of the Private Educational Institutions Law no. 625 in order to enable the learning of the different languages and dialects used traditionally by Turkish citizens in their daily lives;

language classes can be set up with the same objective in these courses and other language courses. The teaching cannot be contrary to the basic characteristics of the Republic as stated in the Constitution and the indivisible integrity of the State with its territory and nation. The principles and procedures relating to the establishment and supervision of these courses and classes shall be set out in a Regulation to be issued by the Ministry of National Education."

"c. The foreign languages to be taught in Turkey shall be determined by the decision of the Council of Ministers."

*Article 24.* Article 4 of the Law on the National Security Council and the General Secretariat of the National Security Council no. 2945, dated 9.11.1983, has been amended to read as follows:

"Article 4. The National Security Council will, within the framework of the definitions pertaining to national security and the state's national security policy as stated in Article 2, take decisions of recommendation on issues concerning the determination and implementation of the State's national security policy, and it will provide its opinions with a view to ensuring the necessary coordination; it will convey those decisions of recommendation and its opinions to the Council of Ministers and will fulfil its duties as set by laws. The Prime Minister may entrust a Deputy Prime Minister with the responsibility of coordinating and following up the implementation of the decisions of the Council of Ministers for the cases where the decisions of recommendation and opinions of the National Security Council are submitted to the Council of Ministers and these are approved by the Council of Ministers"

*Article 25.* Sub-paragraph 1 of Article 5 of Law no. 2945 has been amended to read as follows:

"The Council shall convene once every two months. If necessary, the Council can convene upon the proposal of the Prime Minister or the direct call of the President."

*Article 26.* Article 13 of Law no. 2945 has been amended along with its title to read as follows:

"*The duties and competences of the General Secretariat*

Article 13. The General Secretariat of the National Security Council;

a. fulfils the secretariat services of the National Security Council,

b. carries out the duties entrusted to it by the National Security Council and by-laws."

*Article 27.* Article 15 of the Law no. 2945 has been amended to read as follows:

"Article 15. The Secretary General of the National Security Council shall be appointed upon the proposal of the Prime Minister and the approval of the President. If the appointment in question is envisaged to be made from among the members of the Turkish Armed Forces, the positive opinion of the Chief of General Staff shall be sought."

*Article 28.* The following provisional Article has been added to Law no. 2945:

"Provisional Article 4. In line with the arrangements foreseen in this Law and in the Law on the National Security Council and the Secretariat General of the

National Security Council no. 2945, dated 9.11.1983, a regulation shall be issued within three months following the date of publication of this law within the framework of principles specified in Article 21 of Law no. 2945."

*Article 29.* Additional Article 3 of the Decree Law on the Organisation and Duties of the General Directorate of Foundations no. 227, dated 8.6.1984, has been amended to read as follows:

"Additional Article 3. In cases where international cooperation is deemed to be positive, foundations established in Turkey may become members of foundations or organisations established abroad, with the permission of the Ministry of Interior given in consultation with the Ministry of Foreign Affairs.

The holding of international activities by foundations established in Turkey to realise the objectives specified in their foundation charters, the opening of branches abroad and the cooperation with similar foundations or organisations abroad are subject to the permission of the Ministry of Interior given in consultation with the Ministry of Foreign Affairs.

In cases where international cooperation is deemed to be useful, foundations established abroad can be permitted, on the condition of reciprocity, to undertake activities, establish representations, open branches, set up umbrella organisations, join existing umbrella organisations or cooperate with existing foundations in Turkey with the permission of the Ministry of Interior, given in consultation with the Ministry of Foreign Affairs.

These foundations are subject to the same regulations applicable to foundations established on the basis of the provisions of the Turkish Civil Code."

*Article 30.* Sub-paragraph 2 of Article 7 of the Anti-Terrorism Act no. 3713, dated 12.4.1991, has been amended to read as follows:

"Those who assist members of organisations constituted in the manner described in the sub-paragraph above or those who conduct propaganda in such a manner as to encourage resorting to violence or other terrorist means shall be punished, separately from any other crime that their actions might constitute, with imprisonment of between one and five years and with a heavy fine of between 500 million and 1 billion Turkish liras."

*Article 31.* The expression "of at least seven natural persons" in paragraph 1 of Article 56 of the Turkish Civil Code no. 4721, dated 22.11.2001, has been amended to read "of at least seven natural or legal persons".

*Article 32.* The expression "and legal persons" has been added to follow the expression "natural persons" in sub-paragraph 1 of Article 64 of the Law no. 4721.

*Article 33.* The expression "six months in advance" in Article 66 of the Law no. 4721 has been deleted from the Article text.

*Article 34.* The following sub-paragraph has been added to Article 82 of the Law no. 4721:

"The provisions of the above sub-paragraph shall also apply to persons who will vote on behalf of a legal person."

*Article 35.* The following legal provisions have been abrogated:

a. Last sub-paragraph of Article 6 of the Law no. 2253, dated 7.1.1979, on the Establishment, Duties and Trial Procedures of Juvenile Courts,

b. Sub-paragraph 4 of Article 16, the last sub-paragraph of Article 31 and Article 83 of the Associations Law no. 2908, dated 6.10.1983,

c. Articles 9, 14 and 19 of the Law on the National Security Council and the General Secretariat of the National Security Council no. 2945, dated 9.11.1983,

d. Sub-paragraph 2 of Article 94 of the Turkish Civil Code no. 4721, dated 22.11.2001.

\*\*\*

# Document no. 97

### European Council Decisions in 2003[21]

In the Thessaloniki European Council of June 19 and 20, 2003, the EU welcomed the commitment of the Turkish government to carry forward the reform process, in particular the remaining legislative work by the end of 2003, and supported its on-going efforts to fulfill the Copenhagen political criteria for opening accession negotiations with the Union. However, the EU stated that, even after taking into account progress achieved, significant further efforts to this end were still required. Referring to the revised Accession Partnership, the EU stated that the document has been prepared with the purpose of assisting Turkey to achieve this objective. Finally, the EU stated that "the Accession Partnership constitutes the cornerstone of EU–Turkey relations, in particular in view of the decision to be taken by the European Council of December 2004."

*Brussels European Council Presidency Conclusions, December 12–13 2003*

\*\*\*

*Turkey*

39. The European Council welcomes the considerable and determined efforts by the Turkish government to accelerate the pace of reforms, many of which are significant in political and legal terms. The legislative packages so far adopted, the first important steps taken to ensure effective implementation, as well as the progress in addressing many priorities under the Copenhagen political criteria and in the revised Accession Partnership have brought Turkey closer to the Union. Turkey has also made significant progress in meeting the Copenhagen economic criteria. However, further sustained efforts are needed, in particular as regards strengthening the independence and functioning of the judiciary, the overall framework for the exercise of fundamental freedoms (association, expression and religion), the further alignment of civil–military relations with European practice, the situation in the southeast of the country and cultural

rights. Turkey also has to overcome macro-economic imbalances and structural shortcomings.

40. The European Council underlines the importance of Turkey's expression of political will to settle the Cyprus problem. In this respect a settlement of the Cyprus problem, based on the principles set out in section V below, would greatly facilitate Turkey's membership aspirations.

41. The European Council encourages Turkey to build on the substantial progress achieved so far in its preparations for launching accession negotiations and underlines its commitment to working towards full implementation of the pre-accession strategy with Turkey, including the revised Accession Partnership, in view of the decision to be taken by the European Council in December 2004 on the basis of the report and recommendations of the Commission.

# 14 Year of evaluation for Turkey to start EU accession negotiations — 2004

# Document no. 98

**Introductory comment**

In the Copenhagen European Council of December 12–13, 2002,[1] the European Council had decided to open accession negotiations with Turkey "[i]f the European Council in December 2004, on the basis of a report and a recommendation from the Commission, decide[d] that Turkey fulfils the Copenhagen political criteria." Therefore, the developments in 2004 were very important for Turkey and its chance to start negotiations.

The 2003 Regular Country Report prepared by the European Commission had stated that:[2]

"Over the past year the Turkish government has shown great determination in accelerating the pace of reforms, which have brought far-reaching changes to the political and legal system. It has also taken important steps to ensure their effective implementation, in order to allow Turkish citizens to enjoy fundamental freedoms and Human Rights in line with European standards. Four major packages of political reform have been adopted, introducing changes to different areas of legislation.

Some of the reforms carry great political significance as they impinge upon sensitive issues in the Turkish context, such as freedom of expression, freedom of demonstration, cultural rights and civilian control of the military. Many priorities under the political criteria in the revised Accession Partnership have been addressed.

Progress is being made in streamlining the functioning of public administration and government. The government has, in particular, started reforms with a view to promoting a more transparent management of human resources in the public service. This also serves to strengthen the fight against corruption. The duties, powers and functioning of the National Security Council (NSC) have been substantially amended, bringing the framework of civil–military relations closer to practice in EU Member States. The role of the Secretary General of the NSC has been reviewed and its executive powers have been abolished. There are still representatives of the NSC in civilian boards such as the High Audio Visual Board (RTUK) and the High Education Board (YÖK). Full parliamentary control over military expenditures must be ensured both in terms of approving the budget and in terms of auditing.

More efforts are still needed to enhance the efficiency and the independence of the judiciary. Already, the judicial system has been strengthened with the establishment of a new system of family courts. The competence of military courts to try civilians has been abolished. Positive changes have been made to the system of State Security Courts, in particular the abolition of incommunicado detention. However, the functioning of these courts still needs to be brought fully in line with European standards in particular with the rights of the defence and the principle of a fair trial.

On the ground, implementation of the reforms is uneven. In some cases, executive and judicial bodies entrusted with the implementation of the political reforms relating to fundamental freedoms adopted by Parliament have narrowed the scope of these reforms by establishing restrictive conditions, hindering the objectives initially pursued. The government has recognised that the reforms are not being put into practice systematically and has set up a Reform Monitoring Group in order to ensure their implementation.

Turkey has ratified the Civil Law Convention on Corruption, so that on 1 January 2004 it became a member of the Council of Europe's Group of States against corruption (GRECO). However, in spite of several initiatives, corruption remains at a persistently high level and affects many spheres of public life. Turkey has ratified major international as well as European Conventions such as the International Covenant on Civil and Political Rights, on Social and Economic Rights and Protocol 6 of the European Convention on Human Rights. It is, however, of great concern that Turkey has not executed many judgments of the ECtHR [European Court of Human Rights], by means of ensuring payment of just satisfaction or reversing decisions made in contravention of the ECtHR. One example is the Loizidou case, as it is now five years since the ECtHR ruled on this matter.

The fight against torture and ill-treatment has been strengthened and the Turkish legal system has come closer to European standards in this respect. The scale of torture has declined but there are still reports about specific cases, which continue to cause concern. The reform of the prison system has continued and rights of detainees have been improved. In practice, the right of access to a lawyer is not always ensured. The possibility of retrial has been introduced but in practice few cases have been subject to retrial. In the case of Zana and others, retrial has so far largely resulted in a repetition of the previous trial, leading to persistent concerns about the respect for the rights of the defence.

The adoption of the reform packages has led to the lifting of several legal restrictions on the exercise of freedom of expression. The enforcement of the revised provisions of the Penal Code has led to many acquittals although cases against persons expressing non-violent opinion continue to occur. A number of persons imprisoned for non-violent expression of opinion, under provisions that have now been abolished, have been released.

Notable progress has been achieved in the area of freedom of demonstration and peaceful assembly where several restrictions have been lifted. Nevertheless, in some cases of peaceful demonstration, the authorities have made a disproportionate use of force.

As regards freedom of association, some restrictions have been eased, but associations still experience cumbersome procedures. Cases of prosecution against associations and particularly Human Rights defenders continue to occur. The law on political parties has been amended to make closure of parties more difficult. However, HADEP [People's Democratic Party] has been banned by the Constitutional Court and DEHAP [Democratic People's Party] is facing proceedings with a view to its closure. Concerning freedom of religion, the changes introduced by the reform packages have not yet produced the desired effects. Executive bodies continue to adopt a very restrictive interpretation of the relevant provisions, so that religious freedom is subject to serious limitations as compared with European standards. This is particularly the case for the absence of legal personality, education and training of ecclesiastic personnel, and full enjoyment of property rights of religious communities.

Measures have been taken to lift the ban on radio and TV broadcasting and education in languages other than Turkish. So far, the reforms adopted in these areas have produced little practical effect. The lifting of the state of emergency in the southeast has in general eased tensions amongst the population. There has been greater tolerance of cultural events. The programme for the return to villages proceeds at a very slow pace. Serious efforts are needed to address the problems of internally displaced persons and the socio-economic development of the region in a comprehensive fashion and of cultural rights in general.

In the conclusions of the Thessaloniki European Council, and the Accession Partnership, Turkey is encouraged to strongly support the efforts of the UN Secretary General towards a settlement of the Cyprus problem. Turkey has expressed its support on different occasions for a settlement to the Cyprus problem. Turkey has indicated that an agreement aiming to establish a Customs Union with the northern part of Cyprus will not come into effect.

Relations between Turkey and Greece have continued to improve. Efforts are continuing to put in effect new confidence-building measures. Exploratory contacts on the Aegean between the two foreign ministries have also continued. Turkey decided to give its agreement as a NATO [North Atlantic Treaty Organization] member to the modalities of participation of non-EU European allies in EU-led operations using NATO assets. This has solved a problem which had hitherto hindered the effective launch of the European Security and Defence Policy.

Overall, in the past twelve months Turkey has made further impressive legislative efforts which constitute significant progress towards achieving compliance with the Copenhagen political criteria. Turkey should address the outstanding issues highlighted in this report, with particular attention to the strengthening of the independence and the functioning of the judiciary, the overall framework for the exercise of fundamental freedoms association, expression and religion, further alignment of civil–military relations with European practice, the situation in the southeast and cultural rights. Turkey should ensure full and effective implementation of reforms to ensure that Turkish citizens can enjoy Human Rights and fundamental freedoms in line with European standards.

Furthermore, Turkey should provide determined support for efforts to achieve a comprehensive settlement of the Cyprus problem."

Therefore, 2004 was a very important year for Turkey in that it took steps in implementation of the already enacted legislation and agreed to take additional steps to align its practices with those of the European Union.

# Document no. 99

**Checklist on the status of legislative changes in the political criteria section of the 2001 and 2003 National Programme for the Adoption of the *Acquis*[3]**

| Subject headings | Changes envisaged | Legislative changes realised | Status |
|---|---|---|---|
| *Freedom of thought and expression* | Act no. 3257 on Cinema, Video and Music Works* | Amendment to Articles 3,6 and 9 of the Act no. 3257 on Cinema, Video and Music Works | ✓ |
| | Legislation delineating freedom of expression will be reviewed in the light of the ECHR, especially with regard to the letter and spirit of Articles 10, 17 and 18 of the said Convention Legislative and administrative measures expanding freedom of expression will be implemented effectively Measures will be taken to ensure that the freedom of the press will be applied according to universal norms | Amendment to Articles 159, 426 and 427 of the Turkish Penal Code | ✓ |
| | The provisions on broadcasting in, and learning of, different languages and dialects used by Turkish citizens in daily life will be implemented | Amendment to Articles 4, 15 and 32 of the Act no. 3984 on Radio and Television Broadcasts and adding of one provisional article to this Act | ✓ |
| | | Amendment to Article 2 of the Act no. 2923 on the Education and Teaching of Foreign Languages and the Learning of Different Languages and Dialects by Turkish Citizens | ✓ |

*continued*

| Subject headings | Changes envisaged | Legislative changes realised | Status |
|---|---|---|---|
| | | The by-law on the learning of languages and dialects used traditionally by Turkish citizens in their daily lives (OG no. 25307, 05.12.2003) | ✓ |
| | | The by-law on the broadcasts in languages and dialects used traditionally by Turkish citizens in their daily lives (OG no. 25357, 25.01.2004) | ✓ |
| | Training of members of the judiciary on Human Rights, the European Convention on Human Rights and the jurisprudence of the European Court of Human Rights will be continued and expanded to ensure consistency in implementation | Act on the Establishment of the Justice Academy | ✓ |
| | | Training programmes undertaken at the Ministry of Justice | ✓ |
| | Other | Amendment to Articles 55/A and 149/A of the Act no. 298 on Basic Provisions on Elections and Voters Registrars | ✓ |
| | | Amendment to Article 1 of the Anti-Terrorism Act no. 3713, and adding one provisional article, the repeal of Article 8 and amendment to Article 7 of this Act | ✓ |
| *Freedom of association and the right to peaceful assembly and civil society* | Legislation concerning associations as well as meetings and demonstrations will be reviewed. Provisions in various legislation will be collected into as few laws as possible to provide consistency | Amendment to Articles 1,4, 8, 10, 16, 17, 31 and 38 of the Act no. 2908 on Associations and the repeal of Articles 16/4, 31/final paragraph and Article 83 of this Act | ✓ |
| | | Amendment to Articles 56, 64, 66 and 82 of the Turkish Civil Code and repeal of Article 94/2 of this Act | ✓ |
| | | Amendment to Supplementary Article 3 of the Decree Law no. 227 on the Establishment and Duties of the Directorate General for Foundations | ✓ |
| | | Adding one provisional article to Act no. 2762 on Foundations | ✓ |

*continued*

| Subject headings | Changes envisaged | Legislative changes realised | Status |
|---|---|---|---|
| | The legislative and administrative reforms concerning associations, foundations, meetings and demonstration marches will be implemented effectively | The Law on Relationship of Associations and Foundations with Public Institutions (adopted by TGNA on 22.01.2004) (OG no. 25361, 29.01.2004) | ✓ |
| | | Amendment to Articles 15, 16, 17, 18 and 19 of the Act no. 2911 on Meetings and Demonstration Marches | ✓ |
| | | Ministry of Interior Circular, dated 05.12.2003, on the implementation of amendments to the Act on Meetings and Demonstration Marches Ministry of Interior Circular, dated 09.01.2004, on the international activities of the foundations established in Turkey as well as the activities of the foundations established abroad and foreign non-profit organisations in Turkey | ✓ |
| *Prevention of torture and maltreatment* | Allegations of torture and maltreatment will be investigated immediately and thoroughly, and the offenders will be punished rapidly | Adding one Article to the Code of Criminal Procedure, no. 1412 | ✓ |
| | | Ministry of Justice Circular, dated 20.10.2003, on the investigation of such allegations as urgent matters to be addressed without delay | ✓ |
| | Provisions on the rights of persons arrested, detained or charged to communicate with their lawyers and inform their relatives will be fully implemented | Changing the heading of Article 16 of the Act no. 2845 on the State Security Courts | ✓ |
| | | Repeal of Article 31/1 of the Act no. 3842 Amending Some Articles of the Code of Criminal Procedure and the Act on State Security Courts | ✓ |

*continued*

| Subject headings | Changes envisaged | Legislative changes realised | Status |
|---|---|---|---|
| | Modern investigation techniques and medical monitoring systems to prevent maltreatment and Human Rights violations will be implemented effectively | The by-law amending some articles of the By-law on Apprehension, Detention and Interrogation (OG no. 25335, 03.01.2004) | ✓ |
| | Human Rights training for law enforcement officials will be intensified and expanded | | |
| | Implementation of the measures in the Code of Penal Procedure and the By-law on Apprehension, Detention and Interrogation will be monitored effectively and immediate legal action will be taken against those failing to comply with their provisions | Ministry of Justice Circular, dated 29.09.2003, on the conduct of preparatory investigation personally by the Public Prosecutor | ✓ |
| | The recourse mechanism against responsible personnel for the compensations paid in compliance with the decisions of the ECtHR on cases of torture or inhumane or degrading treatment will be applied effectively | | |
| | Public awareness will be raised on the rights of individuals during arrest, detention, and custody and the procedures for complaint if these rights are denied | By-law on the Establishment, Duties and Working Principles of Province and Township Human Rights Boards (OG 25298, dated 23.11.2003) | ✓ |
| | | By-law Amending Some Articles of the By-law on the Establishment, Duties and the Functioning of Human Rights Advisory Board (OG no. 25298, dated 23.11.2003) | ✓ |
| *Strengthening opportunities to redress consequences of Human Rights violations* | Strengthening opportunities to redress the consequences of Human Rights violations (retrial) | Amendment to Article 53 of the Act no. 2577 on the Act on Administrative Trial Procedures and adding one provisional article to the Act | ✓ |

*continued*

| Subject headings | Changes envisaged | Legislative changes realised | Status |
|---|---|---|---|
| *Training of public servants on Human Rights* | The ongoing Human Rights training of public officials, especially members of the judiciary and law enforcement officials, will be expanded, and training programmes designed to raise awareness on ECHR and ECtHR case law, as well as EC law, will be developed further | | |
| *The functioning and the effectiveness of the judiciary* | Act on the Establishment and Trial Procedures at Military Courts | Article 11 of the Act on the Establishment and Trial Procedures at Military Courts | ✓ |
| | | Act amending the Military Criminal Code and the Act on the Establishment and Trial Procedures of Military Courts (adopted by TGNA on 22.01.2004) (OG no. 25361, 29.01.2004) | ✓ |
| | Entrenchment of the principle of the rule of law in Turkey, as it exists in modern nations that embrace such universal values Provision of effective justice required by modern society Reform of the judiciary Ongoing training programmes on Human Rights and ECHR and ECtHR case law, designed to provide conformity in implementation, will continue in a broadened manner encompassing members of high courts | | |
| | Other | Amendment to Article 6 of the Act no. 2253 on the Establishment, Duties and Proceedings of Juvenile Courts and the repeal of Article 6/ final paragraph | ✓ |
| | | Amendment of the Act no. 2253 on the Establishment, Duties and Proceedings of Juvenile Courts (OG no. 25345, 13.01.2004) | ✓ |
| | | Adding one Supplementary Article to Act no. 832 on the Court of Audit | ✓ |

*continued*

| Subject headings | Changes envisaged | Legislative changes realised | Status |
|---|---|---|---|
| *Abolition of the death penalty* | Abolition of the death penalty in Turkish Criminal Law with the exception of war and the imminent threat of war | Amendment to Article 1/A of the Act no. 4771 Amending Some Acts (death penalties in the Turkish Criminal Code, Act no. 1918 on the Pursuit and Interdiction of Smuggling, Act no. 6831 on Forests and Act no. 4533 on the Gelibolu Historical National Park were abolished) | ✓ |
| | | Act Amending the Military Criminal Code and the Act on the Establishment and Trial Procedures of Military Courts (adopted by TGNA on 22.01.2004) (OG no. 25361, 29.01.2004) | ✓ |
| *Conditions in prisons and detention houses and in custody* | Ensure the effective implementation of the measures adopted for the improvement of conditions in prisons and detention houses | | |
| | Continue the alignment of prisons standards with international standards, in light of the recommendations of the Council of Europe and the Committee for the Prevention of Torture | | |
| | Continue the effective functioning of the Judges of Enforcement and Prison Monitoring Boards | Ministry of Justice Circular, dated 25.12.2003, on the confidentiality of written application submitted to the judges of enforcement | ✓ |
| | Continue to review legislation on the execution of sentences | Repeal of Article 16 of the Act no. 2845 on State Security Courts | ✓ |
| *Full enjoyment by all individuals without any discrimination irrespective of their language, race, colour, sex, political opinion, philosophical belief or religion of all Human Rights* | The legislation concerning freedom of worship will be simplified in implementation in light of the ECHR and its Additional Protocol no. 1, with a view to addressing the needs of different religions and faiths | Amendment to Act on Construction Ministry of Interior Circular, dated 24.09.2003, on the designation of places of worship on municipal settlement plans | ✓ |

*continued*

| Subject headings | Changes envisaged | Legislative changes realised | Status |
|---|---|---|---|
| | The provisions on the learning of and the broadcasting in different languages and dialects used by Turkish citizens in their daily lives will be implemented | See "Freedom of Expression" (fourth line) | – |
| | Appropriate measures will be taken in line with the ILO Convention no. 159 for the Vocational Rehabilitation and Employment for Disabled Persons | | |
| | Emphasis will be given to the application of the ILO Convention for Prevention of the Worst Cases of Child Labour | | |
| | | Amendment to Article 16 of the Act no. 1587 on the Act on Census | ✓ |
| | | Ministry of Interior Circular instructing census bureaus to register names given to their children by parents in accordance with the amendment to Article 16 of the Act on Census | ✓ |
| | | Amendment to Article 453 of the Turkish Criminal Code | ✓ |
| | | Prime Ministry Circular dated 22.01.2004 on respect for the principle of gender equality for recruitment to public service | ✓ |
| | | Prime Ministry Circular dated 24.01.2004 on ensuring the exercise of the right of petition and the right to information | ✓ |
| *Functionality of the Executive* | The consultative status of the National Security Council (NSC) was redefined through constitutional and legislative amendments. The functions of the NSC and the Secretariat General of the NSC shall be harmonised with this definition | Amendments to Articles 4, 5, 13 and 15 of the Act no. 2945 on the National Security Council and the Secretariat General of the National Security Council, adding of a Provisional Article to this Act and the repeal of Articles 9, 14 and 19 | ✓ |
| | | Amendment to Article 1 of the Act no. 2451 on Appointment Procedures at Ministries and Affiliated Agencies | ✓ |

*continued*

| Subject headings | Changes envisaged | Legislative changes realised | Status |
|---|---|---|---|
| *Conventions* | | The By-law on the Secretariat General of the National Security Council (OG no. 25340, 08.01.2004) | ✓ |
| | | Act no. 5017 repealing the articles on the confidentiality of the Staff of and the By-law on the Secretariat General of the NSC (OG no. 25319, 17.12.2003) | ✓ |
| | Signing of the Optional Protocol of the International Covenant on Civil and Political Rights | Signed on 03.02.2004 | ✓ |
| | Signing of Additional Protocol no. 13 to the European Convention on Human Rights | Signed on 09.01.2004 | ✓ |

# Document no. 100

## Constitutional amendments of 7 May 2004[4]

The constitutional amendments adopted by the Parliament on 7 May 2004 constitute yet another significant step forward in the political reform process taken after the endorsement of the first comprehensive package of constitutional amendments of October 2001 and seven legislative reform packages.

These amendments, which reaffirm the political will and commitment in Turkey for EU membership, introduce new provisions on the functioning of the judiciary, the alignment of civil–military relations with European practice and strengthening of civil authority, gender equality, the status of international agreements, the death penalty and the freedom of the press.

It is noteworthy that the constitutional amendments were adopted by an overwhelming majority in Parliament, with a vote of 457 in favour and eight against.

The constitutional amendments are as follows:

1. Article 10 of the Constitution entitled "Equality before the law".

The phrase *"Men and women shall have equal rights. The State has the duty to ensure that this equality is put into practice."* is *added* to the article. With this amendment, gender equality is further reinforced.

2. Article 15 of the Constitution entitled "Suspension of the exercise of fundamental rights and freedoms".

The phrase *"and execution of death penalties"* is *deleted* from the text of the article, abolishing the death penalty in all circumstances.

3. Article 17 of the Constitution entitled "Inviolability of the individual, material and spiritual existence of the individual".

The phrase *"execution of death penalties imposed by the courts"* is *deleted* from the text of the article, abolishing the death penalty in all circumstances.

4. Article 30 of the Constitution entitled "Protection of printing facilities".

The phrase *"except in cases where a conviction for offences against the indivisible integrity of the State with its territory and nation, the fundamental principles of the Republic, and national security"* is *deleted* from the text of the article.

The phrase *"and press equipment"* is *added* to the text of the article.

The amended article now reads *"A printing press established as a publishing house in accordance with the law as well as its annexes and press equipment shall not be seized, confiscated, or barred from operation on the grounds of being an instrument of crime."*

With the amendment, the freedom of the press is further strengthened.

5. Article 38 of the Constitution entitled "Principles related to offences and penalties".

With the first amendment, the phrase *"Except for obligations required by becoming party to the Statute of International Criminal Court"* is added to the last paragraph of the article.

The amended last paragraph now reads: *"No citizen shall be extradited to a foreign country on account of an offence except for obligations required by becoming party to the Statute of International Criminal Court."* The necessary change was made with a view to becoming party to the Statute of the International Criminal Court.

With the second amendment, the phrase *"The death penalty shall not be imposed excluding cases in time of war, imminent threat of war and terrorist crimes. General confiscation shall not be imposed as a penalty."* is replaced with *"The death penalty and general confiscation shall not be imposed as a penalty"*, abolishing the death penalty in all circumstances.

6. Article 87 of the Constitution entitled "Functions and powers of the Turkish Grand National Assembly/General provisions".

The phrase "execution of death penalties imposed by the courts which have become final" is *deleted* from the text of the article, abolishing the death penalty in all circumstances.

7. Article 90 of the Constitution entitled "Ratification of international treaties".

The following sentence is *added* to the last paragraph of the article to clarify the status of international agreements:

"In case of a conflict between international agreements in the area of fundamental rights and freedoms duly put into effect and the laws due to differences in provisions on the same matter, the provisions of international agreements shall prevail."

8. Article 131 of the Constitution entitled "Superior Bodies of Higher Education".

The phrase *"the Chief of the General Staff"* is *deleted* from the text of the article, removing the member of the High Education Council selected by the Chief of the General Staff.

9. Article 143 of the Constitution entitled "State Security Courts".

*Article 143 of the Constitution, which constitutes the legal basis of the establishment of State Security Courts, is repealed.*

10. Article 160 of the Constitution entitled "The Court of Audit".

The last paragraph of the article which reads *"The procedure for auditing, on behalf of the Turkish Grand National Assembly, state property in possession of the Armed Forces shall be regulated by law in accordance with the principles of secrecy necessitated by national defence."* is *deleted* from the text of the article with a view to ensuring transparency in auditing of state property in possession of the Armed Forces.

# Document no. 101

## Brussels European Council Presidency Conclusions, 17–18 June 2004[5]

\*\*\*

### Turkey

27. The European Council welcomes the significant progress made to date by Turkey in the reform process, including the important and wide-ranging constitutional amendments adopted in May. It welcomes the continued and sustained efforts of the Turkish government to meet the Copenhagen political criteria. In this context, the European Council emphasises the importance of concluding the remaining legislative work and of accelerating efforts to ensure decisive progress in the full and timely implementation of reforms at all levels of administration and throughout the country.

28. The European Union will continue to assist Turkey in its preparations and to work towards full implementation of the pre-accession strategy, in particular as regards strengthening the independence and functioning of the judiciary, the overall framework for the exercise of fundamental freedoms (association, expression and religion), cultural rights, the further alignment of civil–military relations with European practice and the situation in the southeast of the country.

29. The Union reaffirms its commitment that if the European Council decides in December 2004, on the basis of a report and recommendation from the Commission, that Turkey fulfils the Copenhagen political criteria, the EU will open accession negotiations with Turkey without delay.

30. The European Council encourages the Turkish government to remain firmly committed to macro-economic and financial stabilisation, including full implementation of the structural reform agenda.

31. The European Council invites Turkey to conclude negotiations with the Commission on behalf of the Community and its twenty-five Member States on the adaptation of the Ankara Agreement to take account of the accession of the new Member States.

32. The European Council welcomes the positive contribution of the Turkish government to the efforts of the UN Secretary General to achieve a comprehensive settlement of the Cyprus problem.

# Document no. 102

**PACE [Council of Europe Parliamentary Assembly] Resolution 1380 (2004): Honouring of Obligations and Commitments by Turkey**[6]

1. Turkey has been a member of the Council of Europe since 1949 and as such has undertaken to honour the obligations concerning pluralist democracy, the rule of law and Human Rights arising from Article 3 of the Statute. It has been the subject of a monitoring procedure since the adoption, in 1996, of Recommendation 1298 on Turkey's respect of commitments to constitutional and legislative reforms.

2. On 28 June 2001, in Resolution 1256 concerning the honouring of obligations and commitments by Turkey, the Parliamentary Assembly welcomed the progress made by Turkey but decided to continue the monitoring process and review progress, pending a further decision to close the procedure.

3. The Assembly notes that, despite a serious economic crisis in 2001, the political instability that led to early elections in November 2002 and the uncertainties caused by the war in Iraq, the Turkish authorities have not deviated from their efforts to implement the reforms necessary for the country's modernisation. Turkey has achieved more reforms in little more than two years than in the previous ten.

4. The Assembly welcomes the adoption in October 2001 of important changes to the constitution, seven reform packages approved by parliament between February 2002 and August 2003 and numerous other laws, decrees and circulars to implement these reforms. It also welcomes the changes made to the constitution in May 2004, which paved the way for the ratification of the Statute of the International Criminal Court.

5. It notes with satisfaction that, despite initial concern in November 2002 about the accession to power of the Justice and Development Party, led by Mr Erdogan, the new government, with the unstinting support of the only opposition party, the Republican People's Party (CHP), has so far made good use of its absolute majority in parliament to expedite and intensify the reform process.

6. With regard to pluralist democracy, the Assembly recognises that Turkey is a functioning democracy with a multi-party system, free elections and separation

of powers. The frequency with which political parties are dissolved is nevertheless a real source of concern and the Assembly hopes that in future the constitutional changes of October 2001 and those introduced by the March 2002 legislation on political parties will limit the use of such an extreme measure as dissolution. The Assembly also considers that requiring parties to win at least 10 per cent of the votes cast nationally before they can be represented in parliament is excessive and that the voting arrangements for Turkish citizens living abroad should be changed.

7. With regard to institutional arrangements, the Assembly congratulates Turkey on reducing the role of the National Security Council to what it should never have ceased to be, namely a purely consultative body concerned with defence and national security. The amendment to Article 118 of the constitution and those to the legislation governing the National Security Council and its secretariat represent fundamental progress that is to be welcomed. With the changes made to the constitution in May 2004, Turkey completed this reform by taking the necessary steps to exclude army representatives from civil bodies such as the Higher Education Council (YÖK) and to establish parliamentary supervision of military activities, particularly from a financial standpoint. The Assembly also calls on the Turkish authorities to exclude any army representatives from the Supreme Board of Radio and Television (RTÜK). Despite Turkey's geo-strategic position, the Assembly also demands that Turkey recognises the right of conscientious objection and introduce an alternative civilian service.

8. The Assembly welcomes the fact that the maximum period of police custody for collective offences has been reduced from fifteen to four days and that all detained persons are entitled to see a lawyer from the first hour of police custody.

9. The Assembly also welcomes the Turkish authorities' decision to abolish the state security courts, following the abrogation of Article 143 of the constitution in May 2004. It strongly urges Turkey, as it did in 2001, to draw on the experience of the Venice Commission for any further constitutional revisions. It believes that the 1982 Constitution, which has already been frequently modified, would gain in coherence and clarity from a complete overhaul. The Assembly also welcomes the fact that the Turkish authorities have started to consider granting individuals direct access to the Constitutional Court.

10. The Assembly also calls on the Turkish authorities to finalise without delay the draft proposal to create an ombudsman institution and congratulates Turkey on the steps taken to improve dialogue with NGOs [non-governmental organisations], particularly via the new composition of regional Human Rights councils and the more flexible legislation on associations. NGOs' freedom of action nevertheless needs to be strengthened.

11. The Assembly welcomes Turkey's determination to fight corruption, particularly through the establishment of several parliamentary committees of inquiry, its approval in January 2003 of an emergency anticorruption plan and its ratification of the Council of Europe Criminal and Civil Law Conventions on Corruption (ETS nos 173 and 174) in September 2003 and March 2004

respectively. It hopes that Turkey will shortly submit the instruments of ratification of the Convention on Laundering, Search, Seizure and Confiscation of the Proceeds from Crime (ETS no. 141), already ratified by the Turkish Parliament on 16 June 2004.

12. The Assembly welcomes the significant advances in women's rights resulting from the constitutional revisions of October 2001 and May 2004, the entry into force in January 2002 of the new Civil Code and the August 2002 Job Security Act, and welcomes the fact that Article 10 of the constitution, as amended in May 2004, now expressly stipulates that the state has a duty to guarantee equality between men and women. Modern states must provide for equality between all their citizens, particularly as regards access to employment, public and elective offices, health and education. It calls on the Turkish authorities to introduce programmes to eradicate female illiteracy, which is essential for women to be able to exercise their rights. The Assembly has noted with satisfaction that the Criminal Code was amended in July 2003 to make it impossible to plead mitigating circumstances for honour crimes. It calls on the authorities to take a clear stand against honour crimes and domestic violence and to offer women support, particularly by increasing the number of refuges.

13. Regarding fundamental freedoms, the Assembly congratulates Turkey for finally abolishing the death penalty, by ratifying Protocol no. 6 of the European Convention on Human Rights in November 2003 and signing Protocol no. 13 in January 2004. Following the changes made to the constitution in May 2004, Protocol no. 13 should be ratified very shortly.

14. It also congratulates Turkey for its commitment to combating torture and impunity — the authorities' zero tolerance policy is starting to bear fruit. Improvements to conditions of police custody, greater safeguards for the rights of the defence and entitlement to a medical examination have been welcomed by the European Committee for the Prevention of Torture and Inhuman or Degrading Treatment or Punishment (CPT), whose recommendations, including those relating to detention conditions, have been systematically implemented. Although the latest report published by the CPT on 18 June 2004 recognises that important progress has been achieved, the Assembly agrees with the CPT that the Turkish authorities must remain vigilant and ensure that their instructions are followed throughout the country.

15. The Assembly considers that, as part of the fight against impunity, abolishing the requirement to secure prior administrative approval to prosecute officials charged with torture or inhuman or degrading treatment, removing the power to suspend prison sentences or commute them into fines, making it obligatory to investigate complaints from victims as a priority and requiring prosecutors to conduct investigations personally all represent considerable progress. It also notes that considerable efforts have been made to improve police and gendarmerie training, with Council of Europe assistance.

16. The Assembly takes note of important measures to liberalise the legislation on freedom of expression: Section 8 of the Anti-Terrorism Act has simply been repealed, Articles 312, 159, 169 of the Criminal Code and Section 7 of the

Anti-Terrorism Act have been amended to make them more compatible with the case-law of the European Court of Human Rights and the legislation on press-related offences has also been amended. However, the Assembly still awaits progress on the offences of defaming or insulting the principal organs of state, which should no longer be liable to imprisonment.

17. The Assembly notes that important progress has been made regarding freedom of association. Under the amended Article 33 of the constitution, only the courts may refuse to register associations' statutes or dissolve or suspend their activities. The 1983 Associations Act has been considerably revised, particularly as regards prior scrutiny of associations' activities. Concerning freedom of assembly, meetings can now be banned only if they pose a clear threat to public order.

18. Turning to freedom of religion and the treatment of religious minorities, the Assembly congratulates the Turkish authorities for amending the legislation on religious foundations and on constructions, which will now allow the bodies concerned to buy and sell property and build new places of worship.

19. Turkey is a secular Muslim state. This unique state of affairs is evidence of its attachment to European democratic values, based on tolerance and mutual respect. Turkey must ensure that the state's neutrality continues to be respected and that the religious sphere does not interfere with the principles of governance of a modern society.

20. The Assembly welcomes the lifting of the state of emergency in the remaining four southeastern provinces where it was still in force, and the passing of the Reintegration Act in July 2003, which has permitted the release, among others, of several thousand Turkish citizens of Kurdish origin and a return to normal life for hundreds of other people who have given themselves up to the authorities. The Assembly also hopes that parliament will shortly approve the draft legislation to compensate the victims of terrorism or of measures taken by the government to combat terrorism. Nearly five years after the end of hostilities, the Assembly believes that the time has come to invest more in the economic and social reconstruction of the southeast. It notes the Turkish authorities' commitment to developing the "village return" programme, with the assistance of the World Bank and the United Nations. The Assembly also welcomes the recent adoption of the law encouraging investments in provinces with low per capita income.

21. The Assembly regrets that Turkey has still not ratified the Framework Convention for the Protection of National Minorities (ETS no. 157) and the European Charter for Regional or Minority Languages (ETS no. 148). Nevertheless, it considers that the first steps have been taken towards recognising the cultural rights of members of different ethnic groups and notably of persons of Kurdish origin. The constitution has been revised and no longer bans the use of languages other than Turkish; it is now possible to open language schools for studying the Kurdish language or languages, radio and television broadcasts are now authorised in Kurdish and parents may choose Kurdish first names for their children. The Assembly strongly encourages the Turkish authorities to

continue promoting cultural and linguistic diversity, and hopes that the measures will have a real impact on the daily lives of those concerned, particularly their access to the judicial and administrative authorities and the organisation of health care.

22. The Assembly notes that the points it made in Resolution 1256 have been dealt with satisfactorily:

i. it congratulates the Turkish authorities for introducing the necessary changes to domestic legislation in 2002 and 2003 to permit the retrial of cases following findings by the Court of a violation of the Convention, which in particular has permitted the reopening of the trial of Leyla Zana and three other members of parliament in the Ankara Security Court. Nevertheless, the Assembly deeply regrets the decision handed down by the Ankara Security Court on 21 April 2004, at the end of the retrial, upholding the prison sentences they were given in 1994. It invites the Turkish Court of Cassation to examine with the utmost care the complaints currently before it concerning the way in which the trial was conducted and is pleased to note the court's decision of 9 June 2004 to release them in the meantime;

ii. it also notes that more than five years after the judgment awarding Ms Loizidou just satisfaction, and in accordance with Article 46 of the Convention by which, like all the other parties to the Convention, it is bound, Turkey has finally agreed unconditionally to make the required payment. It reminds the Turkish authorities that they must still execute the judgment on the merits in the same case, delivered in 1996, and in particular adopt general measures to avoid repetition or continuation of the violations found by the Court. It asks Turkey to continue to cooperate fully with the Committee of Ministers in its difficult task of securing the proper implementation of judgments, particularly in the *Cyprus v. Turkey* inter-State case.

23. The Assembly therefore invites Turkey, as part of its authorities' current reform process, to:

i. carry out a major reform of the 1982 Constitution, with the assistance of the Venice Commission, to bring it into line with current European standards;

ii. amend the electoral code to lower the 10 per cent threshold and enable Turkish citizens living abroad to vote without having to present themselves at the frontier;

iii. recognise the right of conscientious objection and establish an alternative civilian service;

iv. establish the institution of ombudsman;

v. ratify the Convention on Laundering, Search, Seizure and Confiscation of the Proceeds from Crime, the Framework Convention for the Protection of National Minorities, the European Charter for Regional or Minority Languages and the Revised European Social Charter and accept the provisions of the Charter which it has not already accepted;

vi. complete the revision of the Criminal Code, with the Council of Europe's assistance, bearing in mind the Assembly's observations on the definitions of the offences of insulting language and defamation, rape, honour crimes and, more generally, the need for proportionality arising from the European Court of Human Rights' case-law on freedom of expression and association;

vii. undertake, with the Council of Europe's assistance, a comprehensive examination of the legislation dating from the period of the state of emergency, particularly that relating to association, trades unions and political parties, to ensure that as far as possible it reflects the spirit of recent reforms;

viii. reform local and regional government and introduce decentralisation in accordance with the principles of the European Charter of Local Self-Government (ETS no. 122); as part of the reform, to give the relevant authorities the necessary institutional and human resources and arrange redistribution of resources to compensate for the underdevelopment of certain regions, particularly south-east Turkey, and move from a dialogue to a formal partnership with United Nations agencies to work for a return, in safety and dignity of those internally displaced by the conflict in the 1990s;

ix. continue the training of judges and prosecutors as well as the police and gendarmerie, with the Council of Europe's assistance;

x. lift the geographical reservation to the 1951 Geneva Convention relating to the Status of Refugees and implement the recommendations of the Council of Europe Commissioner for Human Rights on the treatment of refugees and asylum seekers;

xi. pursue the policy of recognising the existence of national minorities living in Turkey and grant the persons belonging to these minorities the right to maintain, develop and express their identity and to apply it in practice;

xii. continue efforts to combat female illiteracy and all forms of violence against women.

24. The Assembly considers that over the last three years Turkey has clearly demonstrated its commitment and ability to fulfil its statutory obligations as a Council of Europe Member State. Given the progress achieved since 2001, the Assembly is confident that the Turkish authorities will apply and consolidate the reforms in question, the implementation of which will require considerable changes to its legislation and regulations, extending beyond 2004. The Assembly therefore decides to close the monitoring procedure under way since 1996.

25. The Assembly will continue, through its Monitoring Committee, the post-monitoring dialogue with the Turkish authorities on the issues raised in paragraph 23 above, and on any other matter that might arise in connection with Turkey's obligations as a Council of Europe Member State.

# Document no. 103

**Communication from the Commission to the Council and the European Parliament: recommendation of the European Commission on Turkey's progress towards accession**[7]

## 1. Introduction

EU–Turkey relations have a long history. In 1963 Turkey and the EEC [European Economic Community] entered into an Association Agreement containing a membership perspective. In 1995, a Customs Union was formed and, in Helsinki in December 1999, the European Council decided that Turkey is a candidate for accession to the EU. The Copenhagen European Council in December 2002 concluded that "if the European Council in December 2004, on the basis of a report and a recommendation from the Commission, decides that Turkey fulfils the Copenhagen political criteria, the European Union will open accession negotiations with Turkey without delay". These conclusions were reaffirmed by the European Council in Brussels in June 2004.

For major periods of European history, Turkey has been an important factor of European politics. Turkey is a member of all other important European organisations and has since the Second World War played an important role in contributing to the shaping of European policies.

Within the limits of the mandate received in Copenhagen in 2002, this Communication contains the recommendation from the Commission and, in the Annex, the conclusions of the Regular Report on Turkey. The Regular Report records Turkey's progress towards accession over the past twelve months. It also examines Turkey's track record in respect of the political and economic criteria for accession since the decision by the Helsinki European Council in 1999. The recommendation and the accompanying documents will provide a basis for a decision of the European Council of general political importance for the future of the European Union.

Furthermore, the Commission services have also prepared an assessment of issues arising from Turkey's membership perspective. Its findings are presented in this Communication.

On this basis, a strategy consisting of three pillars is presented. The first pillar concerns cooperation to reinforce and support the reform process in Turkey in particular in relation to the continued fulfilment of the Copenhagen political criteria. This will be based on a revised Accession Partnership, setting out priorities in particular for the reform process, and an upgraded pre-accession strategy. In the second pillar, the specific conditions for the conduct of accession negotiations with Turkey are proposed. A number of preliminary indications are provided for the preparation of accession negotiations, if such a decision is taken by the European Council in December. The third pillar suggests a substantially strengthened political and cultural dialogue bringing people together from EU Member States and Turkey.

Turkey's accession would need to be thoroughly prepared in order to allow for a smooth integration which enhances the achievements of fifty years of European integration. This is an open-ended process whose outcome cannot be guaranteed beforehand. Regardless of the outcome of the negotiations or the subsequent ratification process, the relations between the EU and Turkey must ensure that Turkey remains fully anchored in European structures.

## 2. Assessment of the political criteria

Following decades of sporadic progress, there has been substantial legislative and institutional convergence in Turkey towards European standards, in particular after the 2002 elections. The political reforms are mainly contained in two major constitutional reforms in 2001 and 2004 and eight legislative packages adopted by Parliament between February 2002 and July 2004. Civil–military relations are evolving towards European standards. Important changes have been made to the judicial system, including the abolition of the State Security Courts. Public administration reform is under way. As regards Human Rights, Turkey recognises the primacy of international and European law. It has aligned itself to a large extent with international conventions and rulings, such as the complete abolition of the death penalty and the release of people sentenced for expressing non-violent opinion.

Although some practical restrictions still exist, the scope of fundamental freedoms enjoyed by Turkish citizens, such as freedom of expression and assembly, has been substantially extended. Civil society has grown stronger. Cultural rights for the Kurds have started to be recognised. The state of emergency has been lifted everywhere; although the situation is still difficult, the process of normalisation has begun in the southeast. Finally, on the enhanced political dialogue, Turkish foreign policy is contributing positively to regional stability.

Turkey has substantially progressed in its political reform process, in particular by means of far-reaching constitutional and legislative changes adopted over the last years, in line with the priorities set out in the Accession Partnership. However, the Law on Associations, the new Penal Code and the Law on Intermediate Courts of Appeal have not yet entered into force. Moreover, the decision on the Code of Criminal Procedure, the legislation establishing the judicial police and the law on execution of punishments and measures are still to be adopted.

Turkey is undertaking strong efforts to ensure proper implementation of these reforms. Despite this, implementation needs to be further consolidated and broadened. This applies specifically to the zero tolerance policy in the fight against torture and ill-treatment, and the strengthening and implementation of provisions relating to freedom of expression, freedom of religion, women's rights, trades union rights and minority rights.

In view of the overall progress of reforms, and provided that Turkey brings into force the outstanding legislation mentioned above, the Commission considers that Turkey sufficiently fulfils the political criteria and recommends that accession negotiations be opened.

The irreversibility of the reform process, its implementation, in particular with regard to fundamental freedoms, will need to be confirmed over a longer period of time. Moreover, the *acquis* related to the political criteria is developing, in particular as a result of the Constitution for Europe. Turkey should closely follow this evolution.

Turkey has and continues actively to support efforts to resolve the Cyprus problem; in particular, Turkey agreed to the solution put forward in the peace plan of the UN Secretary General. The European Council of June 2004 invited Turkey to conclude negotiations with the Commission on behalf of the Community and its twenty-five Member States on the adaptation of the Ankara Agreement to take account of the accession of the new Member States. The Commission expects a positive reply from Turkey to the draft protocol on the necessary adaptations transmitted in July 2004. Moreover, it should be noted that any accession negotiations are held in the framework of an Intergovernmental Conference consisting of all Member States of the EU.

The full conclusions of the Regular Report, covering also the progress made by Turkey in meeting the other criteria for membership, can be found in the Annex, Conclusions of the Regular Report on Turkey.

## 3. Assessing the issues arising from Turkey's membership perspective

Accession of Turkey to the Union will be challenging for both the EU and Turkey. If well managed, it would offer important opportunities for both. As the assessment on the issues arising from Turkey's membership perspective shows, the necessary preparations for accession will last well into the next decade. The EU will evolve over this period, and Turkey should change even more radically. The *acquis* will develop further and respond to the needs of an EU at twenty-seven or more. Its development may also anticipate the challenges and opportunities of Turkey's accession.

Based on current EU policies and knowledge, the Commission has identified the following main issues for further reflection and analysis over the coming years:

- Turkey's accession would be different from previous enlargements because of the combined impact of Turkey's population, size, geographical location, economic, security and military potential. These factors give Turkey the capacity to contribute to regional and international stability. The prospect of accession should lead to improving bilateral relations between Turkey and its neighbours in line with principle of reconciliation on which the European Union is founded.

Expectations regarding EU policies towards these regions will grow as well, taking into account Turkey's existing political and economic links to its neighbours. Much will depend on how the EU itself will take on the challenge to become a fully fledged foreign policy player in the medium term in regions traditionally characterised by instability and tensions, including the Middle East and the Caucasus.

- Turkey is at present going through a process of radical change, including a rapid evolution of mentalities. It is in the interest of all that the current transformation process continues. Turkey would be an important model of a country with a majority Muslim population adhering to such fundamental principles as liberty, democracy, respect for Human Rights and fundamental freedoms, and the rule of law.

- The economic impact of Turkey's accession on the EU would be positive but relatively small, due both to the modest size of the Turkish economy and to the degree of economic integration already existing before accession. Much will depend on future economic developments in Turkey. The launch of accession negotiations should help the continued efforts of Turkey to ensure macro-economic stability and promote investment, growth and social development. Under these conditions, Turkey's GDP [gross domestic product] is expected to grow more rapidly than the EU average.

\*\*\* [Economy. Population, agriculture, geopolitical assessment, budgetary concerns, voting allocation in the EU].

## 4. Reinforcing and supporting the reform process with Turkey

Overall, implementation of reforms needs to be vigorously pursued. More specifically, the policy of zero tolerance towards torture should be implemented through determined efforts on all levels of the Turkish state to eradicate remaining instances of torture. Further development of civil society is important. The need to consolidate and broaden political reform also applies to the normalisation and development of the situation in the southeast, including measures to improve the socio-economic situation, initiatives to facilitate the return of displaced people, and to allow for full enjoyment of rights and freedoms by the Kurds. The specific problems of non-Muslim religious communities and trades union rights also need further action.

In order to guarantee the sustainability and irreversibility of the political reform process, the EU should continue to monitor progress of the political reforms closely, on the basis of an Accession Partnership setting out priorities for the reform process. The Commission will, following the analysis in the Regular Report, propose to revise the Accession Partnership in spring 2005. On this basis, a general review of the way in which political reforms are consolidated and broadened will take place on a yearly basis starting from end 2005. To this end, the Commission will present a first report to the European Council in December 2005. The pace of the reforms will determine the progress in negotiations.

In line with the Treaty on European Union and the Constitution for Europe the Commission will recommend the suspension of negotiations in the case of a serious and persistent breach of the principles of liberty, democracy, respect for human rights and fundamental freedoms and the rule of law on which the Union is founded. The Council should be able to decide on such recommendation by a qualified majority.

The enhanced political dialogue and the regular monitoring need to continue after the opening of accession negotiations. As in the past, it will go hand in hand with the expert assistance undertaken by the Commission. The dialogue in the economic field will also need to be pursued, with a clear reference to the *acquis* and in particular the methods of economic policy coordination applied within the EU.

Building on the instruments developed over the past years, such as twinning, peer reviews and TAIEX [Technical Assistance Information Exchange Office], the EU should continue to assist Turkey to achieve the necessary legal and real convergence. The pre-accession strategy for Turkey should be upgraded in order to focus on the priorities outlined in the revised Accession Partnership which will be based on the Regular Report and the assessment of the issues raised by Turkey's prospective accession. Concrete initiatives need to be developed to address the socio-economic development in the southeast, also through the mobilisation of a substantial part of the Community assistance to Turkey.

Until 2006, EU financial and technical assistance to Turkey's preparations will continue to be based on the dedicated pre-accession instrument for Turkey adopted by the Council in December 2001. The Commission has proposed to Council to create a new pre-accession instrument (IPA), from which Turkey would benefit from 2007 onwards, building on the present pre-accession instruments Phare (assistance program for restructuring economies of certain member or candidate states), ISPA (Structural Pre-Accession Instrument [of the EU]) and SAPARD (Special accession programme for agriculture and rural development [of the EU]). In the context of the next financial perspective, the Commission will propose an increase in the amounts to be allocated to Turkey.

## 5. Indications for the conduct of accession negotiations

The assessment summarised above has borne out the fact that both the EU and Turkey will need a considerable amount of time to create the conditions that will ensure a smooth integration of Turkey into the EU. Not only is it necessary to protect the cohesion and effectiveness of the Union, it would also protect Turkey from having to apply policies that may be unsuited for its level of development.

Accession negotiations will take place in the framework of an Intergovernmental Conference where decisions require unanimity. The framework for negotiations will need to reflect the specific challenges related to Turkey's accession. The precise parameters for the conduct of negotiations will be elaborated once the decision is taken to open negotiations, drawing on the broad indications given below.

Immediately after the formal opening of the accession negotiations, the Commission will organise a comprehensive process of examination of the *acquis*, called screening, in order to explain it and to obtain preliminary indications of the issues that may arise during the negotiations. The negotiations will be complex and reflect on the one hand difficulties encountered by Turkey to apply the *acquis* and on the other hand the need for provisions facilitating the harmonious integration of Turkey into the EU.

\*\*\*

The substance of the negotiations will be broken down into a number of chapters, each covering a specific policy area. The Commission will recommend to the Council to open negotiations on each specific chapter once it considers Turkey to be sufficiently prepared.

\*\*\*

Progress in the negotiations will depend not only on Turkey's convergence with the EU. The EU will need to prepare itself because, as stated by the European Council of June 1993, the Union's capacity to absorb new members, while maintaining the momentum of European integration, is also an important consideration in the general interest of both the Union and the candidate countries.

\*\*\*

It is primarily by demonstrating determined implementation of continued reform that Turkey would be able to ensure a successful conclusion of the whole accession process. The conduct of negotiations and the prospect of accession should contribute to further political, social, cultural and economic reform in Turkey. The final outcome will require endorsement by the European Parliament and by the EU countries and Turkey.

## 6. Strengthening the dialogue between the European Union and Turkey

There is a clear need to strengthen the dialogue on a number of issues relating to EU–Turkey relations. Several pertinent questions, which do not immediately relate to the EU as such, need to be addressed. A number of fora should be created, bringing people together from Member States and Turkey, where concerns and perceptions can be discussed in a frank and open manner. This includes a dialogue on difference of cultures, religion, issues relating to migration, concerns on minority rights and terrorism. Civil society should play the most important role in this dialogue, which should be facilitated by the EU. The Commission will present proposals on how to support such a dialogue in future.

## 7. Conclusions and recommendations

In the light of the above, the Commission's conclusions and recommendations are the following:

1. Turkey has substantially progressed in its political reform process, in particular by means of far-reaching constitutional and legislative changes adopted over the last years, in line with the priorities set out in the Accession Partnership. However, the Law on Associations, the new Penal Code and the Law on Intermediate Courts of Appeal have not yet entered into force.

Moreover, the Code on Criminal Procedure, the legislation establishing the judicial police and the law on execution of punishments and measures are still to be adopted.

2. Turkey is undertaking strong efforts to ensure proper implementation of these reforms. Despite this, legislation and implementation measures need to be further consolidated and broadened. This applies specifically to the zero tolerance policy in the fight against torture and ill-treatment and the implementation of provisions relating to freedom of expression, freedom of religion, women's rights, ILO [International Labour Organization] standards including trades union rights, and minority rights.

3. In view of the overall progress of reforms attained and provided that Turkey brings into force the outstanding legislation mentioned in paragraph 1, the Commission considers that Turkey sufficiently fulfils the political criteria and recommends that accession negotiations be opened. The irreversibility of the reform process, its implementation in particular with regard to fundamental freedoms, will need to be confirmed over a longer period of time.

4. A strategy consisting of three pillars should be followed. The first pillar concerns cooperation to reinforce and support the reform process in Turkey, in particular in relation to the continued fulfilment of the Copenhagen political criteria. In order to guarantee the sustainability and irreversibility of this process, the EU should continue to monitor progress of the political reforms closely. This will be done on the basis of a revised Accession Partnership setting out priorities for further reforms. A general review of progress of the political reforms will take place on a yearly basis starting from end 2005. To this end, the Commission will present a first report to the European Council in December 2005. The pace of the reforms will determine the progress in negotiations.

5. In line with the Treaty on European Union and the Constitution for Europe, the Commission will recommend the suspension of the negotiations in the case of a serious and persistent breach of the principles of liberty, democracy, respect for Human Rights and fundamental freedoms and the rule of law on which the Union is founded. The Council would decide on such a recommendation with a qualified majority.

6. The second pillar concerns the specific way of approaching accession negotiations with Turkey. Accession negotiations will take place in the framework of an Intergovernmental Conference where decisions require unanimity and with full participation of all EU Members. The negotiations will be complex. For each chapter of the negotiations, the Council should lay down benchmarks for the provisional closure and, where appropriate, for the opening of negotiations, including legislative alignment and a satisfactory track record of implementation of the *acquis*. Existing legal obligations in line with the *acquis* must be fulfilled before the opening of negotiations on related chapters. Long transition periods may be required. In addition, in some areas, such as structural policies and agriculture specific arrangements may be needed and, for the free movement of workers, permanent safeguards can be considered. The financial and institutional impact of Turkey's accession will be important. The EU will need to define its financial perspective for the period from 2014 before negotiations can be concluded.

Furthermore, the Commission shall monitor during the negotiations the ability of the Union to absorb new members and to deepen integration taking fully into account Treaty objectives as regards common policies and solidarity.

7. The third pillar entails a substantially strengthened political and cultural dialogue bringing people together from EU Member States and Turkey. Civil society should play the most important role in this dialogue, which should be facilitated by the EU. The Commission will present proposals on how to support such a dialogue.

8. The Commission is convinced that the negotiation process will be essential in guiding further reforms in Turkey. By its very nature, it is an open-ended process whose outcome cannot be guaranteed beforehand. Regardless of the outcome of the negotiations or the subsequent ratification process, the relations between the EU and Turkey must ensure that Turkey remains fully anchored in European structures. Turkey's accession would need to be thoroughly prepared in order to allow for a smooth integration which enhances the achievements of fifty years of European integration.

# Document no. 104

**European Commission 2004 Regular Report on Turkey's progress towards accession**[8]

\*\*\*

## A. Introduction

*1. Preface*

The European Council in Cardiff in June 1998 noted that the Commission would present a report on Turkey based on Article 28 of the Association Agreement and the conclusions of the Luxembourg European Council of December 1997. The Commission presented its first Regular Report on Turkey in October 1998, together with the Regular Reports for the other candidate countries.

\*\*\*

As part of the pre-accession strategy, the Commission reports regularly to the European Council on progress made by each of the candidate countries in preparing for membership. Consequently, the Commission has published a series of yearly Regular Reports on Turkey, covering the years 1998 to 2003.

\*\*\*

This Report takes into consideration progress since the 2003 Regular Report. It covers the period until 31 August 2004. In some particular cases, however, measures taken after that date might be mentioned. It looks at whether planned reforms referred to in the 2003 Regular Report have been carried out and examines new initiatives. In addition, this Report provides an overall assessment of the situation for each of the aspects under consideration.

Furthermore, in view of the fact that the 2004 Regular Report provides the basis on which the Commission formulates its recommendation as to whether

Turkey fulfils the Copenhagen political criteria, this Report includes an evaluation of Turkey's track record as regards the political criteria since the Helsinki European Council meeting in December 1999. As regards the economic criteria, the report also provides a dynamic, forward-looking evaluation of Turkey's economic performance.

The Report contains a separate section examining briefly the extent to which Turkey has addressed the Accession Partnership priorities.

As in previous Reports, "progress" has been measured on the basis of decisions actually taken, legislation actually adopted, international conventions actually ratified (with due attention being given to implementation), and measures actually implemented. As a rule, legislation or measures which are in various stages of either preparation or Parliamentary approval have not been taken into account. This approach ensures equal treatment for all the candidate countries and permits an objective assessment of each country in terms of their concrete progress in preparing for accession.

\*\*\*

## B. Criteria for membership

### 1. Enhanced political dialogue and political criteria

The political criteria for accession to be met by the candidate countries, as laid down by the Copenhagen European Council in June 1993, stipulate that these countries must have achieved "stability of institutions guaranteeing democracy, the rule of law, Human Rights and respect for and protection of minorities."[9]

[The report then summarized the general findings of the regular reports from 1998 to 2003]
\*\*\*

The section below provides an assessment of developments in Turkey, seen from the perspective of the Copenhagen political criteria, including the overall functioning of the country's executive and its judicial system. Such developments are in many ways closely linked to developments regarding its ability to implement the *acquis*, in particular in the domain of justice and home affairs. Specific information on the development of Turkey's ability to implement the *acquis* in the field of justice and home affairs can be found in the relevant section (Chapter 24 — Cooperation in the field of justice and home affairs) of part of this Report.

1.1 DEVELOPMENTS SINCE THE HELSINKI EUROPEAN COUNCIL

The decision of the European Council in Helsinki in December 1999 that Turkey is a candidate for membership has proved to be a robust catalyst for Turkey to embark upon a process of far-reaching constitutional and legislative reforms. Following decades of sporadic progress and partly because of a political consolidation after the 2002 elections, there has been a substantial institutional convergence in Turkey towards European standards. Political reforms have introduced changes ranging from improved civil liberties and Human Rights to enhanced civilian control of the military. Civil society has grown stronger. The reform process has clearly addressed major issues and, importantly, highlighted a growing consensus in favour of liberal democracy.

A Department for EU affairs was set up in 2000 to coordinate all Turkey's policies related to the pre-accession process. A National Plan for the Adoption of the *Acquis* was adopted in 2001 and revised in 2003. Political reforms in line with the Accession Partnership have been introduced by means of a series of constitutional and legislative changes adopted over a period of three years (2001–4). There have been two major constitutional reforms, in 2001 and 2004, and eight legislative packages adopted by Parliament between February 2002 and July 2004. Numerous other laws, regulations, decrees and circulars detailing how these reforms should be implemented were issued. In the past few years, the Turkish government has undertaken efforts to ensure effective implementation of the reforms. The Reform Monitoring Group, a body set up under the chairmanship of the deputy Prime Minister responsible for Human Rights, was established to supervise the reforms across the board and to solve practical problems. This body has in particular tried to overcome bureaucratic inertia and bottlenecks, including in the provinces. As regards *democracy and the rule of law*, following some unsuccessful attempts of the previous years, the prospect of public administration reform received new impetus in early 2002. An Action Plan was adopted, which sets out proposals for a major overhaul of the public management system and the restructuring of the relationships between central government, provincial authorities and municipalities. A series of laws reforming public administration and local government were adopted by Parliament in July 2004 although subsequently vetoed by the President.

Civilian control of the military has been strengthened. The duties, functioning and composition of the National Security Council [NSC] were changed. As part of the constitutional amendments, the NSC was made an advisory body with no executive powers and with a majority of civilians. In August 2004, a civilian was for the first time appointed Secretary General of the National Security Council. In order to enhance budgetary transparency the Court of Auditors was granted permission to audit military and defence expenditures.

Extra-budgetary funds have been included in the general budget allowing for full parliamentary control. Military representatives in civilian bodies such as the High Education Board and the High Audio-Visual Board have been removed. The competence of military courts was narrowed and they will no longer try civilians for offences related to criticising the military service. The government has increasingly asserted its control over the military. Although the process of aligning civil–military relations with EU practice is under way, the Armed Forces in Turkey continue to exercise influence through a series of informal channels.

Important changes have been made to the judicial system. The principle of the primacy of international and European Human Rights conventions over domestic law was enshrined in the Constitution. State Security Courts were abolished and some of their competencies were transferred to newly created Regional Serious Felony Courts. Parliament adopted a new Civil Code and a new Penal Code, which will enter into force in April 2005. A draft new Code of Criminal Procedure and draft Laws on the Establishment of the Judicial Police and on the Execution of Punishments remain to be adopted. Other structural changes included the creation of Intermediate Courts of Appeal and a family courts system throughout the country. There has been progress in aligning the rights of the defence with the relevant European standards. A Justice Academy was established and training on international law and Human Rights for judges and prosecutors has intensified. The higher courts, such as the Court of Cassation, have delivered judgments applying the amended provisions adopted by the various packages of political reforms. Nonetheless, there is sometimes still a restrictive interpretation of the reforms, in particular by prosecutors.

\*\*\* [Explaining anti-corruption measures adopted and treaties signed].

As regards *Human Rights and the protection of minorities*, Turkey has signed and/or ratified several international conventions such as the International Covenant on Civil and Political Rights and the International Covenant on Social and Cultural Rights, albeit with reservations. Constitutional amendments were introduced allowing for the signature of the Rome Statute of the International Criminal Court.

Turkey has made increased efforts since 2002 to comply with the decisions of the European Court of Human Rights (ECtHR). The possibility of retrial in civil and criminal cases in which the ECtHR has found violations was introduced. Retrials have taken place and led to a number of acquittals. The case of Leyla Zana and colleagues is emblematic of the difficulties experienced by the different branches of the judiciary when it comes to the interpretation of the reforms.

Based on the fact that Turkey has clearly demonstrated its commitment and ability to fulfil its statutory obligations as a Council of Europe member, the Parliamentary Assembly of the Council of Europe decided in June 2004 to end the monitoring procedure opened since 1996. Turkey will however be subject to a post-monitoring procedure, which will focus on a number of areas pertaining to Turkey's obligations under the European Convention for the Protection of Human Rights and Fundamental Freedoms (the Convention).

The death penalty was abolished in all circumstances according to Protocol no. 13 to the Convention which was signed in January 2004. Turkey also ratified Protocol no. 6 to the Convention and any remaining reference to the death penalty in existing Turkish legislation was removed.

With respect to the enforcement of Human Rights, a number of bodies have been established such as the Human Rights Presidency, the Human Rights Boards and the Human Rights Office within the Ministry of Interior. The Human Rights Committee of Parliament has conducted several investigations leading to the publication of several general as well as special reports. However, the impact of these bodies on the ground is as yet very limited.

Concerning *civil and political rights* more specifically, considerable efforts have been made to strengthen the fight against torture and ill-treatment, in particular through abolishing incommunicado detention and improving the rules for pre-trial detention, access to a lawyer and medical examinations. Nonetheless, on the ground, detainees are not always made aware of their rights by the law enforcement bodies. The authorities have adopted a zero tolerance policy towards torture and legislative measures have been adopted to limit the de facto impunity of the perpetrators of torture. Under the new Penal Code such perpetrators will be more severely punished. Although torture is no longer systematic, numerous cases of ill-treatment including torture still continue to occur and further efforts will be required to eradicate such practice.

Since 2000, the prison system has improved significantly. Institutions such as the Enforcement Judges and Monitoring Boards have been established with a view to enhancing detainees' rights. A number of recommendations of the Committee for the Prevention of Torture have been implemented.

Since 2001, several changes have been made to enhance the general framework for the exercise of fundamental freedoms. The scope of these freedoms has been extended. Various laws, including the Anti-Terror Law, have been amended, lifting several legal restrictions on the exercise of freedom of expression. The situation of people sentenced for non-violent expression of opinion is now being addressed and several persons sentenced under the old provisions were acquitted or released. At the same time, numerous provisions in different laws can still be interpreted to unduly restrict freedom of expression and prosecutors continue to open criminal proceedings against those expressing non-violent opinion.

Constitutional amendments have strengthened the freedom of the press. Press freedom was further improved via the adoption of a new Press Law which abrogates sanctions such as the closure of publications, the halting of distribution and the confiscation of printing machines. However, the frequency of prosecutions against journalists is a cause of concern.

Amendments to the Law on Public Meetings and Demonstrations have led to the lifting of several restrictions on the exercise of freedom of association and peaceful assembly. If adopted, the new Law on Associations, which was initially passed by Parliament in July 2004 and vetoed by the President, will be significant in terms of reducing the possibility of State interference in the activities of associations. New institutions such as the Department for Associations have contributed to the transfer of competencies previously falling under the responsibility of the police to civilians. Measures were taken to end the systematic recording of all meetings and demonstrations and to prevent and punish the disproportionate use of force by security forces. Reports suggest, however, that Human Rights defenders, including Human Rights associations, are still subject to harassment by judicial means.

The Law on Political Parties was amended, limiting the possibility for parties to be dissolved. However, in the last five years, two important political parties were banned, including the main opposition party in 2001. Several provisions of the law fall short of European standards.

As regards freedom of religion, although freedom of religious belief is guaranteed in the Constitution and freedom to worship is largely unhampered, non-Muslim religious communities continue to experience problems related to legal personality, property rights, training of clergy, schools and internal management.

\*\*\* [The Report then analyzed the developments in economic and social freedoms, children's rights, right to organize, and the right to collective bargaining.]

Regarding *minority rights, cultural rights and the protection of minorities*, the Constitution was amended to lift the ban on the use of the Kurdish language. Changes were introduced after some delay allowing radio and TV broadcasting in languages and dialects other than Turkish including Kurdish and the possibility to teach such languages was introduced. Subsequently, Kurdish language courses have opened and television and radio broadcasting in several different languages, such as Kurdish, Arabic and Bosnian, has begun. There has also been greater tolerance towards the use of Kurdish during cultural events in the southeast. While such progress is significant, there are still considerable restrictions on the exercise of cultural rights, including in the areas of broadcasting and education.

The state of emergency, which had been in force for fifteen years in some provinces of the southeast, was completely lifted in 2002. Provisions used to limit pre-trial detention rights under emergency rule were amended. Work has started in cooperation with international organisations in order to address the weaknesses of Turkey's programme aimed at returning internally displaced persons to their villages. However, no integrated strategy aimed at reducing regional disparities and addressing the economic, social and cultural needs of the local population has yet been adopted. A Law on Compensation of Losses Resulting from Terrorist Acts was adopted in July 2004. The Law on Social Reinsertion, which provided partial amnesty for people previously involved in activities of illegal organisations has had limited impact. The security situation in the southeast has considerably improved since 1999, although there have recently been a number of incidents which resulted in casualties. On the ground, the situation of internally displaced persons remains critical. A number of obstacles, including the village guard system and the absence of basic infrastructure, currently prevent displaced people from returning to their villages.

\*\*\* [Under the heading "enhanced political dialogue," the Report assessed Turkish foreign policy and noted positive developments in relations with Greece and Turkey's positive contribution to resolve the Cyprus issue.]

1.2 DEMOCRACY AND THE RULE OF LAW

*The parliament* There has been one parliamentary election since 1999. A clear majority emerged from the November 2002 elections for the AK Party, which enjoys an absolute majority in Parliament. The activities of Parliament have been dominated by political and economic reforms. Since 1999, the Constitution has been amended several times.

Currently, there are 368 AKP [Justice and Development Party], 168 CHP, four DYP [True Path Party], and nine independent deputies in the parliament. There has been a strong consensus between the government party and the main opposition party (CHP) on the policy of pursuing accession to the EU, meaning that many EU-related reforms have been adopted by a large majority. The package of constitutional amendments of May was adopted with 457 votes in favour, many more than the 367 requirement. Similarly, the AKP and the CHP deputies worked closely in the Parliamentary Committees dealing with the reform of the Turkish Penal Code.

Since the previous Regular Report, Parliament has adopted a number of EU-related reforms, related to both the Copenhagen political criteria and the European Community *acquis*. Examples include the Law on the Right to Information (9 October 2003), the Law on the abolition of some of the Articles of the Law on NSC and NSC General Secretariat (10 December 2003), the Law on Public Financial Management and Control (10 December 2003), the Law Amending the Law on Banking (12 December 2003), the Law Amending the Law on the Establishment, Duties and Trial Procedures of Juvenile Courts (7 January 2004), the 8th Harmonisation Package implementing the Constitutional Amendments of May 2004 (June 2004), the amendments to the Law on Public Employees Trade Unions, the Law on Social Insurance (June 2004), the new Law on Associations (July 2004), the legislative package Reforming Public Administration (July 2004), the Law on Compensation of Losses Resulting from Terrorist Acts (July 2004), the new Penal Code (September 2004) and the Law establishing the Intermediate Courts of Appeal (September 2004).

Between October 2003 and July 2004, the Turkish Grand National Assembly adopted a total of 261 new laws. The work of Parliamentary Committees has been central to this process. The EU Harmonisation Committee, which was established in April 2003 to work as a consultative body in the pre-accession process, has given its opinion on numerous pieces of legislation. The Committee invited representatives of the European Commission and of the Council of Europe to some of its discussions, such as on the draft Turkish Penal Code and the Local Administration Law.

The Parliamentary Committee on Human Rights, which monitors the developments in Human Rights issues, has continued its work in the reporting period (see 1.3 Human rights and the protection of minorities).

*The executive* The three-party coalition government which had ruled Turkey since 1999 was, following the early elections in November 2002, replaced by a one-party government. In the last two years, Turkey has enjoyed greater stability, overcoming the consequences of the two serious financial crises of 2000 and 2001. Political and economic reforms received new impetus because of the determination of the government to meet the Copenhagen criteria.

During the last year, the government has clearly given priority to working for the opening of negotiations for accession to the European Union. EU-related reforms and their implementation has been a permanent item on the weekly agenda of the Council of Ministers since December 2003. A Deputy Prime Minister has been appointed to report to the Council on progress in implementing the National Programme for Adoption of the *Acquis*. The cabinet has also received regular briefings about the state of play of the implementation of the reforms.

In order to support the implementation of the Human Rights reforms, the government set up a Reform Monitoring Group in September 2003 (see 1.3 Human rights and the protection of minorities).

The European Union Secretariat General [EUSG] continues to play an important coordinating role as regards the alignment with and implementation of EU norms and standards as well as programming of financial cooperation in support of these objectives. There is some concern that the human and administrative resources of the EUSG are not sufficient to fulfil its mandate.

In the reporting period the President of the Republic exercised his right of veto eight times, in particular in areas connected to reforms of public administration and education. The President continued to chair the NSC and also chaired the extraordinary state summits on Cyprus.

Parliament adopted in June and July 2004 a package on the reform of the public administration. This includes in particular a Framework Law on Public Sector Reform, a Law on Special Provincial Administration, as well as a Law on Municipalities and Metropolitan Municipalities. Taken together, the purpose of the four laws is to reform the division of competences and duties between the four levels of administration (central, provincial, metropolitan and municipal) and to improve performance. In principle, this wide-ranging and ambitious reform aims to convert the country's centralised, hierarchical and secretive administrative system into a decentralised, participatory, transparent, responsive and accountable model.

If successful, this would contribute to modernise Turkey's administrative culture. The broad thrust of the reform is in line with the need to upgrade the public administration to modern standards and practices. A successful reform would underpin Turkey's future EU accession efforts. Nonetheless, it is important that such a challenging set of reforms is both feasible and sustainable. In particular, an impact analysis, an implementation plan and a budgetary and fiscal framework are needed.

Apart from the law on Metropolitan Municipalities, the reforms could not enter into force as several articles under these laws were vetoed by the President on the grounds that they violate the relevant constitutional provisions, in particular those related to the unitary character of the public administration. As a result, Parliament will have to review the legislation.

*National Security Council* Since 1999, civilian control of the military has been strengthened. The constitutional and legal framework has been amended to clarify the position of the armed forces versus the civilian authorities. A number of changes have been introduced over the last year to strengthen civilian control of the military with a view to aligning it with practice in EU Member States.

As regards the duties, functioning and composition of the National Security Council, a Regulation was adopted in January 2004 implementing previous legislative changes of July 2003. The new Regulation abrogates the far-reaching executive powers of the Secretariat of the National Security Council to follow up, on behalf of the President and the Prime Minister, any recommendation made by this body. In particular, the regulation implements the provision which abrogated the following:

"the Ministries, public institutions and organisations and private legal persons shall submit regularly, or when requested, non-classified and classified information and documents needed by the Secretariat General of the NSC."

Under the abovementioned Regulation, the office of the Secretariat General of the NSC is transformed into a body serving the purely consultative function of the NSC. Its role is now limited to the definition of the agenda. The Secretariat is no longer able to conduct national security investigations on its own initiative. It no longer manages directly the special funds allocated to it which are now under the exclusive control of the prime minister. Further changes concern the internal restructuring of the NSC, with a substantial staff reduction and the abolition of some units. In August 2004, a senior diplomat was appointed as the first civilian Secretary General of the NSC by the President upon the proposal of the Prime Minister in accordance with the changes introduced in July 2003.

Under the new Regulation, the frequency of the NSC meetings has been reduced to once every two months, except when it is convened on the request of the Prime Minister or directly by the President. Over the last period, this rule has been respected. Legislation that came into force in December abolished the secret status of decrees governing the activities of the NSC General Secretariat.

\*\*\* [The Report then detailed the developments to enhance the transparency of military and defence expenditure and replace the military under civilian control. However, it concluded that "despite ... developments, there are still provisions on the basis of which the military continues to enjoy a degree of autonomy," and "the armed forces in Turkey continue to exercise influence through a series of informal mechanisms."]

*The judicial system*  Since 1999, some important improvements have been made to the Turkish judicial system. The State Security Courts have been abolished and replaced by Regional Serious Felony Courts (also referred to as Heavy Penal Courts). New specialised courts have been set up in order to improve the efficiency of the judicial system. Legal amendments have improved the rights of defence. A Justice Academy has been established and training on international law and Human Rights for judges and prosecutors has been intensified.

Judges and prosecutors have a considerable role to play in the implementation of the reforms. In June 2004, on request of the President of the Constitutional Court, the Venice Commission of the Council of Europe gave its opinion on a draft constitutional amendment aimed at reforming the Constitutional Court.

As part of the package of constitutional amendments adopted in May 2004, the State Security Courts were abolished. Jurisdiction over most of the crimes falling within the competence of the State Security Courts — principally organised crime, drug trafficking and terrorist offences — has been transferred to newly created regional Serious Felony Courts. Some crimes formerly heard by the State Security Courts, notably under Article 312 of the Penal Code, have been transferred to the jurisdiction of the existing Serious Felony Courts. The rules of procedure applying by the Regional Serious Felony Courts are identical to those applied by other Serious Felony Courts save that the former courts exercise jurisdiction over a wider geographic area and the maximum period which can elapse between detention and charge is forty-eight rather than twenty-four hours. The office of the Chief Public Prosecutor for State Security Courts was also abolished; prosecutions before the Regional Serious Felony Court are handled by the office of the Chief Public Prosecutor. Suspects before both types of Serious Felony Courts enjoy identical rights, including the right to consult a lawyer as soon as they are taken into custody.

The package of constitutional amendments adopted in May 2004 also revised Article 90 of the Constitution, enshrining the principle of the supremacy of international and European treaties ratified by Turkey over domestic legislation. Where there is conflict between international agreements concerning Human Rights and national legislation, the Turkish courts will have to apply the international agreements.

A new Penal Code was adopted in September 2004, replacing the eighty-year-old existing Penal Code. In general, the Code adopts modern European standards in line with the recent developments of criminal law in many European countries. It strengthens sanctions against certain Human Rights violations and introduces new offences reflecting recent developments in international criminal law such as genocide and crimes against humanity, discrimination and abuse of personal data (detailed assessment of the legislation is given in section 1.3 Human rights and the protection of minorities).

The Justice Academy, which was legally established in July 2003, started to operate. The Academy is responsible for training both candidate· judges and prosecutors as well as for the continuing training of serving judges and prosecutors. The Academy also provides training for Ministry of Justice personnel, lawyers and notaries. Between January and July 2004, the Academy trained 210 candidate judges and prosecutors. In September 2004, the Academy will start training a further 239 candidate judges and prosecutors and will provide continuing training for 660 judges and prosecutors. As well as Turkish law and legal procedure, the training will cover the European Convention on Human Rights, EU law and languages.

The Law on Establishing the Intermediate Courts of Appeal was approved by the National Assembly in September 2004 but will come into force only upon the enactment of several related laws, such as the new Penal Code and the draft new Criminal Procedure Code, the latter of which is currently before the National Assembly. The establishment of the Courts of Appeal will substantially reduce the case load of the Court of Cassation and enable it to concentrate on its function of providing guidance to the lower courts on points of law of general public importance.

Two expert advisory missions on the functioning of the judicial system took place in September–October 2003 and in July 2004 respectively. The second advisory mission found that significant progress had been made since the first visit. The Ministry of Justice had followed up on the recommendations produced by the October mission by organising meetings with judges and public prosecutors from throughout Turkey to discuss the suggestions contained in the report. The Ministry has presented a plan of action for implementing many of the suggestions in the report. Moreover, in order to stimulate public debate, the Ministry has posted the report on its website and invited comments from lawyers and NGOs. Many of the recommendations are reflected in the draft Code of Criminal Procedure. The Ministry of Justice has started work on a number of other measures to improve equality of arms between prosecution and defence.

The Law on Notification was amended in March 2004. The amendment provides that written notification to suspects and witnesses in trials will be valid even if the person notified is not found at the given address. This amendment is intended to shorten trials and to prevent prosecutions failing because they exceed the statute of limitation.

The Regulation on Apprehension, Detention and Statement Taking was amended in January 2004 so as to extend the rights of detainees. The medical examination of detained persons must now take place without the presence of the police or gendarmerie unless the doctor requests their presence.

The Law on Juvenile Courts was amended in January 2004 to provide for the establishment of juvenile courts in all cities with a population exceeding 100,000 persons. Currently, however, only sixteen juvenile courts have been established. The Commercial Code was amended in April 2004 so as to establish specialised courts to hear maritime cases.

The Law on Family Courts was amended in April 2004 in order to exclude from the jurisdiction of the Family Courts all non-family law matters. Moreover, the revised law allows unmarried judges, judges without children and judges under thirty to serve in the Family Courts. There are currently one hundred and twenty family courts.

In March 2004, a new Regulation on Legal Aid was adopted, which extends the scope of legal aid to cover court costs.

As regards the functioning of the judiciary, in general trials last for long periods and are subject to repeated adjournments. There has been a reduction in the average trial period in the Serious Felony Courts, the Criminal Courts of First Instance and the Juvenile Courts. Following an increase in the number of civil courts from 3,217 in 2002 to 3,358 in 2003, the average number of cases before each court decreased from 616 in 2002 to 604 in 2003. The average trial period before the Commercial Courts decreased from 434 days in 2002 to 417 in 2003, while the average trial period before the General Civil Courts decreased slightly from 242 days in 2002 to 240 days in 2003. In order to increase the efficiency of the court system, during the reporting period 136 courthouses with an inadequate caseload were closed and 511 judges and prosecutors transferred to work in other courthouses.

The number of judges and prosecutors during the reporting period has remained largely stable; there are currently 9,629 posts available for judges and prosecutors, of which 8,970 have been filled and 659 remain open. The salaries of judges and public prosecutors, although still low, were increased in May 2004 by 27 per cent for junior judges and prosecutors and between 10 per cent and 15 per cent for more senior judges and prosecutors. The National Judicial Network Project has continued to progress. All judges and prosecutors and all courtrooms have been provided with computers and have received information technology training.

During 2003–4, all judges and prosecutors received training on the European Convention for the Protection of Human Rights and Fundamental Freedoms and the case-law of the ECtHR. Moreover, seminars were held throughout Turkey for judges and prosecutors on inter alia EU law, judicial cooperation, intellectual property rights, juvenile criminal justice and organised crime. The Ministry of Justice distributed to courts throughout Turkey a manual on the case-law of the European Court of Human Rights and seven handbooks on Human Rights, including the right to a fair trial and the prohibition of torture. A study on the legal changes introduced by the seven reform packages was also distributed to judges, public prosecutors and law enforcement officials.

Judges and prosecutors have a considerable role to play in the implementation of political reforms. Courts have continued to apply the reforms. The higher courts, such as the Court of Cassation, have delivered judgments applying the amended provisions adopted by the various packages of political reforms. These judgments will guide the lower courts in the application of the reformed legislation. The Court of Cassation has delivered important judgments applying the reforms concerning the use of the Kurdish language, re-trial, torture and freedom of expression.

Since 1 January 2004, more than one hundred judgments have been recorded in which judges and prosecutors have applied the Convention and the case-law of the ECtHR; these cases resulted mainly in acquittals.

As regards prosecutions brought under Articles 159, 169 and 312 of the Penal Code and Article 7 of the Anti-Terror Law, the courts have in many cases acquitted defendants prosecuted under these Articles. The courts have quashed the convictions of persons convicted under Article 8 of the Anti-Terror Law and have reviewed convictions under Article 169 of the Penal Code. However, in some cases in which publications were confiscated under Article 8 of the

Anti-Terror Law, the courts have used other Articles to prolong the confiscation order despite the repeal of Article 8.

So far as prosecutions are concerned, public prosecutors are responsible for supervising all phases of criminal proceedings. However, in practice, they often exercise little or no supervision over police and gendarmerie officers during the investigation of a crime, in part due to their heavy workload. Consequently, many cases come to trial with inadequate preparation. Moreover, prosecutors are reluctant to discontinue evidently unmeritorious cases, in part because they are concerned about possible criticism from judicial inspectors. In 2004, the Ministry of Justice addressed this problem by amending the by-law concerning the judicial inspectors to allow prosecutors greater discretion to withdraw unmeritorious cases.

Following the adoption of the Law on Associations, judges are no longer prohibited from forming professional organisations. However, the draft law to establish an association of judges has not yet been adopted. The principle of the independence of the judiciary is enshrined in the Turkish Constitution but it is to a certain extent undermined by several other Constitutional provisions. The Constitution provides that judges and prosecutors shall be attached to the Ministry of Justice in so far as their administrative functions are concerned. Moreover, appointment, promotion, discipline and, broadly speaking, the careers of all judges and prosecutors are determined by the High Council of Judges and Prosecutors, which is chaired by the Minister of Justice and of which the Under-Secretary of the Ministry of Justice is also a member. The possibility of removal and transfer to less attractive regions of Turkey by the High Council may influence judges' attitudes and decisions. Furthermore, the High Council does not have its own secretariat and budget and its premises are inside the Ministry of Justice building. The High Council is entirely dependent upon a personnel directorate and inspection board of the Ministry of Justice for its administrative tasks.

\*\*\* [Anti-corruption measures.]

1.3 HUMAN RIGHTS AND THE PROTECTION OF MINORITIES

Since 1999 Turkey adopted two constitutional reforms and eight legislative reform packages. The most recent May 2004 constitutional reform addresses a number of issues related to Human Rights. These include: eradicating all remaining death penalty provisions; strengthening gender equality; broadening freedom of the press; aligning the judiciary with European standards; and establishing the supremacy of international agreements in the area of fundamental freedoms over internal legislation. In September 2004 Turkey adopted a new Penal Code, which will have positive effects on a number of areas related to Human Rights, particularly women's rights, discrimination and torture.

Furthermore, a new Press Law was adopted in June 2004 and in July 2004 a new Law on Associations and a Law on Compensation of Losses Resulting from

Terrorist Acts were adopted. A number of regulations and circulars have also been issued by the authorities in order to enable the implementation of legislation.

Turkey has acceded to a significant number of *international Human Rights instruments* since 1999, both within the UN framework and within the framework of the Council of Europe, of which it has been a member since 1949: the UN Covenant on Civil and Political Rights and the UN International Covenant on Social and Economic Rights (although with reservations); Protocol no. 6 to the European Convention for the Protection of Human Rights and Fundamental Freedoms (the Convention) on the abolition of the death penalty; UN Convention on the Elimination of All Forms of Racial Discrimination; the European Convention on the Exercise of Children's Rights and the Optional Protocol to the UN Convention on the Elimination of Discrimination against Women. Moreover, a constitutional amendment has established the supremacy of international agreements in the area of fundamental freedoms over internal legislation.

Turkey has made further progress with regard to international conventions on Human Rights since the last Regular Report. Protocol no. 13 to the Convention, concerning the abolition of the death penalty in all circumstances, was signed in January 2004. The First Optional Protocol to the International Covenant on Civil and Political Rights, providing for recourse procedures that extend the right of petition to individuals, was signed in February 2004. In April 2004 Turkey signed the Second Optional Protocol on the abolition of the death penalty. Turkey ratified the Optional Protocol to the Convention on the Rights of the Child on the Involvement of Children in Armed Conflict in October 2003.

Turkey has not signed the Framework Convention for the Protection of National Minorities or the Revised European Social Charter. The Constitution now enables Turkey to accede to the Statute of the International Criminal Court, but it has not yet done so. Acknowledging the progress achieved by Turkey since 2001 in the area of constitutional and legislative reforms, in June 2004 the Parliamentary Assembly of the Council of Europe lifted the monitoring procedure on Turkey, which had been applied since 1996. Turkey will be subject to a post-monitoring procedure, which will focus on a number of areas pertaining to Turkey's obligations under the Convention.

Turkey has made progress since 1999 in relation to the execution of *judgments of the ECtHR*, particularly over the last year. The payment of just satisfaction was made in the Loizidou case and provisions enabling retrial of cases following judgments of the ECtHR have been introduced. This allowed for the re-trial of Leyla Zana and the other former DEP parliamentarians. Turkey must nevertheless still implement a significant number of other decisions of the Court. Since October 2003, ECtHR has delivered 161 judgments concerning Turkey. On 132 occasions the Court found that Turkey had violated the Convention, and twenty-three friendly settlements were concluded. In two cases, it was found that Turkey was not in violation of the Convention. During this period, 2,934 new applications regarding Turkey were made to the ECtHR.

The constitutional amendment of May 2004 establishing the supremacy of international agreements in the area of Human Rights reinforces the Turkish judiciary's capacity to give direct effect to the Convention. The impact of this change on the judiciary will need to be monitored. According to official sources, since January 2004 over one hundred judgments made reference to the Convention and the case-law of the ECtHR and resulted mainly in acquittals.

\*\*\*

Although considerable improvements have been made, Turkey has not yet taken all the measures necessary to comply with a group of thirty-four judgments related to violations of the right to freedom of expression (see section on freedom of expression). Turkey has also made further progress in executing fifty-five judgments relating to abuses committed by the security forces, although some measures remain outstanding (see section on torture and ill-treatment below). As regards the execution of five judgments relating to the dissolution of political parties, no new developments can be reported.

\*\*\*

As regards provisions enabling retrial in the light of ECtHR decisions, the Turkish courts have received nineteen applications to start retrial procedures. In four cases, the crimes in respect of which the original charges were brought no longer exist and the consequences of the convictions were erased, thus precluding the need for a retrial. Of the remaining fifteen cases, seven have resulted in an acquittal, one in a conviction which was subsequently reversed on appeal, and one in a partial acquittal and partial conviction. Six cases are pending before the courts.

In its judgment delivered on 14 July 2004 relating to the re-trial of the former Democratic Party (DEP) members of Parliament (Sadak, Zana, Dicle and Dogan), the Court of Cassation overruled the 30 March 2004 judgment of the State Security Court, which had upheld the original conviction. Prior to this, in June 2004, the Court of Cassation had suspended the execution of the applicants' sentence and ordered their release upon the request of the Chief Prosecutor. A further retrial will commence in October 2004.

Provisions enabling retrial still do not apply to cases that were pending before the ECtHR prior to 4 February 2003, which includes the case of Ocalan. As the Court has indicated, the most appropriate form of redress would be to ensure that, where applicable, the applicants are given a retrial by an independent court.

In June 2004 the Parliamentary Assembly of the Council of Europe noted that, notwithstanding the progress made, there remained a significant number of cases where the ECtHR decisions had not been implemented and adopted a resolution encouraging Turkey to comply with these judgments.

With regard to the *promotion and enforcement of Human Rights*, Turkey has established a number of bodies since 1999 such as the Reform Monitoring Group, the Human Rights Presidency, the provincial and sub-provincial Human Rights

Boards, the Human Rights Advisory Committee and several investigation boards. This reflects a new approach in developing a constructive relationship between Human Rights organisations and the Turkish State. However, the impact of these bodies has as yet been very limited.

Since January 2004, the Human Rights Presidency has intensified its work to raise awareness on Human Rights, process complaints and address specific cases. Individuals are now able to register complaints of Human Rights abuses by completing a form with a list of questions inspired by the ECtHR, which can be posted in complaint boxes. At the local level, the number of provincial and sub-provincial Human Rights Boards increased from 859 to 931. A regulation published in November 2003 removes representatives of the security forces from these Boards and facilitates greater participation by civil society representatives.

However, the Human Rights Presidency has not yet succeeded in having a nationwide impact; some Boards have received no applications and some have never convened meetings. According to official statistics, 388 individuals filed complaints of Human Rights violations from January to June 2004. Their complaints concerned inter alia torture and ill-treatment and the right to liberty and security. The independence of the Boards has been brought into question, in particular because they are chaired by Governors and include participation from the Governors' administrations. Consequently, two major Turkish Human Rights NGOs, the Human Rights Association and Mazlum-der, still refuse to participate in the work of these Boards.

Since its establishment in September 2003, the Reform Monitoring Group has examined a number of Human Rights violations and exerted influence to resolve specific problems raised by foreign embassies and NGOs. Another monitoring body, the Human Rights Advisory Committee, which is composed of representatives from the authorities and civil society, has held a number of exchanges, but in practice its impact has been limited.

The Parliamentary Human Rights Investigation Committee continued to collect complaints on Human Rights violations and requested that the relevant authorities follow up and redress the situation when necessary. It received 791 complaints between October 2003 and June 2004; of these 322 have been dealt with. The Committee is also providing procedural advice to citizens who would like to apply to the ECtHR following the exhaustion of domestic remedies. The Committee has adopted two reports on issues related to the Human Rights situation.

The gendarmerie's Human Rights Violations Investigation and Assessment Centre has started functioning and as of August 2004 had received 339 applications. In February 2004 the Ministry of the Interior established a Human Rights Investigation Office whose function will include the inspection of police stations.

With regard to training on Human Rights, the Turkish authorities have pursued a number of programmes targeting relevant personnel in the Ministry of the Interior, Ministry of Justice, the gendarmerie and the police. The implementation of the European Commission–Council of Europe joint initiative has allowed for the training of 225 trainers, responsible for training over 9,000 judges and prosecutors. The Human Rights Presidency has benefited from training on the promotion of Human Rights awareness.

As regards the *fight against discrimination*, progress since 1999 has been limited. However, the new Penal Code criminalises discrimination on various grounds, including, gender, ethnicity, race, religion, marital status, political ideas, philosophical beliefs and trades union membership. Additional Protocol no. 12 to the Convention on the general prohibition of discrimination by public authorities has not been ratified.

Despite the adoption of a new Labour Law in 2003, which recognises the principle of equal treatment in employment, Turkey still lacks legislation against discrimination on the basis of all prohibited grounds, such as racial and ethnic origin, religion or belief, age, sexual orientation and disability (see also Chapter 13 — Social policy and employment).

The first periodic report under the UN Convention on the Elimination of All Forms of Racial Discrimination, which was due in October 2003, has still not been received by the UN.

*Civil and political rights* Turkey has abolished the *death penalty* in all circumstances. Protocol no. 6 to the Convention on the abolition of the death penalty except in times of war or the imminent threat of war entered into force in December 2003.

Protocol no. 13 to the Convention concerning the abolition of the death penalty in all circumstances was signed in January 2004. Any remaining references to the death penalty were removed from Turkish legislation as part of the May 2004 constitutional amendments.

With regard to the *prevention of torture and ill-treatment*, most of the legislative and administrative framework required to combat torture and ill-treatment has been put in place since 2002, when the government declared its intention to pursue a zero-tolerance policy against torture. In accordance with various legislative amendments, pre-trial detention procedures have been aligned with European standards; sentences for torture and ill-treatment can no longer be suspended or converted into fines; and the requirement to obtain permission from superiors to open investigations against public officials has been lifted. Although many of the recommendations of the Council of Europe's Committee for the Prevention of Torture and Ill-treatment (CPT) and the relevant UN bodies have been acted upon, a number have still not been followed up by the Turkish authorities. Turkey still needs to pursue vigorously its efforts to combat torture and other forms of ill-treatment by law enforcement officials.

Recent measures include a further amendment to the Regulation on Apprehension, Detention and Statement Taking in January 2004, which strengthened the rights of detainees. Medical examinations of detained persons are now to be carried out without the presence of the security forces, except when the doctor requires otherwise and the custody register and the suspects' rights form were improved. In October 2003 the Council of State clarified that detainees' medical examination reports should not be copied to law enforcement officers. In April 2004 the Turkish Medical Association issued a guideline stating that disciplinary penalties should be brought against doctors who discriminate on the basis of gender, race, nationality, or for any other reason, during medical checks and treatment. Pocket-sized cards setting out a suspect's rights, including his right to see a lawyer, have been distributed to police officers, who have been instructed to read the rights to a suspect immediately upon arrest. Enlarged versions of the cards have been displayed in police stations. The card also reminds police officers that breaching a suspect's rights make them liable for the financial compensation due.

The new Penal Code increases sentences for perpetrators of torture and foresees life imprisonment in cases where the victim has died. An April 2004 circular calls on all law enforcement officials to avoid methods that may engender allegations of ill-treatment of detained persons, such as sleep deprivation, prolonged standing and threats and blindfolding. In October 2003, a circular was issued instructing public prosecutors to carry out, in person, investigations regarding allegations of torture and ill-treatment, which should be considered as priority cases. The amendment to the Military Criminal Code and the Law on the Establishment and Trial Procedures of Military Courts in January 2004 aligned the detention procedures of the military courts with those of other courts.

The government's policy of zero tolerance and its serious efforts to implement the legislative reforms have led to a decline in instances of torture. In the first six months of 2004 the Turkish Human Rights Association received 692 complaints related to torture, a 29 per cent decrease on the first six months of 2003. However, the number of complaints of torture outside of formal detention centres has increased considerably as compared with 2003. Of the total human rights violations claims received by the Human Rights Presidency between January and June 2004, a significant proportion related to "torture and ill-treatment", indicating that such practice remains a problem.

As regards the fight against impunity, according to official statistics, of 2,454 law enforcement agents who were tried in 2003 in relation to allegations of torture or ill-treatment, 1,357 were acquitted and of the 854 defendants that were convicted, 138 were imprisoned. In February 2004, the Minister of the Interior issued a circular aimed at ensuring the attendance of the accused at trials concerning torture or ill-treatment. In some cases, defendants had been able to avoid attending trial for many years, thus causing their cases to exceed the statute of limitation. Concerns remain that despite reforms prosecutors are not always promptly and adequately conducting investigations against public officials accused of torture.

In July 2004 the Court of Cassation overruled a judgment concerning the prison sentence given in 2002 to four policemen found guilty of torture on the grounds that the sanction (eleven months and twenty days' suspended prison sentence) did not adequately reflect the gravity of the offence. Further to this decision a retrial of these policemen will take place.

In March 2004 the CPT published its report, together with the response of the Turkish government, following its field visits to the south and southeast of Turkey in September 2003. The report notes a considerable improvement in detention facilities and in the treatment of people in custody. The use of torture methods such as suspension by the arms and electric shocks is now very rare, although in some police headquarters such methods were reported. Less detectable methods of torture or ill-treatment still occur.

Notwithstanding the January 2004 Regulation, there are still reports of detainees being seen by a doctor in the presence of enforcement officials without the prior request of the doctor. Moreover, the requirement to transmit the medical report to the authorities concerned, without providing copies to law enforcement officials, is also not always met.

In order to help address a lack of forensic experts trained in detecting torture and ill-treatment, a project is currently under way to train 2,500 doctors who work in the western part of Turkey. The training is in accordance with the Forensic Medicine Institution's "Manual on the Effective Investigation and Documentation of Torture and other Cruel, Inhuman or Degrading Treatment" and the Istanbul Protocol. In order to improve the quality of medical examinations, the Forensic Medicine Institute has started to move forensic medicine examination rooms from courthouses to hospitals and health centres.

NGOs have reported that access to a lawyer during pre-trial detention is improving. Official sources indicate that individuals are more inclined to exercise this right; of those accused of crimes related to the State Security Courts in the first quarter of 2004, 46 per cent requested and were given access to their lawyers, whereas the figure for the same period in 2003 was 28 per cent. However, such access varies throughout the country. While the CPT report indicates instances of the security forces discouraging detainees from requesting a lawyer, or not informing them of their right, NGOs have suggested that many individuals may not be inclined to exercise this right even when it is offered because they might fear, for example, that to request a lawyer could be seen as an admission of guilt. While there has been an improvement in informing relatives when suspects are held in custody, this obligation is reportedly still not always respected.

There are still reports of arbitrary detentions, disappearances, abductions, and at least one alleged extra-judicial execution. Some of these cases are under investigation by the Turkish authorities. Prosecutors still require permission to open investigations against members of the security forces when extra-judicial killings and disappearances are alleged.

Following allegations of "systematic" torture in Turkey the Commission undertook a fact-finding mission in September 2004 in order to carry out a further check on the situation vis-à-vis torture and ill-treatment in Turkey. This mission enabled the Commission to confirm that the government is seriously pursuing its policy of zero tolerance in the fight against torture; however, numerous cases of ill-treatment including torture still continue to occur and further efforts will be required to eradicate such practices. The Turkish authorities could further tackle this problem through the establishment of a system of independent monitoring of detention facilities, in line with the recommendations of the UN and the CPT.

With regard to the *prison system* the situation has improved significantly since 1999. Institutions such as the Enforcement Judges and Monitoring Boards have been set up and a number of recommendations of the CPT have been implemented. According to official sources, as of December 2003, there were 64,296 persons in prisons and detention houses, of whom 37,056 were convicted prisoners and 27,240 were prisoners detained on remand. These sources state that there are currently no hunger strikers or "death fasts" in prisons, although NGOs report that some convicts remain on "death fast". In September 2004 a delegation of judges from the ECtHR, accompanied by medical experts, conducted a fact-finding mission to Turkey in relation to applications from around fifty detainees allegedly suffering the after-effects of being on long-term "death fast". An investigation is presently being carried out by the Izmir Prosecutor's office following allegations of systematic torture of juveniles in Buca Prison.

Regarding the court cases related to the December 2000 operations to transfer prisoners to the new F-type prisons, in March 2004 a court found that the state had been at fault with regard to the death of a prisoner during these operations. The court considered that these operations had not been well planned and the use of force had been excessive. Current conditions of detention in F-type prisons are considered to be of a high standard, although the isolation of prisoners remains a serious problem.

The Monitoring Boards continued to carry out inspections. Their work focuses on living conditions, health, food, education and the rehabilitation of prisoners. In the period January to August 2004 the Monitoring Boards made 1,193 recommendations, of which 451 were acted upon. The Monitoring Boards' composition does not currently include a significant representation from civil society and their reports are confidential. As of May 2004, the 140 Enforcement Judges had received 11,923 complaints on actions taken in respect to prisoners and detainees since the establishment of the system in 2001. Of the applications, 3,659 have been accepted and acted upon, 319 have been partially accepted and acted upon and 7,945 have been rejected by the Enforcement Judges. A large number of the applications (5,554) concerned disciplinary punishments. In December 2003, the Ministry of Justice issued a circular clarifying that complaints to Enforcement Judges should be forwarded without any prior screening. The training of Enforcement Judges has, to date, been inadequate.

NGOs have reported that visitors continue to sometimes encounter difficulties meeting prisoners, although intimidating searches have ceased. A circular was issued in June 2004 reminding the gendarmerie that lawyers entering prisons should be searched only if they activate a metal detector and that searches are to be carried out respectfully. There are also reports of prisoners not receiving appropriate medical treatment.

With regard to *freedom of expression*, the situation of people sentenced for the non-violent expression of opinion is now being addressed. Since 2002, the Penal Code, the Anti-Terror Law and the Press Law have been amended to remove restrictions, resulting in a reduction in the number of prosecutions and convictions in cases related to freedom of expression. Nevertheless, there are still a significant number of cases where non-violent expression of opinion is being prosecuted and punished. In the field of broadcasting, radio and television broadcasting in languages and dialects other than Turkish, including Kurdish, has begun.

According to official figures, there has been a decrease in the number of cases filed by public prosecutors and in the conviction rate pertaining to alleged breaches of reformed Articles 159 ("insulting the state and the state institutions"), 169 ("aiding and abetting terrorist organisations") and 312 ("incitement to racial, ethnic or religious enmity") of the Penal Code and Article 7 of the Anti-Terror Law ("propaganda in connection with the (terrorist) organisation in a way that encourages the resort to violence or other terrorist means") between 2001 and 2003. Moreover, all those who had been convicted under the now repealed Article 8 of the Anti-Terror Law ("propaganda against the indivisible unity of the state") have been released from prison and, where applicable, prison sentences have been shortened following the amendment to Article 159. According to official figures, as of April 2004, 2,204 persons have been acquitted as a result of the implementation of the amended provisions by the State Security Courts. As of May 2004, there were 5,809 persons detained for terrorist-related crimes, as compared to 8,657 in 2000, 8,298 in 2001, 7,745 in 2002 and 6,137 in 2003.

Since January 2004, 103 judgments have contained a reference to Article 10 of the European Convention on Human Rights, which led to acquittals. In a recent case of a journalist convicted under Article 312 of the Penal Code, the Court of Cassation overturned the ruling, stating that individuals have the right to support views different from those of the majority and criticise the established order. Despite these positive cases, non-violent expression of opinion is still being prosecuted and punished in Turkey. Moreover when convictions are overturned in line with the amended legislation, full legal redress, such as the restoration of civil and political rights and the deletion of criminal records, is not always guaranteed.

The impact of the reforms has not been uniform throughout the country. The amended articles of the Penal Code and Anti-Terror Law, as well as other provisions, are still used to prosecute and convict those who exercise their freedom of expression. In some cases, prosecutors have reviewed convictions based on the repealed Article 8 of the Anti-Terror Law in order to examine whether the indictment contains grounds to reconvict under alternative provisions. Moreover, numerous legislative and administrative provisions that predate the current reform process could still be used to convict those expressing non-violent opinion.

The revised Article 159 continues to be used to prosecute those who criticise the state institutions in a way that is not in line with the approach of the

ECtHR. In assessing freedom of expression cases, the judiciary should consider whether the expression incites violence, armed rebellion or enmity, what the capacity of the individual or group is to influence the public and what kind of opportunity the target of the expression has to respond.

On the basis of an initial analysis, the new Penal Code, adopted in September 2004, narrows the scope of some articles that have been used to convict those expressing non-violent opinion. The new Article 216 (which largely corresponds with the current 312) states that individuals can be convicted under this article only if their "incitement to enmity and hatred" constitutes a "clear and close danger". Article 305, which penalises those who receive pecuniary benefits from abroad for "activities in contravention of fundamental national interests" has also been limited in scope as compared with Article 127 in the current Code. However, it is of concern that, in the accompanying reasoning, the examples of activities which could be considered in contravention of national interests go well beyond what would be acceptable under the ECHR [European Convention on Human Rights]. The minimum sentence for defamation is reduced in the new Code. Other relevant articles, such as the current 159 and a provision criminalising religious personnel for criticising the state, appear virtually unaltered in the new Code and the penalty for discouraging people from performing military service has been increased.

Overall the new Penal Code provides limited progress on freedom of expression. Articles that have been frequently used to restrict freedom of expression and have been assessed as potentially conflicting with Article 10 of the Convention have been maintained or changed only slightly. The implementation of the new Code will have to be closely followed in order to assess its effect in practice.

In June 2004, the Committee of Ministers of the Council of Europe adopted an Interim Resolution on freedom of expression in which it welcomed the many general measures, including the relevant constitutional reforms, recently adopted. It encouraged Turkey to take further steps towards bringing its domestic legislation in line with Article 10 of the Convention and to further enhance the direct effect of the Convention and of the judgments of the ECtHR in the interpretation of Turkish law. The resolution notes in particular that violations of freedom of expression found as a result of the application of Article 6 of the Anti-Terror Law (which criminalizes inter alia the printing or publication of "leaflets and declarations of terrorist organisations") have yet to be specifically addressed.

As regards *freedom of the press*, notable progress has been made, although further efforts are required to address outstanding issues. Article 30 of the Constitution regarding the protection of printing facilities has been amended so that the confiscation or seizure of the printing equipment of a publishing house is no longer allowed in any circumstances. The new Press Law adopted in June 2004 represents a significant step towards increasing press freedom. Under the new law, the right of journalists not to disclose their sources is strengthened; the right to reply and correction is reinforced; prison sentences are largely replaced by fines; sanctions such as the closure of publications, halting distribution and confiscating printing machines are removed; and the possibility to confiscate printed materials, such as books and periodicals, has been reduced. Moreover, foreigners will now be able to edit or own Turkish publications. However, Article 19, which states that those who publish information concerning ongoing court proceedings shall be punished with a heavy fine, has been criticised for being excessive.

Despite a decrease in sanctions in the new law, fines still constitute an excessive burden, especially on local media. Such fines might contribute to the closure of publications or the continuation of self-censorship, which is particularly widespread at the regional and local level. In addition to the restrictions on freedom of expression foreseen in Article 10 of the Convention, the law includes a reference to "state secrets".

Recent reports indicate that the majority of cases against journalists are not brought on the basis of the Press Law. The provisions most commonly used to prosecute the media are still Articles 159, 169 and 312 of the Penal Code and Articles 6 and 7 of the Anti-Terror Law. Official sources stress the considerable decrease in the number of cases resulting in sanctions. However, whether or not conviction is likely, the regularity with which cases are filed against members of the press represents a significant deterrent to freedom of expression through the media.

Notwithstanding the reduction in convictions, journalists, writers and publishers continue to be sentenced for reasons that contravene the standards of the ECHR. In June 2004, the Turkish Press Council expressed its concern at a recent spate of excessive fines that had been imposed on journalists. Moreover, individuals have been recently imprisoned following the expression of opinion through the press. For example, a journalist was sent to prison in May 2004 on the basis of the 1951 Law on Crimes Against Atatürk. According to the Turkish Publishers Association, forty-three books were banned and thirty-seven writers and seventeen publishers were put on trial in 2003. At least eighteen books were banned in the first six months of 2004.

In the field of *broadcasting* there has been significant progress and previously adopted measures were implemented. The first broadcasts in languages and dialects other than Turkish were aired on radio and television by state broadcasting corporation TRT in June 2004. Broadcasts in Bosnian, Arabic, Circasian and the Kurdish dialects of Kirmanci and Zaza are ongoing. These broadcasts consist of news headlines, documentary, music and sports programmes. Other minorities have reportedly expressed an interest in broadcasts in their languages.

A new regulation was published in January 2004 which established the possibility for private national television and radio channels, in addition to the state broadcaster TRT, to broadcast in languages other than Turkish. This regulation opens the decisions of the High Audio Visual Board (RTÜK) to judicial appeal and removes the requirement that presenters wear "modern" clothing. Notwithstanding these improvements the regulation is still rather restrictive. It sets strict time limits for broadcasts in other languages (for television, four hours per week, not exceeding forty-five minutes per day, and for radio, five hours per week, not exceeding sixty minutes per day).

Local and regional broadcasting is made conditional on the completion of an audience profile by RTUK. Previous restrictions imposed on broadcasters, including the requirement to respect the principle of "the indivisible unity of the state", remain unchanged. The ban on children's programmes is maintained. Some local private television and radio broadcasters have applied to RTUK to broadcast in Kurdish. Although the broadcasters have not yet been granted permission it has been reported that these applications will be assessed favourably. None of the national private television channels is reported to have applied to RTUK for broadcasting in languages other than Turkish.

As regards the Broadcasting Law (RTUK Law), this is still frequently invoked by RTUK in order to impose heavy penalties, including fines and the suspension or cancellation of the broadcasting licence. For example, in March 2004 RTÜK ordered the closure for thirty days of ART TV, a local television channel broadcasting from Diyarbakir, on the grounds that it had violated "the principle of the indivisible unity of the state" when, in August 2003, it broadcast two Kurdish love songs. If this broadcaster is closed for a second time, its licence will be revoked. On a separate occasion, the government successfully challenged RTUK's decision to impose sanctions on a private radio station which had broadcast a song in Kurdish. A further liberalisation of the legislation and a clearer alignment of RTUK's policy with the spirit of the reform process would obviate the need for government intervention in such cases.

As regards *freedom of association*, several legislative reforms undertaken since 1999 have lifted a number of restrictions. The recently adopted new Law on Associations is important in reducing the possibility for state interference in the activities of associations.

A new Department of Associations has been established within the Ministry of the Interior to perform tasks that had previously been entrusted to the Director General of Security. Notwithstanding these important developments, civil society, in particular Human Rights defenders, continues to encounter significant restrictions in practice. The new Law on Associations was adopted by Parliament in July 2004, although the law is not in force due to a Presidential veto. The new law addresses a number of the concerns related to the current law. Limitations on the establishment of associations on the basis of race, ethnicity, religion, sect, region, or any other minority group are removed with the new law. Although constitutional prohibitions which could be used to restrict the establishment of certain kinds of association are invoked in the new law, recent practice suggests that associations are increasingly permitted to open, even when established on the basis of currently prohibited categories.

In addition, the new law removes the requirement to seek prior permission to open branches abroad, join foreign bodies or hold meetings with foreigners. The law also lifts all restrictions on student associations; removes the requirement to inform local government officials of general assembly meetings; and allows for the establishment of temporary and informal platforms or networks for all civil society organisations.

Moreover, the law requires that governors issue warnings prior to taking legal action against associations and the security forces are no longer allowed on an association's premises without a court order.

The new law also permits associations to conduct joint projects with, and receive financial support from, other associations and public institutions and removes the requirement to seek prior permission to receive funds from abroad. However, these are the provisions that have been vetoed by the President on the grounds that they are not in line with the Constitution.

The requirement that associations produce a statute and act only within the field specified therein has been maintained. Such provisions have been used to obstruct the establishment and functioning of associations. However, under the new law, associations acting outside the scope of their statute will receive a fine and will no longer be subject to dissolution.

A regulation will be published in order to provide detailed information concerning the application of the law. This regulation, as well as its implementation in practice, will need to be examined closely in order to ascertain whether full alignment with Article 11 ("Freedom of assembly and association") of the ECHR has been achieved.

Since it was established in August 2003, the new Department of Associations has gradually taken over responsibilities for associations from the Directorate General of Security in seventy-four of the eighty-one provinces, including Ankara, but not Istanbul. Although NGOs have reported that dialogue with the authorities is more open than in the past, these changes have not yet had a significant effect in practice.

The Ministry of the Interior issued a circular in June 2004 instructing the local authorities to deal with demonstrations, marches and press conferences in a way that does not impinge on the rights of peaceful assembly and avoids placing restrictions on the organisers that are not in accordance with the Law on Public Meetings and Demonstration Marches. The circular emphasises that NGOs' activities should not be subject to videorecording unless there is a request from the authorities. Moreover, provided that civil society organisations' public press statements fulfil a number of conditions, such as being less than one hour long and not obstructing traffic or daily life, they will no longer fall under this law. Nonetheless, existing administrative provisions could still allow Governors to restrict public activities in the interest of public order or to regulate the use of slogans and the text on banners. In August 2004 the Ministry of the Interior issued a further circular aimed at both preventing and ensuring the appropriate sanctions for the use of disproportionate force by members of the security forces. The circular encourages Governors to treat this matter as a priority, conduct appropriate studies and ensure disciplinary action is taken where necessary.

In May 2004 the Directorate General for Foundations issued a circular which introduced the restrictive requirement that all foundations, including religious foundations, seek permission prior to submitting applications to participate in projects funded by international organisations, including the European Commission.

On international cooperation of associations and foundations, a circular was adopted in January 2004 which clarifies the necessary requirements for obtaining permission to open branches of foreign associations and foundations in Turkey, and for other international activities and cooperation. Permission is granted on a temporary basis and it is up to the authorities to decide whether the organisations intending to cooperate share similar goals.

Moreover, the requirements include annual reporting to the authorities on all the activities covered. Public meetings with the participation of foreigners require notification to the Directorate General of Security. In practice, some NGOs have continued to face problems as a consequence of their relations with organisations located abroad.

A Kurdish association, the Kurdish Writers' Association, was established in Diyarbakir in February 2004. This was made possible despite an explicit restriction in the current Law on Associations preventing the establishment of an association on the basis of race, ethnicity, religion, sect, region or any other minority group. However, since then charges were brought against this association on the grounds that it held a meeting with representatives of the European Commission without seeking prior permission and the court case is currently ongoing. The association comprises forty-nine Kurdish writers, poets or translators from various professions, including teachers, municipality officers, students, private sector workers and the retired (see section on cultural rights).

While acquittal rates are significantly higher than in the past, Human Rights defenders, including NGOs and lawyers, continue to be subjected to considerable judicial harassment, as illustrated by the number of open investigations and court cases brought against them. For example, between October 2003 and August 2004, ninety-eight court cases and investigations were launched against the Turkish Human Rights Association and fifty-eight are currently ongoing. The majority of these are related to press conferences, which, until June 2004, were treated by the authorities under the Law on Public Meetings and Demonstration Marches, which allows for the attendance of the police.

With respect to peaceful assembly, official figures indicate that public demonstrations are subject to fewer restrictions than in the past: in the first eight months of 2004 twelve demonstrations were prohibited or postponed as compared with forty-one in 2003, ninety-five in 2002 and 141 in 2001. Demonstrations and public meetings are closely monitored by the security forces and cases of intimidation, excessive use of force and detention are still reported. NGOs have indicated that in the first seven months of 2004 the number of detentions related to demonstrations have significantly increased as compared to 2003.

Press conferences and other activities organised by NGOs are routinely subject to videotaping by the local police, especially in the southeast. This includes in many instances the videotaping of participants' identification cards. Those who do not present their identification are often placed in custody.

As regards political parties, no developments can be reported since the last Regular Report. Despite the January 2003 amendments to the Law on Political Parties, which made it more difficult to close political parties, closure cases relating to the Turkish Communist Party (TKP), the Rights and Freedoms Party (HAK-PAR) and the Democratic People's Party (DEHAP) continue. These cases are still pending before the Constitutional Court. In November 2003 the ECtHR found that Turkey had violated Article 11 of the ECtHR when it dissolved the Socialist Party of Turkey in November 1998.

\*\*\* [Freedom of religion, economic and social rights (gender equality, children's rights, trades unions).]

*Minority rights, cultural rights and the protection of minorities* According to the Turkish authorities, under the 1923 Treaty of Lausanne, minorities in Turkey consist only of non-Muslim communities. The minorities usually associated by the authorities with the Treaty of Lausanne are Jews, Armenians and Greeks. However, there are other communities in Turkey, including the Kurds. In this context, Turkey's reservations to the UN Covenant on Civil and Political Rights and the UN Covenant on Economic, Social and Cultural Rights regarding the right to education and the rights of minorities are of concern, as they could be used to prevent further progress in the protection of minority rights.

The 2003 visit of the OSCE [Organization for Security and Cooperation in Europe] High Commissioner on National Minorities to Ankara with the aim of starting a dialogue on the situation of national minorities has not yet been followed up. The OSCE High Commissioner on National Minorities could play a valuable role in assisting Turkey to move towards full compliance with modern international standards on the treatment of minorities.

As stated above, Turkey has not signed the Council of Europe Framework Convention for the Protection of National Minorities and the European Charter for Regional and Minority languages. It has not yet ratified the Additional Protocol no. 12 to the Convention on the general prohibition of discrimination by public authorities. In January 2004 the government abolished the "Secondary Committee for Minorities" established with a secret decree in 1962 in order to carry out security surveillance on minorities. A new institutional body, the "Minority Issues Assessment Board", was set up in order to address the problems of non-Muslim minorities. The Board is composed of representatives of the Ministries of Interior, Education, Foreign Affairs and the Ministry of State responsible for the Directorate General of Foundations. However, the department for minorities established within the Security Directorate of the Ministry of the Interior is still responsible for relations with minorities. Minorities continue to be subject to certain discriminatory practices. Members of minority communities reportedly face difficulties in acceding to senior administrative and military positions.

The history books for the 2003–4 school year still portray minorities as untrustworthy, traitorous and harmful to the state. However, the authorities have started to review discriminatory language in schoolbooks and, in March 2004, a Regulation was issued in which it is stated that school textbooks should not discriminate on the basis of race, religion, gender, language, ethnicity, philosophical belief, or religion. The dialogue with the authorities on the issue of the dual presidency in the Jewish, Greek and Armenian schools (the deputy head of these schools is a Muslim representing the Ministry of Education and has more powers than the head) is ongoing. In May 2004 the Ministry of Education stated that children with mothers from the minority could also attend these schools (previously only those with fathers from the minority could attend).

However, the declaration by parents of their minority status will be subject to an assessment by the Ministry of Education. The Greek community has encountered problems obtaining the approval of new teaching materials and the recognition of teachers trained abroad. Moreover, in contravention of the 2003 Labour Law and in contrast with the situation of their colleagues of Turkish origin, Greek minority teachers are only permitted to teach in one school. The Armenian community has expressed its concern regarding the inadequacy of the teaching of the Armenian language.

Non-Muslim minorities not usually associated by the authorities with the Treaty of Lausanne, such as the Syriacs, are still not permitted to establish schools. The Greek origin minority on the island of Gokceada (Imvros) has encountered difficulties regarding the re-opening of its schools and the current land registry, which has reportedly not been based on fair and transparent procedures and has led to the confiscation of properties.

Legislation preventing Roma from entering Turkey as immigrants is still in force. However, in December 2003 a circular on the Law on Citizenship removed the requirement to state on the citizenship application whether the applicant is a "gypsy". Roma are reportedly socially excluded and experience difficulties in accessing adequate housing.

As regards the protection of *cultural rights*, there has been important progress since 1999. The Constitution has been amended lifting the ban on the use of languages other than Turkish. Legislative changes have been introduced allowing for radio/TV broadcasting in, and teaching of, languages other than Turkish, including Kurdish (see also above on broadcasting). Both broadcasting and teaching began in 2004. More generally, the authorities have shown greater tolerance towards the use of Kurdish. Despite the progress that has been made, there are still considerable restrictions on the exercise of cultural rights.

A Regulation entitled Teaching in Different Languages and Dialects Traditionally Used by Turkish Citizens in their Daily Lives entered into force in December 2003. This allowed for the first time private courses in Kurdish. Six private schools started teaching Kurdish (Kirmanci dialect) in Van, Batman and Sanliurfa in April 2004, in Diyarbakir and Adana in August 2004 and in Istanbul in October 2004. These schools do not receive financial support from the state and there are restrictions concerning, in particular, the curriculum, the appointment of teachers, the timetable and the attendees. Notably, students must have completed basic education and therefore will be older than fifteen. There has been a greater tolerance towards the use of the Kurdish language and the expression of Kurdish culture in its different forms. The Newroz celebrations (marking the beginning of the spring) were authorised and only minor incidents were reported. In December 2003, the Court of Cassation overruled a decision of a local court in Van which had banned the use of posters in the Kurdish language. The Court of Cassation considered that the ban contravened previously adopted legislative amendments.

There have been no changes to the electoral system, which, because of the 10 per cent threshold that political parties are required to reach, makes it difficult for minorities to gain representation in Parliament. There are still restrictions on the use of languages other than Turkish by political parties. NGOs have indicated that a number of individuals were prosecuted for speaking Kurdish during the campaign for the March 2004 local elections and there have been recent cases where Kurdish politicians were convicted. However, in July 2004 (see also section on the Judiciary), the Court of Cassation overruled a judgment, which had sentenced a politician to six months' imprisonment for using Kurdish during a press conference.

Overall the *situation in the east and southeast* of the country, where people of Kurdish origin mostly live, has continued to improve gradually since 1999, in terms of both the security and the enjoyment of fundamental freedoms. The emergency rule has been lifted and the return of the internally displaced persons (IDPs) has continued. Nevertheless, the situation of IDPs remains critical. A Law on Compensation of Losses Resulting from Terrorist Acts was adopted in July 2004. This represents recognition of the need to compensate those in the southeast who have suffered material damages since the beginning of the Emergency Rule period (19 July 1987). Although the criteria on which applications will be accepted and assessed may allow for the possibility of restricting considerably the scope of the law, provision is made for judicial recourse.

Despite a general improvement in the situation in the southeast, the security threat has increased since the Kongra-Gel (formerly PKK) announced the end of the cease-fire in June 2004. Terrorist activities and clashes between Kongra-Gel militants and the Turkish military have been reported.

In March 2004 the Constitutional Court re-established the right of judicial recourse through administrative courts, against Governors' decisions taken during the period of emergency rule. The 2003 Law on Integration to Society offered the possibility for those persons involved in the activities of illegal organisations who have laid down their arms to reintegrate during a six-month period ending in February 2004. The law did not yield significant results. According to official sources, during this period 4,101 applications were made and, of these, 2,800 were from individuals already in prison. Only 1,301 persons applied to the authorities spontaneously. A total of 1,300 persons have so far benefited from the law and were released or received a reduced sentence.

The situation of IDPs is still critical, with many living in precarious conditions. Turkey began a dialogue with international organisations in view of addressing the weaknesses of the "Return to Village and Rehabilitation Programme" which were highlighted by the UN Secretary General's Special Representative for Displaced Persons following his visit to Turkey in 2002. The Turkish government is preparing a survey as a first step in following up on these recommendations.

There have been approximately 1,500 applications to the ECtHR on this subject. In June 2004, the ECtHR found that Turkey had violated Article 1 of Protocol no. 1 ("protection of property"), Article 8 ("right to respect for family life and home") and Article 13 ("right to an effective remedy") of the Convention in the case of Turkish citizens trying to return to their village in the Tunceli region (southeast).

According to official sources, since January 2003, 124,218 IDPs (approximately one-third of the official total of 350,000) have returned to their villages. NGOs suggest that the number of displaced persons is much greater than official statistics indicate (the total number is estimated at 3 million).

The return of IDPs is hampered by the relative economic underdevelopment of the east and southeast. The major outstanding obstacles preventing IDPs from returning to their villages are the government-sponsored village guard system; the problem of landmines; the absence of basic infrastructure; and the lack of capital and employment opportunities.

Public servants who were sent to the west of Turkey during the emergency rule period because it was considered too risky for them to work in the southeast have reportedly not yet been given an opportunity to return. The discretionary power of each provincial Governor also plays a crucial role in the implementation of the legal and administrative provisions regulating return.

Very few Syriac origin citizens have attempted to return from abroad, in particular, because they face harassment from the village guards and the gendarmerie. The issue of the village guards remains unresolved. Notwithstanding the judicial procedures against village guards involved in murders, official figures state that 58,416 village guards are still on duty (as opposed to 58,551 last year). Moreover, although the Turkish authorities state that no village guards have been appointed since 2000, NGOs suggest that new village guards have been recruited in response to the increasing number of clashes between security forces and illegal armed groups. In many cases, authorisation to return to villages is reportedly conditional on the willingness of the returnees to serve as village guards. A petition containing over 30,000 signatures protesting against the village guard system was registered with the Petitions Committee in the Parliament in October 2003.

\*\*\* [Cyprus; peaceful settlement of border disputes.]

1.6 GENERAL EVALUATION

When the European Council of December 1999 decided that Turkey is a candidate for accession, Turkey was considered to have the basic features of a democratic system while at the same time displaying serious shortcomings in terms of Human Rights and protection of minorities. In 2002, the Commission noted in its Regular Report that the decision on the candidate status of Turkey had encouraged the country to make noticeable progress with the adoption of a series of fundamental, but still limited, reforms. At that time, it was clear that most of those measures had yet to be implemented and that many other issues required to meet the Copenhagen political criteria had yet to be addressed. On that basis, the European Council decided in December 2002 to re-examine Turkey's fulfilment of the political criteria at the end of 2004.

Political reforms, in line with the priorities in the Accession Partnership, have been introduced by means of a series of constitutional and legislative changes adopted over a period of three years (2001–4). There have been two major constitutional reforms in 2001 and 2004 and eight legislative packages were adopted by Parliament between February 2002 and July 2004. New codes have been adopted, including a Civil Code and a Penal Code. Numerous other laws, regulations, decrees and circulars outlining the application of these reforms were issued. The government undertook major steps to achieve better implementation of the reforms. The Reform Monitoring Group, a body set up under the chairmanship of the deputy Prime Minister responsible for Human Rights, was established to supervise the reforms across the board and to solve practical problems. Significant progress took place also on the ground; however, the implementation of reforms remains uneven.

On civil–military relations, the government has increasingly asserted its control over the military. In order to enhance budgetary transparency the Court of Auditors was granted permission to audit military and defence expenditures. Extra-budgetary funds have been included in the general budget, allowing for full parliamentary control. In August 2004, for the first time a civilian was appointed Secretary General of the National Security Council. The process of fully aligning civil–military relations with EU practice is under way; nevertheless, the armed forces in Turkey continue to exercise influence through a series of informal mechanisms.

The independence and efficiency of the judiciary were strengthened, State Security Courts were abolished and some of their competencies were transferred to the newly created Serious Felony Courts. The legislation to establish Intermediate Courts of Appeal was recently adopted, but the draft new Code of Criminal Procedure, the draft Laws on the Establishment of the Judicial Police and on the Execution of Punishments still await adoption.

Since 1 January 2004, Turkey has been a member of the Council of Europe's Group of States Against Corruption (GRECO). A number of anti-corruption measures have been adopted, in particular by establishing ethical rules for public servants. However, despite these legislative developments, corruption remains a serious problem in almost all areas of the economy and public affairs.

Concerning the general framework for the respect of Human Rights and the exercise of fundamental freedoms, Turkey has acceded to most relevant international and European conventions and the principle of the supremacy of these international Human Rights conventions over domestic law was enshrined in the Constitution. Since 2002 Turkey has increased its efforts to execute decisions of the European Court of Human Rights. Higher judicial bodies such as the Court of Cassation have issued a number of judgments interpreting the reforms in accordance with the standards of the European Court, including in cases related to the use of the Kurdish language, torture and freedom of expression. Retrials have taken place, leading to a number of acquittals. Leyla Zana and her former colleagues, who were released from prison in June 2004, are to face a further retrial, following a decision by the Court of Cassation.

The death penalty was abolished in all circumstances according to Protocol no. 13 to the European Convention on Human Rights, which Turkey signed in January 2004. Remaining references to the death penalty in existing legislation were removed. Further efforts have been made to strengthen the fight against torture and ill-treatment, including provisions in the new Penal Code. Pre-trial detention procedures have been aligned with European standards, although detainees are not always made aware of their rights by law enforcement officers. The authorities have adopted a zero tolerance policy towards torture and a number of perpetrators of torture have been punished. Torture is no longer systematic, but numerous cases of ill-treatment including torture still continue to occur and further efforts will be required to eradicate such practices.

As regards freedom of expression, the situation has improved significantly, but several problems remain. The situation of individuals sentenced for non-violent expression of opinion is now being addressed and several persons sentenced under the old provisions were either acquitted or released. Constitutional amendments and a new press law have increased press freedoms. The new law abrogates sanctions such as the closure of publications, the halting of distribution and the confiscation of printing machines. However, in a number of cases journalists and other citizens expressing non-violent opinion continue to be prosecuted. The new Penal Code provides only limited progress as regards freedom of expression.

If adopted, the new Law on Associations, initially passed in July 2004 and then vetoed by the President, will be significant in terms of reducing the possibility of state interference in the activities of associations and will contribute towards the strengthening of civil society. Despite measures taken to ease restrictions on demonstrations, there are still reports of the use of disproportionate force against demonstrators.

Although freedom of religious belief is guaranteed by the Constitution, and freedom to worship is largely unhampered, non-Muslim religious communities continue to experience difficulties connected with legal personality, property rights, training of clergy, schools and internal management. Appropriate legislation could remedy these difficulties. Alevis are still not recognised as a Muslim minority.

As regards economic and social rights, the principle of gender equality has been strengthened in the Civil Code and the Constitution. Under the new Penal Code, perpetrators of "honour killings" should be sentenced to life imprisonment, virginity tests will be prohibited without a court order and sexual assault in marriage will qualify as a criminal offence. The situation of women is still unsatisfactory;

discrimination and violence against women, including "honour killings", remain a major problem. Children's rights were strengthened, but child labour remains an issue of serious concern. Trade union rights still fall short of ILO standards.

As far as the protection of minorities and the exercise of cultural rights are concerned, the Constitution was amended to lift the ban on the use of Kurdish and other languages. Several Kurdish language schools recently opened in the southeast of Turkey. Broadcasting in Kurdish and other languages and dialects is now permitted and broadcasts have started, although on a restricted scale. There has been greater tolerance for the expression of Kurdish culture in its different forms. The measures adopted in the area of cultural rights represent only a starting point. There are still considerable restrictions, in particular in the area of broadcasting and education in minority languages.

The state of emergency, which had been in force for fifteen years in some provinces of the southeast, was completely lifted in 2002. Provisions used to restrict pre-trial detention rights under emergency rule were amended. Turkey began a dialogue with a number of international organisations, including the Commission, on the question of internally displaced persons. A Law on Compensation of Losses Resulting from Terrorist Acts was approved. Although work is under way to define a more systematic approach towards the region, no integrated strategy with a view to reducing regional disparities and addressing the economic, social and cultural needs of the local population has yet been adopted. The return of internally displaced persons in the southeast has been limited and hampered by the village guard system and by a lack of material support. Future measures should address specifically the recommendations of the UN Secretary General's Special Representative for Displaced Persons.

In conclusion, Turkey has achieved significant legislative progress in many areas, through further reform packages, constitutional changes and the adoption of a new Penal Code, and in particular in those identified as priorities in last year's report and in the Accession Partnership. Important progress was made in the implementation of political reforms, but these need to be further consolidated and broadened. This applies to the strengthening and full implementation of provisions related to the respect of fundamental freedoms and protection of Human Rights, including women's rights, trades union rights, minority rights and problems faced by non-Muslim religious communities. Civilian control over the military needs to be asserted, and law enforcement and judicial practice aligned with the spirit of the reforms. The fight against corruption should be pursued. The policy of zero tolerance towards torture should be reinforced through determined efforts at all levels of the Turkish state. The normalisation of the situation in the southeast should be pursued through the return of displaced persons, a strategy for socio-economic development and the establishment of conditions for the full enjoyment of rights and freedoms by the Kurds.

The changes to the Turkish political and legal system over the past years are part of a longer process and it will take time before the spirit of the reforms is fully reflected in the attitudes of executive and judicial bodies, at all levels and throughout the country. A steady determination will be required in order to tackle outstanding challenges and overcome bureaucratic hurdles. Political reform will continue to be closely monitored. As regards the enhanced political dialogue, relations with Greece developed positively. A series of bilateral agreements were signed and several confidence-building measures adopted. A process of exploratory talks has continued. On Cyprus, over the last year Turkey has supported and continues to support the efforts of the UN Secretary General to achieve a comprehensive settlement of the Cyprus problem. The European Council of June 2004 invited Turkey to conclude negotiations with the Commission on behalf of the Community and its twenty-five Member States on the adaptation of the Ankara Agreement to take account of the accession of the new Member States. The Commission expects a positive reply to the draft protocol on the necessary adaptations transmitted to Turkey in July 2004.

## 2. Economic criteria

### 2.1 INTRODUCTION

In its 1989 Opinion on Turkey's application for EU membership, the Commission concluded:

"Turkey's economic and political situation, ... , does not convince it that the adjustment problems which would confront Turkey if it were to accede to the Community could be overcome in the medium term."

In its 2003 Regular Report, the Commission found that:

"Turkey has significantly improved the functioning of its market economy, while macro-economic imbalances remain. Further decisive steps towards macro-economic stability and structural reforms will also enhance the Turkish capacity to cope with competitive pressure and market forces within the Union."

In examining economic developments in Turkey since the first Regular Report, the Commission's approach has been guided by the June 1993 conclusions of the Copenhagen European Council, which stated that membership of the Union requires:

- the existence of a functioning market economy;
- the capacity to cope with competitive pressure and market forces within the Union.

In the analysis below, the Commission has followed the methodology applied in the previous annual Regular Reports. The analysis in this year's Regular Report takes stock of developments since 1999.

\*\*\*

### 2.4 GENERAL EVALUATION

Turkey has made further considerable progress towards being a functioning market economy, in particular by reducing its macro-economic imbalances.

Turkey should also be able to cope with competitive pressure and market forces within the Union, provided that it firmly maintains its stabilisation policy and takes further decisive steps towards structural reforms.

Economic stability and predictability have been substantially improved since the 2001 economic crisis ... [However] in order to transform the current positive dynamics into sustained growth and stability, it is of crucial importance to continue the ongoing reform process. \*\*\*

## 3. Ability to assume the obligations of membership

This section addresses the question of Turkey's ability to assume the obligations of membership — that is, the legal and institutional framework, known as the *acquis*, by means of which the Union implements its objectives. Alongside an evaluation of relevant developments since the 2003 Regular Report, this section seeks to provide an overall assessment of Turkey's ability to assume the obligations of membership, and of what remains to be done.

This section is structured in accordance with the list of twenty-nine *acquis* chapters, and incorporates an assessment of Turkey's administrative capacity to implement the *acquis* in its various aspects.

\*\*\*

### 3.2 GENERAL EVALUATION

Turkey's alignment has progressed in many areas but remains at an early stage for most chapters. Further work is required in all areas, new legislation should not move away from the *acquis*, and discrimination against non-Turkish service providers, or products, should be discontinued. Administrative capacity needs to be reinforced. Moreover no Member State should be excluded from the mutual benefits deriving from the alignment with the *acquis*.

\*\*\*

# Document no. 105

**[European Parliament] Resolution on the 2004 Regular Report and the recommendation of the European Commission on Turkey's Progress Towards Accession**[10]

*The European Parliament,*

\*\*\*

1. Welcomes the political reform process in Turkey and the adopted constitutional and legislative changes that have entered into force, as well as the progress made in implementing those reforms since the European Parliament adopted its resolution of 5 June 2003 on Turkey's application for membership of the European Union; nonetheless, is of the opinion that the Turkish authorities still have to adopt and implement further reforms and put current reforms into practice in order to fully meet the political criteria;

2. Welcomes the impressive efforts of the Turkish authorities to achieve substantial legislative and institutional convergence in Turkey towards European standards;

\*\*\*

4. Welcomes the continuing strong motivation and the political will demonstrated by the Turkish government and by the great majority of the representatives elected by the Turkish people to grow closer to the EU; welcomes the significant popular support reflected in poll results;

5. Notes with satisfaction that over the last few years Turkey has fulfilled a number of recommendations and requirements included in Parliament's resolutions regarding in particular, amongst others: the complete abolition of the death penalty, the extension of important fundamental rights and freedoms, reduction of the role of the National Security Council and the lifting of the state of emergency in the southeast; thereby complying with a number of the recommendations set out in Parliament's resolutions; regrets however the reservations expressed on the International Covenant on Civil and Political Rights as well as the International Covenant on Economic, Social and Cultural Rights;

6. Expresses its unconditional support for the civil society organisations and actors operating in Turkey in defence and promotion of fundamental rights and freedoms; calls on the Council and the Commission to strengthen cooperation with such organisations in the process of monitoring Turkey's compliance with the political criteria of Copenhagen;

7. Acknowledges that the reforms implemented by the Turkish authorities have given non-governmental organisations greater scope to take action, in particular as regards the promotion of Human Rights, and calls on the Turkish government to step up its efforts to eradicate all forms of intimidation and harassment of Human Rights activists and organisations;

8. Welcomes in particular the reform of criminal procedure, strengthening the rights of the defence; considers however that Article 305 of the new Turkish Penal Code, which sanctions alleged "threats to fundamental national interests", and the explanatory statement of which targets freedom of expression, in particular related to the Cyprus and Armenia issues, is incompatible with the 1950 European Convention for the Protection of Human Rights and Fundamental Freedoms; calls therefore for its repeal;

9. Welcomes the release of Leyla Zana and her colleagues from the former Democracy Party (DEP), and calls for a fair and equitable retrial and for the immediate release of all imprisoned persons sentenced for the non-violent expression of opinions in Turkey;

10. Welcomes the fact that the Turkish government has introduced legal changes which enable private language centres to offer courses in mother tongues other than Turkish (Kurdish, Circassian, Armenian *et al.*), to broadcast media programmes and to open and operate stations which broadcast in other languages; calls on the Turkish government to lift all remaining restrictions in the area of broadcasting and education in minority languages;

11. Strongly urges Turkey to actually extend these legal changes and the implementation thereof to education and broadcasting for non-Muslim minorities (Greeks, Armenians, Jews, Assyrians);

12. Invites Turkey to drastically improve its perception of ethnic and religious minorities, for instance by highlighting their contributions to the cultural heritage of the country; in particular, requests the Turkish authorities to consider some of these specific contributions such as Hasankeyf, Ani, Zeugma or Aghtamar as suitable for registration in the World Heritage List of UNESCO [United Nations Educational, Scientific, and Cultural Oragnization];

13. Urges, in this respect, the Turkish government to apply EU environmental and Human Rights standards to large-impact projects like the construction of dams in the Munzur Valley and Ilisu, and gold-mining in Bergama, where historical heritage and unique valuable landscapes are at risk;

14. Urges the Turkish authorities to fully implement a "zero-tolerance" approach at all levels and in all aspects to the complete eradication of torture, as cases are still reported to Turkish governmental bodies and Human Rights organisations, and as the zero-tolerance approach is put insufficiently into practice;

15. Suggests to the Turkish government that, when reforming the criminal procedural law, it should abrogate the statute of limitations for all criminal cases when proceedings are opened; calls on the Turkish judicial system, and in particular the prosecutors, to concentrate on cases of alleged torture, given that currently only few judicial investigations and cases against suspected perpetrators are opened; calls on Turkey to increase staffing levels in the public prosecution service in order to achieve results;

16. Calls on the Turkish authorities, in that connection, to redouble their efforts to implement that approach more effectively and, in particular, to take a more resolute approach to the issue of immunity from prosecution, and emphasises the need to step up educational programmes designed to change the attitudes of members of the police and armed forces with a view to ensuring strict compliance with the law;

17. Calls on the Turkish interior ministry to adopt and apply the policy of opening immediately, and as a matter of principle, administrative and disciplinary investigations against any police officer accused of torture or mistreatment;

18. Calls on the Turkish authorities to bring the Law on Associations, the new Penal Code and the Law on Intermediate Courts of Appeal into force and to adopt the decision on the Code of Criminal Procedure, the legislation establishing the judicial police and the law on execution of punishments and measures;

19. Calls on the Turkish authorities to significantly reform the Law on Foundations after consulting — as should be done in the case of all these Laws — those entities affected by this Law such as relevant NGOs and the broad spectrum of religious communities;

20. Calls on the Foreign Affairs Committee and its Subcommittee for Human Rights to follow closely the Human Rights situation in Turkey and in particular the implementation on the ground, especially regarding implementation of the principle of zero tolerance with respect to torture, the return process of displaced people in coordination with international agencies, the implementation of the campaign and the law to eradicate violence against women and the issue of protection and promotion of minority rights, freedom of religion, freedom of expression, press freedom and freedom for trades unions;

21. Reiterates its call for the electoral system to be reformed by reducing the threshold of 10 per cent, thereby ensuring a wider representation of political forces in the Grand National Assembly, including predominantly Kurdish parties;

22. Expresses its concern about the DEHAP trial and the danger of dissolution of the party; calls on the Turkish authorities to respect the right of freedom of expression as well as the right of organisation of democratic political parties such as DEHAP;

23. Regards the drafting of a new Constitution as a further and probably necessary reflection of the very fundamental nature of the changes required for EU membership and notes that a modern Constitution may form the basis for the modernisation of the Turkish State;

24. Reiterates the need for continuing efforts to ensure a competent and independent judiciary and calls on the Turkish authorities to ensure that all

legislative changes are rapidly implemented, especially with respect to the protection of Human Rights, and translated into a change of conduct at all levels of the judiciary;

25. Calls on the Turkish government to reform current inspection services by allocating the tasks involved to independent inspection services which should be given sufficient resources to operate effectively in all regions of Turkey and empowered to investigate any police detention facility at any time while closely cooperating with independent Turkish Human Rights NGOs;

26. Expresses its unconditional support for the civil society organisations and actors operating in Turkey in defence and promotion of fundamental freedoms;

27. Calls on the Turkish authorities to energetically pursue their fight against corruption, which still seriously affects economic, political and social life; welcomes the Turkish authorities' efforts against corruption, including the ratification of the OECD's Anti-Bribery Convention and the UN Convention against Corruption, and membership of the Council of Europe's Group of States against corruption (GRECO);

\*\*\* [gender equality]

31. Urges all parties involved to put an immediate end to the hostilities in the southeast of the country; invites the Turkish government to take more active steps to bring about reconciliation with those Kurdish forces who have chosen to abandon the use of arms;

\*\*\*

33. Stresses that the overall situation in the southeast has improved since 1999, in terms of both security and respect for fundamental rights; calls on the Turkish government to develop plans to enable people who wish to do so to return to their villages and towns in the southeast and to properly address the problems currently caused by the village guard system; urges Turkey to disarm the village guards and disband the village guard system; calls on Turkey to collaborate closely with international bodies, such as the United Nations, the EU and the Council of Europe, to support and speed up the return of internally displaced persons, in conformity with the UN Guiding Principles on Internal Displacement, and urges the authorities to develop an integrated regional development concept to economically develop the southeast as a region and foster the overall modernisation of society;

\*\*\* [International refugee rights, trade unions, child employment]

37. Calls on the Turkish government to limit the political role of the army further through ongoing reforms;

38. Welcomes the fact that the principle of the primacy of international law over national law has been enshrined in the Turkish Constitution as far as the

European Convention on Human Rights is concerned and calls on the Turkish authorities to respect all its provisions and to implement without delay the still outstanding decisions of the European Court of Human Rights;

\*\*\* [Armenia, water requirements of neighbors]

43. Reiterates its call to the Turkish authorities to put an immediate end to all activities discriminating against and creating difficulties for religious minorities and communities, including in the areas of property rights, legal status, schools and internal management, environmental planning rules and the training of clergy, and requests as a first clear sign of implementation the immediate re-opening of the Greek Orthodox Halki seminary and the public use of the ecclesiastical title of the Ecumenical Patriarchate; calls on Turkey, bearing in mind the current difficulties, to act in accordance with the relevant case-law of the European Court of Human Rights; calls for the recognition and protection of the Alevites, including the recognition of Cem houses as religious centres, and for all religious education to be voluntary and to cover not only Sunni religion; calls for the protection of the fundamental rights of all Christian minorities and communities in Turkey (e.g. Greeks of Istanbul, Imvros and Tenedos);

\*\*\* [Cyprus and resolution of any outstanding disputes with neighboring states.]

47. Calls on the Commission to include all the necessary political reforms in the revised Accession Partnership and stresses the need for continued and effective Community assistance based on a revised Accession Partnership and adapted, as far as possible, to Turkey's needs in terms of compliance with the Copenhagen criteria;
48. Requests the Commission, the Council and the Member States to take all necessary steps in order for the European Constitution to enter into force so that the EU can fulfil the preconditions for its smooth functioning and boost its capacity to absorb new Member States;
49. Welcomes the Commission's recommendation to monitor the implementation of the legal reforms, respect for the principles of liberty, democracy, respect for Human Rights and fundamental freedoms and the rule of law, and its commitment to recommend, in line with the Treaty on European Union and the Constitution for Europe, the suspension of the negotiations in the event of a serious and persistent breach of these principles; urges the Commission and the Council to consult the Parliament hereon;
50. Recalls the conclusions of the European Council of 21–22 June 1993 setting out the Copenhagen criteria for EU membership and calls on the European Council, in its decision on starting negotiations with Turkey, to state that the Union's capacity to absorb Turkey as a member, while maintaining the momentum of European integration, constitutes an important criterion for accession, from the point of view both of the Union and of candidates for accession;

51. Encourages the Turkish authorities to continue with the reforms designed to strengthen mechanisms to safeguard Human Rights, such as the possibility offered to members of the public to submit a complaint to an independent body; in that connection, therefore, regards as important the establishment in the near future of the office of Ombudsman;

52. Emphasises, in that connection, the importance of exchange and training programmes for judicial officers and judges and of attendance at the symposiums on Community law which Turkey has started to organise in cooperation with both the EU and some of its Member States and with the Council of Europe;

\*\*\* [Economic criteria]

55. Highlights that only by demonstrating readiness to embrace EU values through determined implementation and continued reform will Turkey be able to ensure the irreversibility of the process of reform and to gather the necessary support amongst the body of EU public opinion; expects the Commission and the Council to demonstrate on the basis of facts that this has been achieved;

56. Calls in this context on the Commission and the Council to report annually to the European Parliament and the national Parliaments of the EU Member States on the progress made by Turkey in fulfilling the political criteria, and to include in this report all verified cases of torture reported in that year and the number of Turkish asylum seekers accepted by the EU Member States during that year;

57. Urges the Commission, once the negotiations on the various chapters have started, to recommend, in the event of a serious and persistent breach of the principles of liberty, democracy, respect for Human Rights and fundamental freedoms and the rule of law, and after consultation of the European Parliament, the suspension of negotiations, in line with the Treaty on European Union;

\*\*\*

63. Stresses that the opening of negotiations will be the starting point for a long-lasting process that by its very nature is an open-ended process and does not lead "a priori" and automatically to accession; emphasises, however, that the objective of the negotiations is Turkish EU membership but that the realisation of this ambition will depend on the efforts of both sides; accession is thus not the automatic consequence of the start of the negotiations;

64. Is of the opinion that in the context of a possible accession it is now up to the Turkish authorities to prove that they can truly fulfil the Copenhagen political criteria and to confirm over a longer period of time that the reform process, which will have to be continued and implemented, is fundamental and irreversible;

65. Calls on the Turkish authorities to encourage frequent visits from and dialogue with the European Parliament, without restrictions;

66. Considers that, regardless of whether or not negotiations are successfully concluded, relations between the EU and Turkey must ensure that Turkey remains fully anchored in European structures;

67. Considers that the opening of accession negotiations is to be recommended so long as it is agreed that:

- in the first phase of the negotiations priority is given to the full implementation of the political criteria; that therefore the agenda of negotiations at ministerial level will start with the assessment of the fulfilment of the political criteria, especially in the area of Human Rights and full fundamental freedoms in both theory and practice, in the meantime opening up the opportunity to put other chapters on the agenda of the negotiations;
- in accordance with the Commission's requirements, six important remaining pieces of legislation are to be adopted and enforced prior to the beginning of negotiations;
- all mechanisms envisaged by the Commission to ensure close monitoring, intensive political dialogue and a possible suspension of negotiations, if necessary, are fully effective;

68. Considering the overall progress outlined in the report of the Commission and taking into account the above provisions of this resolution, calls upon the European Council to open the negotiations with Turkey without undue delay;

69. Instructs its President to forward this resolution to the Council and the Commission, the Secretary General of the Council of Europe, the President of the European Court of Human Rights and the government and Parliament of Turkey.

# Document no. 106

**Brussels European Council Presidency conclusions, 16–17 December 2004**[11]

\*\*\*

## *I. Enlargement*

*General*

4. The European Council welcomed the findings and recommendations presented by the Commission on 6 October 2004 to the Council and the European Parliament in its Regular Reports on Bulgaria, Romania and Turkey, the Strategy Paper on Bulgaria, Romania and Croatia, its Recommendation on Turkey and the document on Issues Arising from Turkey's Membership Perspective.

\*\*\*

*Turkey*

17. The European Council recalled its previous conclusions regarding Turkey, in which, at Helsinki, it agreed that Turkey was a candidate State destined to join the Union on the basis of the same criteria as applied to the other candidate States and, subsequently, concluded that, if it were to decide at its December 2004 meeting, on the basis of a report and recommendation from the Commission, that Turkey fulfils the Copenhagen political criteria, the European Union will open accession negotiations with Turkey without delay.

18. The European Council welcomed the decisive progress made by Turkey in its far-reaching reform process and expressed its confidence that Turkey will sustain that process of reform. Furthermore, it expects Turkey to actively pursue its efforts to bring into force the six specific items of legislation identified by the Commission. To ensure the irreversibility of the political reform process and its full, effective and comprehensive implementation, notably with regard to fundamental freedoms and to full respect of Human Rights, that process will

continue to be closely monitored by the Commission, which is invited to continue to report regularly on it to the Council, addressing all points of concern identified in the Commission's 2004 report and recommendation, including the implementation of the zero-tolerance policy relating to torture and ill-treatment. The European Union will continue to monitor closely progress of the political reforms on the basis of an Accession Partnership setting out priorities for the reform process.

19. The European Council welcomed Turkey's decision to sign the Protocol regarding the adaptation of the Ankara Agreement, taking account of the accession of the ten new Member States.

In this light, it welcomed the declaration of Turkey that "the Turkish government confirms that it is ready to sign the Protocol on the adaptation of the Ankara Agreement prior to the actual start of accession negotiations and after reaching agreement on and finalising the adaptations which are necessary in view of the current membership of the European Union".

20. The European Council, while underlining the need for unequivocal commitment to good neighbourly relations welcomed the improvement in Turkey's relations with its neighbours and its readiness to continue to work with the Member States concerned towards resolution of outstanding border disputes in conformity with the principle of peaceful settlement of disputes in accordance with the United Nations Charter. In accordance with its previous conclusions, notably those of Helsinki on this matter, the European Council reviewed the situation relating to outstanding disputes and welcomed the exploratory contacts to this end. In this connection it reaffirmed its view that unresolved disputes having repercussions on the accession process should if necessary be brought to the International Court of Justice for settlement. The European Council will be kept informed of progress achieved which it will review as appropriate.

21. The European Council noted the resolution adopted by the European Parliament on 15 December 2004.

22. The European Council welcomed the adoption of the six pieces of legislation identified by the Commission. It decided that, in the light of the above and of the Commission report and recommendation, Turkey sufficiently fulfils the Copenhagen political criteria to open accession negotiations provided that it brings into force these specific pieces of legislation.

It invited the Commission to present to the Council a proposal for a framework for negotiations with Turkey, on the basis set out in paragraph 23. It requested the Council to agree on that framework with a view to opening negotiations on 3 October 2005.

***

# 15 Quo Vadis?

After 2004: European Union membership still a rough path

# Document no. 107

**Issues arising from Turkey's membership perspective**[1]

## Table of contents

Introduction and summary
1. Geo-political dimension
2. Economic dimension
3. Internal market and related policies
4. Agriculture, veterinary and phytosanitary issues, fisheries
5. Regional and structural policy
6. Justice and home affairs
7. Institutional and budgetary aspects

## Introduction and summary

In parallel with the preparations of the report and the recommendation requested by the European Council, the Commission services have conducted an assessment of the effects of Turkey's possible accession on the Union and its policies.

The clear position of the European Union with regard to Turkey's status as candidate country and the conditions for the possible opening of negotiations were reconfirmed by the Brussels European Council meeting in June, which concluded that:

"The Union reaffirms its commitment that if the European Council decides in December 2004, on the basis of a report and recommendation from the Commission, that Turkey fulfils the Copenhagen political criteria, the EU will open accession negotiations with Turkey without delay."

Given the suggestion put forward by the European Parliament in March for a study on the impact of Turkey's accession ... [t]he purpose [of this paper] is to give an overview of issues arising from Turkey's membership perspective.

The assessment primarily addresses the effects of Turkey's integration in EU policies. The considerations in the present paper do not constitute additional criteria or conditions to be fulfilled in view of the December decision of the European Council ...

The analysis illustrates the difficulty of undertaking long-term projections and the need for further in-depth studies of specific issues relevant for the conduct of negotiations.

\*\*\*

The first section of the paper focuses on political aspects against the background of Turkey's strategic situation, and attempts to assess the potential implications in the areas of CFSP [Common Foreign and Security Policy] and ESDP [European Security and Defence Policy], in terms of both opportunities and challenges.

The second section addresses the economic effects on both the EU and Turkey as well as the implications of Turkey's participation in economic and monetary union.

Sections 3 to 6 focus on different policy areas — internal market and related policies, agriculture, regional policy and justice and home affairs — and examine the possible effects of Turkey's accession, and the associated challenges and opportunities.

The final section looks at the possible impact on the EU institutions, as well as budgetary implications.

*Summary assessment*

Accession of Turkey to the Union would be challenging for both the EU and Turkey. If well managed, it would offer important opportunities for both. The necessary preparations for accession would last well into the next decade. The EU will evolve over this period, and Turkey should change even more radically. The *acquis* will develop further and respond to the needs of an EU of twenty-seven or more. Its development may also anticipate the challenges and opportunities of Turkey's accession.

Based on current EU policies and knowledge, the Commission has identified the following main issues for the coming years:

- Turkey's accession would be different from previous enlargements because of the combined impact of Turkey's population, size, geographical location, economic, security and military potential, as well as cultural and religious characteristics. These factors give Turkey the capacity to contribute to regional and international stability.

  Expectations regarding EU policies towards these regions will grow as well, taking into account Turkey's existing political and economic links to its neighbours. Much will depend on how the EU itself will take on the challenge to become a fully fledged foreign policy player in the medium term in regions traditionally characterised by instability and tensions, including the Middle East and the Caucasus.

- Turkey is at present going through a process of radical change, including a rapid evolution of mentalities. It is in the interest of all that the current

transformation process continues. Turkey would be an important model of a country with a majority Muslim population adhering to such fundamental principles as liberty, democracy, respect for Human Rights and fundamental freedoms, and the rule of law.
- The economic impact of Turkey's accession on the EU would be positive but relatively small, due both to the modest size of the Turkish economy and to the degree of economic integration already existing before accession ...
- Accession of Turkey, a lower middle income country, would increase regional economic disparities in the enlarged EU in a way similar to the most recent enlargement, and would represent a major challenge for cohesion policy ...
- The integration of Turkey into the internal market would be beneficial. This depends, however, not only on the fulfillment of present obligations under the Customs Union but also on more horizontal reforms, such as strengthening corporate governance and regulatory frameworks, intensifying the fight against corruption, and significantly improving the functioning of the judiciary.
- With over three million, Turks constitute by far the largest group of third-country nationals legally residing in today's EU ... Available studies give varying estimates of expected additional migration following Turkey's accession ... In this context, the EU also has a strong interest in that reforms and investments should be made in education and training in Turkey over the next decade.
- Agriculture is one of the most important economic and social sectors in Turkey and would need special attention ...
- Turkey's accession would help to secure better energy supply routes for the EU. It would probably necessitate a development of EU policies for the management of water resources and the related infrastructure ...
- The management of the EU's long new external borders would constitute an important policy challenge and require significant investment. Managing migration and asylum as well as fighting organised crime, terrorism, trafficking of human beings, drugs and arms smuggling would all be facilitated through closer cooperation both before and after accession.
- The budgetary impact of Turkish membership to the EU can only be fully assessed once the parameters for the financial negotiations with Turkey have been defined in the context of the financial perspectives from 2014 onwards ...
- As to the institutions, Turkey's accession, assessed on the basis of the Constitution, would significantly affect the allocation of European Parliament seats of current Member States, in particular the medium-sized and large countries ...

## *1. Geo-political dimension*

Turkey is situated at a regional crossroads of strategic importance for Europe: the Balkans, Caucasus, Central Asia, Middle East and Eastern Mediterranean; its territory is a transit route for land and air transport with Asia, and for sea transport with Russia and the Ukraine. Its neighbours provide key energy supplies for Europe, and it has substantial water resources. In economic and demographic terms, Turkey is an important actor: it is the world's twenty-first economy in size, and as a member of the EU would be the biggest Member State in terms of population. As a Moslem secular country with a functioning democracy, it is a factor for stability in the region. Through its integration in the western alliance, and membership of many economic and regional organisations, it contributes to the security of Europe and its neighbourhood.

*1.1. Foreign policy implications*

In assessing the impact of Turkey's membership on the EU's external policies, one needs to take account of a number of factors:

- Turkey's relations with countries in the adjoining regions;
- its membership of international organisations;
- its potential contribution to the EU's security and defence policy;
- domestic factors affecting Turkish foreign policy.

*1.2. Turkey's relations with neighbouring countries*

\*\*\*

*1.3. Trans-national issues*

Turkey would be an important model of a country with a majority Muslim population adhering to such fundamental principles as liberty, democracy, respect for Human Rights and fundamental freedoms, and the rule of law. This is particularly relevant given the debate and perceptions which have arisen in the aftermath of the 11 September 2001 attacks.

Fighting *terrorism* constitutes yet another security challenge, where Turkish accession would further enhance already existing cooperation. In recent years, Turkey has suffered several terrorist attacks from extreme-left and radical Islamic fundamentalist groupings. Since the events of 11 September 2001, Turkey has associated itself with several EU initiatives related to the fight against terrorism. Organisations regarded in Turkey as terrorist have been included in the EU list.

As a result of Turkey's accession, the presence of sizeable *Kurdish minorities* in Turkey and in other countries of the region, and the existence of Kurdish *diaspora* in the present EU, could have implications for the EU's relations with these countries.

*1.4. International relations*

\*\*\*

*1.5. European security and defence policy*

\*\*\*

*1.6. Domestic factors affecting Turkish foreign policy*

\*\*\*

*1.7 Assessment*

The assessment of the potential impact of Turkey's EU accession on the EU's external policies faces a number of variables: the uncertain timing of Turkey's possible accession, the fluidity of international developments in general and, in particular in Turkey's immediate neighbourhood, the shape of the European Union over the next ten to fifteen years and not least the course of Turkey's evolution and internal transformation in a similar timeframe.

The EU's enlargement to include Turkey would be different from previous enlargements because of the size of Turkey's population, its economic weight and its geographical position in a region characterised by instability, international tensions, internal conflicts, minority issues and diverging economic and energy-related interests.

The following elements emerge from this analysis:

- Turkey is a strategically important country whose EU membership would have implications for foreign policy in a number of potentially unstable neighbouring regions such as the Mediterranean, Middle East, Caucasus and Central Asia.
- The present Member States of the EU and Turkey have strong interests in these regions, which in many ways converge, but in some cases differ.
- If Turkey pursues its economic modernisation, socio-economic development and regional integration, it would be able to play an important stabilising role in its neighbourhood.
- As an EU member Turkey would have importance for a number of transnational issues (energy, water resources, transport, border management, counter-terrorism).
- With its large military expenditure and manpower, Turkey has the material capacity to make a significant contribution to EU security and defence policy.
- On international issues, Turkey generally aligns its positions to the EU's common foreign and security policy; but on some sensitive issues (Human Rights, the Middle East) this is not yet the case.
- The successful inclusion of Turkey in the European integration process would give clear evidence to the Muslim world that their religious beliefs are compatible with the EU's values.
- However, in the future development of Turkish foreign policy, much will depend on internal developments within Turkey, especially as regards the future role of the military, religion and civil society.
- While Turkey, as potentially the biggest Member State of the EU, would have an important influence in foreign policy, it would be subject to the constraints of membership and common decision-making in the European institutions.

From the point of view of the EU's role in foreign affairs, Turkey's accession brings both advantages and challenges. It could help to stabilise the conflict-prone zone of the Middle East, but it would bring the EU into more direct involvement with the difficult political and security problems of the region. Turkey being a member would give the EU greater weight in regional and world affairs, but it could also make decision-making, especially under unanimity, more complicated. Summing up, Turkey could be a factor for enhancing stability and the role of the EU in the region, but its membership would present challenges as well as opportunities in the field of foreign affairs.

\*\*\*

# Document no. 108

## Developments in 2005 through press reports[2]

### EP [European Parliament] Head Borrell: "Europe must work to dispel anti-Turkish bias" — 7 January 2005

Eliminating bias against Turkey as its European Union membership goes forward is both necessary and beneficial for Europe, wrote European Parliament President Joseph Borrell in a guest op-ed for French daily *Le Figaro* yesterday. Borrell said that the EU had three major homework assignments this year, namely, enlivening the Lisbon strategy, approving the European Constitution and moving Turkey's membership forward. "We need to get used to heated discussions on Turkey's membership bid," he wrote. "This will be a test for our continent. We have to make a serious, concrete effort to dispel prejudices against Turkey. Ankara's membership negotiations will be a long and open-ended process. Ultimately, I believe the Union will benefit from the enlargement."

### Pepe: "Turkey won't forsake its national values" — 10 January 2005

"Turkey will become an EU member without giving up its national values, including its Muslim and Turkish identity," said Environment and Forestry Minister Osman Pepe yesterday. Stating that as it stands now the EU cannot be a global power, Pepe added, "Ankara will join the EU. However, being an EU member doesn't mean giving up our national values, because the EU needs this diversity, cultural richness, and dynamism."

### Turkey is praised — 19 January 2005

The annual report of the Human Rights Watch included positive expressions for the Human Rights practices in Turkey. The report announced in New York said that there had been considerable improvement in the Human Rights practices in Turkey in the last year and the violations of 1990s were left behind.

The report mentioned the amendments in the Turkish Penal Code and the release of Leyla Zana and her friends and the permission given to Kurdish TV stations as well as efforts by the government for the return of people in the southeast to the evacuated villages. (www.turks.us)

## Turkey seeks solutions for EU demands — 24 January 2005

As Turkey prepares to begin negotiations with the European Union (EU), concerns about the possibility that issues like opening the Armenian border and recognizing Alevis and Kurds as minorities will be raised.

All three issues were included in Turkey's report which was approved by the European Parliament (EP) for inclusion in the Accession Partnership Document.

Ankara is concerned that a series of negative issues opposed by Turkey may end up in the three documents that will be prepared between now and October 3 when full membership negotiations officially begin with the EU. During meetings with the European Commission on the negotiations, Ankara expects to face a series of demands born of the Accession Partnership Document, the Framework Text, and the Cultural Dialogue documents including recognition of Cyprus, opening of the Armenian border, and recognition of Alevis and Kurds as "minorities." A Turkish diplomat said Ankara does not want these issues mentioned in the documents and is committed to taking whatever measures are necessary to solve the problem.

Ankara highlights the necessity of preparing a new Accession Partnership Document (APD) that differs from the former APDs and the change in status brought about by the December 17 summit decision to begin full membership negotiations. Under these circumstances, Brussels was told that the opinions expressed in the APD should not include any new additions, but it seems obvious that a series of new demands will be listed in the APD drafts and that, thus, a hard bargaining process will take place between Ankara and Brussels.

According to reports, the statement included in the "Turkey Report" that was accepted by the European Parliament (EP) on December 15, 2004, will also be included in the APD. The final resolution released at the December 17 summit in Brussels stated that the EU Council noted the decision made by the EP on December 15, 2004. As the Parliament asked for an immediate start to full membership negotiations with Turkey, it also made some demands that did not please Ankara. Specifically, the opening of the religious school in Heybeliada and recognition of the Greek Cypriot Administration (GCA) as the nation of "Cyprus" which represents the whole island will also be included in the APD. The EP, furthermore, pointed out the following points in the Turkey report: "Negotiations should be suspended by the EU Commission when necessary. Turkey should solve its problems with its neighbours in line with the United Nations (UN) convention. Restrictions on ships with Greek Cypriot banderol should be abandoned. Alevism should be recognised and preserved. Alevi houses of worship, also known as Cemevis, should be recognised as religious centres. Religious education should be voluntary. The informal system of guardsmanship in southeastern Anatolia should be abolished. Turkey should open its borders with Armenia and both countries' governments should support a mutual peace process." It is expected that the EU, which defines Kurds and Alevis as "minorities," will repeat this in the APD. (www.turks.us)

### Turkish public overwhelmingly backs EU entry — 11 February 2005

The Turkish public overwhelmingly backs Turkey's European Union membership bid, according to a new public opinion poll. Over 70 per cent of Turks surveyed said that if a referendum were held on the bid they would vote yes, while only 16.2 per cent said they would vote no. In the survey, conducted on 6,700 people age eighteen and over, 55.5 per cent also said they believed EU membership would improve their lives.

### Ankara on defensive over EU reform criticisms — 1 March 2005

Faced with charges of losing momentum in its preparations for upcoming membership talks with the European Union, Ankara said EU reforms remained a top priority for the government and told the twenty-five-nation bloc that it had its own expectations from Brussels.

"The primary issue for Turkey is matters related to its EU bid," Foreign Minister Abdullah Gül said after talks with Luxembourg's Minister Delegate for Foreign Affairs and Immigration in Ankara.

Responding to criticisms of slowness in preparations for upcoming entry talks, Gül said Turkey had its own expectations from the EU, too. "There are issues that they have not yet settled", he said.

Ankara expressed its expectations from the EU Commission regarding a number of technical documents that would set out details on the framework of talks. It also aired concerns over recent signals that there could be delays in preparation of these documents. It also pressed the EU to take measures to implement proposed steps to end isolation of Turkish Cypriots. (*Turkish Daily News*)

### Kretschmer: "Turkey should continue its EU harmonisation, including Human Rights reforms" — 7 March 2005

Speaking at a meeting of the Marmara Group Foundation yesterday, European Commission Representative in Ankara Hansjoerg Kretschmer said that Turkey was an important political partner of the European Union, adding that it should harmonise with the Union's *acquis communautaire* and its liberal economic principles. Kretschmer stressed that the EU was a community of values and added, "EU candidates should fulfil certain criteria concerning democracy, Human Rights and the economy which are then taken into consideration during their accession talks." Kretschmer stated that Turkey continuing its reforms was very important. "Among these reforms are ones on Human Rights, women's rights and religious rights and freedoms", he said. "Forging a dialogue between the

Turkish nation and the European public has critical importance." Touching on regional economic imbalances in the country, Kretschmer warned that this could also create political instability. "Ankara will be successful in its EU accession talks if it overcomes this", he added.

### *Gul: negotiations with the EU will be a test for Turkey's resistance and patience — 15 March 2005*

Turkish Foreign Minister and Deputy Prime Minister Abdullah Gul said on Monday that the entry negotiations with the European Union (EU) would be a test for Turkey's resistance and patience, adding, "I believe that Turkey will pass this test successfully."

Speaking at a conference at the London School of Economics, Gul, who is currently paying a four-day official visit to Britain, said, "we are determined to further improve our bilateral relations with Britain."

Referring to Turkey–EU relations, Gul said, "Turkey and the EU have created a synergy in economy and politics. As a result, Turkey became an attractive country for European investors. Recently, diplomatic consultations between Turkey and the EU have increased. Turkey and the EU have also succeeded in creating a joint power to overcome problems such as fundamentalism, racism and anti-Semitism. After the EU decided to open entry talks with Turkey on 3 October, the Turkish government has given priority to the negotiation process with the EU. Therefore, our reforms will continue rapidly."

"We are aware that the negotiation process will not be easy. The negotiation process will be a test for Turkey's resistance and patience. I believe that Turkey will pass this test successfully," he said.

Referring to the Cyprus issue, Gul said, "both Turkey and the Turkish Republic of Northern Cyprus (TRNC) have extended full support to a solution in the island. Turkey's only target is to protect rights and security of the Turkish Cypriots. As you know, Turkish Cypriot people supported United Nations Secretary General Kofi Annan's plan in the referendum on 24 April. However, embargoes and isolation imposed on them have still been continuing."

"Turkey also holds consultations with Azerbaijan, Armenia and Georgia with the aim of providing peace in the southern Caucasus. After Israel withdraws from Gaza, the international community will have to expend more efforts to resolve the economic problems and the issue of security in the region," he said.

Upon a question about Turkey–United States relations, Gul said that relations had been progressing on the right track.

Replying to another question, Gul said, "there is not any problem about signing of the protocol about the Customs Union. However, Turkey's signing the protocol will not mean recognition of the Greek Cypriot side. There are two separate states and two separate nations on the island."

When questioned about the events that occurred during a demonstration in Istanbul marking International Women's Day, Gul said, "we do not approve such events. We have launched an investigation into them. Such events can be experienced anywhere in the world. Turkey has made the necessary reforms; however, it will take time to remove the problems in implementation."

When asked what would happen if the EU Constitution was rejected in referendums in France and the other countries, Gul said, "it may lead to a crisis both in the EU and in those countries. Such a crisis can normally affect Turkey." (TurkishPress.com/London)

## EU Troika meeting press releases[3]

### *Turkey's progress in its rapprochement with the European Union at the centre of talks between the EU and Turkey in Ankara*

Jean Asselborn, Minister for Foreign Affairs and Immigration and current President of the Council of the European Union, led a delegation of the European Troika at a ministerial meeting between the European Union and Turkey held in Ankara on 7 March 2005.

Turkey was represented by the country's Deputy Prime Minister and Minister of Foreign Affairs, Abdullah Gül. On the side of the European Union, the European Enlargement Commissioner, Olli Rehn, and the British Minister for European Affairs, Denis MacShane, also participated in the talks.

The ministerial meeting focused on the progress made by Turkey in its rapprochement with the European Union, and more specifically on reforms in the rights and freedoms of citizens.

The two parties also had an exchange of views on a number of current international matters, such as the peace process in the Middle East, Iraq, Iran, the Southern Caucasus and relations between NATO [North Atlantic Treaty Organization] and the European Union.

At the start of the meeting, Jean Asselborn expressed the concern of the European Union regarding the images of police officers mistreating demonstrators at a demonstration which took place in Istanbul on 7 March.[4] The Turkish side responded favourably to the anxieties expressed by the European Troika and promised a detailed enquiry by competent authorities into the incidents in question.

With regard to the legislative reforms under way in Turkey, Minister Asselborn expressed his appreciation of the presentation by his Turkish counterpart "of a long list of legislative changes which have taken place, which document the irreversibility and the depth of the movement of rapprochement between Turkey and the EU."

However, Jean Asselborn underlined "the importance of maintaining the pace of reforms in order to avoid any risk of losing momentum. Reforms are like a cycle race: as soon as one stops pedalling or brakes suddenly, there is a risk of taking a tumble."

According to the President of the Council, the European delegation indicated that it was expecting to see additional progress in the area of religious freedom, and more specifically in favour of non-Muslim minorities. In the eyes of the

European Union, the new law on foundations should in particular resolve all the problems linked to property of religious communities and freedom of worship.

With regard to the question of the abolition of torture, the European Union noted that the "zero-tolerance" policy was producing results, while stressing the fact that the task now was to develop this policy everywhere, directly in line with the declared intent of the Turkish Government.

The two parties also discussed the situation in the southeast of Turkey. The European delegation stressed the necessity of reducing regional disparities and ensuring the return of displaced persons.

Jean Asselborn also considered that "the progressive use of the languages commonly used in Turkey in the cultural and political domain as well as in education constitutes an encouragement, and I am convinced that this use will grow."

Finally, the President of the Council of the European Union complimented the Turkish Government on its achievements in terms of the Europeanisation of relations between the civil and military powers.

# Document no. 109

**Common future of the EU and Turkey: roadmap for reforms and negotiations[5]**

\*\*\*

The decision by the European Council to open negotiations with Turkey opens a new chapter in the historic process of peacefully unifying the European continent. As a combined result of its population, size, strategic location and economic potential, Turkey has the capacity to make a major contribution to regional and international stability. In a world threatened by the infamous clash of civilisations, it is worth recalling that Turkey is endowed with unique characteristics: the combination of a secular, democratic state with a prevalently Muslim population. I know that there are great expectations in Turkey about the accession negotiations process, and also many questions. The same happened when the EU started the enlargement process with the ten countries which acceded in May last year. The experience gained in the previous enlargement round shows that the process of accession is a powerful engine for political and economic transformation.

Turkey is at present going through a process of radical change, including a rapid evolution of mentalities. It is in the interest of everybody that the current process of transformation continues. At the same time, as shown by the previous enlargement, negotiations can be a difficult exercise. I believe that both the EU and Turkey are perfectly aware that the road ahead will be long and sometimes uneven. We will need a lot of mutual understanding and patience. Then it will be not only a long, but also a winding road, leading to our ultimate objective, which is the accession of Turkey into the EU. On our side, we shall concentrate on the preparation for the opening of accession negotiations in line with the European Council conclusions.

The period between now and the 3 October will be particularly busy. In the next months, on the basis of the European Council's conclusions, we will work on a draft negotiating mandate to be submitted to the EU Member States. This is standard practice: the aim of this document is to set the method and the guiding principles of the negotiations. In the meantime, we will organise information sessions and seminars about accession negotiations. The process of analytical examination of EU legislation, commonly called "screening", will start right after the formal opening of accession negotiations.

On its side, Turkey will also have to get prepared for 3 October. I trust that Turkey will fulfil its commitment by signing in good time the protocol adapting the Ankara Agreement to the accession of the new Member States. This is important since this was attached by the European Council to the start of accession negotiations.

Let me however insist on the utmost importance we attach to the continuation of political reforms with the same pace and with the same intensity as in previous months. The December European Council welcomed the decisive progress made by Turkey in its far-reaching reform process. It also expressed its confidence that Turkey will sustain that process of reform and ensure its proper implementation.

More specifically, the policy of zero tolerance towards torture should be enforced through determined efforts at all levels of the Turkish state to get away with [rid of] the remaining instances of torture. Turkey must also consolidate and broaden political reform to facilitate the normalisation and development of the situation in the southeast, including measures to improve the socio-economic situation, initiatives to enhance the return of displaced people, and to allow for full enjoyment of rights for all Turkish citizens regardless of their origin. Moreover, the specific problems of non-Muslim religious communities and trades union rights also need further action soon.

Besides political reforms, Turkey must further stabilise and reform its economy.

\*\*\*

*Editors' comment:* On January 23, 2006, the Council of the European Union released 2006/35/EC: The Council Decision on the principles, priorities and conditions contained in the Accession Partnership with Turkey.[6] This document enumerates short- and medium-term goals to be reached by Turkey within one to two years and three to four years, respectively. While the document is all-encompassing and covers a wide range of issues pertaining to Turkey's accession, it is important to note that the document includes concerns related to Human Rights, civil rights, judicial issues, and recommendations for the management of the situation in the east and southeast, and requests that certain aspects of these issues be addressed in the short term. Accordingly, the Council of the EU, among other things:

1. Requests that "Turkey align itself with all international and EU Human Rights standards and procedures including international Human Rights law precedents and rulings through the ratification of the optional protocols to the International Covenant on Civil and Political Rights and compliance with the European Convention for the Protection of Human Rights and Fundamental Freedoms."

2. Expects that Turkey will "operationalise these standards through open support of Human Rights institutions, training and education of its law enforcement

agencies in best practice (especially Protocol no. 12 to the European Convention on Human Rights), and open promotion and sound implementation of legislative initiatives to protect these rights."

3. Requests that Turkey "apply a 'zero tolerance' policy for torture and ill-treatment in line with the European Convention on Human Rights and the recommendations of the European Committee for the Prevention of Torture."

4. States that the Istanbul Protocol[7] "shall serve as the set of guidelines for the assessment of persons who allege torture and ill-treatment, for investigating cases of alleged torture, and for reporting such findings to the judiciary and any other investigative body",[8] and requests that no person shall be immune from such orders, as perpetrators will be investigated through an independently operating monitoring institution.

5. Requests that Turkey (i) "recognise and enforce the freedoms of expression and assembly, freedom of religion, and social rights such as those for women and minorities", (ii) "make efforts to promote the status of women in society and guarantee their safety and fair treatment in and outside of the household", (iii) "respect minority rights in accordance with the European Convention on Human Rights and the principles of the Council of Europe's Framework Convention for the Protection of National Minorities and in line with best practice in Member States", (iv) "grant minorities legal protection in line with Protocol no. 1 to the European Convention on Human Rights", (v) "implement an economic development plan to reduce regional disparities in order to ameliorate ethnic and economic tension", (vi) "assist and/or compensate internally displaced persons and those who have suffered as a result of internal insecurity".

For the attainment of these short-term benchmarks for the improvement of Turkey's human and civil rights track records, the Council of the European Union (i) "suggests that Turkey develop and strengthen all legal institutions by training law enforcement bodies, adopting a code of police ethics, using modern investigative techniques and crime prevention strategies, and unifying and consolidating this effort through inter-agency cooperation and communication" and (ii) "recommends the development of a fair and accessible system of justice that ensures that these recommendations are put into effect through legislation, which is immutable in its guarantees of freedom and security".

In addition, in the medium term, the Council of the European Union recommends that Turkey align itself fully with the European Union *acquis* in the areas of asylum and migration, drug trafficking, the development of a customs service with customs cooperation agreements and the introduction of mobile surveillance units, data protection services, border protection and management (to prepare for the abolition of border controls in line with the Schengen Agreement), and prevention of corruption and organised crime as to protect the financial interests of the European Community at large.

# Document no. 110

**Critical developments in Turkey in 2005 and 2006**

*Newroz celebrations of 2005, desecration of the Turkish flag, public and military response*[9]

*Newroz* means "new day" in the Kurdish language. The Newroz celebration is an ancient pagan festival hailing the revival of nature with the spring equinox. Every year, Kurds attempt to mark the arrival of spring with the celebration of Newroz, yet some use the occasion to promote pro-Kurdish politics.

In recent decades, the Turkish military and police have prohibited Newroz celebrations. As changing laws have helped to reduce ethnic tension, Turkish security forces allowed Newroz gatherings in 2005.

According to a newspaper article,[10] in Istanbul, crowds started gathering in the early morning hours to take part in a celebration with folksongs and dancing organised by the main pro-Kurdish party in Turkey — the Democratic People's Party. The gathering was monitored by scores of police. Despite the fact that some of the participants carried a photograph of imprisoned Kurdish rebel leader Abdullah Ocalan, the celebration in Istanbul was peaceful.

However, in the southern Turkish town of Mersin, three police officers and three journalists were slightly injured in incidents involving security forces and teenage protesters who wanted to burn the Turkish flag.

The attempt to burn the flag by a few teenagers led to a patriotic backlash with unprecedented public displays of the national symbol in the following days. According to one article, "the spontaneous reaction to Sunday's incident [had] surpassed even the most patriotic Independence Day displays."

The military's response was swift as well. In a press release, the Office of the Chairman of the Chiefs of Staff stated the following:[11]

"Turkish nation,

Innocent and delightful celebrations taking place to meet the spring have been disturbed by a group of depraved people. These people have tried to burn the symbol of the Turkish nation: the Turkish flag.

The Turkish nation, in its long history, has faced many challenges, victories, losses, and betrayals. However, this nation has never been faced with such a disgraceful act, taking place in its land and carried on by its citizens.

The burning of the flag by a group of *so-called citizens* cannot be comprehended and accepted. This is a treacherous act ...

Friend and foe alike should know this very well: neither this country's indivisible unity nor the symbol of its unity, its flag, is unprotected. First and foremost, the Turkish nation and the Turkish Armed Forces stand ready and sworn to give their lives to protect its flag. We suggest looking at history books to those who misperceive its silence, seriousness and patience, and try to test the Turkish Armed forces' love and respect for its country and flag."

In this message, the Turkish military concisely stated that it would not accept actions against the Turkish state and was ready to start fighting again. Also important is the use of the term "so-called" citizens. As a term used for the first time by the military, it suggests that the people engaged in flag burning cannot be citizens.

*Editors' comment related to 2006 Newroz celebrations:*[12] While most 2006 Newroz celebrations in many cities across Turkey were reported to be peaceful, some news sources reported events similar to those of 2005. In the Aegean city of Izmir, around 5,000 people gathered to celebrate Newroz, and a small group of the demonstrators started fighting with the police. Police used tear gas to break up the fights. Anadolu Agency (Turkey's news agency) reported that police later found a bag containing nineteen Molotov cocktails.

In similar incidents, there was some unrest during celebrations in Diyarbakir (southeast Turkey) where more than 75,000 Kurdish demonstrators gathered. A group hurled rocks at the police, Turkish warplanes flew overhead as monitors of the situation, and at least eight people were injured, and Turkish warplanes flew over the demonstrators. Many of the demonstrators shouted support for the autonomy-seeking PKK and its arrested leader Abdullah Ocalan.

### *Terrorists, not "separatists," in Turkey*[13]

The July 17 news story "Blast in Turkish resort town kills 5" referred to the suspected perpetrators as "separatists" or "guerillas" and called them part of a "civil war" in Turkey. In reality, the Kurdistan Workers' Party (PKK) elements are recognized almost universally — including by the United States — as terrorists.

Turkey has fought terrorism for decades, with little help from allies (except the United States) and within the necessary constraints of our democracy, the rule of law and respect for Human Rights. Terrorists are emboldened when their attacks are referred to as part of a "civil war" or "separatism," implying a just cause for their inhuman acts. Without moral clarity and resolve based on consistent condemnation of all terrorism, the fight against it will falter.

### Increased terror attacks in Turkey by the PKK and abroad by suspected Islamic militants bolster the Turkish intention of revising its threat concept from neighbours to asymmetrical risks[14]

For decades Turkey considered, by rotating rankings, its neighbours to be its top security threat. Not any longer. Recent terror attacks by the Kurdistan Workers' Party (PKK) in Turkey and by suspected Islamist militants abroad have provided enough food for thought for Ankara to seal an already emerging policy change.

Top security officials in the Turkish capital say the recent wave of terror attacks has bolstered intentions to put asymmetrical threats at the centre of an emerging "white paper" security document that government and military leaders will conclude soon.

The paper, which covers the three to four upcoming years, is the key state document that details foreign and domestic security threats, therefore shaping the country's major procurement decisions.

A senior security official said that what has been happening in Turkey, Britain and Egypt proved that asymmetrical threats are the biggest security risk and that this will be reflected in the new threat paper.

The National Security Council (MGK), the country's top security decision-making body, will convene at the end of August to shape the new National Security Political Paper. Turkish leaders are expected to finalise the paper in the next few months.

Following the MGK's next scheduled meeting in late August, the paper will go to Prime Minister Recep Tayyip Erdogan's desk for final revisions and approval.

The PKK and its splinter groups, which Turkey, the United States and the European Union consider terrorists, have in recent months increased remote-controlled mine attacks against military targets as well as bomb attacks against civilians in holiday resorts, killing more than 120 people in the past year ...

"In view of recent terror attacks, it will be more realistic to substitute [Turkey's] conventional concept of terror, which is based on military confrontation with hostile countries," with an approach that emphasises the threat of groups like al-Qaeda, said the same security official.

Last year, Turkey's military leaders indicated they might scrap conventional threat perceptions, saying the real risks were terror and Islamic fundamentalism.

A military official said the new paper will likely pave the way for a fresh, comprehensive anti-terror fight that could include creation of a special anti-terror coordination body, most likely reporting to the prime minister's office. Turkish lawmakers are also mulling revisions in the country's anti-terror laws.

According to Reha Tartici, director for the Istanbul-based research house Consensus, the new threat document also will affect some of Turkey's procurement decisions.

"In a way, it will be a guideline for a future shift to smart weaponry instead of conventional arms", Tartici said. "There already are signs of that. The recently resumed satellite program is a good example."

A month and a half before a deadline to respond to a call from Ankara for the critical satellite military program, scores of local and international manufacturers expressed their intention of bidding on the contract.

Turkey's government had earmarked an initial $138 million for the country's space programme and asked local and international manufacturers to respond to a request for information (RfI), which procurement officials often view as an expression of intention to bid on a contract. But a procurement official familiar with the programme said the eventual cost might exceed $250 million.

As of 29 July, according to Turkey's defence procurement office, the Undersecretariat for the Defense Industry (SSM), 48 local and foreign manufacturers had responded to the RfI. The deadline to respond to the RfI is 26 August.

The programme was shelved in 2001 in response to a punishing financial crisis that slashed Turkey's national income by one-third and prompted the military command to suspend several contracts worth nearly $20 billion.

## Military, government meet to assess terror and "Kurdish problem"[15]

The highest supervisory body for national security, the National Security Council (MGK), convened on Tuesday [August 23, 2005] with terrorism and Prime Minister Recep Tayyip Erdogan's initiative to resolve the Kurdish issue through greater democracy at the top of its agenda.

According to an NTV news report, the MGK General Secretariat, the government, and the military each prepared a report to be submitted at the meeting, with the military referring to the terrorism problem as economic and socially based, not ethnic.

The military was expected to criticise the government's initiative, while Interior Minister Abdulkadir Aksu briefed the council on preparations made for changes to the Anti-Terrorism Law.

The MGK General Secretariat prepared a six-page report on the escalation of Kurdistan Workers' Party (PKK) terrorism and precautions that could be taken to counter it. According to their report, the reason PKK terrorism is escalating is because the organisation is internally divided and fights among PKK leaders have reached unprecedented levels. The report claims the PKK began its recent terrorist campaign just to overcome these problems.

### Erdogan to be warned

Branch commanders of the military, led by Chief of General Staff Gen. Hilmi Oskok, are expected to present a report criticising Erdogan's use of the phrase "Kurdish problem". The military is expected to advise on refraining from making such statements without consulting all relevant state institutions because such acts could harm anti-terrorism efforts, reported CNN-Turk.

The military is expected to call for a combined war on terrorism, with the coordination of military and civilian policies.

Justice Minister Cemil Cicek said on Monday after a Cabinet meeting that Turkey was a unitary state and that Erdogan's statement should be taken within this context.

Cicek accused the opposition of clouding the issue, while Erdogan said fighting terrorism and the Kurdish problem are two separate issues that need to be tackled separately.

\*\*\*

*Opposition keeps up the rhetoric*

Independent Party (HP) leader Yasar Okuyan said, despite all his warnings, that the prime minister continues to refer to the "Kurdish problem". He cautioned that Erdogan might end up facing charges of treason if things continue the as they are.

Speaking at HP headquarters, he said that if the prime minister continued to encourage Kurdish political activism while inadvertently encouraging PKK terrorism, the result would not be something he liked.

Republican People's Party (CHP) deputy Gurol Ergin accused the prime minister of encouraging the PKK, claiming the government's incorrect policy was due to their inexperience. Turkey simply faced terrorism perpetrated by a separatist group, he said.

## Editors' comment regarding other developments

*Revisions to the Penal Code*

The Council of the European Union has requested that Turkey rewrite its penal code as a precondition for accession to the European Union. In accordance with this request, the Turkish Parliament amended the then in force Penal Code with new measures for the protection of Human Rights on September 26, 2004. The new code grants women and children greater protection and places stern penalties on "honor killings." It also criminalizes marital rape, sexual harassment, and toughens punishments for rape, pedophilia, human trafficking, and torture.[16]

Yet some believe the revised code takes away rights, rather than bolstering them. It arguably further limits the expression of anti-government sentiment more than before through Article 301, which states that public denigration of "Turkishness," the Turkish government, the judicial institutions, and the armed forces and its institutions is a punishable offense by up to three years in prison. In the past several years, this article has been used to censor public criticism from the media and penalize internationally acclaimed Turkish writers such as Nobel laureate Orhan Pamuk, and Hrant Dink.[17]

The revised penal code has proven to be controversial on several other fronts as it grants measures for the liberalization of religious instruction.[18] Specifically, the ruling Justice and Development Party tacked on a package of amendments that would reduce the penalties on the teaching of the Quran and the running of clandestine Quran study schools in this strictly secular country.

As a result, of these problems, President Ahmet Necdet Sezer has vetoed the revised penal code.[19] However, his veto was overridden by the Turkish Parliament on June 1, 2005, and the new code passed into law.[20]

*New Anti-Terrorism Bill*

The Anti-Terrorism Law of 1991 (ATL), as discussed in the previous documents,[21] was a major tool available in the Turkish penal system for fighting terrorism. Several commentators have rightfully argued that the law used ambiguous language that allowed for the prosecution of ordinary citizens for crimes of "thought"—"acts, oral or written, that can be considered propaganda, including meetings and demonstrations aimed at damaging the indivisible unity of the state."[22]

On June 29, 2006, the Turkish Parliament passed amendments to the 1991 law in response to the elevation of terrorist incidents and attacks. The proposed amendments would create a new anti-terrorism division in the Prime Ministry that would work in coordination with the Security Affairs Department on counter-terrorism efforts and strategies.[23] The new amendments would also constrain one's ability to criticize the government as the law criminalizes the use and publication of propaganda in support for or in demonstrations for terrorism organizations such as the PKK.[24]

The Istanbul Bar Association and other institutions have argued that this bill is excessively harsh. They believe it will impede on the average citizen's fundamental right of expression as critical newspapers can be penalized and the writing of graffiti can be prosecuted with heavy punishments. Some also claim that the law legitimizes the excessive use of force such as the authority to shoot a suspect.[25] Despite popular dissent, the bill was signed into law by the President on July 17, 2006, but is subject to review by the Constitutional Court.[26]

# Document no. 111

## Problems in the European Union: European constitution and the fading support

*Procedures planned for the ratification of the European Constitution*[27]

Some of the information in this table is subject to change. In particular, certain Member States might decide to hold a referendum.

| Member State | Procedure | Date scheduled | Previous European referendums |
|---|---|---|---|
| Austria | Parliamentary (*Nationalrat* and *Bundesrat*) | Approval by the *Nationalrat* 11 May 2005 Approval by *Bundesrat* 25 May 2005 | 1994: accession |
| Belgium | Parliamentary (Chamber and Senate + Assemblies of Communities and Regions) Indicative referendum ruled out | Approval by the Senate: 28 April 2005 Approval by the Chamber: 19 May 2005 Approval by the Brussels regional parliament: 17 June 2005 Approval by the German Community Parliament of Belgium: 20 June 2005 Approval by the Walloon regional Parliament: 29 June 2005 Approval by the French Community Parliament: 19 July 2005 Approval by the Flemish regional Parliament: 8 February 2006 | No |
| Cyprus | Parliamentary | Approval by the House on 30 June 2005 | No |
| Czech Republic | Referendum. But no final decision so far | Referendum postponed to end of 2006/beginning of 2007 | 2003: accession |

*continued*

| Member State | Procedure | Date scheduled | Previous European referendums |
|---|---|---|---|
| Denmark | Referendum | Referendum postponed (no new date has been set) | 1972: accession 1986: Single European Act 1992: Maastricht Treaty (twice) 1998: Amsterdam Treaty 2000: euro |
| Estonia | Parliamentary referendum unlikely | Approval by Parliament on 9 May 2006 | 2003: accession |
| Finland | Parliamentary | Presentation by the government of a report to the Parliament on 25 November 2005. Ratification expected during the presidency of the Council in the second half of 2006 | Consultative referendum: 1994: accession |
| France | Referendum | Referendum 29 May 2005 negative (No: 54.68%; turn out: 69.34%) | 1972: enlargement EEC 1992: Maastricht Treaty |
| Germany | Parliamentary (*Bundestag* and *Bundesrat*) | Approval by *Bundestag*: 12 May 2005 Adoption by *Bundesrat*: 27 May 2005 | No |
| Greece | Parliamentary, but the Left parties submitted a joint proposal for a referendum | Approval by Parliament: 19 April 2005 | No |
| Hungary | Parliamentary | Approval by Parliament: 20 December 2004 | 2003: accession |
| Ireland | Parliamentary + referendum | Referendum postponed (no date has been set). A White paper has been presented to the Parliament on 13 October 2005 | 1972: accession 1987: Single European Act 1992: Maastricht Treaty 1998: Amsterdam Treaty 2001 and 2002: Nice Treaty |
| Italy | Parliamentary (Chamber and Senate) | Approval by the Chamber on 25 January 2005 and by the Senate on 6 April | Consultative referendum: 1989: possible draft Constitution |
| Latvia | Parliamentary | Approval by the chamber on 2 June 2005 | 2003: accession |
| Lithuania | Parliamentary | Approval by Parliament 11 November 2004 | 2003: accession |

*continued*

| Member State | Procedure | Date scheduled | Previous European referendums |
|---|---|---|---|
| Luxembourg | Parliamentary (two votes) + consultative referendum | Approval by the Chamber (first reading) on 28 June 2005 Positive Referendum on 10 July 2005: 56.52% in favour, 43.48% against Final approval by the Chamber on 25 October 2005 (57 votes in favour, 1 against) | No |
| Malta | Parliamentary | Approval by Parliament: 6 July 2005 | 2003: accession |
| Netherlands | Parliamentary (First and second Chambers) + consultative referendum | Referendum 1 June 2005 negative (61.7%, turn out: 63%) | No |
| Poland | No decision so far | The Parliament failed on 5 July to vote on the ratification procedure. Ratification postponed (no date has been set) | 2003: accession |
| Portugal | Referendum | Referendum postponed (no date has been set) | No |
| Slovakia | Parliamentary | Approval by Parliament: 11 May 2005 | 2003: accession |
| Slovenia | Parliamentary | Approval by Parliament: 1 February 2005 | 2003: accession |
| Spain | Parliamentary (Congress and Senate) + consultative referendum | Referendum 20 February 2005: 76.7% in favour, turnout, 42.3%. Approval of the Congress on 28 April Approval of the Senate on 18 May 2005 | No |
| Sweden | Parliamentary; no referendum envisaged at this stage | Ratification postponed (no date has been set) | Consultative referendums: 1994: accession 2003: euro |
| United Kingdom | Parliamentary (House of Commons and House of Lords) + referendum | Parliamentary ratification process suspended (suspension announced by UK government on 6 June 2005) | 1975: Continued membership of the EC |

***Joint Declaration of President of the European Parliament Josep Borrell Fontelles, President of the European Council Jean-Claude Juncker and President of the European Commission José Manuel Barroso on the results of the French Referendum on the European Constitutional Treaty*[28]**

"The French voters have today, Sunday 29 May 2005, chosen to say no to the ratification of the Constitutional treaty. We take note of this.

We regret this choice, coming as it does from a Member State that has been for the last fifty years one of the essential motors of the building of our common future.

We completely respect the expression of the democratic will that has made itself felt at the end of an intense debate. The result of the French referendum deserves a profound analysis, in the first instance, on the part of the French authorities. The Institutions of the European Union should also, for their part, reflect on the results of the collected ratification processes.

It is important to remember that nine Member States, representing almost half (49 per cent) of the European population have already ratified the Constitutional Treaty, in one case on the basis of a broadly positive referendum and that the majority of Member States have not yet had the opportunity to complete the ratification process.

The tenor of the debate in France and the result of the referendum also reinforce our conviction that the relevant national and European politicians must do more to explain the true scale of what is at stake, and the nature of the answers that only Europe can offer. We continue to believe that a response at the European level remains the best and the most effective in the face of accelerating global change.

We must ask ourselves how each among us — national governments, European institutions, political parties, social partners, civil society — can contribute to a better understanding of this project, which cannot have its own legitimacy without listening to its citizens.

The building of Europe is, by its nature, complex. Europe has already known difficult moments and it has every time emerged from them strengthened, better than before, ready to face its challenges and its responsibilities. Today Europe continues, and its institutions function fully. We are aware of the difficulties, but we have confidence that once again we will find the means to move the European Union forward. Together, we are determined to contribute to this."

***Joint Statement of President of the European Parliament Josep Borrell Fontelles, President of the European Council Jean-Claude Juncker and President of the European Commission José Manuel Barroso on the results of the referendum in the Netherlands on the Treaty establishing a Constitution for Europe*[29]**

The people of the Netherlands, like the voters of France, have chosen to say no to the ratification of the Constitutional Treaty.

This is a choice that we respect. The result of the democratic ballot taken in The Netherlands comes at the end of a rich and intense debate and deserves a profound analysis, to which we must now dedicate the necessary time.

We remain convinced that the Constitution makes the European Union more democratic, more effective and stronger, and that all Member States must be able to express themselves on the project of the Constitutional Treaty.

The fourteen Member States that have not yet had the chance to bring to a conclusion the process of ratification are today faced with a situation in which, although nine member states have ratified the constitutional treaty, two Member States have rejected it. For this reason, the Presidency has decided that the Council of 16 and 17 June could usefully carry out a serious collective analysis of the situation.

Furthermore, we hear the messages sent by the citizens of France and The Netherlands on the European project and we note them well. The European Institutions will listen to the concerns of European citizens and they will come together to offer a response.

We are confident that together and in partnership — national governments, European institutions, political parties, civil society — we will know how to find the means to move the European Union towards an enduring consensus as to its identity, its objectives and its means. As Europe goes on, its institutions will continue to function properly.

## *Process of ratifying the European Constitution is not dead declares Jean-Claude Juncker after British government's decision*[30]

The Prime Minister and current President of the European Council, Jean-Claude Juncker, stated that the process of ratifying the European Constitution "is not dead" after the UK released a decision to suspend its referendum. The British government has not abandoned the process, but has simply announced that "the British government believes that it must wait and see what line of action the other Member States wish to take on the ratification process during the European Council".

"Next week, we are going to hold intensive talks on the issue together with heads of state and government", stated Jean-Claude Juncker while pointing out: "Given that the majority have said that the ratification process must continue, this is an indication of a possible decision to be taken by the European Council."

## *Public opinion in the European Union: first results*[31]

*Table of contents*

Introduction
1. The climate of opinion
2. Being a member of the European Union today
3. Confidence in European institutions

4. Support for a European constitution
5. Support for future enlargement
6. Common foreign and security policy
7. Development towards European political union
8. Democracy in Europe
9. Support for European monetary union
10. The allocation of the European Union's budget
11. The European Union's priorities
Conclusion
Annexes

\*\*\*

*5. Support for future enlargement*

*One in two citizens are in favour of further enlargement of the European Union.*

Half of the respondents in the twenty-five current Member States are in favour of further enlargement of the European Union in future years (50 per cent). This result has fallen by 3 points since last year; at the same time there has been a proportional increase in the level of opposition to the idea (38 per cent).

Support for further enlargement of the European Union is the strongest in the ten new Member States. The size of the difference between the results obtained in the fifteen old Member States and the ten new Member States (27 points) highlights the diversity of opinions as regards the geographical development of the European Union.

For example, support is particularly strong in Slovenia (79 per cent), Poland (76 per cent) and Slovakia (73 per cent), compared with the reservations about and even opposition to further enlargement noted in Germany (60 per cent), Luxembourg (60 per cent) and Austria (58 per cent).

As regards changes in the group of countries most critical of the idea of further enlargement, opposition has grown notably in France (+7 points) and Luxembourg (+6 points), while in Austria the score is 4 points lower than in the previous survey. In the countries next in line for accession, Romania and Bulgaria, seven out of ten persons [people] interviewed support further enlargement. The rate of support is similar in Croatia and Turkey.

A detailed country analysis reveals that there is far stronger support for the accession of current EFTA [European Free Trade Association] member countries, that is to say Iceland and in particular Norway and Switzerland.

One in two citizens are in favour of Croatia and Bulgaria joining the European Union. Opinions, however, seem to be divided as regards the second accession country, Rumania, while a majority of respondents are clearly against Albania and Turkey being granted membership (50 per cent and 52 per cent of interviewees are against membership [respectively]).

Once again, it is clear that citizens of the new Member States are more open and positive as regards [sic] further enlargement than respondents in the fifteen old Member States. The order of preferences is marked by different levels of intensity: thus, after Switzerland and Norway, interviewees in the ten new Member States support clearly possible membership for Iceland and they are also more positive than their fellow Europeans as regards Turkey ...

# Document no. 112

## Terror activities after December 2004 and re-emergence of the Kurdistan Workers' Party (PKK)[32]

### December 2004

10. Five high-level members of the Kurdistan Workers' Party (PKK) were shot and killed in northern Iraq, by unidentified assailants. The occupants of the vehicle also included another Iraqi Kurd, two Iranian Kurds and one Turkish Kurd.
11. Two far-left militants, including one woman, were killed in a clash with Turkish security forces in a remote area of southeast Turkey.

### January 2005

15. Two Turkish soldiers and five leftist rebels were killed in a clash overnight in a remote region of eastern Turkey.
20. Turkish security forces killed five Kurdish guerrillas in a clash in southeastern Turkey after two days of fighting.
25. Kurdish separatists claimed responsibility for a fire at a warehouse of an electronics manufacturer in western Turkey that caused millions of dollars of damage but no casualties.

### February 2005

2. Turkish authorities reportedly found and disarmed a bomb in a nightclub near the entrance to Incirlik Air Base, where hundreds of US troops are based.
15. Kurdish protesters clashed with Turkish riot police in demonstrations across the country to mark the sixth anniversary of the capture of rebel commander Abdullah Ocalan.
16. A Turkish rights group called for a probe into what it called excessive use of force by police in breaking up protests marking the sixth anniversary of Kurdish rebel leader Abdullah Ocalan's capture.

## March 2005

6. Riot police used batons and tear gas to break up a group of leftist demonstrators who refused to disperse during an unauthorized demonstration marking the upcoming World Women's Day.

## April 2005

4. The Turkish military killed nine Kurdish rebels in a five-day operation in the southeast of the country. A soldier was also killed the same day by a mine blast and one rebel surrendered in a large-scale operation backed by helicopter gunships.

7. Two Kurdish guerrillas were killed in southeastern Turkey while attempting to lay a mine in a road used by Turkish soldiers.

11. Turkish troops killed two Kurdish guerrillas in a firefight in the country's troubled southeast.

13. Turkish troops backed by attack helicopters killed twenty-one Kurdish rebels near the Iraqi border overnight in the biggest clash since the rebels declared a unilateral truce more than five years ago.

14. Turkish troops killed at least ten Kurdish rebels in a clash in southeast Turkey; three soldiers died in the fighting.

15. Turkish troops pursued Kurdish rebels in the second day of an operation which has left twenty-five people dead, including twenty-one guerrillas.

27. A village guard was killed and two other people wounded when Turkish security forces clashed with Kurdish separatists in eastern Turkey.

27. Turkish authorities defused a bomb left beneath a heavily used bridge across Istanbul's historic Golden Horn estuary.

30. Five police officers were injured in an explosion as they investigated a suspicious package at a tourist resort in western Turkey.

## May 2005

5. Turkish authorities detained a female suspected of being a suicide bomber in the country's mainly Kurdish southeast during a failed attack on a police station.

11. Turkish security forces killed three Kurdish militants in eastern Turkey, officials said, one day before Europe's Human Rights Court rules on an appeal by the rebel group's leader. The head of the military's land forces also warned that the PKK was planning attacks in rural or urban centers after a large number of rebels smuggled explosives into Turkey from northern Iraq.

13. Two Turkish soldiers were killed and three injured in a clash with Kurdish militants during an anti-rebel operation involving some 10,000 troops in southeast Turkey.

14. Turkish soldiers killed nine Kurdish rebels in Turkey's predominantly Kurdish southeast, heightening concerns about new violence following a

European court judgment that the rebels' imprisoned leader did not receive a fair trial.

16. Two Kurdish guerillas trying to attack the home of a Turkish governor were killed after police fired on them as they approached the building.

17. Four Kurdish rebels and four Turkish soldiers were killed in separate incidents in Turkey's troubled southeast.

25. Kurdish rebels killed four members of the Turkish security forces in an ambush on their vehicle.

25. Turkish authorities detained ten people on suspicion of belonging to a banned Islamist group. The ten are believed to be members of a group known as the Hisb-u Tahrir, which in Arabic means "Party of Liberation."

## *June 2005*

3. Six Turkish soldiers were wounded in a landmine blast, prompting a military crackdown against Kurdish rebels active in the region.

5. Separatist Kurdish militants killed four Turkish soldiers in an ambush in eastern Turkey.

14. Two people were killed in southeastern Turkey when their vehicle hit a landmine which officials accused Kurdish guerrillas of planting.

15. Turkish soldiers killed a guerrilla from the PKK in an operation in eastern Turkey.

16. A leading member of the PKK was quoted as rejecting an appeal from leading Turkish intellectuals for the rebel organization to lay down its arms. A group of one hundred intellectuals including best-selling novelist Orhan Pamuk issued a statement on June 15 demanding the PKK halt all violence "without preconditions" and urging Ankara to seek a lasting peace in mainly Kurdish southeast Turkey. "You cannot ask just one side to disarm ... You have to ask it of both sides. Only then would it make sense," the Europe-based Mesopotamya news agency, which is close to the rebels, quoted senior PKK member Murat Karayilan as saying.

17. Two soldiers and two PKK rebels were killed in renewed separatist violence in Turkey's southeast.

18. Turkish security forces said they had killed seventeen members of an outlawed extreme leftist group in renewed violence in the country's troubled east.

20. A Turkish court sentenced an Islamist cleric to life imprisonment on charges that he plotted to kill members of the country's ruling elite by crashing an explosives-laden plane into a national monument.

21. Kurdish demonstrators clashed with paramilitary police in Van, leaving one protester dead and eight people hurt after police fired into the air. Police dispersed a crowd of around 250 protesters chanting separatist songs and carrying Kurdish rebel banners. They were marching towards a cemetery where two rebels killed by security forces had been buried. Two journalists were among those injured.

21. Three members of the Turkish security forces were wounded when a remote-controlled mine exploded in Siirt.

22. A Turkish soldier was killed and three others were wounded in the southeast of the country after two mines were detonated by suspected Kurdish guerrillas.

23. Three thousand Turkish security forces, backed by helicopter gunships, undertook a sweeping operation in Tunceli.

24. In an operation carried out by the Turkish security forces, some 2,000 soldiers sought to flush out between fifteen and twenty guerrillas active in the southeastern mountains. Five PKK rebel fighters were killed and one Turkish security guard was injured during an armed clash.

## *July 2005*

1. Police shot dead a suspected suicide bomber at Turkey's Justice Ministry after he apparently tried to set off an explosive device.

2. Five soldiers were killed and eight people were injured when a bomb planted by Kurdish guerrillas exploded on a train in eastern Turkey. A second train which traveled to the scene to provide assistance was fired on by militants armed with rifles.

5. A PKK guerrilla was killed and two others were seriously wounded in a clash with Turkish troops in a valley in Mardin during an operation launched late on July 5 against the militants. In another clash in nearby Siirt, two paramilitary police officers were wounded when PKK fighters, armed with automatic rifles, attacked a police station.

6. A former pro-Kurdish politician was gunned down in southeastern Turkey's largest city. It was not immediately clear whether the killing was politically motivated.

7. A Turkish freight train derailed in eastern Turkey when a mine was detonated on the tracks, but no one was hurt. Security sources said the PKK was behind the attack — the second on a train in the region in under a week — but there was no immediate claim of responsibility.

9. Three Turkish soldiers were killed and eight wounded when their vehicle hit a landmine suspected of being planted by Kurdish rebels in Turkey's southeast

10. A bomb blast injured at least twenty people, including at least two foreign tourists, in a popular seaside resort town in western Turkey. The explosive device had been placed in a trash can near a bank. No one has claimed responsibility for the attack so far, but Islamist militants, far-left militants and Kurdish activists have carried out bombings in the past. A previous bomb attack in an Aegean Sea resort in April, in which one police officer was killed and two more injured, was claimed by Kurdish guerrillas.

12. Kurdish rebels kidnapped a Turkish soldier after robbing dozens of vehicles at a rebel roadblock in eastern Turkey.

16. A bomb under a seat of a minibus in a popular Aegean beach resort killed five people, including an Irish teenager and a British woman. No group

has claimed responsibility for that blast, but suspicion also fell on Kurdish guerrillas.[33]

17. Turkish soldiers killed ten Kurdish guerrillas in a clash in a remote area of southeast Turkey. The troops pursued militants from the PKK in a region neighboring Iraq and were involved in a firefight after they failed to surrender. The soldiers seized a rocket launcher, rifles, hand grenades and twenty-five kilograms (fifty-five pounds) of plastic explosives during the four-day operation.

21. Two Kurdish rebels and one Turkish soldier were killed in a gun battle in Turkey's troubled southeast.

23. Five Kurdish rebels, including a woman, were killed in a battle with Turkish security forces in the country's troubled southeast. As a result, the number of dead terrorists seized in the last ten days rose to fifteen.

23. A bomb exploded at an Istanbul cafe frequented by tourists, injuring at least two people. The blast was caused by either a remote-controlled bomb or a bomb with a timer. Police suspected Kurdish rebels were behind the attack.

25. Two soldiers and a Kurdish rebel were killed in a gun battle in a remote corner of southeastern Turkey.

26. A bomb derailed a train in eastern Turkey, but no one was injured — the third attack on a train in the troubled region this month. There were no immediate claims of responsibility and officials did not name any suspects. Kurdish separatist groups have said they were behind the two other attacks.

27. Turkish security forces killed fifteen guerrillas from the PKK and seized a number of arms and documents.

27. Kurdish guerrillas kidnapped the mayor of a town in eastern Turkey and police and troops have launched a search.

28. One police officer and a civilian were wounded in two blasts at the town of Yuksekova, some 100 km (60 miles) from Hakkari.

29. Two Turkish soldiers were killed after a bomb planted in their car detonated in southeastern Turkey.

29. Turkey could come under attack again from al-Qaeda in the next few months, a senior police official said in an interview.

## *August 2005*

2. Two explosions tore through rubbish bins and wounded six people in the southern Turkish resort city of Antalya. Turkey's tourism minister blamed a gas leak for the blasts, which occurred within minutes of each other in separate locations in central Antalya, but police could not confirm this.

3. Kurdish rebels released the mayor of a town in eastern Turkey they kidnapped last week; the mayor said he was in good health.

4. PKK fighters released a Turkish soldier they had been holding captive for nearly four weeks in a remote region of the southeast. The soldier was handed over to representatives of a Human Rights group and was taken to military authorities for debriefing. Paramilitary police detained eleven people, including the four-member Human Rights delegation and five journalists who witnessed the handover.

5. Kurdish guerrillas killed five Turkish soldiers and injured one in a bomb attack on a police station in troubled southeast Turkey.

8. A blast tore through an apartment block in Istanbul, killing two men and wounding five. It was not clear who the two men were.

11. Turkish police detained two Syrians on suspicion of links to al-Qaeda, including one believed to be a go-between for the terrorist network and a Turkish cell that carried out the deadly 2003 bombings in Istanbul.

13. A Kurdish rebel commander declared conditions for a cease fire with Turkey.[34]

13. The governor of Elazig in mainly Kurdish eastern Turkey narrowly escaped death when a landmine blew up as his car was passing by. No one was killed or injured in the blast.

14. One person was killed and one injured overnight when their car blew up in Turkey's east Mediterranean port of Mersin. Officials believed the explosion was caused by a bomb, probably prepared by the person who died. The car exploded near a building used by police.

18. Kurdish rebels are poised to announce a new cease-fire in their armed struggle with Turkey's security forces, Turkish newspapers said. The banned PKK, blamed by Ankara for the deaths of more than 30,000 people since 1984, called off a five-year unilateral cease-fire in June 2004, complaining that the Turkish government had failed to meet its demands.[35]

20. Two separatist fighters were killed in eastern Turkey's mountainous Tunceli despite a cease-fire call from the PKK the previous day.

23. Turkey's top security body, the National Security Council (NSC), said it was determined to fight "terror," in an apparent rebuff to a cease-fire call from banned Kurdish separatist group the PKK. The NSC reiterated its "determination to fight terror which targets our [Turkish] citizens' right to life, security, peace and welfare," the council said in a statement after a meeting.

26. Turkish soldiers killed three Kurdish guerrillas in a clash in a remote part of southeast Turkey overnight. Backed by Sikorsky and Cobra helicopters, security forces launched an operation on Thursday evening after hearing reports of a large group of PKK rebels hiding in a rural part of Batman.

27. Turkish troops killed three Kurdish guerrillas in a clash in southeast Turkey, bringing the total number of rebels killed in the past days to six.

29. One man was killed and five policemen were injured as a group of Kurdish protesters clashed with security forces in Turkey's troubled southeast. The violence flared as a 1,000-strong group from the pro-Kurdish DEHAP party asked authorities in Batman to hand over the corpses of six PKK rebels who had been killed in a battle with the military.

## *September 2005*

7. Two Turkish soldiers were killed and two others injured when a landmine laid by Kurdish guerrillas exploded.

8. Turkish troops killed seven Kurdish rebels in an operation in the east of the country.

11. One Turkish soldier was killed and two others were wounded in an attack on a gendarmerie station in Bingol.

15. Two Turkish soldiers were killed and six wounded when their vehicle hit a mine in Turkey's mainly Kurdish southeast near the borders of Iraq and Iran.

27. Troops killed two rebels after receiving a tip that they were about to launch an attack on a town in the southeastern region. Three policemen were wounded in that clash.

29. Turkish security forces killed two Kurdish rebels in a clash in southeastern Turkey.

## *November 2005*

1. Two Turkish soldiers and a state-sponsored village guard were killed in a clash with Kurdish rebels in southeast Turkey overnight.

2. Kurdish rebels detonated a car bomb in front of security headquarters in a town in southeast Turkey, wounding twenty-three people and damaging dozens of buildings.

9. A bomb explosion in a bookstore in southeast Turkey killed one person and injured several others. After the blast, a group of residents tried to lynch a person suspected of planting the bomb. The unrest spread when residents turned on the police, pelting them with stones.

18. A bomb placed in a trash can outside a bus stop exploded near a fairground in Istanbul, killing one person and injuring twelve.

25. Turkey vowed zero tolerance for Kurdish militants despite concern over actions of its own security forces after a convicted rebel was allegedly targeted in a grenade attack earlier this month.

30. Police detained two members of the security forces implicated in a November 9 bookshop bombing which triggered angry protests in Turkey's mainly Kurdish southeast. The two men are members of the gendarmerie, a military unit responsible for security in rural areas.

## *January 2006*

22. Police officers fired tear-gas grenades and rubber bullets to disperse about one hundred stone-throwing protesters in the working-class district of Dolapdere in Istanbul. The protesters had gathered in support of the jailed leader of the rebel PKK.

30. A blast occurred at a building housing a Turkish–US cultural association in downtown Adana, injuring four people. There was no immediate claim of responsibility for the blast, although leftist and Kurdish militant groups have perpetrated similar small-scale bombing attacks in the past.

## February 2006

9. A hardline Kurdish group claimed responsibility for a bomb blast at an Internet cafe in Istanbul that killed a man and injured sixteen other people, including seven police officers.

13. Six people were injured by an explosion at an Istanbul supermarket; the second blast in Turkey's largest city in four days. A Turkish television station said it had been caused by a bomb for which a hardline Kurdish group has taken responsibility.

15. Kurdish protesters armed with firebombs and stones battled with Turkish police to mark the seventh anniversary of guerrilla leader Abdullah Ocalan's capture.

## March 2006

4. A small bomb wounded one man and damaged dozens of buildings in western Turkey, the state-run Anatolian news agency said. The makeshift bomb exploded in a wheelbarrow near a police station in a mainly Kurdish district of Izmir, Turkey's third biggest city, located on the Aegean coast.

9. Three people were killed and sixteen wounded in an explosion possibly caused by a suicide bomber in the eastern Turkish city of Van, officials said. Police said the blast was near the office of Van's governor. They said an investigation was under way into the cause of the explosion, but gave no further information.

15. A bomb exploded outside a branch of HSBC bank in Diyarbakir, southeast Turkey, where one person was injured, security officials said. The bomb was planted in an automated teller machine and caused serious damage. PKK rebels have recently set off a series of bombs in the mainly Kurdish southeast.

25. Turkish troops killed fourteen Kurdish PKK guerrillas in fighting in southeastern Turkey, local military authorities said. The fighting occurred near the city of Mus.

28. Clashes erupted after funeral ceremonies for fourteen members of the banned PKK killed by troops last weekend.

29. Riot police fired water cannons and used pepper spray to disperse stone-throwing Kurdish rioters in a second day of violence that an official said left at least three people dead and 250 injured in southeastern Turkey. Governor Dijarbakir said 2,500 to 3,000 rioters, including many children, participated in the two days of clashes in Diyarbakir after funerals for Kurdish guerrillas killed by Turkish troops last week.

## April 2006

2. One protester died after police opened fire to disperse Kurdish demonstrators in southeastern Turkey, raising the death toll in six days of street violence to nine, security sources said.

3. Hundreds of Kurds clashed with police in southeast Turkey and in Istanbul three people were killed as they fled a bus set ablaze by protesters, bringing the death toll in violence over the past week to fifteen.

5. Kurdish guerillas attacked a police station in southeast Turkey with shoulder-fired rockets, killing one policeman and injuring seven others.

5. A small bomb exploded at the Istanbul offices of Turkey's ruling Justice and Development Party (AKP) on April 5, injuring two office employees. The bomb was set in the doorway of the building.

7. A woman suicide bomber was killed at a mosque in Turkey's Black Sea city of Ordu and her colleague injured when a bomb they were carrying blew up, media reports said.

10. Police detained two army conscripts at a Burger King restaurant in central Istanbul after a brief hostage drama in protest of the treatment of soldiers in southeast Turkey, the city's police chief and witnesses said. The gunmen, in their early twenties, were detained on the roof terrace of a restaurant after one of them fired his pistol into the air in Taksim Square.

11. Police raided several homes near the capital, Ankara, arresting twenty people suspected of being Kurdish militants allegedly plotting firebomb attacks.

13. Twelve Kurdish rebels and two Turkish troops were killed in clashes in the country's southeastern Sirnak, near the Iraqi border.

17. According to police officials, thirty people were injured in an explosion near a cafe in a suburb of Istanbul, on the European side of the city. The blast occurred near a small restaurant in the Bakirkoy district.

23. A Turkish soldier and three members of the outlawed PKK were killed in a clash in southeastern Turkey. The clash occurred in the remote city of Sirnak on Sunday during the Turkish army's annual "spring offensive" against PKK rebels, who cross into Turkey from their mountain strongholds in northern Iraq.

26. Two soldiers were killed in a clash with PKK militants.

27. Turkey deployed more than 30,000 additional troops in its predominantly Kurdish southeast and along its rugged border with Iraq and Iran to fight Kurdish guerrillas and stop them from coming across the frontier, officials said. The area has some 250,000 Turkish soldiers.

31. One Turkish soldier was killed when he stepped on a landmine in southeastern city of Hakkari. The soldier was walking towards his duty spot when the landmine planted by members of the outlawed PKK exploded.

## *May 2006*

4. A total of fifteen people were injured as a landmine planted by the outlawed PKK exploded on a highway in the southeastern Turkish city of Hakkari.

5. An explosive device detonated on a cargo train that was traveling between Elazig and Tatvan. The blast derailed two of the train cars and damaged others. There were no reported injuries caused.

5. A hand grenade was thrown into the headquarters of the Cumhuriyet newspaper in the Sisli neighborhood of Istanbul. The pin on the grenade was

not pulled, and the device failed to explode. Witnesses report seeing two unidentified assailants throw the device into the garden of the newspaper headquarters before running off. Bomb experts were able to safely defuse the bomb without incident.

7. A resonant bomb detonated under a police vehicle in the Kucukcekmece neighborhood of Istanbul. There were no reported injuries caused in the blast.

11. Three unidentified assailants threw a hand grenade into the headquarters of the Cumhuriyet newspaper, in the Sisli neighborhood in Istanbul. This was the second such device to be thrown at the premises; the first was on May 5. The grenade exploded but caused no casualties and only minor damages.

13. Sources told Anadolu News Agency that a bomb exploded in one of Ulalar's town coffee shops and resulted in the death of two children and the injury of twelve.

17. A deadly assault on five judges in Turkey's highest administrative court underlines the friction that the country faces as it navigates between groups pressing for a greater role for Islam and those that want to protect secular rule. One judge died shortly after a gunman stormed into an Ankara courthouse and opened fire after shouting "God is great!" and "We are God's ambassadors!" He wounded four other judges, and was apparently incensed at a ruling enforcing a strict ban on the wearing of Islamic headscarves.

23. Suspected members of the PKK staged an explosive attack on a natural gas pipeline belonging to the Turkish Petroleum Pipeline Corps (BOTAS). Damage was caused to the pipeline but there were no reported casualties.

24. The Kurdistan Freedom Falcons (TAK) said it was responsible for a fire at the cargo section of Istanbul's Atatürk airport, the hub of international air travel in Turkey, which slightly injured three people and caused delays in air traffic. The Turkish authorities identified an electrical short circuit as the probable cause of the blaze.

31. An explosive device detonated along the Turkish Petroleum Corporation (TPAO) oil pipeline in the town of Yenicaglar. A 10 meter stretch of the pipeline was ruptured by the blast. The attack took place in the Selmo oil field.

## *June 2006*

1. An explosion in the basement of a building injured several people in Istanbul. The explosion occurred in the district of Uskudar on the Asian side of the city. The cause of the blast was not immediately clear.

3. The Kurdistan Freedom Falcons (TAK) claimed responsibility for a major bomb attack in the port city of Mersin. The blast was caused by a grenade which was remotely detonated with a mobile phone. Fifteen people were injured by the bomb, which was planted in front of a buffet.

8. Four police officers were injured when unidentified perpetrators attacked the home of the sub-governor in Kosluk, in Batman. The officers were guarding the home at the time of the attack. The sub-governor was not home at the time of the attack and none of his family was injured.

11. PKK terrorists attacked a military unit in Geyiksu hamlet in the southeastern city of Tunceli. Two soldiers were killed and six other people, including four soldiers, were injured.

13. A group of unidentified perpetrators threw a Molotov cocktail at a national post office in Umraniye, in Istanbul. The device caused a fire, which caused damages, but no injuries. No group has claimed responsibility.

14. Suspected Kurdish rebels set off a small bomb inside a trash container in a busy Istanbul neighborhood injuring at least four people, police and reports said. The explosion occurred near a bus terminal in the district of Eminonu, a busy commercial and historic neighborhood.

16. Three people were slightly injured when a remote-detonated explosive device detonated in a garbage can in the town of Baskale. The blast took place near the Directorate of Meteorology, but it is unclear what the intended target of the blast was. The Meteorology Directorate, as well as other buildings nearby, were damaged by the bomb. Kurdish rebels are believed to be responsible.

18. Suspected Kurdish rebels bombed a freight train in eastern Turkey, causing damage but no casualties. The Turkish state news agency, Anatolian Agency, said the bomb, which exploded as the train passed, flipped over twelve carriages, leaving eight unusable, and wrecked twenty meters of track in the eastern city of Mus. Officials said the bomb may have been activated by remote control.

19. A group of unidentified perpetrators opened fire at the living quarters of civil servants in the city of Sirnak. Witnesses reported seeing four gunmen, who fired on the police checkpoint and living quarters of the premises.

25. The Kurdistan Freedom Falcons group said it was responsible for an explosion that killed four people, including a Norwegian tourist. Local authorities continued to blame the blast on an exploding gas canister.

26. Two people were slightly injured when the passenger minibus in which they were traveling came under gunfire from unidentified gunmen. The attack took place in the Ersin area of Hatay. The gunmen were able to escape without being arrested.

27. A remote-controlled explosive device detonated on the Erzincan–Erzurum railway line, causing damages but no injuries. The bomb was detonated just after an Eastern Express train passed through the area. No group has claimed responsibility.

28. One Turkish soldier died in clashes with the PKK in Hakkari. The PKK members then escaped to Iraq after the clash.

## *July 2006*

2. A police officer died while trying to defuse an explosive device in the town of Kocakoy. No information on the target of the bomb was available.

3. Authorities found five kilograms of C-4 explosives planted along a natural gas pipeline that runs from Iran to Turkey. The explosives were left in the town of Dogubeyazit and were intended to cause damage to the pipeline.

4. A fragmentation bomb detonated in front of the headquarters of the Justice and Development Party (AKP) in Kartal. The bomb was left in a trash can in front of the building and caused some damage, but no injuries. No group has claimed responsibility for the attack.

6. The PKK was responsible for blowing up a delivery truck at the entrance of a military outpost, killing the driver. Local authorities also said on Friday that three soldiers who had stopped the vehicle for inspection were lightly wounded in Thursday's attack in the town of Dicle, near Diyarbakır. Turkish officials believe PKK members placed the bomb in the truck without the driver's knowledge, who was delivering bread to the base.

10. Two police officers were killed by unidentified gunmen in Idil, Sirnak. The attack took place as the officers were on their morning patrol.

11. Four private security guards were injured in a remote-detonated explosive attack along a highway in Silopi, Sirnak. The blast took place as the guards were driving down the road.

12. A small concussion bomb detonated in a trash bin alongside a highway that was to be used by the Turkish Prime Minister on his trip to Malatya. Street-sweepers noticed the unusual package beside the road and threw it in the trash bin, where it detonated later. There was no damage or casualties caused.

13. An explosive device detonated at a building that houses the Justice and Development Party (AKP) in Balcova, in Izmir. There were no reported casualties.

16. A group of unidentified gunmen opened fire at a police checkpoint in the city of Osalp, in Van. One police officer was killed in the attack.

17. One police officer died when an unknown perpetrator opened fire on a police checkpoint in Osalp, Van. Authorities believe the gunman to be a member of the PKK.

24. A group of suspected members of the PKK opened fire on police officers who were guarding the office building of the sub-governor, in Cukurca. One police officer was injured in the ensuing firefight between police and the assailants.

25. Unknown perpetrators threw a hand grenade at the local headquarters of the Justice and Development Party, in the Umraniye area of Istanbul. The blast caused only minor damage. The assailants managed to escape without being caught.

30. A percussion bomb detonated outside an office of the Justice and Development Party in Gaziantep. There were no reported casualties.

30. Six police officers and one civilian were injured when unidentified gunmen opened fire on a police housing unit in Dogubeyazit. The gunmen, suspected members of the PKK, fired on the houses and threw grenades before they were chased out by police.

## *August 2006*

2. An explosive device detonated on a railway line near a train station, in Erzincan. The blast damaged a freight train but caused no casualties.

4. A fragmentation bomb detonated six minutes after a sound bomb, near a bank branch in the city of Adana. The first blast, which only injured two people, drew civilians and police to the scene, where the fragmentation bomb detonated, and injured fifteen others. The second blast also damaged nearby shops and police cars. The Kurdistan Freedom Falcons (TAK) claimed responsibility for the twin attacks and blamed the Turkish government of mistreatment of the PKK leader Abdullah Ocalan, who is in prison. It appears that the first blast was intended to draw Turkish security forces to the scene and maximize casualties. This is the first time the TAK has used this tactic in their attacks.

4. Southern Turkey was hit by a series of blasts when a railway explosion derailed several cars of a freight train and two bomb explosions near a bank left seventeen people injured. A railway blast in Diyarbakir on Friday derailed four of the train's fifteen cars and forced the closure of the railway for repairs, local security sources said. The authorities have blamed the outlawed PKK for similar attacks in the past.

6. An explosive device detonated on rail tracks in Bingol. The blast caused damage to a commercial train that was passing, and injured four security personnel. The train was bound for Elazig.

6. A resonant bomb detonated outside an office of the Republican People's Party (CHP) in Diyarbakir. There were no reported casualties, but the blast caused some property damage.

6. A perpetrator died when the explosives he was attempting to plant near a gendarmerie station in Sirnak detonated prematurely.

12. Five people, including two Algerian nationals, were injured in an explosive attack in the Kumkapi neighborhood of Istanbul. An explosive device was planted in a trash can outside of an Internet cafe, where it detonated. Two men were arrested in connection with the attack and have alleged ties to the PKK.

18. Police fired on a group of suspected PKK members who were preparing an armed attack against the Security Directorate building in Van. The assailants left their small weapons behind, including a light antitank weapon, when they fled the scene.

18. Two police officers were injured when three unknown gunmen opened fire on them while they were patrolling. The attack took place in Istanbul. The perpetrators managed to escape without being arrested.

19. An explosive device, which may have been timed, detonated at the Turkey–Iran natural gas pipeline. The strong explosion caused a major fire that was extinguished by fire brigades. As a result of the attack, the inlet and outlet valves of the pipeline were closed down. There were no reported casualties, though local villagers moved from their houses during the fire. Police are blaming the attack on members of the PKK.

22. Unknown perpetrators opened fire on gendarmerie and police officers near the Bitlis–Diyarbakir road.

25. An explosive device detonated outside an office building in Adana that houses three political party branches — the Republican People's Party, the Freedom and Democracy Party and the Independent Turkey Party — as well as

an office of the Human Rights Association. The blast injured four people and took place after another device exploded at a bank branch nearby.

27. Twenty-one people, including ten British citizens, were injured when an explosive device ripped through a tourist minibus in Marmaris. This was one of three bomb blasts in the city on this day. The Kurdistan Freedom Falcons claimed responsibility for these blasts and another in Istanbul, stating that "It must be realized that the holding in captivity of our historic leader Chairman Apo [Abdullah Ocalan] is in itself the rationale for our destructive acts of revenge against the bloodsucking, colonialist, and fascist TC." One suspect was captured following a tip from his father. The suspect's fingerprints matched those found at the scene of the attack.

28. The Kurdistan Freedom Falcons claimed responsibility for a blast that killed three people in Antalya, one of the country's most popular tourist resorts, while police searched for two people suspected of planting the explosives. The Kurdistan Freedom Falcons, which has threatened to harm Turkey's tourism industry, said on its web site that it carried out the attack and vowed that the "fear of death will reign everywhere in Turkey."

## *September 2006*

3. A remote-controlled bomb exploded in a tea garden in southeastern Turkey Sunday, killing two people and injuring seven others, a local government official said. The bomb was left at a tea garden in Van, a city which borders Iran, a police official said. It exploded as police arrived at the scene to investigate a suspicious package at the open-air cafe. Two people, including a police officer, died of injuries in a hospital. Police suspect autonomy-seeking Kurdish rebels were behind the bombing.

5. A low-intensity resonant bomb was placed in a garbage bin near a Justice and Development Party office in Izmir. The device caused minor damage and there were no reported casualties.

12. Ten people including seven children were killed in Diyarbakir when a powerful bomb went off accidentally in a crowded park, officials said. Tuesday's blast was the deadliest in a string of bombings across Turkey this year. Police said immediate suspicions fell on the separatist PKK, but the rebels denied any role in the blast. "The preliminary investigation established that the blast occurred while the home-made remote-control device, planted in a flask, was being carried (to another location)," the local governor's office said.

12. A remote-detonated explosive device exploded on a railroad track in Bingol damaging three rail cars loaded with coal.

14. A fragmentation bomb detonated near an officer lodging complex in Van. The blast shattered windows in nearby houses but there were no reported casualties.

15. A homemade fragmentation bomb, set by timer, was placed near the wall of a police post in Gaziantep, where it exploded. The blast damaged two cars parked nearby, but caused no casualties.

23. A Kurdish guerrilla group claimed responsibility for a weekend bomb attack that injured seventeen people in eastern Turkey, a pro-Kurdish news agency reported Monday. The armed wing of the PKK said on its web site that it was behind Saturday's attack near a police guest house in the eastern city of Igdir.

## October 2006

1. Three people were injured when a bomb exploded outside a hospital in the southern Turkish town of Mersin, a police official said. The explosion came on the heels of a unilateral cease-fire declared Saturday by the rebel PKK that was to take effect as of Sunday.
1. A member of the outlawed PKK was killed yesterday in an operation in the southeastern city of Mardin.
2. At least fifteen people were injured when unknown assailants threw two grenades into a cafe in Izmir.
4. A landmine planted by terrorists in the rural area of eastern Turkey went off on Wednesday, injuring three soldiers of the Turkish security forces.
10. The General Staff of Turkey's armed forces said that militants of the outlawed PKK had kidnapped four people in Ogulveren village in the eastern city of Van.
10. Three PKK members surrendered to Turkish security forces in the southeastern city of Sirnak.
11. Turkish security forces have killed three members of the outlawed PKK in southeastern Turkey during their biggest military offensive since the group announced a unilateral cease-fire.
14. Two Turkish soldiers were killed and another injured after stepping on a landmine planted by the outlawed PKK during an operation in the southeastern city of Hakkari.
15. Turkish security forces killed a militant of the outlawed PKK in a clash in the southeastern city of Sirnak.
21. Six members of the PKK surrendered to Turkish security forces in southeastern Turkey. Six PKK militants fleeing from the PKK organization proceeded from Iraq to Turkey and surrendered to the Turkish security forces in the Silopi town of Sirnak.
23. Turkish security forces killed three militants of the outlawed PKK in a clash in the southeastern city of Batman.

## November 2006

5. Anti-terrorism police raided an Istanbul branch office of a legal Kurdish party, detaining seven officials. The raid occurred during a morning meeting of the Kurdish Democratic Society Party's branch office in the low-income Bagcilar district. Police, acting on a court-issued search warrant, detained seven party officials and confiscated a number of documents for inspection. Turkish

authorities have accused the party of having links to the outlawed autonomy-seeking Kurdish guerrilla group.

12. Turkish security forces killed three members of the outlawed PKK, in a clash in the Bestler Dereler region in Sirnak, the local governor's office said in a statement, adding that two rifles, fifty-six kilograms of explosives, and 110 hand grenades belonging to the Kurdish rebels were seized in the operation.

13. A soldier was killed in a clash with the outlawed PKK near the border with Iran, despite a unilateral cease-fire proclaimed by the terrorists on October 1. The clash occurred late Monday near the town of Baskale, in the far eastern city of Van. Turkey did not recognize the cease-fire, saying it would continue fighting until all terrorists were killed or surrendered

15. A statement posted on the web site of the Office of the Chief of General Staff said a member of the PKK and also of its political wing Kongra-Gel based in Europe, was captured in the Ümraniye district of Istanbul.

15. A clash took place between security forces and five terrorists in the mountainous district of Kulp in Diyarbakır. Nobody was killed or injured in the clash and the military's operations in the region were continuing. The statement also said a mine placed in the Pervari district of Siirt by terrorists as well as five hundred grams of TNT were seized by security forces during search activities in the area.

16. Turkish Prime Minister Recep Tayyip Erdogan said that Turkey and Iraq have agreed to strengthen their cooperation in fighting against terrorism, including Turkish rebels. Erdogan made the remarks at a joint news conference with his Iraqi counterpart Nouri al-Maliki, who arrived in Ankara Thursday morning for a two-day State visit to Turkey. "During our meeting, we ... reviewed measures to be taken against the terrorist organisation," said Erdogan, referring to the PKK. On his part, al-Maliki said, "We will not allow any formation to jeopardize security of neighbor countries."

17. A clash in a rural area of eastern Turkey on Friday resulted in the deaths of a soldier and three PKK members.

23. One Turkish soldier and three militants of the outlawed PKK were killed in clashes in southeast Turkey. The soldier, a commando sergeant, died on Thursday when rebels opened fire on his unit in a remote mountainous part of Sirnak, it said. A PKK rebel also died in the clash. The other two guerrillas were killed earlier on Thursday in the same region, where security forces have been waging a campaign to flush out the rebels.

## *December 2006*

1. Turkish security forces seized a large amount of explosives and weapons in recent operations against the outlawed PKK in the southeastern city of Sirnak. Security forces launched operations against the PKK in the Bestler Dereler region of the city. A total of 123 kilograms of TNT-type explosives, fifty-two RPG-7 rockets, forty grenades, eighty-four Dokca anti-aircraft ammo and six Kalashnikov assault rifles were seized.

4. Turkish security forces said they killed five Kurdish rebels overnight in clashes in the country's impoverished southeast. The security forces also confiscated nearly four tonnes of food supplies as well as weapons and materials used in mine construction from a cave used as a winter base by the outlawed separatist PKK.

5. Two roadside blasts on Tuesday, blamed on the outlawed PKK, killed four soldiers and injured thirteen more in the southeastern city of Sirnak, Turkey. The first charge went off as the lead vehicle in a convoy passed, throwing soldiers to the ground. A second blast followed, behind the first, causing further damage. The Governor's office said the charges were detonated by remote control.

9. A landmine explosion on a road in southeastern Turkey killed a Turkish soldier and injured eleven others. The mine — believed to have been planted by autonomy-seeking Kurdish rebels — exploded late Friday, on a road near the mainly Kurdish town of Lice.

28. A group of about twenty assailants set fire to an Istanbul Electricity, Tram and Tunnel General Directorate bus in Okmeydani. The group stopped traffic with Molotov cocktails, forced the passengers off the bus and set it on fire. There were no reported injuries caused. The group perpetrated the attack in support of the PKK's leader Abdullah Ocalan, who is in a Turkish prison. They chanted slogans such as "We are together with you in war and peace."

## *January 2007*

19. A prominent Turkish-Armenian editor, convicted in 2005 of insulting Turkish identity, was shot dead outside his newspaper's office in Istanbul.

31. Turkey made a decisive contribution to the Iraq war nearly four years ago when the parliament in Ankara rejected a US request to allow an invasion from the north. The diplomatic fallout is still casting a shadow over the US–Turkish relationship. Now Turkey could be about to make a second dramatic contribution. Amid constant bloody clashes between Turkish troops and PKK Kurdish separatist guerrillas operating out of northern Iraq, Ankara is weighing up a cross-border incursion to attack PKK bases. Turkey, its political leaders insist, has the right and the determination to eliminate threats to its territory wherever they come from.

## *February 2007*

5. In an effort to discourage potential Turkish military intervention into neighboring Iraqi territory, the US pledged to do more against the presence of separatist Turkish Kurdish militants in northern Iraq that threaten the NATO ally's security. Turkish Foreign Minister Abdullah Gul met in Washington with Vice President Dick Cheney on February 5 and Secretary of State Condoleezza Rice on February 6, urging the US to take effective measures against the outlawed PKK based in northern Iraq. He implied that, otherwise, Turkey might take things into its own hands.

22. A court in Diyarbakir, the central city of the predominantly Kurdish southeast, charged Democratic Society Party (DTP) provincial chairman with "inciting hatred" and jailed him pending trial, judicial officials said. Earlier, in the eastern city of Van, DTP provincial chairman and another party activist were jailed pending trial late Thursday, Anatolia news agency reported.

23. A senior Kurdish politician was arrested Friday over remarks that allegedly threatened violence in Turkey, following the arrest of two other Kurdish activists overnight, officials said.

# Document no. 113

**ECtHR — *Ocalan v. Turkey*[36]**

1. The case originated in an application (no. 46221/99) against the Republic of Turkey lodged with the Court under Article 34 of the Convention for the Protection of Human Rights and Fundamental Freedoms ("the Convention") by a Turkish national, Mr Abdullah Öcalan ("the applicant"), on 16 February 1999.

\*\*\*

3. The applicant alleged, in particular, violations of various provisions of the Convention, namely Articles 2 (right to life), 3 (prohibition of ill-treatment), 5 (right to liberty and security), 6 (right to a fair trial), 7 (no punishment without law), 8 (right to respect for private and family life), 9 (freedom of thought, conscience and religion), 10 (freedom of expression), 13 (right to an effective remedy), 14 (prohibition of discrimination), 18 (limitation on use of restrictions on rights) and 34 (right of individual application).

4. The application was allocated to the First Section of the Court (Rule 52 § 1 of the Rules of Court).

5. On 4 March 1999, the Court requested the Government to take interim measures within the meaning of Rule 39 of the Rules of Court, notably to ensure that the requirements of Article 6 were complied with in proceedings which had been instituted against the applicant in the State Security Court and that the applicant was able to exercise his right of individual application to the Court effectively through lawyers of his own choosing.

\*\*\*

8. The Chamber delivered its judgment on 12 March 2003. It held unanimously that there had been a violation of Article 5 § 4 of the Convention on account of the lack of a remedy by which the applicant could have the lawfulness of his detention in police custody determined; unanimously that there had been no violation of Article 5 § 1 of the Convention; unanimously that

there had been a violation of Article 5 § 3 of the Convention on account of the failure to bring the applicant before a judge promptly after his arrest; by six votes to one that there had been a violation of Article 6 § 1 of the Convention in that the applicant had not been tried by an independent and impartial tribunal; unanimously that there had been a violation of Article 6 § 1, taken together with Article 6 § 3 (b) and (c) of the Convention, in that the applicant had not had a fair trial; unanimously that there had been no violation of Article 2 of the Convention; unanimously that there had been no violation of Article 14, taken together with Article 2, in regards to the implementation of the death penalty; unanimously that there had been no violation of Article 3 of the Convention in regards to the complaint relating to the implementation of the death penalty; by six votes to one that there had been a violation of Article 3 on account of the imposition of the death penalty following an unfair trial; unanimously that there had been no violation of Article 3 of the Convention either as regards the conditions in which the applicant had been transferred from Kenya to Turkey or the conditions of his detention on the island of Imrali; unanimously that no separate examination was necessary of the applicant's remaining complaints under Articles 7, 8, 9, 10, 13, 14 and 18 of the Convention, taken individually or together with the aforementioned provisions of the Convention; and unanimously that there had been no violation of Article 34 *in fine* of the Convention. A partly dissenting opinion by Mr R. Türmen was annexed to the judgment.

9. On 9 June 2003 the applicant and on 11 June 2003 the Government requested that the case be referred to the Grand Chamber, in accordance with Article 43 of the Convention and Rule 73.

On 9 July 2003 a panel of the Grand Chamber decided to refer the case to the Grand Chamber.

\*\*\*

11. The applicant and the Government each filed observations on the merits and written comments on each other's observations.

[After a lengthy opinion, the Grand Chamber concluded with the following *dispositif* and declined to change the holdings of the First Section of the Court.]

FOR THESE REASONS, THE COURT

1. *Dismisses* unanimously the Government's preliminary objection concerning Article 5 §§ 1, 3 and 4 of the Convention;

2. *Holds* unanimously that there has been a violation of Article 5 § 4 of the Convention on account of the lack of a remedy by which the applicant could have the lawfulness of his detention in police custody decided;

3. *Holds* unanimously that there has been no violation of Article 5 § 1 of the Convention on account of the applicant's arrest;

4. *Holds* unanimously that there has been a violation of Article 5 § 3 of the Convention on account of the failure to bring the applicant before a judge promptly after his arrest;

5. *Holds* by eleven votes to six that there has been a violation of Article 6 § 1 of the Convention in that the applicant was not tried by an independent and impartial tribunal;

6. *Holds* unanimously that there has been a violation of Article 6 § 1, taken together with Article 6 § 3 (b) and (c) of the Convention, in that the applicant did not have a fair trial;

7. *Holds* unanimously that there has been no violation of Article 2 of the Convention;

8. *Holds* unanimously that there has been no violation of Article 14 of the Convention, taken together with Article 2, as regards the implementation of the death penalty;

9. *Holds* unanimously that there has been no violation of Article 3 of the Convention as regards the complaint concerning the implementation of the death penalty;

10. *Holds* by thirteen votes to four that there has been a violation of Article 3 as regards the imposition of the death penalty following an unfair trial;

11. *Holds* unanimously that there has been no violation of Article 3 of the Convention as regards the conditions in which the applicant was transferred from Kenya to Turkey;

12. *Holds* unanimously that there has been no violation of Article 3 of the Convention, as regards the conditions of the applicant's detention on the island of Imrali;

13. *Holds* unanimously that no separate examination is necessary of the applicant's remaining complaints under Articles 7, 8, 9, 10, 13, 14 and 18 of the Convention, taken individually or together with the aforementioned provisions of the Convention;

14. *Holds* unanimously that there has been no violation of Article 34 *in fine* of the Convention;

15. *Holds* unanimously that its findings of a violation of Articles 3, 5 and 6 of the Convention constitute in themselves sufficient just satisfaction for any damage sustained by the applicant;

16. *Holds* unanimously

a. that the respondent State is to pay the applicant's lawyers in the manner set out in paragraph 217 of the present judgment, within three months, for costs and expenses the sum of EUR 120,000 (one hundred and twenty thousand euros) to be converted into new Turkish liras (YTL) or pounds sterling, depending on where payment is made, at the rate applicable at the date of settlement, plus any value-added tax that may be chargeable;

b. that from the expiry of the abovementioned three months until settlement simple interest shall be payable on the above amount at a rate equal to the marginal lending rate of the European Central Bank during the default period plus three percentage points;

17. *Dismisses* unanimously the remainder of the applicant's claim for just satisfaction.

# Document no. 114

### Negotiating framework[37] (Luxembourg, 3 October 2005)

*Principles governing the negotiations*

1. The negotiations will be based on Turkey's own merits and the pace will depend on Turkey's progress in meeting the requirements for membership. The Presidency or the Commission as appropriate will keep the Council fully informed so that the Council can keep the situation under regular review. The Union side, for its part, will decide in due course whether the conditions for the conclusion of negotiations have been met; this will be done on the basis of a report from the Commission confirming the fulfilment by Turkey of the requirements listed in point 6.

2. As agreed at the European Council in December 2004, these negotiations are based on Article 49 of the Treaty on European Union. The shared objective of the negotiations is accession. These negotiations are an open-ended process, the outcome of which cannot be guaranteed beforehand. While having full regard to all Copenhagen criteria, including the absorption capacity of the Union, if Turkey is not in a position to assume in full all the obligations of membership it must be ensured that Turkey is fully anchored in the European structures through the strongest possible bond.

3. Enlargement should strengthen the process of continuous creation and integration in which the Union and its Member States are engaged. Every effort should be made to protect the cohesion and effectiveness of the Union. In accordance with the conclusions of the Copenhagen European Council in 1993, the Union's capacity to absorb Turkey, while maintaining the momentum of European integration is an important consideration in the general interest of both the Union and Turkey. The Commission shall monitor this capacity during the negotiations, encompassing the whole range of issues set out in its October 2004 paper on issues arising from Turkey's membership perspective, in order to inform an assessment by the Council as to whether this condition of membership has been met.

4. Negotiations are opened on the basis that Turkey sufficiently meets the political criteria set by the Copenhagen European Council in 1993, for the most

part later enshrined in Article 6(1) of the Treaty on European Union and proclaimed in the Charter of Fundamental Rights. The Union expects Turkey to sustain the process of reform and to work towards further improvement in the respect of the principles of liberty, democracy, the rule of law and respect for Human Rights and fundamental freedoms, including relevant European case law; to consolidate and broaden legislation and implementation measures specifically in relation to the zero tolerance policy in the fight against torture and ill-treatment and the implementation of provisions relating to freedom of expression, freedom of religion, women's rights, ILO [International Labour Organization] standards including trades union rights and minority rights. The Union and Turkey will continue their intensive political dialogue. To ensure the irreversibility of progress in these areas and its full and effective implementation, notably with regard to fundamental freedoms and to full respect of Human Rights, progress will continue to be closely monitored by the Commission, which is invited to continue to report regularly on it to the Council, addressing all points of concern identified in the Commission's 2004 report and recommendation as well as its annual regular report.

5. In the case of a serious and persistent breach in Turkey of the principles of liberty, democracy, respect for Human Rights and fundamental freedoms and the rule of law on which the Union is founded, the Commission will, on its own initiative or on the request of one-third of the Member States, recommend the suspension of negotiations and propose the conditions for eventual resumption. The Council will decide by qualified majority on such a recommendation, after having heard Turkey, whether to suspend the negotiations and on the conditions for their resumption. The Member States will act in the Intergovernmental Conference in accordance with the Council decision, without prejudice to the general requirement for unanimity in the Intergovernmental Conference. The European Parliament will be informed.

6. The advancement of the negotiations will be guided by Turkey's progress in preparing for accession, within a framework of economic and social convergence and with reference to the Commission's reports in paragraph 4. This progress will be measured in particular against the following requirements:

- the Copenhagen criteria, which set down the following requirements for membership:
  - the stability of institutions guaranteeing democracy, the rule of law, Human Rights and respect for and protection of minorities;
  - the existence of a functioning market economy and the capacity to cope with competitive pressure and market forces within the Union;
  - the ability to take on the obligations of membership, including adherence to the aims of political, economic and monetary union and the administrative capacity to effectively apply and implement the *acquis*;
- Turkey's unequivocal commitment to good neighbourly relations and its undertaking to resolve any outstanding border disputes in conformity with the principle of peaceful settlement of disputes in accordance with the

United Nations Charter, including if necessary jurisdiction of the International Court of Justice;
- Turkey's continued support for efforts to achieve a comprehensive settlement of the Cyprus problem within the UN framework and in line with the principles on which the Union is founded, including steps to contribute to a favourable climate for a comprehensive settlement, and progress in the normalisation of bilateral relations between Turkey and all EU Member States, including the Republic of Cyprus.
- the fulfilment of Turkey's obligations under the Association Agreement and its Additional Protocol extending the Association Agreement to all new EU Member States, in particular those pertaining to the EU–Turkey Customs Union, as well as the implementation of the Accession Partnership, as regularly revised.

7. In the period up to accession, Turkey will be required to progressively align its policies towards third countries and its positions within international organisations (including in relation to the membership by all EU Member States of those organisations and arrangements) with the policies and positions adopted by the Union and its Member States.

8. Parallel to accession negotiations, the Union will engage with Turkey in an intensive political and civil society dialogue. The aim of the inclusive civil society dialogue will be to enhance mutual understanding by bringing people together in particular with a view to ensuring the support of European citizens for the accession process.

9. Turkey must accept the results of any other accession negotiations as they stand at the moment of its accession.

## *Substance of the negotiations*

10. Accession implies the acceptance of the rights and obligations attached to the Union system and its institutional framework, known as the *acquis* of the Union. Turkey will have to apply this as it stands at the time of accession. Furthermore, in addition to legislative alignment, accession implies timely and effective implementation of the *acquis*. The *acquis* is constantly evolving and includes:

- the content, principles and political objectives of the Treaties on which the Union is founded;
- legislation and decisions adopted pursuant to the Treaties, and the case law of the Court of Justice;
- other acts, legally binding or not, adopted within the Union framework, such as interinstitutional agreements, resolutions, statements, recommendations, guidelines;
- joint actions, common positions, declarations, conclusions and other acts within the framework of the common foreign and security policy;

- joint actions, joint positions, conventions signed, resolutions, statements and other acts agreed within the framework of justice and home affairs;
- international agreements concluded by the Communities, the Communities jointly with their Member States, the Union, and those concluded by the Member States among themselves with regard to Union activities.

\*\*\*

[Compliance with the *acquis* (para. 11–13); participation in the economic and monetary union (para. 14); Schengen *acquis* (para. 15); environmental protection (para. 16); and implementation of the *acquis* (para. 17).]

## Negotiating procedures

18. The substance of negotiations will be conducted in an Intergovernmental Conference with the participation of all Member States on the one hand and the candidate State on the other.

\*\*\*

[Screening process to assess the state of preparation of Turkey for opening negotiations in specific areas (para. 19); breaking down of the *acquis* (para. 20); closure of chapters (para. 21); Turkey's input (para. 22); monitoring progress (para. 23)].

# Document no. 115

**European Commission 2006 Regular Report on Turkey's Progress Towards Accession**[38]

## *1. Introduction*

*1.2. Relations between the EU and Turkey*

*Accession negotiations* were opened with Turkey in October 2005. The first phase of the accession process, the analytical examination of the *acquis* (screening) was completed in October 2006. Negotiations on one chapter, science and research, were opened and provisionally closed in June.

The *enhanced political dialogue* has continued under the United Kingdom, Austrian and Finnish presidencies.

The *Association Agreement* has continued to work in a satisfactory manner.

EC–Turkey trade has continued to expand in the context of the *Customs Union* ...

The revised *Accession Partnership* was adopted in January 2006, setting out priorities that Turkey should address in the short and medium term in its preparations for accession.

## *2. Enhanced political dialogue and political criteria*

*2.1. Democracy and the rule of law*

PARLIAMENT

The Turkish Grand National Assembly, in which six parties are represented, has adopted 148 laws of a total 429 draft bills submitted since October 2005. The next elections are scheduled for November 2007.

\*\*\*

The government submitted a new reform package in June, covering a number of areas related to the Copenhagen political criteria. Parliament passed several laws in the area of the political criteria. However, some legislative proposals included in the government's reform package were not adopted before the end of the reporting period.

Amendments to the Anti-Terror Law were adopted in June 2006 as a response to the escalation of terrorism. Under the new law, the list of what constitutes a terrorist offence was extended and a wide definition of terrorism maintained. The law introduces legal restrictions on freedom of expression, the press and the media. In August, President Sezer applied to the Constitutional Court for the cancellation of Articles 5 and 6, providing for such restrictions. The new Anti-Terror Law reduces procedural safeguards for suspects of terrorist offences. Access to a lawyer may be denied for a period of twenty-four hours, and under certain circumstances security officers may attend meetings between suspects and their lawyer. As regards the defence rights, officials and former officials are granted differentiated treatment. Furthermore they dispose of wider discretion with regard to the use of firearms.

\*\*\*

CIVIL–MILITARY RELATIONS

There has been progress concerning the competence of military courts to try civilians. Under the law amending the relevant provisions of the Military Criminal Code as adopted in June 2006, no civilian will be tried in military courts in peacetime unless military personnel and civilians commit an offence together. The new law also introduces the right of retrial in military courts. Accordingly, if there is an ECtHR decision in favour of military or civilian persons who have been tried before military courts, they can ask for a retrial.

The National Security Council (NSC) has continued to meet on a bi-monthly basis in line with its revised role. It has discussed domestic and foreign policy issues such as counter-terrorism, internal security, energy security, migration, water policy and foreign aid policy. The NSC has submitted reports to the government, including recommendations.

One such document, the revised National Security Policy Document (NSPD), adopted by the government in November 2005, is a classified document and was not discussed by Parliament.

The Armed Forces have continued to exercise significant political influence. Senior members of the armed forces have expressed their opinion on domestic and foreign policy issues including Cyprus, secularism, the Kurdish issue, and on the indictment concerning the Semdinli bombing.

The Turkish Armed Forces Internal Service Law remains unchanged. This defines the role and duties of the Turkish military and contains articles granting the military a wide margin of manoeuvre. Similarly, as reported last year, Article 2a of the NSC Law provides a broad definition of national security. No measures have been taken to enhance civilian control over the gendarmerie. This is part of the army and operates under the General Staff as well as under the Ministry of Interior in terms of law-enforcement duties.

In March, a draft report of the Şemdinli Investigation Commission of Parliament revealed the existence of a secret protocol on Security, Public Order and Assistance Units (commonly called EMASYA). Signed by the General Staff and the Ministry of Interior in 1997, this protocol allows for military operations to be carried out for internal security matters under certain conditions without request from the civilian authorities. Under the protocol, the military can gather intelligence against internal threats.

Reforms in defence expenditures, adopted in previous years have started to be implemented. The budgetary appropriations of the National Intelligence Service, the National Security Council as well as the administrative budget of the under-secretariat in charge of the Defence Industry were all included in the 2006 state budget. However, most procurement projects are funded separately from extra-budgetary funds.

No further progress has been achieved in terms of strengthening parliamentary overseeing of the military budget and expenditures. The Parliamentary Planning and Budget Committee reviews the military budget only in a general manner but does not examine programmes and projects. Furthermore, extra-budgetary funds are excluded from parliamentary scrutiny.

No internal audit of military property has yet taken place pending the adoption of secondary legislation to the Law on Public Financial and Management Control (PFMC). According to Article 160 of the Constitution, the Court of Auditors can carry out *ex post* audit of defence expenditures. However, the Court remains unable to carry out its tasks due to the lack of the relevant implementing legislation.

Overall, limited progress has been made in aligning civil–military relations with EU practices. Statements by the military should concern only military, defence and security matters and should only be made under the authority of the government, while the civilian authorities should fully exercise their supervisory functions in particular as regards the formulation of the national security strategy and its implementation, including with regard to relations with neighbouring countries.

JUDICIAL SYSTEM

The authorities have been focusing on the implementation of the new Penal Code, the Code of Criminal Procedure and the Law on Enforcement of Sentences following the entry into force of these laws in 2005.

In this respect, the Ministry of Justice updated all existing circulars by issuing some one hundred new circulars mainly addressed to public prosecutors in January 2006. ...

Two circulars were issued by the Ministries of Interior and Justice in November 2005 and January 2006, respectively, to clarify the interaction between prosecutors and the judicial police.

Courts have continued to apply the European Convention on Human Rights (ECHR).

\*\*\*

However, a number of issues remain to be addressed. Certain provisions of the Penal Code, in particular Article 301, have been used to restrict the expression of non-violent opinions.

A number of cases have shown inconsistency in the judiciary approach to the interpretation of legislation.

As regards the implementation of the new Code of Criminal Procedure, the establishment of the judicial police has led to some tensions between the law enforcement bodies and prosecutors. Despite the Ministries of Interior and Justice issuing two circulars, prosecutors report difficulties in effective supervision of the judicial police. With regard to the independence of the judiciary, various provisions of the Turkish Constitution and of domestic law guarantee this principle. However, a number of factors are perceived as undermining it. ...

Questions were raised on the independence of the High Council of Judges and Prosecutors in the aftermath of the publication in March 2006 of the indictment on the Semdlinli bombing, which included accusations against the Land Forces Commander and other high-ranking military commanders. The General Staff criticised the indictment in a press statement and urged those bearing constitutional responsibility to take action. In April, the High Council of Judges and Prosecutors reviewed charges against the prosecutor and applied the highest disciplinary sanction, i.e. dismissal from office. The final review by the High Council on this matter is scheduled for November.

Overall, there was continued progress in the area of judicial reform. However, implementation of the new legislation by the judiciary presents a mixed picture so far and the independence of the judiciary still needs to be further established.

\*\*\*

*2.2. Human rights and the protection of minorities*

OBSERVANCE OF INTERNATIONAL HUMAN RIGHTS LAW

Concerning the *ratification of Human Rights instruments*, the Second Optional Protocol to the International Covenant on Civil and Political Rights (ICCPR) on the abolishment of the death penalty was ratified in March 2006. Protocol no. 13 of the ECHR, on the abolishment of the death penalty at all times, was ratified in February 2006. Protocol no. 14 of the ECHR, amending the control system of the Convention, entered into force in May 2006. The UN Convention against corruption entered into force in June 2006.

Turkey ratified the revised European Social Charter on 27 September 2006. The European Social Charter was accepted with reservations on Article 5 (right to organise) and Article 6 (right to bargain collectively) as well as on paragraph 3 of Article 2 (minimum annual holidays) and paragraph 1 of Article 4 (remuneration and decent standard of living). Turkey has lifted previous reservations on the European Social Charter's provisions, namely the right of children and young persons to protection and the right of disabled persons.

Four Additional Protocols to the ECHR remain to be ratified, including Protocol no. 12 on the general prohibition of discrimination by public authorities, signed in 2001. The First Optional Protocol to the ICCPR, signed in 2004, and the Optional Protocol to the UN Convention against Torture (OPCAT), signed in September 2005, also awaits ratification. Ratification of these protocols is a priority in the Accession Partnership.

During the first eight months of the year 2006, the European Court of Human Rights (ECtHR) delivered 196 final judgments finding that Turkey had violated at least one article of the ECHR. In five cases the ECtHR ruled that there was no violation of the ECHR. Most of these judgments refer to cases lodged prior to 1999.

From 1 September 2005 until 31 August 2006 2,100 new applications regarding Turkey were made to the ECtHR. More than two-thirds of the applications introduced to the ECtHR refer to the right to a fair trial (Article 6) and protection of property rights (Article 1 of Protocol no. 1). The right to life (Article 2) and the prohibition of torture (Article 3) are referred to in seventy-eight and 142 cases respectively.

In relation to the situation in the southeast, the ECtHR found in the *Icyer v. Turkey* case that the Law on Compensation and Losses Resulting from Terrorist Acts provides adequate redress to the extent that it is undisputed that the applicant could today return freely to his village. Approximately 1,500 cases relating to the possibility to return to villages have been declared inadmissible by the Court following this decision.

The reforms undertaken by Turkey in 2004 and 2005 have had positive consequences on the execution of judgments of the ECtHR. However, Turkish cases still represent 14.4 per cent of the cases pending before the Committee of Ministers for execution control.

Restrictions in Turkish legislation prevent the re-opening of domestic proceedings following a violation found by the ECtHR under certain circumstances. This prevents the execution of the ECtHR judgment in the *Hulki Gunes* case, as well as in 113 cases related to fairness of proceedings before the former state security courts.

As regards the Ocalan case, the Court left the question of the reopening largely to the evaluation of domestic authorities under the Committee of Ministers' supervision. In July an Istanbul Court rejected the request for a retrial of Abdullah Ocalan. The Committee of Ministers will evaluate the reasons given by the Istanbul Court for rejecting the appeal at one of its upcoming meetings.

Other pending cases before the Committee of Ministers awaiting the adoption of necessary execution measures relate to the control of actions of security forces and effective remedies against abuses (ninety-three pending cases). These cases refer mainly to violations that took place against the background of the fight against terrorism in the first half of the 1990s, but some concern events in the course of normal police activity. A number of positive legal reforms have been adopted since the judgments were issued. The Committee is now closely monitoring their implementation.

Furthermore, 115 cases related to freedom of expression are pending before the Committee of Ministers for execution control. These cases mainly relate to articles of the old Turkish Penal Code which were amended in 2004. Some relate to the provisions of the Anti-Terror Law. Execution of these judgments will however be assessed by the Committee of Ministers in the light of case law of Turkish courts, as well as the practice of prosecutions.

\*\*\*

With regard to the *promotion and enforcement of Human Rights*, the Human Rights Presidency and the 931 District Human Right Boards continued to provide training on Human Rights and process applications on alleged human right violations. Between January and June 2006, 778 applications were received. The vast majority of applications related to health and patients' rights, non-discrimination, right to property, and social security rights.

However, the Human Rights Presidency lacks independence from the government, is understaffed and has a limited budget. Furthermore, a new president has not been appointed since the resignation of the previous one in September 2005. The Human Rights Advisory Board under the Office of the Prime Minister has not been operating since the publication of a report on minority rights in Turkey in October 2004. This is a body composed of NGOs [non-governmental organisations], experts and representatives from ministries.

The Parliamentary Human Rights Committee continued to play an active role in collecting complaints on Human Rights violations and conducting fact-finding visits to the regions. The Committee received 864 applications between October 2005 and June 2006. It has conducted several investigations and finalised three reports since January 2006. The Committee has no legislative role, and is thus not consulted on legislation affecting Human Rights.

Overall, Turkey has made progress on the ratification of international Human Rights instruments and in the execution of ECtHR judgments. However, there is a need to further upgrade the Human Rights institutional framework.

CIVIL AND POLITICAL RIGHTS

With regard to *torture and ill-treatment*, a comprehensive legislative framework is in place. The downward trend has continued in the number of cases of torture and ill-treatment.

The reforms in detention procedures and detention periods have shown positive results on the ground. The regulation concerning the system for the medical examination of persons in police or gendarmerie custody complies with previous recommendations from the Committee on the Prevention of Torture.

However, implementing the legislative reforms undertaken in previous years remains a challenge. Cases of torture and ill-treatment are still being reported, in particular outside detention centres.

With respect to some provisions of the Code of Criminal Procedures and of the Law on Execution of Sentences, the notification of a relative of the detained person and the right to access a lawyer are not uniformly applied. Furthermore, while the Code introduced provisions against the use of statements obtained under torture, concerns remain on statements obtained prior to the enactment of the Code.

Concerns remain with regard to the confidentiality and quality of medical examinations. ...

The Human Rights situation in the southeast raises particular concerns following the violent disturbances that took place in several cities in March and April. Over 550 people were detained as a result of these events, including over 200 children. The Diyarbakir Bar Association submitted more than seventy complaints of ill-treatment to the authorities. Subsequently, investigations were launched into thirty-nine of these claims.

During the events in Diyarbakir, forensic examinations of detainees were carried out in places of detention. This contravenes the rules and the circulars issued by the Ministries of Justice and Health as well as the independence of the medical profession.

The new provisions introduced in June 2006 to amend the Anti-Terror Law could undermine the fight against torture and ill-treatment.

Despite an increase in the number of convictions since 2003, the fight against impunity remains an area of concern.

Overall, the Turkish legal framework includes a comprehensive set of safeguards against torture and ill-treatment. Cases of torture and ill-treatment declined over the reporting period. However, concerns remain regarding cases outside detention centres, Human Rights violations in the southeast and the problem of impunity.

With regard to *access to justice* and right of defence, detainees enjoy the right to legal counsel, and statements made in the absence of lawyers are not admissible as evidence in court under the new Code of Criminal Procedure. However, concerns remain with regard to the lack of review of past statements.

A considerable increase in the appointment of legal aid lawyers has been registered since the new Code of Criminal Procedure entered into force. With regard to the *prison system*, Turkey has adopted regulations to implement the 2004 legislative reforms in this area.

\*\*\*

With regard to *freedom of expression (including the media)*, the Ministry of Justice issued a circular in January 2006, regarding cases of freedom of expression in written and visual media. It instructed prosecutors to take into consideration both Turkish legislation and the ECHR. The circular also established a monthly monitoring mechanism of criminal investigations and court cases against the press and media.

Some progress can be reported in the area of broadcasts in languages other than Turkish at local and regional level.

However, the prosecutions and convictions for the expression of non-violent opinion under certain provisions of the new Penal Code are a cause for serious concern and may contribute to create a climate of self-censorship in the country. This is particularly the case for Article 301 which penalises insulting Turkishness, the Republic as well as the organs and institutions of the State. Although this article includes a provision that expression of thought intended to criticise should not constitute a crime, it has repeatedly been used to prosecute non violent opinions expressed by journalists, writers, publishers, academics and Human Rights activists.

In July, the General Assemblies of the Civil and Penal Chambers of the Court of Cassation established restrictive jurisprudence on Article 301. The Court confirmed a six-month suspended prison sentence for journalist Hrant Dink. This was on the basis of Article 301 of the new Penal Code for insulting "Turkishness" in a series of articles he wrote on Armenian identity.

Against this background, Article 301 needs to be brought into line with the relevant European standards. The same applies to other provisions of the Penal Code which have been used to prosecute the non-violent expression of opinions and may limit freedom of expression. The potential impact of the Anti-Terror Law on freedom of expression raises concerns.

Recent decisions taken by the government in relation to the appointment procedure of the members of the High Audiovisual Board (RTUK) are a cause for concern to the extent that they weaken the independence of the media regulatory body.

Overall, open debate has increased in recent years in Turkish society on a wide range of issues. Notwithstanding this trend, *freedom of expression* in line with European standards is not yet guaranteed by the present legal framework.

As regards *freedom of assembly*, public demonstrations are subject to fewer restrictions than in the past. However, in some cases security forces used excessive force, especially when the demonstrations were carried out without permission.

The administrative investigations have been finalised into the incidents during a demonstration promoting women's rights in March 2005. [Three members of the Istanbul Directorate of Security have been punished with a reprimand and six staff members have been punished with a salary deduction.] ...

Concerning *freedom of association*, the legal framework is generally in line with international standards. The impact on the ground of the legislative reforms concerning associations has been positive, in particular the adoption of a Law on Associations in November 2004.

However, the requirement to notify the authorities in case of receipt of finances from abroad results in difficulties and cumbersome procedures for NGOs. Furthermore, unlike associations, foundations still need permission before applying for projects outside Turkey and funded by international organisations.

Some difficulties related to the registration of associations remain. ... In April 2006, a Kurdish association was ordered to close by a Court in Diyarbakır on the grounds that its statute included the objectives of setting up a Kurdish archive, museum and library and that its activities would be carried out also in the Kurdish language ...

As regards political parties, court cases against several parties, including DEHAP and HAK-PAR, are still ongoing. There has been no progress regarding aligning the Turkish Law on Political Parties with EU practice. Parties are not allowed to use languages other than Turkish. The Law on Political Parties needs to be amended to ensure that political parties are permitted to operate in line with the standards established by the ECHR and the case law of the ECtHR.

As concerns *civil society organisations*, the recent reform environment has led to positive developments. Civil society organisations have become relatively more vocal and better organised, especially since the adoption of the new Law on Associations. There is an increasing variety of organisations in Turkey including approximately 80,000 registered associations, and several hundred unions and chambers (including vocational and professional associations).

As concerns *freedom of religion*, freedom of worship continues to be generally respected. ...

[Generally, freedom of worship continues to be respected. However, no progress can be reported with regard to difficulties encountered by non-Muslim religious communities on the ground. Furthermore, the Alevis continue to face discriminatory practices and the impact of the new Law on Foundations will have to be assessed after its adoption.]

ECONOMIC AND SOCIAL RIGHTS

[Women's rights, children's rights, rights of disabled people, and trades unions' rights.]

MINORITY RIGHTS, CULTURAL RIGHTS AND PROTECTION OF MINORITIES

Turkey's approach to minority rights remains unchanged. ...

The February 2005 visit of the OSCE [Organization for Security and Cooperation in Europe] High Commissioner on National Minorities (HCNM) to Ankara has not been followed up and no progress has been made in starting a dialogue on the situation of national minorities in Turkey. The deepening of such a dialogue between Turkey and the HCNM is necessary. It needs to include relevant areas such as minority education, minority languages, the participation of minorities in public life and broadcasting in minority languages. This would facilitate Turkey's further alignment with international standards and best practice in EU Member States to ensure cultural diversity and to promote respect for and protection of minorities.

Turkey's reservation towards the UN Covenant on Civil and Political Rights (ICCPR), regarding the rights of minorities — to which a number of EU Member States objected as being incompatible with the object and purpose of this Covenant — and its reservation to the UN Covenant on Economic, Social and Cultural Rights (ICESCR), regarding the right to education, are of concern.

Turkey has not signed the Council of Europe Framework Convention for the Protection of National Minorities or the European Charter for Regional or Minority Languages.

There has been limited progress as concerns education. The 2005 recommendations of the European Commission against Racism and Intolerance (ECRI) on school curricula and textbooks as well as on the functioning of minority schools remain valid. Further efforts are needed to remove discriminatory language from textbooks. The management of the minority schools including the dual presidency remains an issue.

[Syriacs and the Greek minority]

As regards *cultural rights*, permission was granted to two local TV channels in Diyarbakir and to one radio in Sanliurfa to broadcast in Kurdish. However, time restrictions apply, with the exception of films and music programmes. All broadcasts, except songs, must be subtitled or translated in Turkish, which makes live broadcasts technically cumbersome. Educational programmes teaching the Kurdish language are not allowed.

The Turkish Public Television (TRT) has continued broadcasting in five languages including Kurdish. However, the duration and scope of TRT's national broadcasts in five languages is very limited. No private broadcaster at national level has applied for broadcasting in languages other than Turkish since the enactment of the 2004 legislation.

Children whose mother tongue is not Turkish cannot learn their mother tongue in the Turkish public schooling system. Such education can be made only by private education institutions. As concerns Kurdish all such courses were closed down in 2004. Therefore, there are no possibilities to learn Kurdish today in the public or private schooling system. Furthermore, there are no measures taken to facilitate access to public services for those who do not speak Turkish.

As reported above, according to the Law on Political Parties, the use of languages other than Turkish is illegal in political life. The court case against the Rights and Freedoms Party (HAK-PAR) regarding a speech in Kurdish continues.

As regards the *situation in the east and southeast*, progress has been made with regard to the compensation of losses resulting from terrorist acts. The ECtHR ruled that the compensation law allowed for the provision of adequate redress for persons who were denied access to their possessions in their place of residence.

The process of compensation is ongoing. The Damage Assessment Commissions established to process the compensation claims have so far received around 215,981 applications. Approximately 33,299 have been processed as of September 2006.

The situation in the southeast has deteriorated since the resumption of violence by the PKK, which is on the EU list of terrorist organisations. During the period between November 2005 and June 2006, there were 774 terrorist attacks reported, which led to forty-four military, five police and thirteen civilian casualties.

In the aftermath of the funerals of some PKK terrorists at the end of March, riots took place in Diyarbakir and spread to other cities in the region. Demonstrators attacked the police, civilian residents and shops. Ten civilians were killed during clashes with the police and security forces, including three children. Many civilians suffered bullet wounds. There are widespread reports of excessive and arbitrary use of force by the security forces, even against ambulances. Investigations are ongoing to determine the causes of these deaths.

The violence triggered by the March riots had a negative impact on the Human Rights situation. Over 700 people were detained and cases of ill-treatment were reported.

A number of security measures have been reinstated as a response to the escalation of terrorism, such as road blocks and checkpoints in some provinces of the southeast. On the legislative side, amendments to the Anti-Terror Law were adopted in June 2006.

The November 2005 Semdinli bombing, which killed one person and injured others, also had a negative impact on the situation in the region. A court in Van imposed heavy prison sanctions on two gendarmerie officers and a former PKK member reported to work as a gendarmerie informer who were found responsible for the bombing. A Parliamentary Committee was established in November 2005 to investigate the Semdinli events. The Committee has not published its report.

The overall socio-economic situation in the southeast remains difficult and there is no comprehensive plan to address this issue. The positive statement of Prime Minister Erdogan in 2005 stressing the need to resolve through democratic means what he called "the Kurdish issue" was not followed up. There is almost no dialogue between the authorities and locally elected politicians. Furthermore, many locally elected politicians face court cases. Moreover, the 10 per cent threshold under the electoral law makes it difficult for all but the nation-wide largest parties to be represented in Parliament.

In spite of the ECtHR ruling in the *Icyer v. Turkey* case of January 2006, the implementation of the Law on Compensation of Losses Resulting from Terrorist Acts raises several concerns. Overall, there seems to be divergences in the methods used by the compensation commissions. They have large discretionary powers and procedures are often cumbersome. As a result, the payment of the amounts due is slow. There are concerns about the level of compensation.

Furthermore, the conditions attached to the eligibility for compensation could leave a large number of potential beneficiaries outside the scope of the Law. There is also a heavy burden of proof on applicants to provide documentation, including property titles, which in many cases have never existed.

The issue of "reconciliation" is not addressed in the compensation approach in relation to past Human Rights violations committed against internally displaced persons — such as the burning and destruction of property, killings, disappearances and torture.

The situation of *internally displaced persons (IDPs)* remains an issue of concern. There has been no further progress on the establishment of a new governmental body responsible for implementing the "Return to village and rehabilitation programme" and to developing policy on IDP return. A study on IDPs carried out by the Haceteppe University should provide a thorough analysis and policy guidance; however, its publication has been delayed.

Several factors affect negatively the return of IDPs: the absence of basic infrastructure, the lack of capital, limited employment opportunities and the security situation. In particular, large numbers of landmines constitute a strong disincentive to return. Moreover, the discretion of the governor plays a crucial role in the implementation of the legal and administrative provisions regulating return.

No progress has been made in addressing the problem of village guards. No action was taken to phase them out.

A return to normality in the southeast can be achieved only by opening a dialogue with local counterparts. A comprehensive strategy should be pursued, to achieve the socio-economic development of the region and the establishment of conditions for the Kurdish population to enjoy full rights and freedoms. Issues that need to be addressed include the return of internally displaced persons, compensation for losses incurred by victims of terrorism, landmines as well as the issue of village guards.

[Roma]

*2.3. Regional issues and international obligations*

[Cyprus, peaceful settlement of border disputes]

## 3. Economic criteria

\*\*\*

[While Turkish markets have certain features which distort the functioning of markets, as a result of structural reforms and the process of macro-economic stabilisation, the functioning of market forces continued to improve.]

## 4. Ability to assume the obligations of membership

\*\*\*

*4.10. Chapter 10: Information society and media*

\*\*\*

Despite progress made in terms of legislation and the entry into force of the new Penal Code, freedom of expression is not yet guaranteed by the current legal framework. Defamation is a criminal offence carrying prison sentences. In addition, the new Anti-Terror Law, recently adopted by the Parliament, expands the scope of crimes punishable as terrorist acts and includes restrictions on the news media. So far, the circulars issued by the Minister of Justice to the judiciary failed to ensure application of the provisions of the Penal Code in accordance with European standards.

\*\*\*

As regards access to radio/TV broadcasting, progress was achieved on broadcasts in languages other than Turkish at local and regional level. However, in accordance with the regulation on TV and radio broadcasting in other languages and dialects used by Turkish citizens (2004), TV broadcasts remain limited to forty-five minutes per day, four hours a week. Radio broadcasts are limited to sixty minutes per day, five hours per week. The Radio and Television Higher Council (RTUK) decided in May 2006 to lift these restrictions as far as music and cinematographic works are concerned. However, as this decision was not officially communicated to broadcasters, they refrained from exceeding the previous limitations for fear of sanctions. News and current events continue to be subject to time limitations. Live broadcasts are not banned, but rendered very difficult in practice by the requirement for subtitles or consecutive translation of all programmes. Broadcasts cannot be educational programmes teaching the Kurdish language or directed at children, and have to be accompanied by Turkish subtitles. An appeal against this regulation is pending. Out of twelve applications, three media outlets received authorisations and started broadcasting in Kurdish dialects.

On the national level, the Public Turkish Radio and Television Corporation (TRT) is broadcasting in Bosnian, Arabic, Circassian, Kirmanji and Zaza. However, these emissions are limited to five days a week, thirty to thirty-five minutes daily and only cover news, sports, music and documentaries, and not, for example, children's programmes.

\*\*\*

### 4.23. Chapter 23: *Judiciary and fundamental rights*

With regard to the *independence of the judiciary*, various provisions of the Turkish Constitution and of domestic law guarantee this principle. However, a number of factors are perceived as undermining it. Judges and public prosecutors are attached to the Ministry of Justice as far as their administrative functions are concerned. The High Council of Judges and Prosecutors, the supreme governing body of the judiciary, does not have its own secretariat and budget. Its premises are still inside the Ministry of Justice building. The judicial inspectors, who are responsible for evaluating the performance of judges and prosecutors, are attached to the Ministry rather than to the High Council. The Minister and the Undersecretary of the Ministry of Justice are two of the seven members of the Council with voting rights. The remaining five are appointed among judges of the Court of Cassation and the Council of State. This composition does not seem to be representative of the judiciary as a whole and, together with the other issues listed above, may create the potential for the executive to influence decisions relating to the careers of judges in Turkey. ...

On 26 June 2006, 501 judges and prosecutors established an *association* called the "Union of Judges and Prosecutors" (YARSAV) [to safeguard judicial independence, impartiality and security of tenure as well as professional rules and ethics].

\*\*\*

In relation to the *professionalism and competence of the judiciary*, the Ministry of Justice and the Justice Academy continued to provide extensive *training* on the new Penal Code and the Code of Criminal Procedure, on prevention of torture and ill-treatment, freedom of expression and effectiveness of the judicial process. Training continued to be provided on foreign languages and on EU and Human Rights law. In this respect, opportunities were given to a number of judges and prosecutors to benefit from periods of training abroad. However, the Judicial Academy should further develop into a strong and independent training provider for the entire magistracy, including at regional level.

Continued progress can be reported on the *efficiency of the judiciary*. As regards implementing measures, in January 2006 the Ministry of Justice updated all existing circulars through the issuing of some one hundred new ones mainly targeting public prosecutors. The move aimed at creating a clearer and more concise framework for the implementation in particular of the New Code of Criminal Procedure and the Law on the Enforcement of Sentences.

\*\*\*

As regards *fundamental rights*, legislative progress is limited. However, implementation of reforms continued. The adoption of the law for the establishment of an *Ombudsman* is a welcome development, in so far as this new institution is expected to contribute to the transparency and accountability of public sector activities.

There were no developments as regards the *institutions* in charge of monitoring and promoting Human Rights, such as the Human Rights Presidency.

With respect to the *right to life* and, in particular, *the abolition of the death penalty*, Turkey ratified, in March 2006, the Second Optional Protocol to the International Covenant on Civil and Political Rights (ICCPR), which aims to abolish the death penalty. Protocol no. 13 to the ECHR, which abolishes the death penalty at all times, was ratified in February 2006. Turkey abolished the death penalty in its national legislation, in all circumstances, in 2004.

As regards *torture and inhuman or degrading treatment or punishment*, the implementation of the legislative framework has continued. Reports of torture and ill-treatment have diminished compared with the previous year. However, cases are still reported outside detention centres. Further, Human Rights violations in the southeast and the problem of impunity remain of concern. The First Optional Protocol to the ICCPR, signed in 2004, and the Optional Protocol to the UN Convention against Torture (OPCAT), signed in September 2005, still await ratification.

[Protection of personal data and freedom of thought, conscience and religion]

In general, open debate has increased in Turkish society. However, certain provisions of the new Penal Code leave a significant margin of interpretation for the judiciary. In particular, the restrictive interpretation of Article 301 led to prosecutions and convictions of people for the expression of non-violent opinion.

Regarding the *freedom of assembly and association*, the trend of diminishing restrictions on civil society has continued. However, there have been reports that security forces have made excessive use of force during demonstrations. Furthermore, there are still some obstacles as regards the establishment of associations representing particular religious or cultural interests.

[Right to education; right to property; anti-discrimination; gender equality and women's rights; and the rights of the child]

[As regards *the right to an effective remedy and to a fair trial*, the average criminal trial period and the duration of civil proceedings increased. The number of cases before the criminal courts remained stable and the pending cases before the civil courts slightly increased.]

Detainees enjoy the right to *legal aid* and statements made in the absence of lawyers are not admissible as evidence in court under the new Code of Criminal Procedure. However, restrictions have been introduced through the new Anti-Terror Law with regard to access to legal aid: access to a lawyer may be denied during the first twenty-four hours of detention. Concerns remain, also, with regard to the lack of review of past cases, where statements were originally made without the presence of legal counsel and where defendants alleged that their testimony had been extracted through torture.

With regard to the right of *defence*, a considerable increase was registered in the appointment of lawyers for free legal aid since the entry into force of the new Code of Criminal Procedure. However, the state fees to lawyers are low. This raises concerns on the quality of legal aid provided. In addition, the Union of Bars and the Ministry of Justice agreed on introducing legislative amendments to limit the scope of legal aid. This would reduce the number of suspects and detainees automatically qualifying for legal aid.

Following the strengthened provisions in the new Code of Criminal Procedure regarding *interpreters* free of charge for legal interpretation between Turkish and languages used by non-Turkish speaking citizens, courts are now required to establish lists of expert witnesses, including interpreters.

Difficulties are reported in the implementation of the principle of *cross-examination*. Efforts are required to provide specific training to both lawyers and judges and to allocate sufficient time to hearings. The capacity to handle the workload of the courts is stretched.

Turkey's approach towards *minority rights* has remained unchanged. There was no progress to further align Turkish practices with international and EU standards.

## Conclusion

As regards the *judiciary*, progress has continued in the implementation of the legislation adopted previously. However, there remain challenges to ensure that the judicial system functions in an independent, impartial and effective manner. Concerns remain regarding the perception of the independence of the judiciary, in particular the influence exerted by state bodies. Efforts are also needed to ensure equality of arms between prosecution and defence before courts.

\*\*\*

As regards *fundamental rights*, limited legislative progress was made, while implementation of reforms of previous years continued. Turkey needs to significantly improve the situation of fundamental rights in a number of areas and address the problems that minorities are facing.

## Editors' comment regarding the European Commission 2005 Regular Report on Turkey's Progress Towards Accession[39]

In its 2005 Report, the European Commission focused on the assessment of the implementation of its previously recommended reforms in the 2004 report, and presented new initiatives for further action. In the 2005 Report, the Commission stated that relations between the EU and Turkey have improved and have resulted in the opening of accession negotiations on October 3, 2005, as planned. It noted that Turkey enacted certain legislation enhancing Human Rights and the functioning of the judiciary, and signed the Adaptation Protocol extending its existing Association Agreement with the EU to all new Member States, including the Republic of Cyprus.

The Report also mentioned a communication, adopted by the Commission in June 2005, on the civil society dialogue between the EU and Candidate Countries. Explaining the long-term objective of the dialogue as "to prepare civil society from the EU and candidate countries for future enlargement," the Report stated that the dialogue will have a special focus on Turkey, as the state of mutual understanding is particularly weak with that country and misconceptions and concerns are more widespread.

After the summarized preliminary statement of the relations, the Report proceeded to discuss Turkey's ability to fulfill the criteria for membership.

Under *enhanced political dialogue and political criteria*, the Report in conclusion stated:

"Political transition is ongoing in Turkey and the country continues to sufficiently fulfil the Copenhagen political criteria. Important legislative reforms have now entered into force and should lead to structural changes in the legal system, particularly in the judiciary. However, the pace of change has slowed in 2005 and implementation of the reforms remains uneven. Although Human Rights violations are diminishing, they continue to occur and there is an urgent need both to implement legislation already in force and, with respect to certain areas, to take further legislative initiatives. Significant further efforts are required as regards fundamental freedoms and Human Rights, particularly freedom of expression, women's rights, religious freedoms, trades union rights, cultural rights and the further strengthening of the fight against torture and ill-treatment. In particular, Turkey should integrate better the reform process into the work of all public authorities. Turkey's commitment to further political reforms should be translated into more concrete achievements for the benefit of all Turkish citizens regardless of their origin.

As regards *democracy and the rule of law*, important structural reforms have been put in place, particularly in the area of the functioning of the judiciary. The six pieces of legislation mentioned in the Commission's 2004 recommendation entered into force. However, implementation on the ground remains uneven. On the one hand, several judgments suggest that the judiciary is increasingly acting in accordance with the case law of the European Court of Human Rights. On the other hand, there have been a number of decisions, in particular in relation to the expression of opinions on traditionally sensitive subjects, which have led to both prosecutions and convictions. Reforms concerning civil–military relations have continued, but the armed forces still exert significant influence by issuing public statements on political developments and government policies.

Concerning the *protection of Human Rights and minorities*, despite some progress, the picture remains mixed. As regards the *fight against torture and ill-treatment* further provisions have entered into force, adding to the comprehensive legislative framework already in place, and the incidence of such practice is diminishing. Nevertheless, reports of torture and ill-treatment remain frequent and those perpetrating such crimes still often enjoy impunity.

Legislative progress has been achieved with regard to the *exercise of fundamental freedoms*, notably through the entry into force of a new Penal Code and a new Law on Associations, and in practice both individuals and civil society organisations enjoy greater freedom than in the past. Nevertheless, individuals continue to be prosecuted and convicted for the expression of non-violent opinion and certain associations continue to face constraints on their activities. In this context court proceedings based on Article 301 will be closely monitored.

There are still reports of the security forces using disproportionate force in the context of demonstrations. ...

Notwithstanding a greater tolerance for the use of languages other than Turkish, the exercise of cultural rights is still precarious. No local broadcasting in Kurdish has yet been authorised, Kurdish language courses have closed down and politicians continue to be convicted for using the Kurdish language in certain contexts. Turkey continues to adopt a restrictive approach to minorities and cultural rights.

Although there is a growing consensus on the need to address the economic, cultural and social development of the southeast, little concrete progress has been made and the security situation has worsened since the resumption of PKK violence. Internally displaced persons continue to face a number of difficulties."

The Report also mentioned *regional issues* (i.e. relations with Cyprus and Greece), *freedom of religion*, and *women's rights* in this section.

Under the *Economic criteria*, the Report stated that Turkey can be seen as a "functioning market economy, as long as it firmly maintains its recent stabilisation and reform achievements. Turkey should also be able to cope with competitive pressure and market forces within the Union in the medium term, provided that it firmly maintains its stabilisation policy and takes further decisive steps towards structural reforms. ***"

Under the heading *Ability to assume the obligations of membership*, the Report stated that "there has been some, though uneven, progress since 2004."

# Notes

## 1 Turkey: country information

1 On January 21, 2008, the populations of Istanbul was released in a press conference by Deputy Prime Minister. The figure is based on Turkish Statistics Institute's census using the address-based population registry. See http://www.milliyet.com.tr/2008/01/21/son/-sontur31.asp?prm=0,5177896. However, many believe that Istanbul's real population, including its surroundings is over 15 million. Istanbul's population is estimated as 20 million by 2045 or 2050. http://www.worldbulletin.net/news_detail.php?id=17045.
2 http://www.cia.gov/cia/publications/factbook/geos/tu.html (last visited April 10, 2007).
3 *Human Development* Report at http://hdr.undp.org/hdr2006/statistics/ (last visited April 10, 2007). The Human Development Index is a comparative measure of life expectancy, literacy, education, and the standard of living (gross domestic product at purchasing power parity in US dollars) on a scale of 1.00 to 0.00.
4 Editors' note: All facts can be attributed to *The Library of Congress Report on Turkey* unless otherwise noted. Some parts of the text have been adopted from *The Library of Congress, Country Studies: Turkey* (1995), at http://lcweb2.loc.gov/frd/cs/trtoc.html (last visited March 2, 2005).
5 The 1924 Constitution vested sovereign power in the Grand National Assembly as representative of the people, to whom it also guaranteed basic civil rights. Under the new document, the assembly would be a unicameral body elected to a four-year term by universal suffrage. Its legislative authority would include responsibility for approving the budget, ratifying treaties, and declaring war. The president of the republic would be elected to a four-year term by the assembly; he in turn would appoint the prime minister, who was expected to enjoy the confidence of the assembly.
6 Minorities have been allowed to establish their own semi-autonomous communities where their language, traditions, religious practice, etc. were accepted and protected by the Ottoman sultanate.
7 A religious Islamic school.
8 Islamic law derived from the Qur'an, Hadith, and other texts.
9 *The Library of Congress, Country Studies: Turkey* (1995), at http://lcweb2.loc.gov/frd/cs/trtoc.html (last visited March 2, 2005).
10 Gunther, John. *Inside Europe Today.* Harper & Brothers: New York, 1961, p. 170.
11 *The Library of Congress, Country Studies: Turkey* (1995), at http://lcweb2.loc.gov/frd/cs/trtoc.html (last visited March 2, 2005).
12 *Political Structure of Turkey* at http://www.byegm.gov.tr/REFERENCES/Structure.htm (last visited April 10, 2007).
13 *The Library of Congress, Country Studies: Turkey* (1995), at http://lcweb2.loc.gov/frd/cs/trtoc.html (last visited March 2, 2005).
14 http://www.wsws.org/articles/2000/sep2000/turk-s27.shtml (last visited April 10, 2007).

15 It should be noted that, although many view their tactics as non-democratic, the Turkish military defines its duty as the preservation of Kemalism.
16 The president is appointed for a single seven-year term and has the power to appoint the prime minister. This individual is a member of parliament (traditionally the leader of the majority party) and must select his cabinet out of the remaining members of parliament.
17 *Background Note: Turkey* at http://www.state.gov/r/pa/ei/bgn/3432.htm (last visited April 10, 2007).
18 While some countries' parliaments accept that this event was genocide, Turkey has never accepted that it took place.
19 *Armenian Terrorism* at http://lcweb2.loc.gov/cgi-bin/query/r?frd/cstdy:@field(DOCID +tr0112) (last visited April 10, 2007).
20 *Armenian Terrorism — A Chronological List, 1973–86* at http://www.atmg.org/Armenian Terrorism.html (last visited April 10, 2007).
21 Controversially, Sezer had served previously as the Chief Justice of the Constitutional Court (*see* Chapter 15 for Sezer's role in recent legislative developments). http://www.cankaya.gov.tr/eng_html/sezer.htm (last visited April 10, 2007).

## 2  1980 Military coup, martial law and state of emergency, and a new constitution

1 Radio address: *Chairman of the Military Chiefs of Staff General Kenan Evren's Radio Address to the Nation on September 12, 1980* (translated by the editors), original available at http://www.ulkum.com/berka/olaylar/1980.htm (last visited May 10, 2005).
2 See *United Kingdom Home Office Country Information and Policy Unit, Country Assessment: Turkey (Apr. 2001)* at http://www.ecoi.net/pub/dh697/01377.html (last visited June 10, 2005).
3 Prepared by the editors. In preparation of the information, the following documents were used and they can be referred to for further information. For general information, see Necla Guney, *Country Report on Turkey*, at http://edoc.mpil.de/conference-on-terrorism/index.cfm. For information on the Special Warfare Office, see *Terörle Mücadele Ve Harekat Dairesi Başkanlığı* (Department of Action against Terrorism) at http://www.egm.gov.tr/temuh/kurulus.html.cfm (last visited August 5, 2005). For official assessments of Turkey's Laws against Terrorism delivered to the United Nations, see *Letter dated 3 September 2003 from the Chairman of the Security Council Established Pursuant to Resolution 1373 (2001) Concerning Counter-terrorism Addressed to the President of the Security Council*, S/2003/856 (September 3, 2003); *Letter dated 21 August 2002 from the Chairman of the Security Council Established Pursuant to Resolution 1373 (2001) Concerning Counter-terrorism Addressed to the President of the Security Council*, S/2002/948 (August 23, 2002); *Report to the Security Council Committee Established Pursuant to Resolution 1373 (2001), Measures Taken Against Terrorism by the Republic of Turkey*, S/2001/1304 (December 2001), available at http://www.un.org/Docs/sc/committees/1373/t.htm (last visited June 15, 2005).
4 *The Martial Law Act*, no. 1402, dated 13 May 1971 (unofficial translation available at http://www.law.qub.ac.uk/humanrts/emergency/turkey/tur5.htm (last modified April 10, 2005)). Dates of decrees and laws referred to in the document are added by the editors.
5 Republic of Turkey Ministry of Foreign Affairs, Turkish Constitutions, at http://www.mfa.gov.tr/MFA/DiplomaticArchives/Constitution (last updated July 29, 2004). For a critical analysis of Turkish constitutional development and the 1982 Constitution, see C.H. Dodd, "The development of Turkish democracy", *British Journal of Middle Eastern Studies*, 1992, January, 16–30; see also H. Tahsin Fendoglu, *Liberty and Turkish Constitutions*, at http://www.dicle.edu.tr/dictur/suryayin/khuka/fendoglu.htm.
6 See Dodd (op. cit., note 10); Fendoglu ((op. cit., note 10). Last visited July 24, 2007.)
7 As promulgated in 1982; available at http://www.hri.org/docs/turkey.
8 *The State of Emergency Law*, no. 2935, dated October 25, 1983 (unofficial translation available at http://www.law.qub.ac.uk/humanrts/emergency/turkey/tur4.htm (last visited June 10, 2005)).

## 3 Emergence of the PKK and Turkey's legal responses to terrorism

1 Republic of Turkey Ministry of Foreign Affairs, PKK/KONGRA-GEL, at http://www.mfa.gov.tr/MFA/ForeignPolicy/MainIssues/Terrorism/PKK_KONGRA_GEL.htm. For a more detailed analysis of the PKK, see Republic of Turkey Ministry of Foreign Affairs *A Report on the PKK and Terrorism*, available at www.ataa.org (last visited March 28, 2005). For the Kurdish view, *see* http://www.pkk.org/MALPER/ (PKK webpage).
2 *Resolution no. 38*, dated March 12, 1987; *Resolution no. 37*, dated March 12, 1987; *Decree Having the Force of Law no. 426*, dated May 18, 1990, available at http://www.law.qub.ac.uk/humanrts/_emergency/turkey/tur8.htm (last visited February 16, 2006). Please note that the resolutions and declarations have been provided as examples and do not represent the whole time-frame in which the state of emergencies have been declared. For a complete list, see Document no. 5 "Martial law and state of emergency in Turkey" in Chapter 2.
3 Originally attached to Turkey's Derogation Notice of August 1990, see Document no. 14.
4 *Letter by the Permanent Representation of Turkey to the Council of Europe* (August 6, 1990), available at http://www.law.qub.ac.uk/humanrts/emergency/turkey/tur9.htm (last visited July 23, 2005).
5 The provinces are Elazig, Bingol, Tunceli, Van, Diyarbakir, Mardin, Siirt, Hakkari, Batman, Sirnak.
6 *Decree having the Force Of Law no. 430*, dated December 16, 1990, (unofficial translation available at http://www.law.qub.ac.uk/humanrts/emergency/turkey/tur7.htm) (last visited July 23, 2005).
7 *Letter by the Permanent Representation of Turkey to the Council of Europe* (January 3, 1991) available at http://www.law.qub.ac.uk/humanrts/emergency/turkey/tur9.htm (last visited July 23, 2005).
8 *The Law to Fight Against Terrorism*, no. 3713, dated April 12, 1991(unofficial translation available at http://www.law.qub.ac.uk/humanrts/emergency/turkey/tur2.htm) (last visited July 23, 2005).
9 Translated excerpt from the Constitutional Court decision of March 3, 1992, in the case brought by the main opposition party to annul several provisions of the ATL *Anayasa Mahkemesi Karari* (Decision of the Constitutional Court), Decision No: 1992/20, dated March 3, 1992, available at (in Turkish) http://www.anayasa.gov.tr/KARARLAR/IPTALITIRAZ/K1992/K1992-20.htm (last visited July 23, 2005).
10 The ATL extensively refers to the Turkish Penal Code (TPC) in stating which crimes are terrorist crimes. The following section consists of the editors' explanatory notes of the mentioned laws in the ATL. For originals in Turkish, see *Turk Ceza Kanunu* (The Turkish Penal Code), no. 765, dated March 1, 1926, available at http://www.idealhukuk.com/index.asp (last visited July 23, 2005).
11 For further information on the State Security Courts see *Devlet Guvenlik Mahkemelerinin Kurulus ve Yargilama Usulleri Hakkinda Kanun* (Law on State Security Courts), Law no. 2845, June 18, 1983, available at http://www.idealhukuk.com/index.asp; see also Report of the Joseph R. Crowley Program/Lawyers Committee for Human Rights: Joint 1998 Mission to Turkey, *Justice on Trial: State Security Courts, Police Impunity, and the Intimidation of Human Rights Defenders in Turkey*, 22 Fordham International Legal Journal 2129 (1999). For the full text of the Turkish Penal Code, see Turk Ceza Kanunu (The Turkish Penal Code), no. 765, dated March 1, 1926, available at http://www.idealhukuk.com/index.asp (last visited February 16, 2006).
12 *Letter by the Permanent Representation of Turkey to the Council of Europe* (May 12, 1992), available at http://www.law.qub.ac.uk/humanrts/emergency/turkey/tur9.htm (last visited August 5, 2005).
13 Unofficial translations of cited portions of laws available at http://www.hrw.org/reports/1999/turkey/turkey993-09.htm (last visited March 10, 2005).

## 4 European system of human rights and fundamental freedoms

1 In preparation of the "introductory comment," the following materials have been used: William Ridgway, Human Rights in the European Union (2002), available at http://www.stanford.edu/class/e297c/Human%20Rights%20in%20the%20European%20Union.htm (last visited July 23, 2005); Vaughne Miller, United Kingdom House of Commons, International Affairs and Defence Section, *Research Paper: Human Rights in the EU: the Charter of Fundamental Rights* (2000), available at http://www.parliament.uk/commons/lib/research/rp2000/rp00(hy}032.pdf (last visited July 23, 2005).
2 See Miller (op. cit., note 1, Chapter 11, pp. 6–8).
3 *The Council of Europe Convention for the Protection of Human Rights and Fundamental Freedoms* (November 4, 1950), available at http://conventions.coe.int (last visited July 23, 2005).
4 Chart of signatures and ratifications of the Convention for Protection of Human Rights and Fundamental Freedoms, available at http://conventions.coe.int (last visited July 23, 2005).
5 Editors' note based on European Court of Justice Rulings.
6 Case 29/69, Erich Stauder v. City of Ulm — Sozialamt, 1969 E.C.R. 419; available at http://www.curia.eu.int/en/content/juris/index.htm (last visited August 4, 2005).
7 Case 11/70, Internationale Handelsgesellschaft mbH v. Einfuhr-und Vorratsstelle für Getreide und Futtermittel, 1970 E.C.R. 1125; available at http://www.curia.eu.int/en/content/juris/index.htm (last visited August 4, 2005).
8 Case 4/73, J. Nold, Kohlen-und Baustoffgroßhandlung v. Commission of the European Communities, 1974 E.C.R. 491; available at http://www.curia.eu.int/en/content/juris/index.htm (last visited August 4, 2005).
9 Case 36/75, Roland Rutili v. Ministre de l'intérieur, 1975 E.C.R. 1219; available at http://www.curia.eu.int/en/content/juris/index.htm (last visited August 4, 2005).
10 List taken from *Protection of Fundamental Rights within the Union;* available at http://europa.eu.int/scadplus/leg/en/lvb/l33021.htm (last visited August 4, 2005).
11 See Miller (op. cit., note 1, Chapter 11, p. 11).
12 See Miller (op. cit., note 1, Chapter 11, p. 13).
13 See Miller (op. cit., note 1, Chapter 11, p. 12, n.20).
14 See Miller (op. cit., note 1, Chapter 11, pp. 12–13).

## 5 European community and human rights

1 OJ L 169, 29.6.1987; available at http://europa.eu.int/abc/obj/treaties/en/entr14a.htm (last visited August 4, 2005) (emphasis added).
2 Case 260/89, Elliniki Radiophonia Tiléorassi AE and Panellinia Omospondia Syllogon Prossopikou v. Dimotiki Etairia Pliroforissis and Sotirios Kouvelas and Nicolaos Avdellas and others, 1991 E.C.R. 260; available at http://www.curia.eu.int/en/content/juris/index.htm (last visited August 4, 2005).
3 Available at http://europa.eu.int/comm/external_relations/human_rights/doc (last visited June 15, 2005).
4 Available at http://europa.eu.int/comm/external_relations/human_rights/doc (last visited June 15, 2005).

## 6 European union and human rights

1 Signed in Maastricht on February 7, 1992; available at http://europa.eu.int/abc/obj/treaties/en/ entoc01.htm (last visited June 15, 2005).
2 Available at http://www.europa.eu.int/european_council/conclusions/index_en.htm. (emphasis added) (last visited June 15, 2005).
3 Available at http://europa.eu.int/comm/external_relations/human_rights/doc (last visited June 15, 2005).

4 Available at http://www.europa.eu.int/european_council/conclusions/index_en.htm (last visited June 15, 2005).
5 *Briefing No. 22 (9 October 1995)*; available at http://www.europarl.eu.int/igc1996/fiches/fiche22_en.htm (last visited June 15, 2005).
6 See CJEC, 14 May 1974, Nold; Case 4/73, ECR 491 CJEC, 28 October 1975, Rutili; Case 36/75, ECR 1219.
7 OJC 103, 27.4.1977.
8 Which reads as follows [sic]: "Determined to work together to promote democracy on the basis of fundamental rights recognised in the constitutions and laws of the Member States, in the Convention for the protection of Human Rights and fundamental Freedoms and the European Social Chapter, notably freedom, equality and social justice".
9 See D. Simon, commentary on Article F of the TEU, In: V. Constantinesco, R. Kovar and D. Simon, "Traite sur l'Union europeene, Commentaire article par article", p. 86, No 11.
10 Ibidem.
11 Institut für Europäische politik, J. Manar et R. Bieber, "Die Unionsbürgerschaft", June 1995, p. 106.
12 Ibidem.
13 D. Simon, op cit., p. 86, No. 11 (Chapter 6, note 9).
14 See paragraph 9.
15 See 1979 Memorandum, supplement 2/79 to the EC Bulletin; and a more recent initiative through its communication SEC (90) 2087 final - C3 - 0022/93.
16 Position expressed during the debate on the Bontempi Report.
17 SEC (95) 0731 final, p. 4.
18 No. 5082/95, 5 April 1995, p. 2.
19 Ibidem.
20 Ibidem.
21 Note on the positions of the Member States of the European Union with respect to the 1996 Intergovernmental Conference", Document by the task force on the IGC, European Parliament, DOC. EN/DV/272/272034, p. 12.
22 *Ibidem*.
23 *Ibidem*.
24 See Task force note, op. cit., p. 28.
25 *Ibidem*, p. 31.
26 *Ibidem*, p. 18.
27 According to the information contained in the only currently existing summary, i.e. the Task Force note quoted above. The document is dated 31 July 1995.
28 97/C 340/02; available at http://europa.eu.int/eur-lex/lex/en/treaties/treaties_founding.htm (last visited June 15, 2005).
29 In the appendix of the Treaty of Amsterdam, "Declaration on the abolition of the death penalty" was proclaimed. The declaration stated: "With reference to Article F(2) of the Treaty on European Union, the Conference recalls that Protocol No. 6 to the European Convention for the Protection of Human Rights and Fundamental Freedoms signed in Rome on 4 November 1950, and which has been signed and ratified by a large majority of Member States, provides for the abolition of the death penalty. In this context, the Conference notes the fact that since the signature of the abovementioned Protocol on 28 April 1983, the death penalty has been abolished in most of the Member States of the Union and has not been applied in any of them."
30 97/C 340/03; available at http://europa.eu.int/eur-lex/lex/en/treaties/treaties_founding.htm (last visited June 15, 2005).
31 Available at http://europa.eu.int/comm/external_relations/human_rights/doc/50th_decl_98.htm (last visited June 15, 2005).

## 7 Turkey–EU relations: 1963–94

1 From the webpage of *The Representation of the European Commission to Turkey*; available at http://www.deltur.cec.eu.int/english/eu-turkey.html (last visited March 10, 2005). The document has been edited to reflect changes in the relations.
2 O.J. (C 113) (1973), available at http://europa.eu.int/comm/enlargement/turkey/pdf/association_agreement_1964_en.pdf (last visited July 25, 2005).
3 Order reported in (1985) *Yearbook of the European Commission on Human Rights 151*, summary provided above; available at http://www.law.qub.ac.uk/humanrts/emergency/turkey/intro.htm (last visited March 15, 2005).
4 SEC (89) 2290 final/2, Brussels, 20 December 1989; available at http://www.deltur.cec.eu.int/english/opinion.html (last visited March 15, 2005).
5 Assembly debate on 30 June 1992 (tenth sitting) (see Doc. 6553, report of the Committee on Legal Affairs and Human Rights, Rapporteurs: Mrs Lentz-Cornette and Mrs Baarveld-Schlaman). Text adopted by the Assembly on 30 June 1992 (tenth sitting); available at http://insanhaklarimerkezi.bilgi.edu.tr/raporlar_avrupa/docs/985.doc (last visited July 14, 2005).
6 4 EJIL 119 (1993); available at http://www.ejil.org/journal/Vol4/No1/art12.pdf (last visited June 10, 2005).
7 Minutes of 29/09/1994, Eur. Parl. Doc. (B4-0111/94); available at http://www.europarl.eu.int/plenary/default_en.htm (last visited July 12, 2005).
8 Minutes of 15/12/1994, Eur. Parl. Doc. (B4-0515/94) (1994); available at http://www.europarl.eu.int/ (last visited July 12, 2005).

## 8 Customs Union decision and the first implications of the human rights problems

1 Minutes of 16/02/1995 meeting, Eur. Parl. Doc. (B4-0171/95); available at http://www.europarl.eu.int. (last visited May 15, 2005).
2 Minutes of 06/04/1995 meeting, Eur. Parl. Doc. (B4-0636/95); available at http://www.europarl.eu.int (last visited May 15, 2005).
3 Assembly debate on April 26, 1995 (thirteenth sitting) (see Doc. 7290, report of the Political Affairs Committee, rapporteur: Mr Bársony; and Doc. 7295, opinion of the Committee on Migration, Refugees and Demography, rapporteur: Mr Cucó). Text adopted by the Assembly on April 26, 1995 (thirteenth sitting); available at http://www.assembly.coe.int (last visited May 15, 2005).
4 1995 ECHR 20 App. No.: 16419/90 (June 8, 1995); available at http://www.echr.coe.int/ (last visited May 15, 2005).
5 19 Eur. Ct. H.R. (1995) App. No.: 16026/90 (8 June 1995); available at http://www.echr.coe.int/ (last visited May 15, 2005). For a more extensive summary of the case, see Netherlands Institute of Human Rights web page; available at http://sim.law.uu.nl.
6 Available at www.tbmm.gov.tr/anayasa/constitution.htm (last visited February 10, 2005).
7 Law No: 4126 of 27 October 1995. Translation of the law from PACE Report: *Turkey's Respect of Commitments to Constitutional and Legislative Reforms* [follow-up to Recommendation 1266 (1995)]. The grounds for the Article and Summary Analysis of the Amendment have been taken from the Ministry of Foreign Affairs (page no longer available on line).
8 Minutes of 15/11/1995, Eur. Parl. Doc. (B4-1419/95); available at http://www.europarl.eu.int/ (last visited May 15, 2005).
9 Minutes of 13/12/1995, Eur. Parl. Doc. (A4-0322/95); available at http://www.europarl.eu.int/ (last visited May 15, 2005).
10 Minutes of 13/12/1995 meeting, Eur. Parl. Doc. (B4-1559/95); available at http://www.europarl.eu.int/ (last visited May 15, 2005).

11 Available at http://europa.eu.int/comm/enlargement/turkey/docs.htm (last visited May 15, 2005).

## 9 After the customs union decision: problems persist

1 Follow-up to Document 45. See also Document 45 (in Chapter 8): Assembly debate on 25 April 1996 (fifteenth sitting) (see Doc. 7445, report of the Political Affairs Committee, rapporteur: Mr Bársony). Text adopted by the Assembly on 25 April 1996 (fifteenth sitting); available at http://assembly.coe.int (last visited May 20, 2005).
2 Minutes of June 20, 1996 — Final Edition; available at http://www.europarl.eu.int/plenary/default_en.htm (last visited June 2, 2005).
3 Minutes of 18/01/1996 — Final Edition; available at http://www.europarl.eu.int/plenary/default_en.htm (last visited June 2, 2005).
4 Minutes of September 19, 1996 — Final Edition; available at http://www.europarl.eu.int/plenary/default_en.htm (last visited June 2, 2005).
5 Minutes of October 24, 1996 — Final Edition; available at http://www.europarl.eu.int/plenary/default_en.htm (last visited June 2, 2005).
6 Minutes of December 12, 1996 — Final Edition; available at http://www.europarl.eu.int/plenary/default_en.htm (last visited June 2, 2005).
7 1996 ECtHR 68, Application no. 21987/93 (December 18, 1996); available at http://www.echr.coe.int/Eng/Judgments.htm. (last visited June 2, 2005).
8 1996 ECtHR 32, App. no. 19092/91 (August 7, 1996); available at http://www.echr.coe.int/Eng/Judgments.htm. For a summary of the case, see Netherlands Institute of Human Rights web page; available at http://sim.law.uu.nl (last visited June 2, 2005).
9 1996 ECtHR 13, App. no. 15530/89 (March 25, 1996); available at http://www.echr.coe.int/Eng/Judgments.htm. For a more extensive summary of the case, see Netherlands Institute of Human Rights web page; available at http://sim.law.uu.nl (last visited June 2, 2005).
10 1996 ECtHR 35, App. no. 21893/93 (September 16, 1996); available at http://www.echr.coe.int/Eng/Judgments.htm. For a more extensive summary of the case, see Netherlands Institute of Human Rights web page; available at http://sim.law.uu.nl (last visited June 2, 2005).
11 1997 ECtHR 37, App. no. 20704/92 (July 1, 1997); available at http://www.echr.coe.int/Eng/Judgments.htm (last visited June 16, 2005).
12 1997 ECtHR 85, App. no. 21890/93 (October 22, 1997); available at http://www.echr.coe.int/Eng/Judgments.htm (last visited June 16, 2005).
13 1997 ECtHR 79, App. no. 21592/93 (October 3, 1997); available at http://www.echr.coe.int/Eng/Judgments.htm (last visited June 16, 2005).
14 1997 ECtHR 45, App. no. 19263/92 (July 9, 1997); available at http://www.echr.coe.int/Eng/Judgments.htm (last visited June 16, 2005).
15 1997 ECtHR 75, App. no. 23178/94 (September 25, 1997); available at http://www.echr.coe.int/Eng/Judgments.htm (last visited June 16, 2005).
16 1997 ECtHR 94, App. no. 18954/91 (November 25, 1997); available at http://www.echr.coe.int/Eng/Judgments.htm (last visited June 16, 2005).
17 1997 ECtHR 95, App. no. 23878–83/94 (November 26, 1997); available at http://www.echr.coe.int/Eng/Judgments.htm (last visited June 16, 2005).
18 1997 ECtHR 97, App. no. 23186/94 (November 28, 1997); available at http://www.echr.coe.int/Eng/Judgments.htm (last visited June 16, 2005).
19 Unofficial translation available at http://www.hrw.org/reports/1997/turkey/Turkey-13.htm (last visited June 18, 2005).
20 Available at http://europa.eu.int/european_council/conclusions/index_en.htm (last visited June 19, 2005).
21 Mehmet Ugur. Testing times in EU–Turkey relations: the road to Copenhagen and beyond. *Journal of Southern Europe and the Balkans*, 2003, 5 (2), pp. 165–84; available at

http://www.gre.ac.uk/~M.Ugur/publications/testingtimes.doc (last visited June 24, 2005).
22 Available at http://europa.eu.int/european_council/conclusions/index_en.htm (last visited June 19, 2005).
23 1998 ECtHR 48, App. no. 22678/93 (June 9, 1998); available at http://www.echr.coe.int/Eng/Judgments.htm (last visited June 19, 2005).
24 Prepared by the editors.
25 Minutes of 17/09/1998 meeting — Final Edition; available at http://www.europarl.eu.int/plenary/default_en.htm (last visited June 2, 2005).
26 Minutes of 3 December 1998 – Final Edition; available at http://www.europarl.eu.int/plenary/default_en.htm (last visited June 2, 2005).

## 10 1999 Helsinki european council and european union membership perspective for Turkey

1 *Information Report Doc. 8300* 15 January 1999 Committee on the Honouring of Obligations and Commitments by Member States of the Council of Europe. Honouring of Obligations and Commitments by Turkey, Eur. Parl. Ass., Doc. no. 8300 (1999); available at http://assembly.coe.int/ (last visited July 5, 2005).
2 Press release, Registry of the European Court of Human Rights, *Judgment in Thirteen Cases against Turkey* (July 8, 1999); available at http://www.echr.coe.int/ (last visited July 6, 2005).
3 Available at http://europa.eu.int/comm/enlargement/turkey/docs.htm (last visited July 7, 2005).
4 Available at http://europa.eu.int/european_council/conclusions/index_en.htm (last visited July 10, 2005).

## 11 After Helsinki: initial developments — 2000

1 Resolution on the Death Sentence on Mr. Öcalan and the Future of the Kurdish Question in Turkey, 1999 O.J. (C 301) 32–34; available at http://europa.eu.int/eur-lex/pri/en/oj/dat/1999/c_301/ c_3011999101en 00320034.pdf (last visited July 25, 2005).
2 The European Parliament Briefing no. 7, *Turkey and Relations with the European Union* (10 February 2000); available at http://www.europarl.eu.int/enlargement/briefings/7a2_en.htm (last visited July 28, 2005).
3 *Kilic v. Turkey*, 2000 Eur. Ct. H.R. 127 (March 28, 2000).
4 Based on the information provided in US Department of State, Bureau of Democracy, Human Rights, and Labor, *Turkey: Country Report on Human Rights Practice 2000* (February 23, 2001); available at http://www.state.gov/g/drl/rls/hrrpt/2000/eur/844.htm (last visited July 28, 2005).
5 *Report on the 1999 Regular Report from the Commission on Turkey's Progress Towards Accession*, Eur. Parl. Doc. A5-0297/2000; available at http://www2.europarl.eu.int/omk/sipade2?PUBREF=-//EP//NONSGML+REPORT+A5-2000-0297+0+DOC+PDF+V0//EN&L=EN&LEVEL=3&NAV=S&LSTDOC=Y (last visited August 5, 2005).

## 12 Turkish reforms on civil rights begin — 2001

1 *Council Regulation (EC) no. 390/2001 of 26 February 2001 on Assistance to Turkey in the Framework of the Pre-accession Strategy, and in Particular on the Establishment of an Accession Partnership*, 2001 O.J. (L.58) 1; available at http://europa.eu.int/eur-lex/pri/en/oj/dat/2001/l_058/l_05820010228en00010002.pdf (last visited July 28, 2005).
2 *Council Decision of 8 March 2001 on the Principles, Priorities, Intermediate Objectives and Conditions Contained in the Accession Partnership with the Republic of Turkey*, 2001 O.J. (L 85) 13;

available at http://europa.eu.int/eur-lex/pri/en/oj/dat/2001/l_085/l_085200103 24en00130023.pdf (last visited July 25, 2005).

3 Available at http://europa.eu.int/comm/enlargement/turkey/pdf/npaa_full.pdf (last visited July 25, 2005).

4 *Law Amending the Constitution of Turkey*, No. 4709; available at http://www.turkishembassy.si/constitution.htm (last visited June 15, 2005).

5 Based on the information provided in US Department of State, Bureau of Democracy, Human Rights, and Labor, *Turkey: Country Report on Human Rights Practices 2001* (March 4, 2002); available at http://www.state.gov/g/drl/rls/hrrpt/2001/eur/8358.htm (last visited July 28, 2005).

6 Parliamentary Assembly Council of Europe, *Honouring of Obligations and Commitments by Turkey*, Doc. 9120 (13 June 2001); available at http://assembly.coe.int/Documents/WorkingDocs/doc01/EDOC9120.htm (last visited June 5, 2005).

7 For a full comparison, see Republic of Turkey Secretariat General for the European Union Affairs, *Studies Within the Framework of National Programme* (December 2001); available at http://www.euturkey.org.tr/abportal/category.asp?TreeID=160&VisitID={C87B542B-B479-4D08-9469-4A037085B94A}&Time=422 (last visited March 15, 2005).

8 See European Council Presidency Conclusions, *Gothenburg European Council, 15–16 June 2001*; available at http://ue.eu.int/ueDocs/cms_Data/docs/pressData/en/ec/00200-r1.en1.pdf (last visited June 15, 2005).

9 *Report to the Security Council Committee established pursuant to Resolution 1373 (2001): Measures taken against terrorism by the Republic of Turkey*, S/2001/1304 (December 2001); available at http://www.un.org/Docs/sc/committees/1373/t.htm (last visited June 15, 2005).

## 13 Turkey's progress on human rights: changes in anti-terrorism-related laws

1 *Law Amending Various Laws*, no. 4744, dated 6 February, 2002; available at http://www.euturkey.org.tr/abportal/category.asp?TreeID=246&VisitID={E59D9075-0630-48A4-8663-F8F60C11232B}&Time=4014 (follow link) (last visited August 5, 2005).

2 Parliamentary Assembly Council of Europe, *Implementation of Decisions of the European Court of Human Rights* (22 December 2001) (text adopted by the Assembly on 22 January 2002); available at http://assembly.coe.int/Documents/WorkingDocs/Doc01/EDOC9307.htm (last visited June 15, 2005).

3 The text of the general reasoning and reasoning of the articles are an integral part of the law.

4 *Law Amending Various Laws*, no. 4748, dated 8 April 2002; available at http://www.euturkey.org.tr/abportal/category.asp?TreeID=246&VisitID={E59D9075-0630-48A4-8663-F8F60C11232B}&Time=4014 (follow link) (last visited August 5, 2005). Analytical notes provided in brackets within the text are taken from the Republic of Turkey Ministry of Foreign Affairs, *Analytical Examination*; available at www.mfa.gov.tr/en/eu (follow link) (last visited August 5, 2005).

5 For the original and explanatory notes, see Council of Europe, *Guidelines on Human Rights and the Fight against Terrorism adopted by the Committee of Ministers on 11 July 2002 at the 804th meeting of the Ministers' Deputies*; available at www.coe.int/T/E/Human_rights/h-inf(2002)8eng.pdf (last visited July 25, 2005).

6 Based on the information provided in US Department of State, Bureau of Democracy, Human Rights, and Labor, *Turkey: Country Report on Human Rights Practices: 2000* (February 23, 2001); available at http://www.state.gov/g/drl/rls/hrrpt/2000/eur/844.htm (last visited July 25, 2005).

7 Parliamentary Assembly Council of Europe, *Implementation of Decisions of the European Court of Human Rights by Turkey*, Doc. 9537 (5 September 2002) (text adopted by the

Assembly on 23 September 2002); available at http://assembly.coe.int/Documents/WorkingDocs/doc02/EDOC9537.htm (last visited August 5, 2005).
8 *Law Amending Various Laws*, dated August 3, 2002; available at http://www.euturkey.org.tr/abportal/uploads/files/Package%20Analysis%20(06.08.2002).doc (last visited August 5, 2005).
9 See European Council Presidency Conclusions, *Seville European Council, 21–22 June 2002*, available at http://ue.eu.int/ueDocs/cms_Data/docs/pressData/en/ec/72638.pdf (last visited August 5, 2005); *Brussels European Council, 24–25 October 2002*, available at http://ue.eu.int/ueDocs/cms_Data/docs/pressData/en/ec/72968.pdf (last visited August 5, 2005).
10 Available at http://ue.eu.int/ueDocs/cms_Data/docs/pressData/en/ec/73842.pdf (last visited August 5, 2005).
11 *Law Amending Various Laws*, dated January 2, 2003; available at http://www.euturkey.org.tr/abportal/category.asp?TreeID=246&VisitID={E59D9075-0630-48A4-8663-F8F60C11232B}&Time=4014 (follow link) (last visited August 5, 2005). For an official topical analysis, see Turkey–EU Relations Directorate General, *Analysis of the 4th Harmonization Package* (January 2, 2003); available at http://www.euturkey.org.tr/abportal/category.asp?TreeID=246&VisitID={E59D9075-0630-48A4-8663-F8F60C11232B}&Time=4014 (follow link) (last visited August 5, 2005).
12 *Law Amending Various Laws*, no. 4793 (January 23, 2003); available at http://www.euturkey.org.tr/abportal/category.asp?TreeID=246&VisitID={E59D9075-0630-48A4-8663-F8F60C11232B}&Time=4014 (follow link) (last visited August 5, 2005). For an official topical analysis, see Turkey–EU Relations Directorate General, *Analysis of the 4th Harmonization Package* (January 2003); available at http://www.euturkey.org.tr/abportal/category.asp?TreeID=246&VisitID={E59D9075-0630-48A4-8663-F8F60C11232B}&Time=4014 (follow link) (last visited August 5, 2005).
13 Ocalan v. Turkey, 2003 Eur. Ct. H.R. 125 (March 12, 2003).
14 Summary of the case taken from European Court of Human Rights Press Service, *Chamber Judgment in the Case of Ocalan v. Turkey* (March 12, 2003); available at http://www.echr.coe.int/Eng/Press/2003/march/Ocalanjudgeng.htm (last visited June 15, 2005).
15 Parliamentary Assembly of the Council of Europe, *Implementation of Decisions of the European Court of Human Rights by Turkey*, Doc. 9537 (September 5, 2002); available at http://assembly.coe.int/Documents/WorkingDocs/doc02/EDOC9537.htm (last visited June 15, 2005)
16 *Reply from the Committee of Ministers of the Council of Europe adopted at the 833rd meeting of the Ministers' Deputies*, Doc. 9754 (March 26, 2003).
17 *EU–TR Association Council Decision of 19 May 2003 on the Principles, Priorities, Intermediate Objectives and Conditions Contained in the Accession Partnership with Turkey*, 2003 O.J. (L 145) 40 (June 12, 2003).
18 *Law Amending Various Laws*, No. 4928, dated July 15, 2003; available at http://www.euturkey.org.tr/abportal/category.asp?TreeID=246&VisitID={E59D9075-0630-48A4-8663-F8F60C11232B}&Time=4014 (follow link) (last visited August 5, 2005). For an official topical analysis, see Turkey–EU Relations Directorate General, *Analysis of the 6th Harmonization Package* (July 15, 2003); available at http://www.euturkey.org.tr/abportal/category.asp?TreeID=246&VisitID={E59D9075-0630-48A4-8663-F8F60C11232B}&Time=4014 (follow link) (last visited August 5, 2005).
19 *Decision of the Council of Ministers*, No. 2003/5930, dated June 23, 2003 *(published in the Official Gazette no. 25178, July 24, 2003)*; available at http://www.euturkey.org.tr/abportal/category.asp?TreeID=246&VisitID={E59D9075-0630-48A4-8663-F8F60C11232B}&Time=4014 (follow link) (last visited August 5, 2005).
20 *Law Amending Various Laws*, dated July 30, 2003; available at http://www.euturkey.org.tr/abportal/category.asp?TreeID=246&VisitID={E59D9075-0630-48A4-8663-F8F60C11232B}&Time=4014 (follow link) (last visited August 5, 2005). For an official topical analysis, see Turkey–EU Relations Directorate General, *Analysis of the 7th*

*Harmonization Package* (July 30, 2003); available at http://www.euturkey.org.tr/abportal/category.asp?TreeID=246&VisitID={E59D9075-0630-48A4-8663-F8F60C11232B}&Time=4014 (follow link) (last visited August 5, 2005).

21 European Council Presidency Conclusions, *Thessaloniki European Council, 19–20 June 2003;* available at http://ue.eu.int/ueDocs/cms_Data/docs/pressData/en/ec/76279.pdf. *Brussels European Council, 12–13 December 2004;* available at http://ue.eu.int/ueDocs/cms_Data/docs/pressData/en/ec/78364.pdf.

## 14 Year of evaluation for Turkey to start EU accession negotiations — 2004

1 See Chapter 13, Document no. 88.
2 *2003 Regular Country Report for Turkey;* available at http://ec.europa.eu/enlargement/archives/pdf/key_documents/2003/rr_tk_final_en.pdf.
3 Checklist on the status of legislative changes in the political criteria section of the 2001 and 2003 National Programme for the Adoption of the *Acquis* (as of February 9, 2004); available at http://www.euturkey.org.tr/abportal/category.asp?TreeID=246&VisitID={E59D9075-0630-48A4-8663-F8F60C11232B}&Time=4014 (follow link) (last visited August 5, 2005).
4 Available at http://www.euturkey.org.tr/abportal/category.asp?TreeID=246&VisitID={E59D9075-0630-48A4-8663-F8F60C11232B}&Time=4014 (follow link) (last visited August 5, 2005).
5 Available at http://ue.eu.int/ueDocs/cms_Data/docs/pressData/en/ec/81742.pdf. (last visited June 15, 2005).
6 Parliamentary Assembly of the Council of Europe, *Honouring of Obligations and Commitments by Turkey,* Doc. 10111 (March 17, 2004) (text adopted by the Assembly on June 22, 2004); available at http://assembly.coe.int/Documents/WorkingDocs/Doc04/EDOC10111.htm (last visited August 15, 2005).
7 European Commission, Com 656 final (October 6, 2004).
8 European Commission, SEC 1201 (October 6, 2004).
9 In the meantime, through the entry into force of the Treaty of Amsterdam in May 1999, the political criteria defined at Copenhagen have been essentially enshrined as a constitutional principle in the Treaty on European Union. Article 6(1) of the consolidated Treaty on European Union reads: "The Union is founded on the principles of liberty, democracy, respect for Human Rights and fundamental freedoms and the rule of law." Accordingly, Article 49 of the consolidated Treaty stipulates that "Any European State which respects the principles set out in Article 6(1) may apply to become a member of the Union." These principles were emphasized in the Charter of Fundamental Rights of the European Union that was proclaimed at the Nice European Council in December 2000.
10 Turkey's Progress Towards Accession, P6_TA(2004)0096; available at http://www.europa.eu.int (last visited August 5, 2005).
11 Brussels European Council, 16–17 December 2004, Doc. No: 16238/1/04.

## 15 Quo Vadis? After 2004: european union membership still a rough path

1 Commission of the European Communities, *Commission Staff Working Document,* SEC (2004) 1202 (October 6, 2004).
2 Office of the Prime Minister, Directorate General of Press and Information; available at http://www.byegm.gov.tr (unless otherwise indicated).
3 Press Release, Luxembourg Presidency of the Council of the European Union, *Turkey's progress in its rapprochement with the European Union at the centre of talks between the EU and Turkey in Ankara* (March 7, 2005); available at http://www.eu2005.lu/en/actualites/communiques/2005/03/07troikatr/index.html (last visited March 25, 2005).

Notes 753

4 In a statement titled "Statement by the EU Troika following incidents during a women's rights demonstration in Istanbul on 6 March 2005," the representatives of the European Union issued the following joint statement: "We were shocked by images of the police beating women and young people demonstrating in Istanbul in connection with International Women's Day. We condemn all violence, as demonstrations must be peaceful. On the eve of a visit by the EU during which the rights of women will be an important issue, we are concerned to see such disproportionate force used against demonstrators. We ask the Turkish authorities to carry out an investigation into this event to prevent similar incidents in the future."
5 Mr. Olli Rehn, member of the European Commission responsible for Enlargement, SPEECH/05/142 (speech delivered in his meeting with business leaders in Istanbul) (March 8, 2005); available at http://ec.europa.eu/commission_barroso/rehn/speeches/speeches_en.htm (last visited August 6, 2005).
6 Full text available at http://europa.eu.int/smartapi/cgi/sga_doc?smartapi!celexapi!prod!CELEXnumdoc&lg=en&numdoc=32006D0035&model=guichett.
7 Istanbul Protocol, *Manual on the Effective Investigation and Documentation of Torture and Other Cruel, Inhuman or Degrading Treatment of Punishment*, submitted to the United National Human Rights Commissioner for Human Rights, 9 August 1999.
8 Available at http://www.ohchr.org/english/about/publications/docs/8rev1.pdf.
9 Prepared by the editors.
10 *Kurds in Turkey mark Newroz spring festival with parties and politics*, AFP (March 20, 2005); available at http://www.flash-bulletin.de/2005/eMarch21.htm (last visited August 6, 2005).
11 "Turk Bayragi" hakkinda Basin Aciklamasi, March 22, 2005; available at http://www.tsk.mil.tr/bashalk/basac/2005/a01.htm (translated by the editors) (last visited February 14, 2007).
12 Prepared based on news reports on or around March 21, 2006.
13 Opinion by Osman Faruk Laloglu, Ambassador of the Republic of Turkey to the United States, published in the *Washington Post*, A 18 (July 25, 2005).
14 *Turkish Daily News* (August 2, 2005); available at http://www.tdn.com.tr (follow link) (last visited August 15, 2005).
15 *Turkish Daily News* (August 24, 2005); available at http://www.tdn.com.tr (follow link) (last visited August 15, 2005).
16 "Turkish parliament overrides presidential veto of penal code"; available at http://jurist.law.pitt.edu/paperchase/2005/07/turkish-parliament-overrides.php.
17 "Turkey: Article 301 is a threat to freedom of expression and must be repealed now"; available at http://web.amnesty.org/library/index/engeur440352005.
18 "Europe adopts new Human Rights law"; available at http://search.ft.com/ftArticle?queryText=turkey+new+laws&y=0&aje=true&x=0&id=050602000864.
19 "Turkey's president uses veto on Koran courses"; available at http://www.iht.com/articles/2005/06/03/news/turkey.php.
20 "Turkish penal code changes cleared"; available at http://english.aljazeera.net/English/archive/archive?ArchiveId=13105.
21 See Documents nos 17 and 18.
22 From The Library of Congress Country Studies, *Turkey: Crime and Punishment*; available at http://lcweb2.loc.gov/cgi-bin/query/r?frd/cstdy:@field(DOCID+tr0115).
23 "New anti-terrorism body to be formed"; available at http://www.turkishweekly.net/news.php?id=31715.
24 Turkish legislative news briefs; available at http://www.legislationline.org/?tid=46&jid=51&less=false.
25 "New anti-terror bill would harm all freedoms"; available at http://www.thenewanatolian.com/tna-5760.html.
26 "Turkish president signs controversial anti-terror bull subject to court review"; available at http://jurist.law.pitt.edu/paperchase/2006/07/turkish-president-signs-controversial.php.

27 See *A Constitution for Europe*; available at http://www.europa.eu.int/constitution/ratification_en.htm (last modified May 10, 2006).
28 Press release, IP/05/627 (May 29, 2005); available at http://europa.eu.int/rapid/searchaction.do;jsessionid=dl11jktbqf3ueoczozawzbnjntujmij1fklplz2yc07e3z0bgqf0!1491408596 (last visited August 5, 2005).
29 Press release, IP/05/653 (June 1, 2005); available at http://europa.eu.int/rapid/pressReleasesAction.do?reference=IP/05/653&format=HTML&aged=0&language=EN&guiLanguage=en (last visited August 5, 2005).
30 Press release, *General affairs and external relations*; available at http://www.eu2005.lu/en/actualites/communiques/2005/06/07jcl-ratif/index.html (last visited August 5, 2005).
31 Standard Eurobarometer, *Eurobarometer 63*; available at http://europa.eu.int/comm/public_opinion/archives/eb/eb63/eb63.4_en_first.pdf (last visited February 12, 2007).
32 Compiled by the editors from various news agency and internet resources.
33 AFP, *Bomb in waist pack triggered Turkey blast* (July 17, 2005); available at http://www.kurdmedia.com/news.asp?id=7270 (last visited August 25, 2005).

Suspicions in a probe into the deadly bombing of a minibus in this Turkish seaside resort have focused on Kurdish separatists, officials said Sunday, as police determined that a bomb in a waist pack hidden in the vehicle caused the blast ... Five people, among them a British and an Irish tourist, were killed and thirteen injured when the explosion tore apart a minibus shuttling between central Kusadasi and a nearby beach Saturday, just one week after a bomb attack injured twenty people in the nearby resort of Cesme ... The Kurdistan Freedom Falcons (TAK), a group the authorities associate with the Kurdistan Workers' Party (PKK), blacklisted as a terrorist organization by the United States and the European Union, claimed responsibility for the Cesme blast and threatened more attacks on tourist targets ... The PKK, which has attacked civilians in the past, denied any role in the blast, rejecting also any links with TAK ... The Turkish army recently warned that PKK militants, who went into hiding in the mountains of neighboring northern Iraq in 1999 after declaring a unilateral ceasefire, were sneaking back, bringing with them large amounts of [explosives] ... Turkish officials, however, believe TAK is a cover for attacks, particularly on civilian targets, which the PKK does not want to claim in order to avoid damaging its claim of defending Turkey's Kurds against state oppression. TAK first emerged last August [2004], weeks after the PKK called off the 1999 truce, claiming responsibility for the bombing of two Istanbul hotels, in which two people died. The group claimed another explosion in Kusadasi in April which killed a policeman, and most recently the Cesme blast.

34 AFP, *Kurdish rebel commander spells out conditions for peace with Turkey* (August 13, 2005); available at http://www.ekurd.net/mismas/articles/misc2005/8/turkeykurdistan252.htm (last visited August 25, 2005).

The Kurdistan Workers' Party (PKK), a rebel group fighting the Turkish government, is ready to lay down arms if the army ends a crackdown on its militants and Ankara guarantees the rights of the Kurds, a senior PKK commander said in an interview with AFP. "For armed action to stop the [Turkish army] operations should end ... If the operations stop, there will naturally be a ceasefire," Murat Karayilan, a right-hand man of jailed PKK leader Abdullah Ocalan, told AFP in a guerrilla camp in the Sinena mountains in northern Iraq late Thursday ... The PKK called off the 1999 truce in June 2004 and has markedly stepped up violence in Turkey over the past several months. Karayilan said Ankara should also guarantee the rights of its Kurdish minority, which comprises about a fifth of the country's seventy million population. "If the values of the Kurdish people are acknowledged and guaranteed by the constitution, there will be no need for arms. We will immediately give up," he said. Karayilan argued that recently intensified PKK attacks were acts of "self-defense." "The PKK says that there is a Kurdish people and that this should be acknowledged. It wants to achieve this through a political and democratic struggle," he said ... Karayilan said it was impossible for the PKK to lay down arms under the current circumstances and "without any guarantees." Besides an end to military operations, the PKK also wants a general amnesty for its militants.

Karayilan rejected PKK responsibility in a series of deadly bomb attacks that claimed at least seven civilian lives over the past month and the Turkish authorities blamed on the group. The worst of them, which blew up a minibus in the seaside resort of Kusadasi on July 16 killed five people, including one British and one Irish tourist. Karayilan said the attacks on civilians were carried out by the Kurdistan Freedom Falcons (TAK), which he described as a group of radical militants who split from the PKK and are no longer under its control. "If positive developments take place in Turkey, some control may be ensured over them," he added.

"We do not favor violence," Karayilan said. "We want dialogue, to discuss problems and resolve them by civilized means." Ankara categorically rejects dialogue with the PKK and has banned several pro-Kurdish political parties for having links with the rebels. Prime Minister Recep Tayyip Erdogan pledged Friday that the Kurdish conflict would be resolved with "more democracy" in a speech in Diyarbakir, the central city of the southeast. He signalled, however, that Ankara would not back down from military action against the PKK, denouncing terrorism and violence as "the worst enemy of the country."

35 Associated Press, Selcan Hacaoglu, *Kurdish rebel group announces truce* (August 19, 2005); available at http://www.washingtonpost.com/wp-dyn/content/article/2005/08/19/AR2005081901859.html (last visited August 25, 2005).

The PKK announced a one-month cease-fire Friday and said it planned to pursue indirect negotiations with the government. PKK said it was ordering its forces to hold fire until September 20, a dramatic step following a string of bombings at Aegean resorts claimed by militants and ambushes of Turkish troops in the southeast ... But the rebels added that they would defend themselves if attacked by Turkish forces ... The Kurdish rebel group has declared several unilateral cease-fires in the past. Turkey has never reciprocated, saying it will maintain its military drive until all rebels surrender or are killed. Turkey has been pressuring the United States to crack down on Kurdish rebel hideouts in neighboring Iraq. The guerrilla group is recognized as a terrorist organization by both the United States and the European Union.

36 *Ocalan v. Turkey*, Decision of the Grand Chamber of the European Court of Human Rights Application no. 46221/99 (May 12, 2005). For the decision of the First Section of the Court, see Document no. 91.

37 Prepared by the European Commission, on file with the editors.

38 The European Commission 2006 Regular Report on Turkey's Progress Towards Accession, SEC 1390, COM 649 (August 11, 2006).

39 Prepared by the editors based on The European Commission 2005 Regular Report on Turkey's Progress Towards Accession, SEC 1426 (November 9, 2005).

# Bibliography

## Books

Abramowitz, Morton, ed. *The United States and Turkey: Allies in Need.* New York: Century Foundation, 2003.
Ahmad, Feroz. *The Turkish Experiment in Democracy, 1950–1975.* Boulder, CO: Westview Press, 1977.
——— *The Making of Modern Turkey.* New York: Routledge, 1993.
Akcapar, Burak. *Turkey's New European Era: Foreign Policy on the Road to EU Membership.* Lanham, MD: Rowman & Littlefield Publishers, Inc., 2006.
American Foreign Policy Institute. *NATO, Turkey and United States Interests.* Washington, DC: American Foreign Policy Institute, 1978.
Anderson, Perry. *Lineages of the Absolutist State.* London: New Left Books, 1974.
Andreades, K.G. *The Moslem Minority in Western Thrace.* Thessalonika: Institute of Balkan Studies, 1956.
Andrews, Peter Alford. *Ethnic Groups in the Republic of Turkey.* Wiesbaden: Dr. Ludwig Reichert Verlag, 1989.
Ankara Journalist Association. *PKK Reality in Turkey and in the World.* Ankara: Gazeteciler Cemiyeti Yayinlari, 1994.
Ansay, Tuğrul and Don Wallace, Jr. eds. *Introduction to Turkish Law.* Denver, CO: Kluwer Law and Taxation Publishers, 1987.
Aral, Berdal. "Turkey's Kurdish problem from an international legal perspective." In *Ethnic Diversity in Europe: Challenges to the Nation State*, edited by David Turton and Julia Gonzalez, pp. 27–53. Bilbao: University of Deusto, 2000.
Arfa, Hassan. *The Kurds: An Historical and Political Study.* London: Oxford University Press, 1966.
Arikan, Harum. *Turkey and the EU: An Awkward Candidate for EU Membership?* Aldershot, UK: Ashgate Publishing Ltd, 2006.
Associations of Solidarity with Western Thrace Turks in Federal Germany and Turkey. *The Drama of the Moslem Turkish Minority in Western Thrace.* L'Institut de Politique Etrangere, 1983.
Ataöv, Türkkaya. "Turkey's expanding relations with the CIS and Eastern Europe." In *Turkish Foreign Policy: New Prospects*, edited by Clement H. Dodd, pp. 88–117. London: The Eothen Press, 1992.
——— "Turkey, the CIS and Eastern Europe." In *Turkey and Europe*, edited by Canan Balkyr and Allan M. Williams, pp. 191–218. London: Pinter Publishers Ltd, 1993.
Aybet, Gülnur. *Turkey's Foreign Policy and its Implications for the West: A Turkish Perspective.* London: RUSI, 1994.

Ayres, Ron. "Turkish Foreign Relations." In Khamsin Collective (ed.) *Modern Turkey: Development and Crisis.* London: Ithaca Press, 1984.
Bahrampour, Firouz. *Turkey: Political and Social Transformation.* Brooklyn: Theo Gaus' Sons, 1967.
Baker, James. *Turkey in Europe*, 3rd edn. New York: Cassell, 1977.
Balim, Çigdem, Ersin Kalaycioglu, Cevat Karatas, Gareth Winrow, and Feroz Yasamee eds. *Turkey: Political, Social, and Economic Challenges in the 1990s.* New York: E.J. Brill, 1995.
Balkyr, Canan and Allan M. Williams, eds. *Turkey and Europe.* New York: Pinter Publishers Ltd, 1993.
Barchard, David and The Royal Institute of International Affairs. *Turkey and the West (Chatham House Papers, No. 27).* London: Routledge and Kegan Paul, 1985.
Berberoglu, Berch. *Turkey in Crisis: From State Capitalism to Neo-Colonialism.* London: Zed Press, 1982.
Bergdoll, Udo. "The relationship between Turkey and Western Europe" (in German). In *IX Deutsch-Türkisches Journalistenseminar*, pp. 101–8. Ankara: Konrad Adenauer Foundation, 1995.
Bianchi, Robert. *Interest Groups and Political Development in Turkey.* Princeton, NJ: Princeton University Press, 1984.
Birand, Mehmet Ali. *Shirts of Steel: An Anatomy of the Turkish Armed Forces.* London: I.B. Tauris and Company Ltd, 1991.
—— *The Generals' Coup in Turkey: An Inside Story of 12 September 1980.* London: Brassey's, 1987.
Blank, Stephen J., Stephen C. Pelletiere, and William T. Johnsen. *Turkey's Strategic Position at the Crossroads of World Affairs.* Honolulu, HI: University Press of the Pacific, 2002.
Bulloch, John and Harvey Morris. *No Friends But the Mountains: The Tragic History of the Kurds.* Oxford: Oxford University Press, 1992.
Burkay, Kemal. "The Kurdish question: its history and present situation." In *Contrasts and Solutions in the Middle East*, edited by Ole Høiris and Sefa Martin Yürükel. Aarhus: Aarhus University Press, 1997.
Center for Middle Eastern and Islamic Studies. *Foreign Policy Issues in the Middle East: Afghanistan, Iraq, Turkey, Morocco.* Durham, NC: University of Durham Press, 1985.
Chaliand, G., ed. *People Without a Country: The Kurds and Kurdistan.* Northhampton MA: Interlink Publishing Group, Inc., 1980.
Chipman, John, ed. *NATO's Southern Allies: Internal and External Challenges.* London: Routledge, 1998.
Council of Europe. *Short Guide to the European Convention on Human Rights.* Strasbourg: Publishing and Documentation Service, 1991.
Cousins, Jane. *Turkey: Torture and Political Persecution.* London: Pluto Press, 1973.
Dahlberg, Robin, Christopher Keith Hall, Rhoda H. Karpatkin, and Jessica A. Neuwirth. *Torture in Turkey: The Legal System's Response.* New York: Committee on International Human Rights of the Bar of the City of New York, 1989.
Danielson, Michael N. and Rusen Keles. *The Politics of Rapid Urbanization: Government and Growth in Modern Turkey.* New York: Holmes and Meier, 1985.
Davison, Roderic. H. *Turkey: A Short History*, 2nd edn. Huntingdon, UK: Eothen Press, 1988.
Deringil, Selim. "Turkish foreign policy since Atatürk." In *Turkish Foreign Policy: New Prospects*, edited by Clement H. Dodd, pp. 1–8. London: The Eothen Press, 1992.
Dodd, Clement H. *The Crisis of Turkish Democracy.* Beverley, UK: The Eothen Press, 1983.
——, ed. *Turkish Foreign Policy: New Prospects.* Huntingdon, UK: Eothen Press, 1992.
Eliot, Sir Charles N. E. *Turkey in Europe.* London: Odysseus, 1965.

Entessar, Nader. *Kurdish Ethnonationalism*. Boulder, CO: Lynne Rienner Publishers, 1992.
Eralp, Atila, Muharrem Tunay, and Birol Yesilada. *The Political and Socioeconomic Transformation of Turkey*. Westport, CT: Praeger, 1993.
Erciyes University. *PKK Reality*. Kayseri: Erciyes University Press, 1992.
Ergener, Rashid. *About Turkey: Geography, Economy, Politics, Religion, and Culture*. Pilgrims Process, Inc., 2002.
Eryilmaz, M. Bedri. *Arrest and Detention Powers in Turkish and English Law and Practice in the Light of the European Convention on Human Rights*. New York: Aspen Publishers, Inc. 2000.
Evin, Ahmet, ed., and Deutschen Orient-Instituts. *Modern Turkey: Continuity and Change*. Oplanden, West Germany: Leske and Budrich, 1984.
Evin, Ahmet and Metin Heper, eds. *The Development of the State in Ottoman Empire and Modern Turkey*. Berlin: Walter de Gruyter, 1988.
Finkel, Andrew and Nükhet Sirman, eds. *Turkish State, Turkish Society*. New York: Routledge, 1990.
Foundation For Middle East And Balkan Studies (OBIV). *Separatist Terror: Menace of The Post Cold War Period, A Case Study Of The PKK In Turkey*. Istanbul: OBIV, 1994.
Frey, F.W. *The Turkish Political Elite, Studies in Comparative Politics Series*. Cambridge, MA: MIT Press, 1965.
Fuad, Jamal. *The Kurdish Question: Missed Opportunities and Future Challenges*. Tallahassee, FL: Badlisy Center for Kurdish Studies, 1993.
Gartler, M., M.W. Benditt, and G.L. Hall. *Understanding Turkey*. River Forest, IL: Laidlaw Brothers, 1962.
Gökalp, Ziya. *The Principles of Turkism*. Translated by Robert Devereux. Leiden, Netherlands: E.J. Brill, 1968.
Graham, E. Fuller, Ian O. Lesser, Paul B. Henze, and J.F. Brown. *Turkey's New Geopolitics: From the Balkans to Western China*. Boulder, CO: Westview Press, 1993.
Graves, Philip P. *Turkey Woos Europe*. London: Allborough Publishing, 1992.
Grothusen, Klaus-Detlev, ed. *Die Türkei in Europa*. Göttingen, Germany: 1979.
Gunter, Michael M. *The Kurds in Turkey: A Political Dilemma*. Boulder, CO: Westview Press, 1990.
—— *The Changing Kurdish problem in Turkey*. London: Research Institute for the Study of Conflict and Terrorism, 1994.
—— *The Kurds and the Future of Turkey*. New York: St. Martin's Press, 1997.
Hale, William M., ed. *Aspects of Modern Turkey*. London: Bowker, 1976.
—— *The Political and Economic Development of Modern Turkey*. New York: St. Martin's Press, 1981.
Harris, George S. "Turkey and the United States." In *Turkey's Foreign Policy in Transition 1950–1974*, edited by Kemal H. Karpat, pp. 51–72. Leiden: Brill, 1975.
Heper, Metin and Ahmet Evin, eds. *Politics in the Third Turkish Republic*. Boulder, CO: Westview Press, 1988.
——, eds. *State, Democracy, and the Military: Turkey in the 1980s*. New York: de Gruyter, 1988.
Heper, Metin and Jacob M. Landau, eds. *Political Parties and Democracy in Turkey*. New York: I.B. Tauris and Company Ltd, 1991.
Heper, Metin and Sabri Sayari. *Political Leaders and Democracy in Turkey*. Lanham, MD: Lexington Books, 2002.
Heper, Metin, Heinz Kramer, and Ayşe Öncü, eds. *Turkey and the West: Images of a New Political Culture*. London: I.B. Tauris and Company Ltd, 1993.
Heyd, Uriel. *Revival of Islam in Modern Turkey*. Jerusalem: Magnes Press, 1968.

Howard, Harry N. *The Partition of Turkey: A Diplomatic History, 1913–1923.* New York: Ferig, 1966.
Hüber, Reinhard. *Turkey: A Way to Europe* (in German). Berlin: Volk und Reich Verlag, 1943.
Hunter, Shireen T. *Turkey at the Crossroads: Islamic Past or European Future? CEPS Paper No. 63.* Brussels: Center for European Policy Studies, 1995.
Hyland, Francis P. *Armenian Terrorist: The Past, the Present, the Prospects.* Boulder, CO: Westview, 1991.
Ince, Nurhan. *Problems and Politics in Turkish Foreign Policy, 1960–1966.* Kentucky: Lexington, 1974.
Ismet, Ismet G. *The PKK.* Ankara: Turkish Daily News Publications, 1992.
Izady, Mehrdad. *The Kurds.* Washington, DC: Taylor & Francis, 1992.
Joseph, Joseph S. *Turkey and the European Union: Internal Dynamics and External Challenges.* New York: Palgrave Macmillan, 2006.
Jung, Dietrich and Wolfango Piccoli. *Turkey at the Crossroads: Ottoman Legacies and a Greater Middle East.* London: Zed Books, 2001.
Karpat, Kemal H., ed. *Turkish Foreign Policy: Recent Developments.* Madison, WI: The University of Wisconsin Press, 1996.
——— *Turkey's Foreign Policy in Transition, 1950–1974.* Leiden: E.J. Brill, 1975.
——— *Politicization of Islam: Reconstructing Identity, State, Faith, and Community in the Late Ottoman State.* Oxford: Oxford University Press, 2002.
Kibritcioglu, Aykut, Libby Rittenberg, and Faruk Selcuk. *Inflation and Disinflation in Turkey.* Aldershot, UK: Ashgate Publishing Ltd, 2002.
Kieser, Hans-Lukas. *Turkey Beyond Nationalism: Towards Post-Nationalist Identities. International Library of Twentieth Century History Series.* London: I.B.Tauris & Company Ltd, 2006.
Kramer, Heinz. *Changing Turkey: The Challenges to Europe and the United States.* Washington, DC: Brookings Institution Press, 2000.
Kreyenbroek, G. and S. Sperl, eds. *The Kurds: A Contemporary Overview,* London: Routledge, 1992.
Kucukaltan, Derman. *Tourism And Terrorism: An Experience of Turkey and the World.* Lincoln, NB: iUniverse, Inc., 2006.
Laipson, Ellen B. *The 98th Congress and Turkey: Attitudes and Actions.* Washington, DC: Congressional Research Service, 1990.
Lake, Michael. *EU and Turkey: A Glittering Prize or a Millstone? Federal Truse Series.* London: I. B.Tauris & Company Ltd, 2005.
Landau, Jacob M. *Pan-Turkism in Turkey: A Study of Irredentism.* Hamden, CT: Archon Books, 1981.
———, ed. *Atatürk and the Modernization of Turkey.* Boulder, CO: Westview Press, 1984.
Larrabee, Stephen F. and Ian O. Lesser. *Turkish Foreign Policy in an Age of Uncertainty.* Santa Monica, CA: The Rand Corporation, 2002.
Lewis, Bernard W. "The United States, Turkey and Iran." In *The Middle East and the United States: Perceptions and Policies,* edited by I. Rabinovich and H. Shaked, pp. 165–80. London: Transaction Books, 1980.
———*Emergence of Modern Turkey.* Oxford: Oxford University Press, 2001.
Lewis, Geoffrey. *Modern Turkey.* New York: Praeger, 1974.
Lovatt, Debbie. *Turkey Since 1970: Politics, Economics and Society.* New York: Palgrave Macmillan, 2001.
Lytle, Elizabeth Edith. *A Bibliography of the Kurds, Kurdistan, and the Kurdish question.* Monticello, IL: Council of Planning Librarians, 1977.
McDowall, David. *The Kurds: A Nation Denied.* London: Minority Rights Publication, 1992.

―― *A Modern History of Kurds*. London: I. B. Tauris and Company Ltd, 1996.
Mackenzie, Kenneth. *Turkey Under the Generals (Conflict Studies, No. 126.)*. London: Institute for the Study of Conflict, 1981.
―― *Turkey in Transition: The West's Neglected Ally – Institute for European Defence and Strategic Studies*. London: Alliance Publishers Ltd, 1984.
Manafy, A. *Kurdish Political Struggles in Iran, Iraq, and Turkey: A Critical Analysis. Federal Truse Series*. Lanham, MD: University Press of America, 2005.
Mango, Andrew. *Turkey, New Nations and People Series*. London: Thames and Hudson, 1968.
―― *Turkey: A Delicately Poised Ally, Washington Papers No. 28*. London: Sage Publications, 1975.
―― "Introduction: Turkish foreign policy." In *Turkey and the European Community*, edited by Ahmet Evin and Geoffrey Denton, pp. 95–100. Opladen, Germany: Leske & Budrich, 1990.
―― *Turkey and the War on Terror*. London: Taylor & Francis, Inc., 2005.
Mango, Andrew and the Center for Strategic and International Studies. *Turkey: The Challenge of a New Role, Washington Papers, No. 163*. Westport, CT: Praeger, 1994.
Mansiali, Erol, ed. *Turkey's Place in Europe: Economic, Political and Cultural Dimensions, International Girne Conferences No. 4*. Istanbul: Middle East Business and Banking, 1988.
Marcus, Aliza. "Turkey's Kurds after the Gulf War: a report from the southeast." In *A People Without a Country: The Kurds and Kurdistan*, edited by Gerard Chaliand, pp. 238–47. London: Zed Books, 1993.
Mastny, Vojtech and R. Craig Nation, eds. *Turkey Between East and West: New Challenges for a Rising Regional Power*. Boulder, CO: Westview, 1996.
Moghadam, Reza. *Turkey at the Crossroads: From Crisis Resolution to EU Accession Occasional Paper 24*. Washington, DC: International Monetary Fund, 2005.
Mortimer, Edward. "Active in a New World role." In *Turkey, Europe's Rising Star: The Opportunities in Anglo-Turkish Relations*. London: Lowe Bell for the Turkish Embassy, 1993.
Müftüler-Bac, Meltem. "Addressing Kurdish separatism in Turkey." In *Theory and Practice in Ethnic Conflict Management: Theorizing Success and Failure*, edited by Marc Howard Ross and Jay Rothman. New York: St. Martin's Press, 1999.
Navaro-Yashin, Yael. *Faces of the State: Secularism and Public Life in Turkey*. Princeton, NJ: University Press, 2002.
Nelson, Daniel N. "Turkish uncertainties: domestic and foreign policy identity in the 1990s." In *Balkan Imbroglio: Politics and Security in Southeastern Europe*. Boulder, CO: Westview Press, 1991.
Ocalan, Abdullah. *Declaration on the Democratic Solution of the Kurdish Question*. London: Mesopotamian Publishers, 1999.
―― *Kürt sorununda çözüm ve çözümsüzlük ikilemi (in Turkish; The dilemma of Resolution and Non-Resolution in the Kurdish Question)*. Cemberlitas, Istanbul: Mem Yayinlari, 1999.
Olson, Robert. *The Emergence of Kurdish Nationalism and the Sheikh Said Rebellion, 1880–1925*. Austin, TX: University of Texas Press, 1989.
――, ed. *The Kurdish Nationalist Movement and its Impact on Turkey in the 1990s*. Lexington, KY: The University Press of Kentucky, 1996.
Özal, Turgut. *Turkey in Europe* (in French). Paris: 1988.
Ozyurek, Esra. *Nostalgia for the Modern: State Secularism and Everyday Politics in Turkey. Politics, History, and Culture Series*. Durham, NC: Duke University Press, 2006.
Radu, Michael S. *Dangerous Neighborhood: Contemporary Issues in Turkey's Foreign Relations*. Piscataway, NJ: Transaction Publishers, 2002.
Robins, Philip. *Suits and Uniforms: Turkish Foreign Policy Since the Cold War*. Seattle, WA: University of Washington Press, 2002.

Rubin, Barry M. *Political Parties in Turkey*. London: Taylor and Francis, 2002.
Saktanber, Ayse. *Living Islam: Women, Religion and the Politicization of Culture in Turkey*. London: I.B. Tauris & Company Ltd, 2002.
Sander, Oral. "Turkey's foreign policy." In *Modern Turkey: Continuity and Change*, edited by Ahmet Evin, pp. 115–30. Opladen, Germany: Leske Verlag, 1984.
Schick, Irvin Cemal and Ertugrul Ahmed Tonak, eds. *Turkey in Transition: New Perspectives*. New York: Oxford University Press, 1987.
Sezer, Duygu B. *Turkey's Security Policies, Adelphi Papers No. 164*. London: The International Institute for Strategic Studies, 1981.
——— "Turkish foreign policy in the year 2000." In *Turkey in the Year 2000*. Ankara: Turkish Political Science Association, 1989.
——— *Turkey's Political and Security Interest and Policies in the New Geostrategic Environment of the Expanded Middle East, Occasional Paper no. 19*. Washington, DC: The Henry L. Stimson Center, 1994.
Steinbach, Udo. "Turkey–ECC relations: cultural dimension." In *Turkey's Place in Europe: Economic, Political, and Cultural Dimensions*, edited by Erol Manisali, pp. 13–24. Istanbul: Uçer, 1990.
——— "The European Community, the United States, the Middle East, and Turkey." In *Politics in the Third Turkish Republic*, edited by Ahmet Evin and Metin Heper, pp. 103–16. Boulder, CO: Westview Press, 1994.
Tachau, Frank. *Turkey: The Politics of Authority, Democracy, and Development*. New York: Praeger, 1984.
Tamkoç, Metin. *The Warrior Diplomats: Guardians of the National Security and Modernization of Turkey*. Salt Lake City, UT: University of Utah Press, 1976.
Togan, Subidey. *Turkey and Central and Eastern European Countries in Transition: Towards Membership of the EU*. New York: Palgrave Macmillan, 2001.
Toynbee, Arnold Joseph. *Turkey: A Past and a Future*. London: Hodder and Stoughton, 1917.
Turkish Democracy Foundation. *Democracy, Human Rights, Terrorism in Turkey*. Ankara: Turkish Democracy Foundation, 1995.
Van Bruinessen, Martin. "Kurdish society, ethnicity, nationalism, and refugee problems." In *The Kurds: A Contemporary Overview*, edited by Paperbackshop.Co.UK Ltd — Echo Library, pp. 35–65. London: Routledge, 1992.
——— *Agha, Shaikh, and State: The Social and Political Structures of Kurdistan*. Atlantic Highlands, NJ: Zed Books, 1992.
Weiker, Walter F. *The Modernization of Turkey: From Atatürk to the Present Day*. New York: Holmes and Meier, 1981.
White, Paul J. *Primitive Rebels or Revolutionary Modernisers?: The Kurdish Nationalist Movement in Turkey*. Atlantic Highlands, NJ: Zed Books, 2001.
Yalcin-Heckmann, Lale. *Tribe and Kinship Among the Kurds*. Frankfurt, Germany: Lang, 1991.
Yavuz, M. Hakan. *The Emergence of a New Turkey: Islam, Democracy, and the AK Parti, Utah Series in Turkish and Islamic Studies*. Salt Lake City, UT: University of Utah Press, 2006.
Yildiz, Kerim. *Kurds in Turkey: EU Accession and Human Rights*. London: Pluto Press, 2005.
Yilmaz, Bahri. *Challenges to Turkey: The New Role of Turkey in International Politics since the Dissolution of the Soviet Union*. New York: St. Martin's Press, 1997.
Zoppo, Ciro Elliot. "Turkey's problems and prospects." In *Southeastern Europe after Tito: A Powder-keg for the 1980s?*, edited by D. Carlton and C. Shaerf, pp. 161–73. London: 1983.
Zürcher, Erik J. *Turkey: A Modern History*. New York: I.B. Tauris and Company Ltd, 1994.

## Articles and reports

Abramowitz, Morton. "Dateline Ankara: Turkey after Ozal." *Foreign Policy* no. 91 (Summer 1993): 164–7.

Ahmad, Feroz. "Military intervention and the crisis in Turkey." *MERIP Reports:* no. 93. *Turkey: The Generals Take Over* (January 1981): 5–24.

—— "The Islamic assertation in Turkey: perspectives and State response." *Arab Studies Quarterly* 4, no. 1–2 (1982): 94–109.

—— "Islamic reassertation in Turkey." *Third World Quarterly* 10, no. 2 (April 1988): 750–86.

—— "Politics and Islam in modern Turkey." *Middle Eastern Studies* 27, no. 1 (January 1991): 3–21.

Ahmet, Salih. "Grievances and requests of the Turkish-Moslem minority living in Western Thrace." *Turkish Review: Quarterly Digest* 3, no. 15 (1989): 37–44.

American University, "The Kurds: search for identity." *An International Conference*, Washington DC, April 17–18, 2000.

Amnesty International. *Turkey: Testimony on Torture.* London: Amnesty International, 1985.

—— *Turkey: Brutal and Systematic Abuse of Human Rights.* London: Amnesty International, 1989.

—— *Turkey: Torture, Extrajudicial Executives, and "Disappearances."* London: Amnesty International, 1992.

—— *Turkey: Dissident Voices Jailed Again.* New York: Amnesty International, 1994.

—— *Turkey: Selective Protection: Discriminatory Treatment of Non-European Refugees and Asylum-Seekers.* New York: Amnesty International, 1994.

—— *Turkey: No Security Without Human Rights.* New York: Amnesty International, 1996

—— *Turkey Constitutional Amendments: Still a Long Way to Go.* New York: Amnesty International, 2002.

——*Europe and Central Asia Summary of Amnesty International's Concerns in the Region January – June 2005.* New York: Amnesty International, 2005.

—— *Turkey Memorandum on AI's Recommendations to the Government to Address Human Rights Violations.* New York: Amnesty International, 2005.

—— *Europe and Central Asia: Concerns in Europe & Central Asia Bulletin July – December 2005.* New York: Amnesty International, 2006.

—— *Turkey: Article 301: How the Law on "Denigrating Turkishness" is an Insult to Free Expression.* New York: Amnesty International, 2006.

—— *Turkey Justice Delayed and Denied: The Persistence of Protracted and Unfair Trials for those Charged under Anti-terrorism Legislation.* New York: Amnesty International, 2006.

Argun, Betigul E. "Universal citizenship rights and Turkey's Kurdish question." *Journal of Muslim Minority Affairs* 19, no. 1 (April 1999): 85–103.

Ataman, Muhittin. "The Kurdish question and its impact on Turkey's foreign policy: from 1923 to 2000." *Journal of South Asian and Middle Eastern Studies* 24, no. 2 (2001): 33–49.

Ataöv, Türkkaya. "A Common European home and Turkey's place in it." *SBF Dergisi* 44, no. 3–4 (June–December 1989): 85–90.

Aybay, Rona. "Some contemporary constitutional problems in Turkey." *Bulletin (British Society for Middle Eastern Studies)* 4, no. 1 (1997): 21–7.

Barchard, David. "Turkey and Europe." *Turkish Review: Quarterly Digest* 3, no. 17 (Fall 1989): 5–13.

—— "Turkey's troubled prospect." *World Today* 46 (June 1990): 107–10.

—— "Turkey: problems and prospects." *Ditchley Conference Report*, no. D (1993).

Barkey, H.J. 1993, "'Turkey's Kurdish dilemma." *Survival* 35, no. 4 (Winter 1993–94): 51–70.

―――― "Turkey, Islamic politics, and the Kurdish question." *World Policy Journal* 23, no. 1 (Spring 1996): 43–52.
―――― "The People's Democracy Party (HADEP): the travails of a legal Kurdish party in Turkey." *Journal of Muslim Minority Affairs* 18, no. 1 (April 1998): 129–38.
Barkey, H.J. and Graham E. Fuller. "Turkey's Kurdish question: critical turning points and missed opportunities." *The Middle East Journal* 51, no. 1 (Winter 1997): 59–79.
Barraclough, Colin. "The Kurds: a fire in Turkey's underbelly." *Insight* 9, no. 43 (October 25, 1993): 6–11.
Batu, Hamit. "A future of the southern flank." *Foreign Policy* 11, no. 3–4 (1984).
Baysan, Tercan. "Some economic aspects of Turkey's accession to the EC: resource shifts, comparative advantage, and static gains." *Journal of Common Market Studies* (September 23, 1984): 15–34.
Bayülken, Ümit Haluk. "Cyprus question and the United States." *Foreign Policy* 4, no. 2–3 (1974).
Belge, Bay Burhan. "Modern Turkey." *International Affairs (Royal Institute of International Affairs 1931–1939)* 18, no. 6 (November 1939): 745–62.
Bölükbasi, Süha. "Ankara, Damascus, Baghdad, and the regionalization of Turkey's Kurdish secessionism." *Journal of South Asian and Middle Eastern Studies* 14, no. 4, (June 1991): 15–36.
Bowder, G. "Turkey at the crossroad." *World Today* 33 (May 1977): 164–8.
Boyle, Elizabeth Heger and Melissa Thompson. "National politics and resort to the European Commission on Human Rights." *Law & Society Review* 35, no. 2 (2001): 321–44.
Bozarslan, Hamit. "Turkey's elections and the Kurds." *Middle East Report*, no. 199 *Turkey: Insolvent Ideologies, Fractured State* (April 1996): 16–19.
Brown, James. "The Turkish imbroglio: its Kurds." *Annals of the American Academy of Political and Social Science* 541 (September 1995): 116–29.
Burrows, Bernard. "Turkey in Europe?" *World Today* 36 (July 1980): 266–71.
Button, Stephen. "Turkey struggles with Kurdish separatism." *Military Review* 75, no. 1 (December 1994–February 1995): 70–8.
Bywater, Marion. "Turkey: a European anomaly." *European Community* (January–February 1977): 26–8.
Çakar, Nezikhi. "Turkey's security challenges." *Perceptions* 1, no. 2 (June–August 1996): 12–21.
Çetin, Hikmet. "The security structures of a changing continent: a Turkish view." *NATO Review* 40, no. 2 (April 1992).
Cicekli, Bulent. "The rights of Turkish migrants in Europe under International Law and EU Law." *International Migration Review* 33, no. 2 (Summer 1999): 300–53.
Çiller, Tansu. "The role of Turkey in the world." *Strategic Review* 12, no. 1 (Winter 1994): 7–11.
Cocks, Peter. "Liberalism or barbarism." *New Perspectives on Turkey* 3, no. 1 (1989): 82–92.
Committee for Democratic Liberties in Turkey. *Minorities and Oppressive Rule in Turkey.* Ankara: Committee for Democratic Liberties in Turkey, 1985.
Committee to Protect Journalists Staff. *Enforced Restraint: Press Conditions in Turkey.* New York: Committee to Protect Journalists, 1990.
Connelly, A. Daniel. "Black Sea economic cooperation." *RFE/RL Research Report* 3, no. 26 (July 1, 1994): 31–8.
Copley, G. "Turkey's bold strategic initiative" and "Interview: Turgut Özal-Bold Moves in Turkey." *Defence and Foreign Affairs* 12, no. 11 (November 1984).
Cornell, Svante E., "The Kurdish question in Turkish politics." *ORBIS* 45 Issue 1 (Winter 2001): 31–46.

Criss, Nur Bilge. "Developments in managing terrorism in Turkey." *Perceptions* 1, no. 4 (December 1996–February 1997): 76–87.
——— "The nature of PKK terrorism in Turkey." *Studies in Conflict and Terrorism* 28, no. 1 (January–March 1995): 17–37.
Cruickshank, A.A. "The international aspects of the Kurdish question." *International Relations* 3, no. 6 (October 1968): 411–30.
Dagi, Ihsan Duran. "Turkey in the 1990s: foreign policy, Human Rights, and the search for a new identity." *Mediterranean Quarterly* 4, no. 4 (1993): 60–77.
Dahlberg, Robin, Christopher Keith Hall, Rhoda H. Karpatkin, and Jessica A. Neuwirth. *Torture in Turkey: The Legal System's Response*. New York: Committee on International Human Rights of the Bar of the City of New York, 1989.
Dikerdem, Mahmut. "A Turkish tug-of-war: the state of Human Rights in Turkey today." *Index on Censorship* 16, no. 6 (1987): 15–19.
Ecevit, Bülent. "Turkey's Security Policies." *Survival* 20, no. 5 (October 1978).
Elahi, Maryam. "Clinton, Ankara, and Kurdish Human Rights." *Middle East Report*, no. 189 (July–August 1994): 22–3.
Ergüvenc, Sadi. "Turkey: strategic partner of the European Union." *Foreign Policy* 20, no. 1–2 (1996): 3–22.
Erkin, Feridun C. "Turkey's foreign policy." *Proceedings of the Academy of Political Science* 24, no. 4 International Tensions in the Middle East (January 1952): 122–33.
Ersan, Tosun. "Turkey's battered democracy: after violence, bloodshed and military coup what are the prospects for the future? Status of human and democratic rights." *Index on Censorship* 11 (February 1982): 11–14.
Evin, Ahmet. "Turkey–EU Relations on the eve of IGC: The social and cultural dimension." *Foreign Policy* 20, no. 1–2 (1996): 35–54.
Fay, James R. "Terrorism in Turkey: threat to NATO's troubled ally." *Military Review* 61, no. 47–48 (1968): 16–26.
Fernau, Friedrich. "Basic principles of Turkish foreign policy" (in German). *Orient* 10, no. 1 (January 1969): 3–8.
Gawarych, George W. "The culture and politics of violence in Turkish society." *Middle Eastern Studies* 22, no. 3 (1986): 307–30.
Grabbe, Heather. "European Union conditionality and the 'Acquis Communautaire.'" *International Political Science Review/Revue internationale de science politique* 23, no. 3 Enlarging the European Union: Challenges to and from Central and Eastern Europe. L'elargissement de l'Union europeenne (July 2002): 249–68.
Gülap, Haldun. "The crisis of westernization in Turkey: Islamism v. Nationalism." *Innovation: The European Journal of Social Science* 8, no. 2 (June 1995): 175–82.
Gumpel, Werner. "Development strategy report: Turkey's devleopment strategy in the light of the economic development in Europe." *Intereconomics* (March–April 1980).
———, ed. "Europa und die Türkei in den Neunziger Jahren." *Südosteuropa Mitteilungen Aktuell* special issue 11 (1991).
Gunter, Michael M. "The Armenian terrorist campaign against Turkey." *Orbis* 27, no. 2 (Summer 1983): 447–77.
——— "Cycles of terrorism: the question of contemporary Turkish counterterror and harassment against the Armenians." *Journal of Political Science* 14, no. 1–2 (1986): 58–73.
——— "The Kurdish problem in Turkey." *Middle East Journal* 42, no. 3 (1988): 389–406.
——— "Kurdish militancy in Turkey: the case of PKK." *Crossroads* no. 29 (1989): 43–59.
——— "The Kurdish insurgency in Turkey." *Journal of South Asian and Middle Eastern Studies* 13, no. 4 (1990): 57–81.

—— "Transnational Armenian activism." *Conflict Studies* no. 229 (March 1990).
—— "The changing Kurdish problem in Turkey." *Conflict Studies* no. 270 (May 1994): 1–29.
—— "Kurdish factor in Turkish foreign policy." *Journal of Third World Studies* 11 (Fall 1994): 440–72.
Güvener, Halit. "Turkey's relations with the West." *Foreign Policy* 9, no. 1–2 (1981): 17–22.
Hadjicosta, Stella G. "The security policies of Turkey." *The Cyprus Review* 2, no. 2 (Fall 1990): 41–54.
Hale, William M. "Turkey, the Middle East, and the Gulf crisis." *International Affairs* 68, no. 2 (Spring 1992): 679–92.
Harris, George S. "Ethnic conflict and the Kurds." *Annals of the American Academy of Political and Social Science*, no. 433 (1977): 112–24.
—— "Islam and State in modern Turkey." *Middle East Review* 11, no. 4 (Summer 1979): 21–6.
Hassanpour, Amir. "The Kurdish experience." *Middle East Report*, no. 189 (July–August 1994) 2–7, 23.
Helsinki Watch Committee. *Human Rights in Turkey's "Transition to Democracy."* New York: Helsinki Watch, 1983.
—— *Freedom and Fear: Human Rights in Turkey.* New York: Helsinki Watch, 1986.
—— *State of Flux: Human Rights in Turkey: December 1987 Update.* New York: Helsinki Watch, 1987.
—— *Destroying Ethnic Identity: The Turks of Greece.* New York: Helsinki Watch, 1990.
—— *Denying Human Rights and Ethnic Identity: The Turks of Greece.* New York: Helsinki Watch, 1992.
Heper, Metin. "Recent instability in Turkish politics: end of a mono-centrist polity?" *International Journal of Turkish Studies* 1, no. 1 (Winter 1979).
—— "Islam, polity and society in Turkey: a Middle Eastern perspective." *Middle East Journal* 35, no. 3 (Summer 1981): 345–63.
Hirsch, Ernst E. "Turkey as a signatory State of the European Convention for the Protection of Human Rights and Basic Liberties" (in German). *Orient* 25, no. 1 (March 1984): 95–106.
Hoffmeister, Frank. "Cyprus v. Turkey. App. No. 25781/94." *The American Journal of International Law* 96, no. 2 (April 2002): 445–52.
International Commission of Jurists. "The Rule of Law in Turkey and the European Convention on Human Rights." *Review: International Commission of Jurists*, no. 10 (June 1973): 7–56.
Karadayi, Ismail Hakki. "The Turkish land forces: duties, responsibilities, and organization." *NATO's Sixteen Nations* 38 (April 1993): 29–34.
Karpat, Kemal H. "Society, economics, and politics in contemporary Turkey." *World Politics* 17, no. 1 (October 1964): 50–74.
—— "The military and politics in Turkey, 1960–64: a socio-cultural analysis of a revolution." *American Historical Review* 75, no. 6 (October 1970) 1654–83.
—— "Turkish democracy at impasse: ideology, party politics, and the third military intervention." *International Journal of Turkish Studies* 2, no. 1 (Spring–Summer 1981): 1–43.
Kemal, Ahmet. "Military rule and the future of democracy in Turkey." *MERIP Reports*, no. 122 (March–April 1984): 12–15.
Kirisci, Kemal. "The challenges of terrorism: a Turkish perspective." *Foreign Policy* 20, no. 3–4 (1996): 1–18.
Kuniholm, Bruce R. "Turkey and the West." *Foreign Affairs* 70, no. 2 (Spring 1991): 34–48.

Kurkcu, Ertugrul. "The crisis of the Turkish state." *Middle East Report*, no. 199. *Turkey: Insolvent Ideologies, Fractured State* (April 1996): 2–7.

Kushner, David. "Turkey and Europe: a relationship of passion of pain." *History of European Ideas* 18, no. 5 (1994): 683–95.

Kutschera Chris, "Mad dreams of independence: the Kurds of Turkey and the PKK." *Middle East Report*, no. 189. *The Kurdish Experience* (July–August 1994): 12–15.

Laber, Jeri. "A new turn in Turkey: recent Human Rights improvement." *New York Review of Books* 33, no. 3 (1986): 18–20.

Laber, Jeri and Lois Whitman. *Destroying Ethnic Identity: The Kurds of Turkey, An Update*. New York: Helsinki Watch Committee, March 1988.

Landau, Jacob M. "The Nationalist Action Party in Turkey." *Journal of Contemporary History* 17, no. 4 (October 1982): 587–606.

Lutz, Russel E. "Claims against Turkey." *American Journal of International Law* (July 1991): 20–6.

MacDonald, Scott B. "Turkey's 1991 elections: democracy renewed or the past revisited?" *Middle East Insight* 8, no. 3 (January–February 1992): 25–30.

Mango, Andrew. "Understanding Turkey." *Middle Eastern Studies* 18, no. 2 (1982): 194–213.

—— "Turkey: democracy under military tutelage." *World Today* 39, no. 2 (November 1983).

—— "Remember the minorities." *Middle Eastern Studies* 21, no. 4 (1985): 118–40.

—— "Turkey's ten-year itch." *World Today* 45 (February 1989).

—— "European dimensions." *Middle Eastern Studies* 28, no. 2 (April 1992): 397–439.

—— "Turkish foreign policy." *Turkologischer Anzeiger* 18, no. 165 (1992): 95–9.

—— "Turks and Kurds." *Middle Eastern Studies* 30, no. 4 (1994): 975–97.

Marguiles, Ronnie. "Turkey and the European Union." *Middle East Report*, no. 199. *Turkey: Insolvent Ideologies, Fractured State* (April 1996): 27.

Martin, Philip, Elizabeth Midgley, and Michael Teitelbaum. "Migration and development: focus on Turkey." *International Migration Review* 35, no. 2 (Summer 2001): 596–605.

Middle East Research Institute. *MERI Report: Turkey*. London: Croom Helm, 1985.

—— "State terror in Turkey: alleged government repression of Human Rights: three articles and three interviews." *MERI Reports*, no. 14 (February 1984): 3–29.

Moraly, Turan. "European security and defence identity and Turkey." *Perceptions* 1, no. 2 (June–August 1996): 132–9.

Müftüler, Meltem S. "Turkey: a new player in Middle Eastern politics." *Mediterranean Quarterly* 6, no. 4 (Fall 1995): 110–20.

—— "Turkey's predicament in the post-Cold War era." *Futuers* 28 (April 1996): 255–68.

Mutlu, Servet. "Ethnic Kurds in Turkey: a demographic study." *International Journal of Middle East Studies* 28, no. 4 (November 1996): 517–41.

Narly, Nilüfer. "The significance of inter-religious dialogue in the course of Turkey's integration with the West." *Zeitschrift für Türkeistudien* 3, no. 2. (1990): 285–94.

Olson, Robert. "The creation of a Kurdish State in the 1990s." *Journal of South Asian and Middle Eastern Studies* 15, no. 4 (Summer 1992): 1–25.

—— "The Kurdish question four years on: the policies of Turkey, Syria, Iran, and Iraq." *Middle East Policy* 3, no. 3 (1994): 136–44.

—— "The Kurdish question and Turkey's foreign policy, 1991–95: from the Gulf War to the incursion into Iraq." *Journal of South Asian and Middle Eastern Studies* 19, no. 1 (1995): 1–30.

Oran, Baskin. "Human and minority rights in Greece: the Ynhanly land dispute file." *Turkish Yearbook of International Relations*, 18 (1978): 19–35.

——— "On minority terror and State terror: the case of Western Thrace." *Public and Private International Law Bulletin* 2, no. 1 (1982): 8–14.
Oxman, Bernard H. and Beate Rudolf. "Loizidou v. Turkey." *The American Journal of International Law* 91, no. 3 (July 1997): 532–7.
Öymen, Onur. "Turkey's European foreign policy." *Perceptions* 2, no. 1 (March–May 1997): 7–14.
Özal, Turgut. "Ankara: European ambitions" (in French). *Politique Internationale* 47 (1990): 233–42.
Özay, Mehmet. "Turkey in crisis: some contradictions in the Kemalist development strategy." *International Journal of Middle East Studies* 15, no. 1 (February 1983): 47–66.
Pamuk, Sevket. "Political economy of industrialization in Turkey." *MERIP Reports*, no. 93. *Turkey: The Generals Take Over* (January 1981): 26–30, 32.
Patton, Marcie J. "Voices from Turkey's southeast." *Middle East Report*, no. 27 (Summer 2003): 42–5.
Perle, Richard and Michael J. McNamara. "U.S. security assistance for Turkey and the challenge of aid for the southern flank." *NATO'S Sixteen Nations* 32, no. 2 (April 1987): 94–7.
Perez, Frank. "Terrorism: lingering threat to Turkey?" *Terrorism* 11, no. 5 (1988): 359–64.
Perry, John R. "Language reform in Turkey and Iran." *International Journal of Middle East Studies* 17, no. 3 (August 1985): 295–311.
Robin, Philip. "The overlord State: Turkish policy and the Kurdish issue." *International Affairs* 69, no. 4 (1993): 657–76.
Rumpf, Christian. "The protection of Human Rights in Turkey and the significance of international Human Rights instruments." *Human Rights Law Journal* 14, no. 11–12 (December 1993): 394–408.
Qureshi, Yasmin. "A review of Turkey's foreign policy." *Pakistan Horizon* 30, no. 1 (1977): 54–71.
Rouleau, Eric. "The challenges to Turkey." *Foreign Affairs* 72, no. 5 (December 1993): 110–26.
——— "Turkey: beyond Atatürk." *Foreign Policy*, no. 103 (Summer 1996): 70–87.
Salt, Jeremy. "Nationalism and the rise of Muslim sentiment in Turkey." *Middle Eastern Studies* 31, no. 1 (1995): 13–27.
Sander, Oral. "Turkish foreign policy: forces of continuity and of change." *Turkish Review: Quarterly Digest* 7, no. 34 (1993): 31–46.
Sayari, Sabri. "Turkey: the changing European security environment and the Gulf Crisis." *Middle East Journal* 46, no. 1 (Winter 1992): 9–21.
Sezer, Duygu B. "Turkey's new security environment, nuclear weapons and proliferation." *Comparative Strategy* 14, no. 2 (April–June 1995): 149–73.
——— "Turkey's security policy: challenges of adoptation to the post-INF era." *Journal of the Royal United Services Institute for Defence Studies* (Winter 1989).
Shah, Syed Imdad. "Turkish foreign policy: an analysis." *Journal of European Studies* 9, no. 2 and 10, no. 1 (1993–94): 79–93.
Skach, Cindy. "Şahin v. Turkey. App. No. 44774/98; "Teacher headscarf." Case no. 2BvR 1436/02." *The American Journal of International Law* 100, no. 1 (January 2006): 186–96.
Smith/Kocamahhul, Joan. "In the shadow of Kurdish: the silence of other ethnolinguistic minorities in Turkey." *Middle East Report*, no. 219 (Summer 2001): 45–7.
Spiliakos, Panos C. "The effect of secular nationalism on recent Turkish foreign policy." *Hellenic Review of International Relations* 1, no. 2 (1980) 480–7.
Tachau, Frank and Metin Heper. "The State, politics, and the military in Turkey." *Comparative Politics* 16, no. 1 (October 1983): 17–33.

Tibi, Bassam. "Die neu Rolle der Türkei." *Die Politische Meinung* 28, no. 284 (July 1993): 57–63.
Trilsch, Mirja and Alexandra Rüth. "Öcalan v. Turkey. App. No. 46221/99." *The American Journal of International Law* 100, no. 1 (January 2006): 180–6.
—— "Turkey and the West: problems and prospects." *Foreign Policy Special Issue* 8, no. 3–4 (1990).
United States Congress Commission on Security and Cooperation in Europe. *The State of Human Rights in Turkey.* Washington, DC: GPO, 1988.
Van Bruinessen, Martin. "The Kurds in Turkey: further restrictions on basic rights." *MERIP Reports*, no. 121. *State Terror in Turkey* (February 1984): 6–12, 14.
—— "The Kurds between Iran and Iraq." *Middle East Report*, no. 141 (July 1986): 14–27.
—— "Between guerrilla war and political murder: the Workers' Party of Kurdistan." *Middle East Report*, no. 153 (July–August 1988) 40–2, 44–6.
—— "Turkey's death squads." *Middle East Report*, no. 199. *Turkey: Insolvent Ideologies, Fractured State* (April 1996): 20–3.
Vaner, Semih. "Die Türkei: Der Schmale Weg." *Europäische Rundschau* 11, no. 4 (1983): 81–92.
Whitman, Lois. *Paying the Price: Freedom of Expression in Turkey (A Helsinki Watch Report)*. New York: Human Rights Watch, 1989.
Wyllie, James. "Turkey adapting to new strategic realities." *Jane's Intelligence Review* (October 1992): 450–1.
Yalpat, Altan. "Turkey's economy under the generals." *MERIP Reports*, no. 122. *Turkey Under Military Rule* (March 1984): 16–24.
Yavuz, M. Hakan. "Turkey's imagined enemies: Kurds and Islamist." *World Today* 52, no. 4 (April 1996): 99–101.
Yilmaz, Bahri. "Turkey as a regional economic power." *Europa-Archiv* 48, no. 24 (1993): 718–24.
—— "The new role of Turkey in international politics." *Aussenpolitik* 45, no. 1 (1994): 90–8.
Yilmaz, Mesut. "Turkish foreign policy." *Foreign Policy* 14, no. 3–4 (1989).

**Web sites**

EurActiv. "EU–Turkey relations." September 23, 2004. EurActiv, http://www.euractiv.com/en/enlargement/eu-turkey-relations/article-129678 (last visited February 6, 2007).
European Commission. "Turkey: country profile." December 6, 2006. European Commission, http://ec.europa.eu/enlargement/turkey/index_en.htm (last visited February 6, 2007).
Human Rights Watch. "Europe/central Asia: Turkey." 2006. Human Rights Watch, http://hrw.org/doc/?t=europe&c=turkey (last visited February 6, 2007).
—— "World Report 2007 essential background: overview of Human Rights issues in Turkey." January 11, 2006. Human Rights Watch, http://hrw.org/englishwr2k7/docs/2007/01/11/turkey14845.htm (last visited February 6, 2007).
Kurdish Human Rights Project. "Home page." January 18, 2007. Kurdish Human Rights Project, http://www.khrp.org/ (last visited February 6, 2007).
Smith-in-Van, Helena. "Human rights record haunts Turkey's EU ambitions" *The Guardian* (2004), http://www.guardian.co.uk/turkey/story/0,12700,1372326,00.html (last visited February 6, 2007).
United States Department of Defense. *Terrorist Group Profiles* (2002), http://www.milnet.com/tgp/tgpndx2.htm (last visited February 6, 2007).

United States Department of State. *Country Reports on Human Rights Practices* (1993–99), http://www.state.gov/www/global/human_rights/hrp_reports_mainhp.html (last visited February 6, 2007).

United States Department of State. *Patterns of Global Terrorism*, (2000–2003), http://www.milnet.com/state/patterns-index.html (last visited February 6, 2007).

# Glossary

**The Ankara Agreement** Agreement establishing an association between the European Economic Community and Turkey.
**CSCE** Commission on Security and Cooperation in Europe.
**The Convention (ECHR)** Council of Europe Convention for the Protection of Fundamental Freedoms and Human Rights).
**CPT** Council of Europe European Committee for the Prevention of Torture.
**CoE** Council of Europe.
**CNS** Council of National Security.
**EC** European Community.
**ECHR (ECtHR in European Council Decisions)** European Court of Human Rights
**ECJ** European Court of Justice.
**EEC** European Economic Community.
**EP** European Parliament.
**EU** European Union.
**AKP or PKPar** Justice and Development Party.
**PKK** Kurdish Workers Party.
**KADEK** Kurdistan Freedom and Democracy Congress.
**KONGRA-GEL** Kurdistan Peoples Congress.
**PACE** Parliamentary Assembly of the Council of Europe.
**SSC (NSC in ECHR decisions)** State Security Courts.
**TAF** Turkish Armed Forces.
**CMUK** Turkey's Code of Criminal Procedure.
**ATL** Turkish Anti-Terrorism Law.
**Decree** Turkish Decree(s) having the force of law.
**GNAA** Turkish Grand National Assembly.
**NPAA** Turkish National Programme for the Adoption of the Acquis.
**TPC** Turkish Penal Code.

# Index

Accession Negotiations, 724
Accession Partnership, 221–22, 421, 426, 429–31, 433–34, 617, 619–20, 622, 625–26, 654, 663, 667–78, 684, 722, 724, 728–29, 749–51
Acquis communautaire, 180, 205, 210, 419, 465, 469, 679, 764
Acquis, 205, 210, 220, 222, 324, 328, 380–81, 394, 396, 419, 426, 429, 430–31, 433, 435, 438, 439, 440–41, 446, 448, 458, 465, 469, 486, 524–25, 528, 532, 570, 580, 581, 618, 620–21, 623–24, 626, 630–31, 658, 672, 679, 685, 721–24, 752, 764
Act on Associations, 504–6, 536, 539
Act on Cinema, Video and Musical Works, 441, 473
Act on Duties and Competencies of the Police, 441, 443, 471, 473
Act on the Coast Guard Command, 441, 443, 471, 473
Act on the Establishment and Procedure of Military Courts, 445, 476
Act on the Establishment and Procedure of the State Security Courts, 443–44, 475
Act on the Establishment of Radio and Television Enterprises, 441, 467, 471, 473
Act on the Military Administrative High Courts, 445
Act on the Organization, Duties and Competencies of the Gendarmerie, 441, 443, 471, 473
Act on the Prosecution of Civil Servants, 442, 444, 475
Act on the State of Emergency, 445, 476
Adaptation Protocol, 739
Aegean Sea Dispute, 325, 402

Agar, Mehmet, 291
Agreement on Illicit Traffic by Sea, 486
Akbulut, Ziyaeddin, 407
Akdivar and Others v. Turkey, 315
Akkus v. Turkey, 318
Aksaray Security Headquarters, 366
Aksoy, Zeki, 295–97, 300–302, 305, 308, 313–14
Alevis, 655, 663, 678–79, 732
Al-Qiada, 480, 484
Amnesty International, 383
Amsterdam Treaty, 141, 215
Anadolu Agency, 687, 708
Andean Pact, 187
Ankara Agreement, 219–20, 232, 241–42, 284, 323, 356, 609, 618, 657, 667, 684
Ankara Police, 238–45
Ankara, 3–4, 261, 265, 368, 373, 677–79, 681, 688, 704, 708, 715
Anter, Musa, 406, 413
Anti-Terrorism Act, 273, 441, 447, 466, 471, 589
Anti-Terrorism Law (ATL), 8, 125–29, 262, 274–76, 289, 366, 402, 612–13, 628, 635–36, 644–46, 689, 691, 724, 729–31, 734, 736, 738
Armed Forces, 6, 7, 26, 30, 33, 45, 48, 58, 60, 63–65, 70, 72, 86, 88, 96–97, 129, 147, 269, 271, 337, 347, 349–50, 355, 358, 369, 408, 455, 466, 504, 586, 588, 608, 626, 632, 654, 661, 687, 690, 713, 725, 740, 757
Armenia, 8, 158, 406, 545, 651, 660, 663, 678, 680,
Armenian Secret Army for the Liberation of Armenia (ASALA), 8
Asselborn, Jean, 681–82
Association Agreement, 219, 233, 431, 433, 724, 739

772  *Index*

Association Committee, 221, 433
Association Council, 191–92, 219–21, 224
Associations Act, 613, 622
Aydin v. Turkey, 318

Baltic Clause, 188–89, 192
Barcelona Declaration, 291
Bayrampasa Prison, 242
Besikei, Ismail, 291
Black Sea Economic Cooperation (BSEC), 484
Board of Inspectors, 405
Brannigan and McBride v. United States, 308–11
Bridal, Akin, 388
Brogan and Others v. United Kingdom, 307, 310
Bulgarian Clause, 188–89, 192
Bylaw on Apprehension, Custody and Interrogation, 442

Cannes European Council presidency conclusions (1995), 196
Capitol Market Board (CMB), 480
Centre for the Research of Societal Problems (TOSAV), 389
Charter of Alliance (Sened-i Ittifak), 38
Charter of Fundamental Rights, 721
Charter of Paris, 172, 191–94, 235
Chief of the General Staff, 25–28, 35, 72, 74, 84, 93, 608, 726–27
Chief Prosecutor of the Republic, 112, 459, 503–4, 519, 523–24, 534–35, 538
Cicek, Cemil, 690
Ciller, Tansu, 8
Civil Law Convention on Corruption, 486, 596
Civil Society Organizations, 732
Code of Criminal Procedure, 33, 98, 298–99, 301, 310–11, 320, 322, 331–32, 334, 336, 341, 343, 345, 408, 612, 614, 617, 622, 627, 634, 654, 661, 726–27, 730, 737–38
Code of Obligations, 409
Commission Communication COM (95) 216, 185
Commission v. Germany, 161
Committee of Ministers, 154–55, 260, 486, 728–29
Committee on Legal Affairs and Human Rights, 234
Committee on the Prevention of Torture, 729

Common Foreign and Security Policy (CSFP), 672
Community Law, 181, 200, 203–4, 210
Confederation Syndicale, 161
Conference on Security and Cooperation in Europe (CSCE), 172, 186–87, 189, 191–92, 194
Conference on the Human Dimension, 172
Constitution of the European Union, 202, 205
Constitutional Court, 35, 40–41, 47, 64, 66–68, 70–71, 79–82, 85, 128, 244, 249, 262, 271–73, 334, 685, 387, 402, 419, 458–59, 462, 469, 503–4, 535, 543, 558, 564, 597, 611, 633, 650, 652, 671, 691, 725, 743–44
Contra-guerilla terrorist groups, 413
Convention for the Elimination of All Forms of Discrimination against Women, 389
Convention for the Protection of Human Rights and Fundamental Freedoms, 165–67, 172
Convention for the Protection of Human Rights and Fundamental Freedoms concerning the Abolition of the Death Penalty, 367
Convention on Laundering, Search, Seizure and Confiscation of the Proceeds from Crime, 485
Convention on the Transfer of Sentenced Persons, 485
Copenhagen Criteria, 324, 327, 354, 358–59, 399, 401, 419–20, 595, 597, 609, 616–17, 625, 630, 653, 660, 663–64, 666, 720–21, 724, 740
Copenhagen European Council, 720
Copenhagen, 172, 182, 425–26, 428, 430, 433, 439
Cotonou Agreement, 185
Council for National Unity, 6
Council of Europe Framework Convention for the Protection of National Minorities, 733
Council of Europe Guidelines on Human Rights and the Fight against Terrorism, 546
Council of Europe Parliamentary Assembly (PACE), 234, 238, 486, 491, 546
Council of Ministers, 19–20, 25, 35, 39–40, 46, 51, 66–68, 70, 72–75, 80, 83, 90–91, 93, 99, 111, 115, 124, 129, 135,

137, 270, 419, 460, 462, 468, 495, 516–17, 518, 524, 588, 631, 751
Council of State, 83, 86, 737
Counter-Terrorism and Warfare Office, 20
Court of Accounts, 271, 458, 726
Court of Cassation, 302, 332, 334, 336–37, 339–40, 346, 350, 503–4, 543, 559, 564, 576–77, 614, 627, 634–35, 638, 641, 652–53, 655, 731, 737
Court of Justice, 200–201, 203–5, 215, 226, 722
Criminal Court, 480
Criminal Law Convention on Corruption, 486
Customs Union Joint Committee, 220
Customs Union, 219–20, 224–25, 232–33, 252 256–58, 260, 279, 281, 284–85, 291–92, 294, 323–25, 353–57, 381, 393–94, 431, 433, 435, 438, 533, 570, 570–71, 579, 592, 597–98, 616, 673, 680, 722, 724, 747–48
Cyprus, 6, 158, 219, 232, 255, 282–83, 293, 323–27, 381, 391–92 395, 430–31, 470, 533, 571, 579, 592, 597–98, 609, 614, 618, 629, 631, 653, 657, 660, 663, 673, 678, 680, 722, 725, 739, 763, 765

Damage Assessment Commissions, 733
Death Penalty, 511, 515, 525, 543–48, 556, 557–61, 562–66, 580
Declaration of Foreign Ministers of the Community on Human Rights (1986), 170, 173
Declaration of Stuttgart, 165
Declaration of the European Union, 213
Decree 285, 110–11, 113–14
Decree 424, 107–9, 115–16
Decree 425, 107, 109, 115
Defense Industry (SSM), 669, 726
Defrenne v. Sabena, 161
Demir, Ahmet, 406
Demirel v. Stadt Schwaebisch Gmund, 168
Demirel, Suleyman, 6–8, 388, 391
Democracy Party (DEP), 249, 252, 289, 292, 467, 637–38, 660
Democratic Left Party (DSP), 384
Democratic Mass Party (DKP), 385, 402
Democratic Party (DP), 5–6
Democratic People's Party (DEHAP), 368, 597, 650, 661, 687, 712, 716
Development and Support Fund, 107, 111

Dicle, Hatip, 291, 638
Dimotiki Etairia Pliroforissis (DEP), 167
Dink, Hrant, 731
Director General for Prisons and Detention Centers, 122
Directorate of Meteorology, 709
District Human Rights Board, 729
Dogan, Orhan, 291
Draft Act of the Indemnification of Losses Resulting from Terrorism and the Fight against Terrorism, 443, 475
Draft Act on Job Security, 442, 471
Draft Act on Public Employees' Trade Unions, 442
Draft Act on the Establishment of Working Principles and Procedures of and Social Council, 442, 471
Draft Act on the Organization of the Directorate General for the Status and Problems of Women, 446, 473
Draft Act on the Organization of the Family Research Institution, 446, 473
Draft Advocacy Act, 444, 472
Draft Turkish Civil Code, 446, 473

Ecevit, Bulent, 391, 402
EC-Turkey Association Council, 284, 429, 431, 433, 570
Elliniki Radiophonia Tileorassi Anonimi Etairia (ERT), 167
Erdogan, Tayyip, 8, 610, 688–90, 714, 734, 755
Euro-Mediterranean Ministerial Council, 197–98
Euro-Mediterranean Partnership (MEDA), 220
Europe Framework Convention for the Protection of National Minorities, 650
European Central Bank, 719
European Charter for Regional or Minority Languages, 33, 468, 650
European Charter of Civil Rights, 141
European Coal and Steel Community, 226
European Commission against Racism and Intolerance (ECRI), 733
European Commission for Democracy through Law, 370, 467
European Commission on Human Rights (UHCR), 219–20, 228, 229–32, 241, 250, 615
European Committee for the Prevention of Torture and Inhuman or Degrading Treatment or Punishment, 235–39, 242, 302, 311, 365, 443, 628, 467, 571

European Conference, 221, 340, 357, 359,
European Constitution, 677, 681, 695–96
European Convention for the Prevention of Torture, 431, 447, 466, 470–71, 685
European Convention of Extradition, 485
European Convention on Human Rights (ECHR), 41–42, 109, 115, 141,181, 187, 200–204, 206, 213–15, 227–28, 234–37, 251, 275, 277–78, 281, 292, 320, 354, 370, 385, 390, 431–32, 441, 443, 446, 463–64, 467–68, 471, 474–75, 612, 627, 633, 635, 637, 644–46 648, 655, 663, 685, 725–29
European Convention on Mutual Assistance in Criminal Matters, 485
European Convention on the Compensation of Victims of Violent Crimes, 486
European Convention on the Control of the Acquisition and Possession of Firearms by Individuals, 486
European Convention on the Exercise of Children's Rights, 387, 637
European Convention on the Supervision of Conditionally Sentenced or Conditionally released Offenders, 486
European Convention on the Suppression of Terrorism, 484–85
European Convention on the Transfer of Proceedings in Criminal Transfer, 485
European Council Nice Summit, 142, 421
European Council Resolution of 9 June 1991, 173
European Court of Human Rights (ECtHR), 131, 148–55, 235, 261, 264, 266, 293, 367, 383, 387, 389–90, 392, 399, 401, 417, 420, 441, 443–44, 467–68, 474, 491, 495, 498, 499–500, 501, 503, 509, 513, 519, 524, 527, 528, 534, 540–41, 543, 547, 566, 571–72, 574, 596, 613, 615, 627, 635, 637–38, 643–45, 650, 653, 663, 665, 700
European Court of Justice, 142
European Economic Community Treaty, 167–68
European Environment Agency, 222
European Free Trade Association (EFTA), 687
European Information and Observation Network (EIONET), 222
European Investment Bank (EIB), 233
European Parliament Sakharov Prize, 420
European Parliament, 165, 182, 186, 188, 190–91, 200–201, 210–11, 220, 226, 235–36, 249, 251–52, 291, 293, 399, 402, 425, 671, 673, 677–78, 695, 721
European Political Cooperation (EPC), 175
European Prison Rules, 447
European Security and Defense Policy (ESDP), 672
European Social Charter, 165, 442, 446, 474, 727–28
European Union Charter of Fundamental Rights, 142
European Union Common Security Policy, 215
European Union-Turkey Customs Union, 292, 323, 325, 352–57, 616, 722
European Union-Turkey Joint Committee, 279, 285
Europe-Turkey Foundation, 421
Evren, Kenen, 15
Execution of Sentences, 122, 583

Fazilet Party, 385
Fight against Terrorism, 546,
Financial Crimes Investigation Board of the Ministry of Finance, 480–81
Financial Protocol, 219, 225, 233
First Constitutional Period (First Meshrutiyet), 38
Force of Law no. 425, 115
Force of Law no. 430, 115
Foreign Affairs Council, 220
Forensic Medicine Institution, 443–44, 471–72
Framework Convention for the Protection of National Minorities, 468

Ganturk, Behcet, 406
Gendarmerie, 20, 72
General Affairs Council, 187, 220, 255
General Directorate of Security, 366
Geneva Convention, 484, 615
Grand Chamber, 150–54, 718
Grand National Assembly, 4–6, 8, 35, 39–41, 51, 65–71, 73–74, 80–82, 86–88, 91, 105, 120–21, 129, 235–37, 241, 245, 249–50, 252, 255–56, 260, 272, 281–83, 289–90, 358, 365–67, 385–86, 400, 402, 407, 440, 445, 459–61, 465–66, 468–69, 476, 483, 491, 504, 515, 523, 525, 537, 557, 581, 608, 661, 724
Grand National Assembly, Conciliation Committee, 418

Greece, 6, 267, 391–92, 542, 579, 651, 657, 660, 663
Greek Cypriot Administration (GCA), 678, 680
Group of Eight (G8), 391
Group of States Against Corruption (GRECO), 654, 662
Gul, Abdullah, 680–81, 715
Gulhane Hatt-i Humayun, 38
Guney, Huseyin, 405, 410, 415
Gursel, Cemal, 6

Haceteppe University, 735
Harmonisation Committee, 630
Harmonisation Packages, 491, 502,515, 534,540,573,583, 581
Helsinki European Council, 401
Helsinki Final Act, 191–94
Helsinki, 190, 192–94, 221, 380, 383, 401, 419, 425, 428–33, 470, 473, 477, 524, 532–33, 570–71, 579, 579, 616, 625, 666–67, 749, 765, 766, 768
Hezbollah, 405, 407, 411, 413, 415
High Audiovisual Board (RTUK), 731
High Commission of Judges, 40
High Commissioner on National Minorities (HGNM), 732
High Contracting Party, 144,148–57
High Council of Judges and Prosecutors, 727, 736
High Military Administrative Court of Appeals, 84
Higher Education Institutions, 271, 506, 531, 534–35,
Hisb-ut Tahrir, 701
Hoechst AG v. Commission, 161
Holy Monasteries v. Greece, 313
Human Development Index, 3
Human Rights Advisory Board, 729
Human Rights Directorate, 442
Human Rights Minister, 369
Human Rights Presidency, 729, 737
Human Rights Watch, 677
Hussein, Saddam, 257

Icyer v. Turkey, 728, 734
Imperial Edict on Justice (Ferman-i Adalet), 38
Imrali, 718–19
Incal v. Turkey, 329
Incal, Ibrahim, 329, 332, 341–43, 345–47, 349
Independence Tribunals, 39
Inonu, Ismet, 5–6

Intergovernmental Conference (IGC) (1996), 200–201, 204–7, 721, 723
Internally Displaced Persons (IDP), 735
International Convention against Torture, 281–82
International Court of Justice, 395, 722
International Covenant on Civil and Political Rights (ICCPR), 432, 474, 596, 627, 650 659, 733
International Covenant on Civil and Political Rights (ICCPR), Optional Protocol, 727
International Covenant on Civil and Political Rights (ICCPR), Second Optional Protocol, 737
International Covenant on Economic, Social and Cultural Rights (ICESCR), 432, 474, 596, 627, 637, 650, 659, 733
International Criminal Court (ICC), 216
International Labor Organization (ILO), 446, 473–75, 721
International Monetary Fund (IMF), 7
International Red Cross, 258, 291–92, 294
International Women's Day, 680, 700
Internationale Handelsgesellschaft, 160–61
Inter-Party Constitutional Harmonization Commission, 440
Iraq, 8, 234, 257–58, 260, 353, 465, 610, 681, 703, 712, 714–15
Istanbul Court, 728
Istanbul Directorate of Security, 731
Istanbul Protocol, 685
Istanbul Stock Exchange, 480

Johnston v Chief Constable of the Royal Ulster Constabulary, 161, 168
Joint Declaration of 5 April 1977, 200
Justice Academy, 737
Justice and Development Party (AKP), 610, 629, 630, 710
Justice Commandos of the Armenian Genocide (JCAG), 8
Justice Party (AP), 6

Kamal, Yasar, 291
Kargili, Captain Cengiz, 415
Kemal Pasha, Mustafa, 4–7, 49, 60, 65, 69, 268, 439, 449
Kemalism, 4, 7, 364
Kenya, 718–19
Kilic v. Turkey, 404
Kilic, Kemel, 404–5, 407, 410–16

Kizilkan, Seyfettin, 292
Klockner-Werke, 161
KONGRA-GEL, 652
Kouvelas, S, 167
Kurdish Writer's Association, 649
Kurdistan Freedom Falcons (TAK), 708–9, 711–12
Kurdistan Worker's Party (PKK), 8, 19–21, 103, 236–37, 249, 251–52, 257–58, 259, 281–82, 291, 293, 295–97, 309, 315, 318, 342, 345, 352, 355, 358, 367, 376–77, 382, 388, 390–91, 399, 404, 411, 413–14, 465–66, 468
Kurds, 3, 6–8, 20, 103, 234, 255, 257–60, 281–82, 289, 291–93, 329–31, 341–44, 352, 355, 357–59, 367, 370–71, 375, 384, 388, 390–92, 542, 559, 564 613, 617, 619, 629, 635, 644, 646–53, 655–56, 660–62

Laeken, 477, 673, 677–79, 686–91, 700–716, 734, 741
Land Forces Commander, 727
Law Concerning Crimes Committed Against Atatürk, 137
Law Concerning Founding and Broadcasts of Television and Radio, 134, 519–20, 529, 573, 575
Law for State of Emergency Regional Governor (no. 2935), 108, 110, 114
Law on Associations (no. 2908), 127, 628, 636, 731, 740
Law on Associations, 127, 507, 516–18, 523, 531, 647, 655, 661
Law on Citizenship, 651
Law on Compensation of Losses Resulting from Terrorist Acts, 629–30, 636, 652, 656, 728, 734
Law on Crimes against Atatürk, 646
Law on Duties and Competence of the Police (no. 2559), 123
Law on Enforcement of Sentences, 726, 730, 737
Law on Execution of Penalties (no. 647), 136
Law on Formation of Criminal Procedure (no.1412), 127
Law on Gatherings and Demonstrations, 127
Law on Internal Affairs of the Armed Forces, 15
Law on Liabilities, 113
Law on Organization and Duties of the Gendarmerie (no. 2803), 26
Law on Political Parties (no. 648), 628, 649, 732
Law on Powers and Duties of the Police, 26
Law on Prosecution of Civil Servants (no. 4483), 121, 365, 386
Law on Protection of Freedom of Conscious and Meetings (no. 6187), 123
Law on Provincial Administration (no. 5442), 110, 137
Law on Public Financial and Management Control (PFMC), 726
Law on Public Housing, 123
Law on Public Meetings and Demonstrations, 628
Law on Repentance (no. 4450), 391
Law on Social Reinsertion, 629
Law on Strikes and Slowing of Jobs, 127
Law on the Establishment of Military Courts and Trial Procedures (no. 353), 32–35, 641
Law on the Fight against Terrorism (LFAT) (no.3713), 479, 481–82
Law on the Foundation of Criminal Procedure for State Security Courts (no. 2845), 118, 120, 129–30
Law on the Freedom of Assembly and Demonstrations, 30
Law on the Prevention of Money Laundering (no. 4208), 479
Law on the Prevention of Offenses against Law and Order (no.1481), 26, 97
Law on the Procedure for Flagrant Offenses (no. 3005), 33, 98
Law on the Prohibition and Prosecution of Smuggling (no. 1918), 37
Law on Weapons, Knives and Other Devices (no. 6136), 130
Loizidou, Ms. 614
Lome' Convention IV, 187, 190
London School of Economics, 680
Luxembourg, 429, 470, 697
Luxembourg's Minister Delegate for Foreign Affairs and Immigration in Ankara, 679

Maastricht Treaty, 182, 200
Mansu v. Turkey, 266–67
Marmara Group Foundation, 679
Martial Law Act, 19, 22
Martial Law Commander, 22–24, 26–27, 29–34, 36–37, 74

Martial Law Military Tribunal, 78
Martial Law, 5, 6, 7 8, 15, 18–19, 22–37, 46, 52–54, 68, 70, 73–75, 78–80, 88, 227–28, 235, 337, 349, 451, 743, 744
Meclis-i Meshveret, 38
MEDA programme, 294, 354
Menderes, Adnan, 5
Mentes and Others v. Turkey, 320
Military Courts (also Martial Law Courts), 27–30, 32–37, 79, 97, 337
Military Criminal Code, 408, 725
Military High Court of Appeals, 83–84
Military Legal Service Act, 337
Military Penal Code, 30, 445, 476
Minister of Foreign Affairs, 383, 681
Ministry of Health, 730
Ministry of Interior, 20, 24, 35, 96–97, 107–8, 111, 114–15, 122–23, 388, 463, 482, 516–18, 526–27, 589, 639, 647–48, 650, 725–27
Ministry of Internal Affairs, 22
Ministry of Justice, 36–37, 77–78, 85, 336–37, 388, 447, 473, 483, 633–34, 636, 639, 643, 726–27, 730, 736–38
Ministry of National Defense, 26–28, 32, 36–37, 337–38
Minority Issues Assessment Board, 650
Mitap and Muftuoglu v. Turkey, 315
Monetary Compensation and Pension, 123
Monitoring Committee, 465
Motherland Party (ANAP), 7, 384

National Defense Ministry, 402
National Intelligence Organization, 22
National Intelligence Service, 726
National Programme for the Adoption of the *Acquis*, 626, 631
National Security Council (MGK), 7, 15, 41–42, 48, 70, 72–73, 87–88, 91, 131, 135, 367, 369, 384, 386, 392, 402, 432, 447, 462, 467, 475–76, 572, 575, 580, 584, 586, 588–90, 595, 626, 631–32, 654, 659, 688, 725–26
National Security Courts, 372,-379, 415–16
National Security Policy Document, 725
Nationalist Action Party (MHP), 6, 384
Necdet Sezer, Ahmet, 8, 725
New System (Nizam-i Cedid), 38
Nold v. Commission, 160, 168
Non-Government Organizations (NGO), 172,174, 216, 220, 729, 731
North Atlantic Assembly, 369

North Atlantic Treaty Organization (NATO), 5, 368, 484, 597, 681
Notice of Derogation, 115–16, 131

Ocalan v. Turkey, 543
Ocalan, Abdulla, 8, 103–4, 131, 382, 385–86, 388–90, 392, 399, 542, 557, 638, 687, 699, 712, 715, 717, 729
Ombudsman, 737
Optional Protocol against Torture (OPCAT), 729, 738
Organization for Security and Cooperation in Europe (OSCE), 189–90, 258, 281, 292, 368, 381, 484, 732
Organization of the Islamic Conference, 484
Ottoman Empire, 3–4, 7, 38–39
Ozal, Turgut, 7–8
Ozgur Gundem, 404, 406, 410–16

PACE Recommendation, 289
Parliamentary Assembly, 149
Parliamentary Human Rights Committee, 729
Parliamentary Inquiry Committee on Human Rights, 365
Parliamentary Investigation Committee Report (1993), 407, 413
Parliamentary Planning and Budget Committee, 726
Passport Law, 483
Pecastaing v. Belgium, 161
Pension Fund, 459
People's Labor Party (HEP), 319, 329, 331, 342, 345, 349
Police Duty and Responsibility Law (no. 2559), 137
Political Parties Act, 87, 441, 473, 503–4
Political Parties Law (no. 2820), 134, 384
Presidential Council, 41
Press Act, 331, 333, 341, 441, 471, 636, 644–46
Press Law no. 5680, 113, 118–19, 136
Prevention of Certain Crimes against the Public Order, 122
Prevention of Terrorism Act, 331–32, 334, 346, 350, 367–69, 373–79, 468
Protection of Human Rights and Fundamental Freedoms, 717
Public Prosecutor, 480

Radio and Television Higher Council, 736
Refah Party, 384

778  *Index*

Reform Monitoring Group, 626, 638, 654
Regional Serious Felony Courts, 632–34
Regulation on Apprehension, Detention and Statement Taking, 634, 640
Regulation on Teaching in Different Languages and Dialects Traditionally Used by Turkish Citizens in their Daily Lives, 651
Reintegration Act, 613
Repentance laws, 20–21
Republican People's Party (CHP), 5, 40, 610, 630, 711
Resolution no. 1187, 546
Resolution no. 1253, 546
Resolution no. 1268, 491
Resolution no. 1297, 513
Resolution no. 37, 105
Resolution no. 38, 105
Resolution no. 426, 106
Rights and Freedoms Party (HAK-PAR), 650, 732–33
Rural Communities Act, 20
Rutili v. Ministre de l'interieur, 160

Sadak, Selim, 291, 638
Sakik and Others v. Turkey, 319, 550, 553
Sargin v. Turkey, 261–64,
Sargin, Nihat, 261–62, 264, 266
Savas, Kutlu, 405
Second Meshrutiyet, 38
Second Regular Commission Report, 402
Security Operation Agreements, 483
Security, Public Order and Assistance Units (EMASYA), 726
Semdinli Investigation Commission of Parliament, 726
Semdlini Bombing, 727, 734
Serious Felony Courts, 654
Settlement Law, 111
Single European Act, 186, 200
Social Welfare and Solidarity Fund, 123
Southeaster European Cooperative Initiative (SECI), 484–85
Special Operations Bureau, 407
Special Warfare Office, 20
State Audit Board, 41
State of Emergency Act, 19
State of Emergency Bureau, 94–95
State of Emergency Coordination Council, 93–95
State of Emergency, 15, 70, 73–75, 90–94, 96–98, 107, 110, 112–15, 298–99, 322, 613

State Security Court, 78, 112, 118, 120, 127, 129–31, 235, 245–46, 251, 261–62, 265–66, 366, 382–83, 385–86, 399, 401, 405, 413, 415, 432, 444, 466, 471–72, 483, 543, 549, 553, 555, 557, 559, 717
State Supervisory Council, 71–72
Statute of the Council of Europe, 155
Stauder v. Ulm, 160
Student Selection and Placement Center (OSYM), 385
Supreme Administrative Court, 408
Supreme Council for Judges and Public Prosecutors, 444, 472
Supreme Court of Appeals, 271, 273, 387, 399, 519, 524, 527–28, 534
Supreme Court, 40, 80–81, 289, 383, 462,
Supreme Election Board, 270
Supreme Election Council, 458
Supreme Military Council, 75
Susurlak Report, 405–7, 411, 413

Tanzimat Reform era, 38
Thessaloniki Regional Court, 167
Trade Unions, 127
Treaty of Lausanne, 370, 389, 650–51
Treaty of Rome of 1957, 141
True Path Party (DYP), 8, 630
Turkey's European Communication Group, 477
Turkish Alcohol and Tobacco Company, 393
Turkish Armed Forces (Internal Service) Act, 26, 96–97, 725
Turkish Armed Forces Personnel Act, 337
Turkish Armed Forces, 129, 269–70, 504, 586, 588
Turkish Civil Code, 113, 477, 507, 524–25, 539, 589, 590
Turkish Communist Party (TKP), 261–62, 266, 650
Turkish Constitution of 1924, 3, 9 40, 742
Turkish Constitution of 1982, 40–41, 275, 290, 334, 611, 614, 743
Turkish Criminal Code, 367–68, 373, 386, 407–8, 413
Turkish High Coordinating Committee for Human Rights, 365, 369
Turkish Human Rights Association, 251, 255, 388–89
Turkish Human Rights Foundation, 251

*Index* 779

Turkish National Programme for the Adoption of the *Acquis* (NPAA), 439–41, 465, 469
Turkish Peace Association, 235
Turkish Penal Code (TPC), 29–30, 32, 35, 110, 113–14, 117–18, 124, 126–30, 132, 275, 365–66, 386, 388–89 399, 419–20, 441–43, 466, 468, 471, 473–75, 479, 481–82, 491–92, 496–98, 505, 515–16, 523, 525–26, 539, 574, 576–77, 585–86, 630, 633–35, 640–41, 644–46, 654–56, 661, 677, 726–27, 731, 736–38, 740
Turkish Petroleum Corporation (TPAO), 708
Turkish Petroleum Pipeline Corps (BOTAS), 708
Turkish Public Television (TRT), 733, 736
Turkish Radio and Television Corporation, 113
Turkish Republic of Northern Cyprus (TRNC), 392, 686+
Turkish Security Organization, 406
Turkish Supreme Coordination Council for Human Rights, 419
Turkish Worker's Party, 261
Turmen, Riza, 718

Union of Bars, 738
Union of Judges and Prosecutors (YARSAV), 737
United Communist Party of Turkey, 344
United Nations Committee against Torture, 311, 314
United Nations Committee against Torture's Summary Account of the Results of the Proceedings Concerning the Inquiry on Turkey, 302
United Nations Convention on the Elimination of All Forms of Discrimination against Women, 474, 637
United Nations Convention on the Elimination of All forms of Racial Discrimination, 446, 472, 637, 640
United Nations Decade of Human Rights Education, 444, 472
United Nations High Commissioner for Refugees (UNHCR), 258, 371
United Nations Register of Arms Transfers, 175
United Nations Secretary General (UNSG), 430–31, 470
United Nations Security Council (UNSC), 479, 483, 487
United Nations Special Rapporteur on Torture's Report of 1995, 302
United Nations Standard Minimum Rules for the Treatment of Prisoners, 432, 447, 474
United Nations, 166, 198, 232, 250, 252, 257–58, 281–83, 391, 395, 473, 495, 524, 529, 546, 558, 571, 580, 722
Universal Declaration of Human Rights, 143–59, 170, 213–14

Wachauf v. Federal Republic of Germany, 168
Working Group on Enforced or Involuntary Disappearances, 387
World Trade Organization (WTO), 197

Yagci, Nabi, Document, 261–62, 264, 266
Yagiz v. Turkey, 315
Yilmaz, Mesut, 292, 325

Zana v. Turkey, 319, 342, 346
Zana, Leyla, 291–92, 353, 355, 358, 420, 614, 627, 637–38, 655, 660

# Index of documents

**Anti-Terrorism Law (ATL)**

Amendment to Article 8 Document 48
Anti-Terrorism Law (Law to Fight Against Terrorism) Document 17
Components Document 18
*See also* Constitutional Court, Laws Against Terrorism, State Security Courts, ECtHR Cases,

**Customs Union**

Ankara Agreement Document 36
Assent procedure
  Document 50
Council of European Parliamentary Assembly Document 45
Developments in Relations Document 64
European Parliament Documents 43, 49
Final Phase Document 52
Iraq Operation (1995) Document 44

**ECtHR Cases**

Compulsory Jurisdiction (Yagiz v. Turkey) Document 57
Effective remedies (Aksoy v. Turkey) Document 56
Exhaustion of Domestic Remedies (Akdivar
and others v. Turkey; Mentes and others v. Turkey) Documents 57, 58
Exigencies of the circumstances (Kilic v. Turkey) Document 72
Failure to protect victims (Kilic v. Turkey) Document 72

Implementation of decisions Documents 86, 92
Inadequate Compensation (Akkus v. Turkey) Document 58
Length of Detention and Criminal Proceedings
(Yagci and Sargin v. Turkey; Mansur v. Turkey;
Mitap and Muftuoglu v. Turkey; Zana v. Turkey &
Sakik and others v. Turkey) Documents 46, 57, 58
No breach by Turkey Document 58
Right of Derogation from the ECHR
(France, Norway, Denmark, Sweden and the
Netherlands v. Turkey; Sakik and others v. Turkey) Document 37
State (National) Security Courts (Incal v. Turkey) Document 62
Torture (Aydin v. Turkey) Document 58
Various decisions in 1998 Document 63
Various decisions in 1999 Document 67
Various decisions in 2001 Document 78
Various Decisions in 2002 Document 86
*See also* Terrorism: Ocalan v. Turkey

**Europe and Human Rights**

Early European Court of Justice Document 23
European Convention on Human Rights (ECHR) Document 22
European System Document 21
Terrorism Document 85
*See also* European Community and Human Rights, European Union and Human Rights

Index of documents 781

**European Community and Human Rights**

Council Declaration Document 26
Council Resolution Document 27
Single European Act Document 25

**European Union and Human Rights**

Amsterdam Treaty Document 33
Copenhagen Criteria Document 29
Euro-Mediterranean Area Document 31
Fundamental Rights Document 32
Maastricht Treaty Document 28
Third Countries (Agreements with) Document 30
Trade Document 30
Universal Declaration of Human Rights Document 34

**Laws Against Terrorism**

Anti-terrorism Law *see ATL*
Code of Criminal Procedure Document 59
Human Rights Document 85
Introduction Document 6
Martial Law *see Martial Law*
Repentance laws Document 6
State of Emergency *see State of Emergency Law*
Turkish Penal Code and the ATL Document 18
Various other laws Document 20
*See also* Legal Changes, Terrorism: Measures taken against

**Legal Changes**

Harmonization Package 1 Document 83
Harmonization Package 2 Document 84
Harmonization Package 3 Document 87
Harmonization Package 3 Document 87
Harmonization Package 4 Document 89
Harmonization Package 5 Document 90
Harmonization Package 6 Document 94
Harmonization Package 7 Document 96
National Programme Checklist Document 99
Turkish Civil Code Document 81
*See also* Laws Against Terrorism, Turkish Constitution, Terrorism: Measures taken against

**Martial Law**

Brief Introduction Document 6
Martial Law Act (with decrees) Document 7
Martial Law by cities Document 5
Martial Law Declarations Document 12

**Military Coups**

1980 Coup Document 4
General overview Document 2

**National Security Courts,** *see State Security Courts*

**Regular Reports by the European Commission**

1999 Regular Report Document 68
2004 Regular Report Document 104
2006 Regular Report Document 115
European Parliament Resolution on the 2004 Report Document 105
European Parliament Resolution on the 1999 Report Document 73

**State of Emergency**

Brief Introduction Document 6
Regional Governor Documents 13, 15
State of Emergency by cities Document 5
State of Emergency Declarations Document 12
State of Emergency Law Document 10

**State Security Courts**

Independence and Impartiality of Document 62
State (National) Security Courts and the ATL Document 18

**Terrorism**

Critical Developments (2005–6) Document 110
Kurdistan Workers' Party (PKK) Activities Document 11
PKK-Abdullah Ocalan Document 70
Measures taken against Document 82
Ocalan v. Turkey (ECtHR) Documents 91, 113

Terror Activities after 2004 Document 112

## Turkey (Country Information)

General Document 1
Historical overview Document 2
Maps Document 3

## Turkey–EU Relations

Accession and regular reports Document 61
Accession Negotiations Document 98
Accession Partnership Agreement Document 93
Accession to the Union (1989) Document 38
Brief History Document 35
Candidacy Document 69
Common Future Document 109
Comparative Analysis (Accession Partnership Agreement,
National Programme and 2001 Regular Report) Document 80
Development of Relations Document 65
Developments in 2005 Document 108
European Parliament (EP) Document 55
European Parliament Briefing regarding relations (1999) Document 71
European Council Conclusions (2004) Documents 101, 106
European Council Decisions (2003) Document 97
European Council Declaration (2002) Document 88
European Union Constitution Document 111
European Union Enlargement Document 35
Honoring of Obligations (CoE–Turkey–PACE Report) Documents 79, 102
Membership Perspective, issues Document 107
National Programme (Turkey) Documents 76, 95
Negotiating Framework Document 114
Obligations of Turkey (CoE) Document 66
Pre-Accession Assistance (2001) Document 74
Pre-Accession Decision (2001) Document 75
Progress Towards Accession Document 103
Trials of Kurdish MPs Documents 41, 42
Turkey's eligibility for membership Document 60
*See also* Regular Reports, Legal Changes: National Programme Checklist

## Turkey and Human Rights

Council of Europe Parliamentary Assembly (PACE) Document 39
Derogations from ECHR Documents 14, 16, 19
European Parliament Document 51, 54
Torture Document 40

## Turkish Constitution

1982 Constitution as enacted Document 9
1995 Amendments Document 47
2001 Amendments Document 77
2004 Amendments Document 100
Constitutional Court and the ATL Document 18
Constitutional History Document 8
PACE Recommendation Document 53

## Turkish Democracy

Brief Political History Document 2
Constitution *see Turkish Constitution*
Military Coups *See Military Coups*
Republican Reforms Document 2

# eBooks – at www.eBookstore.tandf.co.uk

## A library at your fingertips!

eBooks are electronic versions of printed books. You can store them on your PC/laptop or browse them online.

They have advantages for anyone needing rapid access to a wide variety of published, copyright information.

eBooks can help your research by enabling you to bookmark chapters, annotate text and use instant searches to find specific words or phrases. Several eBook files would fit on even a small laptop or PDA.

**NEW:** Save money by eSubscribing: cheap, online access to any eBook for as long as you need it.

### Annual subscription packages

We now offer special low-cost bulk subscriptions to packages of eBooks in certain subject areas. These are available to libraries or to individuals.

For more information please contact webmaster.ebooks@tandf.co.uk

We're continually developing the eBook concept, so keep up to date by visiting the website.

## www.eBookstore.tandf.co.uk